Pillars of Social Psychology

This collection of first-person accounts from legendary social psychologists tells the stories behind the science and offers unique insight into the development of the field from the 1950s to the present. One Pillar, the grandson of a slave, was inspired by Kenneth Clark. Yet when he entered his PhD program in the 1960s, he was told that race was not a variable for study. Other pillars faced first-hand a type of sexism that was hardly subtle, as when women were not permitted into the faculty dining room. Still others have lived through a tremendous diversification of social psychology, not only in the United States but also in Europe and Asia, that characterizes the field today. Together these stories, always witty and sometimes emotional, form a mosaic of the field as a whole – its legends, what drew them into the field, their theories and research, their relationships with one another, and their sense of where social psychology is headed.

Saul Kassin is Distinguished Professor of Psychology at John Jay College of Criminal Justice and Professor Emeritus of Williams College, USA. He has received numerous honors for his pioneering research on false confessions, including the APA Award for Distinguished Contribution to Research in Public Policy (2017) and the APS James McKeen Cattell Lifetime Achievement Award for Applied Research (2021).

Pillars of Social Psychology

Stories and Retrospectives

Edited by

SAUL KASSIN
John Jay College of Criminal Justice, City University of New York

Shaftesbury Road, Cambridge CB2 8EA, United Kingdom

One Liberty Plaza, 20th Floor, New York, NY 10006, USA

477 Williamstown Road, Port Melbourne, VIC 3207, Australia

314–321, 3rd Floor, Plot 3, Splendor Forum, Jasola District Centre, New Delhi – 110025, India

103 Penang Road, #05–06/07, Visioncrest Commercial, Singapore 238467

Cambridge University Press is part of Cambridge University Press & Assessment, a department of the University of Cambridge.

We share the University's mission to contribute to society through the pursuit of education, learning and research at the highest international levels of excellence.

www.cambridge.org
Information on this title: www.cambridge.org/9781009214292

DOI: 10.1017/9781009214315

© Cambridge University Press & Assessment 2022

First published 2022

A catalogue record for this publication is available from the British Library.

ISBN 978-1-009-21429-2 Hardback
ISBN 978-1-009-21428-5 Paperback

Contents

Contributors

Thomas Fraser Pettigrew
University of California at Santa Cruz, USA
(1956; Harvard University; Gordon Allport)

Robert Rosenthal
University of California at Riverside, USA
(1956; UCLA; Bruno Klopfer)

Florence Denmark
Pace University, USA
(1958; University of Pennsylvania; Albert Pepitone)

Elliot Aronson
University of California at Santa Cruz, USA
(1959; Stanford University; Leon Festinger)

Philip G. Zimbardo
Stanford University, USA
(1959; Yale University; Neil Miller)

Jonathan Freedman
University of Toronto, Canada
(1962; Yale University; Carl Hovland)

Anthony G. Greenwald
University of Washington, USA
(1963; Harvard University; Gordon Allport)

Elaine Hatfield
University of Hawai'i, USA
(1963; Stanford University; Leon Festinger)

Bibb Latané
Center for Human Science, USA
(1963; University of Minnesota; Stanley Schachter)

Bernard Weiner
University of California at Los Angeles, USA
(1963; University of Michigan; John Atkinson)

Ellen Berscheid
University of Minnesota, USA
(1963; University of Minnesota; Elliot Aronson)

Alice H. Eagly
Northwestern University, USA
(1965; University of Michigan; Herbert Kelman)

Richard E. Nisbett
University of Michigan, USA
(1966; Columbia University; Stanley Schachter)

Kay Deaux
The Graduate Center City University of New York, USA
(1967; University of Texas; James Bieri)

Wolfgang Stroebe
University of Groningen, The Netherlands
(1966; Univ. of Münster; Wilhelm Witte; 1968; London School of Economics;
Norman Hotopf)

Joel Cooper
Princeton University, USA
(1969; Duke University; Ned Jones)

Michael Harris Bond
Hong Kong Polytechnic University, China
(1970; Stanford University; Albert Hastorf)

Robert B. Cialdini
Arizona State University, USA
(1970; University of North Carolina, Chester Insko)

Edward L. Deci
University of Rochester, USA
(1970; Carnegie Mellon University; Daryl Bem)

Phoebe C. Ellsworth
University of Michigan, USA
(1970; Stanford University; J. Merrill Carlsmith)

James M. Jones
University of Delaware, USA
(1970; Yale University; Robert Abelson)

Claude Steele
Stanford University, USA
(1971; Ohio State University; Thomas Ostrom)

Daniel Batson
University of Kansas, USA
(1972; Princeton University John Darley)

Carol S. Dweck
Stanford University, USA
(1972; Yale University; Dick Reppucci)

Mark Snyder
University of Minnesota, USA
(1972; Stanford University; Daryl Bem and Philip Zimbardo)

Letitia Anne Peplau
University of California, USA
(1973; Harvard University; Zick Rubin)

Hazel Rose Markus
Stanford University, USA
(1975; University of Michigan; Robert Zajonc)

Michael F. Scheier
Carnegie Mellon University, USA
(1975; University of Texas; Arnold Buss)

Margaret Clark
Yale University, USA
(1977; University of Maryland; Judson Mills)

John F. Dovidio
Yale University, USA
(1977; University of Delaware; Samuel Gaertner)

James W. Pennebaker
University of Texas, USA
(1977; University of Texas; Robert Wicklund)

Richard E. Petty
Ohio State University, USA
(1977; Ohio State University; Timothy Brock)

Gary L. Wells
Iowa State University, USA
(1977; Ohio State University; Anthony Greenwald)

Timothy D. Wilson
University of Virginia, USA
(1977; University of Michigan; Richard Nisbett)

Roy F. Baumeister
University of Queensland, Australia
(1978; Princeton University; Ned Jones)

Susan T. Fiske
Princeton University, USA
(1978; Harvard University; Shelley Taylor)

Brenda Major
University of California at Santa Barbara, USA
(1978; Purdue University; Kay Deaux)

William B. Swann, Jr.
University of Texas, USA
(1978; University of Minnesota; Mark Snyder)

Rupert Brown
University of Sussex, UK
(1979; University of Bristol; Henri Tajfel)

Jennifer Crocker
Ohio State University, USA
(1979; Harvard University; Shelley Taylor)

John A. Bargh
Yale University, USA
(1981; University of Michigan; Robert Zajonc)

David M. Buss
University of Texas, USA
(1981; University of California at Berkeley; Kenneth Craik)

Thomas Gilovich
Cornell University, USA
(1981; Stanford University; Lee Ross)

Miles Hewstone
University of Oxford, UK
(1981; Oxford University; Jos Jaspars)

Daniel Gilbert
Harvard University, USA
(1985; Princeton University; Ned Jones)

Mahzarin R. Banaji
Harvard University, USA
(1986; Ohio State University; Anthony Greenwald)

Patricia G. Devine
University of Wisconsin, USA
(1986; Ohio State University; Thomas Ostrom)

Shinobu Kitayama
University of Michigan, USA
(1987; University of Michigan; Robert Zajonc)

1 Introducing the Pillars of Social Psychology

Saul Kassin

In 1978, I received my PhD from the University of Connecticut based on a dissertation titled "Causal Attribution: A Perceptual Approach." I was fortunate to have obtained a postdoc with Lawrence Wrightsman at the University of Kansas. Larry had funding for research on jury decision-making, which seemed a perfect application of attribution theory. In what proved to be a formative year, I will never forget my introduction to KU. Larry graciously hosted a get-together so that I could meet others in the program – Jack and Sharon Brehm, Dan Batson, Michael Storms, Roger Barker, fellow postdoc Rick Gibbons, and others. As soon as I entered, he led me into the living room.

Then without forewarning, he introduced me to an older gentleman I'd never met but who looked familiar at first sight. It was Professor Emeritus Fritz Heider, my hero, the architect of attribution theory. At 82, Heider was brimming with the kinds of insights that filled his writings. Looking through a tome on the history of art, he marveled at "universalities" in form that he believed betrayed aspects of visual perception and human nature. That first meeting was followed by some unforgettable late afternoon tea and cookies in Fritz and Grace's home in Lawrence, Kansas (for a pre-selfies-era photo I took of the Heiders, see www.cambridge.org/pillarsofsocialpsychology). That year, I learned more about the origins of my own work than I ever could have imagined.

What I did not see coming at that time was how relevant all of social psychology would become for my yet unrealized future foray into the study of wrongful convictions, and specifically the invisible phenomenon of false confessions. From the Milgramesque processes of police interrogation, which feature compliance-inducing forms of trickery, foisted upon suspects whose need to belong is frustrated by prolonged isolation, which can pressure even innocent people to produce confessions, which lead judges and juries to commit the Fundamental Attribution Error, inferring guilt despite these situational constraints, the chain of events can cause horrific miscarriages of justice – and fill the pages of a social psychology textbook.

Fast forward forty years. I taught a doctoral level course on social psychology at John Jay College, a branch of the City University of New York. Even before the pandemic stopped us all in our tracks, I thought it would be a great idea to Skype in (pre-Zoom) some of my heroes so that students could humanize the ideas and where they came from. Interacting through a large smart TV on the wall of our seminar room,

Saul Kassin, Distinguished Professor of Psychology at John Jay College of Criminal Justice and Professor Emeritus of Williams College, USA.

I could not believe how much the students (and I) learned from these virtual visits that enhanced my appreciation for this field.

Opening with a discussion of the situationist theme of social psychology, we Skyped in Phil Zimbardo from his home in San Francisco. I had no idea that he and Stanley Milgram were contemporary classmates at the James Monroe High School, in Bronx, New York, in 1948! I could not quite wrap my head around the mind-numbing fact that the two social psychologists whose work most embodies a hardcore situationist perspective – Milgram on the direct power of an authority figure over the individual, and Zimbardo on the indirect power of institutional roles – walked the halls of the same high school at eighteen years old. "He was the smartest kid in the class," Phil told us, but "I was the most popular." Phil fondly recalled that Milgram thanked him after the Stanford Prison Experiment for redirecting the heat on research ethics.

On the topic of stereotyping and prejudice, I Skyped in Mahzarin Banaji, from Harvard, to discuss the development of the universally popular Implicit Association Test, or IAT. Marzu grew up in the cities of Hyderabad and Secunderabad, in India. So I opened with a simple question: What drew you to social psychology? Illustrating Albert Bandura's (1982) point about the fortuitous nature of "Chance Encounters and Life Paths," she talked about being in a train station in India, in 1980, browsing through a book stand, and purchasing the five volumes of *The Handbook of Social Psychology*. That purchase changed her life course. Not long after, she found her way to Ohio State University, where she worked with Tony Greenwald and received her PhD in 1986. The rest is history.

And so it went. We also Skyped riveting visits with Hazel Markus, Martin Seligman, Sheldon Solomon, and Eli Finkel. In each case, I learned something new and interesting about the history and origin of some of our most important perspectives, theories, and programs of research.

Then I had the pleasure of talking with Lee Ross during a visit to Stanford in February of 2020, just before the COVID pandemic struck. In 2018, Lee wrote a terrific article in *Perspectives on Psychological Science* titled "From the Fundamental Attribution Error to the Truly Fundamental Attribution Error and Beyond: My Research Journey." I was in graduate school preparing my dissertation on perceptions of causality when I read Lee's 1977 *Advances* chapter in which he coined the term "fundamental attribution error" to describe our penchant for dispositional explanations. That chapter has had a profound impact on my work to explain why people uncritically infer guilt from confessions – even when they were coerced from innocent people.

I wanted to talk about this article when Lee let me know that he had also written a paper that he has circulated among friends, not necessarily to be published, titled "Dissonance Theory Redux: Re-uniting Leon and Lewin." I read it, I won't give away his main points, or his personal reflections on Asch, Festinger, Schachter, and others, but his insights were extraordinary – and it made me wonder what other high-caliber scholars can cobble together the human stories that now comprise social psychology. What a treat it would be, I thought, to bring these pillars of social psychology together in one place for a retrospective that celebrates the field and provides historical perspectives for students of social psychology.

Sadly, Lee Ross passed away on May 14, 2021. Buried in his inbox at stanford.edu is an email I had sent just two days prior thanking him for his inspiration and asking if he'd be willing to contribute a chapter to this book. What a social psychology legend he was; what a creative genius. Our conversations helped to generate the idea for this book – which is why I dedicate *Pillars* to him along with others, past and current, including today's younger rock stars, who have influenced the field as we know it.

Format and Contents

When I first conceived of this book, I titled it *Historians of Social Psychology*. My aim was to draw from the legends of the field, the children and grandchildren of the founders. Each would serve as a personal historian, reflecting back on their careers in the context of their time and place. Together, I figured, these personal accounts would yield a history of modern-day social psychology. Alas, reviewers of this proposal balked at the title, noting that it is misleading since, after all, the authors are not themselves historians. I argued about imposing such a literal interpretation on the word "Historians" since a history will emerge from the collection. But then I succumbed to the reviewers' consensus like a subject in Asch's conformity experiment. Hence, we are now the *Pillars of Social Psychology*.

As a result of how I had conceived of this book, my intent at the outset was to invite notable social psychologists, starting with those who have populated the field for several decades, to write their memoir, and thereby to compile a repository of stories that provide a sense of our history. Without seeking to impose a boilerplate structure on these legendary figures, I asked them to recount how they found their way into social psychology, what the field was like at the time, who and what inspired their theories and/or research, how the field they influenced has developed over the course of their careers, where they see the field headed, and what advice if any they have for future generations. Again, it was not my desire or intent to create a structurally uniform set of chapters. These questions were designed to serve merely as guideposts. As I indicated to this star-studded group of Pillars, "You will have free rein over your personal narrative."

Introduction to the Pillars of Social Psychology

Providing an historical perspective through today's Pillars is not easy without social psychology's founders, variously born, raised, and educated in Prussia, Poland, Romania, Germany, Austria, Turkey, France, Canada, England, and elsewhere. Kurt Lewin (1890–1947), Floyd Allport (1890–1979), Fritz Heider (1896–1988), Gordon Allport (1897–1967), Muzafer Sherif (1906–1988), Carolyn Sherif Wood (1922–1982), Solomon Asch (1907–1996), Carl Hovland (1912–1961), Kenneth Clark (1914–2005), Mamie Phipps Clark (1917–1983), John Thibaut (1917–1986), Eleanor Maccoby (1917–2018), Irving Janis (1918–1990), Leon Festinger

(1919–1989), Henri Tajfel (1919–1982), Morton Deutsch (1920–2017), Harold Kelley (1921–2003), Stanley Schachter (1922–1997), Erving Goffman (1922–1982), Robert Zajonc (1923–2008), Janet Taylor Spence (1923–2015), Serge Moscovici (1925–2014), Albert Bandura (1925–2021), Ned Jones (1926–1993), Harry Triandis (1926–2019), Stanley Milgram (1933–1984), John Darley (1938–2018), Ed Diener (1946–2021), Lee Ross (1942–2021), Herbert Kelman (1927–2022), and others have passed. But as a genealogy chart would show, their students – and their students – picked up where they left off, often extending into new and important directions.

The riveting collection of memoirs in this book form a mosaic of the field as it developed and where it stands today. As a group, our contributors obtained their PhDs between the years 1956 and 1987, spanning thirty-one years. Five entered the field in the 1950s, eleven in the 1960s, twenty-five in the 1970s, and eight in the 1980s. Together, their average PhD year was 1972 – exactly fifty years ago. In chronological order, the following Pillars tell their remarkable stories.

Contributor	PhD year / Institution / Advisor
Thomas Fraser Pettigrew	1956; Harvard University; Gordon Allport
Robert Rosenthal	1956; UCLA; Bruno Klopfer
Florence Denmark	1958; University of Pennsylvania; Albert Pepitone
Elliot Aronson	1959; Stanford University; Leon Festinger
Philip G. Zimbardo	1959; Yale University; Neil Miller
Jonathan Freedman	1962; Yale University; Carl Hovland
Anthony G. Greenwald	1963; Harvard University; Gordon Allport
Elaine Hatfield	1963; Stanford University; Leon Festinger
Bibb Latané	1963; University of Minnesota; Stanley Schachter
Bernard Weiner	1963; University of Michigan; John Atkinson
Ellen Berscheid	1963; University of Minnesota; Elliot Aronson
Alice H. Eagly	1965; University of Michigan; Herbert Kelman
Richard E. Nisbett	1966; Columbia University; Stanley Schachter
Kay Deaux	1967; University of Texas; James Bieri
Wolfgang Stroebe	1968; London School of Economics; Norman Hotopf
Joel Cooper	1969; Duke University; Edward E. Jones
Michael Harris Bond	1970; Stanford University; Albert Hastorf
Robert B. Cialdini	1970; University of North Carolina, Chester Insko
Edward L. Deci	1970; Carnegie Mellon University; Daryl Bem
Phoebe C. Ellsworth	1970; Stanford University; J. Merrill Carlsmith
James M. Jones	1970; Yale University; Robert Abelson
Claude Steele	1971; Ohio State University; Thomas Ostrom
Daniel Batson	1972; Princeton University; John Darley
Carol S. Dweck	1972; Yale University; Dick Reppucci
Mark Snyder	1972; Stanford University; Daryl Bem and Philip Zimbardo
Letitia Anne Peplau	1973; Harvard University; Zick Rubin
Hazel Rose Markus	1975; University of Michigan; Robert Zajonc

Michael F. Scheier	1975; University of Texas; Arnold Buss
Margaret Clark	1977; University of Maryland; Judson Mills
John F. Dovidio	1977; University of Delaware; Samuel Gaertner
James W. Pennebaker	1977; University of Texas; Robert Wicklund
Richard E. Petty	1977; Ohio State University; Timothy Brock
Gary L. Wells	1977; Ohio State University; Anthony Greenwald
Timothy D. Wilson	1977; University of Michigan; Richard Nisbett
Roy F. Baumeister	1978; Princeton University; Edward E. Jones
Susan T. Fiske	1978; Harvard University; Shelley Taylor
Brenda Major	1978; Purdue University; Kay Deaux
William B. Swann, Jr.	1978; University of Minnesota; Mark Snyder
Rupert Brown	1979; University of Bristol; Henri Tajfel
Jennifer Crocker	1979; Harvard University; Shelley Taylor
John A. Bargh	1981; University of Michigan; Robert Zajonc
David M. Buss	1981; University of California at Berkeley; Kenneth Craik
Thomas Gilovich	1981; Stanford University; Lee Ross
Miles Hewstone	1981; Oxford University; Jos Jaspars
Daniel Gilbert	1985; Princeton University; Edward E. Jones
Mahzarin R. Banaji	1986; Ohio State University; Anthony Greenwald
Patricia G. Devine	1986; Ohio State University; Thomas Ostrom
Shinobu Kitayama	1987; University of Michigan; Robert Zajonc

Finally, I am pleased to note that many Pillars have posted some remarkable photographs. Some of these images are called out in their chapters, most were added later. These images can be found in what feels like a family photo album posted in the Resources tab of a web page created for this book (www.cambridge.org/pillarsofsocialpsychology). So, enjoy this collection of chapters; savor the stories. I will follow up afterward with my own reflections on what it all means and what lessons are to be learned from these extraordinary individuals and their careers.

Suggested Reading

Bandura, A. (1982). The psychology of chance encounters and life paths. *American Psychologist*, *37*, 747–755.

Ross, L. (2018). From the fundamental attribution error to the truly fundamental attribution error and beyond: My research journey. *Perspectives on Psychological Science*, *13*, 750–769.

2   Seven Decades in Social Psychology

Thomas Fraser Pettigrew

You could say I fell into social psychology. Growing up in Richmond, Virginia in the 1930s and 1940s, I did not know what psychology was. In my Scottish-American immigrant family, engineering was the assumed career choice for me. My father had three engineering degrees, invented new heating devices, was elected president of his national engineering association, and obviously loved his work.

My egalitarian father never suggested that I follow his career path, but I knew it would please him. So, I tried my best. I entered his alma mater, Virginia Tech, in 1948 to major in architectural engineering. Tech at the time required you to join its military corps modeled after West Point. I glumly managed the military part, but it took up so much of the day that it severely limited my study time. I survived but received the poorest grades of my life. Apart from the restricted study time, the truth is I lacked the critical skills for engineering. For instance, I could not draw well – a real handicap before personal computers if you wanted to be an architect.

I decided to switch fields and transfer to the University of Virginia (UVA). My father supported the switch and even told me that earlier he had wanted to go to the UVA himself, but had lacked the necessary funds. Needing to tell the UVA what I would major in, I took the Strong Vocational Interest Inventory (now the Strong-Campbell Interest Inventory). It required me to punch holes with a pin in a series of dichotomous choices – such as "I like to draw pictures" vs. "I like to read books." I have forgotten the results, but I was fascinated by the test itself.[1] I asked the administrator, "Who are the people who construct such tests?" He told me that psychologists developed them. That did it! I wrote the UVA that I wished to major in psychology.

Although it had only a six-man staff, the UVA had a highly regarded department of experimental psychology. The staff was strongly biased against social psychology which they regarded from their stern Vienna Circle viewpoint as too "soft" and unscientific. When I later met my old teachers at conventions, they would jokingly ask me, "How are things going in *social work*?"

Thomas Fraser Pettigrew, University of California at Santa Cruz, USA. Brief sections of this chapter are drawn in part with permission from *Contextual Social Psychology* (Pettigrew, 2021b).

[1] My interest in scales has never waned. The best known are the category width scale and the blatant and subtle prejudice scales.

Discovering Social Psychology

In 1950, I encountered social psychology. There were no social psychologists in the department; but the one course in it was ably taught by an expert on the psychology of hearing – Willard Thurlow. Kretch and Crutchfield's *Theory and Problems of Social Psychology* was the text. It featured two pointed chapters on prejudice. Because of my deep racial concerns, I knew at once that I had found the field in which to specialize.

Virtually every chapter in the text and the assigned reader fascinated me. The Newcomb-Hartley reader's seventy-five short articles covered the classics of the time: from Floyd Allport's J-curve of conformity to Sherif's emphasis on norms. Later, the psychology department appointed me an assistant in the introductory psychological course as a junior and senior – a great opportunity that led me to decide to become a university teacher.

I am also grateful to UVA for recommending me for a Rockefeller Foundation Graduate Fellowship that paid for my first year of graduate work. To be nominated for the grant, I had to undergo a stern interview with a committee of three senior and conservative professors of English and history. I worried that that they might view unfavorably my plans to venture north to Harvard to study southern racism. But, as luck and southern White culture would have it, the committee was primarily interested in my name. Did I know about the Confederate General James Johnston Pettigrew? Was I kin to him? Did I know what he did at the battle of Gettysburg? Because my father had taught me all about the general years before, I was able to answer at length their Civil War questions. I later wondered if I had obtained the scholarship more because of my name and the general than of my graduate plans!

Graduate Training

My interest in both psychology and sociology led me to apply to Harvard University's Social Relations Department where I could major in social psychology and minor in sociology. Thurlow had heard that Gordon Allport was writing a book on prejudice and, knowing my interest in race relations, recommended that I apply to Harvard. Innocently unaware of how arrogant it appeared, I wrote in my application that I wished to work with Allport on race relations, otherwise I was not interested in attending Harvard. Fortunately, Allport managed graduate admissions, and my naive impertinence did not prove fatal.

The social psychology doctoral program gave me the extraordinary opportunity to work with Allport, a warm mentor and legendary psychologist, as well as Samuel Stouffer, an inspiring sociological social psychologist who specialized in national surveys. Years later, I annually co-taught a graduate course with Talcott Parsons – a macro-scale theorist of sweeping scope whose work was dominant in the sociology of that period. Repeatedly hearing his lectures furthered my interest in social structure.

Stouffer was an exciting but unorthodox teacher. He could not have been more different from the socially shy, circumspect Allport or the expansive Parsons. Instruction from him was informal and empirical. Intensely engrossed in his work, Stouffer taught by example. You followed him from office to computing room and back, absorbing his excitement and "feel" for survey analysis. I have never lost the sense of excitement and curiosity in analyzing new survey data instilled by these memorable occasions.

Based on my southern experiences, I predicted in my thesis that authoritarianism could not explain the South's heightened racial prejudice. Both Allport and Stouffer encouraged me to pursue this topic. It was an exciting time to be working with them. Allport was writing his classic treatise on prejudice, and Stouffer was conducting national surveys on attitudes toward the fierce Senator Joseph McCarthy.

I almost committed Allport's (1954) *The Nature of Prejudice* to memory. I focused on two chapters in particular – one on conformity, which I viewed as central to southern racial behavior, and the other on the potential of intergroup contact to diminish prejudice. This began my lifelong interest in intergroup contact.

Allport and Stouffer shaped my doctoral thesis. From Allport, I learned to cast my contentions in sharper conceptual focus. From Stouffer, I learned to test them on probability samples with survey methods. In the summer of 1955, I set out with Charles Lamont, my undaunted undergraduate assistant, to sample door-to-door White racial opinions in roughly comparable small towns in the South and North in order to make a regional comparison. To deter trouble, I put Virginia license plates on my old Chevrolet.

In the most deep-South community sampled – Moultrie, Georgia – the tension was palpable. In May 1955 – just before we arrived – the Supreme Court had undercut its historic desegregation ruling with a new and vague "all deliberate speed" order. The White South viewed this order as a sign of weakness, so this second decision heightened opposition to the original decision. Resistance groups called White Citizens' Councils soon mobilized in such towns as Moultrie.

Thus, the survey schedule had to minimize recognition of its purpose. Following Stouffer's suggestion, we asked the White respondents what they thought was "*the most important problem facing the nation.*" The majority of respondents named the salient school desegregation issue as the most important. If they did not, we asked for the second most important problem – if need be, the third most important. By then, the entire sample had named racial issues. Then we introduced the racial attitude questions as a subject they themselves had introduced.

As predicted, the levels of authoritarianism were not significantly different between the southern and northern samples; and it predicted anti-Black attitudes equally well in the two regions. But at the macro-level, authoritarianism could not explain the vast difference in racial prejudice between the regions. Historical, cultural, and normative factors are needed to account for the South's far greater racial prejudice. A later national survey replicated these results.

A Visit to South Africa

In 1956, Allport obtained a grant for me to accompany him for a half-year visit to the University of Natal (now University of Kwa-Zulu Natal) in Durban, South Africa.

I had hoped to repeat my thesis study, but I could only obtain White university student respondents. I replicated my American results with one key difference. Afrikaners *were* more authoritarian as well as more prejudiced against Black Africans than other White South Africans. Still, conformity to rigorously enforced racist norms remained central. The visit had a profound effect on Allport. He stressed personality factors in his prejudice book, and thought I exaggerated the significance of racist norms. But the explicit racism of South Africa made him rethink that position. In his foreword to the abridged edition of *The Nature of Prejudice*, he wrote: "I would, on the basis of my experience in South Africa, give extra weight to the portions of this book dealing with conformity and with sociocultural factors in prejudice" (Allport, 1958, p. vii).

I came back to the United States in August of 1956 and began teaching at the University of North Carolina in Chapel Hill. A year later, I returned to Harvard's Social Relations Department.

A Focus on School Desegregation

While I had published earlier on the subject, by the late 1960s several events led me to focus on the racial desegregation of public schools. In 1966, the US Office of Education issued a tome entitled *Equality of Educational Opportunity* – better known as *"the Coleman Report"* after its sociologist author, James Coleman. Ordered by the 1964 Civil Rights Act, this sweeping look at 650,000 students and teachers and more than 3,000 schools attracted wide interest.

Together with "Pat" Moynihan – then at Harvard, later a US Senator from New York State – I co-chaired a seminar for senior Harvard staff to study and reanalyze the extensive report. A book reported on the group's findings (Mosteller & Moynihan, 1972). Coleman later reentered the school desegregation debate with the claim that it caused massive "White flight" and thus rendered the process impossible. Bolstered by these publicized assertions, conservative judges immediately used it as an excuse to roll back desegregation orders.

The "White flight" argument ignored two major points. First, the Coleman analysis was seriously flawed. While White families did move to the suburbs and private schools more during the *first year* of desegregation, it was basically a *"hastening up" effect*. That is, large urban districts that started school desegregation did not lose significantly more White students over the critical 1967–1976 period than did districts that remained racially segregated. Desegregating districts were already losing White families before the process and after a few years would have lost just as many White families without any desegregation whatsoever.

Second, the first-year loss of White people was especially acute in such huge cities as Detroit where the High Court rejected metropolitan plans for school desegregation in *Milliken v. Bradley*. But in smaller cities, such as Richmond, Virginia and Wilmington, Delaware, metropolitan plans were more feasible.

As court oversight was gradually removed, school desegregation declined. Then in 2006, the US Supreme Court reversed the historic *Brown* decision. A five-judge majority, all Republicans, held narrowly tailored desegregation plans of two school districts – Seattle, Washington and Jefferson County, Kentucky – to be in violation of the Equal Protection clause of the 14th Amendment. They ruled this because a few White children had been denied access to the schools of their first choice due to further racial desegregation and because prior state *de jure* segregation was not involved.

This far-reaching ruling prohibited assigning students to public schools solely for the purpose of achieving racial desegregation and declined to recognize racial balancing as a compelling state interest. These decisions affected hundreds of other desegregated school districts. Earlier, four lower federal courts had consistently upheld the Seattle and Jefferson County plans to be constitutional; but these rulings were overturned.

Two years before, the nation had celebrated the fiftieth anniversary of *Brown* as a great step forward in American democracy. Accordingly, the Seattle and Jefferson County cases that ended *Brown* were great steps backward for American democracy. They made *race* alone to be an unacceptable constraint for limiting school choice, while no such restrictions have ever been explicitly applied to such other categories as gender, religion, social class, and disabilities. These two decisions, together with Detroit's *Milliken* anti-metropolitan decision, marked a partial return to the 1896 infamous *Plessey v. Ferguson* racial segregation decision.

From the 1960s to 1979, I gave more than 100 speeches on school desegregation to various public audiences and published numerous popular articles on the subject. I also testified as an expert witness in federal and state courts on school desegregation in Springfield, Massachusetts, Norfolk and Richmond, Virginia, and Los Angeles, California – primarily relying on intergroup contact theory. With Kenneth Clark, I arranged to have Martin Luther King, Jr. speak at the 1967 convention of the APA. I also served on President Johnson's White House Task Force on Education in 1966.

I began to be called a "public intellectual." But, to be honest, I was quite uncomfortable in this role. I am happiest being a social psychologist, sitting at my computer analyzing survey data and writing. To be sure, I believe strongly that social psychologists should "tell what they know" on important social issues. And you gain valuable insights from these public activities. But such a public role is highly diverting, emotionally draining, and time-consuming. The political world of social policy is hot, controversial, and often divorced from the realities under debate. I learned the hard way that the mass media frequently obscure the issues in pursuit of an attention-getting scoop.[2] And legal logic contrasts sharply with scientific logic.

In 1980, I left Harvard and became a social psychology professor at the University of California at Santa Cruz (UCSC). Harvard's old Social Relations Department, a

---

[2] Consider two examples. One reporter repeatedly assured me over the phone that our discussion was "off the record." It appeared in full on the next day's editorial page. Some reporters learned that one of my adversaries in the desegregation debate was typically drunk by midnight. So, they would routinely call him at that late hour to obtain outrageous quotes that he would never have said while sober. In time, you learn which reporters and news outlets you can trust.

perfect fit for me, was closed in 1972. I regretted leaving such close friends as Herbert Kelman and Freed Bales, but I rejoined two other friends I had known at Harvard – Dane Archer and Elliot Aronson. UCSC also allowed me to take extended leaves to teach and conduct research at European universities.

Three Themes

During my long career, I have tried to contribute to the development of social psychology along three interrelated themes: (1) norms, conformity, and authoritarianism in intergroup prejudice and discrimination; (2) social comparison processes – especially relative deprivation theory; and (3) intergroup contact.

(1) *Norms and Conformity.* From my 1956 thesis to the present, I have studied intergroup prejudice and discrimination throughout the world. Based on growing up in Virginia in the 1930s and 1940s, I began by stressing conformity to racist norms and the role of authoritarianism. More recently, I have viewed these subjects in a three-level contextual framework – the micro (individual), meso (interactive), and macro (structural) levels (Pettigrew, 2021b).

(2) *Relative Deprivation (RD).* Stouffer's use of this theory in the *American Soldier* studies intrigued me. Then the 1966 book on the subject by the British social psychologist Walter Runciman ignited further interest for both me and my Harvard graduate students. At their suggestion, we formed an informal, non-credit, weekly seminar on the subject. Two members of this group went on to make major contributions to the theory – David Gartrell and Joanne Martin. Two other graduate students – Heather Smith and Iain Walker, from a similar group at UCSC – also have greatly furthered the theory's development. Completing my work on RD, an extensive meta-analysis demonstrated the solid effects that RD has on a range of important phenomena (Smith et al., 2012), and that RD functions in similar fashion across nations worldwide (Smith et al., 2018).

(3) *Intergroup Contact.* Allport's chapter on contact and my own early interracial contact led me to take my doctoral special exam on the subject. The test was administered and graded by Allport himself. But his contact chapter's broad and discursive discussion made it difficult to prepare for the examination. So, I boiled the text down to four key factors that enabled intergroup contact to reduce prejudice: (a) equal status between the groups within the situation, (b) common goals, (c) cooperation between groups, and (d) authority support for the contact.

Allport approved of my synthesis, and I used it with his endorsement in later publications. These four factors are now routinely cited as Allport's contact theory even though they are not in his chapter. Yet there are limitations to this approach. It is a "positive factors" approach that proved to be too narrow. Allport assumed that intergroup contact typically *failed* to reduce prejudice. So, he sought to make explicit positive factors that were *necessary* for contact to diminish prejudice.

This approach led writers to add more factors presumed to be required for intergroup contact to have positive results. As the supposedly necessary conditions accumulated, the theory risked becoming meaningless. The ever-increasing list of "necessary" conditions excluded most of the world's intergroup situations. Social psychologists were concentrating on avoiding Type I errors and ignoring Type II errors. My meta-analysis of intergroup contact effects with Tropp later uncovered another limitation of the necessary factors approach – they are highly facilitating but not absolutely necessary (Pettigrew & Tropp, 2006).

The 1960s and 1970s witnessed increasing attention to contact theory as its policy implications became more evident. In 1998, I published in the *Annual Review of Psychology* a reformulated theory of intergroup contact. It emphasized input from various levels of analysis and the time dimension – from initial contact to established contact and finally to a unified single group.

By 2000, it became possible to conduct an extensive meta-analysis of intergroup contact effects (Pettigrew & Tropp, 2006). We uncovered 515 studies with 713 independent samples that met our inclusion rules. These studies span from 1941 to 2000 and contain responses from more than 250,000 participants. The average effect for all studies was $r = -.21$ (Cohen's $d = -.41$). This effect cannot be explained away by participant selection, publication bias, sampling biases, or poorly conducted research. The most rigorous studies actually provide the largest positive effects.

The basic finding is not confined to just those outgroup members who directly participated in the contact. The primary generalization typically extends from the immediate outgroup members who participate in the contact to the entire outgroup. This effect is enhanced when the contact situation makes participants' group identities salient, and when the outgroup members are seen as typical of their group. Contact's effects also normally extend to situations different from the original contact situation. And effective intergroup contact has many positive outcomes in addition to diminishing bias – from supporting pro-minority social policies to participating in collective action on behalf of minority causes.

The review also uncovered evidence for the apparent universality of intergroup contact phenomena across varied settings, ages, and thirty-eight nations throughout the world. We also found significant contact effects for groups that differ in race, ethnicity, nationality, sexual orientation, and physical and mental disabilities. This overall positive trend is remarkably consistent. The universality of the intergroup contact phenomenon suggests that this process reflects the fact that familiarity generally leads to liking – Zajonc's mere exposure effect.

To my surprise and delight, our meta-analysis triggered an enormous increase in intergroup contact research studies around the world. The theory was stretched in new directions. Five general types of indirect contact can diminish prejudice without actually meeting physically: (1) *the secondary transfer effect* to groups not in the original contact situation, (2) *extended contact* – having an ingroup friend who has an outgroup friend, (3) *imagined contact*, (4) *impersonal media contact*, and (5) *virtual contact through computer-generated communication*. Meta-analyses now support each of these contact types as effective prejudice-reducing techniques (Pettigrew, 2021a).

Some commentators wonder whether intergroup contact phenomena operate in areas with intense conflict. But repeated studies show positive results from intergroup contact in such embattled areas as Northern Ireland, Israel, Cyprus, and South Africa. Of course, not all intergroup contact reduces prejudice. Some adverse contact enhances prejudice. But respondents report far more positive than negative contact, and they are best studied together. Both positive and negative contact influence affective dimensions of prejudice, but negative contact has especially strong effects on such cognitive dimensions as stereotypes. Thus, intergroup contact theory – after more than 1,000 studies and eight meta-analyses – has become a major component in the social psychological arsenal of ideas and theories.

These three themes unite as important predictors of the 2016 presidential vote for Trump. Right-wing supporters were significantly more authoritarian, more relatively deprived, and far less likely to have had intergroup contact. These same predictors also proved to be predictive of far-right voting in Europe and the pro-Brexit vote in the United Kingdom (Pettigrew, 2021b).

A Final Word on the Discipline's Developing Global Reach

Today's social psychologists would barely recognize their discipline when I entered it in 1950. Many major universities had no social psychologists on their staffs; only two journals were dedicated to the field; and the discipline of psychology generally held it in low esteem. Moreover, World War II had severely set back the field's development in Europe. I have been greatly heartened over my seven decades in the discipline to witness its rapid growth.

There was a small, flourishing, social psychology in the United States and Europe before World War II. But social psychological programs were not only small but limited largely to North America and Europe. Slowly, following the war, work in the discipline spread throughout much of the world. Finally, by the close of the twentieth century, social psychology had well-established centers throughout much of the world. Often these pioneering social psychologists received their doctorates in North America or Europe, then returned to their homelands to continue their research and teaching. For example, Vanessa Smith-Castro, Professor of Social Psychology at the University of Costa Rica, is fluent in German, English, and Spanish and obtained her doctorate from Germany's University of Marburg.

This broader reach is now routinely reflected in the discipline's publications. David Myers's popular social psychology text has been translated and sold throughout the world with almost one million copies sold in China alone (Myers, personal communication). My book, *Contextual Social Psychology*, cites research from more than fifty different nations. This great variety provides many different cultural and normative contexts for the social psychological processes under study. This offers the opportunity to test just how culturally biased the discipline's basic theory and findings are. The same basic trends are emerging across this new extensive sampling of the world. Varying social contexts, of course, influence these universal trends, but they rarely reverse them.

Consider two examples of cross-national universalism. Susan Fiske's stereotype content model with its focus on competence and warmth operates similarly across vastly different cultures. Second, numerous studies have shown the existence of two different but intercorrelated types of intergroup prejudice – blatant and subtle. Initial measures of these two types were developed using survey data from Western Europe. They have now been successfully employed about different outgroups in many other nations – from Bolivia and Chile to South Africa and Australia. It can now be stated with confidence that social psychological findings and theory are not limited to just Europe and the United States.

Suggested Reading

Allport, G. W. (1954). *The Nature of Prejudice*. Reading, MA: Addison-Wesley.
  (1958). *The Nature of Prejudice*. Abridged edition. New York: Anchor Books.
Mosteller, F., & Moynihan, D. P. (Eds.) (1972). *On Equality of Educational Opportunity*. New York: Random House.
Pettigrew, T. F. (2021a). Advancing intergroup contact theory: Comments on the issue's papers. *Journal of Social Issues, 77*, 258–293.
  (2021b). *Contextual Social Psychology: Reanalyzing Prejudice, Voting, and Intergroup Contact*. Washington, DC: American Psychological Association Press.
Pettigrew, T. F., & Tropp, L. (2006). A meta-analytic test of intergroup contact theory. *Journal of Personality and Social Psychology, 90*, 1–33.
Smith, H. J., Pettigrew, T. F., Pippin, G., & Bialosiewicz, S. (2012). Relative deprivation: A theoretical and meta-analytic critique. *Personality and Social Psychology Review, 16*(3), 203–232.
Smith, H. J., Ryan, D., Jaurique, A., Pettigrew, T. F., Jetten, J., et al. (2018). Cultural values moderate the impact of relative deprivation. *Journal of Cross-Cultural Psychology, 49*(8), 1183–1218.

3   A Career Emerging from an Unnecessary Analysis

Robert Rosenthal

I retired a couple of years ago as a kid in my mid-80s. But I hadn't stopped working. We have a yearlong seminar at UC Riverside, a statistical consulting course. Graduate students can enroll for credit, and we have six or seven faculty members who attend throughout the entire academic year. On Tuesdays from noon to 1 p.m., we would bring data analytic or other methodological questions to that group.

For over twenty years, just about since I got here, I was the secretary for that group. I kept the books and did the advertising and helped people to make up titles for their presentations. And it's a course for credit. So, although I'm an emeritus professor, I'm also an active-duty professor with a new title: Professor of the Graduate Division. One of my great colleagues who was the first to have that title is Howard Friedman, the well-known researcher of nonverbal behavior. He was a Harvard student; he took my courses. But alas, he was not my PhD student. I wish he had been, but now he has the same title. Howard actively participates in the work of the department. He has been here since 1976, making him the longest running academic in our department here at UC Riverside.

I know people have a hard time believing I am still active in these ways. But it's wonderful. I just love to do it. Recently, I received an email from Milan, Italy. There's a university there I hadn't heard of, and they're doing a meta-analysis. And they have a meta-analytic question for me. I just got that question yesterday. And I will have some fun answering that question. I do a lot of informal consulting. And then, sometimes I consult by telephone, too. For the first time ever, I had almost a yearlong seminar with a high school junior who is in an advanced placement (AP) program. I was her external faculty advisor. She was doing a meta-analysis. This was not a one-shot consulting thing. She would send me drafts and ask questions. At 16 years old, she has to be the youngest meta-analyst that I know (and the largest age spread between two people working together on a meta-analysis).

This is the present. Let me now step back in time. I was born in 1933 in Giessen, Germany. We lived in Limburg until 1938 and then left for Cologne, a larger city that afforded greater anonymity (it had become too dangerous for Jews to live in a town where everyone knew who the Jews were and where they lived). Then in 1939, with Hitler in power, we left Germany. We could not get into the United States at the time

Robert Rosenthal, University of California at Riverside, USA. This chapter came about through a joint effort that began when Saul Kassin interviewed me by phone and later composed a first draft.

because of a quota on immigration, but my parents knew that we had to get out as fast as possible. So we boarded a ship as refugees and headed for Rhodesia, then a British protectorate colony that is now Zimbabwe.

We left for the east coast of the United States in 1940. I spent my elementary school years at PS 89 in Queens, New York, then on to Newtown High School, where I ran my first experiment ever – on parapsychology. More on that later. In my senior year, my family moved to Los Angeles. I applied to UCLA's Naval Reserve Officers Training Corps and spent a couple of years there as a beginning naval officer. At that point, I attended the University of California, Los Angeles, where I received my BA in 1953 and my PhD in clinical psychology in 1956.

My Start as a Clinical Psychologist

I was trained and deeply rooted in clinical psychology. My graduate school mentor, Bruno Klopfer, was mentored by the legendary Carl Jung (true to my roots, I did my dissertation research on defense mechanisms). I spent almost four years, predoctoral and postdoctoral, as a full-time clinician at various clinics and VA hospitals in the greater LA area. Then I took an academic position in the PhD program in clinical psychology at University of North Dakota. There were only three faculty members when I got there. It was a wonderful experience to help build a clinical program. It was fun, though the teaching load was five courses each semester. I was also active in the North Dakota Psychological Association and was elected to serve as its president.

After my time in North Dakota, which included a one-year interlude at Ohio State University, I accepted a non-tenure track five-year appointment at Harvard, where I spent thirty-six great years from 1962 to 1999. I went there in the clinical program, in part as a replacement for Timothy Leary, the controversial researcher who used and promoted LSD and other psychedelic drugs for their allegedly therapeutic effects. Leary was fired in 1963. Once I arrived at Harvard, I taught introduction to clinical psychology, psycho-diagnostics, and psychotherapy. Everything I did was clinical. In fact, I think I'd only taken one course in social psychology and that was as an undergraduate at UCLA. And yet, after five years in clinical, I was offered a tenured position in social. How that happened is an interesting story.

From Clinical into Social: The Story of an Unnecessary Analysis

It all grew out of my doctoral dissertation and an unnecessary statistical analysis that I did. My dissertation was on projection, the defense mechanism that Harvard professor Henry Murray studied using the Thematic Apperception Test, or TAT, the projective test that he and Christiana Morgan developed in the 1930s (for an historical overview, see Morgan, 2002). Using photographs of faces, Murray had done an informal study at his daughter's birthday party and observed that children judged the faces to be more fearful or frightening if the children had been playing a game called Murder as compared to an ordinary birthday party activity.

The idea of using faces in this way intrigued me, so for my dissertation at UCLA I gathered a bunch of photographs from magazines of people who looked neither successful nor unsuccessful. My goal was to pretest everybody on how successful or unsuccessful they saw each face. With samples of 36 college females, 36 college males, and 36 paranoid schizophrenic patients, I showed each individual subject one photo at a time (the reason for testing paranoid schizophrenic patients is that projection is a hallmark of the disorder). After pretesting the three groups for their base ratings, I gave them either a success experience, a failure experience, or a neutral experience. My hypothesis was that these experiences would taint how much success they saw in a new set of faces.

With guidance from Joseph Gengerelli, a hardnosed member of my committee and an intellectual hero of mine, I analyzed the data, found some support for my hypothesis, and defended the dissertation, which was accepted. But then, the rest of my career would follow from an unnecessary statistical analysis. I decided to do a separate analysis of the pretest data that was extraneous to the purpose of the research. At that point, the success and failure treatments had not been administered so there should have been no differences among the three groups. Yet what I found were whopping significant differences on the pretest. How can that happen, I wondered. They hadn't had the treatment. But the experimenter (me) knew what the treatment was going to be. I analyzed this pretest, found these huge differences, and thought, "Oh, my goodness." I wrote it up and first used the term experimenter bias in my 1956 doctoral dissertation. I should note that the success and failure groups' instructions had been identical during the pretreatment rating phase of the experiment. The problem, apparently, was that I knew for each subject which experimental treatment he or she would subsequently be administered. As I noted in my dissertation, with some dismay, "The implication is that in some subtle manner, perhaps by tone, or manner, or gestures, or general atmosphere, the experimenter, although formally testing the success and failure groups in an identical way, influenced the success subjects to make lower initial ratings and thus increase the experimenter's probability of verifying his hypothesis" (Rosenthal, 1956, p. 44).

Maybe because misery loves company, I became determined to see if this was a general phenomenon. So I ran a whole bunch of experiments at University of North Dakota that showed, yes, by golly, this is a general phenomenon. The experimenter bias effect was an unintended byproduct of my dissertation. I even incorporated a section on it. A few years later, my North Dakota graduate student and I reported on what we called experimenter bias effects in the training of albino rats to run a maze (Rosenthal & Fode, 1963); a few years after that, Lenore Jacobson, an elementary school principal in South San Francisco, and I found teacher expectancy effects on schoolchildren's academic performance, which we wrote about in *Pygmalion in the Classroom* (Rosenthal & Jacobson, 1968).

Let me get back to those albino rats. During my year at Ohio State, I taught a seminar on experimenter bias, and I speculated as well about interpersonal expectancy effects more generally. In addition to some wonderful students who took my seminar, I was fortunate to have a faculty colleague who sat in on the course. He was a Skinnerian learning theorist named Reed Lawson. He said, "Well, yes, I can even understand how you got that rat result because there's so much handling of the animal that the experimenter might communicate something by the way they handled the rat." With that, he insisted that an experimenter effect would not be found in conditioning experiments using a Skinner box, where the experimenter did not handle the rats much at all, just put them in the box, shaped their behavior, and took them out. So, I said, "Okay, how about we collaborate and try it out on your Skinnerian way?" So we did a second rat study and we replicated the same effect. The so-called bright rats conditioned more quickly – and their experimenters reported being more engaged in the experiment. What happened, we think, is that experimenters with allegedly bright vs. dull rats interpreted ambiguous movements accordingly, and reinforced correct responses more quickly, which facilitated learning (Rosenthal & Lawson, 1964).

My Start at Harvard

Let me also now get back to how I found my way from an untenured position in Harvard's clinical program and into a tenured position in social. Upon arriving at Harvard in 1962, I met a young and brilliant social psychologist, also untenured, by the name of Stanley Milgram. Stanley had received his PhD there in 1961 with Gordon Allport as his advisor. Then he accepted a position at Yale but returned to Harvard for a four-year stint. Harvard junior faculty had little hope or prospect of getting tenure. That was well known. Stanley and I became friends. In 1963 he published his instantly famous but controversial "Behavioral Study of Obedience." Then in 1964, Diana Baumrind published her critique of this study and he spent a good deal of time drafting a reply.

The most amazing thing I remember about Stanley Milgram goes to our very first meeting. When I arrived, we were in different buildings. So, I didn't know him. Then the new William James Hall opened up and we were both assigned offices on the 14th floor. We had never met before and I barely knew what he looked like. We were barely moved in when he came down the hall toward me. As he got right up in front of me, he stopped, clicked his heels, and gave me a Nazi-like salute. I was astonished. He never tried to explain it but after I got to know him I figured that it was something of a brethren gesture: You and I are both Jewish, these Nazis tried to kill us, Hitler is now dead, and we are alive and teaching at Harvard. (Like others who knew Stanley and his research, I also came to appreciate that he loved theater and had quite a theatrical streak.)

Stanley and I had a noncompetitive relationship. He was in the social psychology program, I was in clinical. Then a tenured position opened for a professorship in social for which Stanley was ideally suited. He should have gotten that position but didn't. His work was stirring too much controversy about research ethics, much of it unwarranted. Instead, they gave the position to me. And I wasn't even a social psychologist.

Although I had already accepted a job at Northwestern, which was attractive to me because Don Campbell was there (he was a hero and mentor to me from a distance). But Harvard's offer with tenure was too good to pass up. I remember so well my next interaction with Stanley. He was a very direct guy. He came up to me, looked me right in the eye, and said, "I don't think you're the greatest social psychologist in the world." And I paused and I said, "I agree with you. I think you are." And that was true. At the time, I did think that he was probably the most outstanding social psychologist in the world – not just for the work that he had done, but justified by the work he did afterwards. Anyway, he left to go to the Graduate Center at the City University of New York and we made peace. In fact, in his first year there, he invited me to come and give a talk at the Graduate Center, which I did, then my wife and I had dinner with him and his wife at their home.

The Pygmalion Study

Starting in the mid-1960s, the next step in my research program was to move from studying rats to studying schoolchildren, which brings me to an important figure in my history, Lenore Jacobson. At that point, I had run dozens of studies of experimenter bias using animals and humans. Wanting to make sense of these data sets was how I got interested in meta-analysis. Then in an article I published in the *American Scientist*, in 1963, I reviewed that research and closed with a dramatic practical question: "When the master teacher tells his apprentice that a pupil appears to be a slow learner, is this prophecy then self-fulfilled?" (Rosenthal, 1963, p. 280).

A few weeks after this article was published, I received a letter from Lenore Jacobson, an unlikely correspondent who was principal of a school in South San Francisco, the Spruce School. She said, "Well, when you're ready to graduate to children, have I got a school for you!" So, I got right on the phone, and I called Hank Riecken, the head of the National Science Foundation, Social Science Wing. NSF had been funding my research. I called to see if I could use the balance of funds in my grant to do this study with humans. Always wonderfully supportive, he said, "Yeah, you go ahead."

Within a few weeks of her letter, I was flying out to San Francisco to meet with Lenore to design the study. There were six grades in the school, within each grade there was a fast-track, a medium-track, and a slow-track class. And we got a hold of an IQ test that we were pretty sure that none of the teachers had ever seen – the Flanagan Test of General Ability. We removed the covers of each of the 300-plus tests and replaced them with a new cover that read: "Harvard Test of Inflected Acquisition." At the end of the school year in which we planned the study, all teachers were told that there was a new test from Harvard University that predicted academic blooming in schoolchildren. They were then asked to administer the test to the children in their classrooms. In the fall, when each teacher had just begun classes with their new students, we went to each of our eighteen teachers and said, "You remember that test of intellectual blooming that you administered at the end of last school year? Well, we thought you'd like to know, which are the kids in your new class scored as students poised to bloom intellectually this year." And with that, we gave each teacher the names of from three to six children, chosen completely at random. As reported in Rosenthal and Jacobson's (1968) *Pygmalion in the Classroom*, and in its 1992 updating, the children whose names had been given to their teachers as intellectual bloomers gained significantly more IQ points than did the children in the control group about whom nothing had been told to their teachers.

I'll add two points to the Pygmalion research. First, the idea behind this study was in no way original. One of the things I ran into that I had not heard about was a 1964 book called *Youth in the Ghetto*, or the HARYOU Report, a book about working with kids in Harlem. Kenneth Clark could have been one of the chapter authors – and he proposed exactly what we did, though in the negative, that teacher expectations predicted (and could adversely affect) a student's academic performance. The second point is that interpersonal expectancy effects were reliable and robust. In 1978, Don Rubin and I published a meta-analysis of 345 data studies of interpersonal expectancy effects. The studies varied – involving reaction time tasks, inkblot tests, animal conditioning, laboratory interviews, psychophysical judgments, learning and ability, person perception, and everyday life situations. This research was later extended from experimenters in the animal and human laboratory to teachers, employers, and therapists whose expectations for pupils, employees, and patients may also set into motion interpersonal self-fulfilling prophecies.

Looking Back

Although I set out at UCLA to become a clinical psychologist, an identity I took with me to North Dakota, Ohio State, and my first five years at Harvard, the happenstance that followed from an unintended dissertation data analysis ultimately led me into social psychology. In my second year at Harvard, I was in a small building called the Center for Research in Personality. The Center was headed up by David McClelland. Other colleagues there included Irv Gottesman and Brendan Maher. I then spent from 1967 to 1999 in the social program at Harvard, where I had Gordon Allport as a colleague, Roger Brown, Tom Pettigrew, and Herb Kelman, a warm and wonderful guy.

Over the years, my research branched out in two ways. First my students, colleagues, and I moved from demonstrating the interpersonal expectancy effect across a range of domains, to trying to identify the verbal and nonverbal mechanisms by which these effects came about. I became particularly interested in nonverbal behavior, the inferences observers draw from "thin slices" of such behavior, and the role it plays in mediating these interpersonal expectancy effects. This type of covert communication and influence can be seen not only in the laboratory and in the classroom, but also in health clinics, courtrooms, the military, and corporate work settings. This focus was evident in the work of Judith Hall, one of my many prized PhD students who went on to become a Distinguished Professor at Northeastern University. Then there was

Nalini Ambady, Bella DePaulo, Robin DiMatteo, Alan Hart, and others too numerous to mention. Without a doubt, my proudest contribution to psychology exists in the list of fifty-three PhD students I have been privileged to advise over the years.

The second direction my work took, which could have been predicted by the unnecessary but transformative analysis of pretest data that I conducted for my dissertation, was the importance of research methodology and statistics. Over the years, I have written extensively about issues pertaining to data collection and analysis – much of it with my good friends and colleagues, Ralph Rosnow and Don Rubin. In 1984, for example, Rosnow and I published the first of three editions of *Essentials of Behavioral Research: Methods and Data Analysis* (the third edition was published in 2008); Rubin and I published several papers on meta-analytic procedures in *Psychological Bulletin*. In addition, we all have written about such topics as effect size estimation, the interpretation of statistical interaction effects, the implications of using volunteer subjects in research, and the file drawer problem.

I should add that meta-analysis as we know it today came not only from my work (I had used a form of meta-analysis in a 1966 book I wrote on experimenter effects in behavioral research), but from quantitative psychologist Gene V. Glass, who coined the term in 1976 and later used the procedure to compare educational outcomes and psychotherapy outcomes. That said, I want to give true credit where true credit is due. We were both scooped by many years by Karl Pearson (1904) who, to my knowledge, did the first meta-analysis of correlations between typhoid and mortality and the inoculation status of British soldiers.

Thoughts on Becoming a Social Psychologist Today

After retiring from Harvard in 1999, I accepted a position at the University of California at Riverside. People retire in different ways. I continued to teach. I kept teaching because I enjoyed it – and I was good at it. In fact, I continued to receive university-wide teaching and mentoring awards into my 70s and 80s. And then something happened in 2018 or 2019 that led me to retire. Every year, faculty at UC Riverside, as elsewhere, received post-course student evaluations, which for mine were always high. After this one semester, I got my ratings back and they were barely above the average, a drop of about two standard deviations. Listening to the data, I went to the department chair that week and announced that "I'm retiring."

Part of the problem, I think, is that I had become hopelessly out of date in terms of data analysis. I had reached a point where my graduate students did all the computing for me. And this leads me to a point of advice for up-and-coming social psychologists. Thanks to the ready availability of digital software packages, I think it is too easy for students today to lose sight of what it is they are computing; too often they don't really understand the statistics.

For someone starting out today, the other point of advice I would have is to get to know psychology and related disciplines broadly before deciding on social (as an undergraduate, I took courses in sociology, biology, and genetics). In my case, I had also become interested in parapsychology in high school by reading Joseph B. Rhine, the botanist who founded parapsychology, studied ESP, and opened a parapsychology lab at Duke University. I did Rhine-like experiments while at Newtown High School in 1948–1949. Then, later in life, in the 1980s and 1990s, I published a handful of articles on experimenter expectancy effects, meta-analysis, effect size estimation, replicability, and the file drawer problem in parapsychology research. You never really know where you are headed so it helps to be broadly prepared.

Closing Thoughts

The social and behavioral sciences are currently engaged in vigorous discussion of the topic of replication and its importance to the progress of our sciences. That makes me very happy because I have been fascinated by that topic for many years and had a chapter on replication in my 1966 book on experimenter effects. Let me then close with a suggestion of three dimensions or variables relevant to this discussion. The three dimensions are:

(1) The *target* of the replication: This could be (a) a single study, or (b) the meta-analytically combined results of two or more studies, or (c) both individual and meta-analytically combined studies.
(2) The *metrics* of the replication: This could be (a) p-values, usually expressed as standard normal deviates, the Z associated with the p-values, (b) effect sizes such as d, g, or r, or (c) both p-values and effect sizes.
(3) The *measurement level* of replication outcome: This could be (a) dichotomous – did or did not replicate, or (b) continuous – degree of replication success or failure, or (c) both dichotomous and continuous measures.

The three levels of (a), (b), and (c) for each of the three dimensions (target, metrics, and measurement) produce the 27 cubes of a $3 \times 3 \times 3$ design of which my favorite little cube is the one in which we examine both targets, both metrics, and both types of measurement.

Last word out the door: It would make conducting replications more interesting, more informative, more truly cumulative, and a lot more fun if, whenever we did it we added at least one new variable, such as new treatment condition, that would advance our understanding of the effects being replicated regardless of the degree to which the replication portion of our "Replication-Plus-One" study supports the findings of the original target research.

Suggested Reading

Ambady, N., & Rosenthal, R. (1992). Thin slices of expressive behavior as predictors of interpersonal consequences: A meta-analysis. *Psychological Bulletin, 111*(2), 256–274.

Glass, G. V. (1976). Primary, secondary, and meta-analysis of research. *Educational Researcher*, *5*(10), 3–8.

Milgram, S. (1963). Behavioral study of obedience. *Journal of Abnormal and Social Psychology*, *67*(4), 371–378.

Morgan, W. (2002). Origin and history of the earliest thematic apperception test. *Journal of Personality Assessment*, *79*(3), 422–445.

Pearson, K. (1904). Report on certain enteric fever inoculation statistics. *British Medical Journal*, *3*, 1243-1246.

Rosenthal, R. (1956). An attempt at the experimental induction of the defense mechanism of projection. Unpublished doctoral dissertation, University of California at Los Angeles.

(1963). On the social psychology of the psychological experiment: The experimenter's hypothesis as unintended determinant of experimental results. *American Scientist*, *51*(2), 268–283.

(1966). *Experimenter Effects in Behavioral Research*. New York: Appleton.

(1978). Combining results of independent studies. *Psychological Bulletin*, *85*(1), 185–193.

(1994). Interpersonal expectancy effects: A 30-year perspective. *Current Directions in Psychological Science*, *3*(6), 176–179.

(2003). Covert communication in laboratories, classrooms, and the truly real world. *Current Directions in Psychological Science*, *12*(5), 151–154.

Rosenthal, R., & Fode, K. L. (1963). The effect of experimenter bias on the performance of the albino rat. *Behavioral Science*, *8*(3), 183–189.

Rosenthal, R., & Jacobson, L. (1968). *Pygmalion in the Classroom: Teacher Expectation and Pupils' Intellectual Development*. New York: Holt, Rinehart & Winston.

Rosenthal, R., & Lawson, R. (1964). A longitudinal study of the effects of experimenter bias on the operant learning of laboratory rats. *Journal of Psychiatric Research*, *2*(2), 61–72.

Rosenthal, R., & Rosnow, R. L. (2008). *Essentials of Behavioral Research: Methods and Data Analysis* (3rd ed.). New York: McGraw-Hill.

Rosenthal, R., & Rubin, D. B. (1978). Interpersonal expectancy effects: The first 345 studies. *Behavioral and Brain Sciences*, *1*(3), 377–415.

(1986). Meta-analytic procedures for combining studies with multiple effect sizes. *Psychological Bulletin*, *99*(3), 400–406.

4 Once a Social Psychologist, Always a Social Psychologist

Florence Denmark

I grew up in a large family home in Philadelphia, Pennsylvania. I was always a pretty good student, graduating at the top of my class in high school in 1948. I was eager to begin the next chapter of my academic life as I began in the College for Women at the University of Pennsylvania. Though there were a number of women in my undergraduate class, it always seemed to me that many of them were attending college in the hopes of finding an intelligent husband. On the other hand, while I saw no problem with their dreams of a white picket fence, I loved being enmeshed by the university environment and knew from early on that my future would involve pursuing further education, and hopefully that would lead to an exciting life that would advance the field of psychology.

When attending the University of Pennsylvania as an undergrad, I was a high achieving student, and completed two honors theses in four years. One of these theses was in American history, a subject in which I had always been interested. I wrote about Amelia Bloomer, a woman who revolutionized the way that women could participate in the male dominated workforce by inventing the bloomers, a pantaloon-like garment to be worn under a woman's skirt. This seemingly simple invention allowed women the freedom of movement that they required to participate in activities previously seen as unfit for proper women of the day. With her invention, women were able to make headway into sectors of life and work where the restrictions of their clothing had never previously allowed them.

After completing my honors thesis in American history I found myself ready to tackle another field, and shifted my focus to psychology. I had taken an undergraduate level social psychology course taught by Albert Pepitone, who had recently come to the University of Pennsylvania after studying group dynamics under the great Kurt Lewin. Drs. Pepitone and Lewin's work inspired me greatly. The mentorship of Albert Pepitone began to shape my interest in human behavior and psychology. With his guidance, I completed my second thesis of undergrad, this time in social psychology. Reflecting much of my later work, which largely focused on social behavior of women, my second thesis was written about a study I conducted to observe how men and women experience conformity and how each of these groups adheres to authority figures, specifically noting similarities and differences between them. The

Florence Denmark, Pace University, USA.

pervasive thinking of the time hypothesized that women would conform to authority figures more than would men. To test this, I completed a research study using University of Pennsylvania sorority and fraternity presidents and members. Contrary to the contemporary beliefs, the results of my study did not show that there was a difference between the frequency that men and women conformed to their Greek life president. This study was the first I conducted in social psychology, but certainly wasn't the last and represented an important turning point in my life's path.

Upon graduating from the University of Pennsylvania in 1952, I began to prepare for the next step, graduate school. Though I had enjoyed my social psychology course, and working with Dr. Pepitone during my undergrad studies, I only applied to graduate programs in clinical psychology. At the time I thought clinical research would be better fit for me. The summer after graduating I was set to continue my studies in psychology at Duke University in Durham, North Carolina, when I met my first husband who was completing his dental degree at the University of Pennsylvania dental school. Changing plans last minute, I applied belatedly to the University of Pennsylvania clinical psychology graduate program and was not only accepted, but was granted a teaching and research assistantship.

The field of clinical psychology proved not to be a great fit for me with my inquisitive personality. In one of my early graduate classes I was required to administer the Rorschach technique and interpret the results. By this point the students in my class and I had learned how to score the Rorschach but had not yet learned how to interpret the results of those scores. To complete this assignment I wrote a largely imaginative story that featured a made up interpretation. To my great dismay when I got my assignment back the instructor had given me full marks and the comment "you have the makings of a fine clinician." Upon receiving this feedback on a paper that I felt had more in common with a fairy tale writer than good scientific work, I was upset. My interest in clinical psychology began waning at that point.

A part of the University of Pennsylvania's clinical program at this time included working in the psychological clinic at the school. One day, a young woman came to the clinic complaining of problems with her mother. She confided in me, and I responded with clear directions on how the young woman should proceed. She appeared to understand and agree with my plan of action. When the woman left my office that day, I felt proud for solving the problem, and for delivering such sound clinical advice. However, the next week, much to my chagrin, the young woman was back at the clinic with the same problems she'd had with her mother the week before. It felt like we were back at square one and my interest in clinical psychology waned further. I realized that to be a good clinician I would have to be comfortable making very slow progress and could not expect people to follow my advice or directives. No matter how competent the advice was.

I could no longer deny that my interest lay more in psychological research than in practice. I realized that social psychology was probably a much better fit. I officially made the fateful decision to switch from clinical psychology to social psychology and let the University's program director know. Luckily this decision would not set back my graduate studies at all. Within the offered psychology PhD programs, students could fairly easily switch from one field of study to another because each of the programs opened with the same basic psychology courses. However, it would have been impossible for me to switch to industrial organizational psychology because at the University of Pennsylvania it was considered a masculine occupation, and no women were admitted to the program.

After switching to social psychology, I reconnected with Albert Pepitone through his various courses. Pepitone became an important mentor who introduced me to group dynamics, the area of study in which I truly found my footing. My doctoral dissertation was a test of two theories of group dynamics, Authoritarian Personality Theory and Social Comparison Theory. Though I was always interested in women's issues, the participants in this study were all men. At this time at the University of Pennsylvania, there were five times as many undergraduate men as women, making it much easier to recruit men for the study. After being given a personality test to determine how authoritarian their personality was, the participants would find themselves face-to-face with two confederates who were trained by the researchers to take the opposite stance from the participant on a given issue. These confederates would attempt to influence the participant to agree with this opposing stance. The study investigated if the participant would shift their belief toward the confederate. This would support Social Comparison Theory, but if the participant had an authoritarian personality, the participant would stick with their original position, proving the strength of the Authoritarian Personality Theory. In the end, the results showed that the participants could be swayed to agree with the confederates no matter what their scores were on the personality measures. With these results Social Comparison Theory prevailed.

After obtaining my social psychology PhD in 1958, my first husband and I had our three children in quick succession, the first, Valerie, and a set of twins, a boy named Richard and a girl named Pamela, while my husband opened and grew his dental practice. Shortly after the birth of our first daughter, I began working part-time as an adjunct instructor, teaching in the evenings at Queens College, part of the City University of New York (CUNY) system. Always ready to take on another task, I also worked part-time at the Testing and Counseling Office. It was there where I first had the opportunity to team up with a social psychologist named Marcia Guttentag on a study funded by the US Department of Education. This study, which focused on the effects of racial integration, took place in Manhasset, Long Island where there were three elementary schools, one Black and two White. Marcia and I used this grant to study the effect that racial integration had on the students' grades and self-perceptions before and after. The results of this study showed integration had a positive effect on the grades and self-perceptions of both Black and White children. Not only was this study important to the field of education, but it was personally exciting for me because it was a great opportunity to use my social psychology degree while making way for positive social changes in the world.

Mary Reuder, who had overseen the evening program at Queens College at the time, was impressed with all that I had taken on and my abilities in those roles. Wanting to help advance my career, she had kept her eyes open for a way to hire me to be a full-time faculty member at Queens College. Unfortunately, no positions had come available during my few years there working as an adjunct professor, nor were any positions expected to become available in the near future. Mary suggested that I apply to one of the teaching positions available at CUNY's Hunter College. Though Queens had been a great place for me to start my career, I wanted to put myself in a position to grow, and that meant being on a tenured track.

I was hired at Hunter College in 1964 as a full-time instructor and in my first years there I was assigned to teach courses in general psychology, statistics, and a few different courses on child psychology. In those first years, I was not, however, offered the chance to teach a course in social psychology. One child psych course that I got to teach was called The Exceptional Child. This course was particularly interesting because it was a relatively new class and could be molded however I saw fit. The course looked at intellectual disabilities in children, and I was able to take my class to interesting workshops and even disability wards in hospitals. I was also able to utilize some of the speech and language knowledge that I had gained from taking courses from and student teaching for Dr. Frank Bakes during my graduate studies. I was always interested in giving students the opportunity to interact face-to-face with the population they were studying, so when a student asked if they could bring a friend to the exceptional child class who was both blind and deaf and who operated a type of early computer to communicate, I agreed eagerly. The class spent a memorable afternoon asking questions and learning from this person.

Hunter College was interested in implementing a program titled Search for Education, Elevation, and Knowledge (SEEK) to help students from low-income neighborhoods earn a college degree. I agreed to head up this pilot program, as I had some previous experience working with SEEK at Queens in the testing and counseling center. Working closely alongside the English, Speech, and newly created Academic Skills Departments, I helped them respectively hire additional tutors and counselors. The SEEK program was successful in helping students obtain the credits needed to graduate, and by the end of my two years as director of this program, the average grade of the students who went through SEEK was a C, with each semester boasting a few students who achieved A's in all of their courses.

As much as I loved growing the program and had been grateful for the opportunity to help create something so meaningful, I decided that it was important that this program have a chairperson of color, mirroring the students that this program had been designed to help. So, after two years, I stepped away from the SEEK program to make way for a chairperson of color. Years later, not one, but two students sought me out to thank me for the work I did with SEEK, crediting my participation in creating a foundation upon which they were able to build. Both students eventually obtained their PhDs.

Although I enjoyed the courses I was teaching at Hunter College, I still wanted to be involved in social psychology. The Graduate Center at CUNY had a social psychology program lead by Stanley Milgram, a prominent social psychologist and someone I felt I should get to know. Deciding it was up to me to make this happen, I made the trip down to 42nd Street, where The Graduate Center was located, and spoke with Dr. Milgram. I told him about my academic background in social psychology, my interests, my research, and made it clear that I was interested in being involved in the field. This straightforward tactic worked on Dr. Milgram who agreed to take me on at The Graduate Center to assist with his administrative duties and to teach a course in the history of social psychology. This course was the perfect fit for me as it involved my long-held interest in history as well as social psychology.

After I began teaching this class, a group of students asked if I would teach a course on the psychology of women – a subject I touched on in my history of social psychology course. As someone long interested in the role women play in psychology, I agreed to bring the idea to Dr. Milgram. When first Milgram turned down the idea for this course, my students, not easily deterred, brought it next to the dean of students, who also turned it down. Finally, the students found a receptive audience in the president of The Graduate Center, Harold Proshansky. Dr. Proshansky was himself a social psychologist with whom I had developed an environmental psychology study a few years prior. Seeing that the students were excited to take a course like this, and that I was a great fit for the role, Proshansky mandated that the course be offered during the school year of 1971, though only on a provisional basis. I was quite pleased to have the opportunity to teach what was later determined to be the very first PhD course ever on the psychology of women. I was also impressed with the students who made it happen. In later years, I used the anecdote of this achievement as a teachable moment, showcasing the power that students can have in effecting change. This class, proving popular, quickly became a permanent fixture in the social psychology program of the Graduate Center curriculum. Then in 1972 I became executive officer of the entire multi-campus psychology program at City University, a position I held proudly until 1979.

I first became active in local and national psychological associations during my time at Hunter College and my psychological work grew in scope throughout the duration of my time at The Graduate Center. I first became involved in the New York Academy of Sciences and the New York State Psychological Association in the late 1960s. It was through these groups that I met Virginia Staudt Sexton who introduced me to the rest of the wonderful wide world of psychological organizations. I began taking on more responsibilities in these organizations, starting as the newsletter editor for the Academic Division of NYSPA. After a few years it was suggested that I run for president of that division, and when I did, I won the vote and proudly served as president for a year. Not long thereafter I was elected the president of the Social Psychology Division, of which I was also a member. In 1972 I was elected president of NYSPA. In 1969 I was extended a Letter of Invitation to join the Society of Experimental Social Psychology (SESP), an international scientific organization dedicated to the advancement of social psychological research. I had long been involved in the psychology honors society Psi Chi, and was elected president of that organization in 1978. Psi Chi is now an international psychological honors society.

In 1978, I also campaigned for president of the American Psychological Association (APA). Though I had been involved in the APA for years, notably helping create a permanent Division focusing on the psychology of women (Division 35) in late 1973, I knew it was ambitious to run for president of APA while also serving as president-elect of the National Psychology Honors Society. However, I was confident that I could balance both responsibilities should I win both elections. In July of 1979, I was elected the 88th President of APA, only the fifth woman to hold that position. My second husband, publisher Robert Wesner, who was always supportive, was delighted with my election. The next year I represented the APA at the Inter-American Congress of Psychology as President-elect and, after officially taking the presidential role in 1980, represented the APA at the International Congress of Psychology in Leipzig, Germany, participated in a six-week-long trip through China, and determined that Sun Valley, Idaho would be the location for the APA's annual retreat, chosen in part because Idaho was one of the states that had ratified the Equal Rights Amendment.

Throughout my year as president of the APA I continued to prioritize the psychology of women course I was still teaching at The Graduate Center, returning me to the classroom each week. It was important to me that psychologists and students recognize the contributions women make to the field, and even more generally the importance of women's rights issues. To further emphasize the importance I placed on these issues, during my time as president I would not travel to states that had not ratified the ERA. Additionally I encouraged the growth of the APA's Division 35, which I had co-founded, and which had been renamed the Society for the Psychology of Women. During my presidential term, this division increased its membership significantly. One of the final addresses I gave before stepping down as president in 1981, was the keynote address at the first International Interdisciplinary Congress on Women held in Haifa, Israel. Six years later, I would co-chair the successful effort to bring this event to Hunter College.

Never forgetting my roots, I've always continued to conduct research, teach, and mentor students, even turning down a few opportunities to become a dean and move from the education side of academia to the administrative. In 1975 I published the book *Woman: Dependent or Independent Variable?* with my friend Rhoda Unger, a book about sex-role stereotypes and how women are understood within the bounds of culture. In 1979, I also co-edited a book on *The Psychology of Women: Future Directions in Research.*

During the 1980s I co-authored the first introductory interdisciplinary text on women's studies titled *Women's Realities, Women's Choices*, which contained chapters written by nine women authors from various disciplines. This book was so popular that it was republished in four distinct editions, each with updated information on cultural constructions and issues faced by women. In 2000, I co-authored a book titled *Engendering Psychology*, and in 2010, drawing from my long career as a teacher and mentor, I published *A Handbook for Women Mentors: Transcending Barriers of Stereotype, Race, and Ethnicity*, with Mary Reuder, Carole Rayburn, and Asuncion Miteria Austria. In total, I have authored fifteen published books and numerous articles. I have received six honorary degrees and have earned a number of APA awards (including the Distinguished Leader Award from the Society for the Psychology of Women; the Distinguished Contribution to the International

Advancement of Psychology Award; the Distinguished Contributions to Education and Training Award; and the Gold Medal Award for Lifetime Achievement for Psychology in the Public Interest), along with other remarkable accolades.

I chose to retire from Hunter College as well as The Graduate Center in 1988, after being offered a position as the Chair of the Psychology Department at Pace University. I served as Chair of Psychology there until 2001, when I was given the title of Professor Emerita in Residence; Robert S. Pace Distinguished Research Professor. I have continued to teach and mentor students to this day. Additionally, I continue to participate in various psychological organizations, still serving as the main representative to the United Nations for the International Council of Psychologists. I had been president of that group in 1990, and have enjoyed staying involved.

Throughout my many years observing and participating in the social psychology scene, I've seen many changes to the field. Once a fairly cohesive field, social psychology has found itself branching off into many distinct areas of study, though most remain under the umbrella of social psychology even if only loosely affiliated in practice. A few of these newer areas of social psychological study include health psychology, sports psychology, political psychology, women and gender psychology, and global or cultural psychology.

Looking back, I can say with pride that social psychology has been a very welcoming field. It is both a field that deals in nuanced, even mundane daily happenings, as well as some of the most inspiring instances of human behavior. Social psychology has found itself on the front end of positive, empowering movements, such as the movement toward racial integration in schools, and the equal rights for women movement, and now is taking part in the global movement to combat climate change. These efforts are made stronger through the use of social psychology, and of course, social psychology is stronger because of its involvement in these movements.

As the mentor of countless students over the years, I have both seen a lot and humbly acknowledge that I don't always have the answers. My best advice to newcomers in the field of social psychology, or to any field for that matter, is to work hard and stand up for your own beliefs. I also encourage everyone to say "yes" to opportunities. If an opportunity for a job or elected office arises, the window to take it may be short and could be the only chance you'll get, so if you want to take it, say yes. Even if you don't feel totally ready for it. Once you do, prepare to work hard and rise to the challenge. Looking back over my life and accomplishments, I can confidently say that I have taken this advice through the years and have been better off for it. I am proud of what social psychology is and what it has become, and am very proud to be a social psychologist.

Suggested Reading

Denmark, F. L. (1980). Psyche: From rocking the cradle to rocking the boat. *American Psychologist, 35,* 1057–1065.

(Ed.) (1985). *Social/Ecological Psychology and the Psychology of Women, Selected/Revised Papers.* XIII International Congress of Psychology, 7. Amsterdam: North Holland.

(1994). Engendering psychology. *American Psychologist, 49,* 329–334.

Denmark, F. L., & Paludi, M. (Eds.) (2008). *Psychology of Women: A Handbook of Issues and Theories.* Second edition. Westport, CT: Greenwood Press.

Denmark, F. L., Rabinowitz, V., & Sechzer, J. (2000). *Engendering Psychology: Bringing Women into Focus.* Boston: Allyn & Bacon.

Hunter College Women's Studies Collective (1983). *Women's Realities, Women's Choices.* New York: Oxford University Press.

Rayburn, C. A., Denmark, F. L., Reuder, M. A., & Austria, A. M. (Eds.) (2010). *A Handbook for Women Mentors: Transcending Barriers of Stereotype, Race, and Ethnicity.* New York: Praeger.

Sherman, J. A., & Denmark, F. L. (Eds.) (1979). *The Psychology of Women: Future Directions in Research.* New York: Psychological Dimensions.

Unger, R. K., & Denmark, F. L. (Eds.) (1975). *Woman: Dependent or Independent Variable?* New York: Psychological Dimensions.

5 Abe and Leon and Me

Elliot Aronson

My earliest recollection of thinking like a social psychologist took place long before I knew there was such a thing as social psychology. I grew up in an impoverished, blue-collar area of Revere, a small city a few miles northeast of Boston. Ours was one of the few Jewish families in a virulently anti-Semitic neighborhood. When I was nine years old, while walking home from Hebrew School one particularly dark night, I was waylaid and roughed up by a group of teenagers shouting anti-Semitic slurs. Verbal and physical aggression was not unusual in my childhood, but what made it uncommon for me was what happened immediately afterwards – an event that forms one of my most vivid childhood memories: I sat on a curb and began thinking about what had just happened to me. There I was, nursing a bloody nose and a split lip, wondering why those kids hated Jews so much. Were they born hating Jews or did they learn it from their parents? I wondered how they could hate me so much when they didn't even know me. If they got to know me better and discovered what a sweet and generous little boy I was, would they like me better? And if they began to like me better, would that lead them to hate other Jews less? I did not realize it at the time, of course, but these are profound social psychological questions.

Ten years later, I was a sophomore at Brandeis University, majoring in economics. Why Brandeis? It was the only university that offered me a scholarship, without which college was out of the question. Why economics? Growing up in the Great Depression, I witnessed my father, uneducated, unemployed, and unhappy, in tears over his inability to put food on the table. When it came time to select a major, I found myself overwhelmed by the feeling that I should study something practical. So there I was, on a fine spring afternoon, having coffee with a fellow student, an attractive young woman I wanted to get to know better. When she needed to rush off to class, I walked along with her. We entered the lecture hall, with me hoping we could sit in the back of the room and perhaps even hold hands. I found myself in a large introductory psychology course being taught by some guy named Abraham Maslow.

As it happened, Maslow was discussing the psychological aspects of racial and ethnic prejudice, raising virtually the same questions that I had raised ten years earlier while sitting on that curb in Revere, nursing my split lip and bloody nose. Until that moment, I had no idea that there was a field of study that addressed such questions.

Elliot Aronson, University of California at Santa Cruz, USA

I was so enthralled that I let go of the young woman's hand and started taking notes. I lost the girl but found a different kind of excitement. The next day I officially changed my major from economics to psychology.

As a psychology major, I worked closely with Maslow, whom I found to be both an inspirational teacher and a visionary thinker. His approach to psychology was humanistic, philosophical, and clinical; he was not a rigorous scientist. Thus he was awfully good at speculating about the nature of prejudice but not very good at proposing research that might lead to solutions, short of offering psychotherapy to help "cure" prejudiced people.

From what I began learning of psychology at Brandeis, rigorous science was neither interesting nor important to me. Indeed, experimental psychology seemed pretty drab. The experiments consisted mostly of rats running mazes, pigeons pecking disks in a Skinner box, and college students memorizing nonsense syllables. In contrast, Maslow taught me many important things that stayed with me for the rest of my life. As I look back on it, I realize that what I learned from him was an optimistic orientation toward human beings and their potential; I learned that individuals, and society, could become healthier, more compassionate, and more open minded. From Maslow, I acquired the determination (but not the tools) to apply psychological wisdom and knowledge for the betterment of the human condition.

Maslow was more than a professor to me; he seemed genuinely concerned about my overall welfare. To take just one example, in my senior year, Maslow hired me and one other student to serve as his general, all around assistants/secretaries/errand runners. The other student was a remarkable young woman named Vera. She had grown up in Hungary, survived the Holocaust, and emigrated to America at the age of seventeen. She was not only brilliant, she was also gorgeous and fairly glowed with a quality that I would call serenity. Vera and I always suspected that Abe Maslow was playing matchmaker, and if so, he did a pretty good job: To make a long, wonderful story outrageously short, Vera and I fell in love. We were married shortly after we graduated, in 1954, and here we still happily are, 67 years later.

Maslow was convinced that I stood a chance of becoming an effective college teacher – the kind that might even change lives – and encouraged me to go on for a doctorate. I thought it might be a better idea to proceed in stages, getting an MA first, and so I applied to work with David McClelland at Wesleyan, which had recently initiated a small terminal MA program. He accepted me as the departmental teaching assistant, a position that taught me a great deal about the art of teaching because I was exposed to professors with very different styles. It was a relaxed two years, filled with gentle learning – including learning to be parents for, near the end of our stay, Vera gave birth to the first of our four children. I was ready to move on to the next step, earning a PhD, and was accepted at Stanford.

In August, Vera and I loaded up our VW Beatle with our new baby and our few belongings and drove across the country. I arrived at Stanford in 1956, as a rather insecure student, wondering if I could make it in the big leagues – the same year that Leon Festinger joined the faculty as a distinguished professor. I had no idea he was coming (and, needless to say, he didn't know I was coming either!). He arrived with the reputation of being the world's most eminent young experimental social psychologist. Rumor had it that he was brilliant, angry, and extremely tough on students. Most of the graduate students in my cohort were intent on keeping out of his way. And I managed to do the same – until I didn't.

In the spring quarter, Festinger was scheduled to teach a seminar on a new theory he was developing, called something like "cognitive dissonance." It sounded vaguely interesting so, in spite of serious misgivings, I decided to give it a chance. Only about half a dozen of us enrolled in the course. Within a few weeks it became clear that the rumors about Festinger were true. All of them. He was the smartest, most incisive thinker I have ever met, before or since. And he was intensely impatient, sharptongued, and devastating. He could not abide sloppy thinking and came down hard on anyone who entered his classroom without having thought carefully and thoroughly about the assignment. I remember feeling intimidated and kept pretty quiet during class.

A few weeks into the course, he assigned a term paper, which I dutifully wrote. On handing it back to me, he managed to convey his feelings about my work powerfully and succinctly: he held my paper between his thumb and forefinger, at arm's length, and, with a sour look on his face, said, "I believe this is yours." It took me a while to read the paper because I could only imagine how stinging his marginal comments would be. But, when I finally did, I found not a single mark on it. I squared my shoulders and strode back into his office and said, "Excuse me, Dr. Festinger, you forgot to write a criticism on my paper. How am I supposed to know what I got wrong?" He glared at me long and hard and said, "What? You don't have enough respect for your own thinking to follow your argument through to its logical conclusion, and you expect me to do that? This is graduate school; *you* are supposed to figure out what's wrong with it."

So there I was, at a major choice point: stay in this class or quit? I asked myself, "Is this son-of-a-bitch somebody I really want to work with?" And I realized the answer was yes. "He is a dick, but he is very smart and I love his new theory." Mustering effort, I reread my paper and realized that he was right to dislike it; it was a sloppy, half-baked piece of work. Of course, I wished he had conveyed his distaste in a gentler way, but, hell, I told myself, if that's the way he is, I can handle it. I spent the next few days reworking the paper and then brought it into his office saying, "You might like this one a little more." To his great credit, he must have dropped whatever he was doing because 20 minutes later, he came into the T.A. room, placed my term paper in front of me, sat on the corner of my desk, put his hand on my shoulder, and said, "Now *this* is worth criticizing!"

What Leon was telling me was that if I was not willing to give him my best effort, he didn't want to have anything to do with me. But if I was serious and would give the work everything I had, he was willing to give me his time and the benefit of his criticism. At that moment, Leon and I became teacher and student. Within a few months, he was treating me as a valuable colleague – and eventually we became close friends. He never lost his bite; but it no longer was a problem for me, because it was encased in genuine warmth, caring, and the ability to listen, and listen intently.

Hanging in there with Leon was one of the best decisions I ever made. He could be harsh but he was always honest. In addition, he was a meticulous methodologist – a no-nonsense believer in going the extra mile to design and conduct the most elegant possible experiment to test a given hypothesis. His standards were impeccably high, and I believe that some of them rubbed off on me.

Moreover, dissonance theory was a breath of fresh air that got me excited about framing hypotheses and doing experiments to test them. The theory changed the face of social psychology by showing us that the mind is much more complex and much more interesting than simple principles of reward and punishment could predict. For example, a reinforcement theorist would predict that anything associated with discomfort, pain, or suffering would be disliked and avoided. I was about to turn this notion upside down. Dissonance theory also taught me the great lesson of social influence that guided my thinking for my entire career as a researcher and writer: that although it's true that changing people's attitudes sometimes changes their behavior, if you want a more powerful change to take place, it is far better to get them to change their behavior first; attitudes will follow. In the first experiment I did at Stanford, we showed that people who went through a severe initiation to join a group later liked the group better than those who went through a mild initiation. We didn't try to convince people that the boring group they had just joined was an attractive one; rather, we set up a situation where *they convinced themselves* that the group was attractive.

I not only learned the lesson of the bottom line of that experiment, I also enjoyed every step of the process. Here is how it came about: For a course in anthropology, I was reading John Whiting's work on initiations as rites of passage among indigenous tribes of Africa and South America. In Festinger's seminar, when we were discussing various ramifications of dissonance theory, it dawned on me that perhaps one function of those initiations was to create a more cohesive group, just as people who go through the famously extreme basic training required to join the Marines develop a strong commitment to the Corps. The cognition "I went through hell and high water to get into this group" would be dissonant with any negative aspect of the group. As a consequence, people would minimize the importance of these negative aspects and focus on the positive ones; those who went through the harshest initiation should therefore end up liking the group most.

It was immediately clear to me that to demonstrate causality, an experiment was required because Marines are self-selected. I needed to randomly assign subjects to either harsh or mild initiation conditions. I floated my hypothesis past Jud Mills, a fellow graduate student in the seminar. He was enthusiastic about it, and the two of us spent the next couple of weeks designing an experiment and inventing a workable procedure. The requirements were complex. We had to recruit people willing to join an ongoing discussion group; come up with a credible mild initiation procedure and a credible severe initiation procedure; and rehearse some undergraduates to perform a boring, insipid discussion that we tape-recorded. All subjects, regardless of experimental condition, would listen to the same discussion, which they were led to believe was being held by the group they had just now joined.

I ran the subjects and Jud, remaining blind to their experimental condition, collected the data by asking them a series of questions getting them to rate their feelings about the group. Leon's input was minimal. Through a one-way mirror, he observed me as I ran a few pilot subjects through the procedure. I asked if he had any suggestions. He stroked his chin, smiled, and said, "You're good to go."

I can still remember the exhilaration I felt as the data began to fall into place. Those subjects who underwent the severe initiation liked the group better than those who underwent the mild initiation. It was our first experiment and it became a classic (Aronson & Mills, 1959). I was elated by the realization that human behavior is complex but lawful. My task would be to identify the law, hone it into a testable hypothesis, and create a procedure to get at the essence of that hypothesis. Doing this experiment also showed me that I might have a knack for finding a key to unlock some of the mysteries of human behavior and discover things that no one had discovered previously. It was a great revelation.

While I was partway through the initiation experiment, Leon asked me to come into his office and discuss some research with Merrill Carlsmith, an exceptionally bright undergraduate (who also happened to be Vera's and my favorite baby sitter). Leon and Merrill had designed an experiment aimed at showing that if you paid subjects the paltry sum of $1 for lying to an incoming participant (i.e., for telling him that the tedious task the participant was about to perform was actually interesting and enjoyable), the subject would come to believe his own lie to a greater extent than if he had been paid handsomely, $20, for telling the identical lie. It was an exciting hypothesis but in the pilot testing the experiment wasn't jelling, so Leon asked me to join him to observe Merrill through the one-way mirror as he ran a couple of subjects. Leon asked me what I thought. I said that I thought the procedure was very good but that Merrill needed to be more intense – he needed to get the subject involved in the drama that was unfolding. "Both Merrill and the subjects look like they are sleepwalking," I said. "If the subject doesn't take the situation seriously, there will be no dissonance to reduce." Leon thought for a moment and said, "Okay, train the kid to be more convincing." I did – and Merrill was a quick learner. The resulting experiment (Festinger & Carlsmith, 1959) would be my candidate for the most important senior honors thesis ever done in social psychology.

Writing this about Merrill, and the fun we had turning him into a convincing experimenter, makes me want to pause to lament the shortness of his life. After graduating from Stanford in 1958, he went on to graduate school in social psychology at Harvard, where, one year later, I joined him as an assistant professor. Merrill became my first doctoral student. Together we did some exciting experiments and collaborated on what became an influential chapter on experimental methodology for *The Handbook of Social Psychology* (Aronson & Carlsmith, 1968). Merrill died of cancer – tragically young, at the age of 48. If he had lived, he would undoubtedly have been a contributor to this volume.

I would never have predicted this for myself, but by my second year at Stanford I was becoming enamored of methodology, something I had considered tedious just a few months earlier. But the style of research I was perfecting – a style I dubbed "high impact experimentation" – was both challenging and exciting. At that time, in most experiments, participants had the luxury of sitting back and calmly guessing, how a "normal" person might behave in a given situation – and trying to show they were normal. In our experiments, real things were happening to real people, which enabled us to transcend the fabled artificiality of the laboratory. We plunked people into the middle of a situation that was so real for them that they had to respond as they would have responded outside the laboratory. What I learned from Leon was that it is possible – no, it is essential – to achieve scientific rigor without artificiality or sterility. For the next forty years, that became my mantra as an experimenter.

During my three years at Stanford, Festinger and I agreed on most things (e.g., see Festinger & Aronson, 1960), but we disagreed on two important issues. Leon did not give a fig about making the world a better place. His primary (sole?) interest was in learning how the mind works. One night over drinks, Leon asked me how I first got interested in social psychology. When I told him that I had been inspired by Abe Maslow, Leon was incredulous and disdainful: "Maslow! That guy is a dreamer. His ideas are so vague, they're not even wrong!" I smiled, recalling that Maslow was not exactly a great fan of Leon's either. When I had been at Stanford for a while, Abe asked me who I was working with. When I told him it was Leon he exclaimed, "That guy is a real bastard! How can you stand him?" So there you have it. My two beloved mentors hated each other. And I loved them both. Some might consider this to be a dissonance arousing situation! But I'm not so sure, as you will see.

Our other major disagreement was more substantive. Soon after I received my PhD and was about to depart for the east coast, Leon asked me for a critique of dissonance theory. I told him that something had been troubling me: I felt that the theory was very powerful at its center but fuzzy around the edges; it was often difficult to be sure whether the theory made a prediction at all. Leon reminded me that he had tried to delineate the limits of the theory with a homey example of when dissonance would not apply: A man was driving late at night on a lonely country road and got a flat tire. When the man opened the trunk of his car, he discovered he didn't have a jack. Leon maintained that, although the man would feel frustrated, disappointed, perhaps even afraid, he would not experience dissonance. The example didn't feel right to me. I said, "Of course there is dissonance! What kind of idiot would go driving late at night on a lonely country road without a jack in his car?" "But," Leon countered, "where are the dissonant cognitions? What is dissonant with what?"

That argument clarified my thinking. It dawned on me that the answer was contained in the word "idiot": the driver's self-concept. What was dissonant was (a) the driver's cognition about his idiotic behavior with (b) his self-concept of being a reasonably smart and competent guy. Because most people consider themselves to be reasonably smart, competent, and moral, dissonance is greatest when a person behaves in a way that is stupid, incompetent, or immoral. This simple insight led me to the realization that the theory had been producing clear predictions primarily when an important element of the self-concept was violated, typically when an individual did something that was inconsistent with his or her sense of self. Thus, in the Aronson-Mills experiment, I initially believed that the dissonance was between the person's cognition "I went through a severe initiation to get into a group" and the cognition "the group is worthless." Instead, I now realized, the dissonance was between the cognition "I am a sensible, competent person" and the cognition "I went through a severe initiation to get into a worthless group." That is why the fact that I had warm affectionate feelings for both Abe and Leon, even though they actively disliked each other, did not produce dissonance because their reciprocal disdain had nothing to do with my self-concept. Yes, I would have preferred them to like each other, but their opinions of one another required no justification on my part.

What I first thought was only a minor adjustment of dissonance theory turned out to be a major transformation: from a theory about attitudes into a theory about self-justification. Leon encouraged me to do the research to test my idea, even though he was not exactly ecstatic about it. He believed that my revision limited the scope of the theory; I was convinced that the tightening was worth a minor reduction in scope (see Aronson, 1998).

For the next dozen years, my students and I had a field day discovering interesting things about how the human mind works. We identified phenomena whose names can be Googled easily, such as "gain-loss theory," "the pratfall effect," "the forbidden toy paradigm." Leon had so kindled my excitement about doing basic research that I had lost sight of why I first became interested in social psychology – to find ways to do good in the world. One might say that I had lost sight of Abe Maslow's influence. And then, in 1971, something happened to restore my initial vision.

That year, when I was teaching at the University of Texas, the Austin public schools were ordered to desegregate, and all hell broke loose. Within a few weeks, the schools were in turmoil. African-American, Anglo, and Mexican-American youngsters were in open conflict; fistfights were breaking out among these groups in corridors and schoolyards throughout the city. The situation in Austin was typical, albeit more dramatic, of what was happening across the country. Social psychologists had predicted that desegregation would reduce prejudice and increase the self-esteem and academic success of underprivileged minorities, but the data were showing that our predictions were wrong. Following desegregation, prejudice frequently increased, and the self-esteem and performance of minority kids did not improve.

The assistant superintendent of schools, who was a close personal friend, asked for my help and gave me a mandate to do anything within reason to reduce the conflicts and violence. I wanted to do more than slap a Band-Aid on Austin's problem; I wanted to gain some insight into why, across the nation, desegregation wasn't producing the beneficial effects we had expected.

My students and I began by systematically observing classes in an elementary school. The one thing that leapt out at us was something that anyone who has ever attended traditional public schools simply takes for granted: The typical classroom is a highly competitive place in which students vie with one another for the attention and praise of the teacher. In Austin, as in most communities, in this competition the minority kids were virtually guaranteed to lose. Austin was residentially segregated, the schools in minority neighborhoods were substandard, and their reading skills were approximately one full grade level behind those of the Anglo kids. As a result, the children's existing stereotypes of each other were magnified and confirmed: The Anglo kids saw the minority kids as stupid and lazy; the minority kids saw the Anglo kids as arrogant show-offs.

Accordingly, our intervention consisted of restructuring the dynamics of the classroom from a competitive one to a cooperative one. We invented and implemented a technique that created small interdependent groups, designed to place students of different ethnic backgrounds in a situation where they needed to cooperate with one another in order to understand the material. We called it the jigsaw classroom, because the process was like assembling a jigsaw puzzle (for more detail, see www.jigsaw.org; see also Aronson & Bridgeman, 1979).

Within a week of instituting jigsaw, we could see that the entire classroom atmosphere was changing as kids began to gain respect for one another across racial lines. After six weeks we collected concrete data. The formal results confirmed our casual observations: Compared to students in traditional classrooms, students in jigsaw groups became less prejudiced and more fond of their group mates, both within and across racial boundaries. They also did significantly better on objective exams, showed an increase in self-esteem, and liked school better. (Absenteeism was significantly lower in jigsaw classrooms than in traditional classrooms in the same school.) Finally, students in the jigsaw classrooms developed a greater ability to empathize with others than students in traditional classrooms did (Bridgeman, 1981). My students and I replicated these results in several classrooms in Texas and California.

My work with the jigsaw classroom was as gratifying personally as it was professionally. Not only did jigsaw demonstrate that under the proper conditions, desegregation could be beneficial to minority and majority students alike, but it also answered many of the questions I had raised when I was nine years old sitting on that curb in Revere. Moreover, the research was both a clear example of doing something good for society, and an instance of conducting a series of solid experiments under difficult conditions. As such, I see it as my first success in forging a marriage between my two great mentors, the hard-nosed scientist Leon Festinger and the soft-hearted humanist Abe Maslow. After a slow start, the jigsaw has become a staple of public education in North American schools. However, I must confess to feelings of sorrow that the current political climate seems to be moving away from interracial cooperation and more toward workshops and classroom exercises on "anti-racism" and identity politics. As a social psychologist well versed in the decades of research on the conditions that reduce prejudice or inflame it, I fear that many of these interventions will exacerbate division and hostilities rather than reduce them. I hope I'm wrong; I hope jigsaw will survive and continue to produce the kinds of beneficial effects I first observed half a century ago (Aronson & Patnoe, 1997).

The jigsaw classroom experience encouraged me to continue to step outside of the laboratory, not only to do applied research that would be immediately useful to the participants but that, in addition, might simultaneously teach us something new about how the human mind works. During the 1980s, at the height of the AIDS epidemic, the overwhelming majority of sexually active male college students were reluctant to use condoms even though they knew that condoms would protect them against the

AIDS virus and other sexually transmitted diseases. In other words, they knew condoms were useful, they simply were not using them. My graduate students and I tried a novel approach to overcome their resistance. We recruited sexually active students to video tape a speech about the importance of using condoms, allegedly to be shown in high school sex education classes. Our subjects were happy to do it as a public service – to help keep younger kids safe from STDs. Next, we interviewed half the subjects getting them to talk about their own frequency of condom use and how it was often inconvenient to use them. Thus, they had to confront the fact that they were not practicing what they had just gotten through preaching. Creating dissonance between their behavior and their self-concept as a person of integrity proved to be a highly effective strategy; condom use increased dramatically among young men in the experimental condition (Stone et al., 1994).

That success opened a new paradigm in dissonance research that we dubbed "the hypocrisy paradigm." In a subsequent experiment, during a major drought in California we utilized the hypocrisy paradigm to induce students to take shorter showers. Specifically we got a random sample of students to affix their names, in bold letters, to a poster in the field house which read, "Conserve Water. Take short showers. If I can do it so can you!" The results were stunning. Students in the hypocrisy condition spent an average of 3.5 minutes under the shower – a small fraction of the time spent by students in the control conditions (Dickerson et al., 1992).

I want to end this chapter with a few words about teaching – both in the classroom and via writing books. From the outset, when I was a T.A. at Wesleyan, I have taken teaching very seriously. Indeed, as a 23-year-old, my goal was not to do research but to become a teacher at some small obscure college that did not expect me to publish anything. Even as my professional goals expanded, I have always been most enamored of teaching beginners: My favorite courses were introductory social psychology, where I had the privilege of introducing freshmen and sophomores to the excitement and promise of this field, and the experimental methods course to first-year graduate students, where I got to introduce budding professionals to the art and science of doing experiments. Because I loved teaching in my own personal way, I was never completely happy with existing textbooks. For the graduate course, the solution was easy: I took the *Handbook* chapter that Merrill Carlsmith and I had written in 1968 as a base, expanding it and keeping it up to date by enlisting one of Merrill's terrific students, Phoebe Ellsworth, and one of mine, Marti Gonzales, as co-authors (Aronson et al., 1990).

Writing an introductory social psychology textbook from scratch was more daunting, however, so I would never have undertaken it intentionally. It happened almost by accident. In the late 1960s, I was becoming increasingly impatient with the existing textbooks, which were not addressing the problems that students were most concerned about – the war in Vietnam, the racial divide, political assassinations, and other major events affecting their lives. As a result, my students found the texts dull and irrelevant.

To fill this need, as a supplement to the formal textbook we were using, I prepared a few rough essays on my favorite topics. I duplicated them and gave them away to the students in my course. One rainy day I picked up that collection of sloppy essays and played around with them. Before I knew it, they began to emerge as actual chapters, and after a few months, I could see a book taking shape. I called it *The Social Animal.* It was a personal statement; in effect, I was shamelessly opening my family photo album and sharing it with my readers. It not only described the basic ideas and research in our field, it also included ruminations and conversations with my wife, my kids, my students, and (almost) my dog.

Because the book had first taken shape as a supplement to my lectures, I felt free to write in my own voice, using the first person singular, as if I were talking directly to students. For example, in the first chapter, I enunciated what I rather grandly referred to as "Aronson's First Law: People who do crazy things are not necessarily crazy." (That's just one of my many First Laws; there never was a second.) Of course I was mocking myself by assigning it the status of a First Law – just as physicists, those "real" scientists, do! But the statement itself was dead serious, reflecting what I regard as the essence of social psychology: Namely, that the social situation can exert a powerful impact on human behavior – so powerful that it can make sane people do crazy things, moral people do immoral things, smart people do stupid things, and brave people do cowardly things. If we, the observers, are unaware of the social circumstances that evoked those actions, we are tempted to conclude that they are caused by some deficiency in the character or sanity of the person doing them. Ten years later, my dear friend Lee Ross gave a name to this phenomenon: "the Fundamental Attribution Error." Most of the traditional publishers were not enthusiastic; they considered the manuscript to be too casual, too personal, and (I secretly think) too interesting. But all it takes is one. W. H. Freeman was excited and published it in 1972. From the outset, professors reported that their undergraduates were actually reading it for pleasure. Academic reviewers were lavish with their praise, calling it "a masterpiece" and "a rare gem of a book." APA gave the book its National Media Award. And it is still going strong, fifty years later: One reviewer called the most recent edition (the twelfth), written with my son, Joshua, "better than ever." All this enthusiastic praise for a textbook is, of course, gratifying. By far, most gratifying of all, is being approached, with surprising frequency, at conventions by middle-aged strangers who tell me that it is because of reading *The Social Animal* that they decided to become a social psychologist.

Of the books I've written for general audiences, *Mistakes Were Made (But Not By Me)*, with Carol Tavris, most closely captures the intellectual, political, and personal issues that have intrigued me throughout my life. This book applies cognitive dissonance theory to a wide variety of important issues from our individual lives to the world stage – including memory, marriage, police and prosecutorial misconduct, racism, family rifts, and international conflicts (Tavris & Aronson, 2007/ 2020). I'm pretty sure Abe Maslow would have applauded my having written a book with such clear real-world applicability. And although, initially, Leon Festinger might have resisted being dragged (kicking and screaming!) into the real world, I suspect that, eventually, he would have read the book with appreciation, joy, and even with a modicum of pride.

Suggested Reading

Aronson, E. (1972). *The Social Animal*. New York: Freeman.

    (1998). Dissonance, hypocrisy, and the self-concept. In E. Harmon-Jones & J. S. Mills (Eds.), *Cognitive Dissonance Theory: Revival with Revisions and Controversies* (pp. 21–36). Washington, DC: APA.

    (2010). *Not By Chance Alone: My Life as a Social Psychologist*. New York: Basic Books.

Aronson, E., & Bridgeman, D. (1979). Jigsaw groups and the desegregated classroom: In pursuit of common goals. *Personality and Social Psychology Bulletin, 5*, 438–446.

Aronson, E., & Carlsmith, J. M. (1968). Experimentation in social psychology. In G. Lindzey & E. Aronson (Eds.), *The Handbook of Social Psychology* (Vol. 2, pp. 1–79). Reading, MA: Addison-Wesley.

Aronson, E., Ellsworth, P. C., Carlsmith, J. M., & Gonzales, M. H. (1990). *Methods of Research in Social Psychology*. Second edition. New York: McGraw-Hill.

Aronson, E., & Mills, J. (1959). The effect of severity of initiation on liking for a group. *Journal of Abnormal and Social Psychology, 59*, 177–181.

Aronson, E., & Patnoe, S. (1997). *Cooperation in the Classroom: The Jigsaw Method*. New York: Longman.

Bridgeman, D. (1981). Enhanced role taking through cooperative interdependence: A field study. *Child Development, 52*, 1231–1238.

Dickerson, C. A., Thibodeau, R., Aronson, E., & Miller, D. (1992). Using cognitive dissonance to encourage water conservation. *Journal of Applied Social Psychology, 22*, 841–854.

Festinger, L., & Aronson, E. (1960). The arousal and reduction of dissonance in social contexts. In D. Cartwright & A. Zander (Eds.), *Group Dynamics* (pp. 214–231). Evanston, IL: Row & Peterson.

Festinger, L., & Carlsmith, J. M. (1959). Cognitive consequences of forced compliance. *Journal of Abnormal and Social Psychology, 58*, 203–211.

Stone, J., Aronson, E., Crain, A. L., Winslow, M. P., & Fried, C. (1994). Inducing hypocrisy as a means of encouraging young adults to use condoms. *Personality and Social Psychology Bulletin, 20*, 116–128.

Tavris, C., & Aronson, E. (2020). *Mistakes Were Made (But Not By Me)*. New York: Harcourt.

6 My Contributions to Social Psychology Over Many Decades

Philip G. Zimbardo

I was born during the 1930s depression and raised in the South Bronx, New York, a Catholic second-generation Italian – 100 percent Sicilian, to be precise. A product of the mean streets and the public schools, I loved school and every one of my teachers whose mission I believed was to help Me to succeed in life. I was a really good student, confident, hardworking, socially popular, and happy with my place at James Monroe High School. Then in 1947, for my junior year, my family moved to North Hollywood, California. This imagined paradise turned out to be my social nightmare. For reasons I could not understand, I was shunned by classmates, socially rejected by every one of them. I developed various sicknesses (now known as psychosomatic) that often forced me to stay home from dreaded North Hollywood High School. Why was I being outed?

I discovered the bizarre answer in spring term when I was on the bus headed to a school baseball game from my teammate; I played center field, he was the left fielder, so we often had to share game information. I asked him point blank if he could share the reason for my being shunned. "Sure, most kids are afraid of you; they knew you were the only Italian kid around, and then assumed your family must belong to the Mafia. And the Mafia kills people!" It did not matter that I was a skinny, bright blue-eyed gentle kid, the biased rumor could not be easily undone.

Thankfully, because of my continuing illnesses our family moved back to New York in 1948, enabling me to pick up where I left off for my senior year at Monroe High School. Within two months, I was voted the most popular boy and vice president of the senior class, and my sicknesses vanished!

I told my story of how I went from popular, to shunned, and back to popular again to my classmate, a little Jewish kid named Stanley – Stanley Milgram. After talking about it, we decided that the shift in fortunes was not about me, it was all about the differences in the situation. As Stanley used to say, "How do you know what you would do until you're in the particular situation?" (Hartwig, 2021, p. 18). The conclusion we drew from this conversation was prophetic. In 1963, Milgram published the first of his pioneering but controversial obedience experiments demonstrating the power of authority over the individual. Then some years later, I followed up with the Stanford Prison Experiment (1971) showing that ordinary people can be

Philip G. Zimbardo, Stanford University, USA.

induced to change their behavior, sometimes dramatically so, according to the social roles they are given to play.

One other parallel would join the two of us in this situationist enterprise. Despite the profound implications of Milgram's experiment, he got a lot of flak concerning its ethics because of the extreme stress it induced in many of his participants. Then in 1971, from August 14 to 21, I conducted the prison study, which I talked about at that year's APA convention. Afterward, Stanley came up to me, gave me a hug, and said, "Oh thanks. Now you're going to take all the ethical attacks off my shoulders, because what you did was worse than what I did in my studies." We kept in touch after that for many years, until he died prematurely at only age 51.

Beginnings – Finding My Way to Social Psychology

After graduating from Monroe High School with honors, I was offered a small fellowship from Brooklyn College, an economical but long subway ride from my Bronx home. In my freshman year I took introductory psychology, and it was the most boring course imaginable! Psychology in the 1950s was all about rats running mazes and college kids learning nonsense syllables on memory drums. I got my only C grade in that pathetic course. So, I refocused on sociology and anthropology. Then in my senior year I took a class on research methods in psychology. With a partner, we had to try to replicate many classic experiments. I then realized that I loved doing research more than just reading about it. I went on to complete the psych major in one year. Just as I was gearing up for graduate school in Minnesota to work with Stanley Schachter on a new program of research on social affiliation. I got a call from K. C. Montgomery at Yale University. He made me an offer that I could not refuse. "Yale" was a big name in the Bronx, and closer to home than that Midwestern college. I went to work with Montgomery on a series of experiments on the dynamics of exploration – in rats! I tried to do research with as many different faculty as possible, including Neal Miller, with whom I published articles with such titles as "Facilitation of exploration by hunger in rats" (Zimbardo & Miller, 1958).

As a graduate student at Yale, from 1954 to 1959, initially I was a "rat runner" doing research on their exploratory and sexual behaviors. I then switched into social psychology after reading Leon Festinger's manuscript of his forthcoming book on cognitive dissonance theory, as part of a course taught by Jack Brehm, a new faculty member who had been Leon's first graduate student. I realized the value of being well rounded, so I apprenticed with many different faculty members, among them, Neal Miller, Carl Hovland, Irving Janis, Hal Kelley, Seymour Sarason, and Irv Sarnoff.

I delayed submitting my PhD dissertation for a year (from 1958 to 1959) to avoid being drafted into the Korean War. Instead, I was a postdoc fellow at the West Haven VA. That opportunity broadened my interests in psychopathology and treatment, as I worked closely with individual patients. It also helped broaden the range of my interests throughout my career, enabling me to publish research across nearly fifty totally different topic areas. My eclecticism made writing an introductory psychology text a delightful challenge. I have done successfully over dozens of editions of *Psychology and Life*, as well as *Core Concepts in Psychology*. I also created a PBS video series, *Discovering Psychology*, that has been widely viewed for decades by teachers and students around the world.

The Winding Road into the Stanford Prison

My first academic job in 1960 was a terrible one, at the NYU undergraduate campus in the Bronx. First, there were no graduate students there to assist with my new research endeavors into social affiliation and attitude change. Secondly, there were no colleagues in my area with whom to share ideas. Third, I had to balance any research time with an intensely heavy teaching load of five courses each semester.

My tactic was then to convert a few bright undergrads into viable RAs, so I was able to get some new research conducted and published. The road up the academic ladder to eventual tenure was to publish heavily in peer-reviewed journals. So, I worked my butt off, teaching, researching, writing, advising, and also caring for my newborn son, Adam.

In the mid-1960s, I was delighted to learn of the pioneering new research on obedience by Stanley Milgram, then as a beginning assistant professor at Yale, conducted in the research laboratory that I had built earlier. Curiously, as I noted earlier, Stanley and I had been high school classmates in the Bronx. He was the smartest kid on the block, but uniformly disliked for his arrogance. When I visited the Yale Psych department to give an invited colloquium, I asked Stanley if he could share some information about his new line of research. Surprisingly he said "No." Why? Because "Some people steal others' original ideas." So much for any imagined earlier friendship between us.

In 1967, I was invited to be a one-year visiting professor at Columbia University's social psychology program, to fill in for Bill McGuire who had gone on leave. There I embraced two of the most extraordinary students I had ever known: Lee Ross and Judy Rodin. I gave them a separate tutorial during which we created new ideas about attribution theory and did the first original research in that domain, which we published in 1969. I also taught part time as a visiting professor at Barnard College, the women's side of Columbia. There I was fortunate to interact with a brilliant student, Carol Dweck, with whom I later became a colleague when she joined the Stanford Psychology Department. I managed to get Lee Ross invited to Stanford University shortly after I got there, and he went on to enjoy a brilliant career. I also helped to get Judy Rodin invited to the Yale University faculty the next year. She rapidly moved up the ladder at Yale, and then left to become President of the Rockefeller Foundation.

The gods of research blessings smiled on me shortly after, in the summer of 1967, when I was invited to be a faculty member on the first European Research Graduate Summer Program in Louvain, Belgium. I was the youngest of the American faculty of Bob Zajonc and Harold Gerard. We each had a team of European graduate students with whom we had to design, execute, and prepare for publication an original experiment. We all lived together in a small village. My team won by finishing a complete original experiment on deindividuation using Belgian soldiers as our participants. I later published that research as the start of related studies on anonymity.

My professional and personal life changed dramatically the next year in 1968, when I was invited to become a full professor with tenure at Stanford's psychology department. Over the next forty years, I was surrounded by amazing colleagues, like Walter Mischel, Al Bandura, Eleanor Maccoby, John Flavell, Al Hastorf, Gordon Bower, and so many others. Then we hired Lee Ross, and later Claude Steele, Hazel Markus, Bob Zajonc, Carol Dweck, and Jennifer Eberhardt. What a department!

I did my best research and prolific writing there, while teaching large introductory psych classes to hundreds and even a thousand students. I published vigorously on a dozen different topics. While there, I met and later married Christina Maslach, with whom I will celebrate 50 years of blissful marriage in August 2022. She is a distinguished professor Emerita at U.C. Berkeley and the pioneering scholar in the area of Job Burnout.

In August 1971, I undertook what was destined to become the landmark Stanford Prison Experiment (SPE; see Zimbardo et al., 1973). It demonstrated the power of situational forces to overwhelm otherwise good people to become cruel, when role-playing prison guards, or emotionally overwhelmed as prisoners. Its takeaway message is that most ordinary people, even good ones, can be seduced, recruited, initiated into behaving in evil ways under the sway of powerful systematic and situational forces, both the *evil of* action – to do bad things against others, as well as the *evil of inaction* – to do nothing when they could/should do the right thing, being helpful and compassionate.

The weeklong experiment quickly gained international notoriety following two prison riots that erupted shortly after its conclusion. The day after my study was concluded, there was an alleged prison escape at San Quentin Prison in California by Black activist George Jackson who was murdered along with several guards. Three weeks later in upstate New York's Attica Prison, inmates rioted and took over the entire facility, in part as a testimony to their lost comrade George Jackson. The governor of New York, Nelson Rockefeller, later ordered the National Guard to shoot to kill all prisoners in the open prison yard, which then also included many guards being held hostage.

I was invited as an expert witness before Congressional hearings on prisons held in Washington, DC, and in San Francisco. My testimony on how I believe prisons need to be reformed became part of the Congressional record. Because of that publicity, a national TV program, *Chronolog*, presented the story of the SPE in October 1971. My experiment continued to be influential, most notably during the 2003 Abu Ghraib prisoner abuse scandal. I served as an expert witness for an American prison guard found guilty of abusing Iraqi prisoners during their night shift. My situationally based testimony in support of Sgt. Chip Frederick, head of that shift, at his trial in Baghdad, helped lead the judge to reduce the intended fifteen-year prison term for that soldier to only four years.

In 2007, I wrote about the SPE at length in my book *The Lucifer Effect*, which became an international bestseller. Later, in 2015, it was memorialized in a major Hollywood motion picture, *Stanford Prison Experiment*, which won several awards, and on which I was the major consultant. I then deposited all the materials related to the SPE in Stanford University's historical archives. That included over forty boxes of various information related to the study and its aftermath, as well as all the videotapes and audiotapes we had made during the study. Those materials have been converted into formats available to anyone desiring to know about that experiment in depth and in detail. There is another readily accessible resource of much SPE information at the *Social Psychology Network*, headed by Scott Plous, one of my former Stanford graduate RAs.

Anyone who is interested can review the document my colleagues and I wrote twenty-five years after the SPE for interesting reflections, new research, and legal actions filed over these years (Zimbardo, Maslach, & Haney, 2000; see also Haney & Zimbardo, 1998). Finally, I have compiled an extensive rebuttal to many recent criticisms of the SPE, available at www.prisonexp.org/responses.

Lucifer's Evil

In *The Lucifer Effect*, I explore the dynamic transformations of good people who give into the temptation to cross the line between good and evil, and become perpetrators. It represents a fundamental character alteration of the human personality that has serious personal and social consequences. These transformations are more likely in those contexts where the social forces are powerful enough to overthrow the attributes of personal morality, compassion, empathy, or sense of justice. I asserted that evil is the exercise of power to intentionally hurt physically, harm psychologically, or morally destroy others.

The nucleus of evil is the central process of dehumanization by which certain people or groups are represented as less than human or inhumane; not comparable in personal dignity to those in the power positions that do the labeling. Such dehumanization is a social attribution process, which over time may evolve into transforming ordinary people into vicious perpetrators of evil behavior when they come to accept the stereotyped view of them. This risk is high in some institutional situations such as in prisons, military barracks, or hospitals.

Contemporary social psychology has illuminated the ways in which social situations have the power to constrain individual choices and redirect behavior from positive to negative directions. Situations are the behavioral contexts in which we live out our lives – some for better, others for the worse. Psychology had tended to focus on dispositional factors within individual actors; this situational view puts the actors on a dynamic stage with audiences, co-actors, costumes, stage directions, and more. Some situations are created as power domains where leaders dominate followers and must continually demonstrate their greater control over them. Prisons are the prototypical instance of such power-centric settings, in which prisoners lose their individuality, are dehumanized, deindividuated, and come to be regarded as inferior beings by their controllers – the prison guards and administration. When that change in perception occurs, they may be abused psychologically and physically. At times, many other situations share the basic properties of control and power that typify prisons, such as mental hospitals, schools, summer camps, fraternities, and military training facilities.

The Seven Steps of Descent into Evil

1. *Mindlessly taking the first small step.* Consider the Milgram experiment (Milgram 1974). It began with the subjects only giving a minor 15-volts shock. Later, the vast majority would go all the way up to a possibly deadly 450-volts shock. When a person in a uniform or a lab coat tells us what to do, we tend to do it. We follow authorities' dictates. *Evil starts out small but can up big and bad.*
2. *Dehumanizing others.* In the Stanford Prison Experiment, randomly assigned prisoners were arrested and numbered to dehumanize them. The well-known result was that the experiment went out of control. But a quote from Dennis Burning of Charlie Company concerning the My Lai Massacre in Vietnam more potently illustrates the impact of dehumanization: "I would say that most people in our company didn't consider the Vietnamese human." In that massacre, more than 340 unarmed civilians, women and children included, were killed by members of the US Army's C-company. *Evil involves dehumanizing the subjects of our hate.*
3. *Deindividuation of self.* The violent power of anonymity is highlighted in the work of anthropologist John Watson, who studied twenty-three cultures. He found that if they don't change their appearance before going into battle, only one out of eight kills, tortures, or mutilates the enemy. By contrast, when they do change their appearance in various ways before engaging their enemy, then 90 percent of these warriors kill, torture, and mutilate the other. I wrote about this in a paper on the irresistible lure of deindividuation (Zimbardo, 1969). *When we are anonymous, we become violent and prone to evil acts.*
4. *Diffusion of personal responsibility.* Following the New York City murder of Kitty Genovese in 1964, witnesses were said to have seen the slaying, but did nothing to stop the attack. While the initial number and situation of the witnesses has recently come into question, social psychologists Bibb Latané and John Darley (1970) began research on what has been called the *bystander effect*. This line of research demonstrated a paradox: the greater the number of bystanders, the less likely an individual among them is to help a victim. *If others don't do something, I won't either.*
5. *Blind obedience to authority.* Adolf Eichmann defended his role in the Holocaust by saying he was just following Hitler's orders. He did what he was told to do. But obedience isn't only about hurting others. In 1978, over 900 people committed

suicide or were murdered in a Guyana jungle because they were blindly obedient to their pastor, the Reverend Jim Jones, head of the People's Temple. Mothers even killed their own children on command. *They gave up their lives because a religious authority told them to do so.*

6. *Uncritical conformity to group norms.* The notorious Manson family, responsible for the Tate-LaBianca murders (in 1969, Los Angeles) was a prime example of both blind obedience and conformity to group norms. The group norm was to do whatever Charles Manson said, including many murders, without question. His cadre of female "wives" each said, "Charlie made me do it." *Only doing what everyone else does creates social evil.*

7. *Passive tolerance of evil through inaction or indifference.* In 1972, Dr. Jack Hammond was confronted about the horrific conditions inside Willowbrook State School for learning disabled youth in Staten Island, New York. He responded that "the conditions here are no better or worse than any other facility for the mentally retarded in the state." But now consider that from 1972 to 1987 five children were murdered or disappeared. Andre Rand was the serial killer found responsible. *Cropsey* is a documentary film, by Joshua Zeman, that vividly portrays these evils in action. *Evil thrives on apathy and indifference.*

Converting Evil into Goodness, Villains into Heroes

On the positive side of psychology, it is possible to demonstrate how we can create situations in which people are trained to act courageously against all forms of evil. Adopting a positive psychology orientation, many psychologists are engaged in spreading a strategy that encourages the development of moral outrage and courage against social malignancies.

Currently, my *Heroic Imagination Project* (HIP) helps train ordinary people of all ages and backgrounds how to act courageously in challenging situations in their everyday lives. Programs have been developed and are in use around the world by schools and companies. They first fortify individuals against passive anti-social behaviors, and against the tendency to go along with the group in order to "get along" with the others, even when the group is doing immoral things. Then individuals are encouraged to build heroic action networks that encourage civic engagement and to develop the skills necessary to implement behaviors and habits that have as their goal Community Goodness.

These useful applications of psychology are interventions based on empirical evidence that has clearly demonstrated that those practices, which "humanize" all others, while reducing the power of some situations to encourage evil, are the vital tools essential for spreading social capital among all human beings. Thus, contemporary social psychology demonstrates that we have the inner power to change external evil-generating systems and situations by collective social action in heroic networks where we work together to create new pro-social realities. Please visit www.heroicimagination.org.

Pioneering Research and Therapy on Shyness and on Time Perspective

The year after SPE, while teaching in my introductory psychology class at Stanford, I proposed a metaphor for shyness as a psychological prison. People who are shy put themselves in this prison that limits their freedom of association and speech because they play the dual roles of being the guard who poses those restrictive rules on the prisoner who then reluctantly obeys them. I discovered at that time there was no psychological research on shyness in adolescents or adults, so my students and I went on to develop the Stanford Shyness Research Program.

In this program, we engaged in many kinds of research; cross-cultural, large data collection, experimental, as well as case studies. We then created an experimental shyness clinic to try out different techniques on shy students. We were very effective because we knew exactly what aspects of shyness could be modified in eight-week group sessions. We did not focus on history or etiology, but rather on three features common to shyness: cognitive/negative self-references; social/behavioral problems, not knowing how to talk or act; and excessive physiological arousal. We invite each client to focus in on which of those three conditions set debilitating self-limits, and then we work together on modifying them. Within eight-week group and individual sessions we often achieved 100 percent improvements! We then moved our clinic into the community, where Dr. Lynn Henderson headed it. We renamed it, in positive style, as the *Social Fitness Clinic*. It continues in operation to this day, as does a similar clinic at Palo Alto University. I also wrote a popular trade book titled *Shyness: What It Is, What to Do About It. Shyness* became a national bestseller, with nearly a million readers (Zimbardo, 1977).

Shortly after developing our shyness program, I began doing research on the psychology of time perspective, in part because of my awareness of how time was distorted during the week of the SPE. I created a new way of measuring individual differences in six domains of time perspective, the *Zimbardo Time Perspective Inventory* (ZTPI), that has become the standard in that domain. I then summarized new research my team and I had conducted in *The Time Paradox: The New Psychology That Will Change Your Life* (Zimbardo & Boyd, 2008). Later, other colleagues and I developed an original therapy for PTSD based around different clients' profiles on the ZTPI (Zimbardo et al., 2012). More recently, we extended our view to use what we know about time perspective to enrich all aspects of life, by focusing on living and loving better with time perspective therapy (Zimbardo & Sword, 2017). I also helped to create an International Council on Time Perspective, which has had bi-annual meetings in European cities over the past decade.

Kurt Lewin's Legacy

August 15, 2021 was the golden anniversary of SPE – fifty long, eventful years – during which I have worked to enrich my beloved field of social psychology – by helping to understand the nature of evil and also of heroic goodness. The prison study, and much of my research conducted in its aftermath, were influenced by Lewin's pioneering thinking, experiments, generalist orientation, and social applications. I was recently honored to receive the Kurt Lewin Award (Zimbardo, 2016).

Now as I approach the ripe old age of 89 years, I look back with pride at the accomplishments outlined above, as well as my productivity (over 60 trade and textbooks, along with more than 600 articles and blogs). I was also an energetic President of APA, recipient of many international honorary degrees, along with prized awards for my teaching. I am sure that Mrs. Munvas and my other elementary school teachers at P.S. 25 would be pleased by their vital early contributions to my psychology career.

The Future of the Next Generation of Social Psychology

I will end these reflections by briefly considering what I think is the future path of social psychology. Surely less research on evil and more on positivity, kindness, caring, and heroism are needed. There could be more research on personality trait interactions with social conditions. We need much more cross-cultural research and more well-developed international collaborations. The impact of climate change on our lives across many domains should also be a hot topic.

As our nation, and others, become ever more divided along political lines, social psychologists should be working with political psychologists to study ways for some rapprochements. The same is true for growing major inter-nation global conflicts. Practical persuasion, à la Cialdini, in this time of perhaps a permanent pandemic, is needed to foster greater social adherence to vaccinations and social health habits. More research is needed on younger children's attitudes and beliefs about their uncertain future. Understanding racial and economic diversity is needed in planning better public policies. Cultural sensitivity training should be taught in all police academies. Simply put, it is clear to me that our world needs more well-informed, broadly trained social psychologists able to contribute to the solution of these and other vital issues.

Suggested Reading

Haney, C., & Zimbardo, P. G. (1998). The past and future of U.S. prison policy: Twenty-five years after the Stanford Prison Experiment. *American Psychologist, 53*, 709–727.

Hartwig, D. (2021). *Zimbardo: My Life Revealed*. Florence, Italy: Giunti.

Latané, B., & Darley, J. M. (1970). *The Unresponsive Bystander: Why Doesn't He Help?* New York: Appleton-Century-Crofts.

Milgram, S. (1974). *Obedience to Authority: An Experimental View*. New York: Harper & Row.

Zimbardo, P. G. (1969). The human choice: Individuation, reason, and order versus deindividuation, impulse, and chaos. *Nebraska Symposium on Motivation, 17*, 237–307.

(1971). The power and pathology of imprisonment. *Congressional Record* (Serial No. 15, October 25, 1971). Hearings before Subcommittee No. 3, of the Committee on the Judiciary, House of Representatives, Ninety-Second Congress, First Session on Corrections, Part II, Prisons, Prison Reform and Prisoner's Rights: California. Washington, DC: US Government Printing Office.

(1977). *Shyness: What It Is, What to Do About It*. Reading, MA: Addison-Wesley.

(2007). *The Lucifer Effect: Understanding How Good People Turn Evil*. New York: Random House.

(2016). Carrying on Kurt Lewin's legacy in many current domains Lewin Award 2015. *Journal of Social Issues, 72*(4), 828–838.

Zimbardo, P. G., & Boyd, J. N. (2008). *The Time Paradox: The New Psychology That Will Change Your Life*. New York: Free Press.

Zimbardo, P. G., Haney, C., Banks, W. C., & Jaffe, D. (1973). The mind is a formidable jailer: A Pirandellian prison. *New York Times Magazine*, April 8, pp. 36ff.

Zimbardo, P. G., Maslach, C., & Haney, C. (2000). Reflections on the Stanford Prison Experiment: Genesis, transformations, consequences. In T. Blass (Ed.), *Obedience to Authority: Current Perspectives on the Milgram Paradigm* (pp. 193–237). Mahwah, NJ: Lawrence Erlbaum.

Zimbardo, P. G., & Miller, N. E. (1958). Facilitation of exploration by hunger in rats. *Journal of Comparative and Physiological Psychology, 51*(1), 43–46.

Zimbardo, P. G., & Sword, R. K. M. (2017). *Living and Loving Better with Time Perspective Therapy*. Jefferson, NC: Exposit.

Zimbardo, P. G., Sword, R. M., & Sword, R. K. M. (2012). *Time Cure: Overcoming PTSD with the New Psychology of Time Perspective*. San Francisco: Jossey-Bass.

7   Influences and Dissonances

Jonathan Freedman

As an undergraduate at Harvard, I thought I would become a physicist. I took some great courses in physics, chemistry and math, and did okay in them, but I found it all too dry (and maybe I wasn't good enough in math to pursue physics). Instead, I graduated in 1958 with a major in social relations, which at the time was a combination of anthropology, sociology, and psychology. The psychology faculty were mostly at the social science end of the field, having split from the "hard" psychology department that was focused mainly on psychophysics and Skinnerian learning. The one exception was Dick Solomon who was also in social relations and taught a terrific course on learning.

I took courses and interacted with some famous people – Gordon Allport, Henry Murray, Clyde Kluckhohn, David McClelland, and once, venturing into the psychology department, a seminar with a fairly ancient but still sharp Edwin (Gary) Boring. There were no social psychologists in social relations except I suppose Gordon Allport (who taught my last seminar). In fact, I don't think I knew just what that field was. I have a vague memory that George Mandler, who was an assistant professor, called himself a social psychologist at the time, but that seems implausible so I may be wrong. In any case, there were no well-known or even not well-known social psychologists on the faculty. My one exposure to the field was a course taught by Solomon Asch who was visiting. He taught from his book, which was mostly about Gestalt psychology, but did cover some social psychology. Although it was a pretty small class, I don't think I ever said a word to Asch, but I did get to know the T.A. who happened to be Stanley Milgram (more on him later).

Social relations offered so-called tutors during the last two years and I was assigned to Sarnoff Mednick. I got along with him really well, we did research on stimulus generalization which was his take on what others might call "spread of effect" or just association. I published three papers with Sarnoff and mostly because of him decided that I would go to graduate school in clinical or experimental psychopathology. The idea was that I would do clinical research and maybe become a clinician.

I applied to Yale in clinical and was invited for an interview. I went down to New Haven to meet with Irv Sarason. Psychology was located in the medical school building and as I walked toward it, I saw David Sears riding by on a bike. He and

Jonathan Freedman, University of Toronto, Canada.

I had met as teenagers at camp although we had not been especially friendly. As it happened, I knew that he was a grad student in psychology at Yale because in a casual conversation someone (not a psychologist) on hearing that I was hoping to go to Yale in psychology mentioned that he knew someone there and said Dave's name. So when we met outside the department, I was not totally surprised. Dave was very friendly and helpful and I really liked him. And, to make a long story short, that was how he became the first person who had a big influence on my work in social psychology. We both got jobs in California and did research together for years. I'll return to this.

At Yale I quickly decided that clinical was fascinating but not for me. Instead, I worked with Carl Hovland who I thought was the most brilliant person on the faculty. He got me interested in attitude change and persuasion, which dominated my work for much of my career. Hovland was interested in how one should design a communication to have maximum impact on the recipient's attitudes and behavior. The main point I got from him was what he called latitudes of acceptance and rejection. The idea was that the position taken in the communication would have little impact if it was too far from the recipient's belief. It would simply be rejected.

A good example of this was the Janis and Feshbach (1953) study in which high school students were told what would happen if they didn't brush their teeth properly. The idea was to vary the amount of fear and then assess the impact on their behavior. The "low fear" group was told that not brushing correctly would cause rotting teeth and gums; the "high fear" group was also shown disgusting pictures of rotting teeth and gums. Janis predicted that the high fear condition would produce a boomerang effect and be less influential than the low fear condition and that is what was reported. But I felt then and still do that this was the wrong interpretation. Another way of looking at it is that the supposedly high fear condition was simply rejected by these middle-class healthy high school students. Obviously (to them) they were not going to get rotting teeth by brushing the wrong way. No one they knew had ever had rotting teeth and they weren't going to either. So, they ignored the communication and were not influenced, whereas the low fear communication was more believable and did have some influence.

As an aside, this notion seems to me especially relevant in the current political situation in the United States as it relates to just about everything, particularly vaccinations. Perhaps the best way to convince someone who is against vaccinations to get one, is to find some position that somehow takes into account their opposition. Rather than say that of course vaccinations are the best way to fight COVID and save your life and other people's lives and that they have been shown to be safe and so on, try a more nuanced approach recognizing the hesitation. I'm not sure what that should be, but I think it's important to recognize their resistance to the vaccination no matter how crazy you think it is.

It turned out that Stanley Milgram, my old Harvard T.A., came to Yale as an assistant professor my first or second year there. Stanley and I became friendly. One day I asked him what he was working on. He thought a moment, looked in the hallway and the adjoining offices to make sure no one was around (a tad paranoid perhaps?), and then told me about the obedience study which was about to start. Although the emphasis was quite different, clearly Stanley was influenced by his association with Asch. I was not that impressed by the research (and never was). It was clearly not an experiment but rather a demonstration with no controls, and I doubted Stanley's interpretation of it (I guess I was in the minority on that). On the other hand, I was struck by how cleverly he had devised a situation that was very real to the participants. Whereas the Asch situation was somewhat artificial, the Milgram situation clearly had a real impact on at least some of those involved. He told me that some people got so upset that they ran from the room and threw up. I think this was the first time I realized the importance of making the situation real for the subjects. It wasn't necessary to make them so upset that they vomited, but if you wanted to believe the results, they had to feel the way the experimental manipulation was supposed to make them feel. If you want them to feel fear or anger or guilt or whatever, you better make sure that's what they feel.

Probably the person who had the most influence on me in graduate school was Bob Cohen. He was a young assistant professor and was a genuinely nice person (in contrast to some of the other assistant professors). At some point, Bob introduced me to Festinger's work. It's hard to believe now but I had never read any of Festinger's research or (I think) even heard of him or of cognitive dissonance. So much for being taught social psychology at Harvard. In any case, cognitive dissonance and the research to support it was a revelation (Festinger, 1957).

The research was clever, the reasoning very smart, and the findings both counter-intuitive and fascinating. Imagine showing that larger incentives had smaller effects! Imagine showing that behavior can precede and cause attitude change rather than the other way around! I was struck by all of this because unlike so much of what social psychologists were working on at the time, it was not "obvious." Of course, people and other animals behave so as to increase rewards and avoid punishments; of course, high prestige sources are more likely than low prestige ones to change attitudes. But that people increase their evaluations of something after they have chosen it or that inducing behavior with large rewards was less likely to change their attitudes than if you could induce the behavior with smaller rewards – these ideas were not obvious and the evidence supported them. The idea of affecting behavior with minimal incentives, what I called compliance without pressure, led to my work some years later on the foot-in-the-door effect. Induce people to do something small using little or no pressure, and they were then more likely to agree to do something a lot bigger (Freedman & Fraser, 1966).

Remarkably, after getting my PhD in 1961, my first job was at Stanford working with (under?) Festinger. I said "under" because I heard Festinger's secretary saying to someone on the phone that Professor Festinger was not available but they could talk to his assistant, Professor Freedman. Fortunately for me, that's not how it was. Leon treated me extremely well, took my ideas and comments seriously, helped me design and analyze research, and was generally a very good mentor. He was not always the nicest or most considerate person in the world, but he was awfully nice to me.

Much of my early research was related to or derived from Festinger's work. I studied how cognitive dissonance led to attitude change and behavioral change (e.g., Freedman, 1965). I also challenged some of the ideas from it, especially the notion that people would avoid dissonance by not looking at information that disagreed with their views. I found this not to be true, although most of my work did support the basic idea of the theory.

Festinger influenced me in other ways as well. I was struck by his attention to detail in designing experiments. His research group met weekly and spent a lot of time discussing how to test a particular hypothesis, exactly how to manipulate the key variables and set up the appropriate situation. The focus was on being as certain as possible that the manipulation produced the desired effect and was not open to alternative explanations. Once the results were in, they were analyzed very carefully. But always with the goal of learning what had happened, not on data picking or manipulating the data to get the predicted effect.

If Festinger was my mentor and, in some ways my role model, my closest colleagues were Dave Sears, who was at UCLA and Merrill Carlsmith who came to Stanford from Harvard a year or two after I did. Dave and Merrill were cousins and had more or less grown up together and the three of us formed a close friendship that had a great influence on me that lasted for many years. Dave was very interested in political behavior and became one of the important people in the field of political psychology. I was concerned about politics as it affected the world, but not so much in studying it. Although we did only a few studies together that involved politics, much of our early work was done in collaboration. We spent time thinking of interesting questions and then took turns being the lead author, Dave running studies at UCLA and I running them at Stanford. It worked very well for at least five years before we both branched off into our own separate work.

Although we ran a joint research group, Merrill and I did not do much research together. There was no one smarter or cleverer than Merrill. He was so smart he didn't have to be awake to understand complicated issues. At one of our research meetings at my house, Bob Abelson, who was visiting from Yale, was talking about his work. We were all sitting around on the floor. It was a long meeting, and not very exciting. Merrill had lain back and was obviously asleep. But he suddenly sat up, looked right at Bob and asked the best question of the night. Just how he managed that was not clear, but he was seemingly never out of touch. I should add that as smart as Merrill was, when Dave came up to Stanford, he always beat both of us in our favorite strategy game, Tactics II. No matter how much we planned to get Dave the next time, he somehow had a new strategy to beat us. Merrill influenced me in a different way too. He had a terrific ability to see the weakness in an argument or a set of data. When I look at the results of my research or that of others, I often imagine what Merrill would have said about them and take that to heart. I was sad that after I moved to Columbia, Merrill and I drifted apart, and very very sad when he died.

Dave had a profound influence on my research. This was not so much in terms of the content of the work, but because of his great attention to detail and his always perfect integrity. He never overstated the results, always insisted on pointing out any weakness in the findings and being cautious in the conclusions. I've tried to live up to that and have been greatly disappointed in how often I see others doing just the opposite – exaggerating their results, often even hiding the inconsistencies in the data.

The other person who had a big influence on me was Tony Doob who was the best graduate student anyone has ever had. He was (is) smart, organized, knowledgeable, and focused. We did work on deviancy – how being different affected attitudes and behavior. This was long before the present emphasis on diversity and bias although I think what we did then concerned the same issues. Tony and I talked about what studies to do next, worked out some of the details, and before I knew it the study was completed. He was energetic, smart, and brilliant at research. Later in his career he focused on criminology and became one of the most important figures in that world. When Tony got his PhD, he took a job at the University of Toronto. At the time I thought going to Canada was pretty exotic, little imagining that I would spend most of my career there.

I was also influenced by Daryl Bem, not because I agreed with his outlook but because I strongly disagreed with it. Bem was extremely clever and smart, but he seemed to think that people did not have feelings or real beliefs. He reinterpreted some of the dissonance results in purely cognitive terms by describing the situation to people and asking them to give responses. According to Bem's articles, often people could reproduce the results of the actual experiments done by Festinger. Bem argued that this showed there were no emotions, feelings, or dissonance involved, which was, of course, contrary to the whole idea of Festinger's theory. I did not like this line of research and later wrote an article criticizing the notion that you could find out how things worked simply by asking. I called it "psychology by consensus" and argued that just because people said something, even if lots of psychologists said it, did not make it true unless there were data to back it up. I suppose in some ways Bem's work was the beginning of cognitive social psychology which I have never felt comfortable with – putting me squarely against much of modern social psychology.

One person who had a big effect on my research was, surprisingly, a biologist. I had gotten friendly with a group of biologists including Don Kennedy who later became the president of Stanford, head of the FDA and editor-in-chief of *Science*. I really liked Don but the person who influenced my work was Paul Ehrlich. He was an expert on butterflies but what interested me was his work on population biology. He and I got a huge (for then) grant from the Ford Foundation to fund education and research in population biology and for me to study the effects of crowding. I worked on this for several years finding that under most circumstances, as long as there were sufficient resources, crowding did not have negative effects. I published the research in the book *Crowding and Behavior*. Meanwhile Paul wrote *The Population Bomb*, the blockbuster that argued that the world's increasing population threatened food supply and more. Now, many years later, I realize that Paul was absolutely right about the dangers of overpopulation, but he focused on the wrong problem. Human ingenuity managed to produce more and more food, but has not yet solved the existential problem of the damage to the environment caused by the extra billions of humans.

During this period, I liked and admired Hal Kelly, Ned Jones, and Hal Gerard – three major figures in social psychology at the time. Although I don't think I was influenced by their work, I always liked talking with them and reading their research. I also found Elliot Aronson one of the most engaging and likeable people in the field. Then when I moved from Stanford to Columbia, in 1969, I got to know Stan Schachter. I don't think his research influenced me much, but I was impressed by the number of his students who became stars. In addition to being charming and bright and intuitive, he may have been the most successful teacher of social psychology researchers.

Soon after I got to Columbia, Bob Krauss joined the department. Bob became and still is one of my closest friends. His work on language and communication brought home to me the importance of knowing that what you intend to communicate is what the target of the communication gets. This issue comes up in almost every experimental manipulation or intervention. You say you are manipulating fear (as in the original Janis and Feshbach study) but maybe all you are doing is manipulating plausibility. Years ago, I was defending a gay bookshop against a charge of promoting violence against women. One of the key studies had men watch a neutral movie or the terrific movie *Swept Away*. They found that after seeing the latter, men were more accepting of rape myths and other anti-female beliefs. The authors argued that the effects had been caused by the rape scene in *Swept Away*. That is possible. But an entirely different interpretation of the manipulation is that *Swept Away* is the story of a man and a woman who fall in love on a deserted island and when they are rescued, she totally rejects him in favor of her rich friends. Instead of the rape being central, it might have been the rejection that caused the men who watched the film to resent women.

I've spent the last part of my career at the University of Toronto. During this time, my interests shifted more and more to legal issues. My students and I have studied how jurors are affected by various factors, including pretrial publicity and racial prejudice. Some years ago, I joined the board of Innocence Canada, the main organization in Canada concerned with wrongful convictions, and I became its co-president. I have also spent time reviewing and criticizing research on the effect of violent media on aggression, which I published as *Media Violence and Its Effect on Aggression*. Both interests reflect my feeling that we should be focusing on how social factors affect behavior in the real world, combined with the strong sense that we psychologists better be really certain we know the facts before telling people how to behave.

Social Psychology – Then and Now

Writing about how the world of social psychology has changed makes me feel even more ancient than I am. It sure has changed. In the first place, although this hardly needs saying, there are now women in the field. You will notice that all of the people I mentioned as having influenced me were men. This was because there were almost no women in academic psychology. Dave Sears's mother, Pat Sears, was at Stanford as was Eleanor Maccoby, but not many other women. Consider this true story. Eleanor and I arrived at Stanford at the same time. She was an associate professor and already quite well known. At our first meeting of the otherwise all-male faculty, Eleanor was asked to take notes. (At least she wasn't asked to make the coffee.) It is an enduring embarrassment to me that as the most junior professor, I did not offer to do it instead. It still makes me squirm. Fortunately, much has changed and it seems to me that there are now more women in social psychology than men and that the women are more influential.

Second, although I must admit that I have not kept up with all of the research in the field, I know one major change that has occurred – online data collection. It was not possible in the 1960s or 1970s or 1980s; now it is perhaps the most common type of research procedure. And it sure is efficient. What used to take weeks or even months can be done over the weekend. I've done some myself and it is very rewarding to have a full data set in a few days. However, I wonder if it lends itself to experimental research or even survey-type research involving personal feelings. Online manipulations rarely if ever have the power and validity of those done in person. And although online surveys are great for obtaining lots of information and maybe for predicting elections, they are not so good at investigating actual processes of human and social interaction. They often get "what if" answers to hypothetical questions rather than actual behavior from actual situations.

Changes that I do welcome are more research on racism and sexism, on personal relationships, on sexuality and on sexual and gender identities. This is very delicate and difficult work and it is here, perhaps, that the anonymity of the Internet is helpful. One other change is that there is so much research published that it is very difficult to keep up with it. I suppose that is good, but I am not convinced that this much high-quality research on meaningful questions is being done. That's me being old . . .

Suggested Reading

Ehrlich, P. R. (1968). *The Population Bomb*. New York: Ballantine Books.

Festinger, L. (1957). *A Theory of Cognitive Dissonance*. Stanford, CA: Stanford University Press.

Freedman, J. L. (1965). Long-term behavioral effects of cognitive dissonance. *Journal of Experimental Social Psychology*, *1*(2), 145–155.

(1975). *Crowding and Behavior*. San Francisco: W. H. Freeman.

(2002). *Media Violence and Its Effect on Aggression: Assessing the Scientific Evidence*. Toronto: University of Toronto Press.

Freedman, J. L., & Fraser, S. C. (1966). Compliance without pressure: The foot-in-the-door technique. *Journal of Personality and Social Psychology*, *4*(2), 195–202.

Janis, I. L., & Feshbach, S. (1953). Effects of fear-arousing communications. *The Journal of Abnormal and Social Psychology*, *48*(1), 78–92.

8 From Ideomotor Theory to the IAT in Just 35 Years

Anthony G. Greenwald

The title's 35 years are from June 1963, when I received my PhD, to June 1998, when the article that introduced the Implicit Association Test was published (Greenwald et al., 1998). This chapter will be replete with digressions from the path between ideomotor theory and the IAT. I've italicized the digressions to make them obvious.

Place, Manhattan. Time, early September, 1949, first day of junior high school. I had been "skipped" twice in earlier years, completing Grades 1–4 in two years. In New York's public schools, this occurred commonly for students who progressed rapidly in reading and arithmetic. At age 10, I was two years younger than most of my new 7th grade classmates. I went to my assigned home room, where I was surprised to learn that, with no advance indication to me or my parents, the school had assigned me to an accelerated program that would complete Grades 7–9 in just two years. When the bell rang for students to go to their first classes of the day, I could not follow my homeroom classmates to their first class. I needed to go elsewhere for the accelerated program's first class, but no one had informed me where I should go.

I soon found myself in the emptying hallway of the totally unfamiliar school building, not knowing what to do. When I was at last alone, I did the most reasonable thing – I cried. I was discovered soon by an adult to whom I (sobbing, I'm sure) explained my plight. I was escorted to an administrative office, where I received the additional news that the compressed academic schedule of the accelerated program could not include time for an orchestra class that I was very much looking forward to – I wanted to start playing trumpet. I have no memory of the rest of the school day, but I did learn that I would be allowed to choose between the orchestra class and the accelerated program. When I got home I discussed the choice with my parents. They were as uncertain as I was, and they left it to me. The next day, I started in the orchestra class. This was a decision that likely affected everything significant in the rest of my life.

I discovered ideomotor theory during the most nerdish period of my career. (Not to mislead, I remain a nerd, but not quite so much as when I was a PhD student.) Early on at Harvard, I undertook to learn everything I could about learning–behavior theory, the dominant theoretical paradigm of experimental psychology at that time. I worked

Anthony G. Greenwald, University of Washington, USA.

in the laboratory of a learning theorist, Richard Solomon, in my first year. I was helping him and Lucy Turner, his chief lab associate, with experiments in which the subjects were dogs who were injected with curare (i.e., paralyzed) as part of the protocol for traumatic avoidance learning experiments. A decade or so later, these experiments were discontinued, being regarded as animal cruelty. I confess that I did not question or object to participating in these experiments. It was a different time.

In addition to the standard program for first year social psychology PhD students, my first year of graduate work included a seminar on learning theory taught by Solomon, a lecture course on learning taught by B. F. Skinner, and a following summer spent working in New Haven at the laboratories of Frank Logan, Allan Wagner, and Neal Miller in Yale's Institute of Human Relations Building. In their laboratories, the experimental subjects were rats, mice, and rabbits, and I worked directly with the animals. (In Solomon's lab, my only interaction with the dogs was to feed them, which I'm sure they enjoyed. My main responsibility was to learn about the topics being investigated.) My nerd tendencies got greatest exercise in my course work. I read *everything* that was assigned. Solomon's seminar assigned a lot. Weekly, the syllabus included perhaps twenty articles, most of them published recently in top-tier empirical and theory journals, in addition to lengthy chapters in prominent method and theory texts by Osgood, Woodworth, and Schlosberg, the large handbook by S. S. Stevens, and Ernest Hilgard's learning theory text. Not knowing enough to be selective, I read the assigned readings in entirety for the weekly seminar assignment of writing a 500-word synthesis of conclusions warranted by what I had read. I got interested in the disagreements among the major learning theorists (especially Edwin Guthrie, Clark Hull, and Kenneth Spence), but I was also attracted to Edward Tolman's cognitive learning theory, which was at intellectual war with Hull and Spence.

I also started reading philosophers on the topic of volition. Strangely, the topic of volition was treated not at all by the learning–behavior theorists whose work my courses focused on. Skinner's lecture course was of great interest, but I soon discovered that he shunned theory (I read his 1950 article in *Psychological Review* titled "Are theories of learning necessary?"). Skinner understood that "instrumental responding" (what occurs in Skinner boxes) was a product of "schedules of reinforcement." He felt no need for further conceptual understanding. Apparently, the prior half-century of American behaviorism had made volition an alien topic.

Although Richard Solomon was my formal advisor, informally I was working with Elliot Aronson and Walter Mischel, who were both assistant professors in the Social Relations Department, where the PhD program in social psychology was located. After they left, Merrill Carlsmith, a PhD student one year ahead of me, became not only a good friend, but my informal mentor. I also had very helpful support from graduate students in other departments who were, like me (from my second year on), resident tutors in Harvard's Leverett House. Merrill outdid me in just about everything, except on the squash courts. I wrote about this part of my career in the first several pages of my chapter in Elliot Aronson's 2010 festschrift.

What happened with the junior high school orchestra class? After three years (end of 9th grade) I was a decent trumpet player, enabling me to gain competitive admission to New York's High School of Music & Art (M&A). In my second (junior) year at M&A, two classmates took me under their wing, having concluded it was essential that I learn to play Jazz. Their strategy was to sit me down and play LP records of the major Jazz artists for me. New York was the place to learn about Jazz. The local Jazz clubs (especially Birdland, Basin Street, and Five Spot) would admit under-drinking-age students (I was way under age, in addition to which I was short). As a consequence, I got to repeatedly see and hear the Jazz greats of the Bebop era. Charlie Parker had already died, but he had influenced everyone. I had numerous opportunities to hear live performances by Clifford Brown (my all-time favorite Jazz trumpet player, who tragically died just a few years later, in his late 20s, in a car crash) and also Miles Davis and Dizzy Gillespie, also saxophonists John Coltrane and Sonny Rollins, drummer Max Roach, pianist Thelonious Monk, the Modern Jazz Quartet, and the big bands of Count Basie and Maynard Ferguson.

In my senior year at M&A, I applied to and was turned down for admission by both Yale and Harvard, despite my having the highest grades in my graduating class of close to 500 students. But I did get onto Yale's waiting list. (Much later, I learned that Yale then had a 10 percent cap on Jewish admissions. The quota apparently started in the 1920s and lasted into the 1960s. I graduated in 1959 from Yale in the top 1 percent of my class.) A trombone playing friend of mine at M&A had been admitted to Yale's School of Music and did me the great favor of telling Yale's Director of Bands that there was an excellent trumpet player available to be plucked from Yale's waiting list. That worked. By the time I was a senior at Yale, I was playing solo first trumpet in the University Concert Band (also marching with the Yale Band at all football games). In my last two years at Yale, I also held the 3rd trumpet chair in the New Haven Symphony Orchestra (the first two chairs were held by trumpet majors in the Music School) and I played regularly with a campus Jazz sextet. My trumpet career continued for another 25 years after Yale, into the early 1980s, when I decided that the ten practice hours per week it was taking to keep my lip in shape were taking too much time away from work.

The first scholarly treatment of volition that I read was William James's chapter on "Will" in his two-volume 1890 opus, *Principles of Psychology*. James started a section titled "ideo-motor action" (Vol. 2, pp. 522–528) with a question: "Is the bare idea of a movement's sensible effects [a] sufficient mental cue ... before the movement can follow?" James concluded "yes" and credited that conclusion to the earlier (1852) work by German philosopher-psychologist Hermann Lotze. James's statement of the central thesis of ideomotor theory was that "Every representation of a movement awakens in some degree the actual movement which is its object" (1890, Vol. 2, p. 526).

That last statement is remarkable for expressing what appears to be an empirically testable proposition. When James was writing in 1890, however, there were no methods available to test this Lotze–James ideomotor hypothesis. Seventy years later, when I read James's chapter, methods were available, but no one was using them to conduct tests of ideomotor theory (again, perhaps a residual consequence of behaviorism).

My first ideomotor study used an idea suggested by Lotze's observation that "The spectator accompanies the throwing of a billiard-ball, or the thrust of the swordsman, with a slight movement of his arm" (James's translation from the German original). An experiment done with PhD student Stuart Albert at Ohio State indirectly confirmed Lotze's observation by showing that observers learned more from observing over the shoulder of another subject performing at a discrimination task than when viewing that subject from the side. (The over-the-shoulder subject had superior sensory exposure to the arm and hand movements required by the discrimination task.) This experiment, published in 1968, provided only a minor confirmation of the Lotze–James hypothesis – but it was a start (Greenwald & Albert, 1968).

In the next four years I and grad student co-authors reported four studies showing both that performance was faster when stimuli approximated sensory feedback from required responses (e.g., subjects would say letter names more rapidly in response to hearing them spoken than in response to seeing them printed or, alternately, would write letters faster in response to seeing them in print than to hearing them spoken). Even more convincing experiments came in the next few years, showing that two 2-choice decisions could be made simultaneously without mutual interference, but only when the stimulus for each decision was "ideomotor-compatible" with its required response – for example, moving a lever to the left or right in response to a left- or right-pointing arrow was ideomotor-compatible – while simultaneously speaking the name of a letter heard at the same time the arrow was seen. The apparatus and data-recording requirements for these experiments were challenging in the 1970s. About thirty years later I created a demonstration procedure involving presentations of a visual arrow pointing left or right simultaneously with hearing "left" or "right" in earphones. It is totally simple to make simultaneous rapid decisions of pressing a key with left or right forefinger in response to the arrow stimulus while simultaneously saying "left" or "right" in response to the heard words. In contrast, performance slows greatly (and errors are made) if the spoken words must be given in response to the arrows, with the keypresses made in response to the simultaneously heard words.

The ideomotor compatibility phenomena demonstrated in these experiments revealed automatisms that played roles in voluntary performance. Depending on the assignments of responses to stimuli, these automatisms could either (a) enable perfect timesharing of two decision tasks or (b) cause large interference between the two tasks, greatly slowing performances. In addition to supporting ideomotor theory, this finding provided a significant exception to the (still) widely accepted cognitive psychological principle that choice decision tasks require a limited capacity response selection process that can make only one decision at a time.

My trumpet playing at Yale and my continued development of Jazz "chops" (i.e., technique) had welcome side effects. In the summers after my sophomore and junior years, my job was not in a laboratory, but playing daily and nightly in the band of a Holland–America Line student ship that took eight days for a trip in late June to Amsterdam and likewise to return to Hoboken in late August. The bands were a five-piece Dixieland band ("The Ivy Five") in 1957 and a six-piece Bebop band ("Ivy Five Plus One") in 1958. The eight weeks between trips were spent driving a VW bus around Western Europe with my bandmates, sightseeing in the major capitals, and working as the house band for extended stays in Anzio (at a resort hotel mostly for seniors) in 1957 and at a strip bar frequented by American soldiers in Frankfurt am Main in 1958.

In the summer of 1959, after my Yale graduation, my trumpet playing included a two-week tour of Western Europe with the Yale Concert Band and a scholarship to the two-week session of the Lenox (MA) School of Jazz, where the faculty consisted of major Jazz instrumentalists, composers, and writers. I had the opportunity to perform alongside fellow student, Ornette Coleman, who had just recorded his first album (titled "Something Else"), also to have trumpet lessons with Kenny Dorham, to play with fellow scholarship winners in a sextet led by saxophonist Jimmy Giuffre, and to be lead trumpet player in the school's big band, led by trumpet player Herb Pomeroy. When I moved shortly thereafter to Boston for grad school, Pomeroy "hired" me as fourth trumpet player in his sixteen-piece band that performed two nights a week at The Stables, a bar in downtown Boston. (The sub-minimum-wage pay was based on bar earnings.) I loved every minute of it, playing alongside both veteran musicians and students at Berklee School of Music, three of whom later became well-known Jazz professionals.

The work inspired by ideomotor theory was being done while my primary line of work was on attitudes and persuasion. I decided early in my career that it was desirable to maintain an active line of cognitive research alongside my social psychological research. In the 1970s, I added a third line of research, on methodological topics. My earliest methodological work grew out of an experience of repeated failure in attempting to reproduce others' findings. Although it got some attention, it wasn't very satisfying to publish failed replications. In the 1980s I adopted two plans that I thought were more effective than publishing failed replications. First, I concluded that I (not others) should be responsible for assuring that any results I produced were replicable. Also, when I figured out that a result of $p = .05$ meant that there was only a 50 percent chance of an exact replication obtaining a result for which $p <= .05$, I concluded that I should never base confident conclusions on a finding for which the reported p value was not substantially smaller than .05.[1] I am, alas, aware of one subsequent publication for which I was a co-author in which a non-replicated finding with $p = .05$ was used as the basis for a confidently expressed conclusion. It was quite a few more years before that finding was shown not to be reproducible.

Also on the methodological front, in a paper published with Anthony Pratkanis, Michael Leippe, and Michael Baumgardner (1986), I advocated the challenging strategy of demonstrating within a single publication that a finding of uncertain reproducibility can be reliably obtained under one set of conditions and reliably *not* obtained under a different set of conditions. As difficult as this may sound, it can be done and has been done in at least four publications in which I was involved

---

[1] Greenwald et al. (1996) described why a result of $p <= .005$ could be accepted confidently as a basis for confidence in reproducibility by an exact replication. Subsequent Bayesian treatments have offered similarly strengthened criteria for concluding that a published finding is likely to be reproducible.

(Pratkanis et al., 1988 for the sleeper effect in persuasion; Pratkanis et al., 1994 for effects of subliminal self-help audiotapes; Draine & Greenwald, 1998 for subliminal semantic priming; and Greenwald & De Houwer, 2017 for unconscious classical conditioning).

Two of the four findings just cited were from research in which I investigated cognitive automatisms in a variety of ways. Those accumulating results convinced me that the human mind often makes judgments without awareness of the mental processes that produce those judgments. This was added to in the 1980s by research on what was described by its major innovator, Larry Jacoby, as "remembering without awareness." Larry lost the branding war on this topic to Daniel Schacter who, along with Peter Graf, had come up with the more readily adopted label, "implicit memory" (Graf & Schacter, 1985). Mahzarin Banaji (who started her PhD training at Ohio State in 1980) and I were both very interested in these developments in understanding the operations of memory outside of awareness. That shared interest evolved into an active and long-continuing collaboration that sought to determine when and how those developments could be applied to social cognition. Part of my motivation for this was a long-standing dissatisfaction with social and personality psychologists' near-exclusive reliance on self-report measures for investigating the major social/personality constructs of attitude, stereotype, self-concept, and self-esteem. The problem, at least as I saw it, was evident from well-known findings, mostly obtained in the 1960s, that established artifacts of demand characteristics and self-presentation as contaminants of many self-report measures.

Marzu and I started our collaboration by building on the "false fame" effect described by Jacoby and colleagues in 1989. (Mahzarin became "Marzu" due to my error in pronouncing her preexisting nickname [Mahzu] when she told me of it at our first meeting in 1980 – she was too shy to correct me then; that shyness did not last long.) We wondered if Jacoby's implicit memory effect might be understood as (what we later came to call) an implicit gender stereotype – one of associating male more than female with fame-producing achievement (Banaji & Greenwald, 1995). Our first thought was that this effect might occur primarily for just male names that had acquired familiarity by being encountered on a list that subjects had examined on the preceding day as part of a memory study. When we wrote to Larry asking him whether he had tested for this, he informed us that, actually, almost all of the names used in his false-fame studies were male. When Marzu and I did the obvious experiment of replicating the false-fame study with lists containing equal numbers of male and female names, we found in four replications that the effect was consistently stronger for male than female names. While continuing with other experiments on implicit stereotypes, we put our major effort into producing a theoretically oriented literature review, eventually published (1995) in *Psychological Review*, titled "Implicit social cognition: Attitudes, self-esteem, and stereotypes."

The final sentence of our 1995 article was, "Perhaps the most significant remaining challenge is to adapt these [indirect-measure] methods for efficient assessment of individual differences in implicit social cognition." That sentence was drafted in early December of 1993. In January, 1994 we submitted a proposal to NSF. The first two sections of our proposal described planned research on implicit stereotyping that would be conducted in Marzu's lab at Yale. The third section described research planned for University of Washington on assessment of individual differences in implicit social cognition.

That third section of our NSF proposal had four paragraphs, each describing a distinct procedure based on the methods I had been investigating in my cognitive work of the previous decade. Each offered a possibility to assess cognitive content that might function with conscious cognitive control. The first two procedures (subliminal priming and supraliminal priming) were already known to produce priming effects, although the subliminal effects were weaker and less consistently obtained. Supraliminal priming (i.e., priming by clearly visible stimuli) had been used in research initiated by a 1986 publication by Russ Fazio and colleagues. However, it had not been evaluated as an individual differences measure. These were tested at the UW lab and were judged not to have strong enough potential as individual difference measures. The third ("mixed judgment") method showed itself to be so amazingly effective that it put an end to the search. Its description in the proposal (stated in terms of a measure of gender–attitude associations) was:

[T]wo categories of words are assigned to each of two response keys. Subjects are asked to rapidly press one key whenever the stimulus word is *either* female-associated or pleasant in meaning, and the other key for words either male-associated or unpleasant in meaning. Through the course of a session, pairings of the male and female categories with keys are switched (while left and right are left consistently paired with unpleasant and pleasant, respectively).

Anyone familiar with the IAT will recognize this as a description of the IAT's procedure. A very astute reader may also have noticed the similarity between the last sentence of the above description of the "mixed judgment" task and my description of an experiment involving two simultaneous ideomotor-compatible decisions, which used the contrast between (a) a very easy dual-task setup of pressing a key with the left or right forefinger when seeing a left- or right-pointing arrow and saying "left" or "right" when hearing one of those words and (b) the greatly more difficult task in which spoken "left" and "right" were to be given in response to the arrows and the left or right keypresses in response to the heard words. Both depend on the contrast of an easy combination of tasks with a very difficult combination involving (re-paired) the same stimuli and responses. For the perfect timesharing experiment the two tasks were performed simultaneously, whereas the two tasks were performed singly in the IAT.

The connection between the timesharing experiment and the IAT is more than the structural similarity of their respective tasks. It is also that both involve the automatic activation of mental associations (at least, that's the current best theory). For ideomotor compatible tasks, the associations are links between mental representations of sensory consequences of actions and motor representations theorized to initiate those actions. In IAT experiments, the associations are of mental categories with valences (attitudes), traits (stereotypes), or self (identities). What I see as most important, however, is that both of these paradigms allow observation of automatic operation of associations, meaning that they operate without mental effort or awareness. In the difficult task combinations of both paradigms, the automatically active associations interfere with instructed performance, rather than facilitating it.

In an article we published in 2017, Marzu and I stated that the body of work we had been building was transforming understanding of the relation between conscious and unconscious mental functioning by making much clearer how automatically activated mental associations can shape conscious judgments outside of awareness. We had borrowed that idea from another nineteenth-century German philosopher-psychologist (also a physicist and physiologist), Hermann von Helmholtz (1925), who called it *unbewusster Schluss* (translated: unconscious inference). We used two metaphors to try to capture this: "associations might be understood as mental pigments that operate in combination to construct rich mental images and judgments. A more psychological metaphor is that a mass of associative knowledge acts as a *cultural filter* that elaborates perception and judgment" (Greenwald & Banaji, 2017, p. 868).

Had I not taken the orchestra class in 1949, I would have graduated high school a year earlier, I would not have gone to M&A, and I would not have become a trumpet player. Would I have gotten into Yale? Without the Yale influences, I might have ended up in a discipline other than psychology. I would have gotten my PhD a year later, and I could not conceivably have started a postdoctoral position with Sam Messick's Personality Research Group at ETS in fall of 1963. That last observation is the most significant one. Also arriving at ETS to work as a research assistant in fall 1963 was Jean Alexander, who had graduated from Oberlin as a psychology major two years earlier. Jean and I married six months after our first date. I am crying as I write this, remembering the last fifty-seven years with Jean, who died of leukemia in 2021. Unlike my crying in desperation in 1949, my crying as I write about Jean has a large component of joy. It was Jean's nature for others (not just me) to be happy in her presence. I brought her along to all professional occasions I could persuade her to attend, including quite a few conferences away from home. Early on, I understood that not only was I happier when Jean was with me – my colleagues also seemed much happier to see me when Jean was with me.

Jean influenced a great many things that I did in the past fifty-seven years. Her influence continues. When she and I disagreed, I might try to persuade her of my view. That no longer works. I frequently described Jean to others as "my better 80%." Her death has not changed that. I can't imagine how my choice in 1949 to learn to play trumpet could have turned out any better.

Suggested Reading

Banaji, M. R., & Greenwald, A. G. (1995). Implicit gender stereotyping in judgments of fame. *Journal of Personality and Social Psychology, 68*, 181–198.

Draine, S. C., & Greenwald, A. G. (1998). Replicable unconscious semantic priming. *Journal of Experimental Psychology: General, 127*, 286–303.

Fazio, R. H., Sanbonmatsu, D. M., Powell, M. C., & Kardes, F. R. (1986). On the automatic activation of attitudes. *Journal of Personality and Social Psychology, 50*, 229–238.

Graf, P., & Schacter, D. (1985). Implicit and explicit memory for new associations in normal and amnesic subjects. *Journal of Experimental Psychology: Learning, Memory, and Cognition, 11*, 501–518.

Greenwald, A. G. (2010). Under what conditions does intergroup contact improve intergroup harmony? In M. H. Gonzales, C. Tavris, & J. Aronson (Eds.), *The Scientist and the Humanist: A Festschrift in Honor of Elliot Aronson* (pp. 267–281). New York: Psychology Press.

Greenwald, A. G., & Albert, S. M. (1968). Observational learning: A technique for elucidating S-R mediation processes. *Journal of Experimental Psychology, 76*, 267–272.

Greenwald, A. G., & Banaji, M. R. (1995). Implicit social cognition: Attitudes, self-esteem, and stereotypes. *Psychological Review, 102*, 4–27.

(2017). The implicit revolution: Reconceiving the relation between conscious and unconscious. *American Psychologist, 72*, 861–871.

Greenwald, A. G., & De Houwer, J. (2017). Unconscious conditioning: Demonstration of existence and difference from conscious conditioning. *Journal of Experimental Psychology: General, 146*, 1705–1721.

Greenwald, A. G., Gonzalez, R., Guthrie, D. G., & Harris, R. J. (1996). Effect sizes and *p*-values: What should be reported and what should be replicated? *Psychophysiology, 33*, 175–183.

Greenwald, A. G., McGhee, D. E., & Schwartz, J. L. K. (1998). Measuring individual differences in implicit cognition: The Implicit Association Test. *Journal of Personality and Social Psychology, 74*, 1464–1480.

Greenwald, A. G., Pratkanis, A. R., Leippe, M. R., & Baumgardner, M. H. (1986). Under what conditions does theory obstruct research progress? *Psychological Review, 93*, 216–229.

Jacoby, L. L., & Whitehouse, K. (1989). An illusion of memory: False recognition influenced by unconscious perception. *Journal of Experimental Psychology: General, 118*(2), 126–135.

James, W. (1890). *The Principles of Psychology*, 2 vols. New York: Holt.

Lotze, R. H. (1852) *Medicinische psychologie.* Leipzig: Weidmann.

Pratkanis, A. R., Eskenazi, J., & Greenwald, A. G. (1994). What you expect is what you believe (but not necessarily what you get): A test of the effectiveness of subliminal self-help audiotapes. *Basic and Applied Social Psychology, 15*, 251–276.

Pratkanis, A. R., Greenwald, A. G., Leippe, M. R., & Baumgardner, M. H. (1988). In search of reliable persuasion effects: III. The sleeper effect is dead: Long live the sleeper effect. *Journal of Personality and Social Psychology, 54*, 203–218.

Skinner, B. F. (1950). Are theories of learning necessary? *Psychological Review, 57*(4), 193–216.

von Helmholtz, H. (1925). *Handbook of Physiological Optics* (Vol. 3; J. P. C. Southall, Trans.). New York: Optical Society of America (Original work published 1867).

9   Curiosity

Elaine Hatfield

I was born curious. From the first I can remember, I was like Hermione in *Harry Potter*, always either waving my hand wildly, begging "call on me teacher, call on me" or constantly asking "Why?" Both got me in trouble. I was a gentle, pretty nice child, but it didn't seem to dawn on me that I would be considered a "smart ass" or "really weird" if I was curious about the world.

When my mother warned my sister and me, for instance, that we shouldn't go out on Good Friday because it always rained from 1:00 to 3:00 p.m. (when Christ was crucified) I, of course, had to ask: "Is that true all over the world? Could we get weather reports?" When the Catholic nuns said "birth control was evil because it was unnatural," I asked if I should shun medicine, because that was unnatural too. I was sent to the priest on the assumption that I was being proselytized by Christian Scientists. I was just curious. The nuns were not amused.

Family History

I was born in Detroit in 1937. On my father's side, I am descended from the Hatfields of Hatfield-McCoy fame. (See www.cambridge.org/pillarsofsocialpsychology for a photographic portrait of the family, in which everyone, including the children, have guns!) My father's family was hard-shell Baptist (a very conservative sect that includes snake handlers). But that wasn't conservative enough for my grandfather. So he formed his own sect and called it – the Hatfields. Its membership numbers were, perforce, somewhat limited.

My mother's family was Roman Catholic. They emigrated to Newfoundland and then to the United States during the Great Irish potato famine. I went to Herman Gardens grade school, which educated students in our very low income housing project. I loved that school. When boys called me "teachers' pet," I took that to be a compliment. The teachers loved me and it was a mutual love affair. Schools were my refuge.

It wasn't so nice at home. My father was not fond of women or girls. He was quite gratuitously cruel, a seething cauldron of venom, always ready to explode. He was not my inspiration to study love. My mother was deeply depressed. In all my photos of her, you see this lovely woman staring vacantly into the distance, looking like a sad and wounded child. You can't see those photos without yearning to take care of her.

Elaine Hatfield, University of Hawai'i, USA.

University of Michigan

I escaped the misery of home life at 17, going to the University of Michigan. I majored in psychology and English literature, with generous dollops of anthropology and foreign literature. Bob Zajonc was my mentor and model and remained a friend until his death. There I had a chance to work with Dave Birch (testing Hull's theories with rats) and Gerald Gurin, Sheila Feld, and Joe Veroff (*Americans View Their Mental Health*) which taught me about primitive computers and large survey data sets. How fortunate I was.

Stanford University

When I arrived at Stanford in 1959 (I received my PhD four years later), I signed up to work with Leon Festinger and Douglas Lawrence, who were collaborating on *Cognition, Decision, and Dissonance*, a series of papers arguing for cognitive dissonance in rats. Leon was a delight, totally egalitarian, and always worked hard to foster students' careers.

There was, however, one problem with this natural alliance. I was fascinated by emotions, in general, and the phenomenon of passionate love in particular. One couldn't really be paying attention without noticing that the cognitive-behavioral theorists seemed to be lacking something when it came to explaining powerful emotional experiences.

It was obvious to me that passionate love was a desperately intense motivator for young people. When my friends were besotted with love, they always became a little bit nuts. One fellow student could painstakingly articulate why a certain lovely, bright, vivacious but extremely neurotic woman was poison and why he should stay well away from her. Nonetheless, in spite of his piercing logic, you couldn't help but notice that he kept one eye on the laboratory phone, waiting for it to become free so that he could call her to plead for "just one more chance." (Nobody seemed to be desperately in love with the perfectly sensible men and women who loved them and caused no trouble at all!) Clark Hull and reinforcement theory simply did not do a very good job of explaining such weird (and totally human) behavior. How could I dismiss passionate love as an unimportant topic?

Late in the evening after our work was done, faculty and students often confided in one another about their personal problems – all of which seemed to focus on love and sex. For most, things were not going well; usually they were not going at all! Some of us couldn't find anyone to date. Most were in complicated, confusing relationships. A few of my friends were getting divorces. For my colleagues none of this was trivial. One night, several of my friends complained that they were so discouraged that they sometimes thought about committing suicide. Something profound and unsettling was going on here.

I began to think about conducting research into passionate love. Faculty member Gordon Bower and my fellow graduate students, who were mostly hard scientists interested in constructing mathematical models of rat learning, warned me, in good faith, to avoid such topics. They cautioned me that I had to worry about "career management." Passionate love just wasn't a very important phenomenon (!) and, even if it were, there was no hope of finding out very much about it in our lifetime. Worst of all, the whole topic just wasn't respectable. And it wasn't "hot." (This is ironic.) The topic of the moment was mathematical modeling. Reinforcement theory and math modeling. Perhaps one set of interests (reinforcement and math models) during the daytime and another (passionate love and maybe suicide) in the evenings – as a hobby.

I was always stubbornly interested in what fascinated me rather than with "career management." So I suggested to Leon Festinger, my advisor, that our Thursday night research group should set aside some time now and then for discussing hazy, half-formed ideas. We could discuss the possibilities of doing research on taboo, neglected, and impossible topics like love, sex, and the emotions. He said that sounded like a great idea. I should go first. I decided to speculate about possible links between self-esteem and one's vulnerability to love. My idea was this:

When self-esteem tumbled to an all-time *low*, one should be especially vulnerable to falling in love. There were two reasons why this might be so. First, people with high self-esteem are likely to assume that they have a great deal to offer others; they can afford to "demand the very best." Thus, the higher one's self-esteem, the more one might require from a "suitable" date or mate. Second, when self-esteem is low or has been momentarily shattered, one may well have an increased *need* for the affection and regard of others. The lower one's self-esteem, the more appreciative people should be when anyone seems to love them, and the more likely they should be to reciprocate that affection.

My first step was to check the clinical literature to see if there was any research to support my hypothesis. There wasn't much. In 1944, Theodor Reik had published a wise and witty book entitled *A Psychologist Looks at Love.* He argued that people were most susceptible to passionate love when their self-esteem had been bruised. Novelists seconded his observations. Mary McCarthy, in *The Company She Keeps*, for example, discussed the link between low self-esteem and vulnerability to deeply flawed, misguided love.

But most clinicians (such as Carl Rogers, Alfred Adler, Karen Horney, and Erich Fromm) said Theodor Reik (and I) had things the wrong way around. It was *high self-esteem* people who were most receptive to love. They argued, logically enough: if people can't love themselves, how can they be expected to love anyone else? The sparse correlational data that existed seemed to support *their* contentions and challenge Reik's (and mine).

Leon Festinger agreed with these theorists as well. Dissonance theory predicted that if we think badly of ourselves, we should experience cognitive dissonance if someone assures us we are wonderful. One likely way to reduce such dissonance would be to assume that these Pollyannas must be stupid, confused, or have ulterior motives. Surely when they got to know us better they would change their minds.

On Thursday night, as I stood up to present my half-formulated ideas to the research group, I was stunned to discover that Leon, who had arrived late from a merry faculty dinner at a Greek restaurant, had invited some of the celebrants – Al Hastorf, Gordon Bower, Jon Freedman, and Alex Bavelas – to join in that night's meeting. In terror, I plunged on ahead. It is probably unnecessary to mention that my proposal did not knock the socks off the assembled critics. Many of them agreed that the idea just wasn't a very interesting one. One noted that in the 1940s, theorists had found that rats on partial learning schedules displayed a burst of energy when a reward finally did arrive. Presumably such long-denied rewards were doubly rewarding. The phenomenon even had a name – the Crespi effect. Why bother replicating a well-established finding yet again? People or rats, it didn't matter. An effect was an effect.

One of those wonderful men cautioned me that people's perceptions as to what was rewarding were elusive. Would we find someone who confirmed our opinions rewarding? What if others agreed that we were miserable human beings? Was even that rewarding? Or did we inevitably prefer those who praised us? Who knew? Why bother? Why not stick to basic research? So, of course, I proceeded to do just what I wanted to do anyway. How could I do otherwise? I agreed that I would run traditional, sensible, dissonance and learning experiments in the daytime. But I would do my own research in the evenings and on weekends. And I did.

Stanford was a haven for researchers. I had a chance to work with Alex Bavelas, Jon Freedman, Ernest Hilgard, Doug Lawrence, Pauline and Bob Sears, and of course, dear Gordon Bower. I also learned from fellow students Peter Gumpert, Jane Allyn Piliavin, Ted Rosenthal, and the like.

The world, however, was not so welcoming. When it was time to get a job, Leon asked me, a bit proudly, "Where do you want to teach? You are the best student I've ever had and I can get you a job anyplace." (Probably he said that to all students.) I said "Harvard or Yale," but Leon was to be disappointed. It was the era of Sputnik and there was a plethora of jobs, but not for me. "The times aren't right for a woman. Maybe try one of the women's colleges," a couple of his colleagues suggested.

Over the next five decades I had a chance to work at a distinguished group of faculty and students at first-rate universities. With each move, the faculty's attitude toward women (and me) improved. But first came the University of Minnesota.

The University of Minnesota

Thoroughly chagrined and surprised, Leon called Ben Willerman, the Dean of Social Sciences at the University of Minnesota. There was an opening in the Student Activities Bureau, organizing student activities, Willerman said. "She can have it" – a hilarious irony since at that time I was one of the shyest and least social people on planet Earth. The SAB was very good to me. In truth, I suspect they didn't know who I was or why I was there. Since I was invisible, my colleagues and I were able to run a number of experiments testing how Equity theory affected choice in randomly selected freshmen at computer dances (e.g., Berscheid et al., 1971; for an overview, see Hatfield et al., 1978). Match.com, in embryo . . .

Knowing I was a psychologist, the then Chair of Psychology Jack Darley informed me that: (1) women were not allowed to hang their coats in the faculty cloakroom in Coffman Memorial Union; and (2) they were not allowed to eat lunch in the Faculty Club. At Coffman Memorial Union, there were two dining rooms, separate but unequal. The Faculty Club was stellar: it had high vaulted wood-beamed ceilings. Its walls were glass and they looked out over the Minneapolis skyline and the Mississippi River. It was hushed, elegant, airy, well-upholstered, and intimate. Student waiters, resplendent in starched white jackets, presented the food just-so on the creamy, linen tablecloths.

The Café, on the other hand, was a large public cafeteria that served the lower orders. Young women – the administrative staff, secretaries, and the teaching assistants who helped run the place – ate there. The cafeteria was large and noisy. The clatter ricocheted off the hard surfaces of the tile ceilings, white walls, and tile floors. The food was mediocre and self-service. The steam tables filled the room with damp and heat.

The Chair said that he was sure that I and my new friend, graduate student Ellen Berscheid, would prefer the steam room. Actually, he said cheerily, he wished *he* were free to eat in the Café. "The food is better, the service faster, and the company is certainly a lot prettier." But alas, poor guy, he was condemned to sit with his colleagues. Ellen and I were too polite to mention that he was free to join us anytime he liked.

And so, for a time, Ellen and I ate lunch together every day. We became colleagues and fast friends for life. She was – as I saw it then and see it now – sensitive, brilliant, courageous, and lots of fun. As pariahs, we had a chance to pursue the intellectual interests that fascinated us (passionate love, sex, the importance of looks, Equity and perceptions of social justice) and skip those that bored us to tears. In retrospect, being "forced" to spend so much time with Ellen and deprived of the elegant dining room, turned out to be a marvelous trade-off.

Elliot Aronson, another one-time Festinger student, was head of the lab for Research on Social Relations and he kindly invited me to join the lab (*sub rosa*, of course). I was allowed to team teach with him, work with graduate students (enter my lifelong colleague Ellen Berscheid and Darcy Abrahams) and utilize the UM subject pool. For that I am eternally grateful. When Elliot and his group moved to Texas, Ellen and I moved into their offices. *Don't ask. Don't tell.*

Later, Ellen and I tried to sneak into the Faculty dining room where Paul Meehl, Kenneth McCorquodale, Elliot Aronson, and other luminaries had lunch every day. We asked, "May we sit here?" and promptly did so. They all looked at one another, uneasy and unsettled. "Certainly," they said. But within moments they all "remembered they had a meeting." One by one they left – all were gone within five minutes. We hurriedly finished our lunch, a lump in our throats, and then left too. Talk about leaving a bad taste in one's mouth. It never fully went away.

We didn't give up, though, not completely. The next day, we took a seat at the end of the room. Then, day by day, we moved one table closer. Finally, we were a foot from the Psychology table. (You can see we were secret Skinnerians.) They got used to us close by. We never summoned up the nerve to sit at their table again, however. Our colleagues at Minnesota seemed to have a problem – they found identity between Ellen and me where little existed. They called us "Ellen & Elaine," or "The Gold Dust Twins." Eli Finkel, a favorite of ours, once called us the Thelma and Louise of Psychology.

Sometimes, at the Business School, where Ellen eventually got a job, she was called "Blondie." I suspect the mistaken identities arose from their assumption that "ya seen one lady professor, ya seen 'em all." (Most professors had never seen even one!) To our minds, we possess very different personalities – and our husbands rarely got us mixed up!

Ellen is the elegant and witty one. When I (Elaine) get an email from her, Dick (my husband) will sometimes glance up from his paper and say, "Ah! You must have gotten a letter from Ellen." "How did you guess?" Elaine once asked. "It's obvious," he said. "At the first ping, you start giggling and don't quit until you sign off." Dick is right: Ellen has a very mordant, iconoclastic sense of humor. You can but smile.

University of Wisconsin

Over the next two decades, I team-taught a number of social psychology research courses in which faculty and students speculated about the possible links between passionate love, Equity theory, and physical attractiveness. The *Passionate Love Scale*, first introduced in 1985, was designed to assess the cognitive, physiological, and behavioral indicants of such a longing for union (see Hatfield & Sprecher, 1986). In 1972 Martin Erle invited me to come as a Guest Research Professor to *Sonderforschungsbereich 24*, a collaborative research center in Mannheim, Germany.

One might think I would have worked with Harry and Margaret Harlow given their work on the nature of love in chimps. But Harry was a traditional man, disdaining both Margaret and women in general. During a tenure meeting at the School of Education, he spoke against Margaret's promotion. I argued strongly on her behalf. Indignant, he passed me a little note with a cartoon showing a woman trembling in the corner of a large rat cage and the note: "If you want to be a feminist, why don't you go home and _____." I didn't know exactly what he meant. I still don't. As Kendra Cherry (2020) observed in *History and Biographies*: "After the terminal illness of his wife, he became engulfed by alcoholism and depression, eventually becoming estranged from his own children. Colleagues frequently described him as sarcastic, mean-spirited, misanthropic, chauvinistic, and cruel." (www.verywellmind.com/harry-harlow-and-the-nature-of-love-2795255)

I'd had enough of that with my dad.

The most damaging blow to our research program was yet to come. In 1975, Wisconsin's Senator William Proxmire discovered that the National Science Foundation had granted me $84,000 (over three years) to further my work on passionate and companionate love. He fired off a press release:

I object to this not only because no one – not even the National Science Foundation – can argue that falling in love is a science; not only because I'm sure that even if they spend $84 million or $84 billion they wouldn't get an answer that anyone would believe. I'm also against it because I don't *want* the answer.

An attack on my research project soon followed. Senator Proxmire awarded both Ellen and me the critical "Golden Fleece Award." Subsequently, he gave the same "Award" to dozens of other love and sex researchers, supposedly for "fleecing" the government by conducting research that was "junk." Proxmire's joke could have been worth a chuckle, except that he was deadly serious and damaged many social psychology research enterprises.

The press of course had a field day. My mother's Roman Catholic bishop, the Rt. Rev. Richard S. Emrich, denounced our work in a Detroit newspaper. He reminded parishioners that Christ had told us all we need to know about love in the Holy Bible. We should just follow His orders. The *Chicago Daily News* began a daily series on the debate. They invited readers to call in with their votes. Did readers think our love research was worth $84,000 in tax money or not? The answer of course was a resounding "No!" To illustrate the relative standing of Proxmire and Hatfield in the informal poll, they showed two cartoon characters' heads – his and mine – pasted on little cartoon bodies and balanced precariously on a teeter-totter. Each day, as irate readers called or wrote in, Hatfield's standing or sitting (and position on the teeter-totter) sank lower and lower. The final standing: Proxmire 8, Hatfield 1. Conclusion: love should remain a mystery.

Senator Barry Goldwater, of all people, came to my defense. So did columnist James Reston. In his column in *The New York Times* he wryly agreed that love will always be a mystery. "But if the sociologists and psychologists can get even a suggestion of the answer to our pattern of romantic love, marriage, disillusions, divorce – and the children left behind – it would be the best investment of federal money since Jefferson made the Louisiana purchase."

I tried to explain why the study of love is important. In 1978, I wrote a little book (*A New Look at Love*) to explain why the study of love matters and what social psychologists have learned about passionate and companionate love. In 1979 the book won the American Psychological Association's and the American Psychological Foundation's National Media Award for the best book in psychology.

Today, many people assume that the great debate is an enjoyable memory for me. They make that assumption because the "taboo topics" I thought were fascinating have been taken up by a generation of young researchers. Today, love and emotion are the "hot topics." But I remember those "bad, old days" with no pleasure. The battle, though it had to be fought and despite the agreeable outcome, was never fun.

The University of Hawai'i

I moved to Hawaii in 1981. My University of Hawai'i years have been the happiest time in my life. Shortly after arrival I met and married Dick Rapson, an American and intellectual historian. And I have been happy. Hawaii truly is Paradise.

Funnily, soon after we were married we received a visit from a Hollywood producer who wanted to pitch to us this "great idea" he had for a film he wished to make. It was about this scholar of love – yes, modeled after me – who was supposed to understand how love works, but alas who couldn't find love in her own life. It would be a musical comedy. At this, the guy literally slapped his knees as he laughed at how brilliant his satire was. What did we think? Guess.

Dick is everything I dreamed of in a husband. We share all our intellectual interests. We work together on everything – novels, books, and scientific papers. We are so much Dick & Elaine, that I am often listed as a rising young historian and he as a mature psychologist. We were joint therapists for fifteen years in our free time. Readers of our latest text, *What's Next in Love and Sex*, will see that since my collaboration with Dick my perspective has greatly enlarged, encompassing cross-cultural, interdisciplinary, and historical perspectives (Hatfield, Rapson, & Purvis, 2021). My colleagues in Hawaii have very broad interests, too. These include Ken Cushner (from Semester at Sea), Dharm Bhawuk, Dan Landis, Chuck Mueller, and Tim Naftali. I've learned from my students too: Lisamarie Bensman, Megan Carpenter, Skyler Hawk, Lise Martel, Jeanette Purvis, Ted Singelis, Paul Thornton, and Danielle Young, among others.

I think a richer intellectual future resides with less fragmented and specialized approaches and more with the broader ones. I hope so anyway.

The Future

I stand in wonder to see how things have wildly changed since I was born in 1937. Then there were peddlers parading horse drawn flatbeds, delivering blocks of ice for our iceboxes. Now we count among our friends astronauts like George "Pinky" Nelson, Bob Parker, and Kathy Thornton. We have gone from radios, which broadcast the *Lone Ranger*, *Land of the Lost*, and *Grand Central Station*, to cell phones and streaming movies. Once universities didn't hire women on their faculties; now they make up a much larger number. As late as 1910, people lived forty years on the average. Now they can expect to double that number. Once the study of love was taboo; now people in every field study it.

I have received more than my share of awards for my research on cross-cultural love, passionate love, physical attractiveness, Equity theory, and emotional contagion. But there are scores more doing great research who have not been similarly honored. Awards are a bit of a lottery. As to the future, in *What's Next* we attempted to predict what the world of love and sex will be in coming generations. It addresses such topics as the role of social media in love and sex, an increase in the kinds of love and sex that are considered acceptable (from monogamy to swingers and polyamory), the development of sex dolls and robots, avatars, fantasy sex, virtual pornography, interactive sex, and the benefits and the pain of love.

Predicting the future is, of course, a fool's errand since no one really knows what's coming, whether about love or whether our species will even survive. But with some humor and humility, we tried. Unhappily (or happily) we won't be around to find out whether or not we got it right.

Suggested Reading

Berscheid, E., Dion, K., Walster, E., & Walster, G. W. (1971). Physical attractiveness and dating choice: A test of the matching hypothesis. *Journal of Experimental Social Psychology, 7,* 173–189.

Berscheid, E., & Hatfield, E. (1969). *Interpersonal Attraction.* New York: Addison-Wesley (Revised second edition 1978).

Cherry, K. (2020). Harry Harlow. *History and Biographies.* www.verywellmind.com/harry-harlow-and-the-nature-of-love-2795255.

Hatfield, E., Rapson, R. L., & Purvis, J. (2021). *What's Next in Love and Sex: Psychological and Cultural Perspectives.* New York: Oxford University Press.

Hatfield, E., & Sprecher, S. (1986). Measuring passionate love in intimate relationships. *Journal of Adolescence, 9*(4), 383–410.

Hatfield, E., & Walster, G. W. (1978). *A New Look at Love: A Revealing Report on the Most Elusive of Emotions.* Reading, MA: Addison-Wesley.

Hatfield, E., Walster, G. W., & Berscheid, E. (1978). *Equity: Theory and Research.* Boston: Allyn & Bacon

McCarthy, M. (1942). *The Company She Keeps.* Generic.

Reik, T. (1944). *A Psychologist Looks at Love.* New York: Farrar & Rinehart.

10 The Emergence and Evolution of Social Realities

Bibb Latané

Despite my "foreign" last name, I am an eighth-generation American dating from 1701 when my great[5]-grandfather Lewis Latané, at 14 a refugee from Louis XIV's genocide of French Protestants, at 29 arrived in Tappahannock, VA, newly ordained by the Bishop of London after earning a degree from Oxford, with an annual salary of two hogsheads of tobacco. He promptly used it, no doubt with the full approval of the Church of England, to buy slaves.

My family's living room featured formal oil paintings of Lewis's great-grandson, Henry Waring and his wife Susan Allen Latané, done just before the start of the Civil War. By this time, their slaveholdings had grown to about 200 individuals. Because the land was no longer so suitable for tobacco, these persons were probably used for the breeding of other slaves to sell south to Alabama cotton planters. Their son William, a University of Virginia graduate, physician, and Confederate cavalry officer, was the sole casualty of J. E. B. Stuart's famed reconnaissance raid behind the Union army. William was immortalized in 1864 by a poem in the *Southern Literary Messenger* and a painting called the *Burial of Latané*, showing Black slaves putting his shroud-covered body into the ground while White women and children mourned, and a black-robed matron led the prayers (to view a photo of this painting, see www.cambridge.org/pillarsofsocialpsychology).

A steel engraving of the image, offered free by *Southern Magazine* with the purchase of an annual subscription, became a standard decorative item in late nineteenth-century White southern homes including my family's living room. According to historian Drew Gilpin Faust, recent President of Harvard, the engraving proved integral to creating and sustaining the myth of the Lost Cause, a myth that, although contentious, continues today in the forms of the Confederate flag, MAGA caps, and persistent racism.

Depicting the Civil War from a female perspective, the image also celebrated the so-called loyal and faithful slave as a model of southern race relations. Applauding freedmen who might tearfully mourn their former masters allowed southern Whites to praise those Black people who knew their "place" in the postwar society – those who did not meddle in politics or question the authority of Whites. Thus, the print helped create and communicate *a real, if perverse, social reality*, although one that, thankfully, my family did not share.

Bibb Latané, Center for Human Science, USA.

I am unsure when my mother's side of my family first bought slaves, but it must have been well before my direct ancestor William Wyatt Bibb became senator from Georgia and, in 1817, the first governor of Alabama. I do not know his role as governor in the forced relocation of Native Americans to the West and the brutal practices whereby Black slaves, coffled from Virginia in chains, cleared the land, planted and picked cotton, and brought immense wealth to White Americans north and south. I do know that he was famous for his 1816 US Senate speech opposing a Constitutional Amendment for the direct election of presidents on the ground that it would negate a major southern political advantage – the ability to count 80 percent of their slaves toward the number of electors afforded each state.

Bibbs were important in early Georgia, Alabama and Kentucky (Bibb lettuce was developed in Kentucky in the 1850s). Perhaps the most praiseworthy of my Bibb relatives is the author of the eloquent autobiography, *Narrative of the Life and Adventures of Henry Bibb, an American Slave* (1849) (for the cover portrait of Henry Bibb, see www.cambridge.org/pillarsofsocialpsychology). This book offers a striking reminder of the perverse social realities that fathering a child with a slave produced, not a family member but another slave, and having a mother with one drop of Black blood meant you could be treated as property. Henry Bibb escaped to Canada where he established an abolitionist newspaper and lectured against slavery.

I am proud of my ancestors – many of whom were doctors, lawyers, ministers, professors, and public servants – but not of their slave ownership and I have always been fascinated by how good people can take part in terrible things without being or becoming moral monsters. It seems especially difficult to reconcile their admirable courage and self-sacrifice with their endorsement of and participation in preserving a society based on human bondage. My best explanation is that they were *living under a different social reality*.

Growing Up with Graduate Students

My parents, southerners living in Greenwich Village (where I was born) after going north to Smith College and Harvard Business School, decided in 1950 to come back south to Graduate School at the University of North Carolina, my father in economics, my mother in psychology. I was just starting high school and my sister Julie was in elementary school, and we would all walk around the block to the Carolina Inn cafeteria for dinner, coming home to do our homework together around the dining room table.

It puzzled me that in his economics courses, my father was learning that humans are motivated by the desire to maximize subjective expected utility (von Neumann & Morgenstern, 1947), while in her psychology courses, my mother was learning that humans have a hierarchy of needs leading up to self-actualization (Maslow, 1943). Neither theory seemed very useful in explaining the obvious cultural differences between New York and North Carolina, from whether to put mustard or ketchup/ catsup on a hamburger to speech patterns and the overt expression of racist ideas, and the theories didn't even seem to have much in common.

Culture and Behavior at Yale

I arrived at Yale in 1954 as one of only a few southerners, planning on going to law school and becoming a corporate lawyer. I majored in culture and behavior, hoping to learn about natural social laws before diving into man-made ones. The culture and behavior program offered afternoon seminars with faculty from anthropology, biology, economics, psychology, and sociology, as well as research opportunities. In one, I asked White residents of a New Haven neighborhood into which southern Black families were flooding what they thought of their new neighbors. When I told them "by the way, I'm from North Carolina," their response typically changed from "Oh, they are fine neighbors," to "Oh, then you know how bad they are," an early example of the difficulty of measuring racist attitudes.

Graduating from Yale in 1958, I was accepted at Harvard Law School, famous for its competitive environment, and offered non-work fellowships at Michigan and UNC as well as a research assistantship with Stanley Schachter at the University of Minnesota. As with many of life's choices, rather than reject one alternative, I decided to try for a combination, serving an apprenticeship in group dynamic research methods while gaining some maturity before getting my law degree. I contacted Harvard and was granted a deferred admission.

Social Relations Lab at the University of Minnesota

The Social Relations Lab, one of a number of post-World War II academic efforts to break down disciplinary boundaries, was anchored by psychologists Stanley Schachter and Harold Kelley, with joint appointments from economics, education, philosophy of science, political science, and sociology. Graduate students from psychology, economics (one a future Nobel Prize winner), and sociology were assigned one of about a dozen desks in a large bullpen. Desks, file cabinets, and a coffee pot were arranged to provide some privacy while allowing everyone to see and hear what was going on. Periodically, Stan would stick in his head and summon one of his advisees to meet in his office, where we would often be challenged to a cribbage game as we talked about research plans.

My first seminar with Schachter focused in detail on his thin but rich book *Social Pressures in Informal Groups* (1950), co-authored with Leon Festinger and sociologist Kurt Back. Commissioned by the MIT Housing Authority, this applied survey of attitudes toward a proposed tenants' council at MIT's Westgate married student housing complex resulted in:

- innovative matrix and graphical methods for studying social networks,
- a demonstration that the locations of randomly assigned housing units could shape social interactions and create friendship groups,
- an introduction of the concept of "social reality" as residents developed coherent patterns of beliefs and behaviors about the proposed tenants' council, and
- a group-level theory of "pressures to uniformity" to explain why different courtyards developed different sets of beliefs, or subcultures.

Over the next five to seven years, Stan and Leon published individual-level theories of social comparison and dissonance reduction to explain why and how people influence one another, starting their life-long move away from social dynamics and group processes and toward a focus on individual cognition.

At Minnesota, where I got my PhD in 1963, I got to play the Happy Stooge, hula hooping on a table-top to test Schachter & Singer's (1962) cognitive-physiological theory of emotion and injecting adrenalin into the arms of Stillwater State Prison murderers who were sociopathic vs. those incarcerated for crimes of passion (Schachter & Latané, 1964). I soon realized that I loved what I was doing and notified Harvard I would not be enrolling in law school just yet.

Department of Social Psychology at Columbia University

In the mid-1960s, Columbia University's psychology department was riven by a deep split between statistician Henry Garrett and psychologist/psychiatrist/anthropologist Otto Klineberg. Garrett claimed that every study comparing Black and White populations from whatever part of the country, using whatever measure of IQ, found strong differences favoring the latter – proof, he thought, of a natural White superiority. Klineberg showed that the same data, reanalyzed to compare test scores across regions, found northern Blacks outscoring southern Whites – proof, he thought, that education and other economic disparities explained the differences.

To resolve the conflict, the powers-that-be at Columbia decided to create a new interdisciplinary, graduate-level department built around Klineberg and personality psychologist Richard Christie, but adding Stanley Schachter and William McGuire as core faculty, with joint appointments from anthropology, economics, political science, and sociology.

Within a year, Klineberg was offered his dream position at the University of Paris and I was hired to be his replacement. What an opportunity! With a teaching load of just one graduate seminar per semester, I needed something to teach, but with Bill McGuire covering attitudes and cognitive behavior and Stan covering group dynamics and cognitive behavior, what was left for me? And how could I include a research component? As the social psychology department had no undergraduate students and the psychology department had no requirement for research participation, I cast around for a way to give students some experience designing and conducting research. To be as far away from cognition as possible, I put together a syllabus focusing on animal social behavior and set out to devise a research paradigm using that then-standard tool for psychological research, the albino rat. Columbia agreed to buy a rack of cages for an unused dingy room in the basement and gave me a small budget to *buy* my research participants.

Social Life of the Albino Rat

Norman Munn's *Handbook of Psychological Research on the Rat* (1950) was discouraging – based on repeated demonstrations that rats could not be taught to run to one side of a T-maze or press a bar in order to see another rat behind a mesh screen, Munn concluded that the highly inbred laboratory rat was basically an asocial animal with any sociable tendencies bred out.

With the insight that sociability would best be measured, not from the constrained choices of individual animals, but from *pairs* allowed to interact and play with one another, the class devised an open-field measure of social attraction. Putting two rats at a time into a circular 4-foot space, we simply recorded the location of each animal at 10-second intervals and calculated whether they stayed closer to one another than would be expected by chance. Initial results were quite positive – rats chased one another about, climbed over and under each other, or just huddled together, typically spending about half their time in direct physical contact. This attraction did not depend on stimulus characteristics such as the rat-like smell of the other rat (for example, making rats anosmic did not decrease their attraction and perfumed rats were, if anything, *more* attractive than normal rats), suggesting that inbred lab rats may have lost some of the instinctive underpinnings such as pheromones that may be important for animals in the wild.

In some ways, my research program on animal sociability was the most satisfying of my career. A class could pose a question one week, order a shipment of rats to run the next, collect and analyze data the following week, and draft a brief report by the end of the semester. In the end, my students and I published several dozen papers in *JCPP*, *JESP*, *JPSP*, and Psychonomic Society journals, many not individually major, but together, painting a consistent picture that even the lowly laboratory rat is motivated by a satiable desire for social interaction with properly responsive but not necessarily similar partners (Latané & Werner, 1978), perhaps bringing us full circle to thinking of animal sociability as akin to a cognitive need.

Social Inhibition of Bystander Intervention and the Myth of Apathy

Even more than sixty years later, in part because the research it stimulated is still covered by many high school and college introductory psychology textbooks, people are aware of the midnight murder of Catherine Genovese in the streets of Kew Gardens, NY. Abe Rosenthal, editor of the *New York Times*, started the fascination with the dramatic headline "38 Watch as Woman is Murdered, No One Calls the

Police." Rosenthal's explanation was moral decay, urban alienation, or "apathy," which Rosenthal considered a disease, "a symptom of a terrible reality in the human condition."

In today's terminology, the story went "viral," stimulating massive press coverage, countless sermons and editorials decrying the "fact" that modern urban society had led Americans to become "moral imbeciles," indifferent to the suffering of one another.

Unconvinced by Rosenthal's (1964) claim that "simply by happenstance all thirty-eight did that night what each one alone might have done any night," John Darley, Judith Rodin, Lee Ross, Richard Nisbett, and I designed experiments to test the idea that the number that made the story so sensational may have contributed to its occurrence. As described in *The Unresponsive Bystander* (Latané & Darley, 1970, AAAS Socio-Psychological Prize winner), the resulting discoveries identified three distinct social processes that can be described as the "social inhibition of bystander intervention" (more accurate than the misleading "bystander effect," often misunderstood to mean the victim is more likely to get help the fewer the bystanders).

Far from being a moral illness, failure to respond results from social influence, the understanding of which can be used to help individuals act in closer accord with their moral predispositions. Our discoveries contributed to the emergence of the now prevailing psychological perspective of "situational determinism," the idea that behavior arises not only from within individuals, but from the social pressures they face. Ironically, we now know that Abe Rosenthal's "38 Witnesses" headline was written *after* Ms. Genovese's murderer had been caught as a result of a citizen reporting a crime in progress, and the reason the story went viral was that New York and the nation were in the midst of a decade of *rising*, not falling, concern about social alienation.

Our research on bystander inhibition led, directly or indirectly, to the introduction of the 911 system to make it easier to report a crime and the widespread teaching of the phrase "see something, say something." But still, reporters talk about "apathy" stories, and many people evaluate the actions of our slaveholding forebears in terms of today's morality, forgetting that their actions then were a product of their social environment then.

Behavioral Science Lab at Ohio State University

In 1968, Columbia decided to merge social psychology back into psychology, New York City was becoming increasingly unattractive as a place to raise children, and Chuck Kiesler, before leaving to become APA's Executive Director, convinced the Ohio State University to expand its social psychology faculty from one to four – Tim Brock, Tony Greenwald, Tom Ostrom, and myself. With offices located in the football stadium, the Behavioral Science Lab provided research facilities for political science and sociology, as well as social psychology.

Extending the Social Inhibition Paradigm – Social Loafing, Stage Fright, News Interest Value, and Social Impact Theory

Our research, reliably replicated (Latané & Nida, 1981), showed that social inhibition can result from several simultaneous processes as others can serve as (1) an audience, making people reluctant to make fools of themselves by overreacting, (2) sources of information that if no one is acting, maybe nothing much is going on, and (3) a set of co-actors among whom the onus of responsibility can be shared. From identifying these processes, my students and I extended the research to non-emergency situations such as social loafing (Latané, Williams, & Harkins, 1979, 2nd AAAS Prize) and stage fright (Jackson & Latané, 1981). We also investigated the roles of the strength and immediacy as well as the number of people involved, leading to the SIN formulation of social impact, which envisioned a wide variety of social influences, each with different characteristics, all following some general principles. Like sound, light, and gravity – each with quite different mechanisms of transmission and sensation but each following an inverse square law of distance – this conception can be viewed as a kind of "social physics," whereby impact can be multiplied and/or divided depending on the structure of the situation (Latané, 1981, SPSP Presidential Address).

Professional Activities: The Birth of PSPB and SPSP

During the 1970s, I became active in professional affairs, being appointed or elected to office in the Midwestern Psychological Association and APA's Division 8. A major debate swirled around the publication system, with some people, including the APA Publication Committee and my colleague Tony Greenwald, believing that too much research was being published with too little oversight, and others, including myself and Clifford Morgan of the Psychonomic Society, believing that science was being held back by overzealous editors. As editor and publisher of *Psychonomic Science*, Cliff had shown that it was economically and procedurally feasible to publish quality two-page articles with a very quick turnaround.

As Division 8 representative to the APA Council of Representatives, I was one of the first to learn of its plans to discontinue publication of its *Abstract Guide* for papers selected for presentation at the annual convention, a publication that had been a major resource in finding out what was happening in the field. Searching for a substitute, I discovered that with 4,000+ members and annual dues of $4, Division 8 could afford to publish its own bimonthly journal to be named *Personality and Social Psychology Bulletin* modeled on the *Bulletin of the Psychonomic Society* and distribute it free to the membership starting in 1975. The short-article format and the opportunity to reach such a large audience induced authors to submit papers. Clyde Hendrick as the first editor and Alan Gross as the managing editor managed to keep everything moving, and the journal was an instant success, inspiring us also to add a new publication, *Review of Personality and Social Psychology*, edited by my friend Ladd Wheeler for longer manuscripts.

Concerned that if divisional journals were too successful, APA might swoop in and take over, Marcia Guttentag and I proposed that we incorporate and superimpose a parallel organization to be known as the *Society for Personality and Social Psychology*, which, once it started hosting annual meetings in 2000, now rivals SESP and APA as the leading venue for presenting papers and networking. Unfortunately, this success may have also eroded the interdisciplinary character of social psychology.

Social Science Conferences Inc.

A major problem impeding research in behavioral and social science is the fact that university budgeting practices tend to segregate research into different disciplines, with different jargon, assumptions, methods, and core theories, leading each discipline to race off in different directions with reduced cumulative impact.

In 1982, my father, by then a professor of economics at UNC, and I, concerned by the very different explanations of social behavior between our fields, set up a nonprofit charity with the mission of promoting interdisciplinary communication in behavioral and social science. We each put down $10,000 for a large, ramshackle house on the beach at Kitty Hawk, NC, just across from the First Flight Airstrip – very convenient as I could fly my Cessna directly. All nonprofits need to show public support – in our case not by gifts or grants, but from participants paying their share of the expenses, which, because the house was rented during the summer to pay off the mortgage, were quite low.

Over the next twenty-five years, I hosted almost 150 three- to four-day *Nags Head Conferences*, first in North Carolina, then at the *Sea Frolic* on the Gold Coast of south Florida, another rundown older house on the beach. The conferences attracted over 2,500 participants, mostly university faculty, about a third from outside the country, over half repeat visitors. The meetings were held to a minimal cost so university people could afford to attend, and I drew no salary from running them. Many academics still credit their participation in a Nags Head Conference and the friendships they formed as important influences on their careers. Many of the groups that met regularly at Nags Head Conferences now gather for pre-conferences at the SPSP meetings.

My sister Julie, four years younger than me, started off following my footsteps but branched off to a more activist role. Extremely popular as an undergraduate at UNC, student council member, yearbook editor, dating the most popular boys, she went off to earn a PhD, get married to a fellow student, and land a tenure-track job at a small college in rural Pennsylvania. Frustrated with life as a married woman and professor, she redirected her considerable energy to non-violent direct social action. Hooking up with sociologist Paul Hare, she went with him on missions to protest apartheid in South Africa, to mediate between Greeks and Turks in Cyprus, and to participate in the 1973 occupation by Native Americans of the town of Wounded Knee, SD. Her untimely death at the age of 34 was a great personal loss, and a loss to the field at a time when it was difficult for women to find a place.

Institute for Research in Social Science at UNC-Chapel Hill

My last major interdisciplinary appointment was as Director of an interdisciplinary research institute with a multi-million dollar budget serving the whole university community with a data library, computer lab with terminals to the UNC mainframe, and statistical consultants. Despite some missteps (buying a mini-computer just at the start of the PC revolution), IRSS succeeded in developing CAPS – a computer administered panel survey using a relational database system for presenting questions and collecting and archiving individual responses – and made it available for collaborative research by investigators from different departments. CAPS evolved into KNOW (Knowledge Networking On the Web), which became the basis for *letsKNOW*, conceived as a set of supplements for hybrid courses. *LetsKNOW* consists of a series of "TIQ" slides each with some Text, Images, and a variety of Question formats, including the opportunity to write brief essays. Responses of one participant can be incorporated into questions posed to specific other participants located in an experimentally created social space or network, allowing structured group discussions of any number of topics.

In addition to collecting and archiving individual-level data, the system allows asynchronous group discussion, keeping records of each participant's inputs. Designed to serve as useful infrastructure for research in psychology, political science, behavioral economics, and sociology among other disciplines, the system is uniquely appropriate for testing the large-scale implications of dynamic social impact theory.

Dynamic Social Impact Theory

DSIT assumes that individuals distributed in social space are each influenced in their view of the world by their own individual experience and by their neighbors in proportion to their strength, immediacy, and number. Individuals will switch positions if and only if net persuasive impact is greater than the stabilizing forces of individual experience and net supportive impact. Furthermore, these processes can act independently on each of the variety of beliefs, values, and behavior that comprise subcultures. The question is: what will happen?

A number of studies, using face-to-face and virtual groups and computer simulation, show, surprisingly, that several macro-level phenomena, the "Four C's," emerge from the operation of these micro-level processes: (1) a **consolidation** or reduction in diversity as minority members are necessarily more exposed to contrary positions, (2) a **clustering** of minority positions into spatially coherent subgroups of people protecting each other from exposure to outside influence, (3) a **correlation** of people's initially unrelated positions on different issues as clusters overlap, and (4) an ultimate maintenance of **continuing diversity**, as minority enclaves survive (for an overview, see Latané & Nowak, 1997).

For example, consider a real group of 24 KNOW participants organized into a network of six 4-person teams each communicating electronically with one another

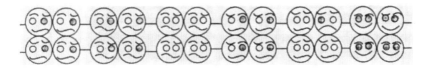

Figure 10.1 Post-discussion norm perceptions for the same actual group
Source: Latané & Bourgeois, (2001).

and with one person from the neighboring team. On each of five rounds, individuals are asked to judge the values of the entire organization on each of six issues. In Figure 10.1, six facial features (left and right eyebrows, eye colors, and smiles) of each person represent their beliefs about six different aspects of the whole organization. The images represent the judgments of real people after five rounds of electronic message exchange (Latané & Bourgeois, 2001).

Similar to the Westgate courtyards studied by Festinger, Schachter and Back (1950), each of the teams has developed its own social reality, with substantial differences between groups and only minor within-team variation of members' perceptions of the views of the organization as a whole. The finding brings us full circle back to the ability to combine individual and group-level processes in a start to a comprehensive theory of human cultures.[1]

Center for Human Science

In 2000, I decided to retire from getting paid as a professor and move back to the house in Chapel Hill, NC where I had grown up, still with the same paintings in the living room. Plans are in flux, but I am thinking of converting the house into the Latané-Gillman-Bibb Center for the Study of Race in America, with space and funding for visiting scholars and guest speakers. Perhaps my long-gone relatives still have something to teach us.

With the proceeds from the sale of the *Sea Frolic*, SSCI was able to add several neighboring houses to create a "campus" of seven structures with two dozen living units on almost two acres adjacent to UNC and downtown. The basic mission is still to bring together people from different backgrounds to share ideas and perspectives. You can find out more about the Center and suggest new directions at www .humanscience.org.

---

[1] Deborah Richardson and Helen Harton developed *KNITS* (Knowledge Networking in Teaching Science) as a classroom demonstration of social influence – students are asked their opinions on a series of issues before and after discussing them with the students sitting to their left and right and displaying the Four C's (Harton et al., 2000).

Closing Questions

Can social psychology still be considered interdisciplinary? How best can we combine individual and group-level processes? Perhaps my greatest professional disappointment has been the failure to get the *letsKNOW* system off the ground.

Suggested Reading

Bibb, H. (1849). *Narrative of the Life and Adventures of Henry Bibb, an American Slave.* Madison, WI: University of Wisconsin Press.

Festinger, L., Schachter, S., & Back, K. (1950). *Social Pressures in Informal Groups: A Study of Human Factors in Housing.* New York: Harper.

Harton, H. C., Green, L. R., Jackson, C., & Latané, B. (2000). Demonstrating dynamic social impact: Consolidation, clustering, correlation, and (sometimes) the correct answer. In M. E. Ware & D. Johnson (Eds.), *Handbook of Demonstrations and Activities in the Teaching of Psychology: Vol. 3. Personality, Abnormal, Clinical, Counseling, and Social.* Second edition (pp. 255–259). Hillsdale, NJ: Lawrence Erlbaum.

Jackson, J. M., & Latané, B. (1981). All alone in front of all those people: Stage fright as a function of number and type of co-performers and audience. *Journal of Personality and Social Psychology, 40,* 73–85.

Latané, B. (1974). The need for a *Personality and Social Psychology Bulletin. Division 8 Newsletter,* July, 16–18.

   (1978). Notes for a talk on our scientific publication system. *Personality and Social Psychology Bulletin, 4,* 22–23.

   (1981). The psychology of social impact. *American Psychologist, 36*(4), 343–363.

   (1997). Dynamic social impact: The societal consequences of human interaction. In C. McGarty & A. Haslam (Eds.), *The Message of Social Psychology: Perspectives on Mind and Society* (pp. 200–220). Oxford: Blackwell.

Latané, B., & Bourgeois, M. J. (2001). Dynamic social impact and the consolidation, clustering, correlation, and continuing diversity of culture. In M. A. Hogg & S. Tindale (Eds.), *Blackwell Handbook of Social Psychology: Group Processes* (pp. 235–258). Oxford: Blackwell.

Latané, B., & Darley, J. M. (1970). *The Unresponsive Bystander: Why Doesn't He Help?* New York: Appleton-Century-Crofts [now Prentice Hall]. (Winner of AAAS Socio-Psychological Prize, and the Richard M. Elliott Memorial Award)

Latané, B., & Jackson, J. (1978). Editors finally outnumber authors. *Personality and Social Psychology Bulletin, 4,* 195–196.

Latané, B., & Nida, S. (1981). Ten years of research on group size and helping. *Psychological Bulletin, 89,* 308–324.

Latané, B., & Nowak, A. (1997). Self-organizing social systems: Necessary and sufficient conditions for the emergence of consolidation, clustering, and continuing diversity. In G. Barnett & F. Boster (Eds.), *Progress in Communication Sciences: Persuasion* (Vol. 13, pp. 43–74). Norwood, NJ: Ablex.

Latané, B., & Werner, C. (1978). The regulation of social contact in laboratory rats: Time, not distance. *Journal of Personality and Social Psychology, 36,* 1128–1137.

Latané, B., Williams, K., & Harkins, S. (1979). Many hands make light the work: Causes and consequences of social loafing. *Journal of Personality and Social Psychology, 37,* 822–832. (Winner of AAAS Socio-Psychological Prize)

Maslow, A. H. (1943). A theory of human motivation. *Psychological Review, 50*(4), 370–396.

Munn, N. L. (1950). *Handbook of Psychological Research on the Rat: An Introduction to Animal Psychology.* Boston: Houghton Mifflin.

Nowak, A., Szamrej, J., & Latané, B. (1990). From private attitude to public opinion: A dynamic theory of social impact. *Psychological Review, 97*(3), 362–376.

Petty, R. E., Williams, K. D., Harkins, S. G., & Latané, B. (1977). Social inhibition of helping yourself: Bystander response to a cheeseburger. *Personality and Social Psychology Bulletin, 3,* 579–582.

Rosenthal, A. M. (1964). *Thirty-Eight Witnesses: The Kitty Genovese Case.* New York: McGraw-Hill.

Schachter, S., & Latané, B. (1964). Crime, cognition and the autonomic nervous system. In M. R. Jones (Ed.), *Nebraska Symposium on Motivation 1964* (pp. 221–273). Lincoln: University of Nebraska Press.

Schachter, S., & Singer, J. (1962). Cognitive, social, and physiological determinants of emotional state. *Psychological Review, 69*(5), 379–399.

Von Neumann, J., & Morgenstern, O. (1947). *Theory of Games and Economic Behavior.* Second edition. Princeton, NJ: Princeton University Press.

11 The Good Old Days

Bernard Weiner

In this abridged autobiography, I ask if I was born in the twenty-first century instead of 1935, how would my educational and professional life have differed from my actual experiences? That is, I consider some environmental conditions that influenced my life course. I also briefly examine a major research shift in my career that was not caused by environmental changes. I proceed in a life-span temporal sequence.

The Pre-Psychology Years

As an undergraduate at the University of Chicago, I was part of a Great Books curriculum. There were no majors or electives. For physics, a year was spent reading Newton and Galileo. I do not know how a light bulb works but I still remember Newton's laws of motion. Psychology was included within a year-long course in the social sciences; we read two of Freud's books. I assumed that fully represented the field.

My education at the University of Chicago, which started in 1952, was fantastic and altered my life but left me little prepared to choose a graduate field or place of study. I remained at the university, as did many of the undergrads, because we were guaranteed acceptance into graduate school. I entered the Business School with an interest in industrial and labor relations. A seminar was offered in industrial psychology, my only psychology course prior to later entrance into a graduate psychology program. That class was taught by Harold Leavitt, a student of someone I later came to revere by the name of Kurt Lewin. I subsequently became Leavitt's research assistant and found immortality when he put my name in the footnote of one of his publications. I was quite proud when I first saw that!

Shortly after graduation, while searching for an industrial job, I was drafted into the Army. This was not a surprise; many friends in my Chicago neighborhood also received their Army notifications. I spent two years honing my skills at ping-pong, improving my bridge game, and pondering what I really should do in life. I decided I wanted to be like Leavitt – obtain a PhD in organizational psychology and enter the field of education. One obligation I needed to fulfill was to take the graduate school

Bernard Weiner, University of California at Los Angeles, USA.

entrance exams. I was stationed in Huntsville, Alabama; the closest test administration was hours away at the University of Alabama. I left my barracks very early, drove a number of hours, and eventually was put into a closet of a room with some exam booklets. The one I most remember was called the Miller analogy test. It contained items such as: Pear is to Apple as Peach is to (Watermelon, Plum, Melon, Papaya). I won't tell you the answer. My scores on the other exams were 1240 and 1210 respectively for the math and verbal scales. These mediocre results, along with my B average from the Great Books undergraduate immersion, one psychology class in business school, one footnote, an absence of evidence of leadership skills (although I never understood what that means), and the trump card of a strong letter of recommendation from Leavitt, got me accepted into the University of Michigan, the only psychology program to which I applied! I was naïve and in a barracks in Alabama, far from advice.

So far, does this sound different from what I need to do or would do today to be admitted into a top graduate program? At that time, we were concerned but not consumed by thoughts and anxieties about college grades, graduate school entrance exams, or premature publications.

Psychology Graduate School

When enrolled in Leavitt's seminar in industrial psychology, I was exposed to a number of articles written by professors at the University of Michigan. Especially impressive were papers by Daniel Katz. He was the main reason I applied to Michigan; I had no idea what a great faculty it had and that it was considered the top, or near the top, psychology department in the country.

After moving to Ann Arbor, Michigan and barely settled, I went to Katz's office to introduce myself. I was, of course, quite apprehensive. However, my emotions were soon to change. On his office door was a note reading something as follows: "On sabbatical. Returning in September, 1960. Have a great year. Dan Katz." I was stunned and staggered away, my future plans in disarray. I immediately went to the psychology office and was casually informed that my advisor was John Atkinson and I was to be a research assistant to Melvin Manis.

After recovering, I went to meet with Atkinson, little imagining our future relationship. I had never heard of him and was unaware of his reputation as a motivation psychologist. He had me enroll in his course during my first semester. I later became Atkinson's research assistant, was accepted into his research group, and completed my doctoral dissertation under his direction. At that time, shifting from industrial psychology to personality, where Atkinson was listed, involved little other than informing a secretary. In my time later as a faculty member at UCLA, a student changing major areas required something akin to a letter from the President! Such inflexibility was not part of the Michigan culture; students switched majors from clinical to experimental psychology, and vice versa. In general, specialization and placement into a particular track too early was avoided.

Much of my graduate school life was spent in the library. This was prior to computers and the assigned reading was on library reserve, typically for two hours. After walking home for a quick supper, it was back to the library, hopefully returning before the other students, to read the required material. The library also was a meeting place for socialization. During one of my library evenings, I noticed a thoughtful girl sitting next to me, deep into her studies. After a period of time I took a risk and asked if she wanted a coffee break. To my delight, she agreed and we chatted in the library lounge for a short time before returning to our books. She then accepted a request for a date and a few days later I drove to her address. She was living in a faculty residential area of Ann Arbor, which was somewhat surprising. I assumed she was renting a room in a house. I rang the bell and a friendly man opened the door and held out his hand to shake, saying: "Hello, I am Dan Katz, Susie's father." I turned pale, stuttered, and said: "Hello, I am Bernie Weiner. I came here last year to study with you."

I immediately considered the great fortune of him becoming my father-in-law, and a Katz & Weiner, or even better, a Weiner & Katz, publication. However, the date was somewhat of a disaster and my fantasy was not to be. On the other hand, Katz took a fatherly interest in my career and when we crossed paths he thoughtfully asked about my progress. There is a coda to this episode: as editor of the prestigious *Journal of Abnormal and Social Psychology*, Katz rejected the first manuscript I submitted for publication, which concerned a Lewinian theme regarding task recall (the so-called "Zeigarnik effect"). However, his letter was so positive and encouraging that I felt it had been accepted!

I presume that today the library no longer has a dating service nor is a gathering place to exchange ideas and problems with fellow graduate students. I regard this as a great loss; just one of the deprivations of being in a computer culture. I experienced a similar loss later as a faculty member when other faculty began working at home on their computers rather than coming to the office.

On Securing an Academic Position

During my final year in graduate school, I began to pursue an academic placement. I closely examined all the advertisements. To my great fortune, the University of Minnesota had an opening to join The Center for Personality Research, which was directed by Norman Garmezy, known for his work on schizophrenia. I spent two happy and productive years there, enjoying Minneapolis and being an Assistant Professor. On some days, I was able to walk to school with Paul Meehl, the only genius I have ever met!

One morning, Garmezy called me into his office and strongly suggested that I leave the department. I was shocked because I thought my research was going well and that I had established good relationships with the other faculty. He said that, unbeknownst to me, the department was in turmoil and many were going elsewhere in the coming year because of conflicts regarding the Departmental Chair and other political issues.

He was correct: In the following year Elliot Aaronson and Gardner Lindzey, well-known social psychologists, were among the departed. Garmezy recommended I consider UCLA. I was unsure what that meant since I did not know if they had an opening or a personality area.

A short time later, I received a call from the Chair of the psychology department at UCLA, asking if I would be interested in a position. Garmezy had contacted his co-researcher at UCLA, Eliot Rodnick, who spoke to the Chair, and the next thing I knew I had a job offer. This was the old-boy network at its worst (or, for me, its best). The Assistant Professor salary ($7,500 yearly) was slightly higher than the amount I was receiving at Minnesota. I asked if I could first visit the department before deciding. No job talk was required, only suggestions regarding how I would like to spend my time! I left on this calling in March when the temperature in Minneapolis was below zero, arriving in Los Angeles on a smog-free, 75-degree day in 1965. I was convinced to move before arriving on campus. It was my final permanent position. I remained on the UCLA faculty for almost fifty years, leaving occasionally for sabbaticals or short leaves of absence to other universities. Today, fifty-six years after my arrival in 1965, I maintain active connections with the university.

In general, at the time of my graduation, academic jobs were available. Of course, not everyone obtained his or her top choice. But I do not recall students at Michigan fearing unemployment or having to leave academics or seek postdoctoral arrangements because there were no available academic positions. Job anxiety was much lower than it is today.

On Research

In the 1960s, the experimental study of psychology was in its infancy; social psychology was a relatively new field of study with learning and motivation the most established areas of research. I identified as a motivation rather than social psychologist, and this remains true today.

Researchers at that time faced some of the same problems and issues they confront now: where to obtain experimental participants; whether their findings generalize to populations other than college students; how to fund the assistants who conducted the research; how to deal with publication demands and rejection; and on and on. On the other hand, there also were some important differences between research in the past and the present. Foremost among these is the availability of computers for data analysis and writing. Some of my early research relied on non-parametric statistics, in part because computing correlations and t-tests required hours in front of one's calculating machine, with its annoying ching-chong sound (I cannot think of an adequate description). Analysis of variance was just being introduced and elicited excitement. Since the more complex regression and path analyses were yet to be introduced, certain research designs were not considered. Other obstacles were faced because the required technology remained to be created. I am unsure if this made research easier or more difficult to conduct.

There was another important difference between then and now regarding research, and it may have been especially characteristic of motivation research, although it applies as well to social psychology. Namely, the research was top-down, that is, directed by and deduced from larger theories. Hence, it was not only the specific research hypotheses that were being tested but also the underlying theory. In social psychology, the dominant theories involved cognitive consistency, including Heider's theory of balance and Festinger's theory of cognitive dissonance (these were theories of motivation as well). For motivation psychology, the conceptual networks were the so-called grand theories proposed by Hull (drive theory), Tolman (expectancy-value theory), and Lewin (field theory). There were also less influential theories such as Atkinson's theory of achievement motivation, Rotter's social learning theory, and others.

My own career was shaped by the notion that research should service theoretical development and confirmation. One striking illustration of this occurred during a talk I was giving on poverty. A socially conscious person in the audience inquired how I happened to become interested in this essential topic. I replied that I had no special interest in poverty and could have just as readily given a talk about wealth but it was less amenable to an attribution analysis, which was my theoretical home. I was focused on theory building, independent of the specific content area.

The field of motivation had its experimental origin in animal research and behaviorism. When this area first embraced cognition, the primary and virtually only mental construct was the expectancy of success. But this resulted in little relational fertility; the field needed more cognitive constructs to branch out and predict behaviors other than the speed of a rat running down a maze (the focus of Hull and Tolman) or choice from tasks differing in difficulty (Atkinson's primary concern). This was the backdrop that guided me to my association with attribution theory for the remainder of my career – it supplied a construct to enlarge the domain of motivation research and was extremely fruitful in generating new research directions.

Attribution theory is based upon the layperson's perceptions of causality. In the achievement domain, for example, failure can be attributed to a lack of ability, a lack of effort, or factors external to the individual. Which of these is accepted by the failing individual greatly influences subsequent motivation. Also, the causal beliefs of other individuals determine how they react to this person. Among the questions I pursued were, what are the common properties of causes (their location as internal or external to the actor, as enduring or unstable over time, and whether the actor has control or no control over the cause). These properties, in turn, influence emotional reactions and then action. For example, personal failure ascribed to lack of ability gives rise to low personal esteem, humiliation, low expectancy of future success, and withdrawal from achievement activities. Yet if others perceive the failure is due to lack of effort, they experience anger and exhibit anti-social reactions. Similar analyses were made for other types of motivated behavior, including aggression and help giving, and a causal analysis was extended to impression formation, political ideology, social rejection, reactions to the stigmatized, and more.

I cannot claim to be the first to embrace causal beliefs as central to behavior. Well-known prior psychologists associated with attribution theory include Fritz Heider, followed by Edward Jones and Harold Kelley. But they were primarily interested in causes as dependent variables, that is, for example, under what conditions might another person be blamed for failing. As social psychologists, person perception was the focus. As a motivation psychologist, however, I concentrated on causal beliefs as independent variables, that is, what beliefs give rise to what behaviors. For summaries of this research, see Weiner (1985, 1995, 2006, 2018), where each publication captures my view of attribution theory during that decade.

On Longevity

I obtained my PhD in 1963; my first publication was in 1965, around sixty years ago, and my last will be in 2022, hence spanning seven decades! During that time period, much has changed regarding the field of psychology. Some of the largest alterations had little apparent impact on my academic life and career. For example, the field shifted from predominantly male to mainly female; the percentage and number of clinical psychologists greatly increased, in part due to the advent of professional schools; some areas of research disappeared (e.g., verbal learning) whereas others flourished (e.g., neuropsychology). Some changes have been to my benefit, some may have hindered my career, and others have had both effects.

One of the most evident shifts regards the so-called "hard-soft" separation of the fields of psychology. When I first became an Assistant Professor, the areas of clinical, personality, and social psychology were labeled as "soft," that is, quasi-experimental. They were lower in a hierarchy of perceived "real" sciences, which included the study of learning, perception, sensation, and motivation (which was primarily examined among sub-human populations). This indeed had some negative consequences during my early career inasmuch as the Chairperson at UCLA had little tolerance for the study of "soft" fields and hindered my advancement (or, attempted to do this). However, at UCLA the areas of clinical and social psychology were rated higher than those in the other experimental fields so that any hierarchy dissolved by around 1980. This movement toward equality was true at other universities as well, perhaps facilitated by the marriage of clinical and social psychology to neuropsychology and genetics.

A personal change: A shift also occurred during my lengthy period in academics involving my research focus. In the time following my PhD and when first arriving to UCLA, I concentrated on the study of achievement motivation (although as a "hobby" I also engaged in research on motivation and memory). First, I embraced Atkinson's approach, while later shifting theoretical allegiance to attribution theory. But around 1980, about twenty years after my PhD, I changed course from achievement to a variety of interpersonal topics, some mentioned earlier, including help giving, impression management, reactions to the stigmatized, perceived responsibility (including within achievement contexts), political ideology, and others that fit within my particular attribution framework. This shift was in part because studies in the achievement area typically use performance as the main dependent variable. This creates obstacles inasmuch as performance is greatly affected by ability, which can overwhelm the manipulated variables in accounting for the research findings. Furthermore, this turn greatly increased my range of possible research directions. I ultimately proposed two attribution theories: one for intrapersonal behavior (primarily achievement striving) and a second for interpersonal behavior (primarily, but not exclusively, for helping behavior). I regard these as intimately related for both achievement-related behavior and help giving are greatly affected by beliefs about causality (Why did I, or they, fail?" and "Why does he or she need help?").

A Final Word

As I was writing this manuscript, I began to wonder if I were an undergraduate student today, would my career have been less successful? I immodestly start with the belief that I have attained a reasonable degree of success, given that I was invited to contribute to this book.

First, as an undergraduate, I would not have had the opportunity to be educated in a Great Books program without a major. The University of Chicago taught me how to think and read. Also, in today's competitive environment I would not have been accepted to the University of Chicago or the University of Michigan, given my mediocre records. This conclusion also holds true regarding my initial position at the University of Minnesota – I had no publications as a graduate student, which would have eliminated me as a current candidate. Continuing with this litany of likely rejections, I needed the "old-boy network" for my position at UCLA. Of course, I do not credit all my success to the external causes of good luck or easy circumstances. There were internal attributions as well, especially hard work. But I do feel my life would have been substantially more difficult in the current environment and quite likely not as successful. Perhaps that is a misattribution and everyone shares such doubts and dire predictions about their own lives. Wow, I may have hit upon a new research direction for attribution theory, hypothesizing that when looking backward, external or circumstantial causes of success including good luck are perceived as more important than internal attributions such as ability and effort! Is there any university out there that will hire me?

Suggested Reading

Weiner, B. (1985). An attributional theory of achievement motivation and emotion. *Psychological Review*, 92(4), 548–573.
    (1995). *Judgments of Responsibility: A Foundation for a Theory of Social Conduct*. New York: Guilford Press.
    (2006). *Social Motivation, Justice, and the Moral Emotions*. Mahwah, NJ: Lawrence Erlbaum.
    (2018). The legacy of an attribution approach to motivation and emotion: A no-crisis zone. *Motivation Science*, *41*(1), 4–14.

12 "What Ever Happened to that Blond Girl?"

Ellen Berscheid

When I graduated from high school in Reno Nevada in the mid-1950s, Betty Friedan had yet to publish *The Feminine Mystique* (1963), which is often credited as sparking a second women's revolution equal to that of suffrage. At this time the revolution was already in progress, for I, along with many other young women, had already adopted many of the views Friedan was to express. We had rejected the assumption that all women would find their life's fulfillment in domestic household chores and caring for a husband and children. I agreed with Friedan before she wrote it that women who married immediately after graduating from high school were volunteering to stint their lives at an early age.

Although I knew what I did *not* what to do out of high school, I had no idea what I *did* want to do. Most women were still marrying young and those who didn't usually went to work as a cashier, waitress, or store clerk until some suitable man proposed. I was not interested in any of these jobs, seemingly leaving only the alternative of continuing my education. But I did not want to go to college. I wasn't troubled by my lack of direction and purpose at the time but it concerned my parents. My father wanted me to attend Stanford University but not only did I not want college, I especially did not want Stanford. They had turned down one of my girlfriends, who was brilliant, had a stellar high school record, and desperately wanted to go to Stanford. Yet they admitted another girlfriend whose "C" quality mind and dismal record would not get her in anywhere else. My suspicion that her father's status as a Stanford alumnus had something to do with this odd admission decision only increased my dislike of the place.

One summer morning, my father told me to ditch my usual Levi's and put on a dress. He wanted to take me downtown to have lunch with him and a friend of his. I immediately suspected he was up to no good. He was. The friend turned out to be the head of the Stanford Alumni Association. When I heard the friend say to my father, "She's perfect for Stanford," I smugly pointed out that I couldn't possibly go because their applications had been due many months previous and I had not applied there or anywhere. "Not to worry," the man said, "I'll take care of everything." This cemented my dislike of Stanford.

Ellen Berscheid, Regents' Professor of Psychology Emerita, University of Minnesota, USA. The title of this chapter is a quotation from Harold Kelley (1960).

My mother, who also was concerned with my aimless drifting, had been pressing me to go to the University of Nevada. No one understood that I did not want college. Escape from the mounting pressures at home seemed possible when my mother's sister and husband visiting from our native Wisconsin suggested I ride back with them. I happily took off. Because I had to have a good reason to stay in Wisconsin, I enrolled in a small private college there. College meant that I had to choose a major. I decided on mathematics. The aptitude tests I had taken years earlier showed that I had an aptitude for math, which was confirmed by my performance in high school math classes. More importantly, I enjoyed math.

Unfortunately, I managed to anger my new college math professor. It happened at the first college dance, which freshmen were required to attend the Saturday night before classes. Assuming he was simply one of the young men at the dance, I politely rejected his unwanted and persistent attentions by saying that I didn't dance (in fact, I didn't know how) but he was clearly insulted. When I next saw him again at the head of the room of my first math class I shrunk the moment he recognized me. His harassment, designed mainly to fluster me, continued. By the end of the first semester I was so anxious I could barely add 2 plus 2. My state of mind in that class was reflected in the grade of "C" I received. Fortunately, my other grades were high and put me on the "Dean's List."

Thinking that Nevada might not be so bad after all, I returned home, much to my mother's delight, enrolled in the university, and changed my major to English literature. I discovered that the university required a course in introductory psychology. I was not interested but decided to get that nuisance out of the way. That semester the course was taught by Paul Secord. I did not find it particularly interesting but saw that next semester Secord was offering a seminar titled "Perception and Cognition." Oddly, I thought it would be a course in extrasensory perception and precognition, so I signed up. Secord started talking not about the occult but about Fritz Heider's views of phenomenal causality, the "new look" in social perception, and interpersonal attraction. I was fascinated – and I was hooked (for life, as it turned out).

Secord (1958) had just presented a paper on "Facial Features and Inference Processes" at the seminal 1957 Harvard-ONR Symposium on Person Perception. He had also received a grant from the National Institutes of Health, which included funding for one research assistant. He asked me if I would be interested, and I was. After a month on the job, I was stunned to hear that I would be paid for my time! To be paid for doing something so enjoyable seemed wrong. I did not know until the end of that year that Secord was criticized by other faculty for giving that one precious research assistantship to me, not to a graduate student in their Master's program. Even worse, he gave it to an undergraduate who was not even a Psych major. The next year, in order to keep my research assistantship (I surmised), Secord asked me if I would change my major to psychology. I said that I would add it to my English lit major, which I did. Thus, I later was to graduate with the two majors, but not without first having to take a course in physical education!

Mandates to take phys ed had been the bane of my life since junior high school and I now vigorously balked at taking such an unnecessary course in college. Because

I really didn't care if I got an official paper diploma or not, I stood fast. Secord, however, did care. He entered the fray and in the end the administration transferred the task of finding a solution to the head of the phys ed department, Jake Lawler, the much loved and celebrated football coach (and whose name now is atop the University of Nevada sports stadium). Lawlor happily offered me not just one but two ways to solve the problem. The first was that for a semester I could sit in his office weekly and listen to phonograph records of other people doing calisthenics! The second was that I could take the only course that still had an opening: "Beginning Tap Dancing"! I opted for the latter and learned to tap dance to the tune of "Three Blind Mice." I also continued taking psych courses and graduated in 1960 with both a Bachelor and Master's degree in psychology.

Earlier, when I was his research assistant, Secord insisted that I apply for a Public Health Service Predoctoral Research Fellowship. The award could be taken to any university that admitted the recipient to a doctoral program and it would not only pay the university for training the recipient but also provide a stipend for the recipient to live on. After filling out the form, I completely forgot about the fellowship because the probability that I would actually receive the award seemed close to zero to me. Few universities admitted women to their doctoral programs, so it seemed doubtful that a woman would be given a research fellowship. A second reason I forgot about the fellowship application was that I had just married a veteran who was graduating from the University of Nevada with high honors in journalism. He had applied to the best graduate journalism programs in the country and we were sifting through the many assistantships offers he'd already received. One of those offers was from the University of Minnesota, not far from my native Wisconsin and family there. He tentatively decided to accept Minnesota's offer.

Because continuing my own education was far from my mind, I was surprised at the news that I'd been awarded the fellowship and could pursue a PhD at any university that would take me. Secord immediately suggested Duke (which had an excellent social psychology program) so I dutifully filled out the Duke admission forms. When I got to the end of the last page, however, I read at the bottom and in small print: "Applications accepted from men only." Secord seemed to know that more applications to other universities likely would produce more disappointments and did not press me further. But he didn't give up. When I told him that my husband had accepted the Minnesota offer, he called his friend Harold Kelley at the University of Minnesota's Lab for Research in Social Relations and asked him if he would take me with my research fellowship. Kelley agreed and said that I should contact him when we arrived.

Kelley's greeting to me at our first meeting seemed lukewarm at best. I was also having difficulty adjusting to marriage and a death in the family, so I gave up the idea of continuing in the program. I never went back to speak with Kelley again; I just disappeared. Sometime later I learned that he had asked the graduate students in his lab, "What ever happened to that blond girl?" They didn't know, of course. In the meantime, I gave my precious research fellowship back to the government and with my husband in graduate school I got a job at Pillsbury in their Research and

Development Department. Many years later, Hal Kelley invited me to work with him. He went on to become a good friend and advisor for life. I miss him still.

I enjoyed my time at Pillsbury. I especially enjoyed working on the development of the first disposable baby bottles. But when it came time to persuade hospital administrators to try our bottles, I was taken off the project. I knew that I did not look the part (I kept being mistaken as "the mail girl"). A gray-haired man, who knew little or nothing about the bottles but looked like one of those popular doctors on TV, was hired to get our bottles into hospitals. Although I had been promoted to the position of market research analyst (viewed as a "man's job"), Pillsbury really couldn't find anything for me to do and so, once again bored, I quit. The time wasn't wasted, however, because my Pillsbury stint was an important factor in my later getting a temporary professorship in the Marketing Department of the Business School at the University of Minnesota.

After quitting Pillsbury, I heard that many changes were taking place at the University's Lab for Research in Social Relations. Kelley left for a professorship at UCLA and Jack Darley, who had resigned the presidency of the American Psychological Association (APA) in DC, returned to Minnesota. The university wanted to make organizational changes and chose Darley to execute them. The Social Relations Lab at that time was a free-standing unit, separate and located some distance from the Psych Department building, but its social psychologists had their professorships in psychology. Darley took an office in the Lab before assuming the chair of psychology and would bring the Lab into psychology when the department moved into its new building. With Kelley's departure, Darley hired another social psychologist, Elliot Aronson, a student of Leon Festinger.

I had heard that Aronson was looking for a research assistant so I applied for the job. Our initial conversation did not go well. We had a vigorous exchange of opinions on the role of women in higher education. I ended the interview by standing up and stomping out, expecting never to hear from him again. A few weeks later, however, I received a crisp letter from him. He said he had looked at all the applications and I was the most qualified, so if I wanted the job, I should show up at the Lab on such and such a day. I did.

The research assistant position with Aronson seemed almost too good to be true. It was. Just before fall semester began, Aronson got a message from the Graduate School saying that a research assistant had to be a "graduate student in good standing." I wasn't a graduate student of any standing so, he said, "You have to take some courses." "What courses?" I asked. "Just copy whatever the other students are doing." I took the minimum number of courses I could, just enough to stay in good standing so I could keep the research job I loved.

The next year my job was in jeopardy again. The Lab was short of assistantship money (a not unusual condition, I was to learn). When Aronson and Darley told me that they did not have the money to keep me on, Darley made the ludicrous comment: "In any event, we want to see how serious your husband is about you having a career." I almost laughed out loud. I knew he meant that if my husband wanted me to have a career, he'd have to pay for it. I replied, "I can tell you right now what my husband thinks about my so-called career. He would be delighted if I quit coming here!"

My reply was met with silence but then, changing the subject, Darley said, "I see that you once had a PHS pre-doctoral research fellowship. You should try to get it back." I protested, "Why would they ever give it back to someone who was so unable to cope as to feel forced relinquish it; they would never do that and I would be embarrassed to even ask." He said, "Well, trying to get that back is your only chance to continue here. I will write a supporting letter and perhaps that will help." So, I did, he did, and wonder of wonders, I got the fellowship back! I then became a real graduate student in good standing, and I continued to copy what the other students in the Lab were doing (except taking all the courses they did). When the others took their written doctoral exams, I did also. I passed them. When they presented a thesis, I did also. It was accepted and later published. In other words, I had earned a PhD but doubted I would ever receive it (and didn't much care). I was right to doubt. The Graduate School told Aronson that they could not give the doctorate to someone who had taken so few courses in psychology (but so many courses in statistics, they did not add). But Aronson went to bat for me. He wrote a blistering letter back to the Graduate School, pointing out that their rules made their doctorate essentially an "examination degree." They assumed that taking some number of courses was necessary to pass their examinations but there was nothing in their rules that said they *had* to be taken. He concluded by saying, "I don't know where Berscheid got the information to pass those written exams and meet your other requirements but she did and so you have to give her the degree." They did. Then they quickly changed their rules.

In the Business School's marketing department, I was the only female professor and all my students were male as well. The faculty were pleasant and helpful to me but the temporary dean of the Business School quickly tried to get rid of me. He charged that I had "mutilated university property" by removing from the employment bulletin board in the lobby a notice for "research analyst" at Pillsbury that listed "male" as a requirement. He called me into his office late one afternoon and shouted vulgarities and profanities at me. Among other things he said I had jeopardized Pillsbury's financial support and that only men were suitable for the jobs placed on the employment board. My friend Elaine Hatfield was in my car out in the parking lot waiting for me to drive her home. When I got to her, I was crying so hard she couldn't understand me. This is the only time in memory I ever cried about anything that had to do with my work. Elaine offered to drive me home but I still had the presence of mind to understand how dangerous that would be. Elaine did not know how to drive but, fearless, I knew she would go ahead and try.

Elaine was another student of Leon Festinger. She was working in the Student Activities Bureau and also attended our weekly lab meetings when I was Aronson's research assistant and then his graduate student. Her story was not very different from mine. Even though she was Festinger's star student, no one wanted to hire her. Finally, Festinger called an old friend of his, the Dean of Students at Minnesota, who found her a position in the Student Activities Bureau (sororities and fraternities and other student events and organizations were under its jurisdiction). While I was in the Business School and Elaine in the Student Activities Bureau, we both had "adjunct" professorships in psychology. As Jack Darley, put it, we were to regard psychology as our "spiritual" home even though we had to live our earthly lives elsewhere.

When I went into the Lab one day to clear out my books and papers, Elaine was there. All the Lab faculty, including Aronson, had moved to greener pastures and their offices were empty. Elaine said, "Why don't you take that office and I'll take this one." I was horrified, certain we would be tossed out. But with her usual elan, Elaine said, "Oh, no one will notice and someone has to care for the graduate students who were left behind." Elaine was persuasive so I left my books there and visited my "squatter" office almost every day afterward as did Elaine. It was there that we started to work together and that is how it happened that she was waiting for me in my car that day I was called into the Business School Dean's office.

When Elaine secured a "real" job (as she called it) at the University of Rochester, she persuaded the Dean of Students to hire me for her job in the Student Activities Bureau. I was grateful because my days were numbered at the Business School. I had survived the "mutilation" of the employment board charge but the grant supporting my job was running out. Later, and while I was at the Student Activities Bureau, Jack Darley, who by that time had risen to be the head of the psychology department, called me one Monday morning in 1969 to say that I now was an associate professor in the psychology department and no longer was working in the Student Activities Bureau. It was never clear how he had arranged to do that. Many people at the university were as surprised as I was by the news and asked the Dean of the college how it happened. All the Dean would ever say is, "One morning Jack Darley got out of bed, went to the window, pulled up the shade, and said 'Let there be woman!'" That was good enough for me, but I later suspected that the passage of the 1964 Civil Rights Act might have had something to do with it.

For a time, I was not just the only woman in the psychology department but also the only social psychologist so there were efforts to move me to the sociology department. Fortunately, social psychology had matured enough to distinguish itself from sociology and to justify its rightful place in psychology departments. Of relevance to my own work, the study of interpersonal attraction had become of special interest when I was an undergraduate and Secord's research assistant. This interest was fueled by Heider's (1958) newly published book and then the publication a year later of Thibaut and Kelley's (1959) book on interdependence theory.

When I was Elliot Aronson's research assistant I met John Darley, of later bystander effect fame, who then was a grad student at Harvard and often came home to see his father on holiday breaks. John and I published in *Human Relations* a test of the Heiderian hypothesis that people would increase their liking of another person as a result of "anticipation of personal contact" (Darley & Berscheid, 1967). Two years later, Elaine and I published the first edition of *Interpersonal Attraction* (Berscheid & Hatfield, 1969). As Anne Peplau and I would later observe, a science of relationships was emerging (Berscheid & Peplau, 1983).

About the interpersonal attraction book: I really became interested in attraction through Elaine. She was in her new position at the University of Rochester and I was still in her old job in the Student Activities Bureau. She had been interested in equity in relationships so we were focusing on that when her former classmate, Chuck Kiesler (another Festinger student at Stanford), invited her to participate in his new book series called "Topics in Social Psychology." Each short book was to be written by an "expert." He asked Elaine to write a book on attraction. I was surprised when she accepted the invitation and even more so when she asked me to help her write it. So I took my first airplane flight (very scary) to Rochester to work with Elaine on the book. Lo and behold, it turned out to be a success. It was revised in a second edition published in 1978 and translated into Japanese, Portuguese, German, and Spanish. Both Elaine and I went on to write many other articles and chapters on interpersonal attraction. For example, Lindzey and Aronson asked me to write the chapter on interpersonal attraction for their 1985 edition of the *Handbook of Social Psychology.*

When Jack Darley removed me from the Activities Bureau and somehow made me a professor in the psychology department, my life changed. I then had graduate students and a secretary; I taught seminars; and I could apply for funding. I went on to receive a grant from the National Science Foundation, which was later renewed. In my last renewal application, I indicated a desire to explore the topic of love and romantic relationships. Unbeknownst to me, Wisconsin Senator William Proxmire had been battling with NSF to no effect and started to attack its principal investigators. He got all the publicity he hoped for when he attacked my NSF grant with his "Golden Fleece" award. It was a terrible time for me and because I received so many death threats I did fear for my life. Just dealing with the bags and bags of mail from people all over the world who wanted to know more about love and all sorts of emotions in relationships was time-consuming and often heart-breaking. I did not have the information they wanted and neither did the field. A few years later, Hal Kelley received a grant from NSF to assemble a small group to study relationships. His invitation to me to be part of that select group returned my life to normal. Working in that group was one of the happiest times of my life.

Both my and Elaine's professional lives were fraught with surprises, good and bad, so much so that some went on to call us the "Thelma and Louise" of social psychology. But that is not really an accurate appellation; neither of us ever was so discouraged that we wanted to drive our career over the cliff. We both are still here, retired from what I remember to be a truly wonderful life.

Suggested Reading

Berscheid, E. (1985). Interpersonal attraction. In G. Lindzey & E. Aronson (Eds.), *Handbook of Social Psychology*. Third edition (pp. 110–168). New York: Random House.
    (1994). Interpersonal relationships. *Annual Review of Psychology, 45,* 79–129.

Berscheid, E., & Hatfield, E. (1969). *Interpersonal Attraction*. New York: Addison-Wesley (Revised second edition 1978).

Berscheid, E., & Peplau, L. A. (1983). The emerging science of relationships. In H. H. Kelley et al. (Eds.), *Close Relationships* (pp. 1–19). New York: Freeman.

Darley, J. M., & Berscheid, E. (1967). Increased liking as a result of the anticipation of personal contact. *Human Relations, 20*, 29–40.

Friedan, B. (1963). *The Feminine Mystique.* New York: W. W. Norton.

Heider, F. (1958). *The Psychology of Interpersonal Relations*. New York: John Wiley & Sons.

Thibaut, J. W., & Kelley, H. H. (1959). *The Social Psychology of Groups*. New York: John Wiley & Sons.

13 A Quest for Social Psychology That Spans the Psychological and the Social

My earliest insight that I might become a social psychologist emerged in 8th grade when I prepared an oral report to fulfill a class assignment to give a talk on an occupation. I chose social scientist. Although my knowledge of that occupation was limited to what I had learned from a relevant magazine article, the idea that human behavior could be the subject of science was enticing and entirely new to me. The seed was planted.

I was already interested in science but had studied only physical and biological science. In high school, I thought that I might become a chemist because the field seemed interesting and accessible. However, that idea did not last long once I was in college. At Radcliffe College, Harvard's coordinated women's college, I soon settled on an interdisciplinary major known as social relations. Its curriculum offered an enthralling mix of social science disciplines – from social, developmental, and clinical psychology to sociology and anthropology.

The social sciences were in transition during my college years, 1956–1960. Some grand theorizing was still alive with, for example, attention to Freud in psychology and Talcott Parsons in sociology. Simultaneously, social psychology was quickly gaining visibility with the publication of Festinger's (1957) *Theory of Cognitive Dissonance* and Heider's (1958) *The Psychology of Interpersonal Relations.*

Given this rising profile of social psychology, I decided to go to graduate school in this specialization. The field appealed to me as potentially integrative, at least of psychology and sociology. In large part because the University of Michigan offered a social psychology program sponsored jointly by sociology and psychology, I applied to this program and was admitted to start my graduate work in 1961. In the year intervening between my undergraduate and graduate studies, I spent a year at the University of Oslo on a Fulbright scholarship.

Despite the efforts of Michigan's outstanding senior faculty, including Theodore Newcomb, Albert Reiss, Daniel Katz, Herbert Kelman, Guy E. Swanson, and Helen Peak, this so-called "joint program" in social psychology was in its waning days; it was becoming more difficult to integrate psychology and sociology in a single coherent curriculum. Among those graduate students identifying mainly with psychology, their research increasingly concentrated on individual processes, and

Alice H. Eagly, Northwestern University, USA.

experimental research methods were becoming more popular. Most of these students were not much interested in studying Marx, Weber, Parsons, and other social theorists and thinking deeply about the social structural and cultural context of behavior. In fact, the joint program folded a few years after I completed my graduate work, and thereafter graduate students in social psychology at Michigan pursued degrees in either psychology or sociology. Nevertheless, in this somewhat unsettled academic environment, I produced a dissertation on involvement and persuasion, a topic that was of some importance in attitude theory of the 1960s. My excellent and encouraging graduate school mentors consisted of Professor Herbert Kelman, who directed my dissertation, and Professor Melvin Manis who directed some of my research earlier in my graduate program.

Allure of the Psychology of Attitudes

With my PhD in hand in 1965, I obtained an assistant professor position, first at Michigan State University for two years, and then at University of Massachusetts in Amherst, where I remained until 1980. I mainly settled into studies of attitudes and persuasion in the 1970s and subsequently at Purdue University in the early 1980s. For example, some projects investigated attributions about why communicators take positions on issues and the effects of these attributions on the persuasiveness of messages. Gradually the research broadened to consider dual processes in persuasion (Chaiken et al., 1989).

Beyond producing research on attitudes and persuasion, I had the goal of insuring that *attitude* retained its status as core integrative concept linking the individual and the social environment. When broadly defined, attitude encompasses phenomena such as interpersonal attraction and social values. Attitude theory pertains to affect and emotion, cognitions and beliefs, and the prediction of behavior. It was this breadth that inspired me to write a book that would help bring this field of research and theory into one big tent, so to speak. I also desired to help reverse a certain decline of appreciation for attitude research starting in the late 1970s, which reflected in part a lessening of interest in cognitive consistency theories. To help counter this trend, I began a book on attitudes, with the superb collaboration of Shelly Chaiken, a former graduate student during my stay at the University of Massachusetts who was then a faculty member at the University of Toronto (Eagly & Chaiken, 1993). This writing project spanned a six-year period in often-intense collaboration with Shelly. The resulting volume, *The Psychology of Attitudes*, communicated the integrative value of attitude theory and the scope of the field's varied research programs. The book's approximately 20,000 citations (according to Google Scholar) attest to its success.

Other empirical projects also filled these years. For example, one project consisted of a meta-analysis of research on memory for attitude-relevant information, and subsequent experiments probed this topic. My earlier interest in psychological involvement led to an integrative meta-analysis with Blair Johnson on the varied approaches to studying involvement and persuasion (Johnson & Eagly, 1989).

Discovery of Meta-Analysis

In the 1980s, my research skills expanded by incorporating meta-analysis, then an emerging method for integrating research across studies. This method helped to address an important problem often faced by psychologists: the apparent lack of replicability of many research findings. The tradition of laboratory experiments, in particular, raised questions about both generalizability and replicability. Therefore, it was not uncommon that a research topic would elicit a flurry of interest, but subsequent findings in the same paradigm inconsistently replicated the initial findings. Given this situation, one of the appeals of meta-analysis was its potential to discover larger patterns in what might otherwise seem to be a confusing mix of findings. When appropriately analyzed across studies, research findings often became more interpretable and cumulative as the presence of moderating variables became apparent.

In a formative experience that introduced me to meta-analysis, I had published a narrative review on sex/gender differences in conformity and social influence (Eagly, 1978). Then I produced a meta-analysis of the same research literature that clarified the findings well beyond the earlier review (Eagly & Carli, 1981). This learning experience gave me at least moderate facility in wielding a new, powerful tool for integrating research. Yet, adopting this new method brought many challenges. Intellectually, I had to learn to think beyond individual studies to consider entire research literatures. Methodologically, I had to probe many researchers' methods and the relations between their methods and study outcomes. And statistically, I had to understand the new meta-analytic statistics as well as the wide range of statistical methods that appeared in research articles entering into meta-analyses. Having gained these skills, my subsequent research career was punctuated by the publication of meta-analyses along with other types of research. The emphasis of most of this research gradually changed from attitudes to the social psychology of gender as I transitioned in 1995 from Purdue University to Northwestern University.

Research on Gender

When I began my work on the psychology of gender, this topic was a blind spot in social psychology. Most of the theory and academic research on the psychology of women and gender had been developmental or pertained to individual differences in gender identity. The traditional message of social psychology – the power of the situation – seemed to be largely missing from these accounts.

The context of my early interest in gender was the women's movement of the 1970s, which posed many unanswered questions about men and women. Because there was only a limited body of research to draw on, this area struck me as open to discovery and innovation, somewhat in contrast to the attitudes field, which was already well stocked with theory and research. Therefore, relatively modest contributions to scholarship on gender could receive recognition. For example, to my surprise, my 1978 *Psychological Bulletin* narrative review of gender and influenceability

(Eagly, 1978) won two prizes, one from the Association for Women in Psychology (Distinguished Publication Award) and the other from the Society for the Psychological Study of Social Issues (Gordon Allport Intergroup Relations Prize).

Encouraged by this early success, meta-analyses on sex/gender differences and similarities in social behavior were an obvious direction for additional research. In particular, I tackled projects on altruism and aggression, the good and the bad of social behavior. After these two projects, I turned to the socially important topic of leadership, which offered the interdisciplinary mix of scholarship that first brought me to social psychology as an undergraduate. Moreover, the underrepresentation of women in leader roles was then (and still remains) an important barrier to gender equality and thus warrants continuing research.

These leadership meta-analyses appeared in journals between 1990 and 2011. The first four projects compared women and men in leadership styles, their emergence as leaders in initially leaderless groups, their effectiveness as leaders, and the evaluations they received when their attributes were experimentally equated. Subsequent meta-analyses pertained to the cultural stereotype of leaders and the transformational and transactional leadership styles of women and men. These projects provided the backbone of the book for general readers that I wrote with the very skillful collaboration of Linda Carli: *Through the Labyrinth: The Truth about How Women Become Leaders* (Eagly & Carli, 2007).

Social Role Theory

Beginning in the 1980s while conducting my first research on sex/gender differences (Eagly & Steffen, 1984), I developed social role theory, initially published in a book based on lectures that I gave at the University of Alberta (Eagly, 1987). Although I have developed this theory further in subsequent years, with the crucial collaboration of Wendy Wood, even this early version had success in bringing a distinctively social psychological theory to the study of sex and gender.

According to social role theory, to the extent that the men and women of a society are differently positioned in the social structure, a variety of mediating processes conspire to make the two groups psychologically distinctive in ways that facilitate performance of their typical roles. Yet, the tendency for many roles to be segregated reflects multiple causes, including biological differences between women and men. For example, men's greater size and strength gives them preferential access to strength-demanding roles. Temperamental differences between men and women likely are relevant as well.

These typical roles, yielding a gender division of labor, are the main source of each society's *gender roles*, which are consensually shared expectations about men and women. These expectations emerge from observation and cultural learning – that is, from people's everyday experiences with what women and men do in their daily lives. People thus come to believe that men and women have distinctive psychologies, based on observing them engaging in differing types of activities and inferring that corresponding traits account for these activities. For example, if people commonly observe women performing nurturing activities in caretaking roles (e.g., as mothers, nurses, and teachers of young children), they assume that women tend to be warm, nurturing, and caring – at least more so than men. Moreover, the traits of women and men are in fact shaped to some extent by socialization for the roles that they occupy, thus supporting people's assumptions that corresponding traits underlie observed social roles. In summary, psychological sex/gender differences reflect influences arising from membership in the general social category of men or women, as mediated by socially constructed social roles, socialization, and individual psychological processes that include expectancy confirmation, self-regulation, and psychophysiological responses.

The emphasis on social roles in this theory follows from the consideration that, role, like attitude, is one of the central integrative concepts of the social sciences. Role expectations thus exist in the minds of individuals and are also shared with other people who typically endorse them. They are thus truly social psychological constructs that exist at both the individual and the social levels of analysis.

One extension of social role theory followed from my research on gender and leadership. Specifically, the *role congruity theory* of prejudice against female leaders (Eagly & Karau, 2002), which analyzes leaders as occupying both a gender role and a leader role. When women occupy both of these two roles, people's expectations are often in conflict because the communal qualities expected in women do not match the largely agentic qualities expected in leaders. This mismatch, or *role incongruity*, fosters a prejudicial lowering of the evaluation of women as potential leaders and actual leaders, compared with their male counterparts. Yet, the strength of this prejudice varies with moderators such as the extent of male domination of a leader role.

With gender becoming a growth area of research, other theorists entered the picture – most notably, evolutionary psychologists, who analyzed sex/gender differences in mate selection and other psychological attributes mainly in terms of sexual selection theory (see Geary, 2020). This perspective became increasingly popular in the 1990s, although in my opinion it oversimplifies a complex set of questions. Social role theory thus argues that the psychology of women and men stems, not primarily from the evolved dispositions postulated by evolutionary psychologists, but from the processes that follow from the social roles occupied disproportionately by women and men (Zentner & Eagly, 2015).

The popularity of evolutionary psychology provided a challenge to seek an alternative evolutionary analysis based on social psychological principles (Wood & Eagly, 2002). Relevant to the division of labor between men and women, Wood and Eagly identified physical differences between the sexes – primarily female reproductive activity and secondarily male size and strength – as important determinants. Invoking mainly research from anthropology, we showed that the effects of these physical characteristics depend on societies' socioeconomic and ecological environment. A key principle is that the effects of female reproduction and greater male size and strength are much diminished in postindustrial societies because of low birthrates and a relative absence of high-status occupational roles that are very physically demanding. In this work, led in large part by my excellent collaborator Wendy Wood, this analysis became the *biosocial theory* of the origins of sex differences.

Research on Gender Stereotypes and the Magnitude of Sex/Gender Differences

My research then turned to gender stereotypes, a key component of social role theory. Anne Koenig and I produced an improved empirical case supporting the argument that group stereotypes, including gender stereotypes, follow from their members' typical role occupancies (Koenig & Eagly, 2014). This research successfully predicted stereotypes of many social groups from the attributes ascribed to the group members' typical occupational roles. Further work carried out with Anne described the "vicious cycle" of stereotypes and social roles whereby members of social categories defined by attributes such as sex, race, and age occupy certain types of social roles much more than members of other social categories do. The qualities that define these roles become associated with the category as a whole, thus forming a stereotype. In a vicious cycle, this stereotype then hinders category members' movement into roles with different demands because their stereotype portrays them as well matched to their existing roles but not to these new roles (Eagly & Koenig, 2021).

Stereotypes change over time but only if people's everyday observations of groups change. Although Amanda Diekman and I showed that people predict that the stereotypes of women and men will converge over long time spans (Diekman & Eagly, 2000), the actual changes over time have proven to be more complex, as shown in analyses of public opinion data on gender stereotypes spanning 1946–2018 (Eagly et al., 2020). Although communion stereotypes became more pronounced over time and agency stereotypes showed little change, competence stereotypes did converge. For example, in one 1946 poll, only 35 percent of those surveyed thought men and women are equally intelligent, and of those who believed there is a difference, more thought men are the more competent sex. In contrast, in a 2018 poll, 86 percent believed that men and women are equally intelligent, 9 percent believed women are more intelligent, and only 5 percent believed men are more intelligent. People's observations fueling this shift in competence stereotypes pertain to women becoming the more educated sex and increasing greatly in paid employment, including in higher status occupations in management and the professions. Following this theme of stereotype change, my current collaborative research on gender stereotypes compares them across time in many nations as well as across language groups within Switzerland.

Finally, working with my colleague William Revelle, I have addressed one of the most fundamental questions about sex and gender: Are the psychological differences between women and men, small or large relative to other psychological phenomena? The innovations of effect sizes and meta-analysis might seem to have solved this problem but actually not sufficiently. Critical issues pertain to the aggregation of research findings over measures of psychological attributes. The Eagly and Revelle (in press) article clarifies this issue by demonstrating that larger and smaller sex/gender differences can reflect differing ways of organizing the same data. For single psychological constructs, larger differences emerge from averaging multiple indicators that differ by sex/gender to produce scales of a construct's overall typicality for women versus men. For example, averaging self-ratings on personality traits more typical of women or men yields much larger sex/gender differences on measures of the femininity or masculinity of personality. In addition, in psychological domains such as vocational interests that are composed of many variables, at least some of which differ by sex/gender, the multivariate distance between women and men is typically larger than the differences on the component variables. These psychometric analyses reveal the interdependence of similarity and difference in psychological data and should foster greater understanding of sex and gender.

Career Advice, Tentatively Offered

Although there are many paths to rewarding careers in social psychology, I offer some advice based on my own history. For me, it has proven valuable to follow my own interests and not be overly constrained by what topics are most popular at the moment. Had I followed the crowd in the critical period of my early career, I would have taken up then-current topics in social cognition and not written *The Psychology of Attitudes* or learned to meta-analyze or investigated the social psychology of gender. By taking these less traveled paths, I was able to exert intellectual leadership and become more visible than I would have on the more traveled paths, which were already crowded with very talented investigators. I thus suggest that young researchers consider investigating topics that are not pursued by many researchers if these seem appealing, although of course embarking in new directions does entail risk. Yet, the risk I took in studying gender, for example, was hardly foolish, given its obvious importance in individuals' lives.

I also encourage young social psychologists to increase their breadth, both methodologically and theoretically, beyond the traditional confines of social psychology. I developed breadth in the interdisciplinary contexts of my undergraduate and graduate education, and this intellectual background enhanced my ability to expand my focus to the social psychology of gender.

Finally, it is obvious that one's career benefits from outstanding collaborators. My career would not have gone at all well without helpful mentors and extraordinarily talented graduate students and colleagues, with whom I developed ideas and studies. Without the collaboration of Shelly Chaiken, Wendy Wood, Linda Carli, Blair Johnson, Valerie Steffen, Steven Karau, Amanda Diekman, Anne Koenig, Paul Eastwick, David Miller, Sabine Sczesny, William Revelle, and many other outstanding researchers, my research career would have languished. Together, we labored on studies, articles, chapters, and books. It is thus wise to work cooperatively with collaborators who complement one's own skills. Also, personal resilience is essential because productive researchers inevitably encounter rejections of their submissions to journals and sometimes negative evaluations that seem entirely unfair. Pause, learn from these experiences, and continue on. With persistence and the support of talented collaborators, a research career in social psychology can yield important contributions to this most vigorous and exciting of scientific fields.

The Promise of Social Psychology

Reflecting on my long career in social psychology, I have to ask myself if I made the right career choice. I think, given my particular strengths and interests, social psychology was an excellent choice, although I might have been happy as a sociologist or perhaps a personality psychologist or anthropologist. Part of the pleasure of my social psychological career has come from the field's growth in theory and research well beyond anything I had imagined sixty years ago. I read the field's journals with constant admiration for the sophisticated and interesting work that my colleagues have accomplished. The methodological growth is impressive as is the increasing number of topics that are pursued. It is also encouraging to see obvious problems such as the replication crisis addressed by improvements in scientific practice. I do remain troubled by the difficulties of negotiating scientific discoveries on topics that pertain to politically volatile issues of race, social class, and gender, where ideological orthodoxy sometimes can stifle viewpoint diversity. Yet, negotiating such challenges is part of what makes social psychology important as well as merely interesting.

Suggested Reading

Chaiken, S., Liberman, A., & Eagly, A. H. (1989). Heuristic and systematic processing within and beyond the persuasion context. In J. S. Uleman & J. A. Bargh (Eds.), *Unintended Thought* (pp. 212–252). New York: Guilford Press.

Diekman, A. B., & Eagly, A. H. (2000). Stereotypes as dynamic constructs: Women and men of the past, present, and future. *Personality and Social Psychology Bulletin, 26,* 1171–1188.

Eagly, A. H. (1978). Sex differences in influenceability. *Psychological Bulletin, 85,* 86–116.

(1987). *Sex Differences in Social Behavior: A Social-Role Interpretation.* Hillsdale, NJ: Lawrence Erlbaum.

Eagly, A. H., & Carli, L. L. (1981). Sex of researchers and sex-typed communications as determinants of sex differences in influenceability: A meta-analysis of social influence studies. *Psychological Bulletin, 90*(1), 1–20.

(2007). *Through the Labyrinth: The Truth about How Women Become Leaders.* Boston: Harvard Business School Press.

Eagly, A. H., & Chaiken, S. (1993). *The Psychology of Attitudes.* Fort Worth, TX: Harcourt Brace Jovanovich.

Eagly, A. H., & Karau, S. J. (2002). Role congruity theory of prejudice toward female leaders. *Psychological Review, 109*(3), 573–598.

Eagly, A. H., & Koenig, A. M. (2021). The vicious cycle linking stereotypes and social roles. *Current Directions in Psychological Science, 30*(4), 343–350.

Eagly, A. H., Nater, C., Miller, D. I., Kaufmann, M., & Sczesny, S. (2020). Gender stereotypes have changed: A cross-temporal meta-analysis of US public opinion polls from 1946 to 2018. *American Psychologist, 75*(3), 301–315.

Eagly, A. H., & Revelle, W. (in press). Understanding the magnitude of psychological differences between women and men requires seeing the forest and the trees. *Perspectives in Psychological Science.*

Eagly, A. H., & Steffen, V. J. (1984). Gender stereotypes stem from the distribution of women and men into social roles. *Journal of Personality and Social Psychology, 46*(4), 735–754.

Festinger, L. (1957). *A Theory of Cognitive Dissonance.* Evanston, IL: Row, Peterson.

Geary, D. C. (2020). *Male, Female: The Evolution of Human Sex Differences.* Third edition. Washington, DC: American Psychological Association.

Heider, F. (1958). *The Psychology of Interpersonal Relations.* New York: Wiley.

Johnson, B. T., & Eagly, A. H. (1989). Effects of involvement on persuasion: A meta-analysis. *Psychological Bulletin, 106*(2), 290–314.

Koenig, A. M., & Eagly, A. H. (2014). Evidence for the social role theory of stereotype content: Observations of groups' roles shape stereotypes. *Journal of Personality and Social Psychology, 107*(3), 371–392.

Wood, W., & Eagly, A. H. (2002). A cross-cultural analysis of the behavior of women and men: Implications for the origins of sex differences. *Psychological Bulletin, 128,* 699–727.

Zentner, M., & Eagly, A. H. (2015). A sociocultural framework for understanding partner preferences of women and men: Integration of concepts and evidence. *European Review of Social Psychology, 26*(1), 328–373.

14 Reasoning

Richard E. Nisbett

On my sixth birthday, June 1, 1947, I moved to El Paso to live in a tiny house made of rock and surrounded by cottonfields irrigated from the Rio Grande, which I frequently rode to on my bike. Half a mile away was a barrio where Mexican braceros lived in growing season, and which I visited occasionally. I roamed the fields, the surrounding desert, the irrigation ditches with crayfish, and the canals with muskrats and catfish. Heaven, in other words.

On my wanderings I did lots of thinking. I read recently that one of the very few things known to be correlated with success as a scientist is the amount of time spent being sick as a child. Lots of time for thought as well as reading, which I also did a lot of.

I debated at Austin High School and was good at it. I also did a lot of acting. In a one-act play contest I played the ragpicker in *The Madwoman of Chaillot* by Jean Giraudoux. When my portrayal was over, I sat down in the audience, pleased by my excellent performance, to watch El Paso High's play. Within five minutes, I was mortified. Their male lead was absolutely fantastic, a gifted actor. I realized I had been a rank amateur by comparison, which the judge verified in his critique of my performance. El Paso High's lead was F. Murray Abraham, who decades later won the Academy Award for his portrayal of Salieri in *Amadeus*.

I was brought up in Methodist churches. By the time I had been an agnostic for a few years I was confident my religious upbringing had no influence on me. Then, in mid-life, I read Weber's *Protestant Ethic and the Spirit of Capitalism*. The book, written 100 years ago, describes the Methodism of England's John Wesley 100 years before Weber's book was written. The shock of recognition was great. I realized that the God part aside, I was ethnically Methodist. For example, I always knew I had to have a calling. Don't ask me who's doing the calling, I wouldn't have an answer.

I was always ambitious, by which I mean *ambitious*. I calculated the odds that I could become president of the United States. I started by noting that of 200 million people in the country I could immediately remove half from competition on the grounds of gender. Then I could remove half the men because they were too unattractive, another large percentage because they were not white, another fraction because they weren't very smart, but I could never reach odds better than one in a thousand.

Richard E. Nisbett, University of Michigan, USA. Excerpted from *Thinking: A Memoir*.

Shortly after my coming to recognize that I was not going to be president, I read Calvin Hall's *Primer of Freudian Psychology*. It was lock and key. The heck with being president.

"Are you stupid?" asked the stunned baggage handler at Boston's South Station. These were the first words spoken to me above the Mason-Dixon Line.

It was my turn to be dumbfounded. I had merely asked a simple question: "How do I get to the subway?" Responding to my slack jaw, the baggage handler asked, "How do you think you're going to get three trunks on the subway?" Well, I hadn't actually thought about it. And what was I doing with three trunks? My mother and I had piled into them everything that seemed to one or the other of us to be essential for life at a New England college, which I felt included my record player and a large stack of records and my mother felt included a white dinner jacket. The baggage handler helped me into a cab to go to Tufts.

I went to New England in 1959 thinking I would fit among people there – a reasonable but mistaken deduction from the fact that I didn't fit among people in Texas. However, the fit turned out not to be with Christian New England. The interesting people I met tended to be Jews from the New York area, so nearly all my friends were Jewish – from then on.

Several experiences I had at Tufts led to research I was to do later.

I frequently found it difficult to get to sleep. I finally bought some Sominex, which I took just before bedtime one night and proceeded to toss and turn while waiting for the blessed drug to take effect. Which it didn't. I had a particularly bad bout of insomnia. Years later Michael Storms and I gave insomniac college students a placebo which I told them was a pill that would reduce physiological arousal at bedtime. I anticipated that the fact that their arousal was about the same as usual despite taking the pill would arouse them still further. Sure enough, such subjects reported taking longer to get to sleep than usual. And subjects told the drug would increase their arousal got to sleep more quickly on the nights they took the drugs (Storms & Nisbett, 1970).

The insomnia study made a big splash, but no one could replicate it. Years later someone did replicate the study – for subjects with high need for cognition. Subjects with low need for cognition did not show the effect. My original study was done with Yale students; subsequent ones were done at schools that likely had fewer students with high need for cognition. An important lesson for our time: Failures to replicate don't establish that the original finding was spurious.

My senior year I took an American literature course. I experienced doing the reading as tedious work. I puzzled over this fact because until I went to college, reading the sort of book assigned in the course was high entertainment. I drew on this experience later in my research showing how easy it can be to turn play into work. With Mark Lepper and David Greene, I asked nursery school children to draw with magic markers for a chance to get a "good player award" They played less with the markers on subsequent occasions than children not offered a contract (Lepper et al., 1973).

I also noticed early on that people seemed to be more impolite in the Northeast than in Texas. Paradoxically, the level of homicide in the South and Southwest is higher than in the Northeast. My observation of the paradox played a role in the theory

I ultimately came up with to explain regional differences in homicide. The North was settled mostly by farmers; the South mostly by herders. Herders present an aggressive face to the world to make it clear they are not to be trifled with. Insults are sometimes met with lethal aggression. Dov Cohen, Norbert Schwarz, and I insulted Michigan students, with resulting increases in testosterone and cortisol for southerners and no changes in those hormones for northerners. I am proud to say the abstract was the first in *JPSP* history to contain the word "asshole" (Cohen et al., 1996).

After graduating with a major in psychology, I went to Columbia University, where I got my PhD in 1966. It was wonderful to work with Stan Schachter. He was a gifted and generous teacher. The technique Schachter used to teach students how to do science was the grunt method. "Ehh" meant your idea was not a very good one. "Mmm" meant "probably not but I won't rule it out just yet." "Ahn!" meant "by Jove, you've got it!" Early in my teaching career I decided I wouldn't force my own students to induce correct principles of scientific thinking from mere grunts. I would take the trouble to explain to them why an idea they had was good or bad. This tended to produce endless discussions about philosophy of science. I soon came to employ the grunt method exclusively.

Lee Ross became Schachter's student through my good offices. Within weeks of meeting Lee, who arrived at Columbia my last year there, it was clear to me that this was a brilliant person who had the potential to be a great psychologist. I told Schachter he should work with Lee, but Schachter said he already had too many students. I then told Schachter he *had to* work with Lee. Some people would have bristled at such pushiness. But fortunately for Lee, Schachter, and the field of psychology, Schachter agreed to work with him. The good turn I did Lee was paid back a hundredfold in friendship, intellectual pleasures, and big contributions to literally all the ideas I've worked on.

Whether because of Schachter's example or because I'm built that way, I have usually made friends with my students. I think the importance of the emotional bond between student and advisor is underappreciated.

My first job was at Yale. This was the era of the old boy network. In those days, when the top departments had an opening, they called the best researchers in their field and asked them if they had any good men (!) coming out. Schachter would be on everyone's list to call, and I was his fair-haired boy the year I was to get my PhD.

I did not love Yale. Many of the faculty members were pretentious. The subtext of a lot of conversations was, "I'm this smart, how smart are you?" The one time I was in a senior faculty member's home I looked at a drawing on the wall and my host said, "The master told me an interesting story about this sketch when I saw it in his workshop in Paris." The master being referred to was Picasso.

But I made good friends among the graduate students, including Mark Lepper, Michael Storms, Shelley Taylor, Carol Dweck, David Kanouse, Leslie Zebrowitz, and Mark Zanna. All of those people were to make major contributions to psychology.

In 1969, Hal Kelley wrote to the National Science Foundation asking it to pay for a six-week conference at UCLA for six psychologists to work on developing attribution theory. Remarkably, NSF did provide the rather considerable sum that was necessary.

Participants included Ned Jones, Bernard Weiner, David Kanouse, and Schachter students Stuart Valins and me.

It was fascinating for me to have the opportunity to engage at close range with Kelley and Jones. Hal Kelley seemed preternaturally calm, rational, and kindly – one of the most Apollonian figures I've ever encountered.

Ned was friendly, thoughtful, and straightforward. Lee Ross once heard Ned put forward a very interesting hypothesis, and Lee suggested a punchy experiment to test Ned's idea. Ned said, "Oh, that kind of razzle-dazzle is not my style." Ned had nothing against other people doing sexy experiments, he just wasn't going to stoop to doing it himself.

The six of us wrote a book together showcasing attribution theory (Jones et al., 1972). I wrote a chapter with Stu Valins on people's explanations of their own behavior and another chapter with him on clinical applications of attribution theory. Ned announced that he wanted to write a chapter for our book that would compare the causal attributions of the "actor," or individual who engaged in a particular behavior, and the "observer" of that behavior. I invited myself to join with him in working on the chapter. He graciously welcomed my participation.

Early in the collaboration with Ned the idea occurred to me that there was often a profound difference between the actor and the observer in attributions for behavior. The actor will normally attribute behavior to situational factors while observers attribute the behavior to presumed dispositions of the actor. I sketched the idea and sent it to Ned, who made many interesting observations and amplifications of the basic idea that would never have occurred to me. I carried out several studies showing that there can be marked differences along the lines we had speculated about.

Right after I came up with the actor-observer hypothesis I told it to Lee, who instantly said: "Great idea, Dick. But it misses the more basic point, which is that everybody, including even the actor, *overattributes* behavior to dispositions of the actor." He labeled this concept the Fundamental Attribution Error. The FAE idea and the demonstrations in that era by Walter Mischel and others that personality traits are typically a poor predictor of behavior ultimately gave rise to the book *The Person and the Situation* by Lee and me.

At the end of my third year at Yale, I asked that I be considered for promotion to associate professor without tenure, which had been done for my two social psychology predecessors. I was turned down, because, I was told, I didn't have many publications. This shocked me. The senior faculty knew, or should have known, that my work was getting a lot of attention. When a tenure offer came the next year from the University of Michigan, I was receptive.

My interview at Michigan took place on an extremely cold day in February of 1971. Dirty snow lay in patches on the ground. I don't believe the Dean said a word during my visit with him. (I subsequently found out that he was in the middle of dealing with a student uprising that was threatening to become violent.) Nothing of interest was discussed during my meeting with the department's Executive Committee. The person who spent the most time talking to me was an utter bore.

None of this mattered to my decision. I had made up my mind to go to Michigan because everything I had heard about the university, the department, and the town was positive. My one-day exposure would be a trivially small evidence base. Good thinking!

People at Michigan are accommodating and unpretentious. There are no levers for a prima donna to press. No accident that the intellectual environment at Michigan was more exciting than what I routinely experienced at Yale or Columbia. Then and now, lunchtime conversation ranges from gossip to intellectual topics to shop to movies to yes, football, without any attempt at point scoring. Because people are not terribly worried about being evaluated or one-upped, they try out ideas that might be viewed as silly. And if you can't risk seeming silly, you're going to get less out of conversation.

The non-evaluative climate results in constant formation of faculty seminars involving people across several disciplines. This is undoubtedly aided by the fact that Michigan, more than I believe any other major university, is riddled with centers and institutes that throw people of different disciplines together. It was out of such seminars that the fields of evolutionary psychology (Randy Nesse, David Buss) and judgment and decision-making (Ward Edwards, Amos Tversky) developed. The most important group to me was the Culture and Cognition program, founded by psychologist Hazel Markus, anthropologist Larry Hirschfeld, and me. The program included at various points luminaries including social psychologists Shinobu Kitayama and Phoebe Ellsworth, anthropologists Joan Miller, Dan Sperber, and Joe Henrich, developmental psychologists Susan Gelman and Harold Stevenson, and cognitive psychologists Doug Medin and Edward E. Smith. The modern field of cultural psychology originated in this group.

Bob Zajonc played a big role in making me quickly happy at Michigan. Bob was 48 when I met him, and I was 30. I never really felt that Bob was older. His physical condition and his enthusiastic approach to psychology, as well as the sciences generally, music, sports, and the arts made him seem more adolescent than middle-aged. Bob was a great leader. Even when Bob was chewing a person out, they were aware that they were in some sense still in his good graces.

Much of the work I did at Columbia and Yale showed that people often have no idea, or only a largely incorrect idea, of the reasoning processes which caused them to behave in a particular way. Tim Wilson and I did systematic research showing that people can be quite mistaken about their reasoning processes, even about the most routine matters. Our conclusion that much of behavior happens as the result of unconscious processes was accepted by the field without a fight. This was partly due to Danny Kahneman. The *Psychological Review* paper reporting the work (Nisbett & Wilson, 1977) was extremely long. Two of the reviewers insisted that it be cut. Danny insisted that everything in it was needed in order to be completely convincing.

Even before I went to Michigan I had begun to realize that there was a missing field – that of empirically based epistemology. I developed a graduate course looking at various philosophical treatments of how people gain knowledge, or should gain knowledge. My work with Gene Borgida on people's frequent failure to make use of base rates, their inadequate appreciation of the law of large numbers, their errors in causal reasoning, and their overweighting of information acquired personally was included in the course (e.g., Nisbett & Borgida, 1975).

When I gave a talk on that work at Stanford, Lee Ross told me I should look at work by Tversky and Kahneman. Indeed. I began to use their heuristics and biases ideas to frame my own research. My work on reasoning and Lee's, as well as that of Tversky and Kahneman, were described in 1980 in the book *Human Inference: Strategies and Shortcomings of Social Judgment.* The book also reviewed the enormous difficulty we have in assessing correlations between events, the concept of confirmation bias, the limits of our ability to analyze the causes of events, the ways in which self-knowledge can be flawed, and our inability to view our cognitive processes.

Working with Lee was as important to me personally as it was intellectually and professionally. For more than fifty years Lee was my closest friend and personal therapist. Shortly before his death I asked Lee why he was able to solve people's problems and social conflicts so well. He told me it was because he didn't reflexively look at a problem in the same way as the person he was trying to help, but rather looked at the problem as he imagined it would appear to other actors. "Here's the way Joe is probably perceiving the conflict. Here's what you could do to change his perceptions."

Decades after the books I wrote with Lee, he wrote a wonderful book with social psychologist Tom Gilovich called *The Wisest One in the Room: How You Can Benefit from Social Psychology's Most Powerful Insights.* As it happens, I had written a textbook on social psychology with Tom and in the process came to realize that he was also one of the wisest and most humane people I have known. Lee and Tom deserved the title of their book.

Here's a fact that will seem strange to readers who are not yet of a certain age. Most psychologists in the 1970s and 1980s believed that psychologists have no right to criticize people's judgments. That's a job for philosophers and theologians. It's presumptuous, even immoral, for psychologists to arrogate powers of criticism to themselves. Many psychologists and philosophers attempted to show that the heuristics and biases work was inappropriately judgmental and empirically wrong. From Oxford philosopher L. J. Cohen: ". . . our fundamental epistemic principles and habits, whatever ones they turn out to be exactly, are *good* principles . . ."

So when are you justified in saying that someone's reasoning is produced by flawed principles? With now-famous philosopher Paul Thagard, I argued that it's permissible to judge people as less than fully rational if you have an empirically justified account of what they're doing when they violate normative standards of reasoning.

With another now-famous philosopher friend Steve Stich, I wrote a paper arguing that the justification of an inductive argument requires that the principle we used to make it is endorsed by people we acknowledge to be expert about the kind of inference in question. This introduces a social consideration into the problem of induction. Inductions are good only if the right people would say they are.

To see whether people can improve their reasoning by learning to use abstract general principles such as statistical rules, principles of experimental science, and cost-benefit principles, Darrin Lehman and I created a package of everyday-life problems for which the right answer involved applying one or another correct formal principle. We gave the problems to Michigan students at the beginning of their first semester and again to those same students and others at the end of their last semester.

We were amazed to find that for our package of problems there was a 25 percent gain in ability to apply these inductive reasoning concepts for natural science majors and humanities majors. For social science and psychology majors, there was a 65 percent gain! It's no exaggeration to say that fundamental change occurred to their inductive reasoning principles.

Work I did with David Krantz and Geoffrey Fong showed that you could teach people statistical principles in brief sessions which they were able to apply weeks later even when the test consisted of questions asked in the context of what they believed to be a poll of political opinions. In my belief that rules for statistics, probability, scientific methodology, and microeconomics can be taught with only a little effort I recently wrote *Mindware: Tools for Smart Thinking* and created a free online course called *Mindware: Critical Thinking for the Information Age* (www.coursera.org/learn/mindware).

"There was a light shining out of him," the great statistician Persi Diaconis was wont to say of Amos Tversky. That was certainly the way I felt. I had the great good luck to be able to spend a lot of time with Amos because he was at Michigan for a couple of extended periods, and once when he was ensconced at Stanford and I was there working with Lee.

Amos was tremendous fun to be with. Like Lee, he would take an idea I might offer up and give it a workout. Whether the upshot was a reframing and extension of the idea or a decision to abandon it, conversation with Amos was always helpful. Like Lee, he had exquisite taste in ideas.

Amos was generally considered to be the smartest person one knew. By one, I mean everyone. I had a joke about Amos, which was that meeting him afforded a measure of your own IQ. The smarter you were, the quicker you realized he was smarter than you were.

In contrast with Amos, Danny is sometimes moody or labile, and that can make him less than a joy to be around. But he can also be a great raconteur and a dazzling conversation partner. There's a certain expectant, almost pixie-ish smile that Danny radiates when he's in a conversation which he thinks is really going somewhere.

Danny, like everyone else in the world but Amos, could be wrong. But I don't think always being right is necessarily a virtue. A labile temperament can cause you to leap to some ridiculous conclusions, but such a temperament is a constant goad to thought. And there's this: The more I got to know Amos and Danny the more I began to feel that without Danny, Amos might have been the world's greatest mathematical psychologist. Period.

Around the time I started work on *Culture of Honor*, I dropped into Hazel Markus's office to tell her I was going to teach a graduate seminar on cultural psychology.

I expected her to say, "Only dopes study culture." Instead, she said, "No you're not. I'm going to teach it." Unbeknownst to me, Hazel had been at work on a paper with Shinobu that was to become one of the most cited ever in psychology and would become the founding document of the new field. It established that there were profound differences between East Asians and Westerners in basic social orientation.

Of course Hazel and I taught the seminar together. And it turned out to be the most exciting educational event of my career. The first students included the astonishingly talented Dov Cohen, Michael Morris, Kaiping Peng, Incheol Choi, Rick Larrick, and Ara Norenzayan. Not surprisingly, with that kind of brain power the course was electrifying. It was perfectly clear to everybody that there was an orchard here filled with low hanging fruit.

The first crew of students was followed in quick succession by yet another batch of truly remarkable students: Li-Jun Ji, Taka Masuda, Yuri Miyamoto, Hannah Chua, Jan Leu, and Jeffrey Sanchez-Burks.

Early on Kaiping tipped me off to the idea that Asians think holistically more than do Westerners, who think more analytically. Kaiping and Mike showed that Chinese explanations of an individual's behavior were likely to invoke situational factors including the behavior of other people, whereas explanations of the same behavior by Americans tended to invoke traits and motives.

Asians actually see more of what there is to see in the environment. Taka Masuda and I showed underwater scenes to Japanese and Americans and then asked them to report what they had seen (Masuda & Nisbett, 2001). Japanese reported about the same amount of information about the attributes of the largest, most salient fish as Americans did, but the Japanese reported 60 percent more information about the environment (rocks, plants, small animals) and twice as much about relationships (the big fish was swimming toward the smaller fish). Other work showed that Asian perception of the world focuses on relationships among objects and similarities between them, whereas Western perception is more likely to be based on categories of objects and rules that govern objects' behavior (Nisbett, 2003).

Kaiping and I showed that whereas logical thought is common for Westerners, Easterners favor dialectical reasoning. We presented Chinese and Americans with choices between types of argument. One argument was always logical in nature, applying the law of noncontradiction, and one was holistic or dialectical. For each argument pair, Chinese participants preferred the dialectical argument and Americans preferred the object based on avoiding contradiction (Peng & Nisbett, 1999).

My work on reasoning left me in a good position to critique the way intelligence was understood by professionals from the middle of the twentieth century to the early twenty-first. In my 2009 book, *Intelligence and How to Get It: Why Schools and Cultures Count*, and an *American Psychologist* article with James Flynn, Eric Turkheimer, and others I argued that intelligence is a far broader concept than is captured by IQ tests, that heritability estimates for IQ markedly underestimate the role of the environment, that schooling and early childhood environment are very import-ant, that people have been getting smarter at least since the mid-twentieth century, that the IQ difference between blacks and whites owes nothing to genes and is narrowing, that there is no evidence that young Asians have higher IQs than young Westerners and there are clear environmental factors producing greater Asian skills in later life, and, most important, it's both possible and urgently important to boost the intelligence of poor minority children. It's now been twelve years since *Intelligence* was published and none of its major conclusions have been contradicted by any systematic critique.

Saul asked me to end by reflecting on social psychology today. The most striking thing to me is that social psychology has gone over the course of my career from being a small and obscure enterprise to one having a major impact on the world. The concepts of cognitive dissonance, FAE, confirmation bias, groupthink, hindsight bias, and many others are known to the great majority of educated people and taught not just in psychology departments but in philosophy, sociology, and economics as well as business schools, law schools, public health schools, and engineering schools. Many of our concepts are taught to intelligence analysts and to future military officers. Social psychologists have created effective interventions at every educational level from grade school to college, and our methodologies have been employed to change medical practices and to debunk interventions such as "scared straight" and "grief counseling." No social psychologist of my generation would have guessed that our field could make such an impact on the world.

Suggested Reading

Cohen, D., Nisbett, R. E., Bowdle, B. F., & Schwarz, N. (1996). Insult, aggression, and the southern culture of honor: An "experimental ethnography." *Journal of Personality and Social Psychology, 70*(5), 945–960.

Gilovich, T., & Ross, L. (2015). *The Wisest One in the Room: How You Can Benefit from Social Psychology's Most Powerful Insights.* New York: Free Press.

Jones, E. E., Kanouse, D. E., Kelley, H. H., Nisbett, R. E., Valins, S., & Weiner, B. (1972). *Attribution: Perceiving the Causes of Behavior.* New York: General Learning Press.

Lepper, M. R., Greene, D., & Nisbett, R. E. (1973). Undermining children's intrinsic interest with extrinsic reward: A test of the "overjustification" hypothesis. *Journal of Personality and Social Psychology, 28*(1), 129–137.

Masuda, T., & Nisbett, R. E. (2001). Attending holistically versus analytically: Comparing the context sensitivity of Japanese and Americans. *Journal of Personality and Social Psychology, 81*(5), 922–934.

Nisbett, R. E. (2003). *The Geography of Thought: How Asians and Westerners Think Differently . . . and Why.* New York: Free Press.

  (2009). *Intelligence and How to Get It: Why Schools and Cultures Count.* New York: Norton.

  (2015). *Mindware: Tools for Smart Thinking.* New York: Farrar, Straus & Giroux.

  (2021). *Thinking: A Memoir.* Ann Arbor, MI: Aqora Books.

Nisbett, R. E., & Borgida, E. (1975). Attribution and the psychology of prediction. *Journal of Personality and Social Psychology, 32*(5), 932–943.

Nisbett, R. E., & Cohen, D. (1996). *Culture of Honor: The Psychology of Violence in the South.* Denver: Westview Press.

Nisbett, R. E., & Ross, L. D. (1980). *Human Inference: Strategies and Shortcomings of Social Judgment.* Englewood Cliffs, NJ: Prentice-Hall.

Nisbett, R. E., & Wilson, T. D. (1977). Telling more than we can know: Verbal reports on mental processes. *Psychological Review*, *84*(3), 231–259.

Peng, K., & Nisbett, R. E. (1999). Culture, dialectics, and reasoning about contradiction. *American Psychologist*, *54*(9), 741–754.

Ross, L., & Nisbett, R. E. (1991). *The Person and the Situation: Perspectives of Social Psychology*. McGraw-Hill.

Storms, M. D., & Nisbett, R. E. (1970). Insomnia and the attribution process. *Journal of Personality and Social Psychology*, *16*(2), 319–328.

15 Chance and Choice
My Career in Social Psychology

Kay Deaux

In the sixty years since I took my first psychology course, much has changed. Wars have begun and ended, the US population has nearly doubled, and fifty new countries appear on redrawn world maps. Nor has social psychology stood still. The Society of Experimental Social Psychology was founded in 1965; the European Association of Experimental Social Psychology followed suit the next year (later dropping Experimental from its name). In 1974, the Society of Personality and Social Psychology (SPSP) was formed, building on the history of Division 8 of the American Psychological Association. The Association for Psychological Science (originally the American Psychological Society) came into being in 1988, and hosted the initial meetings of SPSP that evolved into an independent convention. These six decades establish the context for my development as a social psychologist on a path shaped by both chance and choice.

Finding the Start of the Path

When I entered Northwestern University in 1959, I doubt if I had any idea what psychology was. High schools didn't teach the course at that time and newspapers weren't filled with reports of psychological findings. My early choices reflected subjects I had liked in high school. Math was my first major, but despite a subsequent career in which I happily did statistics and pored over data, the more abstract aspects of math did not appeal and I quickly (but temporarily) pivoted to French. It was in the final quarter of my sophomore year that I took an introductory psychology course and I was immediately hooked. From then on I immersed myself in psychology, running verbal learning experiments on memory drums in Ben Underwood's lab, working on library research and writing for Donald Campbell and his co-authors in their development of *Unobtrusive Measures*, developing an experiment with then-graduate student Barry Collins to pit learning theory against cognitive dissonance theory (never published), conducting an observational study of black and white seating patterns at O'Hare airport for my sociology minor – and figuring out what to do next.

A small honors class for senior psychology majors was a natural springboard for graduate school, but only for the men in the class, it seemed. The professor in charge

Kay Deaux, The Graduate Center City University of New York, USA.

was quite clear that he would never accept women as graduate students and suggested I find other paths. Somehow I came up with the idea of graduate study in social work, not to become a practicing social worker, but rather to get a doctorate in social work that would allow me to focus on research with people in social settings. And so my next stop was the Columbia University School of Social Work. But as was true with my earlier ventures into math and French, I soon realized that social work was not the answer either, and I left Columbia after one year in the two-year program. A desire to live a bit longer in New York City before beginning a PhD program led me to enter the Master's psychology program at Brooklyn College in 1964. Happily, I was back in social/personality research, working as a research assistant for James Bieri. During that year, however, Bieri accepted a job offer from the University of Texas (UT) and suggested that I transfer there as well. Soon I was on the move again, this time to Austin, Texas and its on-the-rise psychology department.

Entering the UT doctoral program in the fall of 1965, I needed to develop some focus and make some choices. Multiple pieces were part of the puzzle of what kind of psychology I wanted to do. From my early training in Underwood's lab, the principles of experimentation as a route to knowledge were solidly laid down. Coexisting with them were the varied approaches to knowledge that Don Campbell had introduced (in some cases, ideas that I did not fully comprehend at the time). Added to the mix was my minor in sociology. Then there was the brief involvement in social work, with its broader view of society and its focus on the betterment of individuals, groups, and social systems. The year at Brooklyn College was a counterbalancing act between experimental personality work on concepts of cognitive complexity with Bieri and the passionate advocacy of socially relevant research that Hal Proshansky offered.

At UT, I initially continued to work with Bieri, who was nominally my major advisor, but with my own NIMH fellowship I was free to develop whatever line of research engaged me. Learning theories were a dominant theme in the department, and as part of my qualifying exams I had to familiarize myself with Hull-Spence theory and with the newly emerging math models, among other examples (which did not include the still-nascent versions of social learning theory). None of what I learned in those classes seemed very social to me. Elliot Aronson had recently arrived in the department and cognitive dissonance was the primary emphasis in the social psychology program. Yet despite the intellectual enthusiasm surrounding cognitive dissonance in the mid-1960s and the charismatic presence of Aronson in the UT program, I could not fully engage in that research model, with its emphasis on creating impactful and often dramatic manipulations in laboratory settings, frequently involving high levels of deception. I settled on a more traditional field of attitude change in my dissertation work, using Sherifian concepts of latitudes of acceptance and rejection to explore a newly identified phenomenon of anticipatory attitude change.

But what would the next step be? I thoroughly enjoyed the research process and felt that social psychology was the right field for me. I also had some teaching experience in the summer between Brooklyn and Texas, so I understood that teaching and research typically went together. At the same time, neither at Northwestern nor Texas was there a single woman on the psychology faculty, so it is not clear why

I assumed that would be a path available to me. There were some other women in my graduate classes at Texas, but the feminist movement had not yet begun at that time and place and I don't remember any discussions of whether and how women could attain academic positions. And so in 1967, with my PhD in hand and four refereed journal articles on my beginner's CV, but with considerable naiveté about what the future might entail, I continued on the path to professordom.

Getting an academic position was challenging but ultimately successful. With marriage to a fellow graduate student, we were a two-career couple looking for compatible positions at a time when the availability of any position was communicated mainly through word of mouth and the "old boy network." My advisor of record was not in social psychology and my husband's major advisor had unexpectedly died before our job search began, so the challenges were even greater. But eventually we did get two assistant professor positions in the same geographic area, and I began my career at the newly established Wright State University in Dayton, Ohio. The psychology department consisted of a small group of young assistant professors, chaired by an old-timer who gave us ample space to develop our careers. Three years later (and no longer married), I moved to Purdue University, my identity as an academic now firmly established and my commitments clear.

The Purdue Years (1970–1987)

I arrived at Purdue at the age of 28 and left when I was 45. During that seventeen-year period, I developed my research skills, identified issues that would engage me for years to come, and defined my place in the broader academic world. I also now had graduate students to work with and quickly learned how rewarding those collaborative relationships can be, both professionally and personally. Some of those early students are still close friends today.

My research interest in gender, begun in earnest soon after I arrived at Purdue, is a clear example of an interaction between person and environment. As a woman in academia, I had experienced gender discrimination, including the discouraging advice from my undergraduate honors professor as well as a substantial pay differential at Wright State University when I was hired (that I learned about only later). The growing women's movement was unquestionably a powerful influence on defining issues and underlining the importance of understanding more about gender stereotypes and discriminatory judgments. And the dearth of relevant scientific work on these questions was apparent.

A significant factor facilitating my focus on gender was the support of the department chair, Jim Naylor. Though it is unlikely that Jim considered himself a feminist, his support for me was evident in his actions. Doing good research was important to him, and if I could show professional recognition of my work, through traditional markers such as publication in recognized journals, he would defend me on all occasions. (A Ford Foundation Fellowship in Women's Studies in 1973 also helped to establish my credentials.)

One important professional and personal relationship that developed during my Purdue years was with Janet Taylor Spence. Although Janet was at UT during the two years I was there, she was not in the psychology department (due to nepotism rules, which precluded her from being in the same department with Kenneth Spence) and I knew her only slightly. It was more than a decade later, when we both were then doing gender research, that Janet and I began to interact regularly. An empirical paper, a handbook chapter, and a lasting personal relationship emerged from those interactions (the latter included a purely pleasure trip to Hong Kong and Singapore together, aided by frequent flyer miles that Janet had accumulated as president of APA!).

While at Purdue, my skill and confidence as a researcher and a writer grew considerably. I began my research program by building on theories of social psychological predecessors, notably attribution theorists such as Fritz Heider and Bernard Weiner. Using their theoretical models we were able to predict and show how judgments of the performance of women and men varied and how women and men themselves used different explanations for their successes and failures. We then turned our attention to the content and structure of gender stereotypes, as well as more general considerations of the pervasive role of gender in thought and action. This work contributed to the theoretical framework that Brenda Major and I developed in our 1987 *Psychological Review* paper, as well as to an amicus brief filed by APA in the case of *Price Waterhouse v. Hopkins* (Fiske et al., 1991).

In the review paper written with Brenda (earlier a student of mine at Purdue, at this point an associate professor at SUNY Buffalo) we offered an interactive model of gender-related behavior as an alternative to the traditional sex differences model. In our view, many observed differences are a product of both others' expectations and contextual cues, interacting with self-systems of the individual. This was an intrinsically social and dynamic model that, although not presuming to be a rigorous, easily tested theory, offered an important framework for further theoretical development.

The amicus brief focused on gender stereotypes and their adverse consequences for judgments of women in the workplace. Susan Fiske had first been brought in by lawyers to testify at the district court level in the *Price Waterhouse v. Hopkins* case; when the case went to the Supreme Court, APA asked three other psychologists (Eugene Borgida, Madeline Heilman, and me) to join Susan and attorney Donald Bersoff in preparing a supporting brief for Hopkins. In their decision in favor of Hopkins, the Court clearly attended to the psychological evidence, establishing its value for future judicial proceedings.

While at Purdue, I expanded my methodological toolbox, feeling a need to occasionally go beyond the lab in search of more general populations and more realistic activities, as exemplified by a study of game choices at county fairs. In a more ambitious project, done in collaboration with a professor in the business school, we analyzed the position of women in the basic steel industry, both from the perspective of the women themselves and from those workers and managers who were interacting with this new population of steelworkers (Deaux & Ullman, 1983).

I also learned new ways to write to a wider audience. My ability to write the basic scientific report was well-honed by the time I left graduate school, but writing a book seemed far more daunting. Yet my belief that a summary of where we were (or more often, were not) in terms of understanding the similarities and differences between women and men made me eager to write in a more accessible form for a broader audience. From this belief emerged my first book, *The Behavior of Women and Men* (Deaux, 1976). In this slim volume, I reviewed standard social psychological topics through a gender lens, which I developed by digging through the existing literature to find reported sex differences (often relegated to footnotes). Even then, a decade before the Deaux and Major model, I argued for a more situational analysis of gender differences. My hope for a wider audience was also achieved, as the book was both adopted in undergraduate courses and used as a graduate-level reference in a field that was still understudied.

Textbook writing was a next step, facilitated by Larry Wrightsman. I first linked up with Larry to write a single chapter on sex roles for the second edition of his best-selling social psychology textbook. In the third edition (1981) he took me on as a second author; in the 1984 fourth edition I became the first author and continued in that role for two more editions. Textbooks can introduce very large numbers of undergraduate students to social psychology and the impact can be far greater than one realizes – a consequence that I realized most vividly when visiting a bookstore in Helsinki, Finland and finding our book on the shelf!

Assessing and Reorienting the Path (1987)

The year 1987 brought major transitions and life changes for me, as I moved from Purdue to the Graduate Center of the City University of New York. Preceding that move, I had spent the 1986–1987 academic year at the Center for Advanced Study in the Behavioral Sciences (CASBS) at Stanford. Two features distinguished this year from my previous stint at the Center (1983–1984): first, this time I was part of a formal working group comprising sociologists and psychologists who had weekly discussions of issues of self, affect, and society; and second, the residency was planned in conjunction with Sam Glucksberg (a psychology professor at Princeton University), who would become my husband at the end of that year.

As I contemplated a move from Purdue, I had time to think about the career path I had staked out, as well as to consider what opportunities might lie ahead. Given my Lewinian belief in the interaction of persons and situations, both an assessment of my own skills and preferences and an evaluation of the new environment were in order (though admittedly, this analysis is more easily seen in retrospect than I had articulated at that time).

My career had developed with an appreciation of different emphases and possible paths within social psychology. As a first-year graduate student at Brooklyn College, I had joined the Society for the Psychological Study of Social Issues (SPSSI), undoubtedly influenced by Hal Proshansky. Later that same year, I began my decades-long subscription to the *Journal of Personality and Social Psychology* with its 1965 inaugural volume. I went on to be active in both sponsoring organizations throughout my career. I also looked frequently to the sociological literature to help me analyze a problem. Working on gender almost inevitably impelled me to consider structural factors such as social norms, organizational climate, and legal policies. Somewhere along the way I became familiar with the writings of Sheldon Stryker, who throughout his career argued forcefully for bridges between sociological social psychology and psychological social psychology, and the 1986–1987 work group at CASBS gave me a year of lively interaction with Shel and other major researchers from the sociological side.

Another early influence on my thinking about the social psychological enterprise, and in particular the implicit (and often explicit) assumption of the universality of our findings, was Israel and Tajfel's (1972) book, *The Context of Social Psychology*. Authors in this European edited volume questioned standard practices in the field, raising questions about cultural differences in theoretical assumptions and priorities for research. Though many details of the book have been forgotten, the basic message remained a latent influence on my thinking. One likely effect was my growing attention to social psychological research in Europe, reacting in part to what seemed to be the narrowing focus of attention in the United States. The Europeans appeared to have a broader concept of social psychology, one that gave more attention to social interactions and contextual influences and accepted more permeable boundaries between laboratory and field research, such that both could be considered valid sites for basic research (in contrast to the assumption that lab = basic and field = applied).

Later I would become a member of the European Association of Social Psychology and frequently participate in their triennial conventions in places like Oxford, San Sebastian, Stockholm, and Amsterdam. I also spent a sabbatical year at the University of Kent in Canterbury to become more familiar with social identity theory, at that time little recognized in the United States. Numerous international research collaborations developed over the years. But most of this was yet to come, awaiting developments in the next phase of my career.

The CUNY Years (1987–2009)

In 1987, I moved to the CUNY Graduate Center and my physical, intellectual, and lived environment all changed, in some ways dramatically. The Graduate Center was and is different in many respects from a traditional academic psychology department. First, I would now teach only graduate students, in seminars and one-on-one meetings. Second, the facilities and resources for laboratory research were minimal and "subject pools" were non-existent. At the same time, the structure of the Graduate Center meant that interdisciplinary contact and interchange was not only easier for both faculty and students, but in fact was in some ways normative. Further, New York City, with its diversity of people and settings, challenged me to think more broadly about the human experience. The opportunity structure presented by my new environment definitely shaped choices I made. In teaching, the interdisciplinary climate encouraged co-teaching, which I did twice with sociologist Cynthia Epstein (courses on women and work and on self and identity), as well as the development of a course on gender and the law with Maureen O'Connor, a professor at John Jay College, a branch of CUNY that trained in both social psychology and law. Within the social-personality program, Suzanne Ouellette and I for years taught a combined first-year course that included a historical perspective on both areas.

I also redefined my research agenda, shifting my focus from gender to immigration, mediated by a continuing interest in questions of identity. In the closing paragraphs of Deaux and Major (1987), we recognized that gender is only one of numerous identities that can influence behavior. My interest in the multiplicity of self was further nurtured by the previous year's CASBS working group. Thus when I arrived at the Graduate Center I was ready for a deep dig into identity, beginning with developing a seminar on social identity and then designing research projects to explore phenomena of interest. Over the next decade, I published a series of chapters and papers probing the structure and function of multiple social identities. In some cases, the work can be directly traced to the activities of a five-year-long working group of social and developmental psychologists organized by Jacque Eccles, Diane Ruble, and myself and funded by the Russell Sage Foundation (RSF).

My focus on immigration emerged from these more general investigations. When I thought about influential identities other than gender, the diversity of New York City made ethnicity an obvious candidate for further exploration. From there, the move to research on immigration was almost inevitable. With identity as a conceptual center-piece, I saw immigration as a site for the application of a variety of social psycho-logical concepts and theories. This broader conceptualization culminated in my book, *To Be an Immigrant* (Deaux, 2006), published by RSF.

The importance of RSF to this stage of my career is considerable. Led for many years by Eric Wanner, RSF is committed to supporting social science research that increases knowledge about critical issues in society and informs social policy. My first contact with RSF was a funded grant to study stereotype threat among first- and second-generation West Indian immigrants, done together with Claude Steele and a diverse team of researchers. I received funding from RSF several times over subse-quent years, both as an individual and as co-leader of the previously described working group. Later I served on RSF's advisory committee on cultural contact for nearly ten years. In that capacity, I helped to develop collaborative relationships between social psychologists and immigration researchers from sociology and polit-ical science to tackle key issues in immigration.

That activity reflects another aspect of my professional life that includes adminis-trative service. Although on several occasions, both at Purdue and CUNY, I served as area head of the social psychology program, becoming a department head was not something I was drawn to. Nonetheless, in 1994, I accepted the request of Graduate Center president Frances Horowitz (a developmental psychologist) to serve as Executive Officer of Psychology, a position unique to the Graduate Center. Serving a three-year term made it clear that research was far more important to me than what often seemed like a thankless job in a Byzantine structure, and I happily returned to a life of teaching and research.

At the same time, I was consistently drawn to work with psychological organizations, from my early involvement with the Midwestern Psychological Association (on Council for six years followed by the presidency in 1981–1982) to later stints with social organizations such as SESP, SPSP, and SPSSI, as well as the broader-based Association for Psychological Science. In most cases, I saw these positions as opportunities for social psychology (or in the case of APS, psychology more generally) to develop its potential and strength as a discipline and to use its knowledge base to understand and improve the larger society. In this regard, I was acting in accord with the missions of SPSSI and of RSF, convinced that social psychology had importance beyond the academic journals.

And Now?

It is 2021 as I write this. I retired from the CUNY Graduate Center in 2009. From 2008 to the present, I have had a renewable position as Visiting Scholar in the Psychology Department at New York University, where I interact with a stellar group of faculty and students in the social psychology program. Although I no longer teach, I have continued to collaborate on research and writing projects with colleagues around the world.

That world has of course changed since I first entered the field, not only at the global level of populations and nation states, but more particularly in the size and sophistication of the social psychology community. Now there is more of everything social psychological: more academic programs, more social psychologists working in more locations, more journals, more specialized societies. There are many more options for study design and statistical analysis of data (consider that ANOVA was state of the art when I was in graduate school!). Computer programs allow for complex analyses of large data sets that were inconceivable in the days of the Monroe calculator and early-stage computers. The Internet has created an immensely broader network to make our findings readily available across discipline and national boundaries, an availability that also makes multisite collaboration much easier. And the open science movement has given us more confidence in our collective findings and more credibility in the larger arena – credibility and accountability that are important in an era when social psychological findings often have an audience far outside of the academy, appearing regularly in newspaper reports, television interviews, Twitter feeds, and trade books.

I can look with some satisfaction at changes in the substantive topics that social psychology now addresses. Gender and diversity have become central concerns of the field, both in defining research agendas and in assuring representation of all those who might become leaders in the field in the future. From my sixty-year perspective, this is a major change for a field that consisted almost solely of white males and a general assumption that findings from one group would necessarily be true for all, whatever their location. I see change as well, though perhaps lesser in magnitude, in the sharpness of the boundary drawn between laboratory and field research. Though the challenges and constraints differ, theories can be tested outside of the lab and many social psychologists have found both intellectual and practical rewards in doing so.

I also find satisfaction in the greater frequency of collaboration across disciplines – a process that is never easy but can have considerable rewards, particularly if one is concerned with the applicability of one's work to a societal context. Work on gender has often demonstrated the value added by crossing disciplinary lines; immigration is a developing area where a social psychological perspective can contribute significantly to a full understanding of an important social and policy area.

If you spend several decades in a career line, the field that you leave is not the one that you entered. New perspectives and theories, new and redefined problems, advances in methods and analyses will all emerge. During a long career, it is essential to take advantage of the progress and capabilities that have developed. Hopefully, one can also contribute to the field in ways that outlast one's own participation. Yet in making the most of the new, it is also important to appreciate the old. Earlier studies may seem primitive and flawed in methodology and design, given current standards and options. But good ideas can have remarkable longevity and contemporary applicability. I would always advise investigators to take a look at earlier expressions of the ideas that seem intriguing, as well as to consider how other disciplines may be approaching similar issues.

Unchanged for me, over sixty years in the field, is my belief that social psychology is the right path for me to have chosen. Whatever combination of chance opportunities and personal inclination got me on that path, it has been a terrific journey.

Suggested Reading

Deaux, K. (1976). *The Behavior of Women and Men.* Monterey, CA: Brooks/Cole.
    (2006). *To Be an Immigrant.* New York: Russell Sage Foundation.
Deaux, K., & Major, B. (1987). Putting gender into context: An interactive model of gender-related behavior. *Psychological Review, 94,* 369–389.
Deaux, K., & Ullman, J. C. (1983). *Women of Steel: Female Blue-Collar Workers in the Basic Steel Industry.* New York: Praeger.
Fiske, S. G., Bersoff, D. N., Borgida, E., Deaux, K., & Heilman, M. E. (1991). Social science research on trial: Use of sex stereotyping research in *Price Waterhouse v. Hopkins. American Psychologist, 46,* 1049–1060.
Israel, J. & Tajfel, H. (Eds.) (1972). *The Context of Social Psychology: A Critical Assessment.* London: Academic Press.

16   Looking Back on a Charmed Career

Wolfgang Stroebe

My first encounter with the concept "stereotype" was during my final oral exam in social psychology at the University of Tübingen, when Professor Wilhelm Witte asked me what I knew about it. In those days, the psychology training for us ten psychology students was a bit patchy. On the positive side, Witte gave an excellent lecture series on experimental psychology, and we had required courses on the anatomy of the central nervous system and in philosophy. But all other topics were taught by adjunct faculty from nearby pedagogical institutes. For social psychology we had a seminar on group dynamics, and attitudes seemed to have played no role in group dynamics. Witte kindly informed me that attitudes were considered major determinants of social behavior.

Witte, who had moved to the University of Münster, had accepted me as a PhD student to do an empirical dissertation on the size-weight illusion. The perception of the weight of an object is strongly influenced by its size: If two objects of the same weight are of different size, the smaller one will be perceived as heavier. My task was to quantify this dependence. I had three sets of cubes of different dimensions, but with the same weight range. Ten psychology students spent 30 hours each, comparing pairs of weights. I had to sit in a small room for 300 hours to hand out weights and to note down their judgments. At the end, I decided that I was ready for a career change.

I remembered what Witte had said about attitudes and thought that the study of social psychology might be interesting. In 1966, only three German universities offered social psychology, but none as a special degree course. I therefore decided to go abroad. I was reading Dahrendorf's book on *Class and Class Conflict in Industrial Society* and saw on the back cover that he received his PhD at the London School of Economics. Since London seemed a nice change after Münster, I applied at the LSE for their master program in social psychology and as a prospective PhD student. A decade earlier, Sherif and Hovland had published their interesting study of how judges' attitudes toward an issue influenced their rating of attitude statements about that issue. I decided to do my dissertation research on that topic, because my familiarity with psychophysical theories of judgment would be helpful. Since Dick Eiser, a Tajfel student, was also doing his dissertation on judgments of attitude statements, we became close friends and worked jointly there for two years.

Wolfgang Stroebe, University of Groningen, the Netherlands.

A great feature of the LSE department was that social psychologists, who spent their sabbatical there, were asked to teach a course. As a result, I had a course on attitudes by Marty Fishbein, a course on leadership by Judson Mills, and a course on social power by John Schopler. When John asked for student helpers in conducting experiments, Dick and I volunteered and received our first introduction into the art of doing (real) social psychology experiments involving cover stories and deception. Sadly, we also learnt that most studies do not work.

When I submitted my dissertation to my PhD supervisor Norman Hotopf, he did not think it was good enough. Because I already had a PhD, I would have accepted his judgment. But Dick disagreed and suggested I sent my manuscript to Henri Tajfel, an internationally recognized expert on that topic. Because I had not read any of his work, I thought it wise to do so, before sending him my manuscript. To my surprise, I discovered that Tajfel's theory of "perceptual accentuation" could explain an aspect of my data, which none of the psychophysical theories could explain. Thus, I added a section on the application of "Tajfel's theory of 'perceptual accentuation' to judgments of attitude statements." Tajfel was appointed as external examiner and Hotopf had agreed that he would accept my dissertation, if Tajfel did.

The first thing Tajfel did when entering Hotopf's office was to offer me a contract for a book on social judgment in a new European book series he was editing. He then criticized Hotopf for not approving my dissertation. This developed into a heated argument and lasted for approximately forty minutes. When Hotopf finally suggested that it was really I who should defend my dissertation, Tajfel replied that he had a committee meeting and left.

By 1966, I had two PhDs, but no publications and no job. I was therefore delighted when I received a letter from John Schopler asking me to join the department of social psychology at the University of North Carolina at Chapel Hill as visiting assistant professor. My predecessor on that position had on very short notice accepted a job at another university. Furthermore, John Thibaut was interested in social judgment. I developed a friendship and close working relationship with Chet Insko, who taught me how to conduct experiments and write manuscripts. However, even though the Chapel Hill department was a great place, with great colleagues and bright graduate students, it was less ideal for a young bachelor. I had increasingly the feeling that life was passing me by. So when Tajfel offered me a postdoc position at the University of Bristol (UK), I accepted and moved to Bristol in 1970.

In those days, Bristol was the center of social psychology in Europe. There were typically several international scholars spending their sabbaticals at Bristol. The Tajfels also invited a group of us for breakfast most Sundays and I met more eminent social psychologists at those breakfasts than on any other occasion. Tajfel had hoped I would get down to writing the social judgment book. Although I was distracted by courting Maggie Harrold, one of Tajfel's graduate students, whom I married in 1972, Dick Eiser (who had joined me as co-author) and I managed to finish the book that year (Eiser & Stroebe, 1972).

In 1972, I accepted a position as lecturer in social psychology at the University of Sussex. Because I did not particularly enjoy that job, I was delighted when my friend

Steve Reisman, a former Chapel Hill graduate student, who was assistant professor at the University of Massachusetts, asked me to join them for a year as visiting associate professor. I happily accepted, even though it meant giving up my tenured position for a one-year job. The plan was that I would replace Alice Eagly, who intended to go on sabbatical. For some reason, Alice was unable to leave. As a result, I had to teach personality instead of social psychology. Having never had a personality course myself, I was totally ignorant of that literature. I had to read up while I went along and often ran out of material before the end of my lecture. It was a total disaster. But I was not at UMass until 1986 at that time was a fascinating place with a great faculty: Alice Eagly, Icek Ajzen, Susan Fiske, George Levinger, Ivan Steiner, Jim Averill, Seymour Epstein, Erv Staub, and Ronnie Janoff-Bulman. In 1972 I also went to my first meeting of the Society of Experimental Social Psychology at the University of Kansas, which took place in Sara and Chuck Kiesler's living room (!!). Harold Kelley gave a talk on his attribution theory and Fritz Heider was the discussant.

This was an exciting period for social psychology, with major theories being developed. Consistency theories were still widely tested and dissonance theory was being challenged by Bem's self-perception theory. The small group area was dominated by Thibaut and Kelley's exchange theory. Nobody would have predicted that the field would enter into a crisis only a few years later. That crisis had been developing for some time, but it burst into the open with Gergen's article on "Social psychology as history" (Gergen, 1973). Although many people would agree with his history argument today, I still remember several crises conferences, organized by Lloyd Strickland at Carleton University (Canada), where senior colleagues were shouting at Gergen that he would be responsible for social psychology no longer receiving any research funding. It is ironic that an awareness of Gergen's argument might have prevented the more recent crisis, which *actually* undermined the ability of social psychologists to obtain research grants. This recent crisis was partly caused by the fact that *exact* replications often failed to replicate original research findings. It follows from Gergen's argument that operationalizations in social psychology derive their meaning from historical, social, or cultural context. As a result, exact replications may fail to reflect the same theoretical variables that were manipulated or measured in the original study, a problem that can be addressed by conducting *conceptual* replications (Stroebe, 2019; Stroebe & Strack, 2014).

But getting back to spring 1973, when at the end of my stay at UMass, I was again without a job. I had applied for numerous professorships in Germany, where social psychology had become a growth area, but had only received rejection letters (in ugly blue envelopes of recycled paper). However, when I visited Brighton toward the end of our Amherst period I learnt that there were letters for me at the department. Among them was another of the ugly blue envelopes. When I opened it on my flight back to the United States, I learnt to my surprise that I had been appointed professor at the University of Marburg and civil servant for life at the State of Hessia. As I later discovered, Marburg's first choice had decided to stay at his home university. Since Marburg had been certain he would come, they placed me second without ever having seen me. Once he did not accept, the ministry automatically offered the position to me.

The Marburg department was one of the best psychology departments in Germany and my stay had a lasting influence on my approach to social psychology. The professor of methodology, Hartman Scheiblechner, a specialist on measurement theories, despised rating scales and missed no opportunity to let me know. Even more important were the Marxist students, who formed the majority of the student body. They organized a seminar accompanying my social psychology lecture. Their main point of critique was that social psychology was useless and could at best explain changes on rating scales. Although I tried to convince them otherwise, this critique, which admittedly was not totally unjustified, had a lasting impact on my own work.

During that period, a career-changing event happened on a wine buying tour with our friends the Gergens. It was a rainy day and the breakfast room of our hotel overlooked a cemetery. Maggie started talking about research showing that the death of a marital partner often resulted in the premature death of his or her spouse. Since German tombstones display the birth and death dates of both partners, we decided to conduct an empirical test of this hypothesis. We planned to compare the difference in death dates of real couples with that of randomly formed couples. With hotel umbrellas to protect us against the pouring rain, we noted down the birth and death dates on all tombstones. However, when we tried to test the "broken heart hypothesis," we realized that in a cemetery used for hundreds of years, the difference in death dates of randomly formed couples would always be more divergent than that of real couples. Fortunately, we later discovered that instead of traipsing around graveyards, one could get this information from published statistics. This led to our first publication on that topic (Stroebe et al., 1981). What I loved about this research was the idea that mortality dates would be much "harder" measures than rating scales. To my disappointment, my Marxist students were uninterested in this research: It did not improve the lot of the working class.

In 1978 the University of Tübingen advertised a position for a professor of social and personality psychology. I applied and was offered the job. My qualification in personality was that I had taught a personality course at the University of Massachusetts. I could hire two assistants and appointed Michael Diehl, who in Marburg had been my research assistant on a project on how social support moderates the effects of counter attitudinal behavior on attitude change (Stroebe & Diehl, 1981). (This project taught me that social psychological theories are not refuted, but forgotten, because people get bored with them.) I chose Klaus Jonas for the other position. Both stayed with me during my time at Tübingen, and both had successful careers later.

Michael Diehl and I started a research project on group brainstorming. I had been puzzled by the finding that individuals are less creative when brainstorming in groups rather than individually. At that time I had become a member of a small interdisciplinary group that met twice a year to discuss social science topics. The two members of our group who influenced me most were Hans Albert, a philosopher of science and leading proponent of a Popperian vision of epistemology in Germany, and Bruno Frey, a Swiss economist. Through Bruno, I read Mansur Olson's (1965) *The Logic of Collective Action* and became convinced that the lower productivity of brainstorming groups was due to the fact that group products were "public goods." Unlike private goods, which can *only* be consumed by the individuals who produced them, public goods (e.g., clean air) can also be utilized by people who contributed nothing to their production. This creates a temptation to "free ride" on the contribution of others (Stroebe & Frey, 1982). The theory explained the pattern of brainstorming findings so perfectly that I felt no need to test it empirically. But when Bruno invited me to publish an article on brainstorming in an economic journal he co-edited, I decided to test my public goods interpretation. Although manipulating the extent to which group brainstormers expected that we would analyze their ideas individually (versus combining them into a group product) did influence productivity, the effect was minor.

This left mutual production blocking (the assumption that group members cannot be productive while listening to other members' ideas) as the major culprit. This explanation was difficult to test: Was it the content of other people's ideas that was inhibiting production or was it the fact that group members had to delay presenting their own ideas until other members had finished? It seemed impossible to separate these two aspects. However, we finally came up with a simple solution: We had each of the four members of a brainstorming group sit in a separate room, with a set of four lights in front, one green and the others red. When one member talked, a voice-activated system lit the red lights of the other three members. When the member was finished, these lights went off, and another member could talk. In one of these traffic light conditions the four members had earphones and could hear the ideas that were presented. However, in the crucial condition, participants had no earphones and experienced blocking, without being exposed to other ideas. When we compared the productivity under these conditions to that of a normal group brainstorming session, it turned out that blocking was the crucial factor; exposure to other ideas did not make a major difference (Diehl & Stroebe, 1987).

In addition to staff members, I also had a number of postdocs. One of them was Miles Hewstone, who became a life-long friend and co-editor of a social psychology textbook and the *European Review of Social Psychology*. Both book projects had been planned by the Executive Committee of the European Association of Experimental Social Psychology during my term as president (1981–1983). At that time the Association had great financial problems. We therefore decided to develop publications to earn money for the Association. I asked Miles whether he would join me as co-editor. Miles agreed and turned out to be a fantastic editor. We jointly published twenty-five volumes of the *European Review* and seven editions of an introductory textbook. Ironically, the plenary meeting of the Association did not want their executive committee to become editors and rejected our offer.

During this period, I was also approached by Arie Kruglanski, then professor at Tel Aviv University, who suggested that we should organize Israeli–European conferences to establish links between Israeli and European researchers. These conferences became a great success and, in addition to many European and American colleagues who visited the Tübingen department, we increasingly had Israeli colleagues staying with us.

As an aftereffect of our breakfast meeting with the Gergens, Maggie and I decided to apply for a research grant to conduct a longitudinal study of recently bereaved men and women to assess the physical and psychological consequences of partner loss. Although none of our hypotheses about the buffering effect of social support worked out, the study provided a rich data source, leading to publications on bereavement over two decades. These later publications were only possible because of Georgios Abakoumkin (now a professor of social psychology in Greece), our research assistant in Tübingen on a second grant that allowed us to further analyze the data. Georg was not only a fantastic research assistant, but his familiarity with the data allowed us to continue using the study as a source for testing new hypotheses (e.g., Stroebe et al., 1996).

In presenting our bereavement research at conferences, it dawned on us that our professional identity had expanded and we were increasingly considered to be health psychologists. We began writing a book on social psychology and health and I started to teach a health psychology course. However, although I had fulfilled my life's ambition to become a professor at Tübingen University and was doing interesting research, I began to wonder whether this was all I wanted to do for the remainder of my career.

I was therefore receptive when Hans Adriaansens, Dean of Social Sciences at Utrecht University, approached me with the suggestion to found a Research Institute of Health Psychology and to succeed my old friend Jaap Rabbie, who was retiring. Since German professors who move abroad lose most of their pension, I doubted that I would accept the offer. But Hans was persuasive and, after spending a sabbatical there, we decided to move to Utrecht. Dutch faculties were then required by the government to form interuniversity research institutes and Utrecht had decided that their institute should focus on health psychology. This was a risky decision, because hardly anybody in Utrecht was doing health psychology. Fortunately we succeeded in persuading the psychology departments of Tilburg and Leiden to join us and, to everybody's surprise, the research committee of the Dutch Royal Society of Science accepted our proposal. Thus, I became founding director of this institute. I created the position of deputy scientific director and left most of the day-to-day administration in the capable hands of Henk Schut (who also worked with us on the bereavement project) and his outstanding administrative support team. This allowed me to stay on as chairperson of the social psychology group.

One day I was approached by Bernard Nijstad, whose Master's thesis I had supervised, about doing a PhD project on brainstorming. I told him that after the Tübingen research, there was nothing more to discover. He disagreed and argued that we had failed to develop a theory of brainstorming and therefore did not really know what was going on. I said he was free to develop such a theory and a month later he returned and presented a new theory (Search for Ideas in Associative Memory). His dissertation, co-supervised with Hein Lodewijkx and Rainer Wippler, received the dissertation award of the Society of Experimental Social Psychology.

In order to be assigned a PhD student from the research institute, I had to write a research proposal. As I was working on the chapter on eating in the social psychology and health book, I had become interested in Herman and Polivy's elegant "Boundary Model of Restrained Eating." Restrained eaters are chronic dieters, who find it difficult to resist palatable food and therefore often overeat. Although I was fortunate to appoint an excellent PhD student, none of our hypotheses worked out. This convinced me that the boundary model was not valid and I began to think about alternative theoretical explanations of why some chronic dieters are unable to resist the temptation of palatable food. Since I am a life-long restrained eater (a great advantage in an eating researcher), I was struck by the fact that palatability was not a variable in this model. I had also discussed goal system theory with Arie Kruglanski, who had spent his sabbatical at Utrecht. Stimulated by these ideas, I developed the "Goal Conflict Theory of Eating Behavior." According to that theory, restrained eaters hold two conflicting goals: to enjoy good food and to control their weight. As long as they are in an environment with few food cues, they will be successful in pursuing their weight control goal. However, when they are extensively exposed to cues signaling the availability of palatable food, their eating enjoyment goal increases in cognitive accessibility and finally becomes the dominant goal.

Because it was obvious that social cognition methods had to be used to test this theory, a methodology with which I was not familiar, I asked my colleague Henk Aarts, who is an expert social cognition researcher, to collaborate on that project. In our first joint study, we subliminally primed our participants with either palatable food (e.g., ice cream, pizza) or neutral words. We then used a lexical decision task to measure the ease with which they recognized words that reflected weight control (e.g., weight loss, diet) compared to neutral words. With a lexical decision task, subjects are presented with words or non-word letter sequences and have to decide as fast as possible whether they had been presented with a word. The assumption is that subjects will recognize words that are highly cognitively accessible faster than less accessible words. In support of the goal conflict model, palatable food primes decreased the recognition response time for dieting-related words (but not control words) for restrained (but not unrestrained) eaters.

Henk Aarts and I applied for a four-year research grant, which was approved in 2006, the year I turned 65 and had to retire. Fortunately, the faculty had given me a five-year honorary professorship, so I had continued access to all facilities. We were extremely fortunate to appoint Guido van Koningsbruggen, a highly competent researcher, as postdoc. Most tests of that theory were successful resulting in publications, which we finally summarized in an article in *Psychological Review* (Stroebe et al., 2013).

At the end of my honorary professorship, it became clear that my days at Utrecht were numbered. Thus, I was glad when in 2011 Tom Postmes, then chair of the social psychology group at Groningen, asked me to join the Groningen department as visiting professor. Since Maggie received a similar invitation from the clinical group, we were delighted to accept. I had become interested why so many Americans insisted on owning guns. I had written two review articles, but saw no possibility to conduct empirical research. One day, standing at the printer, which social psychology shared with organizational psychology, Pontus Leander, who was also waiting, mentioned that he was interested in gun-related issues. It turned out that Pontus was not only a brilliant social psychologist (wasted on organizational psychology), but also knew how to collect data from US gun owners through Amazon Turk or Qualtrics Panels. Together with his excellent graduate students Max Agostini and Jannis Kreienkamp, we started a gun research program and tested my theory of gun ownership (Stroebe et al., 2017) and Pontus's theory of displaced aggression (see: https://gunpsychology.org).

Final Observation

The reader might have wondered about the diverse topics I studied during my career. This was not a career-enhancing strategy, because by the time I had become known in one area I had already left it and studied something else. The reason for this seemingly erratic choice of research topics was that I always studied problems that puzzled me. And what was intended as a single theory-testing study (e.g., one brainstorming study to test my public goods interpretation), often developed into a decade-long research program until I was satisfied that I had learnt the answer either to my original question or to the new questions that arose during the course of that research (Stroebe et al., 2010). That social psychology enabled me to study any topic that interested me is the reason why I never regretted my decision to become a social psychologist.

Suggested Reading

Diehl, M., & Stroebe, W. (1987). Productivity loss in brainstorming groups: Towards the solution of a riddle. *Journal of Personality and Social Psychology, 53*, 497–509.

Eiser, J. R., & Stroebe, W. (1972). *Categorization and Social Judgment*. London: Academic Press.

Gergen, K. J. (1973). Social psychology as history. *Journal of Personality and Social Psychology, 26*, 309–320.

Stroebe, M. S., Stroebe, W., Gergen, K., & Gergen, M. (1981). The broken heart: Reality or myth? *Omega, 12*, 87–106.

Stroebe, W. (2019). What can we learn from Many Labs replications? *Basic and Applied Social Psychology, 41*, 91–103.

Stroebe, W., & Diehl, M. (1981). Conformity and counterattitudinal behavior: The effect of social support on attitude change. *Journal of Personality and Social Psychology, 41*(5), 876–889.

Stroebe, W., & Frey, B. S. (1982). Self–interest and collective action: The economics and psychology of public goods. *British Journal of Social Psychology, 21*, 121–137.

Stroebe, W., Leander, N. P., & Kruglanski, A. (2017). Is it a dangerous world out there? The motivational bases of American gun ownership. *Personality and Social Psychology Bulletin, 43*, 1–15.

Stroebe, W., Nijstad, B. A., & Rietzschel, E. F. (2010). Beyond productivity loss in brainstorming groups: The evolution of a question. *Advances in Experimental Social Psychology, 43*, 158–210.

Stroebe, W., & Strack, F. (2014). The alleged crisis and the illusion of exact replication. *Perspectives on Psychological Science, 9*, 59–71.

Stroebe, W., Stroebe, M. S., Abakoumkin, G., & Schut, H. (1996). The role of loneliness and social support in adjustment to loss: A test of attachment versus stress theory. *Journal of Personality and Social Psychology, 70*, 1241–1249.

Stroebe, W., van Koningsbruggen, G. M., Papies, E. K., & Aarts, H. (2013). Why most dieters fail but some succeed: A goal conflict model of eating behavior. *Psychological Review, 130*, 110–138.

17 My Train Ride to Social Psychology

Joel Cooper

The train rocked back and forth as it carried me on my journey to school. I was riding a New York City subway, making my way to class at the City College of New York. I was dimly aware of the D-train stopping and starting again on a trip that I had made hundreds of times before. This time, however, I found myself not at CCNY but in midtown Manhattan, well past the college. The culprit: an article in a social psychology journal on cognitive dissonance. The authors tried to persuade me that people who expend a high degree of unpleasant effort to join a fictitious club actually like that club better than people who do not expend effort. Although the prediction seemed altogether impossible, it fit so nicely with the theory that generated it. How fascinating, how exciting, how relevant! And so, a boy from the Bronx jettisoned his would-be career as a mathematics major and became a social psychologist – or at least a social psychology wannabe.

My professor at CCNY who had assigned this career-changing article to the class was the late Barbara Dohrenwend, an expert in community psychology and mental health. Although not a social psychologist, she was enamored by the elegance of Leon Festinger's dissonance theory and we spent many class sessions discussing the new research and its criticisms. I was hooked. I switched from mathematics to psychology. A few other students from the class joined me in designing some original research that, in retrospect, was less than memorable. What I learned was that research is hard – and that research is fun.

CCNY had been a wonderful place. Classroom education was excellent, and the chances for student activism were even better. It was the 1960s and we spent more energy advocating for social justice, civil rights, and opposing the war in Vietnam. By contrast, the opportunity for advice for graduate education in psychology was more difficult to come by. My interest in dissonance theory suggested an application to Festinger's lab at Stanford. After all, Festinger had been a New York City boy like me, attended the City College of New York like me, and had constructed the theory that had lit a fire in me. But that thought came to a crashing halt when I discovered that Festinger had changed his research from social psychology to understanding eye blinks. That was not for me. Instead, I headed to Duke University where Jack Brehm, one of the key players in the foundation of cognitive dissonance, was headquartered. It had never

Joel Cooper, Princeton University, USA.

occurred to me to call or write to Jack to find out if he was interested in working with me or, for that matter, whether he was still interested in exploring dissonance theory. The answer to both questions turned out to be no, and although Jack and I eventually became friends, my budding career as a dissonance researcher seemed stalled.

The Duke Years

There is no question that I owe my becoming a social psychologist to my advisor, Edward E. Jones. He was the most wonderful human being, with a marvelous family and a healthy outlook on life – qualities that made me not only like him, but also want to be like him. He was an incredibly productive and innovative scholar. Truth is, when I went to Duke, I had no idea who he was. He studied something called person perception and he had written a book on ingratiation. There was a manuscript in press called, "From acts to dispositions" (Jones & Davis, 1965). That paper was to become one of the major theoretical insights into the processes of attribution and solidify his position as one of the most significant psychologists of his generation. I did not know any of this.

Ned was not a dissonance researcher and I scrambled to find something to do in the field of person perception that he would find interesting. In the meantime, social psychologists around the world continued their criticisms of cognitive dissonance. Irving Janis, Herb Kelman, Milton Rosenberg, Natalia and Alfonse Chapanis hammered away at dissonance theory while Aronson, Abelson, Mills and Brehm, among others, provided full-throated responses. An empirical dilemma occurred in a 1965 publication in which Rosenberg conceptually repeated the procedure that had initiated the forced compliance paradigm but did not replicate Festinger and Carlsmith's (1959) results. Instead, he reported results consistent with reinforcement theory: The greater the incentive for writing a counterattitudinal essay, the greater the attitude change.

Harold B. Gerard, a well-known University of California Riverside social psychologist who had collaborated with Ned Jones on their seminal textbook in social psychology, made a phone call to Ned. He thought he had figured out why Rosenberg's findings directly contradicted Festinger and Carlsmith. Hal told Ned and Ned told me and it was my task to turn those conversations into a laboratory study. Like the game of "Telephone," when one person tells the next person who tells the next who tells the next ... the statement gets distorted, sometimes in hilarious ways. And so it was that I apparently got Hal's idea all wrong. To this day, I do not know what Hal's idea was but when Ned watched me run the study, he was amused that I was testing a different idea. But he let me continue, and the study turned out to be the first step in launching my career.

We tested the role of choice as a necessary condition for dissonance to be aroused. The hypothesis was that acting contrary to one's beliefs causes dissonance if and only if the actor believes he or she was free to act or not act. Without choice, incentive functions in the fashion of a reward but with choice, it acts to increase the magnitude of cognitive dissonance. So, either result was possible, but dissonance would prevail if free choice was present. In the social psychology climate of the mid-1960s, we thought we had struck theoretical gold and sent the work out to *JPSP*.

I Lose a Publication and Learn a Lesson

A quick look at our major journals in the 1960s and 1970s will show that it was not uncommon for publications to include only a single empirical study. Our single study was accepted for publication. But at the same time, I was enrolled in a research methods course taught by an exciting new professor, Darwyn Linder. Darwyn received his PhD under the guidance of Elliot Aronson and was sympathetic to dissonance theory. For our final project in the seminar, I suggested a follow-up study to the one that Ned and I had submitted. When that study worked, Ned and Darwyn realized they should be packaged together. *JPSP* granted Ned's request to un-accept our manuscript and replace it with the two-study manuscript. As a graduate student at the time, it was almost heartbreaking to combine two studies into one manuscript and end up with a single publication. Faculty and graduate students today would share no sympathy for my plight since manuscripts with only two studies are rare at our major journals. Nonetheless, it was the 1960s, and I had to admit that the manuscript published by Linder, Cooper, and Jones (1967) was a far more substantial contribution than either study taken alone. Lesson learned.

Social or Clinical Psychology?

Another lesser known fact about my graduate career is that I was nearly a clinical psychologist. My brother Allan was a practicing clinician and I had a real interest in doing clinical work. When I came to Duke, I asked if I could also participate in the clinical training program. With some reluctance, the clinical director allowed me to join and I was trained in psychoanalytically based psychotherapy. There came a point, however, when I had to choose. I asked myself how I could reconcile the enjoyment I had designing and running experiments compared with helping people overcome psychological difficulties. Again, it was Ned who came to the rescue. We do social psychology, he said, precisely because it is fun. It is the enjoyment of identifying the nuances of how people relate to each other and the ability to confirm that identification. We create theories to help us understand how people act in a social environment, ascertain the truth of those theories by doing subtle experiments. Best of all – there is an audience that actually values that activity. I was sold and never looked back.

The Colleagues

You make friends in graduate school. You support, challenge, and learn from each other as you make your way through the graduate school years. Sometimes, you make friends for life. My friends included George Goethals, Steve Worchel, Kelly Shaver,

Russell Jones, and Bob Wicklund among others. We played touch football, talked about life, and formed very close social bonds. We also argued about research. Many of my publications came from those arguments and disagreements. We either disagreed with each other about predictions from our own work or we collectively argued with findings in the literature that we wanted to extend or prove wrong (mostly, prove wrong). Most of my publications from the Duke days include the names of friends from the graduate school and were likely more a tribute to my friends' thinking than to mine.

The Politics

Many years after I was hired at Princeton, I discovered that Ned Jones's recommendation for me included a caution that he would not have been surprised if I jettisoned psychology for politics. This warning had a history in my career at Duke and was not completely wrong. It was the late 1960s, and the war in Vietnam could not be ignored by anyone. Hundreds of thousands of young people were fighting in Southeast Asia. Even in the academy, the war was personal. Some PhDs were being drafted immediately after graduate school and the dreaded draft lottery was just around the corner. No one could avoid the war, and most of us at universities considered the war to be both misguided and immoral. We protested peacefully on campus and were chased by the North Carolina state police. We engaged in silent protests in the center of town. We stood in silent contemplation for an hour in front of the county courthouse while FBI agents in trench coats that seemed borrowed from a Humphrey Bogart movie, snapped our pictures with the implied threat that we were enemies of the state. Admittedly, being photographed by the FBI for a silent protest seems amusing in retrospect, but seemed deadly serious at the time. A small band of psychology graduate students even devised a scheme to send anti-war delegates to the 1968 Democratic National Convention in Chicago. It was a small victory, but a satisfying one, when we watched the state of North Carolina cast one vote for the anti-war candidate Eugene McCarthy.

As a postscript, my later involvement in the political process began and ended with nine years on my local school board. Asked to run for election to the state legislature, I thought how close to reality Ned's warning had been about my penchant for politics. I turned down the offer, and was never tempted again.

My First Job, My Only Job

When I was in my fourth year of graduate school, it was time to go on the so-called job market. The field of psychology was transitioning from an "old boy network" to a more open search in which positions were posted in journals and other official publications. Too bad, I thought, because Ned Jones was well connected in the hierarchy of social psychologists and, a few years prior, could have picked up the phone and arranged a job. Still, there were good jobs available in 1969. I recall that Harvard, Rutgers, and Dartmouth had positions that seemed attractive. They all had established programs and a history of commitment to social psychology. I would have been honored to be at any of them.

Then there was Princeton, a university that had enormous prestige as an undergraduate institution but almost no history in social psychology. Its reputation for research was centered in sensation and perception with such giants in the field as Frank Geldard and Ernest Glen Weaver. Hadley Cantril had been their one social psychologist and the rumor was that Princeton wanted to keep it that way. I applied, and it was the first university to offer an interview. In the context of saying that I would have been delighted to get any job as a real, bona fide professional psychologist, I could not get excited about interviewing at a place that did not support social psychology. However, I did believe that interviewing at Princeton would be good practice for later interviews at places that had more established programs in social psychology. So I drove to Princeton for practice. I came away sold that this was the place for me – if they would have me.

Here is another lesson: Institutions change before their reputations catch up. Often, places that are well known in particular fields have hit the decline before their reputation catches up to them. In Princeton's case, the delayed reputation went in the other direction: Changes were underway that put me on the ground floor of a place that would become one of the best programs in social psychology. Call it luck or call it John Darley.

John Darley had been brought to Princeton to build a social psychology program. The prior year, the university had selected a new chairperson to rebuild the department. That chair, Leon Kamin, often told us that he knew nothing about social psychology but thought a good department should have it (whatever it was). He snared Darley from NYU and gave him carte blanche to begin to recruit social psychologists. John was committed to creating an experimental social psychology program and I was the first recruit. My indebtedness to John cannot be overstated. Neither can the strength of our friendship be overstated that spanned the many decades until his death in 2018.

So, in 1969, I was hired in a department that was in dire need of more recruits in social or personality psychology. Because of my flirtation with clinical at Duke, I regularly taught personality and abnormal psychology, leaving the teaching of social to Darley. We recruited more young people to help fill out a program. Mark Zanna came to us from Yale, Tory Higgins from Columbia, Diane Ruble from UCLA. Then came the break that allowed us to transition from a band of young social psychologists to a program with heft and focus. Ned Jones signaled that he might be interested in leaving Duke. We pounced, and successfully recruited him to Princeton. By that time, I had tenure and the three of us – Jones, Darley, and me – set out to make Princeton a center for experimental research in social psychology.

The 1970s in Social Psychology: White and Male

I attended my first meeting of the Society of Experimental Social Psychology in 1974 at the University of Illinois in Champagne Urbana. I admit that I was a star-struck young social psychologist and could not imagine that I was sharing a drink with the likes of Harold Kelley, Walter Mischel, or Bob Zajonc. These were people whose work I had read in textbooks and now I was chatting with them in person. I needed to pinch myself to see that it was real. It was almost as though I belonged there – but not quite.

In 1974 there was a "crisis in social psychology." Some of our most productive scholars were asking, were we relevant? Did our science matter? Did we design experiments whose answers were so obvious that only data in support of our hypotheses could be published? I listened to my peers and my heroes debate the crisis but for people of my age, designing and conducting experiments was so much fun that the issue seemed very odd. Some of us went home more determined than ever to try fill our journal pages with what we thought were theoretically interesting experiments and leave the consternation about the crisis to the senior generation.

In retrospect, I believe there was a crisis in the 1970s, but it was not about our science. It was about our insularity. One could not avoid the observation that there were virtually no women or people of color in the group. I confess I had never given much thought to gender or race as I read articles in *JPSP* or *JESP*. Looking at a few score of my famous colleagues in Champagne Urbana, it was apparent that we were a field locked in a restricted demographic space. We studied issues of prejudice, but we could only do that from the perspective of a White, privileged point of view. We studied interpersonal attraction but primarily from a very male perspective. Our discipline needed to diversify if it was to fulfill its destiny as a science of how all people are affected by their social situations. And it did diversify. Sitting in a much larger auditorium at the SPSP conference in New Orleans in 2020, I realized that we had not only grown larger but that we had grown so much stronger by attracting a vibrant new group of social psychologists, diverse in ideas and methods as well as in ethnicity, race, and gender.

The Colleagues

As much as I might like to think that my contributions to psychology were largely of my own creation, it is far from true. From the outset, my work has been the product of collaborations. Some came from conversations and arguments that I had with my friends and students about cognitive dissonance. Some came from putting our heads together to think of new avenues of research. My current colleagues, including Susan Fiske, Nicole Shelton, Stacey Sinclair, Betsy Levy Paluck, Diana Tamir, Katherine Olson, Alin Coman, and Eldar Shafir, continue to be the source of inspiration not only for my own research but also for my confidence that our field is robust and diverse.

In the early days of my Princeton career, I collaborated with my friend Mark Zanna. He had unparalleled creativity and I often remarked that one way to a successful career was to just walk with Mark and pick up the ideas that he did not have time to test on his own. One of my favorite, most cherished studies that I conducted with Mark was the dissonance-and-the-pill series. Mark and I each had an invitation from Jerry Suls to contribute to a volume he was editing on attribution. A major challenge to dissonance theory in the early 1970s was whether the provocative findings beginning with

Festinger and Carlsmith's and including the Linder, Cooper, and Jones studies could be accounted for by a rational attribution process rather than the motivational concept of cognitive dissonance. In true Zanna style, Mark suggested that we collaborate on a single chapter and, instead of writing about any of our prior work, we design a series of new studies designed to show whether the uncomfortable arousal state of dissonance was necessary to produce the results predicted equally well by dissonance and attribution theory. We designed a series of novel studies in which we had students ingest a pill that they thought (incorrectly) would cause uncomfortable arousal when it was in fact only a placebo and a companion experiment in which we had students ingest a pill they thought (incorrectly) was a placebo but was actually either amphetamine or a sedative. We found that dissonance required arousal: Exacerbate the arousal with amphetamine and dissonance effects increase. Diminish it with a sedative and dissonance is reduced. Allow people to misattribute their arousal to a pill and dissonance effects disappear. Attribution theory could not account for those results, which seemed to resolve the debate in favor of dissonance theory (Zanna & Cooper, 1974).

Generating the New Look Model

A few years later, my first stellar graduate student arrived in Princeton. Russell Fazio was the kind of student who changes your career. He was too smart and too creative to allow anyone to stay static. Together, we created the so-called "New Look" of dissonance theory, in which we took the position that dissonance occurred not from inconsistent cognitions per se, but rather from feeling responsible for bringing about unwanted consequences (Cooper & Fazio, 1984). We did not set out to invent a new position but it seemed clear to us that the antecedent conditions that caused dissonance were not those that Festinger had specified. Although inconsistency often leads to dissonance, it does so because acting inconsistently typically brings about the responsibility-for-consequences dilemma that is the true instigator of dissonance.

The true story of the New Look began with a challenge from the sociologist Paul Secord who was visiting Princeton in the 1970s. He remarked that it used to be easy to understand cognitive dissonance when it was about inconsistency. However, the ensuing decade of research had added so many caveats that one needed a road map to decide when inconsistency resulted in dissonance. There seemed to be multiple "if and only if conditions" that prevailed: Inconsistent cognitions led to dissonance under conditions of free choice, commitment, responsibility, aversive consequences, and so forth. It was in response to Secord's challenge that Fazio and I decided to make such a road map and, in so doing, realized that a new theoretical account of dissonance had emerged. That new theory had its share of critics and led to some energetic exchanges that are beyond the scope of this reflection. Suffice it to say that we were gratified when Festinger spoke at the annual convention of the American Psychological Association held in New York City in 1987 in celebration of the thirtieth anniversary of cognitive dissonance theory. He singled out the New Look version of dissonance theory for special praise. Fazio and I were thrilled.

Research ideas continue to evolve and the graduate students responsible for encouraging me to change with them are too numerous to mention, but include Diane Mackie, who first directed my interest to the study of social groups, Dan Gilbert, Bob Croyle, Adam Galinsky, Mike Norton, Roy Baumeister, John Fleming, James Hilton, Fred Rhodewalt, and Joe Avery. Postdocs and colleagues from other institutions also changed the course of my career. At an SESP meeting in the early 1990s, the dissonance pioneer, Elliot Aronson, mentioned that he had a superb graduate student seeking a postdoctoral position. The student was Jeff Stone and the two of us set off on a multi-year friendship and research excursion. I sympathized with Jeff's dilemma: He had worked on dissonance with Aronson whose theoretical claim was that dissonance necessarily involved self-esteem. But he was coming to work with someone whose New Look theory took a very different slant on the issue. Jeff managed to thread the theoretical needle and from the arguments and discussions that ensued, the Self-Standards Model, our final integration of decades of dissonance research, emerged (Stone & Cooper, 2001). The good luck of having good students, postdocs and colleagues continued.

A Trip to Australia and a New Direction

I had the opportunity to take a sabbatical leave in 1995 and had my heart set on seeing Australia. I wanted to be as close to the Great Barrier Reef as possible and so wrangled an invitation from the northernmost of the major Australian universities – the University of Queensland. That is where I ran into Mike Hogg, and my research took a new twist. We came from two such different perspectives: Hogg theorized about the role of group membership on people's attitudes and I concentrated on how individuals bring about changes to their own attitudes based on their idiosyncratic behaviors. And yet we found common ground and common challenges. We speculated that people in groups might experience dissonance vicariously on behalf of other group members. Because of the importance of group membership, the idiosyncratic action of one member of a social group might be experienced as though it were one's own action. We embarked on a series of studies that eventually embraced the ingenuity of a number of outstanding graduate students including Mike Norton and Benoît Monin and began a new venture on "vicarious cognitive dissonance" (for an overview, see Cooper & Hogg, 2007). Thank goodness for proximity to the Great Barrier Reef!

A Ride on Today's D-Train

Decades ago, while riding the D-train to the refrain of my first dissonance article, my career path took a turn toward becoming a social psychologist. If I were a passenger on that train today, there would be so much more that could have grabbed my attention and made me a convert to social psychology. The field has grown and expanded in so many ways. We are a much more diverse field than we ever were, both substantively and methodologically. We use our theories and our methods to study health, prejudice, aggression, law, persuasion, and so much more. We combine a new-found ability to deal with big data with our traditional stock-in-trade – the experiment. Our numbers have grown and, with it, a diversity of approaches and perspectives.

While I celebrate almost all of the trends that I have seen in the growth of our discipline, there is one that I lament. It became apparent to me when during the seven years I served as editor of the *Journal of Experimental Social Psychology*. I truly loved seeing the creativity of our colleagues and was impressed by the topics they studied and the methods they created to study them. Sometimes, work that could not be published was as creative as the manuscripts that I accepted for publication. What disturbed me as I read the hundreds of papers that were submitted to the journal was the frequency with which authors seemed not to be aware of the prior literature or ignored major seminal papers in their field. A science needs to build on itself. It needs to take established findings and expand them, limit them, or transfer them to new areas. A science that does not build on its own foundations spends too much time rediscovering the proverbial wheel, hindering rather than facilitating a cumulative discipline.

As I reflect on my own path, I see clearly the impact of serendipity and plain old good luck in my professional path. I am certain there are scholars who knew from an early age what they wanted to pursue and had the determination and intelligence to succeed. To the extent that I deserve a place in this volume, it is due in more than equal part to the people that I was fortunate to interact with and the help they gave me along the way.

Suggested Reading

Cooper, J., & Fazio, R. H. (1984). A new look at dissonance theory. *Advances in Experimental Social Psychology, 17*, 229–245.

Cooper, J., & Hogg, M. A. (2007). Feeling the anguish of others: A theory of vicarious dissonance. *Advances in Experimental Social Psychology, 39*, 359–403.

Festinger, L., & Carlsmith, J. M. (1959). Cognitive consequences of forced compliance. *Journal of Abnormal and Social Psychology, 58*, 203–210.

Jones, E. E., & Davis, K. E. (1965). From acts to dispositions: The attribution process in person perception. *Advances in Experimental Psychology, 2*, 219–266.

Linder, D. E., Cooper, J., & Jones, E. E. (1967). Decision freedom as a determinant of the role of incentive magnitude in attitude change. *Journal of Personality and Social Psychology, 6*(3), 245–254.

Rosenberg, M. J. (1965). When dissonance fails: On eliminating evaluation apprehension from attitude measurement. *Journal of Personality and Social Psychology, 1*(1), 28–42.

Stone, J., & Cooper, J. (2001). A self-standards model of cognitive dissonance. *Journal of Experimental Social Psychology, 37*, 228–243.

Zanna, M. P., & Cooper, J. (1974). Dissonance and the pill: An attribution approach to studying the arousal properties of dissonance. *Journal of Personality and Social Psychology, 29*(5), 703–709.

18 The Making and Remaking of a Cross-Cultural Psychologist in Six Acts
A Character in Search of Four Co-authors

Michael Harris Bond

The initial mystery that attends any journey is: how did the traveller reach his starting point in the first place? ... I can hardly remember how ... There must be, however, some reasonable explanation for my presence here. Some step started me toward this point, as opposed to all other points on the habitable globe. I must consider; I must discover it.

Louise Bogan, *Journey Around My Room* (1980)

How was it that I reached this stage in my personal journey to be asked by Saul Kassin to contribute my story to this shared quest for professional self-understanding that he has orchestrated? I eagerly took up the opportunity to join this group of esteemed social psychologists in my explicit, and perhaps our implicit, quest to answer Bogan's haunting challenge; the time to do so had come again, for I had tried to answer her challenge before, but the passage of time has shaped new apprehensions and the passing of too many colleagues in the last decade has added urgency to my quest to fathom an answer at this late stage of my career.

So, what follows is a personal self-unfolding that has been helpful to chart for myself, and, I hope, useful for those who journey along with me through the rest of this retrospection. I will try to be open and fair-minded in combing through my memories to achieve some satisfactory sense of closure; I want especially to show good faith to my many companions who joined me along this way. For, emerging from the kaleidoscopic details infusing the travels of this cross-cultural psychologist is the fundamental drama of my slow and still-growing awareness of *Ubuntu*, viz., the understanding that "a person becomes a person through other persons." If my mandate is to focus on my progress in becoming a cross-cultural psychologist, then I have identified six acts in my development and four colleagues whose openhearted and openminded companionship were crucial to my arriving here, now – Harry Triandis,

Michael Harris Bond, Hong Kong Polytechnic University, China.

Geert Hofstede, Kwok Leung, and Peter Smith. I offer this essay as some measure of my thanks to them, as we traveled along our separate ways sometimes together.

The "Mise-en-Scène" – Enculturing an Innocent

The life paths that realistically become open to (humans) are also partly determined by the nature of the cultural agencies to which their development is entrusted.

Bandura (1982, p. 747)

If the journey of interest for this collection lies in my becoming a cross-cultural psychologist, then its preparation began with my halcyon boyhood in 1940s Toronto, a city bequeathed with an Anglo-Christian heritage, represented to me in the stern photograph of my paternal great-grandfather, a Methodist circuit minister in Southern Ontario. I wanted to be "good" in the terms of this cultural drama, difficult as that proved to be, but derived some hope from my paternal grandfather's annual Christmas gift of a bible, inscribed with the cryptic message that, "Money and the bible go together like ham and cheese." Grandfather's folksy message encouraged me to believe that maybe I could have it all, "rendering unto Caesar what is Caesar's, and unto God what is God's," to recall an exhortation from that Bible. Balancing ideologies against practicalities would exercise me always.

Canada had emerged from the devastation of World War II relatively untouched by the burden of that savagery, alive with halcyon postwar possibilities awaiting an energetic and curious youngster. Of course, I was innocent of this historical perspective and simply got on with life's job of figuring out where I fit. My openness to experience was continually refreshed by my love of reading, especially tales of adventure in exotic places, the Oxford dictionary close to hand. By nature, I was ambitious for recognition and used my intellectual and athletic gifts, such as they were, to find a place where my talents would be recognized and appreciated.

That place was at school – primary, secondary, and then university, a particular environment that for me, "Charmed magic casements, opening on the foam of perilous seas, in faery lands forlorn," as Keats wrote. Libraries, sports teams, specialist clubs, courses with inviting content, and knowledgeable teachers whom I held in awe, these drew me into the academic life. I had been sequestered at a boy's-only secondary school and the presence of smart women, glistening with youth, was a welcome bonus! The possibilities on offer seemed endless . . .

My career course was set by four years studying psychology in the honors program at the University of Toronto. The allure of scientific precision had drawn me into studying psychology, and social psychology with its focus on how people live their lives captured my imagination; I had always been intrigued to learn how regular people navigated their daily lives with one another. Having endured dreary summer jobs in banks and companies, I knew that I wanted to live an intellectual's life instead, earning a living by teaching about and researching the mystery of being human. That future required a PhD.

Act 1 – Striving for a PhD in Psychology

Individuals contribute to their own destiny by developing potentialities that afford access to particular social milieus.

Bandura (1982, p. 750)

Having done well academically as an undergraduate, but unsure about my credentials, I applied to seven American universities. Given the allure of California and Stanford's lofty reputation, I went West. Little did I realize then that this "road taken" was my first cultural self-posting – I had become an immigrant for the first time, "a stranger in a strange land," where the institutional requirements to study in America, living as a renter in East Palo Alto, driving on California freeways, and shopping in local supermarkets, were fraught with novelty. (As I soon discovered, so too was the American version of the English language, both spoken and written, accent and vocabulary!)

My living circumstances as a financially supported graduate student were benign, so I adapted well enough to focus on my major of psychology. In retrospect, I now realize that my future approach as a cross-cultural psychologist was shaped by three professors, Walter Mischel, Phil Zimbardo, and Albert Hastorf. Walter taught us from the galley proofs for *Personality and Assessment* (1970), which soon alerted the psychological world to the weakness of personality tests in predicting behavior beyond obvious baselines and signaling the need to consider the circumstances a person was confronting in order to improve the predictability of his or her behavior; Al had co-authored with Cantril the seminal paper, "They saw a game" (1954) and was ever alerting me to the ways our perceptions of others shaped our behavior toward them or the group they represented; Phil was exploring the power of situational trappings of uniforms and social roles in his work on deindividuation (1969). All three served on my PhD committee.

In 1968, I had been stunned by Rosenthal's work, *Pygmalion in the Classroom*, realizing that interpersonal outcomes could be altered by a person's beliefs about the other. To test this concept in short-term social encounters, I designed my thesis to explore the so-called self-fulfilling prophecy in conversations between strangers by giving one of the partners credible information that a future partner was warm or cold. To my amazement, our analysis of videotaped records revealed instead a self-reversing prophecy that I struggled to understand and explain in three subsequent publications over the next four decades. In consequence of this early surprise, I have remained alert to disconfirmations throughout my subsequent career, even welcoming them as intellectual gadflies. Studying culture provided many!

That struggle to understand and explain my early surprise engendered an appreciation of the social actor's active role in shaping her interpersonal environment. I also recognized the importance of the other's beliefs about us in shaping our responses in return. How were these beliefs about one another established, and how did features of an interpersonal encounter channel how social actors behaved toward one another? These early questions prepared me for an academic career of thinking about and exploring how our birth culture and the cultural groups whose members we encounter throughout our lives contribute to the persons we become.

Act 2 – Go Further West, Young Man, to the East

Psychology does not have much to say about the occurrence of fortuitous intersects except that personal bents and social structures and affiliations make some types of encounters more probable than others.

Bandura (1982, p. 749)

I failed to find a job in Canada after completing my postdoctoral fellowship at Michigan State University. Having become a member of the Bahá'í Faith with its vision of ecumenical harmony through service, I decided with my adventurous American wife to find work "in alien corn," beyond the US–Canada borders that we knew. We found employment in Japan, a country whose ecology, history, financial regulations, transport systems, cuisine, housing, spoken language and script were a total mystery to both of us. Fortunately, we were hired as teachers of English, a respected occupation of high status in Japan, and were happily presumed to be Americans, much admired for defeating the Japanese in World War II and then for providing a benign postwar administration of Japan's economic, social, and political recovery. Again, my adaptation challenges were buffered by a supportive cultural system.

Committed to psychology and the academic life, I conducted social psychological research and taught personality and research methods at Kwansei Gakuin University through the good offices of a faculty member and interpreter, Dr. Ken Takeda. With his PhD from Michigan State University, Ken became my cultural mediator into Japanese culture, good-humoredly explaining its reflections in my interpersonal exchanges with the office personnel and my graduate supervisees. I was in a new cultural kindergarten.

Here, I ventured into my first cross-cultural studies by collaborating with colleagues from graduate school at Stanford. Our comparison of Japanese and American student responses to the Rotter I-E scale measuring internal-external control was a sobering experience. Professor Takeda and my team of graduate students first struggled mightily with a series of translations and back-translations. Then, and crucially, when we factor analyzed our results separately in both cultural groups, we could not "force" the expected one-factor solution from each culture. Instead, a two-factor solution produced item groupings that were comparable in both cultures, so that factor scores could be calculated, and American and Japanese responses could then be legitimately compared.

Throughout this laborious and unsettling process, I learned some important lessons for any cross-cultural aspirant: (1) orchestrating, then running, analyzing, and interpreting a cross-cultural result took three and possibly four times as much human resource as running a within-culture study; (2) the question of equivalence in meaning – in the measures, in the participants, and in perceptions of the measurement situation – was contentious and would be ever nipping at our heels from editors, reviewers, and interested colleagues; (3) not many colleagues were interested in reading about "iffy" cross-cultural comparisons; and (4) the few interested colleagues were typically members of the cultural systems being compared, and often complained that the authors had "got my culture wrong" or "hadn't quite understood my culture fully" (the latter challenge coming from colleagues of cultures with more respectful conversational norms!). Such challenges intimated my forthcoming confrontation with the infamous "emic versus etic" (culture-specific versus culture-general; distinctive versus universal) issue in Hong Kong with Chinese psychologists. Was I ready for this added struggle?

Act 3 – Meeting the Master

In a chance encounter the separate chains of events have their own causal determinants, but their intersection occurs fortuitously.

Bandura (1982, p. 747)

While navigating these treacherous cross-cultural shoals, I met Harry Triandis. Our paths converged in 1972 at a conference in Tokyo held by the International Council of Psychologists; we were later to intersect at such international conferences throughout Harry's long and prolific career. He was Greek by birth, multi-lingual, and an accomplished social psychologist, energetically promoting the scientific perspective in cross-cultural psychology. Always a reliable and responsive communicator, Harry kept in regular contact, and proved to be an ideal guide for me, as we traversed the "realms of gold" for the next forty-plus years of our colleagueship.

Among his many publications, Triandis's landmark *Interpersonal Behavior* (1977) became my inspirational lodestone because of its cross-cultural grounding and synoptic view of so many cultures. Its contents introduced me to the concept of the subjective culture adopted by individuals, its variation across different national-cultural traditions, and its implications for the social behavior of a culture's members. Our culture of socialization shaped our personalities within the constraints and affordances provided by our cultural system. Our encultured personality revealed itself in our daily exchanges but was especially evident when we interacted with someone from a different cultural-linguistic heritage.

Triandis impressed this social-psychological perspective of the individual as "structured-by-culture" and inspired me to adopt it in my subsequent, co-authored integrations of the emerging literature in cross-cultural social psychology (e.g., Smith et al., 2013). But I was also impressed by Harry's personal example, as I observed him interacting graciously and conscientiously with numerous colleagues across the globe. His extensive interpersonal network inevitably afforded Harry opportunities to serve international organizations in administrative and editorial capacities, responsibilities he assumed with energy and focus. For me, he became the contemporary Ulysses who could best claim, "Much have I seen and known; cities of men [a]nd manners, climates, councils, [and] governments" (*Ulysses* by Tennyson). Harry Triandis became and remains my academic hero.

Act 4 – Opening and Examining the Chinese Puzzle-Box

Marco Polo describes a bridge, stone by stone. 'But which is the stone that supports the bridge?' Kublai Khan asks. 'The bridge is not supported by one stone or another,' Marco answers, 'but by the line of the arch that they form.' Kublai Khan remains silent, reflecting. Then he adds: 'Why do you speak to me of the stones? It is only the arch that matters to me.' Polo answers: 'Without stones there is no arch.'

Italo Calvino, *Invisible Cities* (1972)

By 1974, I had come to love almost everything about living in Japan, except for my distaste at needing to teach English to support my wife and newly born daughter, Mieko. However, research support from the Canadian government had run dry, and I could not find a job teaching psychology in Japan, so I began looking elsewhere. Receiving a job offer from both Australia and Hong Kong, my wife and I decided on a contract from the Chinese University of Hong Kong (CUHK). The lure of the East was irresistible, and I have subsequently spent the last forty-seven years entranced by "things Chinese."

I intuited early that I could enhance my chances of being tenured and promoted at CUHK by contributing something distinctive to my university's mission of providing a bi-cultural education. Surveying the scattered literature on Chinese society and its interpersonal dynamics, that distinctive something turned out to be gathering together knowledge about Chinese cultural dynamics and conveying that knowledge to English-reading psychologists intrigued by Chinese culture. I set about doing so and have continued refining that agenda for the last four decades, the latest offering in Huang and Bond (2012). While Marco Polo was gathering the stones to assemble the bridge, Kublai Khan was searching for the arch that characterized the bridge.

That agenda was initiated in the summer of 1979, when Kwok Leung knocked on my office door. He was an undergraduate majoring in biology and had taken my courses in social psychology to fulfill his minor requirements in psychology. Fascinated by what he heard and then crafted in a group project, he offered to work with me to write up his class project on group-serving attributions for publication. Kwok's initiative set in motion a series of conversations about Hong Kong Chinese culture that resulted in twenty-nine joint publications over the next thirty-eight years until his untimely passing in 2017. Marco Polo and Genghis Khan had begun conversing about cross-cultural bridges.

From the outset, Kwok and I worked to integrate our different cultural heritages to ensure that whatever research design we initiated and whatever explanation we offered for its results were *true for both of us*, i.e., made sense from each of our cultural perspectives and life experiences. What were the underlying social-psychological processes that could be deployed to best represent the experienced reality of our research participants? Initially, our concern was mono-cultural, focusing on Hong Kong Chinese, but soon became bi-cultural, American-Hong Kong Chinese, and eventually multi-cultural as our range of collegial contacts grew through our mutual networking. When we progressed to crafting multi-cultural studies, we likewise insisted that our colleagues ensure that their respondents' cultural realities were incorporated into the measures and analytic procedures used. Kwok and I conscientiously tried to avoid any form of intellectual-cultural imperialism in our work. That respectfulness in approaching all cultures was realized in our multi-cultural study of social axioms where all our collaborators contributed items from their cultural heritage to our measure of beliefs (Leung et al., 2012).

So, too, in our relationship. Kwok was fourteen years my junior and we began working together when he was an undergraduate and I a tenured professor; I always worked in my first language, but he in his second, ever-improving English. This status imbalance could easily have undermined our search for cultural truth had I not proceeded cautiously and he persistently. Procedural fairness and mutual accommodation were the keys we used in our shared search to unlock the Chinese puzzle-box. Looking back, I realize how important was the fact that Kwok and I respected one another and enjoyed each other's company – playing basketball, eating Cantonese food, and laughing together, especially about our misunderstandings. I miss him deeply.

Act 5 – Another Dutch Mercator Maps the Known World

Once established, binding relationships serve as a vehicle for personal changes that can have long-range effects.

Bandura (1982, p. 750)

Another fortuitous confluence that shaped the flow of my work was confronting Geert Hofstede at the 1980 conference of the International Association for Cross-Cultural Psychology (IACCP) held in Bhubaneswar, India. He had traveled there from Holland to promote his soon-to-become-foundational tome, *Culture's Consequences*; I had ventured from Hong Kong to present a cross-cultural comparison of Rokeach values at the most appropriate venue for such comparative psychological research, the IACCP.

Geert attended my talk, then announced to me and other members of the audience that, "Unfortunately, you have analyzed your data incorrectly." After the session, I sought him out to try and discover my mistake. So began a fifteen-year collaboration in co-authorship where I developed the Chinese Value Survey as a cultural counter-point to his IBM-based Values Survey Model, adding the dimension of "Confucian work dynamism" to Hofstede's four (Chinese Culture Connection, 1987).

Under Hofstede's tutelage, I slowly figured out the difference between individual-level and cultural-level analyses of data derived from multiple cultural groups. These two levels of analysis needed to be distinguished since they had their separate logics and produced their distinct nomological networks of constructs. Kwok Leung and I continued to probe the distinctions between individual and (national-)cultural levels of logic in our research into beliefs about the world decades later (Leung et al., 2012). So, prior discoveries unearthed with Geert segued into my ongoing work with other colleagues and continue to do so. "I am part of all that I have met," to quote again from *Ulysses*.

Act 6 – Nuancing by Culture

The man truly conversant with life knows, against all appearances, that . . . every wall
is a gate.

Ralph Waldo Emerson, "Natural History of Intellect" (1871)

How were we to bridge this difference in levels of analysis and move from culture to
the individual? The answer slowly emerged over the course of my almost four-decade
partnership-in-culture with a British social-organizational psychologist, Peter
B. Smith. Peter entered my career trajectory in the mid-1980s as he was passing
through Hong Kong on his way to assume a Canon fellowship and compare British-
Japanese leadership in teams. I was intrigued by the applied nature of Peter's interest,
and, as we continued to converse, struck by his scholarly integrity and personal
sincerity. I volunteered to collect parallel data from Hong Kong for his project
on teams.

The Smith project incorporated data from four nations/territories on team member
perceptions of their leader's behaviors, relating these behaviors to their leader's
performance and maintenance styles of leading. In looking at these perception–
behavior linkages culture by culture, it became evident to Peter and me that certain
behaviors consistently predicted team member perceptions in every national culture,
but other behaviors were not consistently linked. On occasion, the behavior linked to
one style in one cultural group, but to the other style in the other culture. Surprises
abounded!

So, there was a different strength of linkage between two measured constructs
across cultures, and on rare occasion that linkage reversed in sign. Across four books,
Peter and I reviewed the emerging literature in cross-cultural social-personality psychology to produce integrations of findings then bubbling up, the latest Smith et al.
(2013). Over time, we began noticing other "moderation-by-culture" outcomes. We
concluded that a respondent's cultural background sometimes produced an enhancement effect making certain individual-level predictors of individual outcomes more
powerful in some cultural systems than in others, a moderation-by-culture effect. But
how to explain these scattered enhancement effects?

Diener and Diener, other teachers along my way, set the standard with their 1995
multi-cultural study. They found that a measure of national individualism correlated
with the *size* of the correlation between personal self-esteem and satisfaction with life
pan-culturally, but more so for individuals born into individualistic national cultures.
They had demonstrated that an aspect of person's cultural heritage, its individualism,
"nuanced" the strength of a so-called "universal" effect, enhancing the precision of
how well an individual measure of personality, self-esteem, predicted an individual
outcome, life satisfaction.

A template had finally been presented to show how culture-level constructs and
their measures could be meaningfully linked to individual-level concepts and measures, demonstrating the importance of an individual's particular cultural heritage. The
race to explore these cross-level relationships was on – the twenty-first century

brought accessible data sets from representative samples of persons from more and more societies along with more sophisticated statistical tools to examine these cross-level relationships. Researchers began broadening their appreciation of what constituted a culture and started considering the cultures of smaller size than the nation, like provinces; corporate cultures; team or family cultures, even social roles being played, as creating a culture for individual enactments (Smith & Bond, 2019). A perspective shift was emerging...

Coda

When you reach an advanced age and look back over your lifetime, it can seem to have had a consistent order and plan ... Events that when they occurred had seemed accidental and of little moment turn out to have been indispensable factors in the composition of a consistent plot ... And just as people whom you will have met apparently by mere chance became leading agents in the structuring of your life, so, too, will you have served unknowingly as an agent, giving meaning to the lives of others.

Joseph Campbell, *The Power of Myth*

I continue to do cross-cultural research in social psychology, feeling rejuvenated by the possibilities for exploring how our birth and current cultures shape us to become who we now are. My faith in how our individual personalities will shape this process has been revitalized by recent advances in genetics and culture-fair measures of personality. I now consider that cultures constitute the recurring situations in which we function according to Levine's formula of Behavior = f(Personality.Situation). Cultural groups act on persons at different proximities and often simultaneously; these multiple "situations" operate with different strengths relative to an individual's personality as it evolves over the individual's life span. There is much intriguing research waiting to be done by using this enlarged and evolving understanding of the interface between individuals and their multiple cultural memberships (Morris et al., 2015). I, for one, am ready!

> There lies the port; the vessel puffs her sail:
> There gloom the dark, broad seas ...
> Old age hath yet his honour and his toil (Tennyson, *Ulysses*)

Suggested Reading

Bandura, A. (1982). The psychology of chance encounters and life paths. *American Psychologist, 37*, 747–755.

Chinese Culture Connection (1987). Chinese values and the search for culture-free dimensions of culture. *Journal of Cross-Cultural Psychology, 18*, 143–164.

Diener, E., & Diener, M. (1995). Cross-cultural correlates of life satisfaction and self-esteem. *Journal of Personality and Social Psychology, 68*, 653–663.

Hastorf, A. H., & Cantril, H. (1954). They saw a game: A case study. *Journal of Abnormal and Social Psychology*, *49*, 129–134.

Huang, X., & Bond, M. H. (Eds.) (2012). *Handbook of Chinese Organizational Behavior: Integrating Theory, Research and Practice*. Cheltenham, UK and Northampton, MA, USA: Edward Elgar Publishing.

Leung, K., Lam, B. C. P., Bond, M. H., Conway, L. G., Gornick, L. J., Amponsah, B., . . . Zhou, F. (2012). Developing and evaluating the social axioms survey in eleven countries: Its relationship with the five-factor model of personality. *Journal of Cross-Cultural Psychology*, *43*(5), 833–857.

Mischel, W. (1968). *Personality and Assessment*. New York: John Wiley & Sons.

Morris, M. W., Chiu, C.-Y., & Liu, Z. 2015. Polycultural psychology. *Annual Review of Psychology*, *66*, 631–659.

Rosenthal, R., & Jacobson, L. (1968). *Pygmalion in the Classroom: Teacher Expectation and Pupils' Intellectual Development*. New York: Holt, Rinehart & Winston.

Smith, P. B., & Bond, M. H. (2019). Cultures and persons: Characterizing national and other types of cultural difference can also aid our understanding and prediction of individual variability. *Frontiers in Psychology*, *10*, 2689. doi:10.3389/fpsyg.2019.02689.

Smith, P. B., Fischer, R., Vignoles, V. L., & Bond, M. H. (2013). *Understanding Social Psychology across Cultures*. Second edition. London: Sage Publications.

Triandis, H. C. (1977). *Interpersonal Behavior*. Monterey, CA: Brooks/Cole.

Zimbardo, P. G. (1969). The human choice: Individuation, reason, and order versus deindividuation, impulse, and chaos. *Nebraska Symposium on Motivation*, *17*, 237–307.

19 A Professional Past of Arranging to Be Compelled

Robert B. Cialdini

My first publication was in the journal *Science* (which allows me to joke that my publication history has been downhill from there); oddly, for someone in my position, the article didn't involve social influence or social psychology or even human behavior. It concerned ethology, and it emerged from an observation I'd made in an undergraduate laboratory class in which we were recording the conditioned responding of earthworms to electric shock. Things weren't proceeding well with the earthworm I was trying to condition; so I secured a second worm, putting it into the same small box where the first had been repeatedly buzzed and had secreted a creamy precipitate from its skin. Soon, *I* became the shocked party, as I witnessed my new subject begin trying frantically to escape up the walls. After getting the same reaction from a third and fourth worm, I called over the lab instructor to watch. Wide-eyed, he said, "I think we've found an alarm pheromone (a chemical signal certain animals send out to alert conspecifics to danger) that hasn't been recorded before." With a pair of his graduate students, we explored the reliability and functionality of the phenomenon, after which we successfully submitted a report to *Science*.

Armed with an in-press paper in a prestigious outlet and good GRE scores, I applied for graduate training to several strong ethology programs. At the same time, I had a girlfriend who was taking a social psychology class where there was an empty chair next to hers. I filled the seat. By the end of the term, I was more enamored of social psychology than of ethology – and, as these things go at around this age, of the girlfriend. I promptly began researching social psychology doctoral programs and hit on the University of North Carolina at Chapel Hill as right for me because its faculty was editing the *Journal of Experimental Social Psychology* at the time. I remember thinking, *Experimental*, that's what I've been trained in and *Social Psychology*, that's what I want to study. Perfect."

At UNC, and then during a postdoctoral stint at Columbia University, my approach to research was affected profoundly by three mentors: Chester Insko, John Thibaut, and Stanley Schachter. Of course, there were others who influenced me greatly at the two institutions. Still, it can be safely said that these three individuals delivered the greatest impact. They did so differently, though.

Robert B. Cialdini, Arizona State University, USA.

It wasn't that Chet, John, and Stan held fundamentally different values regarding the discipline of social psychology or of the scientific enterprise more generally. However, they sought to realize those fundamental values in ways that stood apart from one another. I've cast about in my mind for the right term to characterize the variances in approach I observed. "Style" is too superficial, "context" too general, "preference" too narrow. "Tenor" may be best. The tenor of their research orientations differed significantly from one another.

The Three Tenors

Chet Insko's Influence

Chet Insko was my major advisor during the three years I spent in Chapel Hill – three golden years from 1967 through 1970. From the outset, he taught me how to track down important questions as well as the answers to those questions through precise logic. Together, we distilled hypotheses from theories, derived tests from those hypotheses, and held the theories accountable from the results of those tests. No sloppy thinking was allowed, no superficial analysis was accepted. Chet got to the heart of things via inescapable deduction. From him, I acquired the tools of the logician's trade.

The implications of this kind of tutelage went beyond a deep understanding of the hypothetico-deductive method for uncovering testable ideas. Chet's lessons in stripping away the nonessential aspects of a thing have helped me in two professional domains: research implementation and teaching. In the first, the lessons have proven invaluable in the vital arena of operationalization. Getting one's experimental operationalizations right is tricky business. It means selecting one particular form of a variable from the many forms it could be made to take. Precision is the key. Miss the heart of the concept in your operationalization and your experiment tests something other than you intended.

The benefit of learning to recognize or construct proper exemplars of a central concept has paid dividends in the teaching realm as well. Truth be told, the thing students remember best about the theories, studies, and data covered in our classes is the stories we've told to illustrate them. It's become clear to me that those illustrations have to be *apt* ones to do the job optimally. Cute anecdotes with multiple engaging features (e.g., personal disclosures, embarrassing incidents, racy components) may well hold an audience's attention but may make the wrong (i.e., irrelevant) aspects of the tale memorable. It's a mistake to embellish a story with various attention-grabbing details that are oblique to the main purpose of the account. It's an even bigger mistake to settle for stories that are only roughly related to the conceptual point we are trying to make. I now view the aptness of the illustrations I employ in the classroom as the single most important determinant of my overall teaching effectiveness. As with the process of developing the right operationalizations in the research arena, precision is the key. Although Chet never provided a word of counsel to me regarding teaching (as my research advisor, it wasn't his job), I know that, nonetheless, he trained me to do it better.

John Thibaut's Influence

Whereas Chet Insko showed me how to track down phenomena in logical, linear ways, John Thibaut taught me how to circle in on them in concentric fashion. John was never my principal advisor but in classes and research meetings, I was impressed with the breadth of his knowledge, which he mined to provide uncommon and instructive starting points for a program of inquiry. Let's say the question at hand was "How do people bargain differently when they are negotiating for themselves versus when they are representing others and, thereby, accountable to them?" John might begin by asking what any of the great novelists had said about this. Next, he might ask, "Well, what have the philosophers said about the question?" So, we might move from Henry James to William James. Then, he'd press us to think about what the perspectives of our sibling disciplines – sociology, political science, anthropology – could add. Finally, John would tighten down the circle of inquiry to the thinking of other social psychologists who had reported their findings in the literature of our discipline. It struck me that this endpoint would have been my starting point without John's insistence that we begin the search for answers with a more diverse store of information.

An upshot of my exposure to John's far-flung circles approach was a desire to build a broad array of perspectives into research questions, especially at the early stages. One way has been to accept graduate students from a wide variety of backgrounds. I've tried to be especially receptive to non-North American students, to applicants who have been in the working world for a time, and to candidates whose undergraduate majors were not in psychology. It may take these students a bit longer to get their minds around the core of the discipline, but the value they bring has made the trade-off more than worth it.

Stan Schachter's Influence

If Chet Insko taught me how to snare effects, and John Thibaut taught me how to encircle them, then Stan Schachter taught me how to chase them wherever they manifestly led. He let the data steer him, and he took their counsel like no one I'd ever worked with. For instance, his classic program of work on affiliation started as an investigation of human isolation. When I asked him about this shift in focus, he explained that he had quickly recognized that isolation – he waved his hand dismissively as he said the word – was too rare in the repertoire of human responding to warrant his continued attention. Now, *affiliation*, that was another story. We are an intensely affiliative species and that's where the power is, he assured me. Accordingly, that's where he went. I recall being impressed by his willingness to get off the horse he was riding and get on one going in the opposite direction – in midstream – because he would rather follow powerful effects than his preconceptions or initial interests.

Although my exposure to Stan's heat-seeking missile model was relatively short – involving a year's postdoctoral fellowship at Columbia – the impact on me was considerable. It didn't just teach me to prepare to be steered by powerful effects; it taught me to seek them, indeed, to organize myself to register and be captured by them. Once that was accomplished, I could use the lessons of my earlier mentors to help properly select and attack important questions regarding those powerful effects. Thus, within my developing orientation to research, systematically arranging to be compelled became the first step to take.

But, how *does* one organize to encounter and be swept by powerful phenomena? How does one even know where to look? Let's use a metaphor. If we can conceive of the flow of human behavior as a river, we might also conceive of "hip deep" as the optimal way to register its force. That is, the best-situated observer may not be the one who stands, dry on the shore, recording from a distance. Instead, it may be the one who "wades in" to feel the rush close up and personally. In this regard, I can point to a pair of methodologies: (1) *participant observation*, which has been employed more frequently in disciplines outside of our own (e.g., anthropology and sociology) and requires that investigators immerse themselves in a research setting to analyze it and (2) *field research*, which is conducted in naturally occurring settings while optimally possessing a rigorous scientific component. I've engaged in both, preceded in each case by a lone, career-changing decision.

Stepping from the Avenues to the Streets

Let's employ another metaphor. As members of the academic research community, we don't operate in the streets – the cluttered, chaotic, congested streets. We do our work primarily in the neat, ordered, traffic-controlled avenues. There's nothing wrong with this division of labor; in fact, there's much to recommend it. Staying with our metaphor, producers from the streets often supply raw materials to those on the avenues who sort, clarify, purify, and package the materials before placing them on offer. If done well, everyone wins. Early in my career, though, I became concerned that as avenue-dwellers, we weren't participating properly in the exchange. Increasingly, mostly for reasons of convenience, we weren't going to the streets for the basic goods of human social behavior. Instead, we were simply trading our refined versions of those goods with one another to be refined still further at each step. I worried that, with each new subtlety, the effects we were obtaining were more delicate and less representative of those of the street – that rather than *distilling* the effects (to their essence), we were progressively *denaturing* them (in potency and character). I have employed the methodological approaches of participant observation and field research to head first to the streets to try to avoid this problem.

Participant Observation

Although it's fine to stand ready and waiting to be struck by powerful naturally occurring phenomena worthy of scientific pursuit – indeed, I'm on record as encouraging it – there is no reason to be only reactive in these matters. This is especially the case in an area like social influence, where there are all sorts of organizations dedicated to influencing us to comply with their requests. It's possible to study these units from the inside to observe the effective techniques they employ. The findings are likely to be highly valuable, because effects that appear consistently across a range of different compliance practitioners are likely to be particularly influential ones. That is, these organizations serve as natural proving grounds for procedures that work. Their business is to make us comply, and their livelihoods depend on it. Those who don't know how to get people to say yes soon fall away; those who do, stay and flourish. Therefore, when we bring their street practices back to the avenues and examine them in controlled settings to learn why they work, we can do so with the knowledge that these are genuinely powerful phenomena worth studying.

This is what I resolved to do. In a nearly three-year study, I became a spy of sorts, infiltrating the training programs of as many influence professions as I could get access to and learning how people can be led to say yes within them. Through it all, I watched for parallels. I thought that, if I could identify which psychological principles were being used successfully by individuals selling insurance and industrial machinery and computer equipment and portrait photography and if these were the same principles being used successfully by negotiators and fundraisers and recruiters and lobbyists, then I would know something important. I would know that *these* must be the most powerful and applicable principles of influence available, because they worked across the widest range of influence professions, influence practitioners, and influence opportunities.

My intent with this program of inquiry was to find principles and practices that were clearly powerful but not clearly grasped. I was looking for strong effects for which multiple possible explanations coexisted. It's important to recognize that even though compliance professionals know the procedures that work in the streets – that, after all, is their job – they don't necessarily know why they work. That is *our* job. It's what we are equipped to do on the avenues. I set about the task with the purpose of identifying such potent street practices and then taking them to controlled settings, where I could unpack their underlying causes – something I loved doing. Yet, it wasn't long before I recognized that another, larger purpose could be achieved as well. There was a book to be written. It wasn't to be a book for the academic community, though. It was to be for the popular reader, who could benefit from what I'd learned.

The idea to write for a general readership sprang from a long-standing sense I had that social science as a profession and social psychology as a discipline were not holding up their end of an implicit contract with the larger society. The public was expected to fund social scientific research and, in turn, researchers were expected to describe – in a much more elaborated and ongoing fashion than has ever actually been the case – what society had received for its money.

Because society had paid for our research, it was as much theirs as ours; consequently, we should be devoting our efforts not so much "to giving psychology away" as to giving psychology a *way* – a *way* to communicate our science widely to the society in a professionally responsible fashion. That was something I attempted in the resultant book, *Influence*, which persists in that attempt up to the present (Cialdini, 2021). Fortunately, myriad social psychologists are now finding ways to communicate our worth to the nonacademic community in blogs, podcasts, columns, videos, and (still my personal favorite) general readership books. It is a trend, as well as a disciplinary responsibility, I hope never to see fade.

Field Research

As instructive and consequential that my period of participant observation was for me, it would be naive to advocate its wide use by social psychological investigators. The opportunities for it are rare. Its barriers in terms of logistics, financial costs, and informed consent are daunting. Besides, it seldom results directly in publications; it's more of a feeder program for insights that, when tested scientifically, lead to publications. Fortunately, there's a second, more feasible route to keeping research effects "street-real" that I can endorse: field research. A definition is in order. A while ago, I established a prize for the best example of field research published each year. Conveniently, we can use the prize's language for our definition, which assigns the label to research conducted in naturally occurring settings in which participants can expect to find themselves under normal life circumstances and in which they are unlikely to suppose they are research participants. Investigations conducted under such conditions bring the investigators immediately and inexorably to effects characteristic of the streets.

The advantages are several. The obtained behavior patterns are those that have withstood the battering influences of all manner of other powerful phenomena that naturally inhabit the settings. Thus, the surviving effects are more replicable in other research domains, as well as more actionable and appreciated within non-research contexts. For a full explication of the advantages/disadvantages of field research and a systematic treatment of field research methods, see Paluck and Cialdini (2014). For now, it would be better to trace the course of one program of my field research that provides a rich set of illustrations.

Field Research into Pro-Environmental Action

All my professional life, I've been a social influence researcher, studying the factors that, if incorporated into a persuasive appeal, spur people to say yes to it. At around the midpoint of my career, I decided to focus my research on what I thought might well be the most important social influence question facing us at the time and still today: How to influence people to engage in pro-environmental activity. Initially, my team and I began to study a relatively minor form of environmentally related conduct – littering in public places such as parking lots, dormitory lobbies, amusement parks, and building staircases. From there, we advanced to a more objectionable action – the theft of environmentally sensitive artifacts from a US national park. Finally, we moved to the more societally consequential behaviors of household recycling and of commercial and residential energy conservation. It is on the last of these behaviors, residential energy conservation, that I'd like to spend our remaining time, as it offers the greatest opportunity for impactful large-scale interventions. However, readers interested in an overview of the entire three-decade-long program of work can find one in Cialdini (2012).

Throughout, we sought to test a theoretical formulation, the Focus Theory of Normative Conduct (Cialdini et al., 1990). The formulation has a pair of central postulates. First, there are two main types of social norms: (a) *descriptive norms*, which refer to what is typically done in a situation and that motivate by informing individuals of what is likely to be adaptive action in that situation and (b) *injunctive norms*, which refer to what is typically approved/disapproved in a situation and that motivate by promising to provide or withhold social acceptance. Second, each type of norm is likely to guide behavior only to the extent that it is focal (salient) in an actor's attention at the time. In this sense, we can view social norms as functioning not like an ordinary magnet with a regular constant pull but, rather, like an electro-magnet that can lie dormant, exerting little or no force until current is sent into it in the form of a norm's salience, thereby activating and strengthening its pull.

In a particularly generative set of studies, with a team led by my colleague Wes Schultz and along with our graduate students, Jessica Nolen, Noah Goldstein, and Vladas Griskevicious, we examined the effects of focusing people on the perceived descriptive norms of household energy conservation. In one study, once a week for a month, on door-hangers, residents of a suburban San Diego neighborhood received one of four messages that asked them to reduce their energy consumption. Three of the messages contained a frequently employed reason for conserving energy – the environment will benefit; or it's the socially responsible thing to do; or it will save you significant money on your next power bill – whereas the fourth played the social norm card, stating (honestly) that most of your fellow community members do try to conserve energy at home. At the end of the month, we recorded how much energy was used and learned that the social norms-based message had generated 3.5 times as much energy savings as any of the other messages.

I'd like to make a couple of additional points about these findings. First, we obtained the data by having our undergraduate research assistants go into the yards of the homes, braving the presence of household dogs and rogue watering systems, to read the power meters. (I am happy to report than no research assistants were harmed or sacrificed in the conduct of this research.) Second, despite our encouraging results, we were left with an important pragmatic question: How could we scale these social norm effects to a national level that would make a societal difference? It turned out the answer was to engage the private sector in the process.

I should say that I didn't go looking for a way to engage the private sector as a partner; it came looking for me. A pair of young entrepreneurs, Dan Yates and Alex Laskey, who'd learned of our energy conservation research proposed (successfully) that, for a three-year period, I become the part-time chief scientist for their then-startup firm, Opower, which would team up with utility companies to send residents information about how much energy their household was using compared with their neighbors. A crucial feature of the information was that the comparison was not with *any* neighbors but, instead, was with neighbors whose homes were nearby and comparable along dimensions such as size – hence, "homes just like yours." The results, driven mainly by householders reducing their energy consumption if it was greater than their peers', have been truly consequential. There are several remarkable indicators of the favorable effects of these reports on recipients' energy consumption and, therefore, on the greater good – such as $700 million each year in residential customer bill savings, and 23 trillion fewer watts per hour of electricity expended. But, there is one that's my favorite: Over the past ten years, these peer comparisons, now sent to customers of over 100 power companies, have saved more than 36 billion pounds of CO_2 emissions from entering the atmosphere.

Coda

So, how did I get from placing hangers on doors in a suburban neighborhood to such outsized outcomes? It required a different partnership than I'd ever employed. No university I've been associated with has had the wherewithal to scale-up my findings to societal levels; and government agencies are too encumbered by administrative and political constraints. It required a partnership with the private sector – something, as a social scientist, I'd never thought I'd want to forge. It turns out I was wrong. In any effort to scale-up the results of my work to greater-good levels, I wouldn't make that mistake again. When I began my academic career, I didn't know what to predict for my future. But I did know that after I retired, I wanted to be able to look back and smile. I am retired now, and I can say that the field research I've done, especially within this last-described program of work, has allowed me to broaden that smile considerably.

On the subject of predicting the future, I am sometimes asked where social psychology is headed in terms of research topics. I always reply that I don't know. However, I do think I know where best to look for the answer. It is in the unrestricted research interests of our graduate students. I've always thought that graduate students are the oracles of our discipline. Researchers, in interactions with their advisees, are invariably in the position of providing counsel. On this particular dimension, though, they'd be well advised to take the counsel of their students – many of whom I hope to meet out on the streets.

Suggested Reading

Cialdini, R. B. (2012). The focus theory of normative conduct. In P. A. M. Van Lange, A. W. Kruglanski, and E. T. Higgins (Eds.), *Handbook of Theories of Social Psychology* (pp. 295–312). Thousand Oaks, CA: Sage Publications.
    (2021). *Influence: The Psychology of Persuasion (New and Expanded)*. New York: Harper Business.
Cialdini, R. B., Reno, R. R., & Kallgren, C. A. (1990). A focus theory of normative conduct: Recycling the concept of norms to reduce littering in public places. *Journal of Personality and Social Psychology, 58,* 1015–1026.
Paluck, E. L., & Cialdini, R. B. (2014). Field research methods. In H. Reis & C. Judd (Eds.), *Handbook of Research Methods in Social and Personality Psychology* (pp. 81–97). New York: Cambridge University Press.

20 A Social Psychological and Personality Approach to Human Motivation

Edward L. Deci

After I graduated from high school, in 1960, I was a student for four years at Hamilton College. Mathematics was my major, but I became increasingly interested in psychology during that period. Many years before I was at Hamilton, B. F. Skinner had been a student there, and by the time I got there the psychology faculty's research was based entirely on Skinner's operant theory, which was focused primarily on rewards, although they were called reinforcements. Similarly, the psychology program for students was entirely operant-theory-based.

My introductory psychology course was two semesters long and used programmed learning materials instead of textbooks or articles. Further, I had a three-hour laboratory each week during which I would typically get my rat from its cage and put it in a Skinner box to be conditioned on one type of reinforcement schedule or another. Occasionally I would try to apply the theory to humans by getting a fellow student to be a participant and conditioning him (Hamilton was all male at that time) by nodding my head or saying "yeah" when he did the behavior I was trying to strengthen. I found the operant-based course very interesting, in part because I had no idea what other types of psychology there might be. As far as I can recall, I had not even heard of "cognition" at that point.

When I graduated from Hamilton, I had no idea of what path I wanted for my future. I knew I didn't want mathematics, and when I thought of psychology, although it was interesting, it did not cut it for me because I could not see how I would use operant theory to make meaningful changes in the world. So, I decided to take a trip to London, to see a different part of the world, and to think more about my future. While I was there, I took a few courses at the London School of Economics. Some of the classes were in human resources, which seemed a lot like psychology, although fortunately it was not just operant psychology. In fact, what stood out the most for me were the ideas that seemed like motivation. I found the course materials both very interesting and very applicable, so when it was time for me to return to the United States I decided to pursue an MBA degree at the Wharton School with a focus on organizational behavior.

I have never had any interest in becoming a businessperson, but I was increasingly interested in motivation, which I was finding in the organization courses.

Edward L. Deci, University of Rochester, USA.

Then one day I had a conversation about my interests with my favorite Wharton professor, Dean Berry. He suggested that I read the book *Work and Motivation*, which had recently been published by his friend, Victor Vroom. That did it for me! I knew then that I wanted to go on studying psychology, and motivation in particular. I then figured out that if I went into the social psychology PhD program at Carnegie Mellon University (CMU) I could study motivation with Victor who was a faculty member in that program along with Daryl Bem, Joel Goldstein, and Herb Simon. So that is what I did, and it suited me perfectly from the very beginning, with Victor as my primary mentor.

An important thing that happened for me when I was in my second year at Wharton was that I got a job teaching statistics to Wharton undergraduates. I had been a math major in college with six semesters of calculus and a course in probability and statistics, and I had also taken the Wharton graduate statistics course in my first year of the MBA program, so I was given the teaching job when one of the teachers was in an accident the day before classes began and there was no one else around to teach it. It was a year-long course that met three times a week and I loved teaching it. Fortunately, I got the highest student ratings of any of the statistics teachers that year. It was clear from that experience that I wanted university-level teaching to be part of my future.

When I got settled at CMU, I did a couple of studies mostly just to learn how to do a social psychology experiment. I also co-edited a book with Victor titled *Management and Motivation.* Doing that allowed me to learn a great deal more about motivation theories, which excited me considerably. I was particularly interested in Harry Harlow's (1950) research on intrinsic motivation in monkeys, which led me to Robert White's (1959) theory of competence and motivation. At that time, I was also reading about many social psychology experiments and theories, and what I wanted for my future was finally becoming clear. I wanted to do motivation research using social psychological and personality perspectives, and I wanted to teach it for undergraduate and graduate students.

One of the most famous theories of that time was Festinger's cognitive dissonance theory with its phenomenon of "insufficient justification." The gist of that phenomenon was that, if people did an uninteresting activity and did not have sufficient justification for having done it, they might convince themselves that they found the activity interesting and enjoyable so they could justify to themselves having done it. Stated differently they might experience new-found interest and enjoyment, which would become their motive for doing the activity. When reading that, it occurred to me that the intrinsic motivation I had read about in Harlow's and White's work might be very similar to the interest and enjoyment (i.e., the intrinsic motivation) that could be brought about by dissonance-related motivational processes. That started me thinking about intrinsic motivation in different types of social situations and how various social psychological processes might affect people's intrinsic motivation. It turned out that that was about the time I needed to do a doctoral dissertation to complete my program at CMU, and I knew that something about intrinsic motivation would certainly be involved in my dissertation research.

Social Psychological Experiments on Intrinsic Motivation

So I designed a set of social psychological experiments, starting with the question: If a person were intrinsically motivated to do an activity and someone began to pay the person for doing that activity – that is, if someone provided the person with extrinsic rewards for doing it – what, if anything, would happen to the person's intrinsic motivation for the interesting activity? Would it be enhanced, diminished, or left unchanged?

In my experiments I had undergraduates work on very interesting puzzles – that is, intrinsically motivated puzzles. In one study, half of them were paid one dollar for each puzzle they solved and the other half worked on the same puzzles but nothing was said about extrinsic rewards (i.e., the dollars). My results indicated that when people were paid for each puzzle they solved, they lost some of their intrinsic motivation for the puzzle activity relative to the other half of the participants who did the same puzzles with no mention of monetary rewards. In short, I had found that when people did an interesting activity for monetary rewards, their intrinsic motivation (i.e., their interest and enjoyment for the activity), appeared to be somewhat diminished. I referred to that as an undermining effect.

These results were very exciting to me, although they were substantially counter to what I had learned several years earlier when studying operant theory at Hamilton College. So I replicated these results to be sure they would appear again, and then several other people began to replicate them using not only money but also gifts and other extrinsic influences. This indicated to me that the undermining effect was at least somewhat valid even though many psychologists were very quickly criticizing it strongly, and the operant theorists were outraged about it and did what they could to make people believe it was invalid. This set of experiments represented my doctoral dissertation, immediately after which I took a faculty position in the psychology department at the University of Rochester, where I stayed for forty-eight years. When I first got to Rochester I published the dissertation studies in the *Journal of Personality and Social Psychology* (Deci, 1971).

That article got a tremendous amount of attention and very soon numerous other researchers had replicated the findings using varied methods. That allowed me to feel certain that there was indeed an undermining effect. So I thought about it carefully, wondering why this effect might have happened, and it occurred to me that the undermining of intrinsic motivation by extrinsic rewards could be caused by people feeling controlled by the rewards even though they wanted them, because rewards had likely been frequently used to control them throughout their lives. That then could diminish their feelings of personal freedom or autonomy and in turn undermine their intrinsic motivation.

Another experiment I did in this group indicated that positive verbal feedback, also known as verbal rewards, could enhance rather than undermine people's intrinsic motivation, presumably because it leaves them feeling competent as Robert White had talked about, without leaving them feeling controlled.

In 1999, when more than 120 articles examining the effects of extrinsic rewards on intrinsic motivation had been published, I did a meta-analysis in collaboration with

Richard Koestner and Richard Ryan, and we found that the undermining effect was supported, and the enhancement of intrinsic motivation by positive feedback was also supported. The meta-analysis was then published in *Psychological Bulletin.*

All of those experiments and various others led to the formulation of *Cognitive Evaluation Theory* (CET) which was considered a mini-theory that could explain how both interpersonal and intrapersonal events could affect people's intrinsic motivation by influencing their experiences of autonomy and competence (Deci & Ryan, 1980).

Attributions and Energy

Some of the researchers who replicated the undermining effect interpreted it in terms of attributions, which essentially means that they considered the undermining to be caused simply by a change in thoughts, or self-perceptions, as Bem's (1972) self-perception theory would suggest. For me, however, that was not enough. Motivation involves energy, and it is important to consider energy when studying human motivation. Hence, although the concept of attribution is extremely important for explaining many social psychological happenings, I did not find it adequate for providing meaningful explanations of intrinsic and extrinsic motivational phenomena.

Organismic Psychology

At about that time, after I had done quite a few intrinsic motivation experiments and had written the book *Intrinsic Motivation* (1975), I began having vigorous discussions with my colleague Richard Ryan who became a faculty member in the psychology department at the University of Rochester. Richard had studied philosophy and organismic psychology intensely. His thinking, in line with Piaget's, focused on the inherent integrative tendency within human beings. Stated differently, Ryan suggested, and I agreed, that all humans have an innate developmental process, and that that integrative tendency is very much in accord with the idea of energy being fundamental to motivation. Ryan then used the concept of inherent integration to explain how extrinsic motivation might function effectively.

Up until that time, with respect to extrinsic motivation, I had focused primarily on the negative aspect of extrinsic motivation undermining intrinsic motivation. However, Ryan's argument made clear that, under certain conditions, it is possible to internalize and integrate extrinsic motivation. More precisely he argued that internalized and integrated extrinsic motivation could become autonomous and part of the person's true self. The research based on these ideas led to *Organismic Integration Theory* (OIT), which was the second mini-theory, following CET, in our work on intrinsic and extrinsic motivation. At this point, then, I have discussed intrinsic motivation which is autonomous by nature, and also internalized extrinsic motivation, which is also considered autonomous when it has been fully integrated. Together these two types of motivation represent the overall idea of autonomous motivation, and an enormous amount of research has shown that autonomous motivation yields well-being and positive performance.

Psychological Needs

Consistent with our belief that energy is crucial for motivation, various approaches to studying motivation have used the concept of "needs" as a primary source of energy. However, the concept of psychological needs has two quite different forms. One view is that needs are learned. This occurs, for example, in the theory of David McClelland whereby people are said to learn to need achievement, or to need affiliation, or to need power, and the results of their learnings are individual differences in how much of each of those learned needs they will require in their lives. The alternative form of needs, which is more consistent with the type of motivation I have been talking about and with the inherent integrative tendency that Ryan suggested, is that all human beings have three fundamental and basic psychological needs – the need for autonomy, the need for competence, and the need for relatedness. These needs are not learned; they are inherent to human beings, and they are essential for wellness in all people. Our accepting these needs as critically important for all individuals' wellness has emerged empirically, which is to say that we have found through an enormous amount of research that the degree to which people get these three psychological needs satisfied does, in fact, determine whether they behave excellently and experience healthy lives.

Self-Determination Theory

The overall theory that I and Ryan co-founded, and that we titled *Self-Determination Theory* (SDT) currently comprises six mini-theories, of which CET and OIT were the first two (for an overview, see Ryan & Deci, 2017). The functioning of the psychological needs represents the content of a third mini-theory, *Basic Psychological Needs Theory* (BPNT). A fourth is *Causality Orientations Theory* (COT) which is concerned with motivations as personality orientations in people's lives. For example, people may have strong general personal *autonomous* orientations and they will likely have more positive outcomes than people who have strong general personal *controlled* orientations.

The fifth mini-theory is *Goal Contents Theory* (GCT) which deals with people's goals or aspirations and how effectively the goals function as a result of satisfaction of the people's basic psychological needs and the strength of their different types of motivational orientations. For example, research indicates that if people's primary life goals are what we call extrinsic goals such as attaining huge amounts of money, becoming famous, and looking very attractive and trendy, they are likely to evidence less wellness than if their primary aspirations are what we call intrinsic goals, such as affiliating with others, being physically fit, and growing and developing as individuals. The sixth of the mini-theories in SDT is *Relationships Motivation Theory* (RMT) which is concerned with how people's close personal relationships can be deeply gratifying, for example when their basic psychological needs are being satisfied and there is mutuality in their autonomous motivations.

Applications of the Theory

Another very important aspect of our work, done in collaboration with many dozens of international SDT scholars has had a focus on the applications of the theory to varied life domains, including: parenting; education; organizational behavior; psychotherapy; health behavior change; sports; other physical activities; and virtual environments among many others. Applications of SDT have been done in many ways. One of the most important ways that it is applied involves at least two people where one of them is, to some degree, an authority figure. For example, parents can be considered authority figures for their children. Similarly, that can be said about teachers and students, coaches and athletes, managers and employees, as well as people in other such relationships. It is often said that it is the job of authority figures to motivate others, but we in SDT do not see it that way, because that tends to imply extrinsic controls. We would rather say that it is the job of the authority figures to *support* the autonomous motivation – that is, the intrinsic motivation and the integrated motivation – of the others. Further, both the theory and research have indicated that the support for autonomous motivation comes by supporting the basic psychological needs of the others – that is their autonomy, competence, and relatedness.

Concretely speaking, examples of how to support the basic psychological needs of others include: (1) relating from the others' perspectives, not just from your own; (2) encouraging the others' self-initiation and exploration; (3) offering choices to the others rather than telling them what they have to do; (4) providing a meaningful rationale when requesting behaviors from the others or when setting limits for the others; (5) giving both positive and constructive feedback to the others; and (6) refraining from using controlling language in conversing with the others.

Methods in SDT

As is clear from this chapter, the research in SDT began with social psychology experiments, particularly ones involving intrinsic motivation. However, we and our colleagues and students soon began to supplement the experiments by developing psychological metrics that assessed various concepts of the theory – types of motivational orientations, types of goals, degrees of internalization and integration, and numerous other constructs especially for use in the applied research. In order to disseminate the growing body of SDT research and methods, we developed a website (https://selfdeterminationtheory.org) to make available psychometric materials and other resources.

In the spring of 1999 we decided to invite about twenty faculty members from various universities who had done research on SDT to join us at the University of Rochester for a small conference at which each invitee presented their research. In all, there were approximately one hundred faculty and students who attended the event. Since then we have had a conference about every three years, with increasing numbers of people attending each one. The most recent conference was in the Netherlands in 2019 which was attended by 800 SDT researchers and practitioners.

Center for Self-Determination Theory

With SDT growing exponentially in terms of scholarship and impact across life's domains, in addition to public interest in our website content and the multitude of inquiries about the theory, it became clear that we needed an entity to support the work. We therefore created the Center for SDT (CSDT), which is a not-for-profit organization focused on advancing the development and dissemination of SDT. Shannon Cerasoli, who had been working with Richard Ryan and me for a number of years, became Director of the Center which is based in Celebration, Florida. CSDT's online presence presents the results of worldwide research as well as other resources and events that are relevant to SDT.

Conclusion

Over the past half century, the research and theory of psychological science has been continually changing, from a behavioral orientation to a more cognitive orientation, to an orientation that is somewhat motivational. Among the early motivation theorists who worked with a general social psychological orientation was Victor Vroom who trained and supported me for several years and has remained my close friend ever since. Subsequently, after I had begun doing intrinsic motivation experiments, I partnered with Richard Ryan and facilitated an expansion of the field of human motivation in the form of SDT, which is a macro-theory of human motivation comprising six mini-theories that express a very person-centered approach. It examines human growth and autonomy as well as human defense and control. It has employed elements from social psychology and personality to create an understanding of motivation that can be applied to facilitating effective behavior and wellness among humans. This approach is widely used for improving the lives not only of individuals, but also of close personal relationships, groups, organizations, and societies. Further, research is now ongoing at each of these levels of generality (Ryan & Deci, 2017).

Suggested Reading

Bem, D. J. (1972). Self-perception theory. In L. Berkowitz (Ed.), *Advances in Experimental Social Psychology* (Vol. 6, pp. 1–62). New York: Academic Press.

Deci, E. L. (1971). Effects of externally mediated rewards on intrinsic motivation. *Journal of Personality and Social Psychology, 18*(1), 105–115.

(1975). *Intrinsic Motivation*. New York: Plenum Press.

Deci, E. L., Koestner, R., & Ryan, R. M. (1999). A meta-analytic review of experiments examining the effects of extrinsic rewards on intrinsic motivation. *Psychological Bulletin, 125,* 627–668.

Deci, E. L., & Ryan, R. M. (1980). The empirical exploration of intrinsic motivational processes. In L. Berkowitz (Ed.), *Advances in Experimental Social Psychology* (Vol. 13, pp. 39–80). New York: Academic Press.

Harlow, H. F. (1950). Learning and satiation of response in intrinsically motivated complex puzzle performance by monkeys. *Journal of Comparative and Physiological Psychology, 43*(4), 289–294.

Ryan, R. M., & Deci, E. L. (2017). *Self-Determination Theory: Basic Psychological Needs in Motivation, Development, and Wellness*. New York: Guilford Press.

Vroom, V. H. (1964). *Work and Motivation*. New York: John Wiley.

White, R. W. (1959). Motivation reconsidered: The concept of competence. *Psychological Review, 66*(5), 297–333.

21 Wandering into Psychology and Law

Phoebe C. Ellsworth

Some people have a passion for a single topic that motivates and engages them for life. I'm not one of them. I can get interested in almost anything, and my career looks more like a random walk through a candy store than a single-minded pursuit of a goal. I am both a theorist and researcher in the field of emotion and a contributor to the application of psychology to legal issues. In this piece I will focus on my work in psychology and law. A review of my research on emotion can be found in Ellsworth and Scherer (2003).

I was the first-born child in a family that believed in education, and my father had a passion for teaching. He probably would have been happiest as a teacher in a high school or prep school, but instead, during my childhood, he was first a graduate student in sociology, then an assistant professor at Yale, where his passion for teaching so consumed him that he failed to publish enough to get tenure. He taught me to be interested in everything. He and I made scrapbooks of animal species, collected stamps and learned about their different countries, studied prehistoric hominids, and diagrammed football games. In the meantime, both parents gave me works of literature that were generally at the edge of my capacity – *Pride and Prejudice* when I was ten, *Moby Dick* when I was thirteen. That was what was fun: learning stuff.

My family assumed that their children would go to college. They also pretty much assumed that the girls wouldn't have jobs but would be well-educated, suitable wives to well-educated, successful men. So when I was asked what I wanted to be when I grew up, I would say an artist or a writer – something where you worked from home and didn't actually have a job. This was basically the world view for upper middle-class women in the 1950s and it didn't occur to me to question it.

I started college at Bryn Mawr in 1961. Bryn Mawr women were seen as high on intellectual skills but low on social skills, and that was true of me. At Bryn Mawr there was a tacit assumption that college was not the last step in becoming a well-educated interesting wife, but the first step toward making a contribution in the world. Its second president, M. Carey Thomas, famously said, "Our failures only marry." I don't remember ever having a moment of sudden insight when it occurred to me that I might have a career; it just gradually came to feel like a normal thing to

Phoebe C. Ellsworth, University of Michigan, USA.

do. I thought I'd major in anthropology, perhaps because it had long been a field where women had succeeded.

After my sophomore year, I transferred to Harvard, following an unsuitable man. The relationship didn't last long and neither did my major, as the Harvard anthropology department didn't think I was qualified. I was later told that it was a notoriously sexist department and would do anything it could to discourage women. So I floated along, replaying my childhood by always taking more courses than were required, but in such a wide range of topics that I didn't have enough to make up a major in any field.

I was not particularly interested in either law or psychology. I thought law was dull, and I was suspicious of psychologists. Like most undergraduates, I thought of psychology as clinical psychology. Several of my folk-singing, counterculture, would-be beatnik friends had been pushed into therapy by their parents, sometimes inpatient therapy, and I thought it was evil to equate nonconformity with mental illness.

Back home for the summer, I looked for a job, knocking on doors at Yale and asking whether anyone was looking for an undergraduate assistant. In the 1960s, funding for psychological research was easy to come by, but I was hired by the psychology department to work as "office help" for three social psychologists – Chuck Kiesler, Barry Collins, and Norman Miller. I had neither the skills nor the temperament to make a good secretary. When I proofread a manuscript, I was more likely to question the ideas than the spelling, so I was repurposed as a research assistant. I ran subjects, I attended research meetings, and soon I was helping to design studies and write grant proposals. They were working on cognitive dissonance and attitude change, and while I wasn't deeply interested in the topic, I was excited by the idea that you could answer questions by designing experiments. I loved the formal design part of it – figuring out what control groups and control measures were important, and I loved the procedure part – figuring out how to turn your concepts into events and measures that would be meaningful and involving for the participants.

Back at Harvard at the time, social psychology (along with sociology and cultural anthropology) was part of a department called social relations. They were extremely liberal about the courses they would accept as part of the major, allowing not only my course on physiological psychology, but also my course on *Beowulf*, so all I had to do was take a few more psychology courses and write a senior thesis. In my always passionate perusal of that garden of earthly delights – the new course catalogue – I came upon a course that combined psychology and law, taught by a visitor named Hans Toch. I probably took it because I had a law school boyfriend at the time. Although its approach was fairly clinical, I loved it, and it opened up a whole new world of questions I had never thought about. Most of all, I was shocked by the realization that legislators and judges regularly made decisions based on their understanding of human behavior without bothering to educate themselves about what was *known* about human behavior.

This first struck me when I discovered that in creating laws involving defendants who were mentally ill, judges didn't bother to learn anything about mental illness, but devised a rule of their own that defined "legal insanity." This meant that even if psychiatrists and psychological researchers agreed that a person was seriously adrift from reality, he might be "legally sane" and could be sentenced to prison or death. The common legal definition of insanity, the M'Naghten rule, was established in the 1840s, and remained the standard despite over a century of scientific and medical research on mental illness. When I asked how this could be so, I was told about the idea of *precedent*, by which courts are bound by previous legal decisions. This struck me as a crazy requirement for any decisions that involved science.

In the fall of my senior year my advisor, Ken Gergen, suggested that I apply to graduate school. The idea hadn't occurred to me, but I'd always liked being a student and had recently come to like research, so I thought, why not? I thought I'd probably stay at Harvard, but it turned out that they had decided not to accept any women that year because someone on the faculty had done a study showing that women did not have the stamina to complete the PhD. So after graduating from Harvard in 1966, I went to Stanford. On my application I said that I was interested in nonverbal communication of emotion, cultural differences, and psychology and law. No one at Stanford was interested in any of these topics, but I had very high GRE scores and had graduated *summa cum laude*, and they assumed that if I was that smart, I would soon learn to recognize an acceptable topic.

I never did. I did experiments on nonverbal communication, and once I had actual data, the faculty seemed to think that was acceptable enough. I ran studies for my advisor, Merrill Carlsmith, and he let me run studies of my own. Psychology and law stayed in the background until my second year of graduate school, when I met Robert Levy, a lawyer who was at the Center for Advanced Study in the Behavioral Sciences. He was working on drafting a uniform code for child custody adjudication. This struck me as a topic that cried out for collaboration with developmental psychologists, and I asked him whether he was talking to any of them. He said no, but to his credit, he said he thought it would be a good idea. I told him I'd ask Eleanor Maccoby, who was in the Stanford psychology department. I bounced into her office, full of enthusiasm about this exciting opportunity to influence the law, but her response was one of disdain. "This is Stanford," she said. "We don't do *applied* research here." Later, in the 1990s, she became an important contributor to the literature on child custody.

So I offered to review the developmental research myself, and Levy and I ended up writing an article together in the *Law and Society Review* (Ellsworth & Levy, 1969). That was my first publication in psychology and law – way out of my field of expertise, but not bad anyway. The psychology department seemed to be pretty much unaware of this work, and I had pretty much given up on getting any guidance from the faculty. On the other hand, I was doing well in my other research, and neither Merrill nor anyone else did anything to dissuade me. I think this must have been partly because I was a woman, so it didn't matter what I did. Although the department was very good about accepting women graduate students (unlike Harvard), they didn't actually expect us to get jobs, so they didn't make any effort to make us marketable. They might have paid more attention if I were a man, and worked harder to persuade me that getting involved in psychology and law would hurt my career chances.

I took courses at the Law School. My professor in criminal law was Tony Amsterdam, and meeting him changed my life. Once or twice in your life – if you're lucky – you meet someone who seems to exist on a whole new higher level of intelligence. That was Tony. I knew immediately that I wanted to work with him and learn from him. He was working on developing test cases to challenge capital punishment. I neither knew much nor cared much about capital punishment, but that didn't matter. Some of the issues at the time, such as whether the death penalty deterred homicide, involved empirical evidence, and I offered to review these studies for him. He agreed, and I became an acolyte in the community of death penalty litigators and scholars and a Tony Amsterdam disciple.

One day in my fourth year of graduate school, Merrill mentioned to me that Bob Abelson had called him because Yale was looking to hire an assistant professor and he wanted to know if Merrill had any good students. That was how people got academic jobs at elite schools in those days – through the old boy network. Merrill told Abelson that he had a real tiger but she wouldn't be interested. "Hey boss," I said, "where did that part about not being interested come from?" It came, of course, from the general assumption that women would not want full-time jobs. Only one female Stanford social psychology PhD, Elaine Hatfield, had ever done so. To his credit, Merrill called Abelson back right away, I was invited to give a job talk, and was offered a job at Yale. I started there in 1971.

Yale was good to me. They treated me like any other assistant professor, never assigning me courses like "Psychology of Women" but giving me the same graduate and undergraduate classes as anyone else. I taught the graduate social psychology course my first year, and quite a few senior graduate students decided to take it, probably figuring that they might have to teach it very soon in their jobs and that they could save themselves a lot of work by using my course as a template. For me it was a classic case of Impostor Syndrome, as Reid Hastie, Shelley Taylor, Ellen Langer, and I think Carol Dweck all took it, and most knew at least as much as I did. Yale also let me teach a new course on psychology and law, which quickly became hugely popular, probably because the undergraduates thought (falsely) that it would help them get into Law School.

The Russell Sage Foundation had a Law and Society program with a branch at Yale, and there I met Neil Vidmar, and we wrote an article reviewing all the research on public opinion and the death penalty, and concluded that very little of it was relevant to the issues raised by *Furman v. Georgia* (1972), a highly controversial death penalty case. In *Furman*, the US Supreme Court invalidated all the death penalty laws in the country, but held that capital punishment might be constitutional if jury verdicts were guided by rules that limited the unguided discretion they had previously exercised. This meant that simply expressing support for the death penalty was uninformative, because there was no way to tell whether it signaled support for legal or illegal capital punishment.

In 1973, I was back at Stanford as a visiting professor. I'd become good friends with Lee Ross, who had joined the Stanford faculty when I was a senior graduate student. When I went to Yale, Lee took over my role as on-the-spot consultant to Tony

Amsterdam. By then Tony's group had decided that we weren't likely to make much progress in the abolition of capital punishment as long as it continued to have such strong public support (around 60 percent in 1973). So Lee and I decided to do a survey to find out the reasons that people supported or opposed the death penalty, figuring that knowing the reasons for the attitude would make it easier to identify strategies that might change it.

At that time, surveys mostly just asked whether people favored or opposed the death penalty. We asked which crimes they favored it for, whether they favored mandatory or discretionary capital punishment, how well-informed about the death penalty they were, and several other questions designed to assess their attitudes in the light of *Furman.* We listed every reason we had heard of for favoring or opposing the death penalty, and asked if their opinions were based on that reason. It was a wonderful survey, far more complete than any other that had been done, but our effort to find out why people favored or opposed the death penalty completely failed. People who favored the death penalty endorsed *every* reason for favoring it; people who opposed it endorsed every reason for opposing it. This led us to conclude that the attitude was more important to people than the reasons, that death penalty attitudes were symbolic, emotionally based elements of people's ideological self-image (Ellsworth & Ross, 1983).

In the fall of that year a much smaller, more personal incident arguably had a greater impact than our research on the field of psychology and law. A defense lawyer in San Jose called the Stanford psychology department asking for someone who could serve as an expert witness in a case that he thought involved eyewitness misidentification. The department referred him to me, since I was the psychology and law person. I had never heard of anything like this, but since I was such an advocate of basing legal decisions on psychological research when it was relevant, I agreed. Working from the literature on person perception, I presented data on how expectations influence perception and on stereotyping (the defendant was a Latina accused of shoplifting).

When I got back to Stanford after testifying, I ran into my old friend and Stanford classmate, Beth Loftus. I told her about my courtroom experience, and after a long pause, she said, "Phoebe, why did they ask *you*? You don't know anything about perception or memory." I said I supposed it was because of my interest in psychology and law. "Well, *I* really want to do that," she said. "How do I get them to ask *me*?" I told her that there was hardly any research on eyewitnesses, that I'd just cobbled together research from person perception in general, and that I'd love it if she did work that focused more specifically on sources of eyewitness error. The rest is history.

Along with eyewitness testimony, one of the first big topics in psychology and law at that time was juries. In the early 1970s the Supreme Court handed down two decisions on juries that galvanized the young field of psychology and law. In *Williams v. Florida* (1970) they held that six-person juries are constitutional, in part because they saw no difference in how deliberations would play out in groups of six versus twelve. Then in *Apodaca v. Oregon* (1972), they used similar reasoning to hold that non-unanimous juries were fine – deliberations would be the same whether or not the jury was required to reach unanimous agreement. Research psychologists were shocked because these were empirical questions, and the Court had set binding legal precedents without considering any empirical evidence. On the other hand, there actually wasn't much empirical research on group size or unanimity, and a number of psychologists quickly began to study these questions. If judges had an obligation to consider empirical evidence relevant to legal questions, we had an obligation to provide it.

In 1968 the Court had decided *Witherspoon v. Illinois*, a case that involved both juries and the death penalty. In capital cases, people who said they opposed the death penalty were automatically disqualified as jurors for fear that they might be unwilling to sentence the defendant to death. Since the same jury decides both guilt and punishment, these jurors were also excluded from the jury that decides whether the defendant is guilty or innocent.

In Witherspoon's case, nearly half the prospective jurors were disqualified because of their attitudes about the death penalty. He argued that such a "death-qualified" jury was unconstitutionally biased toward a guilty verdict, compared to the juries that try all other crimes. His lawyers actually presented evidence from three unpublished studies that supported this claim. The Court concluded that this evidence was "too tentative and fragmentary" to reverse Witherspoon's conviction; however, in an unusual move, they also acknowledged that the question was an empirical one, and that their decision might be reversed if future research showed that death-qualified juries were "less than neutral with respect to *guilt.*"

Of course the Court's suggestion that it might be influenced by future empirical research was catnip to me, and I regularly asked my psychology and law class to design research that might be persuasive. In 1978, my old hero, Tony Amsterdam, along with Sam Gross, a young lawyer who worked with the National Jury Project, and other abolitionist lawyers were gearing up to prepare a comprehensive test case on death qualification. Obviously a centerpiece of that case would be providing new research. They asked me to organize the research effort, and I agreed.

Several extremely smart and dedicated graduate students were committed to the project – Bob Fitzgerald from Berkeley, and Bill Thompson and Claudia Cowan from Stanford – and we worked intensively with Tony and Sam on designing research that would satisfy not only scientists, but judges. For example, it took us more than a month to come up with the crucial question that would identify the people who would be excluded as jurors. The lawyers thought my initial question was way too simple and conversational to match the legal definition; I thought that their legally correct question would be incomprehensible to survey respondents, so their answers would be worthless. But in this context, more than in any work I've done as an expert, the lawyers and the social scientists were enormously respectful and patient, listened carefully to each other, and never gave up until we were all satisfied.

We began with a survey to find out how many people would be excluded and how they differed in their demographics and their attitudes from the death-qualified jurors.

(This was done in the county where we planned to hold the evidentiary hearing, so the judge could not dismiss it as irrelevant to that jurisdiction.) The other really important study was an experiment in which we showed eligible jurors a videotape of a homicide case and then divided them into juries that excluded strong opponents of the death penalty (the usual death-qualified juries) or included them and looked at their tendencies to vote for guilt and at the quality of their deliberations. And we did smaller studies on specific issues like perceptions of the credibility of defense and prosecution witnesses and perceptions of the insanity defense. We found that the excluded jurors were more likely to be Black, more likely to be female, and more likely to favor the defense. Including them on juries produced discussions that were more balanced and more thorough. Craig Haney joined us and did a study that showed that the very process of being grilled about their attitudes toward the death penalty made people think the defendant was probably guilty.

In August 1979, the evidence was presented at an evidentiary hearing on death qualification in Oakland. It was a very big deal for all of us. It went on for over three weeks and almost everyone who'd ever done any research on the topic testified as an expert witness. The idea was to create a complete record of the evidence which could then be used in future appellate cases all the way up to the US Supreme Court. In addition to presenting my own research, my job was to provide a mini course on research methodology and statistics, so that future judges would have the information they needed to evaluate the research and the arguments. Having recently co-authored a textbook on research methods in social psychology (Carlsmith, Ellsworth, & Aronson, 1976), I had plausible credentials. Sam had the task of preparing me. We spent weeks planning how to fit all the background material in, arguing over whether to include information that was scientifically essential (I thought) but legally not persuasive (he thought), creating graphs and other materials in big notebooks for the judge and opposing counsel, practicing my testimony over and over again, and buying impressive outfits to wear in court.

When I took the stand, the judge said, "You're much too young and pretty to be a doctor." I was not about to assert women's rights – I took it as a sign that he might let me go on and on about research methods and data analysis, and he did. Most people in the courtroom seemed pretty bored – I could tell because at that time the sports pages of the *San Francisco Chronicle* were green, and during that part of my testimony I felt as though I were in a bowl of lettuce. But the important thing was to get it into the record, not to amuse the present audience.

The lawyers on the other side had no idea that this hearing was going to be such a big deal, so they had to scramble at the last minute to dig up experts to refute our evidence. We were worried that experts sometimes relax their standards of accuracy when they get into a courtroom and say things they would never say if they were being judged by other scientists. So, to keep them honest, I asked Merrill Carlsmith and Lee Ross to come up from Stanford and sit in on the hearing during their testimony. Merrill and Lee were well known and respected in the field, and I hoped their presence would raise the experts' standards of scientific accuracy. So, on the day that they took the stand, Merrill and Lee introduced themselves and said that they were interested in observing the presentation of scientific evidence in the courtroom. It worked. The criticisms were mild, and mixed with praise.

As I said, Sam and I spent hundreds of hours working together as a team, and we both felt that we had never worked with anyone so competent and so rewarding. One day I said I wanted to spend a few hours not talking about the case or the research – and that's all it took for us to realize that we were in love. Then we went back to working on the case, which took so much time and effort that any sort of prolonged courtship or preparation for a life-long relationship was out of the question. As soon as the hearing was over, Sam moved in with me at Yale.

The issue of death qualification slowly moved through the lower courts. We kept working on them, though of course I was no longer available for expert testimony, as marrying Sam had reduced my credibility to zero. In the meantime we expanded our collaboration to include our whole life. In 1981 our first child, Sasha, was born, and we took jobs at Stanford. My colleagues and I continued to research and publish data indicating the biasing effects of death qualification (e.g., Cowan et al., 1984; Thompson et al., 1984).

In 1986, the issue of death qualification finally reached the US Supreme Court in the case of *Lockhart v. McCree*. Sam argued the case, and I worked on an *amicus* brief for the APA. We lost. Rehnquist, ignoring the concept of convergent validity, managed to find a flaw in fourteen of the fifteen studies we presented, dropped them from consideration, and concluded that the single remaining study was not sufficient basis for a constitutional decision. And just for good measure, he held that future empirical evidence that death-qualified juries were biased was irrelevant: As long as the twelve people on the defendant's particular jury were impartial, it didn't matter what groups in the population were left out.

That was disappointing, although not unexpected, given the Court's support for the death penalty. In the meantime, I was pregnant again, though I didn't notice for the first couple of months because we were so busy preparing the case. Emma was born in August of 1986, and a year later we moved to the University of Michigan, where we've been ever since. Our collaboration, in work as well as life, has remained as intense and rewarding as ever.

Suggested Reading

Carlsmith, J. M., Ellsworth, P. C., & Aronson, E. (1976). *Methods of Research in Social Psychology*. Reading, MA: Addison-Wesley.

Cowan, C., Thompson, W., & Ellsworth, P. C. (1984). The effects of death qualification on jurors' predisposition to convict and on the quality of deliberation. *Law and Human Behavior, 8*, 53–79.

Ellsworth, P. C., & Levy, R. J. (1969). Legislative reform of child custody adjudication: An effort to rely on social science data in formulating legal policies. *Law and Society Review, 4*, 167–233.

Ellsworth, P. C., & Ross, L. (1983). Public opinion and capital punishment: A close examination of the views of abolitionists and retentionists. *Crime & Delinquency, 29*, 116–169.

Ellsworth, P. C., & Scherer, K. R. (2003). Appraisal processes in emotion. In R. J. Davidson, H. Goldsmith, & K. R. Scherer (Eds.), *Handbook of Affective Sciences* (pp. 572–595). New York: Oxford University Press.

Furman v. Georgia, 408 U.S. 238 (1972).

Lockhart v. McCree, 476 U.S. 162 (1986).

Thompson, W. C., Cowan, C. L., Ellsworth, P. C., & Harrington, J. C. (1984). Death penalty attitudes and conviction proneness: The translation of attitudes into verdicts. *Law and Human Behavior, 8,* 95–113.

Witherspoon v. Illinois, 391 U.S. 510 (1968).

22 My Meandering Journey into Social Psychology

James M. Jones

It started when I realized that going to college was a better choice than getting a job! Fortunately, I lived in Elyria, Ohio nine miles from Oberlin (which happened to be my dad's birthplace), was a good athlete, and was offered an "athletic" scholarship – which meant that I was expected to play sports but was not obligated to. I suppose I would have been considered a "jock" in that I loved sports – played and lettered in all of them; football, basketball, baseball, and golf – but I did not have a jock sensibility. By my senior year, I had quit football, golf, and baseball, and was working as a research assistant in Norman Henderson's behavioral genetics lab. That was the beginning of my fledgling career in psychology.

But in some respects, my career began earlier as an inheritance from my maternal grandfather – William Thomas Hayes. He was born on a plantation in North Carolina in 1856. He was a slave until he was freed by the Emancipation Proclamation in 1865. He died in 1924, when my mother was only three years old. Grandpa Hayes was an extraordinary man. The mistress of the plantation taught him to read and in gratitude, he adopted the owner's name – Hayes. He was never formally educated but he believed strongly in education as the pathway to the betterment of the race and fulfillment of one's human potential. He was a natural leader and a dedicated servant of his people. He became a minister in the African Methodist Episcopal Church, leading congregations in Kentucky and Ohio. With three different wives, he produced seven children, six of whom lived to adulthood. He demanded that they get college educations and that the oldest should help the next one, until all of them attained college degrees. His proclamation was fulfilled – all of Grandpa Hayes's children graduated from college. The last college graduate, my mother, Eliza Marcella, graduated in 1972 at the age of fifty.

The other aspect of my narrative is a diversity story. My mother's mother, Ella Elizabeth Pace, was born in 1880 in North Carolina to a Cherokee Indian mother and a Black father. I know less about my paternal side, but I do know that my paternal great-grandfather was an immigrant from Jamaica. His wife, Anna Marti, was an immigrant from Switzerland who landed in Wisconsin to work with her brothers in a cheese business. Great Grandpa Jones was a chef on a boat that carried ore and other manufacturing products to ports on the Great Lakes. He met Anna Marti on one of

James M. Jones, University of Delaware, USA.

his trips. They settled in Oberlin, Ohio, and produced ten children one of whom, John Harold Jones, sired my father Arthur McCoy Jones. Slave, immigrant, Indian, Black, White, conjoin in an alchemy of circumstance and context to produce me and shape my destiny.

This history is sobering to me. I learned of this legacy late in life, after I had obtained my PhD. I had made a variety of decisions that gave direction and purpose to my life, and believed the path I followed into higher education, a desire to both understand and educate others about race, and human decency, were the creation of my personhood. These goals defined me as a Black man in America. I now realize that my steps were also guided from an energy, a spirit, a powerful force of strength, spirituality, belief, and profound humanity beyond my personal history.

But it also tells me of the duality of our historical dilemma. As Gunnar Myrdal put it in 1944, the *American dilemma* was created by the coexistence of the American liberal ideals of freedom and the miserable, oppressive situation of Black people. My grandfather was a slave – saying that aloud is chilling and gives resonance to a past that is dishonored by those who proclaim its irrelevance or its demise as a factor in contemporary life. This past is a blight on an American narrative of freedom and justice for all, and I, as a Black man in America, am also blighted by it. I knew that despite my athletic and academic accomplishments, and my decency and friendly nature, because I was Black, I would have to challenge, surmount, or circumvent limits. But, in my mind, and with directed energy from my grandfather beyond, I would overcome any obstacle placed in my path. His dreams turned out to be my destiny.

My Career in Social Psychology: Beginnings

Back to Oberlin. I loved working in the rat labs, raising, shocking, testing, and sacrificing them. But it was clear that was not a place I wanted to go. With a nod from Norm Henderson, I was hired by the Franklin Institute Research Laboratories (FIRL) in Philadelphia as a human factors researcher, assisting in a study of personality characteristics of highly skilled air traffic controllers. Again, it was interesting, and I learned a lot about research methods and statistical analysis and scientific writing. Again, this was not my path. I enrolled in a Master's program at Temple University while working for FIRL and, under the guidance of Tom Shipley, studied inhabitants of skid row to determine what personal characteristics best predicted their likelihood of returning to a more conventional place in society. We used a battery of personality tests and created profiles that we linked to various outcomes. Again, it was fun, and I was "doing psychology," but it did not define a path for me.

Inspiration for My Academic Journey

In 1965, I read an article in the *New York Times* magazine in which Dr. Kenneth Clark reported on his work in Harlem – known as HARYOU (Harlem Youth Opportunities

Unlimited). This work addressed educational reform including recruiting educational experts to reorganize Harlem schools, providing preschool programs and after-school remedial education, and employment programs for dropouts. President Lyndon Johnson allocated $110 million to implement many of the recommendations from Dr. Clark's work.

His work inspired me. I thought to myself, I want to get a PhD so I can play a role in addressing the needs of Black people specifically, and American society more generally. I was a classmate of Clark's daughter, Kate, at Oberlin, and was quite familiar with the famous "doll studies" he conducted with his wife Mamie Phipps Clark (e.g., see Clark & Clark, 1939). Their results were cited by the US Supreme Court in the 1954 *Brown* decision as an argument for why the "separate but equal" doctrine of *Plessy v. Ferguson* was wrong, and that legalized racial segregation was *inherently* unequal. Interpretation of the meaning of their research for the psyches of Black children continues to fuel debate, but its role in providing a rationale to overturn *Plessy* is undeniable.

So, in 1965, I applied to graduate schools with strong social psychology programs and after some interesting misadventures, I began my professional journey in 1966 at Yale University. As a coda to this overture, I (with Tom Pettigrew) wrote the obituary for Dr. Clark for the *American Psychologist* when he passed away in 2005.

Yale Years: Psychologist in Training

I arrived on the campus of Yale University in 1966 – the first ever Black graduate student in the psychology department – accompanied by my wife Olaive and our three-year-old daughter Shelly.

I entered Yale to *become* Ken Clark! However, my training as an *experimental* social psychologist, presented a challenge. I learned early on that, according to some of my colleagues, experimental social psychologists were not interested in *people*, only in *variables*! And the kicker – race was *not* considered an "experimental" variable! How could I become Dr. Clark in this environment of raceless variables? So, I adapted and applied my training in social cognition to the analysis of the cognitive factors that made things funny. This led to a dissertation on humor and, along the way, a meeting with Alan Funt of *Candid Camera*, a guest appearance on *What's My Line*, and a chance to have the former senator Al Franken as one of my students. It also enabled me to obtain a prestigious Guggenheim Fellowship to study humor in Trinidad. My Trinidadian experience played a significant role in my thinking about Black culture and sources of resilience.

Harvard Years: Beginning a Social Psychology Career

I got my first academic job because of affirmative action. In the late 1960s, Harvard's affirmative action approach was to call Yale and ask if their lone Black graduate student would be interested in coming to teach at Harvard. My advisor, Bob Abelson, asked me if I'd be interested, and I said noncommittally and uncertainly, "sure!" The result was that we (including an embryonic energy who would become our second daughter Nashe) arrived at Harvard in the winter of 1970 to begin my academic career.

Social psychology was in transition from hot (dissonance theory) to cold (attribution theory), from overt race prejudice to more subtle, symbolic, and aversive forms. I experienced this transition during my Yale years, but now at Harvard, I wanted to get back on my journey to *become* Ken Clark. My teaching reflected this effort. I created a course called "Social Psychology of Afro-American History" in which I sought to make my background in social cognition applicable to Black experiences. I distrusted some of the data science on Black psyches – the so-called self-hate thesis, as well as the flawed understanding of motivation from a Black experiential context. So, I taught "Black Lives" in which I used autobiographies of a variety of Black people to show a range of experiences, approaches to coping with racial adversity, and the foundation for individual and collective advancement and success. Finally, I co-taught a course with my colleague, social anthropologist Claudia Mitchell Kernan in which we combined our social psychology and anthropology perspectives to understanding Black life and culture. The point here is that in many ways, I invented my approach to social psychology to afford me the opportunity to shape my work from a Black and personal point of view.

A Career-Defining Moment: Prejudice and Racism

I arrived at Harvard with a contract to write a book about prejudice that jump-started my intellectual and academic life. My other Yale advisor, Chuck Kiesler, was editor of a social psychology book series and invited me to write this book. That book became *Prejudice and Racism* which was published in 1972 and launched my career.

When I began writing this book in June of 1970, I was trying to understand the 1960s. The Kerner commission had concluded that White racism was responsible for the urban riots. Stokely Carmichael and Charles Hamilton had introduced the notion of "institutional racism." The Civil and Voting Rights Acts had passed and Affirmative Action was launched as a corrective for the historical wrongdoing in American history. The Immigration Act of 1965 had ended racial and national quotas, ushering in what Richard Frey (2014) calls a *diversity explosion* which, in his analysis, was remaking America. By the end of the decade, however, John and Bobby Kennedy, Malcolm X, Martin Luther King, and Medgar Evers were gone, assassinated for bending the arc of the moral universe toward justice? The Black Panther party was created to protect Black people in Oakland – resistance and resilience continued to define the struggle for civil and human rights.

So, I thought, prejudice is an affliction of individuals – negative beliefs about groups that are generalized to individuals in these group. There was no doubt that racial prejudice was really a blight on the rights and freedoms of Black people, but for me, it represented an incomplete account of oppression and marginalization that had persisted for four centuries and continued to actively bend the arc of the moral universe *away* from justice.

Institutional racism perpetuates oppression, discrimination, and the cumulative consequences of marginalization, disadvantage, and inequality. This dynamic was seeded by our racist history. It not only *informed* institutional structures, practices, and policies, it was their *raison d'être*. Importantly, institutional racism was not limited to the intentional actions of individual racists to create racist outcomes, but institutions could do it by themselves as an everyday *standard of practice*! We now use terms like "systemic racism" but that was the idea I was proposing in the 1972 edition of *Prejudice and Racism*. In my view, institutional racism, whether *de facto* or *de jure*, was driven by a culture founded simultaneously on principles of freedom and acts of oppression. This duality was noted by de Tocqueville and formalized by Gunnar Myrdal (1944) as the *American dilemma*.

For me, culture was the overarching driver of institutional racism, and responsible for prejudice and racism of individuals. It wasn't until twenty-five years later in the second edition of *Prejudice and Racism* that I formalized this nexus as shown in Figure 22.1. This figure captures what I believe to be the foundation of systematic racism and its building blocks.

Kroeber and Kluckhohn (1952, p. 86) define culture as follows:

Culture consists of patterned ways of thinking, feeling and creating, acquired and transmitted mainly by symbols, constituting the distinctive achievements of human groups, including their embodiments in artifacts; the essential core of culture consists of traditional (i.e., historically derived and selected) ideas and especially their attached values. Culture systems may ... be considered products of action, [or] as conditioning elements of future actions.

The divide we are experiencing is sewn into the fabric of this nation – divergent histories beget divergent perceptions, symbols, values, beliefs – buildings, monuments, flags, role of the Supreme Court. Cultural narratives supply values that become rationales for acts of aggression, marginalization, neglect, protest, resistance, activism.

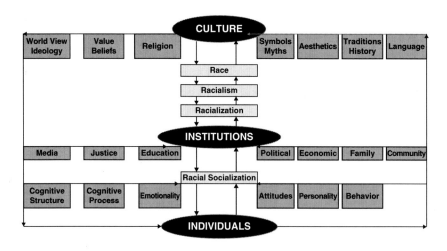

Figure 22.1 Cultural building blocks of institutional racism
Source: Jones (1997).

I do not believe racism will ever disappear, it cannot. It is woven into the fabric of our society and our psyches. And as cultural psychologists tell us, "culture and psyche make each other up!" We can, though, resist it, mitigate its pernicious effects, and cope with it by developing creative ways to achieve goals and express our humanity despite it. In so doing, we create a new version of our culture that moves us closer to that more perfect union.

Resistance and Resilience

Racism spawns resistance. It also necessitates resilience. I was interested in how Black people could survive our history, and continue to insinuate ourselves in a society which, at minimum, is ambivalent about our merit and right to belong, and at maximum, tries to keep us down and out. So, I began developing psychological ideas about resistance to oppression and factors that promoted resilience – the ability to endure and find agency in circumstances that seemed bleak if not hopeless. The foundation for these adaptive, coping mechanisms could be found in elements of African culture, transformed over time by the oppressive experiences in America. These searches led me to the Universal Context of Racism (UCR) and a psychology of resilience and agency that could be extracted from perspectives on Time, Rhythm, Improvisation, Orality and Spirituality – TRIOS (Jones, 2003).

UCR makes the simple assumption that in a society where racism is so widely practiced and impacts the lives of so many people, it is a universally accessible and available explanation for a Black person's negative experiences. Racism is not *always* an explanation for negative experiences, but it always *could* be the explanation – hence the universality. What is complicated is determining when racism is or is not a factor, and what one should do about it. Our research identified three facets of the UCR: **Salience** – the psychological attention paid to and explanations of potential occurrences of racism; **Transcendence** – the personal belief that one could achieve one's goals despite the obstacles posed by racism; and **Racelessness** – the motivated attempt to ignore race as a factor in one's life. Our research showed that UCR-Salience was associated with greater anxiety and depression, lower self-esteem, and reports of more frequent racial hassles. Paying close attention to race and the possibilities of racism can bring with them significant psychological costs.

TRIOS emerged from my research on racial differences in sports, travels, and research in Trinidad, and examination of anthropological, historical, and cultural writings on Africa and the diaspora. TRIOS signals psychologically meaningful characteristics that have important, interconnected influences on behavior. The confluence of these psychological traits enables resilience based in *Time*, the capacity to live in and benefit from the present, and an ability to use the past as a guide for the future; the *Rhythmic* capacity to flow with the context and circumstance, connect internal and external rhythms to maximize interactions with others around you and promote setting and reaching personal and collective goals; *Improvisation*, a means of controlling one's circumstances in contexts that are uncertain, and potentially dangerous. Improvisation gives rise to self-confidence and self-expression that enhances one's personal since of agency. *Orality* provides a means to forge strong bonds with similar others. Coded communication is often nonverbally delivered, significant information, knowledge, and values are delivered over time and space, and barriers are erected that establish protective boundaries that mitigate incursion of outsiders and potential harm-doers. Humor, language, and gestures all operate to strengthen ties with others for communal cohesion and action. *Spirituality* situates a person in a broader context in which power and control are shared with a spirit world that is intimately connected to a person's daily life. This connection permits a level of calmness and peace that is both self-protective and exalting of the personal spirit.

Our research shows that intersection of these TRIOS facets is associated with lowered anxiety and depression, and higher levels of self-esteem, and are unrelated to self-reported experiences of racial hassles. The resistance/resilience formula merges UCR and TRIOS where UCR is a vigilance system, prone to resistance and self-protection. TRIOS is an adaptation system, providing the qualities that enable one to move through a life of marginalization and discrimination with strength, confidence, and a belief in one's ability to set, pursue, and reach goals that define one's purpose and humanity.

Where Is the Field Now and Where Is It Going? From Prejudice to Systemic Racism

From my perspective the most important evolution in the study of race since I began my work in 1970 is theorizing about and examining the interconnectedness and reciprocal influences of individuals, institutions, and cultures. These interconnections are recognized as a means of transmitting racial disadvantage over time, with minimal intentional direction from individuals who may or not be prejudiced – *systemic racism* has been "discovered."

A *PsycINFO* search of publications from 1972 to the present that are classified broadly as social psychology ("Social Perception & Cognition," "Social Processes & Social Issues," "Social Structure & Organization," "Social Psychology") returns 156 entries of the term" systemic racism" appearing anywhere in the publication. The entries consisted of 63 journal articles, 17 books, and 74 dissertations. Evidence of a recent focus on systemic racism is demonstrated by the distribution of the publications – 0 between 1972 and 1992; 7 between 1992 and 2006; and 149 since 2006, a full 95 percent! If we think of dissertations as a pipeline of theorizing and research on systemic racism, it is reasonable to expect that the trajectory from the last fifteen years will continue upward.

I see four challenges to social psychological work on systemic racism. First, the individual as the unit of analysis complicates our ability to examine systemic influences. Nevertheless, finding creative ways to make connections across levels of analysis and teasing out causal relationships in a multidimensional space has emerged as a necessary and vital direction for social psychology.

A second challenge is recognizing that contemporary conflicts and inequalities are embedded in events, decisions, and experiences from the past. Further, that the salience of these events and awareness and reactions to them alter their meaning across racial groups. Recent studies have shown how differing views about historical "facts" of racial experiences shape contemporary attitudes and beliefs about racial discrimination. Understanding racial history is critical to understanding how people think and act, and how institutions perpetuate racial inequities.

A third challenge is understanding the reciprocal influence of experiences of marginalization and privilege and how they foster divergent perceptions of the state of things and their meaning. For example, White people believe that Blacks *used* to be more discriminated against than Whites were. But they now believe that they are *more* discriminated against than Blacks are. Black people feel entitled to *reparations*, and that White people have been privileged as a result of their power and Whiteness for centuries. Black people thus feel entitled (I call it *psychological reparations*) by this persistent unfairness and White people feel resentment at the prospects of losing their privilege to what they consider to be underserving "others." Focusing on the divergences in attitudes and beliefs, values and expectations across racial groups is a challenge that must be met. Again, recent research is taking up some of these issues.

Fourth, examining the reciprocal connections between targets and perpetrators, "privileged" and "underserved," Us and Them requires a transactional analysis to properly examine the simultaneity of cross-racial interactions and their reciprocal consequences. Pluralistic ignorance is one example of this approach. Intergroup interaction is a staple of social psychological approaches to race relations and will continue to be in a multidimensional approach to racism.

An important aspect of this reciprocal analysis is to focus attention on the ways in which people who are targeted by racial animus, indifference, or unfairness adapt and cope with their circumstances. How they respond to these circumstances signals resilience that disrupts the poor circumstances leading to poor outcomes expectation. My work with the UCR and TRIOS approaches to self-protection and self-enhancement is an attempt to identify sources of psychological and cultural capital.

If I Were to Give Advice to Future Generations ...

As I look back on fifty years of writing about race and racism, I see how the relative scientific innocence I brought to writing the first edition of *Prejudice and Racism* enabled me to think freely and draw heavily on my own and friends' experiences in laying out the issues I felt needed to be addressed (the second edition in 1997 was a much different story; by then I knew a lot, the field had grown exponentially, and while I used the same basic analytical narrative and structure, the details and examples were much more voluminous and current). I gathered the existing scholarship across disciplines to assist in my analysis and knew that the substantive issues resonated with my lived experiences and with those of other Black people.

My advice to the pipeline of researchers interested in understanding and disrupting systemic racism is to trust yourself to employ the methods and approaches of social psychology to assist you in reaching your professional career goals. The problems are there but their essence or means of redress are not always what the field has defined them to be. Use your own observations, intuitions, experiences, and "due diligence" to ferret out the important considerations and put them under your analytic microscope. I advise being flexible, creative, courageous, and self-confident enough to let your training help to get you where you want to go, not necessarily where others have been and are going.

The beauty of social psychology is that virtually no problem is beyond its purview, and the methods we use to study them are constrained only by imagination, dedication, and a desire to understand and make better the world in which we live. That is a noble calling which I invite future generations to sign up for.

Suggested Reading

Brown v. Board of Education of Topeka, 347 U.S. 483 (1954).

Clark, K. B., & Clark, M. K. (1939). The development of consciousness of self and the emergence of racial identification in Negro preschool children. *Journal of Social Psychology, 10*, 591–599.

Frey, R. (2014). *Diversity Explosion: How New Racial Demographics Are Remaking America*. Washington, DC: Brookings Institution Press.

Jones, J. M. (1972). *Prejudice and Racism*. Reading, MA: Addison-Wesley.

(1997). *Prejudice and Racism*. Second edition. New York: McGraw-Hill.

(2003). TRIOS: A psychological theory of the African legacy in American culture. *Journal of Social Issues, 59*, 217–242.

Jones, J. M., Dovidio, J. E., & Vietze, D. L. (2014). *The Psychology of diversity: Beyond prejudice and racism*. Chicester, UK: Wiley-Blackwell.

Jones, J. M., & Pettigrew, T. F. (2005). Kenneth B. Clark (1914–2005). *American Psychologist, 60*, 649–651.

Kroeber, A. L., & Kluckhohn, C. (1952). Culture: A critical review of concepts and definitions. *Papers. Peabody Museum of Archaeology & Ethnology, Harvard University, 47*, 223.

Myrdal, G. (1944). *An American Dilemma: The Negro Problem and Modern Democracy*. New York: Harper & Row.

23   A Career in Ten Episodes

Claude Steele

1

In the first lecture in my first psychology class at Hiram College in Hiram, Ohio, the professor, James Marcia – then a clinical psychology graduate student at The Ohio State University and now a well-known psychologist of identity development – said that psychology was not the science of the mind, but the science of behavior. And since behavior was seen to be largely under the control of reinforcement contingencies and incentives, I took hope from this statement: If you could just arrange the incentives of your life artfully enough you could be, or achieve, just about anything you wanted to.

It was spring, 1964. I was 18, an African-American kid from a working-class black town off the south side of Chicago. I was one of only eight African-Americans on the Hiram campus – part of an early wave of blacks integrating in American higher education. I was looking for hope. And that was a charm of the behaviorism of that day. B. F. Skinner was its guru. His book *Beyond Freedom and Dignity* broadly disseminated this view. Reputedly he'd raised his children – at least part of the time – in a "Skinner Box" that could deliver the right incentives at the right time to elicit the most felicitous pattern of development. Of course, this seemed cold, mechanistic. But to my ears at the time – and to those of many others – it seemed like psychology was on to something empowering, hopeful. I didn't get that feeling in my other courses.

2

Ralph Cebulla was the most engaging professor of my time at Hiram. Red-haired, a bit freckled, a fairly big man who loved ideas. He lectured with an engrossing intensity. And his lectures on this new field of social psychology were riveting. The textbook in the course was Roger Brown's *Social Psychology*. It read like a good novel. And like novels, the grist of this science was not the molecule or the economy or outer space, but everyday life. Ralph's gift was to make that connection vivid. This was at the height of the Civil Rights movement. College students everywhere were joining

Claude Steele, Stanford University, USA.

Freedom Rides to desegregate public facilities in the South and going to Mississippi to register black voters. We read sections from Gordon Allport's *The Nature of Prejudice*, from James Baldwin's *Notes of a Native Son*. We talked about Kenneth and Mamie Clark's doll studies. I was enthralled ... with a field no more than twenty years old at the time. I applied to graduate school, something I'd never thought of for myself. When I came to college and people asked what career I wanted, to appear serious, I'd say dentistry. My childhood dentist was named Claude. Apparently, for me at the time, that's what passed for career planning. But after Ralph's course, I knew what I wanted to do.

3

Hiram ignited my interest in social psychology, but offered little research experience. It was through good fortune that I eked my way into the newly redesigned graduate program in social psychology at The Ohio State University in 1967, just as its new faculty – Tim Brock, Tony Greenwald, Tom Ostrom, and soon to follow, Bibb Latane – had arrived. I'm not sure this brilliant young faculty felt blessed by the talents of us incoming graduate students. But they had a growth mindset. With rigorous training, they seemed to believe they could make us solid soldiers of this new science. Gone were the heady discussions about psychology and social change I'd had at Hiram. This was Midwestern, hard-nosed science training. A statistics minor was required. The PhD qualifying exam – comprising multiple eight- and four-hour sit-down sections, take home papers, and an oral exam – went on for weeks.

I worked with Tom Ostrom testing predictions from the Reference Scale Theory of Attitude Change that he had developed with his advisor, Harry Upshaw, at the University of North Carolina. In multiple ways, we tested the theory's main prediction: that you could change a person's position on an issue by changing the reference scale they used to locate how extreme the position was. For example, you might make people more favorable toward Lyndon Johnson's Poverty Program if you framed the issue with reference scale anchors that made that program seem normative, not extreme (Steele & Ostrom, 1974).

I liked this research. But these were heady times. In my first year of graduate school, I got drafted to fight in Vietnam. In another miracle of good fortune, I eventually got out of that through a medical deferment. But Martin Luther King and Bobby Kennedy got assassinated within months of each other in my second year. I felt an obligation to be doing something more contributive than graduate school – helping with voter registration in the South perhaps. Tom sympathized. But somehow, against my unpreparedness, against cultural and class differences between me – a Chicago South Sider – and the program, against the trauma and distraction of the Vietnam War, against a sense of intimidation (stereotype threat) I felt in the program, and a sense of obligation that I should contribute somewhere else, *Tom led me to identify with the science of social psychology*. How he did that, how he built trust across our identity divides, would become, many years later, a research focus of mine and my students. His practices would become testable hypotheses.

4

I have a distinct memory of the drive from Columbus to Salt Lake City in the late summer of 1971 to take my first academic job at the University of Utah. Driving slowly across the endless Midwestern plains (the U-Haul I drove had a governor that limited its speed to 45mph) with my new PhD in hand, with my wife awaiting me in Salt Lake having flown ahead because she was too far pregnant to join me in the truck, with the realization that I was on a better path than my origins gave me the right to expect, a certain image kept coming to mind – of the kids I'd gone to elementary school with; boys trying to be cool or hit a ball farther than anyone else; girls who could run faster than the boys, pretty faces, dark beautiful skin, with wood matchsticks in their ear lobes to prepare for the gold studs they'd get for Christmas. Innocent, we were. Relatively unknowing of the societal devaluation that awaited us. We had inklings of course. Not being allowed to try on clothes in department stores. Being allowed to swim in public pools only on Wednesday afternoons, allowed in the roller rink only on Thursday nights. Strict housing, school, and relationship segregation. We had each other. But what would happen when we engaged the larger society, the economy, the Big Chill of adolescence and adult life? How does one receive and manage the full weight of one's lower position in the social order? I came to a certainty: that somehow this would be a focus of my research life. There was just one problem. I had no idea how to do that.

I eventually got to Salt Lake. My daughter was born five days later. I began teaching in a friendly department. The closest research I could come up with that fit my cross-country vision, was a series of telephone studies testing whether name-calling – a devaluation – would provoke behaviors aimed at refuting the name, in this case, compliance with a help request. Yes, it did, the study found. But it also found something interesting that, years later, would inform my research on self-affirmation processes: being seen negatively based on one's identity (in this case residency in a neighborhood of Salt Lake) led to image-restoring actions even when the actions, while affirming overall self-regard, did nothing to refute the provoking name. The note-to-self: After a devaluation, it's general self-regard, not psychological consistency that people are after – giving us great flexibility in how we maintain self-regard.

I was buoyed by these results and their later publication in *JPSP* (Steele, 1975), but not by the racial climate in Salt Lake City at the time. This was when the Mormon church, in this majority Mormon city, wouldn't grant full membership to African-Americans. We faced housing discrimination in our first days in town. Blessedly, in 1973, the University of Washington made a job offer. My wife and I left for Seattle with a great sense of gratitude. It would be our home, and where I would go through the academic ranks over the next fourteen years.

I'd like to report that things went smoothly in those early Seattle years. We loved our new city. I got some research out. I enjoyed teaching. But under tenure pressure, my focus scattered. My cross-country research vision got back benched. Racial experience was a completely marginal topic in social psychology at the time, as was gendered experience. I got drawn into salient topics of the day – attribution processes, the effectiveness of high-fear messages in deterring alcohol abuse. Tom Ostrom and I published our Reference Scale research. Gratefully though, I got tenure – buoyed by good teaching ratings and having gotten a large grant on alcohol messaging. A huge relief – let there be no doubt. Still, I felt unfocused, without a clear research identity in the field.

5

Then I figured something out. Without thinking too much, I had assumed that a researcher was supposed to have an insightful idea about a psychological issue – usually one getting attention in the literature – operationalize that idea, and then test it. If the study supported the idea, good, you'd made your point. If the research didn't support the idea, then ... move on to a better idea. How one selects research ideas, or moves from one experiment to the next isn't codified in the field. I'd fallen into an approach that, as I said, scattered my focus.

Preparing for class one day, I read an article by Stanley Schachter and others (1977) on the nature of nicotine addiction. I noticed something. They didn't start with an idea or theory. He started with a question, a problem, and then designed research to answer the question. For example, does stress cause smoking? Well ... his thinking went, let's put smokers under stress in the lab (e.g., a near painful level of noise) and see if they smoke more. Simple. If they don't smoke more under stress, then perhaps stress doesn't cause smoking. You'd probably want to try other operationalizations before settling on that conclusion. But right away, you'd learned something, and gotten a follow-up question. If they did smoke more under stress, you'd also learned something. You'd probably then want to see what mediated the effect, and eventually whether the effect is situationally moderated, and if so, what those moderators are, and so on.

This approach positions the researcher not as a "knower," invested in a particular insight, but as a "seeker," using research to learn about a phenomenon or process. Theory is *deduced* from the unfolding revelations of the research itself. And the importance of the research is not carried by the importance of a preordained idea, but by the importance of the question it addresses. The pressure in this approach is simply to design research that gives you non-trivial, non-biased results. Then you can be fairly sure you'll learn something that carries the process forward. With this approach, my research life changed. It became more secure, meaningful, fun. And, if I dare say so, it enabled the ideas I eventually published to be far more interesting than the ideas I'd had before the research began.

6

One such question: How does drinking alcohol become so reinforcing that people often get addicted to it despite its being, physiologically, a depressant? Alan Marlatt, a friend and colleague who happened to be a leading addictive behaviors researcher, made me aware of this question. Once you have an interesting question, the kind of thinking you do, in my experience, is a lot like figuring out where you lost your keys. You generate hypotheses and test them against available facts. And the facts can come from anywhere – relevant research literatures for sure, but also from government and institutional statistics, qualitative accounts, observations of your own and others' behavior, lab group discussions, newspapers, etc.

So off we went, and by "we" I mean Lillian Southwick Bensley, Robert Josephs, and Barbara Critchlow – graduate students at the time, and Mahzarin Banaji – then a postdoc. As if looking for keys, we came up with questions. Maybe drinking alcohol is reinforcing because it lifts mood. No. As I said, it's a depressant. Well, maybe it's alcohol's impairment of thinking, the myopia it causes – the inability when intoxicated to see the larger significance of things, or how actions square with moral standards, or the consequences of one's actions, etc. – that rewards drinking. But when people drink alone, or with nothing to do, they can wind up crying in their beer. With nothing to distract them, the myopia of alcohol intoxication focuses people in on their troubles, making it harder for them to get perspective – a problem not uncommon among the elderly living alone. No, the keys aren't there either. Well then maybe it's the myopia plus distraction that lifts affect and makes drinking reinforcing by freezing one's worries out of consciousness. The experiments we did testing this question hit the mark. This is where the keys were. It's the myopia plus distraction that makes drinking alcohol reinforcing enough to launch one on a path to addiction (e.g., Steele & Josephs, 1990).

7

During these same years, another question presented itself – one more theoretical. Do we humans really have the need for psychological consistency that so many social psychology theories, most prominently cognitive dissonance theory, say we have? Having lectured on these theories for years, this question nagged me. Yes, often we rationalize our self-inconsistencies – suggesting a need for psychological consistency. But sometimes we don't. I've known smokers, for example, who know fully the inconsistency between smoking and its health risk, but long ago stopped rationalizing it. A need for consistency didn't seem to fully explain the motivation behind rationalization. But if not a need for consistency, then what? Where are the keys? Elliot Aronson, a student of dissonance theory's founder, Leon Festinger, had already shown that it was *self*-inconsistencies, not just any inconsistent cognitions, that most reliably provoked rationalization. Tom Liu, a graduate student at the time, and I thought about all of this and came to a simple proposal: Rationalizations that were apparently consistency-restoring were actually aimed at affirming an overall perception of oneself as good and competent. It was the threat to this perception, not a motivation for consistency per se, that drove rationalization. If we were correct, then allowing people to affirm their overall moral and adaptive adequacy after an inconsistency would preempt their need to rationalize it. We tested this idea in several dissonance and attribution experimental paradigms. The results were consistent: Self-affirming experiences reduced people's rationalization of their inconsistencies even though the affirmation did nothing to resolve the provoking inconsistencies per se (Steele & Liu, 1983). Remember the name-calling experiment. People sought affirmation of their broader self-image, not consistency per se. Derived from this research I was able to develop a broader theory of self-affirmation, one that supplanted a need for psychological consistency with a need to perceive the self as morally and adaptively adequate as the chief motive underlying human rationalization and defensiveness more generally (Steele, 1988).

I am proud of the insight this work brought to light. But I am equally proud of the extensions of that insight into real-life, practical areas. For example, would a self-affirmation help people be more accepting of self-threatening but important information such as health warnings, critical career feedback, or mask mandates? Would it increase compliance with health recommendations? Could it be used to help students contending with negative stereotypes about their abilities in school? Research exploring the real-world implications of self-affirmation theory by former students and new colleagues – Geoff Cohen, David Sherman, Julio Garcia, Valerie Purdie-Greenway, Kevin Binning, Peter Harris, Greg Walton, David Creswell – is research about which I am especially proud and gratified. It transformed research of primarily theoretical significance into research of practical significance – an accomplishment I could hardly have imagined as this research began (e.g., Cohen & Sherman, 2014; Easterbrook et al., 2021; Sherman & Cohen, 2006).

8

In 1987, I moved from the University of Washington to the University of Michigan where yet another question presented itself, one closer to my cross-country research vision. At the first meeting of a university committee on minority student experience, I saw an intriguing graph: At each level of entering SAT score for Michigan students, black students got lower subsequent grades at Michigan than other students at the *same* SAT level. In the psychometric literature this is known as "underperformance" (UP). Before seeing these data, I thought students with the same preparation for college would get roughly the same grades in college. Yet, something in the experience of black students was causing them to "underperform." We soon found the same thing happened to women in advanced STEM courses at Michigan; they got lower grades in these courses than men with the same SATs. Hmmm ... Then we found these patterns weren't just at Michigan. They were a national pattern, long known about in the psychometric literature. The consequences of underperformance can be tragic – in its impact on mental health, career choice, even future income.

But it also struck me as an especially interesting social psychological problem – a view that many lunches with Dick Nisbett further reinforced for me. Dick, as this readership knows, is among our field's most distinguished psychologists ever. I trusted his judgment; these underperformances were important to understand, and social psychology might have the tools to do it. More generally, the Michigan social psychology program of this era was incredibly adventurous – with, for example, Hazel Markus, Shinobu Kitayama, and again, Dick Nisbett – incubating a new look at cultural psychology. I felt licensed to take up a new problem. With the move from Washington to Michigan, I'd already backed off a bit from alcohol research. And it faded to the background even more as I obsessed over this new question: What on earth was causing these mysterious patterns of underperformance throughout American higher education?

So, joined by especially Steve Spencer, a new graduate student, also by Robert Josephs, a student who had come with me from Washington, and not much later, Josh Aronson who would vigorously join in when I moved to Stanford in 1991, we were off looking for lost keys – with regular kibbitzing from Dick. We looked everywhere – reading broadly in and out of the field, digging into administrative data, talking to test makers, to academic advisors, to colleagues, to students themselves and conducting exploratory experiments. Eventually, two or three years along, in an experiment that would become part of Steve Spencer's dissertation, we found something: that women strongly identified with math underperformed in relation to equally skilled men on a truly difficult math test – replicating in the lab the standard underperformance effect – but not when we made the stereotype about women's math ability irrelevant to the test: "You may have heard that women don't do as well as men on difficult standardized math tests, but that's not true for the test you are taking today. It's a test on which women always do as well as men." With the threat of being judged stereotypically removed in this way, their performance went up to match that of equally skilled men. Underperformance gone. Josh and I found similar results in a series of experiments examining the effects of stereotype threat on African-Americans' performance on a difficult section of the GRE verbal test. Could stereotype threat (ST) be a factor in group underperformances? These early experiments suggested the possibility and launched a cottage industry of studies testing stereotype threat effects in many different identity groups, in relation to different stereotypes, and in relation to different types of performance (from academic to athletic performances). Stereotype threat effects became among the most conceptually replicated phenomena in the field.

Stereotype threat theory (e.g., Steele, 1997; Steele & Aronson, 1995) specifies the conditions under which this threat is most likely to impair performance, that is, the factors that moderate its effect. Most fundamentally, stereotype threat is a *situational predicament* in which (1) you are in a situation or doing something for which a negative stereotype about one of your social identities is relevant, (2) you are strongly invested in the performance, and (3) the task you are performing is sufficiently difficult, capacity-consuming, and frustrating as to make you feel at risk of confirming the stereotype. When these conditions are met, you know you could be reduced to a stereotype in an area you care about – a prospect that can be upsetting enough to interfere with performance. ST is not a personal trait like, say neuroticism, that goes with you, in some degree or another, from situation to situation. It is a situational predicament or pressure *that does not exist when any one of the elements of the predicament are not present, but that can have big, even life-shaping effects when those elements are present, especially when they are persistently present in a domain of life that is important to the person.* Research supporting this conception came from a number of Stanford students and colleagues I was blessed to work with during this period: Mary Murphy, Geoff Cohen, Valerie Purdie-Greenway, David Sherman, Valerie Taylor-Jones, Paul Davies, Dian Quinn, David Nussbaum, Sapna Cheryan, Toni Schmader, Michael Inzlicht, Taceta Thomas, Phillip Goff, Kristen Stoutemeyer, Kelli Keough, Joseph Brown, and Bonnie Brown.

By this time there have been multiple meta-analyses of ST effects on performance. In trying to get an estimate of its overall effect in particular areas of the ST literature, these analyses generally average over all condition comparisons in which a given stereotype could have an effect. This often includes contrasts in which one or more of the elements of the ST predicament are not present – where the participants are not invested in the performance, or where the performance is not difficult enough to be frustrating, or when the research was done in a society, era of time, or part of the population for which the stereotype is weak or absent. These are contrasts, of course, in which no ST effect is predicted. Yet even including these contrasts, these meta-analyses show meaningful overall ST effects that range from $d = .17$ to $d = .52$ (e.g., Spencer et al., 2016). I like to be cautious; whereas recent meta-analyses rule out questionable research practices as contributing to ST effects, some publication bias is almost inevitable (better done studies are more likely to find an effect when one is there *and* be more likely to be published) and can push effect sizes upwards – not nearly enough to explain away ST effects in this broad literature, but perhaps enough to inflate estimates in a subarea. Most importantly, *the effect sizes are substantially larger for contrasts in which the elements of the ST predicament are present.* Similarly, as ST theory has stressed, replication is most expected when the conditions of the ST predicament are met.

An especially pertinent view of ST's effect on performance – its strength as well as how it plays out in real-life schooling contexts over substantial periods of time – comes from research testing how much real school performance improves when an intervention relieves ST (research led by former students and colleagues such as Greg Walton, Mary Murphy, Geoff Cohen, David Yeager, and others mentioned above). A recent meta-analysis combing 251 effect sizes from 181 experiments yielded an overall effect size of $d = .44$ (Lui et al., 2021) for these interventions. Especially for students whose intellectual abilities are negatively stereotyped in our society – based on their race, income level, gender, ethnicity, etc. – these interventions can significantly improve their school performance. This research expands our understanding of some of the nation's most tenacious educational and social challenges and is developing a suite of tactics to address them. Recalling images from that long ago cross-country drive, these findings are especially heartening.

9

More recently, as part of a book project, I am focused on a different question: how to make diversity work in the communities of our lives, schools, classrooms, institutions, corporations, etc. It's a question that came from my experience as a university administrator, particularly in two stints as a university provost in which I had significant responsibility for fostering an inclusive campus climate. In this project, I'm using the word "churn" to denote the anxiety we can all have over how our identity will play out in a diverse setting. Think of a young African-American man trying to succeed in a corporation. He knows our society's history and the stereotypes of his group that come down from that history. He could worry that, in this important setting, he'd be seen stereotypically – as less prepared for example – and not given the benefit of the doubt in critical decisions. He's in churn. As might be a white American in this same setting. He too knows the stereotypes of his group. And *in a diverse setting* he could worry that he'd be seen that way. One misstatement or one unfavorable decision about a black colleague, and he could be seen as "racist." He too is in churn. For both parties there's a tension between remembering and forgetting in diverse settings; between remembering how one's identity group can be seen and using that memory to interpret what is happening to them in the setting, versus forgetting how one's group can be seen and simply trusting the setting. Churn is a state of suspended trust – vigilance as to whether trust in the setting is a good idea. The argument I am developing is that *the identity and stereotype threats that cause churn make it difficult for us to* trust *each other in diverse settings . . . and that it is this fragility of trust that makes identity integration (diversity) difficult – uncomfortable, even polarizing.*

Importantly though, Churn has a kryptonite: Things that enable us to trust that we won't be stereotype-diminished – by this person, in this relationship, in this setting, in this institution – can reduce, even kill churn. The road to successful diversity, the argument goes, is paved as much by things that build trust in a setting as by things that mitigate prejudice itself – important as that is. Trust-building is an underappreciated tool in the pursuit of a successfully diverse society.

If this is so, there should be evidence that building trust across identity divides enables people of multiple identities to flourish in diverse settings. And there is. For members of ability-stereotyped groups, a host of tactics have been shown to foster trust – such as having their potential recognized early on; using cues that signal their belonging in the setting; giving people an opportunity to reveal their self-defining values so they know they are accepted and that their acceptance doesn't depend entirely on their assimilating to an imposed culture in the setting. Also, in organizations where people of different identities flourish more or less equally, there is often evidence of their having taken these tactics to scale – of having affirmed people's potential to succeed as they enter the organization, of their trusting people's promise in the organization before expecting them to trust the organization, of their giving concrete support to people tied to their real needs and in a way that reflects how valued they are in the organization, of their having clear markers of progress in the organization to diminish ambiguities that otherwise allow one to churn over how one's identity affects one's progress.

Research also shows how, *as individuals*, we can inspire trust across identity divides – much of which boils down to taking a learning/curiosity mindset toward identity differences. And there is the American tradition of the "beloved community," which embodies principles from our social psychological literature such as the unifying power of a superordinate identity – our shared human identity – and equal status contact between people of different identities.

Getting better at making diversity work is something I believe our field can help with. Trust-building joins our field's insights about mitigating prejudice. And it has a particular advantage; it's a game played on the ground: across the divides of difference, give trust to get trust; listen, listen again in a learning mindset; and then, show up with sustained, trusting support. This is a scalable blueprint. It can be hard work. But it's not magic. And anyone can do it. Tom Ostrom did.

10

A closing thought. I feel the forward movement of social psychology as a science depends less on the research hygiene preoccupations of the day as important as they are (e.g., preregistration, new statistics, the deterrence of data inflationary practices) than on fulfilling the field's founding Lewinian mission of helping society understand social psychological functioning and solve its social problems. That is certainly what drew me to the field, as I hope this chapter has conveyed. It's through trying to understand and solve real problems that I eventually got to meaningful theory – just as Lewin promised. It is what has made a life in this field, for me, always meaningful and at times exciting.

Research hygiene is a necessity, but not a sufficiency. When it becomes the dominant lens through which we see our science, it can make the field insular, weaker methodologically (as in replacing research that puts participants in real psychological situations with "as if" research that asks them to surmise what they would do in those situations), and disengaged from the concerns that are the field's *raison d'être*. Of course, this can be seen as a "senior" view. And I suspect that among the authors of this volume, I am a member of the chorus, not a solo voice. Still, it is probably time now to incorporate the wisdoms and best practices from this era of anxiety over research – we've had others in the past and will again – and get on with the vision that made most of us want to be social psychologists.

Suggested Reading

Cohen, G. L., & Sherman, D. K. (2014). The psychology of change: Self-affirmation and social psychological intervention. *Annual Review of Psychology, 65*, 333–371.

Easterbrook, M. J., Harris, P. R., & Sherman, D. K. (2021). Self-affirmation theory in educational contexts. *Journal of Social Issues, 77*(3), 683–701.

Lui, S., Lui, P., Wang, M., & Zhang, B. (2021). Effectiveness of stereotype threat interventions: A meta-analytic review. *Journal of Applied Psychology, 106*(6), 921–949.

Schachter, S., Silverstein, B., Kozlowski, L. T., Herman, C. P., & Liebling, B. (1977). Studies of the interaction of psychological and pharmacological determinants of smoking: IV. Effects of stress on cigarette smoking and urinary pH. *Journal of Experimental Psychology: General, 106*(1), 24–30.

Sherman, D. K., & Cohen, G. L. (2006). The psychology of self-defense: Self-affirmation. *Advances in Experimental Social Psychology, 38*, 183–242.

Spencer, S. J., Logel, C., & Davies, P. G. (2016). Stereotype threat. *Annual Review of Psychology, 67*, 415–437.

Steele, C. M. (1975). Name-calling and compliance. *Journal of Personality and Social Psychology, 31*(2), 361–370.

   (1988). The psychology of self-affirmation: Sustaining the integrity of the self. *Advances in Experimental Social Psychology, 21*, 261–302.

   (1997). A threat in the air: How stereotypes shape the intellectual identities and performance of women and African Americans. *American Psychologist, 52*, 613–629.

Steele, C. M., & Aronson, J. (1995). Stereotype threat and the intellectual test performance of African-Americans. *Journal of Personality and Social Psychology, 69*, 797–811.

Steele, C. M., & Josephs, R. A. (1990). Alcohol myopia: Its prized and dangerous effects. *American Psychologist, 45*(8), 921–933.

Steele, C. M., & Liu, T. J. (1983). Dissonance processes as self-affirmation. *Journal of Personality and Social Psychology, 45*(1), 5–19.

Steele, C. M., & Ostrom, T. M. (1974). Perspective mediated attitude change: When is indirect persuasion more effective than direct persuasion? *Journal of Personality and Social Psychology, 29*(6), 737–741.

24 Getting Lucky

Daniel Batson

Luck had a lot to do with my landing in social psychology – and landing where I did. As an undergraduate psychology major in the early 1960s with plans to become a Presbyterian minister, I took a course in social, although you probably wouldn't recognize it as such. It was closer to a course in personality. The textbook was titled *Social Psychology*, but it was written by a clinical psychologist who collaborated with sociologists, and the instructor's main research interest was Raymond Cattell's 16PF, a self-report measure of personality dimensions or factors. I learned virtually nothing about experimental social psychology. I don't think I knew such a discipline even existed. Blissfully ignorant, I headed to seminary.

A Lost Call

By the second year at Princeton Theological Seminary, it was clear that I wasn't cut out to be a minister. I had no right to inflict my idiosyncratic (and possibly heretical) religious views on other people, especially not on a Presbyterian congregation. Meanwhile, my interest in psychological research had grown. I did an independent study class on measures of religious attitudes. I read Festinger, Riecken, and Schachter's *When Prophecy Fails* (1956), and for my term paper in a psychology of religion class, I conducted and reported a study that used boys and girls in church youth groups to test the Festinger et al. claim that being confronted with belief-disconfirming information would lead religious believers to affirm their beliefs more strongly, not less. A report of that study later appeared in *JPSP*.

In my third and last year in the Bachelor of Divinity (i.e., ministerial training) program at the seminary, I applied to graduate programs in clinical psychology, thinking clinical would be a good way to combine my interests in psychological research and helping people in need. The three clinical programs to which I applied didn't share this thought. Each rejected my application. (Admittedly, I had a suspect record – three different undergraduate schools, some Bs on my transcripts, even one C, and the stigma of seminary.)

Daniel Batson, University of Kansas, USA.

Thinking Again

Having foolishly assumed a Plan B wasn't necessary (or was it now Plan C?), I found myself in a quandary until hitting on the rather bizarre idea of pursuing two different doctoral degrees over the next five years. One doctorate was to involve continuing work with Jim Loder, a faculty member at Princeton Seminary, reading broadly across disciplines – especially philosophy and psychology – to come up with an interdisciplinary analysis of religious creativity. In essence, it was to be a graduate-level liberal arts degree. The second doctorate, in psychology at Princeton University, was to provide an empirical research focus to test aspects of the religious-creativity analysis.

But there was a hitch. Neither the seminary nor the university allowed students to be enrolled in another institution at the same time, so I had to pursue the two degrees sequentially not simultaneously. The plan was to do the degree at the Seminary first, then the one at the university. Fortunately, Harry Schroeder, a social psychologist at the university who did research on cognitive complexity, was willing to serve on my doctoral committee at the seminary and to direct my readings and course work in psychology while I worked on the seminary degree. Harry also said he would be willing to supervise my doctoral work in psychology if/when the time came.

Three years later, while working on my dissertation at the seminary, I applied as planned to the graduate program in psychology and was accepted – only, I suspect, because Harry was willing to supervise an oddball applicant from the seminary. But then, another hitch. Between the spring when I was accepted and the fall when I matriculated, Harry left Princeton.

Finding a Home

The psychology faculty turned down my request to have Harry serve as an in-absentia advisor, which he was willing do. They said that if I was going to pursue a degree at the university, I needed to shelve my planned research on cognitive complexity of religious beliefs and find a new advisor. At that time (September 1970) there were three young social psychologists on the faculty, none of whom I knew anything about: Joel Cooper, John Darley, and Mark Zanna. I needed to find a mutual interest with at least one.

Luckily, that was easily done. Reading up on each, I encountered Joel's important experiments on dissonance, Mark's early work on attribution theory, and, most importantly, I read *The Unresponsive Bystander: Why Doesn't He Help?* by Latané and Darley, which had just been published. My immediate reaction to this little book was delight and amazement. Here was a scientific approach to studying ethical behavior. It had never occurred to me that experiments could be done to test hypotheses about helping others in need. I discovered that not only could such experiments be done, some had been done, and one of the people doing them was at Princeton.

Camelot?

In a 1994 retrospective review for *Contemporary Psychology*, I compared my first encounter with *The Unresponsive Bystander* to opening a window on Camelot:

Here is a world of maidens in distress, dragons of misinformation and misunderstanding, and social-psychological knights courageously wielding the powerful two-edged sword of conceptual analysis and hypothesis-testing experimentation to make matters right. It seems a world in which, truly, "by eight, the morning fog must disappear." (Batson, 1994, p. 941)

Along with the decision-tree analysis of cognitive steps necessary for a bystander to provide help and the well-known experiments on pluralistic ignorance and diffusion of responsibility, there were (a) studies that demonstrated the ambiguity and impotence of norms (e.g., by having people on the subway overhear a confederate give a lost soul wrong information about which direction the train was going, or by starting Frisbee games in waiting rooms at Grand Central Station only to have someone disapprove and then either stay or leave), (b) studies that replicated laboratory effects in the field (e.g., by staging thefts of a case of beer in a liquor store), and (c) studies that tested the effect of environmental familiarity on helping (e.g., by creating the same accident in LaGuardia Airport versus a local subway station).

Not only was I drawn to the substance of the conceptual analysis and reported research, I was also drawn to the style. I sensed that the design, running, and write-up of these experiments were accompanied by many sly smiles and even a little glee. Here were two research psychologists, their colleagues and students, having a lot of fun. Of course, they weren't just having fun; they were showing how ethical action could be studied scientifically using psychological theories and experimental methods. As Richard Burton intoned in the Broadway play: "I know it sounds a bit bizarre, but in Camelot, Camelot that's how conditions are."

Or a Golden Age?

Actually, I don't think Camelot is the most apt metaphor for my experience of *The Unresponsive Bystander* – nor, more generally, for my experience of experimental social psychology in the late 1960s and 1970s. Even better, especially in retrospect, is to call it a Golden Age.

Art historian Kenneth Clark, in his classic TV series *Civilisation*, mused from time to time on what civilization is and on what makes a Golden Age possible. There needs to be some wealth and comfort, he said, but not too much. More importantly, there needs to be vision and confidence in pursuit of the true and the beautiful – not in pursuit of fortune, fame, or fulfillment.

In the late 1960s, social psychology had the marks of civilization. Jobs and grants, while neither lavish nor plentiful, were available. And there was vision and confidence in pursuit of truth (if not beauty). In part, vision was thrust on the discipline by the pressing social issues of the day. It was the Vietnam era, the time of the Civil Rights movement, Black Power, the War on Poverty, drugs, sex, and rock and roll. Conflicts roiled over racial equality, patriotism, civil disobedience, alternative lifestyles, and more. But to have vision means to see solutions as well as problems, and at that time, social psychologists saw solutions by looking through the eyes of Kurt Lewin.

Lewin's vision was three-dimensional: (a) address real and important social issues by (b) conceptual analysis (theory) that involves getting beneath surface empirical relations to underlying psychological processes (as Lewin said, look to genotypes rather than phenotypes), then (c) test the conceptual analysis using experimental manipulations plus random assignment of individuals to conditions to examine predicted causal relations (in Lewinian terms, do Galilean not Aristotelian science). As in the research done by Latané and Darley, the experimental situations employed often involved elaborate deceptions reminiscent of the then-popular TV show *Candid Camera*, which touted itself as revealing "people caught in the act of being themselves." This Lewinian vision had produced marvelous works in the hands of Festinger, Schachter, Milgram, and others. In the late 1960s, it was clear what a social psychological perspective involved. It was also clear that this perspective was unique and that it could provide valuable new insights. Vision and confidence.

Producing insight into social problems in the Lewinian tradition was neither easy nor automatic. Nor was it without critics and crises. It required that one be willing and able to trust conceptual analysis – that is, to trust turning your back on the very phenomenon to be explained in order to reflect on the dynamics of the underlying psychological processes at work. It also required that one trust the logic of experimentation, including one's instantiation both of the phenomenon at issue and of the relevant independent and dependent variables, and that one recognize the necessity of using experiments to test one's conceptual analysis. As good students of the Lewinian tradition, Latané and Darley (1970) knew that all this should be done. They also knew it could be done. Vision and confidence.

I felt I had found a disciplinary home.

More Luck

Fortunately, John agreed to be my advisor, and we set about designing our first (and, as it happened, our only) study together. We examined the effect of three factors on helping: norm salience, religious devotion, and being in a hurry. That study – what's come to be called the Good Samaritan study – was my minor research project, the equivalent of a Master's thesis (see Darley & Batson, 1973). The next year, my dissertation (which Mark Zanna graciously chaired because John was away on sabbatical), drew on attribution theory to examine cognitive biases that influence both the ways we perceive other people's problems and the help we provide.

In the spring of that year, I found myself giving a job talk at the University of Kansas on attribution as a mediator of bias in helping, feeling thrilled and a little terrified to have Fritz Heider, the father of attribution theory, in the audience. After the talk, the Heiders hosted a reception in their home. I was more than a little pleased and impressed.

Toward the end of the reception, Fritz was sitting quietly alone in the midst of the crowd. Emboldened by a drink or two, I went over, sat down, and asked him what he thought of the talk. Speaking softly and slowly, as he almost always did, he said, "Very interesting . . . there was so much . . . I'm not sure I got it all . . . but it seems to me you're trying to take a matter of the heart and turn it into a matter of the head."

I was stunned – to hear this from one of the pioneers of the cognitive revolution, a patron saint of cool analyses of "hot" processes! Didn't he understand the implications of his own ideas? His comment violated my expectations, as well as the zeitgeist, so I did what any eager (and cocky) young scholar would do. I tried to forget it. Only several years later, after I had joined the faculty at Kansas and after a very bright first-year graduate student (Jay Coke) convinced me that we should look at the effect of empathic emotion on helping, did I begin to understand and appreciate Fritz's comment. Although not ignoring the head, I've focused on matters of the heart ever since, on motives, emotions, and values.

A Surprise and Long Search

Jay and I (and Katherine McDavis) used a high-impact deception experiment of the sort dominant in social psychology at that time – and virtually non-existent in social psychology today – to test whether feeling empathy increases helping. We weren't willing to rely on people's reports of how prone they are to feel empathy. Nor were we willing to accept their reports of how helpful they had been in the past, would be in the future, or could be in some hypothetical situation. We felt we had to confront our research participants, undergraduate men and women, with a specific person in need for whom they could feel empathy. We also felt we had to experimentally manipulate whether they felt high or low empathy in response to the need, and to randomly assign them to experimental condition. Then we had to give them a plausible and feasible opportunity to help address the empathy-inducing need.

Not wanting to put an actual person in need, we created a fictitious needy person and led participants to believe that she was real. Each participant listened to a taped pilot radio newscast that presented the situation of Katie Banks, a senior at the university. Ostensibly, Katie's parents and a sister had recently been killed in an automobile accident, and because her parents didn't carry life insurance, Katie was struggling to provide for her surviving younger brother and sister while finishing her last year of college. She badly needed money, but she also needed transportation to the grocery store and laundry as well as sitters to stay with her younger brother and sister while she attended her two night classes. The announcer then interviewed Katie. In a grief-stricken voice, she explained that her primary concern was to graduate so that she could get a job that would enable her to support her younger brother and sister. Without a good job, she'd have to give them up for adoption.

We manipulated empathic feelings for Katie through perspective-taking instructions – either imagine how Katie felt about her situation (high empathy) or observe the broadcasting techniques used to make the newscast impactful (low empathy). After hearing the newscast, each participant was unexpectedly given an opportunity to help Katie by offering to run errands, sit with her brother and sister while she attended her classes, and so on. A cross-cutting misattribution-of-arousal manipulation checked that any effects of the perspective manipulation on helping were due to empathic emotion rather than to differences in attention or in cognitive processes (for more procedural detail, see Coke et al., 1978).

I was surprised by what we found in this experiment. Not by the pattern of helping – participants in the high-empathy/no-misattribution condition helped more than those in the other three conditions, as we expected. My surprise came after the chance to help and just prior to debriefing, when we asked participants about their reactions to the study. Many of the high-empathy participants seemed genuinely concerned about Katie's welfare.

I couldn't believe these participants actually cared about Katie. Like the vast majority of psychologists at the time, I assumed that it was naive to think we humans care for another person for his or her sake rather than for our own – such thinking overlooks the variety of ways we can benefit from such care. As the wise and witty Duke de La Rochefoucauld put it long ago: "The most disinterested love is, after all, but a kind of bargain, in which the dear love of our own selves always proposes to be the gainer one way or other" (Maxim 82, 1691).

I suspected our participants were either fooling themselves or trying to fool us. They'd probably been taught that they should feel concern for those in need and would feel guilty if they didn't. Or perhaps hearing about Katie's distress caused them distress, and they wanted her distress to end in order to end their own. After all, isn't that what empathic concern is, our discomfort caused by another's?

Still, what the participants said gave me pause. Could it be that when we feel empathic concern for a person in need, we care about that person for his or her sake, not ours? I wasn't ready to abandon the widely held assumption that we care only about ourselves, but the apparent concern for Katie raised doubts.

Those doubts led me to think more carefully about what altruism is and whether it might exist. (My earlier reading in philosophy, especially the Scottish Enlightenment, proved very helpful here.) This thinking, in turn, led to a long series of experiments. I wanted to know if empathy-induced helping is motivated by concern for the person in need or is – as I thought more likely – somehow, in some way, motivated by concern for the helper's own welfare. To find the answer to this question wasn't quick or easy; it took years and over thirty experiments (see Batson, 2011, for a review). But I think we now have the answer, albeit necessarily a tentative one. And I think we owe this answer to the approach to science that flowered in the social psychology of the 1960s and 1970s.

Looking Back – and Ahead

Camelot evokes admiration and wistful envy, but also an awareness of make-believe. It's a fantasy world in which we cannot, indeed must not, live. To look back on a

Golden Age is quite a different matter. Looking back on the social psychology in which I landed in 1970 is less like opening a window on Camelot than like the experience of a monk in the Dark Ages struggling to decipher an ancient Greek scroll. It's something wonderful – beautiful and elegant – but also something that seems out of touch with the current reality, something no longer possible, almost incomprehensible. Social psychology of the 1960s and 1970s was a product of and testimony to vision and confidence, traits that seem lacking in social psychology today. As such, it renders both a judgment and a challenge.

My sight may be clouded by geriatric nostalgia, but looking back leads me to doubt that the way out of our current dark times is through preregistration, meta-analysis, online studies, new statistical techniques, more publishing outlets, or seeking empirical discoveries. Instead, I think the next Golden Age is likely to be founded on a rediscovery of Lewin's vision of addressing real social problems through careful conceptual analysis and experimental hypothesis-testing.

I encourage younger social psychologists who only know the works of the 1960s and 1970s secondhand to take the time to read some of the original texts – to marvel and reflect. There are lessons to be learned, both substantive ones about social psychological processes and methodological ones about how to arrive at substantive insights. Of course, living in a different world, we can't simply resurrect this past civilization and shouldn't try. Still, we can hope for renaissance. Perhaps reflection on that Golden Age will be a step toward a new expression of vision and confidence.

As for me, I was lucky enough to wander into social psychology at that time, have my attention directed to a basic question about human nature to which I really wanted to know the answer, and find the experimental methods to answer the question scientifically. It would be greedy to ask for more.

Suggested Reading

Batson, C. D. (1994). Looking back at *The Unresponsive Bystander*: Camelot or the Golden Age? *Contemporary Psychology, 39*, 941–943.

(2011). *Altruism in Humans*. New York: Oxford University Press.

Coke, J. S., Batson, C. D., & McDavis, K. (1978). Empathic mediation of helping: A two-stage model. *Journal of Personality and Social Psychology, 36*, 752–766.

Darley, J. M., & Batson, C. D. (1973). "From Jerusalem to Jericho": A study of situational and dispositional variables in helping behavior. *Journal of Personality and Social Psychology, 27*(1), 100–108.

Festinger, L., Riecken, H. W., & Schachter, S. (1956). *When Prophecy Fails*. Minneapolis: University of Minnesota Press.

Latané, B., & Darley, J. M. (1970). *The Unresponsive Bystander: Why Doesn't He Help?* Englewood Cliffs, NJ: Prentice Hall.

25 Mindsets
From Bathtubs to Hot Beliefs to Social Change

Carol S. Dweck

I entered graduate school in the late 1960s, but not as a social psychologist. I'm not sure exactly when I became one or when I came to be considered one. As you will see, I had identity issues (and conformity issues), which made me a different kind of social psychologist and which I sincerely hope in the end added to any contributions I have made to the field.

I Was Not Obedient: The Early Do's and Don'ts of the Field

From childhood, I had a habit of not really listening when people told me what I could or couldn't – or what I should or shouldn't – do. When I entered graduate school, I was told women probably couldn't be professors. Hmm. Later, we were told that motivation was not really a topic of interest any more. I thought: How could that be? How could motivation – the very thing that drives and organizes all of human functioning – how could that no longer be central to psychology? Would we just study cognition, affect, and behavior in isolation and not try to understand how they work in concert as people pursue their goals? It just didn't make sense.

Still later we were told that research on real-world topics, and especially research that sought to have an impact on real-world issues, was frowned upon. And that making our research accessible to the public was not what good scientists do. Writing books was a no-no.

Happily, many of the "don'ts" of the earlier time are things that have become valued pursuits. I couldn't be more excited that social psychology is now turning its considerable arsenal of tools toward social problems – such as inequality, under-achievement, mental health, or poverty – and is working toward solutions. I hope my disobedience played some role.

My Love of Science and My Refusal to Partition Psychology

I always loved science. I started reading *Scientific American* in 7th grade. I loved that you could do experiments to address the deepest questions about how things work.

Carol S. Dweck, Stanford University, USA.

So when I found out in college that you could use these same methods to study behavior, I was hooked.

The next thing I knew, I was a graduate student in psychology at Yale. At first, I studied animal learning with Allan Wagner and Bob Rescorla. I was in the thick of things as the new (and still highly influential) Rescorla-Wagner theory of learning was born. But something was wrong. I failed the bathtub test. No, no, don't worry. This is simply a one-item test that I invented and it goes like this: Do you think about your research topic in the bathtub (or shower, as the case may be)? If you don't, it's not your topic.

I was an avid participant in the many lab discussions, I contributed lots of ideas to the enterprise, and I spent a ton of time on my research (e.g., Dweck & Wagner, 1970), but I didn't think about it in the tub. So, after my second year, I switched areas. Or more accurately, I removed myself from the area system entirely and, with the blessing of the director of graduate studies, I became a citizen of the department. (In fact, my new advisor was in the clinical psychology program.) I have remained a citizen of the field of psychological science ever since.

Where many people see divisions, I try to see connections. For example, many social psychologists view personality as something quite separate – but personality is very much about a person's history in their cultures and contexts and how it has shaped their current ways of seeing and being in the world. And, in fact, I recently published a theory of personality with this social psychological viewpoint at its core (Dweck, 2017).

I've also recently used a social psychological perspective to address another question that cuts across psychology: As humans, what makes us so smart? What is the true seat of intelligence? Many psychologists and neuroscientists would say that it's the cool, cognitive parts of the brain (such as the prefrontal cortex) that make us smart. However, with Matt Dixon, I have a new article that places the motivation-related areas of the brain (such as the amygdala) in an equal partnership with the cooler, more "cognitive" areas when it comes to intelligent decision-making (Dixon & Dweck, 2021). The motivation-related areas represent what we value and what we seek, an issue that has always been of deep concern to social psychologists.

Finally, I am working with AI/machine learning researchers to help solve the problem of why the skills they program into their agents often don't generalize to new situations. As a social psychologist, I bring to the table the critical idea of context and the extent to which skills generalize when new contexts make contact with an agent's motivations and support the use of those skills to fulfill the agent's goals. Skills don't simply generalize because they are programmed into your repertoire.

I am proud to be called a pillar of social psychology, but I am also proud to bring our social psychological way of thinking to other areas of psychology.

My Introduction to "Hot" Beliefs

OK, back to graduate school. I left the animals behind, but I was still interested in how organisms (now people!) come to function in their world. I was both daunted and thrilled by the fact that humans don't just record reward contingencies; they bring their arsenal of beliefs to bear in choosing goals and reacting to outcomes.

One question in particular came to intrigue me: Why do some people take on challenging goals and persist, or even thrive, in the face of setbacks – while others, with virtually the same abilities, shy away from difficulty and give up quickly? The answer could help us understand why some people reach their goals in life and others do not. I knew this was bathtub worthy.

I sought the answer to my question in people's beliefs. But how do you find a way to study those beliefs and understand their impact? As luck would have it, attribution theory was developing in social psychology. Attributions are answers to the question of why something happened, of what caused it. I was especially taken with Bernie Weiner's approach (Weiner & Kukla, 1970) because it put attributions in a motivational framework. It wasn't just a cool and logical cognitive process of figuring out causes, as it was depicted in other approaches. It was a hot process, often undertaken in the heat of a failure and with potentially important motivational consequences. Moreover, people could differ from each other in the attributions they favored, which could then push their thoughts, feelings, and actions in different directions.

Attributions were a perfect place to start my journey into the study of people. They could be precisely assessed and experimentally manipulated, giving greater insight into mechanisms and processes. They had measurable consequences for motivation and performance. Before I knew it, we were using attributions to understand individual differences (including gender differences) in reactions to failures, mapping (and experimentally simulating) the antecedents of these differences, and putting the whole process as it unfolded under the microscope (e.g., Diener & Dweck, 1978; Dweck & Reppucci, 1973). We were showing that retraining these attributions could change reactions to setbacks, even in those who had previously shown strong negative responses. Aside from the impact and origins of different attributional tendencies, my students and I also explored attributional effects in social relationships, as well as the way in which different "achievement goals" could predict or cause different attributions.

The Emergence of Mindsets

But I still wasn't satisfied. I kept asking more and more questions about why people with similar abilities would interpret their setbacks in such different ways, with some condemning their abilities and others simply stepping up their effort and trying new strategies. For example, why would people with ample ability take one failure to mean they were incompetent and then flee? Were there more fundamental beliefs that could help us understand the whole process?

Out of this persistent questioning, our work on mindsets was born. In this work, mindsets (or implicit theories) are people's beliefs about whether their most fundamental qualities, like their intelligence or their personality, are simply fixed or, instead, can be developed (Dweck, 1999; Dweck & Leggett, 1988). Over time we found that holding more of a *fixed mindset* made people worry about how their fixed trait would be judged, and tended to lead to less challenge-seeking, more negative self-attributions for failures, and a lesser tendency to persist in the face of difficulty. More of a *growth mindset*, with its emphasis on developing one's abilities, seemed to foster the opposite. Moreover, experimentally manipulating the mindsets created similar patterns. In other words, these "hot" beliefs seemed to set the stage for a cascade of effects.

The research went on to show how mindsets were at the heart of person perception (Dweck et al., 1995) and how believing that people's core traits were fixed could play a key role in stereotyping and prejudice (Levy et al., 1998). Mindsets were shown to influence such important and diverse phenomena as the course of close relationships, the exertion of willpower, and the development of interests. And exciting new work, led by Mary Murphy, is showing that organizations, and not just individuals, can embody a mindset (Canning et al., 2020). Organizations can believe in and revere fixed talent or they can believe in and promote the growth of everyone's abilities – creating quite different cultures, ones that can magnify or reduce inequities.

Well, if we could study and even create these effects in the lab, why not the real world? Mindset beliefs seemed like a prime target for interventions.

Mindset Interventions

So, the next steps seemed clear. Why not offer people, say students, a new way to think about their abilities – as malleable – and see whether this could alter their actual academic outcomes and not just their performance on laboratory tasks?

Joshua Aronson, Catherine Good, and their colleagues were the first to take the plunge. They created mindset programs that raised the grades and achievement test score of students, especially those from underrepresented groups. We soon followed suit, culminating in a recent study, led by David Yeager, that took mindset interventions to a national level (Yeager et al., 2019). Working with a nationally representative sample of students who were making the challenging transition to high school, we tested whether a carefully crafted, well-tested 50-minute program, sent out over the Internet, and self-administered by the students could possibly (a) raise grade-point averages at the end of the year for lower achieving students and (b) increase the overall number of students who elected to take advanced math a year later. The answer was yes on both fronts.

Of course, the effects seemed modest compared to the effects of lab experiments or interventions with small samples, or interventions with simple or immediate outcomes. But they were meaningful, exceeding the effects of most long-term and costly educational programs that have been evaluated with large diverse samples in fully randomized controlled experiments. And it was kind of remarkable to achieve anything with such a short program at this scale. We were also inspired by the call for the highest, most rigorous level of scientific practice (Dweck & Yeager, 2019). So, in this study, we took many steps to ensure the validity and generalizability of our findings:

The hypotheses and analyses were massively preregistered, the sample was large and nationally representative, and the data were collected, prepared, and analyzed by three separate research organizations.

In other intervention research, David Yeager and Jessica Schleider have each taken mindset interventions into the realm of adolescent mental health, now a huge societal problem (Miu & Yeager, 2015; Schleider & Weisz, 2018). They have shown that short, self-administered programs can meaningfully decrease the onset of clinically significant mental health problems, such as depression or anxiety, and can reliably decrease the levels of depression and anxiety in clinical populations. This is extremely exciting in a time when the demand for help is enormous and the availability is so limited or costly.

Are these interventions just demonstration projects with little scientific value added? No. These interventions are testing theory, testing mechanisms, and testing the conditions under which a phenomenon holds – all of which feed back into our psychological understanding and then allow us to hone our theory and create improved interventions.

Indeed, over the past ten years the whole social psychology program at Stanford has coalesced around addressing social problems: developing programs that increase academic outcomes, guide policing, support economic initiatives, promote juvenile justice, and enhance physical and mental health. Virtually all of these are relatively short programs that influence people's psychology by offering them another way of seeing things, and thereby allowing them to act and react to their worlds in more effective ways – in ways that make them more likely to reach their own goals and help others reach theirs. These programs of research highlight the ability of social psychology to identify the psychological components of social problems and are testimony to the power of social psychology to play a role in alleviating them.

I Did Write a Book: Reflections on *Mindset*

When I published my book *Mindset* (Dweck, 2006), very few academic researchers were writing books for the public. As I noted above, it wasn't encouraged. Plus, Malcolm Gladwell seemed to be writing the books for us – taking social psychological research and bringing it to a wide audience. And, since I didn't really know how to write in that way (yet), I sort of hoped he would write my book too. However, my students had been urging me for a while to bring our work to the public and finally I heeded their request.

The book took vast amounts of time, thought, and work. Among other things, I had to learn how to use my real-life speaking voice in written form. I had to find many, many real-world examples of mindsets in action and interweave them with the research findings in a natural and compelling way. I had to decide whether to put personal material into the mix. (I decided I would in order to relate to the reader on a deeper level.) The effort was well worth it. The book seemed to strike a responsive chord. I think people really love our field, especially when it's put into a form that's accessible and when they can think about how research findings relate to their lives. Over time, the book was widely read by individuals, business and sports organizations, educators, and parents. It was translated into forty languages. Needless, to say, this was extremely gratifying.

However, over time we've come to realize that it's one thing to describe in a book how a growth-mindset organization, team, or classroom functions and quite another thing for people to understand how to implement that organizational mindset in reality. In a wonderful feedback loop, this realization has greatly informed our current research. Led by Mary Murphy, David Yeager, and Stephanie Fryberg, we are analyzing the active ingredients in growth-mindset cultures and, in a series of field experiments, figuring out how to help people systematically build them.

A Message for Future Researchers

My message for future generations of researchers is simple. Psychology, maybe especially social psychology, is a field that allows your research to grow as your knowledge, interests, and values develop. You can put key social and psychological issues under the microscope with careful smaller-scale experiments and then go out and try to do something about them.

In short, social psychology is a field that allows you to make a difference. So, my advice to young people is to ask yourself what contribution you would like to make to our world, which so urgently needs it. And then use your considerable abilities and scientific tools to work toward that contribution.

Suggested Reading

Canning, E. A., Murphy, M. C., Emerson, K., Chatman, J. A., Dweck, C. S., & Kray, L. J. (2020). Cultures of genius at work: Organizational mindsets predict cultural norms, trust, and commitment. *Personality and Social Psychology Bulletin, 46,* 626–642.

Diener, C. I., & Dweck, C. S. (1978). An analysis of learned helplessness: Continuous changes in performance, strategy and achievement cognitions following failure. *Journal of Personality and Social Psychology, 36,* 451–462.

Dixon, M. L., & Dweck, C. S. (2021). The amygdala and the prefrontal cortex: The co-construction of intelligent decision making. *Psychological Review.* https://doi.org/10.1037/rev0000339.

Dweck, C. S. (1999). *Self-Theories: Their Role in Motivation, Personality, and Development.* New York: Psychology Press.

(2006). *Mindset: The New Psychology of Success.* New York: Random House.

(2017). From needs to goals and representations: Foundations for a unified theory of motivation, personality, and development. *Psychological Review, 124,* 689–719.

Dweck, C. S., Chiu, C., & Hong, Y. (1995). Implicit theories and their role in judgments and reactions: A world from two perspectives. *Psychological Inquiry, 6,* 267–285.

Dweck, C. S., & Leggett, E. L. (1988). A social-cognitive approach to motivation and personality, *Psychological Review*, *95*, 256–273.

Dweck, C. S., & Reppucci, N. D. (1973). Learned helplessness and reinforcement responsibility in children. *Journal of Personality and Social Psychology*, *25*, 109–116.

Dweck, C. S., & Wagner, A. R. (1970). Situational cues and correlation between CS and US as determinants of the conditioned emotional response. *Psychonomic Science*, *18*(3), 145–147.

Dweck, C. S., & Yeager, D. S. (2019). Mindsets: A view from two eras. *Perspectives on Psychological Science*, *14*, 481–496.

Levy, S., Stroessner, S., & Dweck, C. S. (1998). Stereotype formation and endorsement: The role of implicit theories. *Journal of Personality and Social Psychology*, *74*, 1421–1436.

Miu, A. S., & Yeager, D. S. (2015). Preventing symptoms of depression by teaching adolescents that people can change: Effects of a brief incremental theory of personality intervention at 9-month follow-up. *Clinical Psychological Science*, *3*, 726–743.

Schleider, J., & Weisz, J. (2018). A single-session growth mindset intervention for adolescent anxiety and depression: 9-month outcomes of a randomized trial. *Journal of Child Psychology and Psychiatry*, *59*, 160–170.

Weiner, B., & Kukla, A. (1970). An attributional analysis of achievement motivation. *Journal of Personality and Social Psychology*, *5*, 1–20.

Yeager, D. S., Hanselman, P., Walton, G. M., Murray, J., Crosnoe, R., . . . Dweck, C. S. (2019). A national experiment reveals where a growth mindset improves achievement. *Nature*, *573*, 364–369.

26 Social Psychology and Me
The Ties That Bind

Mark Snyder

Although I don't carry calling cards with "Mark Snyder, Social Psychologist" embossed on them, it is fair to say that, after some five decades of doing social psychology, I am a social psychologist. It is also fair to say that, after five decades, the ties that bind social psychology and me are strong and enduring ones. As I look back over my life and times as a social psychologist, I am struck by several recurring themes that have characterized my interests and that are reflected in the problems that I have tackled in my research. Looking back, I am also struck by the ways that social psychology (and the social sciences more generally) has changed in meaningful ways that, as I look forward, point the way to the next generations of theory, research, and application. With this preamble done, let me tell you about how I became a social psychologist, and how the kind of social psychologist that I am has evolved over time.

Before I even entertained the notion of studying psychology, I was struck by the ways that people are social beings, going to great lengths to fit in with others, conforming to the norms of their groups, and fulfilling the expectations of their roles. I saw it in friends, family, and even in strangers; I saw it in "real people" and in characters in books, movies, plays, and television programs; and, with some reflection, I even saw it in myself. Then when I began studying psychology (as an undergraduate at McGill University in the mid-1960s, where Mick Rothbart was my honors thesis advisor, and as a graduate student at Stanford University in the late 1960s and early 1970s, where Daryl Bem and Phil Zimbardo were my doctoral dissertation advisors), I learned about a discipline devoted to the scientific study of how people are influenced by the social contexts in which they operate, with people being, in so many areas of life, creatures of their situations.

Learning about social psychology during my student days was largely a matter of reading books and journals (yes, in my youth, I spent a lot of time in libraries) as well as working on research projects with my faculty mentors and my fellow students (to this day, I still believe in the power of learning by doing). For whatever reasons, I never took an actual course in social psychology. However, I have taught courses in social psychology all my working life (from my early years on the job when I taught "Introduction to Social Psychology" every winter, to the present day; as I write this

Mark Snyder, University of Minnesota, USA. This chapter was prepared with the support of the Center for the Study of the Individual and Society at the University of Minnesota.

essay in fall semester 2021, it's "Principles of Social Psychology" and, next semester, it will be "Self and Identity"). What better way to learn about the field, and to stay up to date with the latest developments, than to teach it!

When I began the transition from student to researcher, especially when it came time for my doctoral dissertation (which I completed in 1972) and in my early years at the University of Minnesota (whose faculty I joined that same year), the questions to which I was drawn were in large measure sensitive to the concerns of the times, especially the concerns in social psychology about the weak and inconsistent relations between attitudes (one of the field's core bedrock concepts) and behavior and the parallel concerns in personality psychology about the consistency between traits (arguably the most fundamental of building blocks of personality) and behavior. Quite simply, there could be striking gaps, inconsistencies, and even contradictions between who people *are* (as defined by their attitudes, identities, and personalities) and what people *do* (as reflected in their behavior in social situations). I wanted to understand those gaps, inconsistencies, and contradictions – to discover their meaning, their origins, and their consequences.

Long story short, I found that understanding of the relations between the public appearances of people's words and deeds and the private realities of their underlying attitudes and personalities in the construct of self-monitoring (for an overview of theory, research, and applications on self-monitoring, see Snyder, 1987), which proposes that people vary meaningfully in the ways that they rely on information from social situations and information from personal dispositions in guiding their self-presentation and social behavior. Some people, known as high self-monitors, are highly sensitive to how they appear in social situations and work to control the images that they project to others, choosing to present themselves in ways that best fit the circumstances at hand, whether or not it matches who they really are. By contrast, other people, known as low self-monitors, are not so concerned with constantly assessing the social climate around them, instead expressing what they really think and feel, consistently acting on their attitudes, and accurately displaying their personalities.

To identify these contrasting interpersonal orientations (which I thought would be the key to understanding the "who, when, and why" of gaps and contradictions between the public appearances of the self that people display to the world and the private realities of the inner self that only they experience), I created and validated (with a variety of converging methods in the laboratory and in the field) the Self-Monitoring Scale, a 25-item self-report instrument, which can be readily used in laboratory and field research (Snyder, 1974).

The takeaway message from research in many domains of life (including friendships and romantic relationships, jobs and careers, leisure time pursuits, choices of consumer products, voting habits, and more), is that high self-monitors are creatures of their situations. As they tell us in their responses to this illustrative item of the scale, and as their dealings with other people confirm, "In different situations and with different people, I often act like very different persons." In contrast, low self-monitors are products of their personalities. As they reveal in their responses to this item of the scale and in their words and deeds, "My behavior is usually a reflection of my true inner feelings, attitudes, and beliefs."

As it happens, both high self-monitors and low self-monitors are actively involved in structuring their lives in ways that are conducive to their self-monitoring orientations. By probing the underlying mechanisms of self-monitoring, my colleagues and I (e.g., Snyder, Gangestad, & Simpson, 1983) found that this structuring is achieved through our choice of friends (high self-monitors choose friends that make it easy to play a role; low self-monitors choose friends that make it easy to be themselves) and by our choice of situations (high self-monitors choose situations that are scripted; low self-monitors choose situations that allow them to display their own attitudes and personalities). These choices make it easier for high self-monitors to be high and for low self-monitors to be low; moreover, these choices help to ensure that highs remain highs and that lows remain lows.

The more I thought about these processes of choosing friends and structuring situations, the more I realized that not only have I learned something about the dynamics of self-monitoring, but also that I have learned something about the larger processes by which individuals actively choose, influence, and even create the social worlds in which they live. Indeed, this idea of the active role that individuals play in constructing their social worlds shows up thematically in so much of my work. As I have examined the effects of expectations on behavior in studies of behavioral confirmation in social interaction, and as I have explored the ways that people address the problems of society through volunteerism, I have increasingly come to see these as phenomena that invoke considerations of the impact of individuals on their social worlds.

Work on behavioral confirmation has focused on how, in the course of social interaction, people lead others to behave in accord with their preconceived beliefs and expectations. By treating the targets of their expectations as if these expectations were true, thereby inducing the target to behave as if these expectations were true (even if initially false or exaggerated), people can effectively turn social beliefs and interpersonal expectations into self-fulfilling prophecies. Typically, in studies of behavioral confirmation, two people who have never met before have a brief getting-acquainted conversation, with one member of the pair (the "perceiver") being given an expectation about the other person (the "target"). In one study, Beth Tanke, Ellen Berscheid, and I arranged for perceivers to have a telephone conversation with targets they believed to be physically attractive (as a result of seeing a Polaroid instant photo, ostensibly of the target, but actually chosen by random assignment). Those targets came to behave in more friendly, outgoing, and sociable ways than targets interacting with perceivers who believed them to be physically unattractive. These differences in the behavior of the target were readily apparent to outside observers who listened in on the target's contributions to the conversations and knew nothing about the perceiver's expectations (Snyder, Tanke, & Berscheid, 1977; for an overview of research on behavioral confirmation, see Snyder, 1984).

Perhaps somewhat ironically, this process of behavioral confirmation in social interaction is the product of a motivated agenda in which people actively try to use social interaction as a vehicle for discovering whether the expectation really "fits" and whether it serves well to predict what the target will be like and serve as a useful guide to how to handle the interaction. In fact, even when Bill Swann and I gave people the explicit task of treating their beliefs about others as hypotheses and putting those hypotheses to test in social interaction with the targets, they nevertheless treated others as if their hypotheses were true and elicited actual confirmation for those hypotheses (e.g., Snyder & Swann, 1978). At times, the more motivated people are to find out whether their beliefs about others are accurate (perhaps because they are in positions of power and making consequential decisions), the more they treat other people in ways that produce the appearance of accuracy. This "belief creates reality" scenario represents, to my mind, a powerful instance of the impact that individuals have on their social worlds. What begins as a *belief* in the mind of one person becomes, by virtue of the dynamics of behavioral confirmation in social interaction, *reality* in the behavior of another person.

Furthermore, this process of individuals acting on their social worlds is something that we have seen in our work on volunteerism and other forms of social action. Every year, millions upon millions of people around the world volunteer to provide services such as companionship, tutoring, counseling, and health care to those in need; as well, volunteers donate their time and invest their energies to address the challenges of society by donating their time and investing their energy in causes such as human rights, social justice, and the environment. For many people, volunteerism is an important source of identity – it's not just something that they do, but also something that defines who they are, that gives meaning and purpose to their lives, and that is a source of great personal pride.

Why do people get involved in volunteerism, and why do so they stay involved in it? To some extent, it is a matter of the values and ideals of service to others and society. But, more so than having these values is what volunteers actually do with these values. Research has revealed that what seems to characterize volunteers and distinguish them from non-volunteers is the integration of these values into an *agenda for action* that links the good done for others to good done for the self. With these agendas for action, at one and the same time, volunteers act both on behalf of *others* (volunteering to alleviate the problems of homelessness, poverty, illiteracy, etc.) and on behalf of *themselves* (e.g., volunteering to make friends, to acquire new skills, to boost self-esteem, and/or to affirm personal values). That is, many of the motivations for volunteer service are ones that bring together a mutual concern for benefiting others and for benefiting oneself. As my long-time collaborator Allen Omoto and I have seen in studies in which we have followed volunteers over the course of their ongoing service to see who sticks with it for the long haul, and who abandons it when the going gets tough (e.g., Omoto & Snyder, 1995; Snyder & Omoto, 2008), it is often self-oriented motivations that are powerful predictors of how long one serves as a volunteer. Moreover, these self-oriented motivations can be harnessed to promote volunteerism with persuasive appeals matched to the specific motivations important to potential volunteers.

Thus, it appears that the essence of volunteerism is people forming and carrying out agendas for action. Just as with self-monitoring, where individuals can and do construct social worlds conducive to their interpersonal orientations, and just as with behavioral confirmation, where individuals construct social worlds fashioned in their images of other people, volunteerism illustrates how people who embark on a course of service as a volunteer play out an agenda that links self-relevant concerns to actions (whether helping individuals in need or addressing social issues and societal challenges) that change the worlds around them.

Not only does the proposition that individuals actively create their own social worlds serve as a unifying theme for these programs of research, but it also makes clear how much my long-standing core identity as a social psychologist is intimately intertwined with another important and deeply rooted identity, that of personality psychologist. In accord with Kurt Lewin's (1936, p. 12) well-known proposition that "Every psychological event depends upon the state of the person and at the same time on the environment, although their relative importance is different in different cases," I have come to realize that if we are to understand people and their actions, we need to know about them as individuals *and* as social beings, to understand their personalities *and* their situations, to be both a personality psychologist *and* a social psychologist. As much as I appreciate social psychology's core tenets about the power of situations to influence social behavior, I am also mindful that people often choose to be in situations conducive to their personalities; that is, the very situations that appear to influence behavior actually may have been chosen by people themselves. By the same token, for me, being a good personality psychologist means, at times, adopting a situational perspective. As much as I appreciate the fact that traits and dispositions serve as sources of regularities and consistencies in behavior, as a social psychologist I am also mindful that regularities and consistencies in the situations in which people find themselves can also lead to regularities in their behaviors that, in turn, may be internalized into corresponding identities and dispositions.

In accord with this dual identity, my work has straddled the boundaries between personality and social psychology. The investigative strategy that I employ is something of a hybrid between the two approaches. It brings together personality's concern with the psychology of the individual and social psychology's focus on the influence of the situation. Over the years, the boundaries have grown increasingly permeable as many scholars have also crossed back and forth, integrating theoretical perspectives and methodological orientations of both fields, such that being both a social psychologist and a personality psychologist has very much moved into the mainstream.

The results of this intertwining of perspectives, I am pleased to say, have been productive and generative of bridges between social and personality psychology. In hopes of solidifying those bridges, Kay Deaux and I have edited *The Oxford Handbook of Personality and Social Psychology*, now in its second edition (Deaux & Snyder, 2019). To do so, we invited a diverse group of scholars to think deeply and generatively about the ways that integrating the two perspectives can lead to a rich understanding of the many and varied phenomena of interest to psychological science. Of course, as Tom Pettigrew (2019) has noted in an insightful historical analysis in that volume, personality and social psychology have a long history of moving together and moving apart, with efforts to bridge the disciplines encountering obstacles and barriers, along with the support that has sustained those efforts along the way. Nevertheless, with the pillars provided by advances in theoretical perspectives and investigative strategies of the form demonstrated by contributors to the *Handbook*, who have pushed beyond the traditional boundaries in their innovative work, there is reason for optimism about the prospects for an integrated social-personality psychology and, quite possibly, a hybrid discipline of personality and social behavior.

That today's social psychology is much closer to, and more integrated with, personality does not mean that it has become any less "social" over the years. To the contrary, the field today is, in many ways, an even *more social* psychology than what I had first encountered all those years ago, concerned not only with how people are influenced by their social situations but also how people influence the social situations they encounter. Moreover, the increased attention to social relationships, made possible by advances in theorizing about close relationships (e.g., interdependence and attachment theories) and advances in methodological and statistical techniques for studying reciprocal influences (e.g., the Actor Partner Interdependence Model and multilevel modeling techniques), we know much more about social processes, especially the reciprocal effects of members of social relationships influencing and being influenced by each other and the growth and development of these reciprocal influences over time.

With advances in neuroscientific and cultural psychology, today's social psychology is also very much a multi-level enterprise, spanning events that play out at the most micro of levels deep within human biology to events that play out at the most macro of levels on the worldwide stages of nations and cultures. Increasingly, and in line with larger trends in scientific exploration, social psychology is a collaborative venture, with individual researchers bringing together different theoretical and methodological skill sets in teams that are more than the sum of their parts, producing research that might not be possible for individual researchers to conduct on their own. As many who have tried it have discovered, there is an exciting, energizing, fulfilling, and even joyful side to collaborative work (for "behind the scenes" looks at collaboration in social psychology, see the inspiring collection of essays edited by Richie Zweigenhaft and Gene Borgida, 2016). As a result of these exciting trends, social psychology is now very much an interdisciplinary enterprise, manifested in such bridge-building ventures as political psychology, legal psychology, and relationship science.

Coupled with this collaborative, bridge-building spirit of today's social psychology is a growing commitment to doing research that addresses pressing social problems and societal challenges. As such, the field seems to be coming back to an "action research" tradition in which basic and applied science are linked in a reciprocal relationship, mutually complementing each other and guided by the Lewinian proposition that "There is nothing so practical as a good theory" (Lewin, 1951, p. 169). Within this tradition, researchers need not choose between being basic or applied, as research can be both at the same time. Within this tradition, researchers easily move back and forth between laboratory and field setting in coordinated scientific ventures that have the potential to advance the state of theory and improve the well-being of individuals, communities, and society at large.

These trends in social psychology over the years are, for me, very welcome ones. So too is the increase in the diversity of the field as well as its investment in the principles and practices of open science. These trends have made social psychology an increasingly appealing field, one whose population has grown substantially as more and more scientists and practitioners have been welcomed into its ranks. One index of this growth is the large and growing membership of its professional societies. As of October 2021, according to their websites, the Society for Personality and Social Psychology (SPSP) had over 7,500 members, the Society of Experimental Social Psychology (SESP) had over 3,000 members, and the European Association of Social Psychology (EASP) had over 1,200 members.

Closer to home, the social psychology program of which I am a member at the University of Minnesota has quadrupled its faculty size over the years. However, I must confess that, as much as I truly love the size and diversity of our program today, and all that it does to enhance our research and teaching portfolios, I do have fond nostalgia for the days when my colleague Ellen Berscheid and I were the totality of social psychology faculty in our department of psychology, somehow doing it all. In those days, everyone in the social psychology program – faculty and students – could easily and comfortably gather around a modestly sized table in a conference room on the third floor of Elliott Hall for our weekly get-togethers. These days, the conference room is still there, and although the furniture has long been replaced it continues to be the site of lively discussions and research meetings with faculty and student colleagues, collaborations with whom are my proudest accomplishments.

To draw this retrospective essay to a close, let me turn from looking back to looking ahead. Forecasting the future is, all too often, a perilous enterprise, so I won't try to predict what is in store for social psychology and for me. However, I do know what I hope for and what I will continue to work for; and, just maybe, my efforts can in some small way help nudge the field along. I look forward to a future where social psychology continues to welcome a diversity of researchers with a diversity of perspectives, working on a diversity of problems with the best of scientific practices, with the identity of social psychology itself reflecting these many forms of diversity, and the labors of social psychologists contributing meaningfully to the well-being of society and its members. No doubt, if I were starting over, I would do it again, perhaps this time with calling cards embossed with "social psychologist" on them!

Suggested Reading

Deaux, K., & Snyder, M. (Eds.) (2019). *The Oxford Handbook of Personality and Social Psychology*. Second edition. New York: Oxford University Press.

Lewin, K. (1936). *A Dynamic Theory of Personality*. New York: McGraw-Hill.

(1951). *Field Theory in Social Science: Selected Theoretical Papers* (D. Cartwright, Ed.). New York: Harper & Row (original work published 1944).

Omoto, A. M., & Snyder, M. (1995). Sustained helping without obligation: Motivation, longevity of service, and perceived attitude change among AIDS volunteers. *Journal of Personality and Social Psychology, 68*, 671–686.

Pettigrew, T. F. (2019). The intertwined histories of personality and social psychology. In K. Deaux & M. Snyder (Eds.), *The Oxford Handbook of Personality and Social Psychology*. Second edition (pp. 11–33). New York: Oxford University Press.

Snyder, M. (1974). Self-monitoring of expressive behavior. *Journal of Personality and Social Psychology, 30*(4), 526–537.

(1984). When belief creates reality. In L. Berkowitz (Ed.), *Advances in Experimental Social Psychology* (Vol. 18, pp. 247–305). Orlando, FL: Academic Press.

(1987). *Public Appearances/Private Realities: The Psychology of Self-Monitoring*. New York: W. H. Freeman.

Snyder, M., Gangestad, S., & Simpson, J. A. (1983). Choosing friends as activity partners: The role of self-monitoring. *Journal of Personality and Social Psychology, 45*, 1061–1072.

Snyder, M., & Omoto, A. M. (2008). Volunteerism: Social issues perspectives and social policy implications. *Social Issues and Policy Review, 2*, 1–36.

Snyder, M., & Swann, W. B. (1978). Hypothesis-testing processes in social interaction. *Journal of Personality and Social Psychology, 36*(1), 1202–1212.

Snyder, M., Tanke, E. D., & Berscheid, E. (1977). Social perception and interpersonal behavior: On the self-fulfilling nature of social stereotypes. *Journal of Personality and Social Psychology, 35*(9), 656–666.

Zweigenhaft, R., & Borgida, E. (Eds.) (2016). *Collaboration in Psychological Science: Behind the Scenes*. New York: Worth Publishers.

27 My Life as a Social Psychologist

Letitia Anne Peplau

A half century ago a young woman fell in love with social psychology and started on a path to an amazing career. I've been helped along the way by countless remarkable teachers, students, colleagues, and friends only some of whom can be included in this short story of my journey.

I was raised by a single mother who was a strong independent career woman. Hilda Peplau was a pioneering leader in psychiatric nursing and a university professor. When I was a child, my babysitters were often her graduate students. Since I felt at home in school, I never doubted that I, too, would go to graduate school. I was a serious student but liked to do my homework listening to rock music. At the time, social critics fretted about the dangers of TV and pop music on young minds; I was not convinced. For my high school science project, I designed an experiment to study the effect of pop music on problem solving. I randomly assigned students to work individually to solve a series of anagrams either listening to a rock music tape or in silence. I carefully computed the mean scores of the two groups which looked remarkably similar. But then the flaw in my project emerged: I didn't know how to do a statistical test to demonstrate that there were no significant group differences. Clearly, I had much more to learn about conducting research.

At Brown University, I took a year-long introductory psychology seminar with Professor Frances Clayton, the only woman on the psychology faculty. By the end of the year, I was pretty sure that psychology would be my career. My social psychology class confirmed that decision. We read Roger Brown's *Social Psychology* (1965). Unlike more recent textbooks (including ones I've co-authored), Brown's book had no bells and whistles – no photos, boxes, key terms, or videos. The beautifully written chapters are leisurely explorations of such topics as the basic dimensions of interpersonal relationships, the authoritarian personality, and impressions of personality including one's own.

My social psychology professor also assigned Tom Pettigrew's *Profile of the Negro American* (1964) which I read with great interest. I had gotten my first lesson in prejudice as a young child living in Manhattan. I loved to ride the city buses and my favored seat was the back bench. When my mother and I visited North Carolina and took a public bus, I immediately raced to the back of the bus. The irate bus driver

Letitia Anne Peplau, UCLA Distinguished Professor of Psychology, emeritus, University of California, USA.

yelled repeatedly that I couldn't sit there – it was for Negroes only. The family story goes that when we returned to New York and took a bus, I loudly proclaimed that I liked it here because anyone could ride in the back of the bus. In 1957 when we got our first television, I watched as Black students trying to attend a public high school in Little Rock, Arkansas had to be protected against angry White crowds by federalized National Guard troops. In 1965 I joined a group of Brown University students who traveled by bus to Alabama to participate in a large civil rights march from Selma to the state capital, Montgomery, to protest racist suppression of Black voting rights. I witnessed first-hand the amazing courage of Black people who braved violent attacks to challenge White power. In Montgomery, Dr. Martin Luther King, Jr.'s speech inspired us all. Reading Pettigrew's book suggested that social psychologists could use their skills to understand and perhaps help ameliorate social injustice. At this point, my path was clear: I would apply to graduate school at Harvard to study with Tom Pettigrew.

Fortunately, I was accepted by the social relations department to study for a PhD in social psychology. In 1968, the Harvard department was interdisciplinary, encompassing social, developmental, and clinical psychology as well as sociology and anthropology. I arrived on campus with funding from the NSF and joined a group of gifted classmates. There were several women in my cohort, a very recent change from the history of discrimination against women in higher education.

Our program was heavy on coursework: four courses a semester for two years and then more seminars. My first year I took Pettigrew's lecture course on race relations. Tom was an engaging lecturer and wonderful storyteller. Later I worked as his teaching assistant. I also took a proseminar in social psychology from Pettigrew and Bob Rosenthal, both great teachers. For our first research project, all the social psychology students were asked to replicate a classic study. I chose the Asch conformity study and used his methods with a student sample from a local state university. My project failed miserably, finding no evidence of conformity. This was my introduction to the so-called replicability crisis in social psychology, a controversy that has recurred periodically during the intervening years.

During graduate school, protests against the war in Vietnam intensified. At the time, all young men had to register for the draft and some were chosen randomly to serve. Many young men feared being drafted to fight in a war they vehemently opposed. The 1971 national draft lottery, held live on TV and radio, unexpectedly influenced the direction of my future research. Assistant Professor Zick Rubin decided to use the widely publicized lottery to test ideas about young men's "belief in a just world." Would randomly receiving a "good" outcome (low probability of being drafted) versus a "bad" outcome (high probability of being drafted) affect perceptions of oneself and others taking part in the lottery? Zick asked me to be his research assistant for the project (Rubin & Peplau, 1973). We worked well together, published two papers on the Belief in a Just World, and began a long-lasting and very productive collaboration.

Zick was a wunderkind who sprinted through school. Only a year older than me, Zick impressed with his intelligence and creativity, not his seniority. At Harvard, he obtained funding from the NSF to conduct a two-year longitudinal study of more than 200 college-age dating couples. The Boston Couples Study was ground-breaking for the time. It integrated multiple research methods to characterize many features of beginning relationships and to understand which couples stay together and which break up over time. I and Chuck Hill were Zick's main collaborators. With my growing interest in feminism, I eagerly investigated power relations in couples, sexual intimacy, and the impact of sex-role attitudes on relationships. An important way in which research in the early 1970s differed from today was the use of computers. Data for the Boston Couples Study were laboriously keypunched onto computer cards, then taken to a central computing facility to be returned a day or two later unless, of course, there was a bug in the program. Today, the same analyses could be done on a laptop computer in minutes.

While I was in graduate school, the women's movement increased in national prominence. In 1970, the Equal Rights Amendment was introduced in Congress and the American Psychological Association established a Task Force on the Status of Women in Psychology. Harvard hired Assistant Professor Matina Horner, who studied achievement in women and argued for the harmful effects of "fear of success" on talented women. I enthusiastically enrolled in Matina's graduate seminar on the psychology of women. For the seminar, I wrote a term paper on homosexuality, trying to compile and critique the scant available literature. I chose this topic because several good friends were deeply closeted about being lesbian, fearful that disclosure would derail their professional careers. This included my professor at Brown, Fran Clayton, who became a friend after I graduated. In 1970, Fran left academe to begin a decades-long relationship with acclaimed poet, essayist, and civil rights activist Audre Lorde. At Harvard, a lesbian classmate and I had long talks about her experiences and spent hours together reading newsletters of the Daughters of Bilitis, a lesbian organization that published member surveys and articles about discrimination. Sadly, the stress of concealing her identity ultimately led my classmate to leave Harvard. (Only decades later did Roger Brown's autobiography reveal that he, too, was gay.)

In my third year in graduate school, I was appointed as a sophomore tutor to teach a year-long seminar to a small group of undergraduates on any topic in "interdisciplinary social relations." I developed a course on sex roles, using readings from anthropology, sociology, and psychology. About this time, I also had the opportunity to write two chapters for an introductory psychology textbook, one on sex roles and one on intergroup behavior.

My last year at Harvard I worked to finish my dissertation, an experiment testing the impact of sex-role attitudes versus "fear of success" on the performance of women who either cooperated with or competed against their boyfriend on an intellectual task. As predicted, women with traditional attitudes performed significantly better when working as a team with their boyfriend than when working in individual competition; non-traditionals showed an opposite pattern. Fear of success was unrelated to performance. When I applied for academic positions, one job seemed tailor made for me: UCLA advertised for a social psychologist who could teach an undergraduate course on sex differences. At this point, I had taught a course on sex roles for two years, had published a chapter on sex roles, and was doing relevant research. When I was offered the position, my advisors encouraged me to accept. A visit to campus convinced me to give UCLA a try. What began as a five-year trial became my life-long academic home.

When I arrived at UCLA in 1973, my office had hand-me-down furniture that look like army surplus. It also had a lovely view of campus. Today assistant professors at research universities often negotiate generous start-up packages and reduced teaching. In contrast, the department lent me $300 for supplies until I got a grant. Without discussion, the chair assigned me to teach a large lecture class at 8 a.m. in the fall. I was the first woman faculty member in social psychology and only the third in a department of sixty-five faculty. My male colleagues were welcoming but in different life stages – most were married with children. It was the graduate students who befriended me, introduced me to local restaurants, and showed me around the city. I also sought out women faculty in other departments. In 1974 I joined a committee chaired by Lena Astin, a psychologist in the School of Education, that successfully lobbied the university to start an interdisciplinary program in women's studies. In 1983 a new committee developed a proposal to start a research center on women. Ultimately, the UCLA Center for the Study of Women was approved by the UC Regents and became the first among UC campuses. Early on, I served as Associate Director and then Acting Co-Director of the Center.

I continued publishing findings from the Boston Couples Study for several years (e.g., Peplau et al., 1993) but knew that I needed to start my own independent line of work. At Harvard I had attended a fascinating talk by sociologist Robert S. Weiss about loneliness. As a relationship researcher, I understood that loneliness results from inadequate social ties. It seemed a worthy topic for empirical work. I invited Dan Russell and other graduate students to launch a program of research on loneliness. Initially, we developed a questionnaire measure of loneliness and did studies to demonstrate that loneliness is distinct from related psychological experiences such as depression. When I told my mother about this new project, I learned that twenty years earlier she had published a paper on loneliness based on her own clinical observations. In 1976, Dan Perlman began a sabbatical at UCLA. Over coffee, we discovered our shared interest in loneliness and discussed ways to conceptualize loneliness and understand its origins. By the end of the year, Dan and I decided that a conference bringing together scholars doing relevant work would be productive. With funding from the NIMH, the conference was held in 1979. Subsequently Dan and I published an edited book that examined theoretical perspectives on loneliness, loneliness across the lifespan, and ideas about ways to help lonely people. In the forty years since, the UCLA Loneliness Scale has become a citation classic and loneliness research has blossomed (Russell et al., 1980). Newer research including studies in social neuroscience has consistently documented the detrimental impact of loneliness not only on psychological well-being but also on immune function, physical health, and mortality. In January 2021, as the COVID-19 pandemic raged, *Harvard Magazine*'s cover story was "Loneliness: The psychology and social costs of isolation."

My UCLA colleague Hal Kelley was influential in my career. Hal invited me to join a group of nine psychologists who met on campus for three weeks in the summer of 1978 to assess the current field of close relationship research and suggest directions for future work. The group included Ellen Berscheid, Ted Huston, George Levinger, and others. As a junior professor, the opportunity to work so closely with leaders in the field was both a bit scary and deeply rewarding. I had long admired the work of Ellen and her collaborator, Elaine (Walster) Hatfield, and had used their book on interpersonal attraction in classes at UCLA. In 1974 Ellen had received a "Golden Fleece" award from Senator Proxmire who ridiculed her NSF-funded research on love as a waste of taxpayer money. We hoped that our project would make a strong case for the value of relationship research.

Ultimately the close relationships group met for three summers to "go back to basics" to understand the essential phenomena of close interaction. Our long days of talking about ideas were punctuated by trips to Hal's Malibu beach club, lunch at the UCLA Sculpture Garden, and dinners at people's homes. A book presenting our conceptual framework and its application to such topics as emotion, power, love, and conflict appeared in 1983. The book began by observing that each person's dependence on others is a fundamental fact of the human condition. It emphasized that a science of relationships would be enriched by research and theory from multiple disciplines. And it argued that although the development of a science of relationships is a formidable task, it is ultimately "do-able." Today it is safe to say that this once fledgling field now has a sound foundation.

In 1994, the International Society for the Study of Personal Relationships was formed to foster interdisciplinary relationship research. To enhance the stature of this new organization, Hal Kelley, then a member of the National Academy of Sciences, agreed to serve as the first president. The next four elected presidents were Ellen Berscheid, Ted Huston, me, and Dan Perlman. Over time the organization, now renamed the International Association for Relationship Research, has thrived. New cohorts of leaders have emerged. Young researchers and graduate students have found a welcome home in IARR. Conferences, two academic journals, and a book series have further encouraged new scholars and international collaborations.

A final major focus of my research has concerned same-sex relationships and sexual orientation. Although I developed an interest in this topic in graduate school, I didn't begin research until I was at UCLA. How that came about is a bit unusual. In teaching the undergraduate class on the psychology of sex differences, I lectured about the Boston Couples study, a topic that many students found interesting. What I didn't anticipate was that gay and lesbian students in the class would approach me to ask why I didn't talk about their experiences. I was impressed that these young people felt safe enough to disclose their orientation but, I suggested, there was little research and much of it was harmful. Indeed, it wasn't until 1973 that the American Psychiatric Association removed "homosexuality" from the Diagnostic and Statistical Manual of Mental Disorders (DSM).

The students repeatedly suggested that I should undertake a project and offered to help me recruit participants. With this offer of assistance, I invited several graduate students to work with me on a project that would ask the same kinds of questions we used in the Boston Couples Study to characterize lesbian relationships. Through word of mouth, we identified people in the community who might be willing to participate. The next step was to convince reluctant participants. I remember vividly meeting in the home of a local nurse with a group of her lesbian friends. Why should they trust me, they asked? I described my background and invited them to look at the anonymous questionnaires we had brought that asked about love, commitment, and other relationship issues. Fortunately, they all agreed to take part and we were able to recruit a community sample of lesbians. Over the next thirty-five years, I and various collaborators published a range of journal articles and book chapters about same-sex couples and sexual orientation. I knew that this topic had gained some respectability in mainstream psychology when I was invited to write a chapter for the *Annual Review of Psychology* (Peplau & Fingerhut, 2007).

Research on sexual minority issues grew quickly from the 1980s on. In 1985 APA Division 44 was established as the Society for the Psychological Study of Lesbian and Gay Issues. Since renamed Psychology of Sexual Orientation and Gender Diversity, the expanded division publishes a journal, a book series, and a newsletter. Today, researchers studying same-sex couples and sexual minority individuals use a wide range of methodologies including representative national surveys, longitudinal studies, and observational studies of couple interactions. Much of academia has become more welcoming to sexual minority students and faculty.

My interest in sexual orientation led me in another direction. In 1986 I met and became friends with Evelyn Hooker, a retired psychologist living in Santa Monica who had conducted pioneering research on gay men. In 1957 Evelyn published the first community-based study comparing the psychological health of matched samples of gay and heterosexual men. Using the best psychological tests available in the 1950s, she demonstrated that trained clinicians could not distinguish between the two groups. This research, widely acclaimed by the gay community, was part of the evidence that led to homosexuality being removed as a clinical diagnosis. I was fortunate to be included in Evelyn's "kitchen cabinet," along with Linda Garnets and Jackie Goodchilds. We gathered regularly in Evelyn's living room to share food, wine, and lively discussions about psychology, current issues, politics, and more. In the 1990s, Evelyn established the Wayne F. Placek Award program at the American Psychological Foundation, initially funded by a bequest from one of Evelyn's research participants. This program supports research to increase public awareness about sexual orientation and to alleviate the stress experienced by sexual minority individuals. From 1995 to 2000, I served as a member of the Scientific Review Panel for this program.

I have often thought about comparisons between Evelyn's career and my own. We both wanted to teach but UCLA offered Evelyn only the opportunity to teach in Extension, not a full-time position. We both began research on sexual orientation at the urging of students who helped us gain entrée to the gay/lesbian community. We were both heterosexual, married women which, at the time, meant that our research couldn't be criticized as "self-interested." Although Evelyn studied mental health and I studied close relationships, we both were in on the ground floor of scientific inquiry that has since matured and expanded. Finally, we have both, in small ways, contributed to changes in social policy.

In 2008 I was asked by the ACLU to testify as an expert witness in a Florida court case about adoption. At that time, state law prohibited adoption by gay men and lesbians although they were permitted to be foster parents. To challenge this law, Frank Gill, an openly gay man, petitioned the court to adopt two boys that he and his partner had been raising as foster children for several years. The ACLU represented Gill. I and other expert witnesses testified that based on scientific research gay men and lesbians can and do form close, caring, and stable relationships. Further, there is no evidence that children are harmed by being raised by gay or lesbian parents. Amicus briefs supporting Gill were filed by APA and other professional organizations. Ultimately, the Florida law was overturned. I was also involved in similar successful legal challenges in Arkansas and Montana.

In addition to these significant legal changes, polls consistently show that public approval of gay adoption has increased over time. In 2008, voters in California passed Proposition 8, a law prohibiting same-sex marriage. Soon after, two same-sex couples challenged the legality of this new law in a widely publicized court case with high-profile attorneys Ted Olsen and David Boies in the lead. The plaintiffs relied heavily on scientific research findings and called many expert witnesses including four psychologists: Greg Herek, Michael Lamb, Ilan Meyer, and me. Preparation for the trial was extensive. I spent countless hours working with attorneys fine-tuning a written statement of my opinions and doing practice sessions for depositions and the trial itself. Based on a then substantial body of research, I testified that same-sex couples closely resemble heterosexual couples in terms of the quality of their relationship and the processes that affect their relationships. Same-sex couples would benefit physically and psychologically from legal recognition of their relationships as do heterosexuals. Such recognition would likely strengthen the stability of committed same-sex couples as it does for heterosexuals. Further, there is no reason to believe that permitting same-sex couples to marry would harm the institution of heterosexual marriage.

There was great public and media interest in this trial. Because the court prohibited the public from viewing a recording of the actual trial, Hollywood actors volunteered to recreate the trial verbatim from the court transcript on YouTube. I was ably portrayed by Adrienne Barbeau, an actress known for the TV sitcom *Maude* and such movies as *Swamp Thing* and *Escape from New York*. Subsequently those involved in the trial were invited to a reading of Dustin Black's play *8* by George Clooney, Brad Pitt, and others in Hollywood. Most important, this case was ultimately followed by a US Supreme Court case, also argued by Boies and Olsen, that finally established same-sex marriage as a legal right throughout the country. Our expert statements were cited in that federal case. Recent national polls show that more than 60 percent of Americans now support marriage equality. When I chose a career in social psychology, I never imagined that research would play a part in bringing about these dramatic changes.

Several people have been uniquely important to me. At UCLA I met Steve Gordon, a sociologist and my husband of forty-plus years. Steve has been a constant source of support and made it possible for me to take advantage of many professional opportunities while raising our now grown son David. Steve's humor and vast intellectual curiosity have greatly enriched my life. At Harvard, I met Shelley Taylor, then a young assistant professor. I also worked briefly with Chris Dunkel Schetter, who spent a year as a research assistant on the Boston Couples Study. It was my good fortune that both women eventually joined the UCLA faculty. They are treasured friends who have traveled with me through such challenges as promotions, child rearing, and now aging. One of the biggest rewards of being a professor was the opportunity to work with and get to know so many talented graduate students. I miss them.

I retired from UCLA in 2011 but continued part-time as Vice Chair for Graduate Studies. In 2018, I emptied my office, cheerfully disposed of mountains of files, packed the books, and ended a career that had nourished me for forty-five years. I may never stop viewing the world as a social psychologist but I was ready to leave academia.

Suggested Reading

Brown, R. (1965). *Social Psychology*. New York: Free Press.

Peplau, L. A., & Fingerhut, A. W. (2007). The close relationships of lesbians and gay men. *Annual Review of Psychology, 58*, 405–424.

Peplau, L. A., Hill, C. T., & Rubin, Z. (1993). Sex-role attitudes in dating and marriage: A 15-year followup of the Boston Couples Study. *Journal of Social Issues, 40*(3), 31–52.

Pettigrew, T. F. (1964). *A Profile of the Negro American*. Princeton, NJ: Van Nostrand Publishers.

Rubin, Z., & Peplau, L. A. (1973). Belief in a just world and reactions to another's lot: A study of participants in the national draft lottery. *Journal of Social Issues, 29*(4), 73–94.

Russell, D., Peplau, L. A., & Cutrona, C. E. (1980). The revised UCLA loneliness scale: Concurrent and discriminant validity evidence. *Journal of Personality and Social Psychology, 39*(3), 472–480.

28 You Can't Be a Self by Yourself

Hazel Rose Markus

I was born Hazel Rose in London, England to an English Catholic mom and a Jewish American dad who had grown up in England. Our family immigrated to sunny, orange-scented, anything-was-possible Southern California; first to Los Angeles and then to San Diego. My mother, father, uncles and aunts all became public school teachers. It was at San Diego State University that I became certain that social psychology was my path. I had planned on a major in English and journalism. As the editor of my high school newspaper, I was convinced that my passion was rigorous reporting and clear writing that would deliver the truth of important events to inquiring minds. Then in my sophomore year I took Psychology 101. The professor divided the room into two groups and positioned us so that the groups were out of each other's earshot. He told my group a story about shopping for shoes and how it was often difficult to find a shoe that fits. He moved to the other side of the room and told the second group a story about the excitement of travel in North Africa.

The professor then positioned himself between the two groups and asked everyone to write down exactly what he said next. He uttered several sounds and collected our responses. From my group, 22 of 30 people heard *Triple E* (a designation for wide shoes and boots). In the second group, 26 of 33 people heard *Tripoli* (the capital of Libya). The event was identical for both groups, but their responses were strikingly different. A mundane example to be sure, yet one from which I experienced nothing less than the construction of social reality. The meaning of the uttered sounds for me and the others in my group – our truth – took form through the professor's story. Those across the room hearing a different story experienced a different reality – their truth.

I began to worry about journalism and my intention to report the truth. In retrospect, I learned to never underestimate the power of an in-class demonstration. I decided to major in psychology. I was following the writings of 1960s philosopher Alan Watts on Buddhism and marching against the Vietnam War with my soon-to-be husband, Greg Markus, a political science major. I was also caught up in second wave feminism. The rallying call of "the personal is political" made an impression that stayed with me. I knew it meant that questions of who should do the housework and the care of children were not just women's individual problems but also problems of

Hazel Rose Markus, Stanford University, USA.

power and patriarchy. Yet from my beginner's perspective, there was even more to this already provocative statement. I was taking social psychology and our text was *Social Psychology: An Experimental Approach* by R. B. Zajonc which defined social psychology as the study of the interdependence – the mutual and reciprocal influence – among individuals. So if there was a *mutual and reciprocal relation* between the personal and the political, then the political was also personal.

I knew that my experience of the world – for example, what I heard in a story about shoe shopping – depended on what I brought to that situation to make sense of it. And what I brought to the situation depended to some degree on both immediate and past experience; I was OK with this level of social influence. Yet the thought that what I heard, saw, and thought, my ways of being a person, being a woman, were in fact being crafted by the political ideas and practices of people in the past made me feel constrained and controlled. It seemed that there was very little I could do about it. Could it really be that the more you peer inside the personal, the more you discover the context, culture, and history? This tension was the source of my fascination with the relationship between culture and agency. Culture for me was an umbrella term for all types of social categories – regions of the world or the country, ethnicity, race, religion, gender, class, occupation, etc. Agency meant ways of acting in the world.

The notion that I was not fully my own creation was disturbing. The foundational individualism of the United States was taking on a new and heady but extreme form: People go their own way and do their own thing (or as we say now, you do you). Personal freedom and growth and self-expansion were the sanctioned goals. If relationships were constraining your individual pursuits, ditch them. The shared cultural task and the individualist norm of my cohort became to *find* your *true* self; it was there to be discovered. In 1970, Greg and I left San Diego for graduate school in Ann Arbor. (Our undergrad mentors Rosalind and Ivo Feierabend, a political scientist and a social psychologist, insisted that given our interests we could do our own thing better at the University of Michigan than at Berkeley or North Carolina – our other options.) I thought I might figure out if being a self was really a personal project or more of a group one.

Ann Arbor

I did eventually find an answer in graduate school. But not at first. At the University of Michigan, I proposed several research topics centering on the links between those big social categories that seemed to organize the world and sometimes the self. What about the role of gender in shaping the self? Given women's traditional roles and the expectations through which they lived their lives, it made sense that some aspects of being a person would take a different and a more relational form for women. My advisors, all men, said that wasn't a topic. They said, "What was a self?" "Why gender?" They went on: the topic was "marginal" and "I wouldn't get a job."

I remember thinking how nice it must be to get to say what is a topic and what is marginal. That seemed a special kind of power indeed. I proposed race and the self.

My experience in San Diego had been a segregated one, both in the city and in the university. Ann Arbor was different. Discussions of race and diversity were at the top of the intellectual agenda. When I would meet James Jackson who was organizing the first nationally representative study of Black Americans in the halls of the Institute for Social Research, I would say "Hi, how's it going?" He would respond with a smile and say, "It's your world, I'm just paying rent." It took me more years than I care to admit to understand what he meant.

Patricia Gurin who helped me understand so much about race and gender explained that thinking about group differences at a time when women were marching to underscore that they were equal to men was awkward because no matter the theoretical setup, a different self would be invariably cast as a lesser self. The same would be true for differences in self by race. The field didn't know how to think about group differences. I could understand this, but it frustrated me. If social psychology was concerned with mutual and reciprocal influence among people, the connections between cultural formations like gender and race and self seemed like excellent topics.

I followed the advice of my advisors. So instead of comparing the selves of men and women or of European Americans and African-Americans, for my dissertation I worked on "the basic self." I understand now that I was coming up against psychology's hegemonic view of the agency and implicit idea that there was one right and good way to be a person – the way exhibited by European American middle-class white men. Departures from this model were irrational or inferior. A field's embrace of the idea that differences in behavior can be construed as assets, strengths, and resources would be a long time coming.

I was looking to theorize about the self in ways that didn't cast it as mystical or epiphenomenal. I didn't want to say "self-concept." The self is an organization of past behavior to be sure, but it is more than just a static category. I was interested in self as a process. The self is the part of you that attends, perceives, thinks, feels, imagines, remembers, decides, and acts. It is a story you are writing whether you know it or not. A self strings together thoughts, feelings, motives, and actions; it connects you to your past and future and lets you know that the person who went to bed last night is the same person who woke up this morning. If you lose the plot, you're in trouble.

The self and selving process needed some solid empirical referents. I decided to theorize the me-in-the-middle as a system of self-schemas or interpretive structures that help you make sense of your experiences and figure out what to do next. These studies showed that self-schemas facilitate judgments and decisions about the self. For example, if you described yourself as highly independent, you would later push a "me" button for ideas related to independence with shorter latency than if you weren't sure about your independence. Other tasks revealed that self-schemas contained easily retrievable behavioral information, provided a confident basis for the self-prediction of behavior, and made people resistant to information that suggested they weren't independent (Markus, 1977).

After I finished my dissertation, I got a job at the UM, first as a lecturer and then as an assistant professor. It was 1977, I was likely a recipient of the affirmative action of the time. It felt good to do my small part to redress the decades long imbalance in favor of affirmative action for men. Greg also got a job as an assistant professor in political science. We were lucky. Still our marriage came apart. The cultural winds of the 1970s blew strong. We remained on good terms. I kept Greg's name, but made sure to always use my birth name as well. The personal was political and vice versa.

In the 1980s, the Cognitive Revolution was fully underway. Michigan social psychologists were an incredible group – Bob Zajonc, Nancy Cantor, Dick Nisbett, Gene Burnstein, Pat Gurin, Mel Manis, James Jackson, Claude Steele, Phoebe Ellsworth, and Camille Wortman. We talked constantly in threes and fours in the bays of the Institute for Social Research. We ate lunch together, stopped for coffee at 3 p.m., and pot lucked on Friday night. Like virtually everyone in the field, we were drawn to the computer as a metaphor for the mind and the self. At the same time we struggled with trying to stuff the whole mind and self into the head. We took deep dives into many types of cognitive and affective representations and how they lend meaning and coherence to our worlds and construct experience – schemas, proto-types, life tasks, scripts, construals, hypotheses, theories, heuristics, frames, sets, plans, goals, motives, attitudes, beliefs, attributions, stereotypes, and more. These interpretive structures have some differences, but they are all built up from past interactions in our many social worlds, and they all fashion our current realities, not after the fact of perception, but during it; they are necessary for it. We read Allport, Mead, Asch, Bruner, Gibson, Kelly, Lewin, Neisser, Berger and Luckman, Moscovici, Tajfel, and Kelley. I hope newcomers to the field will continue to take time for these foundational texts.

With grad students Keith Sentis, Paula Pietromonaco, Jeanne Smith, Geoff Fong, Lisa Brown, and Elissa Wurf, we carried out studies revealing the influence of self-schemas. We showed that people quickly attend to, learn, and remember what is relevant to their needs, goals, and interests (e.g., what is me) and ignore what is not-me. Together these studies demonstrated that what I see as relevant to my self takes on a special glow and has behavioral significance. Adding a future oriented component of the self, Paula Nurius, Susan Cross, Daphna Oyserman, and I then investigated the role of possible selves – what people hope for or fear for themselves (e.g., Markus & Nurius, 1986). We saw these aspects of the self as a bridge from the cognitive to the motivational and the behavioral. We also began to explore how gender shapes the self. We saw that women and men tended to make the me/not me divide in different ways and reasoned that women were more likely to have a connectedness self-schema and men a separateness self-schema. This distinction was consistent with demonstrated differences in spatial abilities, intuition, and moral reasoning (Cross & Markus, 1993; Markus & Oyserman, 1989).

These self-schema studies were a partial answer to my culture and agency problem. Culture does not completely determine the personal and does not shape everyone in the same way. There is plenty of room for uniqueness and personal orientations. When men and women, or even members of the same family, are in what appears the exact same situation, they may have surprisingly different responses depending on the schema through which they construct that information. Agency depends on one's self-schemas which are a function of where and how attention has been previously deployed, that is, where and how you have been encouraged, or encouraged yourself, to see, hear, think, believe, or feel.

We demonstrated the powerful role of the self in organizing behavior. Yet, we also encountered a great deal of resistance, primarily from cognitive psychologists who claimed that a schema about a self was no different than a schema about a chair – just a cognitive representation of an object in the world, nothing special. We argued the self is not just another cognitive representation. It was one that could mediate and regulate all the other psychological processes in a way other categories do not. That which is "me" is used as a benchmark for organizing, evaluating, and understanding the rest of the world. As Anaïs Nin is said to have written, "we don't see the world the way it *is*, but as the way *we are*."

These were exciting times. The magic of Michigan was that it served up a heady mix of people, projects, theories, and visions for social change. The social was real. The social sciences mattered. Everyone knew this; no one had to be convinced. Bob Zajonc and I married in 1982 – the influence was mutual and reciprocal. We talked and argued about psychology, politics, and how to fix the world. Nobody I had encountered thought like Bob. These conversations changed when Bob passed in 2008, but in many ways they continue and inspire me to this day.

Japan

As part of a long-standing scholar's exchange program between the Research Center for Group Dynamics and the University of Osaka, I had the opportunity to visit and lecture in Japan, an unbelievably fascinating site for a student of the self and social behavior. This is when I met Shinobu Kitayama who had come from Japan to graduate school in the United States. He also worried about culture and agency. He noticed that Americans seemed to believe that agency or the motivation for action came from inside the person rather than from relations with others. He wondered how he could get such an agent – not one who would book him speaking gigs – but an ongoing sense of an internal force that fueled his behavior, the one that seemed common in many Americans. I immediately understood his concern. Finally, someone who could talk about a different way of being and who wasn't worried that his type of agency might be cast as a less good one. Even with his less than perfect English and my non-existent Japanese, we communicated easily and seamlessly. Shinobu was full of ideas and brimming with plans for experiments. And he was confident. Of course, agency could be relational. Again, by way of quick historical context, this was the period of "Japan is number one." Its cars were problem-free, its workers productive, and its children high-scoring. Americans wanted to know about the Japanese way of doing things. The political does impact the personal.

We began conversations and a collaboration that has spanned decades. As we speculated and traded observations, we began to ask questions. Why was it, I asked, that after weeks of lecturing in Japan to students with a good command of English, no one said anything – nothing – no questions, no comments? Where were the arguments, debates, and signs of critical thinking? And if you asked a straightforward question such as "Where is the best noodle shop?" why did the answer tend to be an audible intake of air followed by the response, "It depends." Didn't Japanese students have their own preferences, ideas, opinions, and attitudes?

Shinobu listened and then asked his own questions. He was curious about why students shouldn't just listen to a lecture and why American students felt the need to be constantly active, to talk all the time, often interrupting and talking over each other and the professor? And why did the comments of his fellow students reveal such strong emotions and have such a competitive edge? What was the point of this arguing? Why did intelligence seem to be associated with getting the best of another person, even within a class where people knew each other well?

Sure, it was true, I responded, that some Americans were on the extroverted edge. However, wasn't that better than the reticence and low self-esteem of Japanese professors and students? Why, for example, did Japanese visiting scholars begin their talks with an apology? "I'm sorry, but I am not the best qualified person to give this presentation and I hope that you will forgive the fact that I may waste your time."

Shinobu asked why American psychologists began their talks with a joke, even in important settings. And why do friends of the speaker gather around afterward and give hugs and say the talk was "fantastic." Why the constant evaluation? Why the superlatives? And why the effort to make the speaker and the audience feel good? And, he continued, why at the party after a talk do hosts bombard their guests with questions and choices? Do you want wine or beer or soft drinks or juice or water, or would you rather have something hot, coffee or tea? Wine? Do you want red or white? What was the point of burdening guests with these trivial decisions?

These questions about the details and peculiarities of everyday life in different cultural contexts led to all types of larger questions that were tractable and that became the basis of our research programs. These highly speculative conversations and the edgy questions we asked and answered will never appear in journal publications, but such exchanges are critical in developing new ideas in uncharted terrains. To make such exchanges both meaningful and productive, however, one needs collaborators one trusts and confides in. Collaboration we discovered requires a great deal of the very phenomenon we began to examine – interdependence.

As we explored these questions, the answers were surprising. It became clear that people in the United States and in Japan were making sense of their everyday experience with very different interpretive frameworks – a little bit like the difference between shopping for shoes and traveling in Northern Africa. In a paper we published at the time, we called these frameworks *self-construals* (Markus & Kitayama, 1991). In North American and many Western contexts, the obvious, taken-for-granted, and "right" way to think about a person is as a separate and stable individual who freely chooses their actions and exerts influence on their environment. People's actions in the world (their agency) are largely understood as independent of other people and circumstances and driven by personal preferences, beliefs, and goals. In Japan, the equally obvious and default way to think about a person is quite different. A person is less a free agent and more one who is flexible, committed to others, and an interdependent part of a larger social unit. People's actions are always in relation to some others and require being aware and responsive to their needs and expectations.

Where do these differences in self-construal come from? They come from the many cultures that organize our lives and guide our actions. We generally have little awareness of their influence. We found that what people are doing in the "same" situation – a classroom, a restaurant, a baseball field, a party – was often surprisingly different. We analyzed self-reports, social interactions, institutional policies, and cultural products, as in ads, websites, songs, books, newspapers, and themes began to emerge. We analyzed culture in terms of four levels – ideas, institutions, interactions, and individuals that comprise a dynamic called the culture cycle (Markus & Kitayama, 2010; see Markus & Conner, 2013).

Shinobu had taken a job at the University of Oregon but over the years and in between other projects, we kept thinking together. We elaborated a theory of the mutual constitution of culture and self, or in the more resonant phrase of Rick Shweder (1991): "how culture and self make each other up" (Markus & Kitayama, 2003, 2010). We described how the various ideas and practices of cultures can give rise to different types of selves, and how selves in interaction with each other reinforced and fostered the cultures. It was not that people live in the same world and view it through different lenses. Instead, people often live in different social realities because through their actions they shape their cultures to align with their construals. Shweder's (1991) book, *Thinking through Cultures*, had a lasting influence on us both.

What became most clear was that Western psychology is still grounded in an independent model of agency commonly found in what Henrich and colleagues (2010) have branded Western, Educated, Industrialized, Rich, and Democratic or WEIRD contexts. This is not a neutral or an empirically derived model, but instead a philosophical and historical construction. Baked into this model is the idea of the authority of the individual – a product of Western Enlightenment thinking, Christianity, the Protestant Ethic, the Declaration of Independence, the frontier, the American Dream, and all the formal and informal institutions and daily interactions that animate these ideas. The personal, the self, the psyche, thinking, feeling, acting were in some large part political, as well as historical, cultural, economic, and social. As a field we had a good grasp of selves and minds in one context, but what about in others? With shared enthusiasm, Dick Nisbett and I developed a cultural psychology class and a culture and cognition program in which we explored other contexts and other psychologies.

Palo Alto

When I moved to Stanford in 1994, I was lucky enough to become interdependent with another group of amazing social psychologists (Claude Steele, Lee Ross, Mark Lepper, Jennifer Eberhardt, Greg Walton, Carol Dweck, Dale Miller, Benoît Monin) and wonderful graduate students who eagerly took up cultural psychology. These students expanded the range of cultural contexts, methods used, and behaviors observed to study how culture and selves make each other up. Some examples: Glenn Adams (2005), after several years in the Peace Corps in Sierra Leone and Ghana, discovered why people in West Africa are sure that they have enemies, while Americans are equally sure they do not. Heejung Kim (2002), annoyed with widespread reports that East Asian students do not contribute in class, showed that while Americans confuse talking with thinking, East Asians do not. Stephanie Fryberg and others (2008) found that exposure to Native mascots depresses self-esteem and possible selves in Native students. Vicky Plaut and others (2002) found that regions of the United States are distinct subcultures that can shape self-concepts and well-being. Annie Tsai (2005) examined hierarchy as evil to be subverted in the United States, but as necessary for societal integration in China. Alyssa Fu discovered why East Asian but not European American moms can motivate performance (Fu & Markus, 2014). Alana Snibbe Conner carried out the first experiments on how social class shapes preference and choice (Snibbe & Markus, 2005). Krishna Savani and others (2010) demonstrated that North Americans who carry out the exact sequence of actions as South Asian Indians think they have made twice as many choices.

During this time, with my colleagues Claude and Dorothy Steele, historians Al Camarillo and George Fredrickson, and literary critic Paula Moya I had the chance to develop the Center for Comparative Studies in Race and Ethnicity. Race became the cultural formation that focused my interests. I had always thought that if social psychology was the field that took seriously the influence of other people's views on the individual's behavior, then race was the single best example. It is a social construction that changes the perceiver's and the target's social realities in the most powerful ways. How could you *not* be interested in race?

Claude Steele and his lab were revealing the consequences of being a target of a stereotype, and how this phenomenon can be examined in simple but powerful laboratory studies. And on a daily basis, the students in my diverse lab group helped me to take the target's perspective and the need to think about my own race. One example from 1995 stayed with me. I had taken my daughter to see the newly released Disney movie *Pocahontas*. I suggested to the students that it was a pretty good cultural product. Stephanie Fryberg, who is Native and at that point a grad student, gave a loud sigh and said, "Yeah, white people would think that." Although it has now become common to identify as "white" and to describe people as "white," it was not then. White people were the unmarked standard of neutral. With Stephanie's comment I experienced being the target of a "white American" stereotype. (I know, white tears.) Even though I was so taken with the idea that we see the world *as we are*, I came to understand that I was still in habit of construing the world from one invisible to me but racialized perspective. I thought back to the greeting of James Jackson when I was in graduate school and realized that coming to terms with my own race and my responsibility for current racial dynamics is an essential and ongoing task.

At the turn of the century, startup culture saturated Stanford. You should innovate, do things differently, do it quickly, and change the world. And if you happen to break things or fail or disappoint, that's OK, good even. It was the US independent model of the self on steroids. One good fall-out from these broader contextual trends was that social psychologists were now free to go back to Lewin's future and address themselves to pressing societal problems. In my Ann Arbor days, researchers studied social problems. Applying these findings, fixing problems, and changing the world was not basic science. That was someone else's job.

Grad students quickly picked up on these more practical trends. Nicole Stephens and colleagues (2012) found that first generation college students had relatively interdependent selves and struggled in university contexts primarily designed for continuing generation students with more independent selves. Tiffany Brannon and others (2015) found that incorporating interdependent aspects of African-American culture within an independent university setting enhanced the persistence and performance of African-Americans on achievement-related tasks.

Together with Paula Moya, I edited a book called *Doing Race: 21 Essays for the 21st Century* (2010) in which we challenged the then and still popular idea that race doesn't matter. These essays reveal how race is made real at every level of culture and how achieving a just society requires us to continually take account of race. Alana Conner and I wrote *Clash! How to Survive in a Multicultural World* (2013) in which we argued that a root cause of many conflicts of ethnicity, gender, social class, race, region, religion, occupation is, in fact, the clash between independence and interdependence. We described how we can use both our independent and interdependent selves to bridge these cultural divides.

Now with my colleagues Jennifer Eberhardt and Mar Yam Hamedani, we direct a Center called Stanford SPARQ. We are a "do tank." We partner with industry leaders and changemakers in criminal justice, health, economic development, education, and media who hope to reduce societal disparities and bridge divides. A major focus in this research is on illuminating cultures and inviting people to claim their roles in culture making and changing (Eberhardt et al., 2021; Hamedani & Markus, 2019).

In Closing or TL;DR

It turns out you can't be a self by yourself. For me personally, my self and my work are the result of many rich and rewarding collaborations, only some of which I have hinted at here. And more generally, we are all culturally shaped shapers. Who we are, what we care about, what we are supposed to do, what moves us to action, what is possible, what happens to us, how we are seen and treated is influenced by our many crisscrossing sociocultural contexts – all of which give us schemas to make meaning and to construct our worlds. The self is a dynamic group project. The full consequences are still to be realized, theoretically or empirically.

Given that my analysis of myself reveals that the self is a dynamic group project, my advice to those entering the field is to seek out advisors and friends who inspire and help you and to whom you commit to do likewise. Increasingly, high impact research will center on pressing societal problems. Progress on any of these challenges from climate change, immigration, poverty reduction, public health, political polarization to racial justice will require an understanding of how people make sense of themselves and others in particular situations. I predict a bright and practical future with careers for social psychologists in universities, governments, and corporations as this essential understanding becomes ever more apparent and widespread.

Suggested Reading

Adams, G. (2005). The cultural grounding of personal relationship: Enemyship in North American and West African worlds. *Journal of Personality and Social Psychology*, *88*(6), 948–968.

Brannon, T. N., Markus, H. R., & Taylor, V. J. (2015). "Two souls, two thoughts," two self-schemas: Double consciousness can have positive academic consequences for African Americans. *Journal of Personality and Social Psychology*, *108*, 586–609.

Cross, S., & Markus, H. R. (1993). Gender in thought, belief and action: A cognitive approach. In A. E. Beall & R. J. Sternberg (Eds.), *The Psychology of Gender* (pp. 55–98). New York: Guilford Press.

Eberhardt, J., Markus, H. R., & Hamedani, M. (2021). Bringing the world into our science. *APS Observer*, *34*(4). www.psychologicalscience.org/observer/into-our-science.

Fryberg, S., Markus, H. R., Oyserman, D., & Stone, J. (2008). Of warrior chiefs and Indian princesses: The psychological consequences of American Indian mascots. *Basic and Applied Social Psychology*, *30*(3), 208–218.

Fu, A. S., & Markus, H. R. (2014). My mother and me: Why tiger mothers motivate Asian Americans but not European Americans. *Personality and Social Psychology Bulletin*, *40*, 739–749.

Hamedani, M. G., & Markus H. R. (2019). Understanding culture clashes and catalyzing change: A culture cycle approach. *Frontiers in Psychology*, *10*(700), 1–7.

Henrich, J., Heine, S. J., & Norenzayan, A. (2010). The weirdest people in the world? *Behavioral and Brain Sciences*, *33*, 61–83.

Kim, H. S. (2002). We talk, therefore we think? A cultural analysis of the effect of talking on thinking. *Journal of Personality and Social Psychology*, *83*(4), 828–842.

Markus, H. (1977). Self-schemata and processing information about the self. *Journal of Personality and Social Psychology*, *35*, 63–78.

Markus, H. R., & Conner, A. C. (2013). *Clash! Eight Cultural Conflicts that Make Us Who We Are*. New York: Penguin (Hudson Street Press).

Markus, H. R., & Kitayama, S. (1991). Culture and the self: Implications for cognition, emotion, and motivation. *Psychological Review*, *98*(2), 224–253.

  (2003). Culture, self, and the reality of the social. *Psychological Inquiry*, *14*(3–4), 277–283.

  (2010). Cultures and selves: A cycle of mutual constitution. *Perspectives on Psychological Science*, *5*(4), 420–430.

Markus, H. R., & Moya, P. (2010). *Doing Race: 21 Essays for the 21st Century*. New York: W. W. Norton.

Markus, H. R., & Nurius, P. (1986). Possible selves. *American Psychologist*, *41*, 954–969.

Markus, H. R., & Oyserman, D. (1989). Gender and thought: The role of the self-concept. In M. Crawford & M. Gentry (Eds.), *Gender and Thought* (pp. 100–127). New York: Springer-Verlag.

Plaut, V., Markus, H. R., & Lachman, M. (2002). Place matters: Consensual features and regional variation in American well-being and self. *Journal of Personality and Social Psychology, 83*(1), 160–184.

Savani, K., Markus, H. R., Naidu, N. V. R., Kumar, S., & Berlia, N. (2010). What counts as a choice? U.S. Americans are more likely than Indians to construe actions as choices. *Psychological Science, 14*(3), 391–398.

Shweder, R. A. (1991). *Thinking through Cultures: Expeditions in Cultural Psychology.* Cambridge, MA: Harvard University Press.

Snibbe, A., & Markus, H. R. (2005). You can't always get what you want: Social class, agency and choice. *Journal of Personality and Social Psychology, 88*(4), 703–720.

Stephens, N. M., Fryberg, S. A., Markus, H. R., Johnson, C. S., & Covarrubias, R. (2012). Unseen disadvantage: How the American universities' focus on independence undermines the academic performance of first-generation college students. *Journal of Personality and Social Psychology, 102*, 1178–1197.

Tsai, A. Y. (2005). Equality or propriety: A cultural models approach to understanding social hierarchy. Unpublished doctoral thesis, Stanford University.

29   Getting to Here from There

Michael F. Scheier

First, a disclaimer. I am not a bona fide social psychologist. I have taken social psychology courses at both the undergraduate and graduate level. I have also published research on topics that clearly fall within the purview of social psychology. Still, my formal training is not in social psychology, but in personality psychology, and the bulk of my research falls within the personality domain. Given my background, the perspectives offered in this chapter might differ somewhat from those offered by others, especially so concerning things to do going forward.

Now that that is done, I can begin to describe how it was that I got to "here" from "there." The difficulty, of course, is knowing exactly where "there" should begin. My formative years were largely unremarkable. I spent most of my time in California, living in Redondo Beach (a beach town south of Los Angeles) and in Carmichael (a suburb of Sacramento). I am particularly fond of my time in Redondo Beach, where I spent my summers fishing off the local pier in the morning and lying on the beach in the afternoon "working on my tan." At that point in time, school was only something that I was required to do in the cooler months of the year.

Finding My Way: The Drift from Political Science to Clinical Psychology to Personality

Santa Clara University

I went to Santa Clara University (in 1966) after graduating high school. My plan was to major in political science, as one of my high school teachers thought I would be good at it. It became quickly apparent, however, that political science was not for me. I started to explore other majors.

About this time, I took a self-paced course in introductory psychology. I really enjoyed the class. The concepts were a lot of fun to work with, and I found myself using them regularly to better understand myself and the social world around me. Interestingly, a few years later, I had the occasion to take the California Psychological Inventory. The highest score that I received on any of the scales, by far, was the one

Michael F. Scheier, Carnegie Mellon University, USA. The author would like to thank Carsten Wrosch and Karen Matthews for reading and commenting on a prepublication version of this chapter.

that assessed "psychological mindedness." Soon after the course ended, I switched my major to psychology.

The University of California at Berkeley

I also decided to switch institutions to the University of California, Berkeley. It was an outstanding decision! I immersed myself in psychology, taking courses on a variety of different topics. Along the way, I started to think seriously about getting an advanced degree in clinical psychology. My mother was diagnosed with major depressive disorder when I was in high school. Her illness was a significant burden on the family, even though my father did his best to hide her condition from me and my two siblings. I thought it would be great if I got the training needed to help people like my mother.

In the fall of my senior year, I applied to ten graduate programs that offered PhD degrees in clinical. Shortly after, I got ten rejection letters. It was time to regroup. After talking to some relevant folks, I decided that my failure was due to two aspects of my resume. First, in my personal essay, I stressed helping others rather than doing research as the major reason for seeking a clinical degree. Second, I did not have any relevant research experience, which likely explains why I did not think to push harder on it.

I could always rewrite the personal essay. What I really needed to do was gain some research experience. Donald Riley and his graduate student, Linda Warren, were running a project on discrimination reversal training in small, coastal shelf octopuses and were seeking an undergraduate research assistant to help with the study. I applied for the position and got lucky. They hired me. Working in the lab allowed me to learn what doing experimental research was all about, as well as excellent training on how to do it (my first empirical paper, co-authored with Warren and Riley, described the work coming out of this project). I owe much to them.

I loved working with the little octopuses, so much so that I began toying with the idea of getting an advanced degree in comparative psychology rather than clinical. At the same time, the little octopuses also pushed me in the direction of personality psychology. The octopus is a very basic critter. Yet, the animals in the lab differed from each other in fundamental ways. Some were bold and sociable. Others were timid and shy. The fact that even octopuses had personalities suggested to me that individual differences of this sort were a basic aspect of life.

A second experience reinforced my interest in personality. I continued to work in Riley's lab after graduation, which enabled me to continue to take courses. I happened upon a course on personality taught by Lewis Goldberg. Goldberg is a very energetic, animated person, whose enthusiasm about life (in general) and personality psychology (in particular) is infectious. Goldberg's course further increased my interest in pursuing personality as a field of study.

As a result of these experiences, I decided to apply to a program in experimental personality that was being offered by the University of Texas, at Austin. I was accepted, so (in 1971) off to Texas I went.

Graduate School: The University of Texas at Austin

The Separate Programs in Personality and Social Psychology

Social and personality were organized in a rather unique way. They were completely independent. The two programs had separate faculty, admitted separate students, taught separate courses, and had their own separate area requirements for graduation. The two programs were even housed in separate buildings. The only element they seemed to have in common was the quality of the faculty in the two areas. The social program had the likes of Elliot Aronson (a contributor to this volume) and Robert Wicklund. The core personality program was centered around Arnold Buss and Lee Willerman, with a supporting cast provided by several behavior geneticists, including Jan Bruell.

I gave no thought to this separation between programs, but I have come to believe that it was and is extremely rare. This separation between the two areas did have the consequence of causing me to perceive greater differences between social and personality than might really exist. It also led to an engaging sense of competitiveness among the students in the two areas, an "us versus them" mentality. The competitiveness among the area faculty was also apparent.

Outstanding Quality of Students in the Program

Part of what made my experience at Texas truly transformative was the quality of the graduate students who comprised the social and personality areas. It is unclear how such cohorts form, but Texas would not have been the exciting place that it was, if those students had not been there. The social students included people such as James Pennebaker (also a contributor to this volume), David Krantz, and Fredrick Gibbons. Besides me, the personality students included people such as Robert Plomin, Charles Carver, and Karen Matthews. It was a remarkable, lively group of students. As a marker of how exceptional this group was, five students from this combined cohort went on to receive distinguished scientific contribution awards from APA.

Meeting Charles S. Carver

One of the first persons I met when I arrived in Austin (next to Karen Matthews, who later became and is my wife) was Charles Carver. I remember the meeting clearly. Carver was sitting on the floor outside of Buss's office. Buss was Carver's advisor and soon become my advisor too. Carver looked a bit grumpy and not entirely interested in being where he was or in meeting anyone else who was there. What was not to like, right? From this auspicious start, our professional careers would become intertwined for the next forty-six years, continuing to his death in the summer of 2019.

Early Work on Self-Awareness
Although both Carver and I were advisees of Buss, we spent a fair amount of time talking together about Wicklund's theory of Objective Self-Awareness. The idea was

that self-awareness made people feel bad because, as they reflected upon themselves, they invariably found a self-dimension for which there is a negative discrepancy between their perceived and ideal selves. The basic question we asked was why self-awareness was necessarily an aversive state. Why did people not just alter their behavior when they could to bring it into alignment with their ideal selves? We started doing experimental research manipulating self-awareness and found that self-attention did in fact cause closer alignment between the behavior people were emitting and the principles that were guiding it.

These experimental studies went on for a year or so, at which point Buss called me into his office for a heart to heart. He pointed out, rightly so, that I was in fact enrolled in a personality program. Yet, I spent my time doing social psychology. He suggested to me, somewhat bluntly, that it was time to start doing some personality research. My response was to work with Allan Fenigstein to develop, with Buss's guidance, the *Self-Consciousness Scale*. The idea was that there exists in people the disposition to be self-attentive, some people being more introspective than others. The scale was designed to assess these differences.

Armed with a scale to assess the disposition to be self-aware, a very interesting methodology began to evolve. We would use one technique to cross-validate the effects of the other. That is, if the scale assessed the same underlying dynamics as did experimental exposure to self-awareness inducing stimuli, similar findings should be obtained for each. Low and behold, this did in fact seem to be the case. I have often thought this cross-validation technique should be used more widely in personality and social psychology. It is difficult to think of many social psychological mechanisms that do not have some type of dispositional counterpoint.

Moving from Self-Awareness to Behavioral Self-Regulation

While the research on self-awareness was going on, Carver happened to audit a class on control theory. Control theory provides a framework for thinking about self-regulating systems. When people think of self-guiding systems, they usually think of things like room thermostats, guided missiles, or maybe homeostatic mechanisms in the body. At some point, Carver had an epiphany. This same set of principles might also apply to human behavior.

It was Carver's insight that first started us thinking about the work we had been doing on self-awareness in terms of behavioral self-regulation. That is, the research findings on self-awareness were showing that the behaviors people engaged in were more closely aligned with their intentions and goals when they were more self-aware. This sounded a lot like something a self-regulating system would do, operating in ways that kept the person's behavior tightly coupled to the intentions, values, and goals that were governing it. Our confidence in the utility of reframing our work in this way was buoyed by the work of William Powers, who was also using control theory to describe how the human nervous system might be organized to produce human actions.

Starting and Ending a Career at Carnegie Mellon

Finding a job after graduate school was an interesting proposition. The work that Carver and I were doing had become completely intertwined. We decided that it did not make sense to compete for positions. Rather, we would look at the positions open and then decide who would apply to each, taking into consideration our assessment of the quality of the institution, geographical location, personal preferences, and so on. We had a hard time deciding how to assign the University of Indiana and Carnegie Mellon University. We decided to flip a coin, heads Carver applied to Carnegie Mellon, tails I applied to Carnegie Mellon. The coin came up heads, so I applied to the University of Indiana.

How did I get to Carnegie Mellon? The department there really wanted to hire someone who focused on personality. On paper, I looked more like a personality psychologist than did Carver. The department decided to call some other programs just to see if they had missed someone. Consequently, Richard Schulz called Steven Sherman at Indiana. Sherman identified me as an applicant on their list. Shortly after, Schulz gave me a call to see why I had not applied and to ask if I was interested. After getting consent from Carver, I applied, visited, and was offered the position. The job situation could have easily ruined our emerging collaborations. It did not. If anything, it strengthened the personal bonds between us and made us even more interested in working together. So, in 1975, we both went our separate ways (geographically speaking only), Carver to Miami and me to Pittsburgh.

Ultimately, Carnegie Mellon was one of the best places I could have landed. The department was (and still is) incredibly supportive of new junior faculty, and the faculty itself was of extremely high quality. The social and personality group was going through a transition period when I arrived, and several other people had or would be hired. They all made my professional life more interesting in one way or another. Most notable among this group were Schulz, Margaret Clark, and Susan Fiske (the latter two are contributors to this volume).

Elaborations on a Theme

The first part of my career at Carnegie Mellon was spent trying to flush out and expand upon our ideas about behavioral self-regulation. Carver and I wrote grants together and conducted a host of interlocking studies. Having Carver and I at separate institutions not only allowed us to play dispositional assessment and experimental manipulations against each other, but it allowed us to replicate the work in two geographical locations as well. The work we did during this period is summarized in two research monographs (Carver & Scheier, 1981, 1998).

Expectancies and Dispositional Optimism

In considering what behavioral self-regulation involved, Carver and I were drawn to the important role played by outcome expectancies. Clearly, self-regulation does not always unfold smoothly. Sometimes people struggle to do what they want to do or intend to do. What happens during times of adversity depends on the nature of the outcome expectancies people come to hold. Positive expectancies are associated with confidence and lead to a continuation of behavior directed toward goal-attainment. Negative expectancies result in feelings of doubt and result in a tendency to disengage from goal-directed effort. Concomitantly, positive expectancies produce positively toned emotions, whereas negative expectancies produce emotions that are more negative.

Early on, we focused on outcome expectancies in a limited way. Our intent was to test the validity of the ideas. We did this by conducting studies in which we manipulated situation-specific expectancies to determine their impact on behavior and emotion. Often, we manipulated self-awareness as well (or identified people high and low in introspectiveness) to see how self-reflection influenced the process.

After several years, we began to broaden the ways in which we thought about expectancies. Carver and I were both surrounded by people who played an instrumental role in founding what has become known as health psychology. Sheldon Cohen had become a colleague of mine at Carnegie Mellon. Matthews, Schulz, Stephen Manuck, and Andrew Baum were colleagues at the University of Pittsburgh, a quick twenty-minute walk away. Carver and Neil Schneiderman were colleagues at Miami. Carver and I both knew Krantz from Texas. Collectively, they challenged us to apply some of our ideas about expectancies to real-world contexts, especially those that might be relevant to physical health.

Of course, one could easily study outcome expectancies in health settings and still target expectancies that are limited in scope (e.g., the expectation held by a patient of walking again after a car accident). About the same time that we felt the push from our health psychology colleagues, I started to hear the voice of my advisor again, reminding me that I had been trained in personality research. As a result of these forces, Carver and I started to think about expectancies in a broader way. We started to entertain the possibility that people come to hold rather stable, generalized tendencies to expect positive versus negative outcomes across a range of life domains. In brief, we found ourselves interested in dispositional optimism.

We first looked in the literature to see if there was already a scale that assessed dispositional optimism in a way that was consistent with how we viewed the construct. Not finding anything that was right on the mark, we set out to construct our own self-report questionnaire to measure dispositional optimism. After spending a few years constructing a scale, we began to explore the implications of optimism for physical health. Our first study explored the development of physical symptoms in a group of undergraduates during a particularly stressful portion of the academic semester. It turned out that optimism was associated with the development of less intense physical symptoms over time.

Carver and I were fortunate to get the description of the scale, our guiding theoretical framework, and the results of our initial undergraduate symptom study all published in one place, *Health Psychology* (thanks to Howard Leventhal, the action editor, for helping to get this paper through the system). Publication in *Health*

Psychology was important, as it enabled health psychology researchers to become familiar with the scale, findings, and ideas. There is now a wide-ranging literature linking dispositional optimism to physical well-being (for a review of this work, see Scheier & Carver 2018; for a description of the scale currently used to measure dispositional optimism, see Scheier et al., 1994).

The Work on Coping

While studies on optimism and physical health accrued, a parallel literature was being developed exploring associations between optimism and psychological well-being. Conceptually, similar associations were emerging there. Given the research on physical health being done, it is not surprising that many of the studies conducted on subjective well-being and optimism were embedded in physical health contexts (e.g., patients responding to diagnosis and treatment for various kinds of illnesses, injuries, and diseases).

As studies accrued, Carver and I started to think about why these associations were emerging. Guided in part by behavioral self-regulation theory, we were drawn to the idea that there might exist differences in the ways in which optimists and pessimists dealt with adversity. Specifically, the notion was that optimists tended to confront problems head on, engaging in various strategies relevant to problem-focused coping, whereas pessimists were more likely to avoid problems through denial or to disengage from coping efforts prematurely. Subsequent work has shown that coping is in fact an important mediator of the associations that are observed between dispositional optimism and physical and psychological well-being.

There is an amusing anecdote about our work on coping. As was our *modus operandi*, we began our work in this area by constructing a questionnaire to assess the variable of interest, in this case coping (Carver et al., 1989). When we got to the copyright stage of production, the copyeditor informed Carver that we had to use the full title for the scale (Coping Orientations to Problems Encountered) and not just the acronym (COPE) in all the tables. Carver thought this was a stupid rule. The two of them went round and round. Finally, Carver recanted, by pulling the formal scale title out of the paper. The scale was just called the COPE. It was a brilliant move, which allowed them to both walk away happy, but Carver clearly walked away the happier. He would not have to put the full title of the scale into the table titles as the copyeditor wanted.

The Pittsburgh Mind-Body Center

In the year 2000, the health psychology researchers at Carnegie Mellon and the University of Pittsburgh joined forces to respond to a call for proposals from the National Institutes of Health (NIH). The NIH was allocating 50 million dollars of special congressional funding to create five centers to study mind-body interactions and physical health (10 million dollars/center). The review panel liked our proposal, and we received funding for an initial five years, which was later renewed to provide additional funding for a second five-year period.

Connections between personality, social psychological processes, and physical health would have been made in any event. The existence of the centers, however, accelerated that process tremendously. (A side bar: One of the fun parts of the center was that I got to co-direct it with Matthews, who, as you might recall, was and is my wife.)

Goal Adjustment Processes: Goal Disengagement and Goal Re-engagement

In 1998, Schulz was back in town after leaving Carnegie Mellon, but he was now at the University of Pittsburgh. That summer, he arranged a meeting between me and Carsten Wrosch, a postdoctoral fellow visiting his research group. A couple of years later, Wrosch decided to return to Pittsburgh and do an additional two-year postdoctoral fellowship with me. As a result of our somewhat chance encounter (once again Schulz plays the role of intermediary in my life), I have spent the last twenty (and final) years of my career collaborating with Wrosch on goal adjustment processes. The basic idea is that when goal attainment becomes impossible, the adaptive response is to disengage from goal pursuit. We identified two critical components of successful goal disengagement: reduction of effort to attain the goal, and, perhaps even more importantly, withdrawal of commitment to the goal.

Goal disengagement is a necessary part of life. It prevents the person from experiencing repeated failure and frees resources for other activities. A life without goals, however, is a life devoid of meaning and purpose. To move forward successfully, the person also needs to re-engage in new goals. We identified three components of successful goal re-engagement: identification of new goals to pursue, commitment to those new goals (in the sense of truly coming to value them), and the expenditure of effort toward those new goals. The capacity to re-engage in new goals is thought to reduce thoughts and feelings of failure, and more importantly, create new ways to find purpose in life.

As you might have come to expect, Wrosch and I began our work by developing a scale to assess goal adjustment processes, the *Goal Adjustment Scale*. The scale is intended to be context free and to capture the person's general ability to disengage and re-engage from unattainable goals. We have used the scale to study the adaptive nature of both goal disengagement and goal re-engagement, documenting the positive impact each has on subjective well-being and physical health (for a review of the work done by ourselves and others, see Wrosch & Scheier, 2020).

What I Wish for Social and Personality Psychology Going Forward

I have spent forty-plus years doing research in the personality and social psychology domains. I have some sense of the directions I would like to see research go in the future. Here is a short wish list that identifies what I would like to see occur:

- That people would stop thinking in terms of personality *or* social psychology, but rather in terms of personality *and* social psychology. Thinking in terms of both can lead to a richer and more complete view of human behavior. For example, if you are doing research on a particular social psychological process (say self-handicapping), ask what kinds of people might engage in this process more intensely than others (say people low versus high in self-esteem), and then see if stratification on the personality factor produces the differential effect you might expect.
- That people decompose and not aggregate. Huh? My advisor used to say that there are two types of theorists in the world: "lumpers" and "splitters." Lumpers try to aggregate variables and concepts together. Splitters tend to divide existing constructs into underlying components. A lumper would produce something like the Big 5 mega-factors. A splitter would produce the underlying facets. I believe that much information is lost in aggregation. The problem is that when you find a relationship between a mega-factor and some outcome, you do not know which of the mega-factor components is producing the finding. Maybe all facets are adding something. Maybe the effect was just due to one critical facet. It is better, in my view, to decompose rather than aggregate.
- And finally, that people stop judging a personality scale by its title. When we use a scale, say a scale that measures trait anxiety, we assume that the scale in fact measures anxiety. This is a reasonable assumption. The real question, however, is what, if anything, the scale is also measuring. When you look at scales from this perspective, it becomes readily apparent that many (maybe most) scales measure additional constructs. A scale that purports to assess anxiety might also have items that measure self-esteem, depressive symptomatology, or optimism. These factors might be related to the focal factor, but they are not the primary factor itself. This creates the same problem of interpretation as was outlined in the prior suggestion about aggregation and decomposition. The solution, I think, is also the same: break down the items from the scale into the underlying components to see which of the components is producing the finding. If nothing else, such item level analyses will provide a much deeper understanding of the finding.

A Career in Retrospect

Looking back, I am struck by the impact that certain events and experiences had on my career. Sometimes I did things (or seemingly did things) to cause the events to occur. Other things I just stumbled into. The experiences were important not only when they happened, but they were important far after the episode ended. Each put me on a trajectory that led to other possibilities that would not have been presented had the earlier experience not occurred.

Here are the critical turning points in my journey. Had I not taken that undergraduate psychology course, I likely would not have majored in psychology. Had I not moved to Berkeley, I would not have interacted with Goldberg and Riley. Had

I not been surrounded by health psychologists in mid-career, the work on optimism and physical health might not have happened. Had Wrosch not joined me for a postdoctoral fellowship, I might not have thought hard about goal adjustment processes (and been as prepared as I was for my own retirement). The most critical event of all, however, was meeting Carver at Texas. No Carver, no forty years of collaboration and friendship.

Life is filled with pivot points, bifurcations that lead in different directions, each providing different opportunities. My professional life has certainly been filled with such pivot points. I would be very surprised if there were not similar pivot points in the lives of most of the other contributors to this volume. Given my perspective on life, it should not come as a complete surprise that I am quite fond of a quote that is generally attributed to Yogi Berra (a catcher who played for the New York Yankees from the mid-1940s into the early 1960s). The quote is, "When you come to a fork in the road, take it."

Suggested Reading

Carver, C. S., & Scheier, M. F. (1981). *Attention and Self-Regulation: A Control Theory Approach to Human Behavior*. New York: Springer-Verlag.

(1998). *On the Self-Regulation of Behavior*. New York: Cambridge University Press.

Carver, C. S., Scheier, M. F., & Weintraub, J. K. (1989). Assessing coping strategies: A theoretically based approach. *Journal of Personality and Social Psychology, 56*, 267–283.

Scheier, M. F., & Carver, C. S. (2018). Dispositional optimism and physical health: A long look back, a quick look forward. *American Psychologist, 73*, 1082–1094.

Scheier, M. F., Carver, C. S., & Bridges, M. W. (1994). Distinguishing optimism from neuroticism (and trait anxiety, self-mastery, and self-esteem): A re-evaluation of the Life Orientation Test. *Journal of Personality and Social Psychology, 67*, 1063–1078.

Wrosch, C., & Scheier, M. F. (2020). Adaptive self-regulation, subjective well-being, and physical health: The importance of goal adjustment capacities. In A. J. Elliot (Ed.), *Advances in Motivation Science* (Vol. 7, pp. 199–238). New York: Elsevier.

30 A Relational Life

Margaret Clark

Growing up in a very small New England town, in the 1950s and 1960s, I didn't imagine a life in academia. Now, I cannot imagine a different life and am grateful for the opportunities and experiences I've had.

My family valued education but with some gender-based expectations. That is, my brother's education was to a pathway to a career. My sister and I should just *be* educated at a good liberal arts college. Yet pursuing a career was not out of the question either. I could do what I wanted. If my early teachers were engaging, I focused on learning; if not, not so much. As for unofficial mentors, my paternal grandfather was the best. He lived close by and later in life with our family. He knew about geology and water systems, and very early on, was concerned about threats to the environment. He was happy to teach me about those things and to challenge me to Scrabble.

School itself wasn't so interesting. I recently came across an early report card noting that I spent too much time day-dreaming; that seems accurate to me. I regularly spent time at the shore in Rhode Island in the summers (and loved that) and I took some summer school science courses at a local preparatory school in Connecticut not so much out of ambition but because there was little to do in my Connecticut town in the summer. I headed off to college intending to major in political science probably due to one terrific high school teacher of government and also all that was going on politically in the late 1960s.

A Small, Influential, Liberal Arts College Experience; During a Turbulent Time

I went to Franklin & Marshall College, a small liberal arts college in Pennsylvania. My government professors were interesting and passionate, but the courses did not capture my interest so much as the small group of dedicated psychology professors there did. I had naively thought of psychology only with regard to clinical practice and was not interested in that. Then, upon taking a popular introductory psychology course, I became interested. The course was team taught. There was no one text;

Margaret Clark, Yale University, USA.

rather the faculty used a newly published series of separate paperback books each covering a different topic. The series included Ellen Berscheid's and Elaine (Hatfield) Walster's (1969) new bright pink book entitled *Interpersonal Attraction.* (I still have my copy.) I don't think there was a social psychologist teaching that first year but the interpersonal attraction book was assigned and a fellow, more advanced, undergraduate who would later become a social psychologist, William (Bill) Graziano was my very enthusiastic teaching assistant. Other books in that course and other professors focused on perception, learning and memory, motivation, human development, and animal behavior with instructors who were passionate about those topics and research and about psychology as a science.

I was captured by the experimental nature of psychological research and the creation of new knowledge. The term cognitive psychology was not yet common but we read Ulric Neisser's also new at the time book, *Cognitive Psychology* (1967). *Every* course was a lab course. The lab in introductory psychology involved doing canned experiments (conditioning rats in Skinner boxes). Thereafter, we were required to design an original experiment with one or two fellow students for every course, actually conduct the study, analyze the results and write the work up in APA style. (There were no IRB approvals to be secured; we just presented the study to the professor who had to approve it and we went out and got the work done.) There was no graduate program; the focus was on the undergraduates and we received lots of feedback on our work. Some of the projects we did were trivial but one project led to a publication in the *Bulletin of the Psychonomic Society* (Clark et al., 1974) and two others resulted in my being a co-author on two *Journal of Personality and Social Psychology* papers (Isen et al., 1976, 1978). The latter two projects both focused on mood and helping and were overseen by Alice Isen who had recently received her PhD from Stanford and taken a job at my college. I now realize how unusual it was for faculty members to spend so much time with undergraduates doing such work.

The only lab I did not care for was one associated with a course on animal behavior. Despite the small size of the college and department, there was a primate lab. This was likely due to one professor having been a Harry Harlow student. The monkeys in that lab had come from Harlow's lab. I don't know for sure, but have always wondered if they were some of the ones deprived of early maternal care for they were definitely not pleasant beings and I did not enjoy working with them. On the other hand, I loved my statistics course. The statistics professor had us design sixteen different studies in one semester and submit them to him. He then made up data (building in some challenges, violations of statistical assumptions and such) for all those studies and we analyzed those data by hand or by writing our own code, punching cards and running them through a mainframe computer (with many failed attempts – I did not like that part). I learned a lot. Years later, upon thanking that professor for the course, he laughed and said he taught the class that way only once given complaints about the workload.

I kept my government major and slid into completing a psychology major as well. As a senior I was surprised to win the psychology department's prize for overall academic achievement. Still I did my senior thesis in government and recall criticism for this choice from my psychology professors who warned that the choice could hurt my chances of getting into graduate school.

The quality and intensity of the psychology faculty at the small school and the attention they paid to individual students was crucial to my pursuing and enjoying psychology. Equally impactful, in a different way, were national events. In the spring of my first year, colleges and universities across the country closed early in the wake of the Kent State shootings. I participated in civil rights protests, protests of the Vietnam War, and emergent women's discussion groups. Watergate happened. Now the country once again faces many important issues and engagement remains important.

Graduate School

I landed at the University of Maryland for graduate school both because my future spouse was in the area studying law at Georgetown University and because my eventual PhD advisor, Judson Mills, was willing to accept me to the program despite recommendations that may have included cautionary comments about me not having elected to conduct a senior research project in psychology. My fellow entering grad students, Carolyn Gotay, Robert Gould, and Paul Brounstein were great. Jud Mills was a quiet man but also a fabulous person and devoted mentor. He loved social psychology, insisted on conceptual clarity, developing theory, and doing truly experimental work. He was unusually flexible, I realize in retrospect, in terms of what I could study. He was an attitudes guy, trained under Leon Festinger and still interested in attitude formation and change. I was interested in relationship functioning but had no clue as to how to pursue that interest. Jud was willing to let me pursue my own topical interest and also willing to teach me how to do so experimentally.

At the time, right along with the rest of psychology, social psychologists were firmly focused on individual functioning. Although there certainly had been work on group processes in the past, social cognition was "the" emerging area in which to be. Relationship research was not yet a thing. Social psychologists, even those interested in attraction, focused on a single individual at a time who might be asked to interact with another person in a laboratory setting who was a stranger to that individual or, commonly, a hypothetical other person. As Ellen Berscheid wrote later, psychologists – even *social* psychologists – were busy studying reactions to people with whom they "had never interacted in the past, were not actually interacting in the present, and did not expect to interact in the future" (Berscheid, 1999, p. 262). Psychologists certainly weren't studying relationships as they actually existed – with pasts and anticipated futures. We weren't studying individual differences in people's approaches to relationships.

Still, in the fall of 1973 I had an interest in the functioning of close relationships combined with the good fortune to have an advisor who was okay with helping me with the firm caveats that I must do so experimentally and that the work must be theoretically driven. Although Jud had not done work on attraction and relationships he knew and respected the research of Ellen Berscheid and Elaine Hatfield (both represented in this volume). He pointed to their work as examples good experimentation on relationships. He simultaneously urged me to read Erving Goffman's *Presentation of Self in Everyday Life* and I did. In that book, Goffman drew a distinction between social and economic exchange. It was not quite the distinction we wished to make but it was the inspiration for it. Jud urged me to refine the distinction and do experiments to test it. One could not randomly assign people to be friends or romantic partners with one another and correlational work was out of the question if I were to get a degree in experimental social psychology. But, Jud said, I could develop manipulations that would lead people to desire one type of relationship or the other and I could then observe the effects of those manipulations on judgments and behavior.

I developed my initially simple theoretical distinction between communal and exchange relationships with benefits being given non-contingently on the basis of needs in the former type of relationship and on a tit-for-tat basis in the latter type of relationship. Then it was time to test it. Our idea was that if people could be led to desire one or the other sort of relationship then we could assign them randomly to "relationship" conditions, have a confederate give a participant help, and later ask for repayment or not. We could then observe our participants' reactions. Did they like that confederate better when she repaid them or when she did not? This led to experiments that supported the notion that people follow distinct norms when they desired friendships or romantic relationships versus wishing to remain acquaintances. Those experiments formed the basis of my Master's and PhD theses as well as many more experiments (see Clark & Mills, 1979, 1993).

Only much later at Carnegie Mellon University (CMU) did I even think of doing a non-experimental study on record keeping comparing real pairs of friends to pairs of strangers and I did so only after having done the same type of work experimentally. Later still, Michael Scheier, who was trained in personality psychology, inspired me to develop communal and exchange orientation scales to study individual differences in people's approaches toward relationships. My first such work was published in the same year Hazan and Shaver (1987) published their work on attachment styles. Their individual differences work had a huge impact on the field; mine had a small one. It is also the case that it was only long after conducting my initial studies that I realized that it was very likely due only to Jud making me do true experiments that my initial findings on the distinction between communal and exchange relationships were as clear cut as they were. When people desire close relationships but do not yet have them, they bend over backwards to follow norms appropriate to those relationships (for signaling and self-promotion purposes). They also bend over backwards to avoid any appearance of wanting a transactional relationship. The distinction holds later as well but people relax a bit when it comes to adhering to the norm.

The success of my first and early experiments was encouraging and exciting. (It was nice that those first experiments worked. Later I'd have many other, more frustrating research experiences.) Then after four years in graduate school and marriage to a lawyer practicing in Washington, DC, along with some interesting summers spent working in Washington, DC at the IMF, World Bank, and Department of Agriculture, and watching Watergate unfold, which included attending impeachment hearings in the House office building, I got my PhD. Jud knew and liked my spouse but voiced the opinion that getting married might end my career. My spouse, however, *was* supportive and up for moving but wished to be in or near a city so that he could pursue his own career.

In 1977, many social psychologists were newly on the job market – Shelley Chaiken, John Cacioppo, Jack Dovidio, Mark Leary, Richard Petty, Jamie Pennebaker, Gary Wells, and Tim Wilson among them. (Note that 1977 is the most frequently represented PhD year in this book.) I am glad that I wasn't nearly as aware then as I am in retrospect just how tough my competition was. Fortunately, I did receive invitations for interviews but most involved universities and colleges far from cities – in Maine, North Carolina, Georgia, Kansas, and Missouri. Eventually, I received a call for an interview at Carnegie Mellon. I turned to my spouse and said – "it's in *Pittsburgh*. That's a city." I initially was called by two psychologists who had recently moved to CMU: Michael Scheier (also represented in this volume) and Richard Schultz. I could not tell who was who on that call (nor, indeed, for a time afterwards as well; they were just two guys who were clearly friends and who finished each other's sentences). I knew almost nothing about the university or the city. I did know I was their ninth interviewee, which worried me. If they didn't like the first eight people, why would they like me? Yet I received the job offer and moved to Pittsburgh. It was a good decision. (As an aside, I interviewed at University of Kansas and had an opportunity to meet Fritz Heider there. I had no clue he would be at my talk. He was. When I mentioned his work in my talk he made a comment to the effect that "Heider did not *quite* think that." Embarrassing. Yet it was an honor to meet and talk to both Fritz Heider and his wife Grace.)

I joined the faculty at CMU in the fall of 1977. It was in many ways an ideal place to launch and pursue a career and Pittsburgh was a good place to raise a family. The department members were devoted to research. Almost everyone had an active, ambitious, and successful research program, most often with grant support. That was inspiring. The teaching load was light relative to other places; the undergraduates were good; there was a PhD program. Especially at the start, cognitive psychology (as represented by many senior faculty members) was clearly valued over social or personality psychology (which, when I arrived, included no senior faculty members). I recall being urged by my first department chair to set aside the relationship and emotion work I was doing and to at least study social cognition. Still, there *was* a group of social psychologists there: John Carroll (who left for MIT a year after my arrival), Rich Schultz (who also left shortly thereafter), and Michael Scheier to start. Susan Fiske arrived a year later, then, in order, Charles Kiesler, Sheldon Cohen, Vicki Helgeson, and Brooke Feeney arrived. A healthy health psychology group emerged within the social area and included close ties to the University of Pittsburgh. It was strong and distinct from the cognitive psychology group. Karen Matthews came to University of Pittsburgh and became a good friend and there was a larger group of social psychologists at University of Pittsburgh whose campus was adjacent to that of CMU.

At the time, I did my own research on relationships and emotion. I taught social psychology, research methods courses, and seminars. I was happy to receive grants and publications and to receive a college wide and then a university wide teaching award. Sheldon Cohen had interests in social support; Vicki Helgeson in unmitigated communion. As noted, Michael Scheier inspired me to think about individual differences in orientations toward relationships. In time, Brooke Feeney, a fellow relationships researcher, arrived. My husband joined and became a partner in a Pittsburgh law firm. The suburb of Fox Chapel where we lived was a good place to raise our two children. Notably, CMU had no maternity leave and I sometimes taught with a sleeping infant in a carrier attached to me. Later, the university president asked me to chair a committee with the hope of showing that maternity leave was unnecessary to succeed at the university. I declined. He responded saying that he supposed being able to decline that was what tenure was about. Indeed. I loved my twenty-nine years there – the students, colleagues, and friends both at CMU and at the University of Pittsburgh.

The Trajectory of Relationship Science

During my early postgraduate school years, doing research on relationships remained rare. Two years into my graduate training, as I tentatively began to explore relationship dynamics, in 1975, Senator William Proxmire from Wisconsin began giving out what he called "Golden Fleece awards" for wasting taxpayer (grant) money on what he called frivolous research. With much fanfare he gave Ellen Berscheid and Elaine Walster the first one, asserting that no one wanted scientists to study relationships. He said love and relationships were domains best left to be explored by novelists and poets.

For years thereafter it was important to carefully word titles and abstracts for our grants to avoid capturing his attention. Much later, when Berscheid and Walster won SESP's distinguished scientist award, I recall Harry Reis introducing them and reveling in the fact that while Proxmire had since faced relationship problems including a divorce, Ellen and Elaine had thrived (and continued to do so). Importantly, four years after Proxmire's first Golden Fleece award, Berkman and Syme (1979) reported on a large epidemiological study which clearly documented the benefits to physical health of people who have close relationships. Other similar studies and findings followed. Such work was crucial for basic research on relational processes becoming valued. It was important then and today to know why having relationships is so very good for people over and above many other factors linked to health.

Early on, a small group of quite young and then still quite rare relationship researchers (John Holmes, Art Aron, Harry Reis, Caryl Rusbult, and me) formed an informal group initially because Harry Reis knew each of us and urged us to tack on a brief get-together-vacation to a relationships research meeting in the Netherlands.

Harry had spent a sabbatical there and suggested visiting an island in the North Sea. We did and for a long time thereafter and still continuing today small, tacked on jaunts became a tradition. We eventually labeled ourselves the Gang of Five, spent much time discussing relationship research and sometimes collaborated with one another. Although we lost Caryl to cancer over ten years ago, the original group still gets together, albeit on Zoom during the pandemic. Others have joined in. Ellen Berscheid and Elaine Walster were consistently supportive of newer relationship researchers. I would be invited to do this or that only to learn that it was Ellen Berscheid who suggested me. I was and will be forever grateful for her support.

And the relationships field grew: first greening (Berscheid, 1999), then ripening (Reis, 2007), and, finally, blossoming (Campbell & Simpson, 2013). In the early 1980s interdisciplinary conventions on relationship research began to meet, and small pre-conferences on relationship research preceded larger social psychology meetings; these grew and eventually relationship work was regularly featured in the main conferences as well. Colleges and universities began to offer courses on the psychology of attraction and relationships, statistical techniques were developed for analyzing dyadic data with people such as Dave Kenny and Niall Bolger being leaders in this regard, a choice of textbooks to support relationship courses appeared, and, most importantly, generations of strong, productive, and new relationship scholars emerged and thrived.

Two Very Different Universities: CMU and Yale

In 2005 I moved from CMU to Yale where I've now been for fifteen years. John Bargh was instrumental in hiring me, a fact for which I am very grateful, and new colleagues included Marianne LaFrance, and then Jack Dovidio, Jennifer Richeson, Maria Gendron, and Melissa Ferguson. The move in 2005 entailed coming home to the state in which I grew up, being closer to extended family members and friends and also closer to that spot on the Rhode Island coast where I'd vacationed all my life. It also involved coming to a very different institution.

What was gained and lost in the move was (and is) very salient. I lost daily ties with those scholars with whom I had grown up academically and alongside whom I had raised a family. I left a place that was narrow in its foci and great in depth in the fields that were represented. It's notable that anthropology and political science departments did not exist at CMU, but fine arts, computer science, and psychology were robust areas of scholarship and had lots of depth. I left a place where classes were uniformly small and committee and administrative work was minimal. I left many friends (but still keep up with most of them).

I arrived at a place with a long history of being, at its heart, a liberal arts college, one with a wider array of departments, and one with many associated professional schools. It was also one with some colleagues who were and are public intellectuals and others who are not, a place where classes can be huge or tiny, as well as a place where students are involved intensely in extra-curricular activities that are often more competitive for them than their classes. I came to a place with outstanding financial aid and, hence, a more diverse (in many ways) student body as well as a place with generous funding for graduate students (a big plus) and much more committee work (not a plus).

One committee assignment involved working closely with the Dean of Yale College (Mary Miller at the time) and that work pulled me in an unanticipated direction. In 2013 I was asked if I wished to serve as master (now head) of one of Yale's residential colleges. I accepted, live right in the center of the campus and have gotten to know students, faculty, and visiting scholars engaged in a wide variety of domains that has broadened me. At the same time, I remain at heart a social psychologist, teacher, and researcher. Between serving as head of a residential college, teaching, doing research and a new part-time job as Dean of Academic Affairs, I've never worked as hard in my life. Yet it all is interesting and challenging and gives rise to new research ideas. I'm glad I didn't do administrative work earlier in my career; but I'm grateful for the opportunity to have done it now, especially my job serving as head of a college.

Some Overarching Thoughts

Reflecting back, I would not make many different career choices. I would decline more invitations to serve on committees, I'd start longitudinal studies earlier and keep them going longer, and I'd include more diversity in participant samples with regard to race, age, culture, and socioeconomic status. I'd also make more time for my own relationships.

Lots of work remains to be done. To this day, most psychological studies, even on topics such as cooperation, morality, and selfishness, typically do not take relationship context into account. If others are involved they typically remain strangers or even hypothetical people just as Berscheid lamented long ago. I firmly believe that almost all psychological research should consider relational context (Clark et al., 2017).

Existing relationship work should also be integrated. Doing so is important in and of itself and, undoubtedly, will reveal gaps to be filled. To give one example within relationship science itself, it is now clear that a lack of trust in partner care and responsiveness (likely arising from poor experiences in prior relationships) is a major impediment to forming and maintaining high quality communal relationships. Currently social and clinical relationship researchers have *many* overlapping constructs and measures that appear to capture such low trust: low self-esteem, rejection sensitivity, avoidant attachment, anxious attachment, and social anxiety to name just a few. Programs of research using these terms are fairly siloed. What do these constructs share in common and what they do not? These research programs themselves should be integrated. To give another example, agreement is high that "people need to belong" but many means of striving to belong (including forming communal relationships) have been proposed. When and for whom does each apply? Which ways work? Do they work additively or interfere with one another?

Relationship researchers have moved from studying individuals to studying dyads, which is great, but now we ought to be expanding our work. We need to study more types of relationships. In 1988, Harry Reis and I wrote an *Annual Review* piece bemoaning the lack of research on romantic couples; now such work is flourishing but what about adult child–parent relationships, sibling relationships, boss–employee relationships? Are there optimal *networks* of relationships for individuals? How are dyadic relationships themselves shaped by the larger social and non-social contexts in which they exist?

Suggested Reading

Berkman, L. F., & Syme, S. L. (1979). Social networks, host resistance, and mortality: A nine-year follow-up study of Alameda County residents. *American Journal of Epidemiology*, *109*(2), 186–204.

Berscheid, E. (1999). The greening of relationship science. *American Psychologist*, *54*(4), 260–266.

Berscheid, E., & Walster, E. (1969). *Interpersonal Attraction*. Reading, MA: Addison-Wesley.

Campbell, L., & Simpson, J. A. (2013). The blossoming of relationship science. In J. A. Simpson & L. Campbell (Eds.), *The Oxford Handbook of Close Relationships* (pp. 3–10). New York: Oxford University Press.

Clark, M. S., Lemay, E. P., & Reis, H. T. (2017). Other people as situations: Relational context shapes psychological phenomena. In J. F. Rauthmann, D. C. Funder, & R. Sherman (Eds.), *The Oxford Handbook of Psychological Situations* (pp. 40–61). New York: Oxford University Press.

Clark, M. S., & Mills, J. (1979). Interpersonal attraction in exchange and communal relationships. *Journal of Personality and Social Psychology*, *37*(1), 12–24.

(1993). The difference between communal and exchange relationships: What it is and is not. *Personality and Social Psychology Bulletin*, *19*(6), 684–691.

Clark, M. S., & Reis, H. T. (1988). Interpersonal processes in close relationships. *Annual Review of Psychology*, *39*, 609–672.

Clark, M., Stamm, S., Sussman, R., & Weitz, S. (1974). Encoding of auditory stimuli in recognition memory tasks. *Bulletin of the Psychonomic Society*, *3*(3A), 177–178.

Goffman, E. (1959). *The Presentation of Self in Everyday Life*. New York: Anchor Books.

Hazan, C., & Shaver, P. (1987). Romantic love conceptualized as an attachment process. *Journal of Personality and Social Psychology*, *52*(3), 511–524.

Isen, A. M., Schwartz, M., & Clark, M. S. (1976). Duration of the effect of mood on helping: Footprints on the sands of time. *Journal of Personality and Social Psychology*, *34*(3), 383–393.

Isen, A. M., Shalker, T., Clark, M., & Karp, L. (1978). Affect, accessibility of material and behavior: A cognitive loop? *Journal of Personality and Social Psychology*, *36*, 1–12.

Neisser, U. (1967). *Cognitive Psychology*. Englewood Cliffs, NJ: Prentice-Hall.

Reis, H. T. (2007). Steps toward the ripening of relationship science. *Personal Relationships*, *14*(1), 1–23.

31 Planning Is Overrated
A Case Study

John F. Dovidio

I was taught by my parents and teachers that having an explicit plan is essential to success. While I still agree that this is wise counsel, I also have come to believe that planning is overrated. One reason is that much in life is out of our control, which frustrates even the best of plans. Another reason, which both experience and research have informed me, is that we are guided in many thoughts, feelings, intuitions, and inclinations that are not specified steps in the formal logic within "the plan." We may not even be aware of these influences: These are implicit processes. However, it is not an "either/or" to decide to be planful, deliberate, and explicit in your reasoning *versus* being oriented, directed, and pushed and pulled by implicit processes that you cannot fully articulate. While these two types of influences can operate independently and move us in different directions, they also can function in a complementary fashion that guides us along a chosen path but alerts us to new, even more rewarding opportunities. Recognition and acceptance of implicit influences have been core themes in my research and, as I illustrate through personal experiences, my life.

How I Became Interested in the Field

Being a social psychologist was not at all part of my life plan as I entered college. In fact, I was totally unaware that there was such a thing as social psychology. I grew up with a blue-collar background in a working-class city (as my accent signals, just outside of Boston). There were no psychology classes offered in my high school. As I entered college, my plan was a simple one: Get a good education, then get a good job, and then make good money. I ended up drifting into social psychology not by design but by a series of seemingly minor events that slowly, imperceptibly, but steadily shaped my career and life.

I entered Dartmouth College in 1969 intending to major in mathematics. From my first semester, I jumped right into the sequence of courses leading to that major. However, like many other first-year students for whom course offerings tend to be limited, the large introductory psychology class with virtually unlimited enrollment was inviting. The content of that course was very different than anything I had experienced in the past. I was intrigued by the material but not quite hooked. So,

John F. Dovidio, Yale University, USA.

I dabbled with other psychology courses, as well as related classes in sociology and education. For one semester, I had an off-campus internship in which I lived with and tutored high school students (mostly Black and Latinx students) from educationally disadvantaged areas across the country enrolled in the A Better Chance (ABC) program. This offered me a new perspective on life in America and made a lasting impression.

I sensed that I was moving in a direction away from a major in mathematics. My passion for psychology intensified with every course I took. Most of that was the material. Another element was my fascination with research that allows people to ask and answer questions. A substantial part was the quality of teaching. Still another significant part was something more informal. I got to meet with and know faculty members. They inspired me with their intelligence and commitment, but most of all with their obvious love for what they were doing.

Midway through my senior year, as I followed my original plan of getting a good education and then a good job, I applied for many, many jobs. The opportunities that came my way were basically of two types – either jobs that paid well but did not interest me at all or jobs that interested me but did not pay much. Then, a pivotal moment occurred. My undergraduate advisor, Bill Morris, asked me if I had considered pursuing graduate school in psychology. I said no, because I had already spent too much of my parents' and my money for college and could not take on the cost of more education. He then explained that I might qualify for a fellowship or teaching assistant position, which would include a tuition waiver and some additional funding. I never heard of or imagined such a thing; it was a transformational moment. It was already February, and most graduate school application deadlines had passed, but I did find a few schools and scurried to apply. So, by late spring I had three options: (a) a good paying job that seemed unfulfilling, (b) a couple of jobs in areas related to social justice that did not pay enough for me to live anyplace but with my parents, and (c) a funded admission to a PhD program in psychology. I chose Plan C. There was clearly something invisible to me that was drawing me into psychology and, eventually, academia.

I arrived at graduate school at the University of Delaware still quite clueless about what I was getting into. I met my graduate advisor, Dr. Sam Gaertner, who became my mentor and soon my lifelong friend. I marveled at his creativity, but I was particularly astounded by his passion for the profession. He created a sense of partnership from the beginning, saying things like, "I will tell you what I am interested in; you tell me what interests you. Then you get me interested in what you want to study, and I will do the same with you." So, we began doing research on racial attitudes (his main interest) and helping behavior (my initial interest). As time went on, our interests became more intertwined, and we developed a collaborative relationship into which we brought different but complementary interests, skills, and strengths. It was largely through this relationship that the invisible pull of a career in psychology became a clearly perceptible tug. I was hooked. I committed fully to a new life plan.

One of the most exciting parts of research for me was that the studies I conducted usually answered some of the questions I was asking, but they also revealed that I had so much more to learn. I came to appreciate that my participants were smarter than me: When they did not conform to my expectations, what they were doing was "right." Persisting in my latest plan (i.e., my original hypotheses) would likely lead me to a dead end, whereas being open to following the leads my participants provided often guided me to new, more productive directions.

Adopting this perspective early in my professional career, my studies of helping behavior and racial attitudes spawned new ideas and produced new questions to answer. One of the topics was aversive racism. Aversive racism involves a subtle bias among "well-intentioned" White Americans who consciously endorse egalitarianism but unconsciously harbor negative racial feelings and beliefs. My collaborative work with Sam further documented the validity of this framework, frequently blended with our interests in prosocial behavior. Early on, for example, we found that whereas White participants would help Black people in need as often as White people when the right thing to do was clear, they would help a Black person less often when they could rationalize not intervening on the basis of some factor other than race – such as when the need was ambiguous, or others were available to help instead (Gaertner & Dovidio, 1977).

While the supporting evidence was reassuring, it was a "loose end" that particularly piqued my interest. We had been hypothesizing the role of the unconscious feelings and beliefs that aversive racists harbor, but we did not test that premise directly because we did not know how to measure what lies outside of a person's awareness. Sam had initially considered this question using a particular cognitive measure (a lexical decision task), but I felt that there were still important issues to consider. Thus, beginning years before the introduction of the Implicit Association Test, the challenges of measuring unconscious bias and understanding how explicit and implicit racial biases of White Americans combine to influence how they treat Black Americans fueled my work for decades (Dovidio & Gaertner, 2004).

Even as my research helped answer these questions, it also flooded my mind with new questions. One important insight, which seemed to elude me for years, was that race *relations* are not solely the product of the behavior of White people toward Black people; it involves the attitudes and perceptions of Black people and reciprocal relations in interracial exchanges. We discovered, for example, whereas White participants' explicit (self-reported) racial attitudes predicted behaviors, such as verbal behavior, that were relatively controllable, implicit attitudes predicted spontaneous behaviors, such as nonverbal behaviors (Dovidio et al., 2002). The inconsistency between aversive racists' verbal behavior, which was seemingly positive, and their nonverbal behavior, which signaled negativity, led Black participants to perceive bias (that White participants did not see) and to accentuate their racial mistrust – a finding that resonated with the experiences described by my Black and Latinx students at the ABC house. In more recent years, collaborations with another friend and colleague, Dr. Louis Penner, have shown these effects can produce lower quality healthcare for Black Americans and contribute to the significant racial disparities in health that persist in the US (Penner et al., 2016).

As we discovered answers to our questions about implicit bias, a new question emerged: How do you reduce a bias that people may not know they have? Moreover, as subsequent research has shown, there is no known intervention that reliably reduces implicit racial bias in an enduring way. So, we focused not on changing the implicit intergroup bias but on altering the process that activates this bias – social categorization. In the common ingroup identity model (Gaertner & Dovidio, 2000), we proposed that whereas categorizing others mainly in terms of their different group memberships ("we's" and "they's") creates intergroup bias, recategorizing others as members of a common ingroup (e.g., viewing Black and White students as students at your university) can redirect the forces of ingroup favoritism and reduce bias.

One of the scholarly challenges I have had is distinguishing "me-search," which is the often implicitly motivated quest to further understand particular experiences or events in my own life, from truly theoretically-based research. A danger of me-search is that, particularly around socially sensitive issues such as racism, it is easy for ideology to distort the types of questions posed and the interpretation of findings. I have tried to strike a balance between being theory-based while also being informed my relevant experiences.

Thus, I ended up in a place in my research that I did not anticipate. These scholarly pursuits, in turn, opened new doors professionally. After twenty-seven years at Colgate University, an undergraduate liberal arts college, I moved to the University of Connecticut (UConn) and then to Yale University. When a door opened, I needed to see what was on the other side of it. I am here not by plan but by serendipity, trusting "my gut," and benefiting from the ways other people have lifted me throughout my career. Plans do facilitate purposeful movement through life, but rigid plans put blinders on people that create tunnel-vision and can lead to devastating frustration when obstacles are encountered. Every obstacle is an opportunity – but only if you are willing to explore new directions.

The Field as I Entered It and How It Has Changed

I entered graduate school in 1973 and received my PhD in 1977. The field at that time was substantially defined by the individuals who were the luminaries. The classic works by Leon Festinger on cognitive dissonance, Stanley Schachter on emotions and attributions, and Stanley Milgram on obedience to authority were already embedded in the lore of social psychology. More recent additions included the pioneering work of John Darley and Bibb Latané on emergency intervention, Harold Kelley on attributional processes, and Lee Ross and Richard Nisbett on attributional biases. Their work and stature have had an enduring influence on the field. The phenomena they brought to the forefront of the field influenced what generations of social psychologists studied. However, they also conveyed implicit messages about the field including both professional and social dimensions. A key element of many of these classic works was the counterintuitive findings they revealed. Soon, in a discipline that preached logical derivation of hypotheses from existing research and theory, creativity of perspective and counterintuitive findings became a desired standard for major research publications and, ultimately, eminence.

In many ways it was a golden age of discovery in social psychology, encouraging of creativity. However, there was a tarnished side, too. Both the kind of work that was celebrated and the general research practices employed in the field set the stage for some relatively immediate and more distant crises in the discipline. One prominent example was how the Milgram obedience studies (along with the discovery of exploitation of participants in medical studies) raised issues of ethics. The public outcry stimulated the establishment of formalized ethics committees for research – a consequence that strengthened research practices and helped restore the stature of social psychology in the views of the public and the profession.

Another example was that the emphasis on counterintuitive results contributed, at least in part, to research practices that eventually led to the "replicability crisis" in social psychology (Simmons et al., 2011). One such practice, which was actually recommended in articles instructing how to write psychological papers (Bem, 1987), was to describe the rationale in the introduction of the study in terms of what makes the most sense based the results, not on the original hypothesis. This approach makes unexpected results appear to be predicted and thus inflates the number of false positives (Type I errors) – which have little chance to be replicated – in the published literature. Awareness of problems with this practice and with other common research practices at the time produced new standards in publishing (e.g., full disclosure of materials and preregistration of hypotheses and analyses). Again, crisis stimulated important innovation. For example, currently the Open Science Framework offers guidance and structure for facilitating open collaboration and improving reproducibility in social psychology and other fields. In fact, a general strength of the field has been its resilience in the face of periodic crises and its adaptability, profiting from the best of its past while advancing in new directions.

The demographic profile of eminence that existed in the field also had a significant, largely unintended impact. The acknowledged leaders of the field were primarily White men who worked at the most prestigious institutions in the United States. This helped define social psychology as a White man's profession, and the vast majority of those entering the field were, like me, White men. It should be noted, for example, that one of the most prestigious awards in social psychology, the Distinguished Scientist Award from the Society for Experimental Social Psychology (SESP), had its first female recipients (Ellen Berscheid and Elaine Hatfield) in 1993, following a string of twenty honoring men. The first Black recipient (Claude Steele) was recognized in 2009.

This is not meant to imply that the SESP selection process was biased; it is intended to illustrate the skew in the profession as a result of numerous processes and biases that have shaped the pipeline and limited the perspectives represented in the field. While in my professional cohort (those who received PhDs in the late 1970s), there are many eminent female scholars, which gave the impression of a major change in the gender profile of the discipline, that impression was misleading. Women were still substantially underrepresented in social psychology into the new millennium. Moreover, many of the women in my cohort have stories to tell of obstacles and experiences related to gender bias. People of color on the eminence shortlist were also rare. They have stories, as well. These stories are essential, but often untold, elements of the history of social psychology. Some of the obstacles were egregious insults and violations; others were more subtle, perhaps driven by implicit rather than explicit bias. This regular exposure to bias, subtle as well as blatant, is professionally and personally corrosive. It is also damaging to the field because it excludes important voices and ideas that would produce more comprehensive perspectives on social behavior. Currently, a substantial majority of those entering social psychology are women, and diversity along multiple dimensions is increasing.

Another aspect of the skew in eminence in the field was the dominance of US social psychology in the profession. Although many people assert that science is value free, culture shapes the ways people see the world and what they believe important. Because of the prominence of scholars in the United States, which represents a highly individualistic culture, a core emphasis of social psychology through the 1970s was on the individual. However, starting in the 1960s but attracting more widespread attention toward the end of the 1970s, a new and vibrant interest in collective identity and intergroup behavior began in the European social psychology community (Dovidio et al., 2012). In the area of intergroup relations, the pioneering ideas and research of Henri Tajfel at the University of Bristol in England were beginning to take hold. Building on his studies of how the mere classification of people into ingroups and outgroups creates intergroup bias, Tajfel, in collaboration with John Turner, introduced social identity theory (Tajfel & Turner, 1979). This perspective distinguished between personal identity, viewing the self as a distinct individual with particular motives and goals, and social identity, one's view of the self that is derived from group membership. Social identity theory has stimulated generations of research and thousands of empirical studies. Importantly, it also made social psychology an international science: It redefined the field socially as well as intellectually.

Where the Field Is Headed

As I have tried to illustrate in the previous section, social psychology is constantly evolving. This evolution is guided not only by new perspectives within the field but also by general social changes and current events. Because of the more expansive perspective it brings, greater diversity within social psychology has already proved to be an important force for change. Because of the deep tradition in individualism in the United States, it is unlikely that social identity theory could ever have developed from US scholars alone; similarly, stereotype threat research, which also has had dramatic theoretical and practical impact, would not have emerged from a social psychology community of only White men.

Greater diversity is also represented in broader access to new populations of research participants. The availability of global online participant-recruitment platforms and the capacity to present sophisticated experimental protocols online are expanding the geographical reach of social psychology. The social psychological study of prejudice was traditionally shaped by work on racial bias in the United

States, a particular form of bias that is grounded in a unique history of race relations. Studying more forms of intergroup bias involving different groups across cultures will help identify potentially universal dynamics while recognizing systematic cultural variation. However, social psychology is still dominated by researchers, participants, and consumers from Western, educated, industrialized, rich, and democratic (WEIRD) societies, which constitute only about a tenth of the world's population. There is substantial opportunity for growth of perspective.

Social psychology is a unique gateway science that studies a broad range of phenomena from cells to societies to illuminate the dynamics of human behavior, and it is poised to expand its connections to allied disciplines using both smaller and larger levels of analysis. Much of the energy of the field has been in the expansion of social psychology in the direction of more micro-level analysis, adopting tools such as fMRI and EEG. Less visible have been the links between social psychology and other disciplines that typically employ more macro-level approaches to human behavior. Although some bridges have already been established (e.g., by political psychology), social psychology's connections to disciplines such as public health and economics are still works in progress. These connections offer reciprocal benefits to the fields. Social psychological research and theory, for instance, provides insight into individual-level processes (e.g., implicit bias) that contribute to racial disparities in health and healthcare. Disciplines such as political science and public health and medicine call our attention to policies and structural factors that shape human behavior and outcomes. Becoming a stronger ally with other disciplines that have theories, methods, and a well-developed language to study systemic influences will have enormous benefit for social psychology in the quality and breadth of its research products.

Advice for Future Generations

In closing, I offer just two broad strands of advice. Both are derivative of key threads in this chapter. The first is about pursuing your passions through high-quality, rigorous work in social psychology (in teaching and application as well as in research). Planning and logical calculation *are* valuable for shaping your career path. However, there is also important, guiding information in implicit signals that you may not be able to articulate. Just because you cannot explicitly explain why you have a preference does not mean that such a preference is not valid. Humans have evolved robust implicit thinking systems because of their benefits in orienting and guiding our attention, action, and effort. Clearly, some conscious checks and balances are needed. As the research on aversive racism shows, implicit biases can compromise our conscious egalitarian values if we are not careful. Nevertheless, we do not always need to know why something makes us feel happy to benefit from the happiness it brings. These intuitions, which can draw you to the field of social psychology (as they did me), can also lead you to study something that is especially meaningful to you, which can produce unique insights because of how you see the issues. Here, your implicit drive is also of particular value. It provides the additional fuel to go the extra mile(s) to pursue your questions in a deep and programmatic way.

The second piece of advice is about the social aspect of social psychology. This has two elements. One is, even though there are many forces within the profession that encourage scholars to emphasize their scholarly independence, it is important to recognize the contributions of others to your success and to remember all of assistance you have received. As I have tried to illustrate, so much of my journey was shaped by the kindness of others. Sometimes it was a generous investment of time and energy; other times it was incidental, such as an off-hand comment. The second element of this advice is, whether you are a student, an early-career scholar, or someone firmly established in the profession, to understand that what you do daily has meaning for those around you – even when it does not seem significant to you. Think of all that people have done to help you and "pay it forward." Use these encounters as opportunities to extend to others the kindness, encouragement, and support that have benefited you. Create a legacy not simply of research productivity but of investment in the field through others.

Suggested Reading

Bem, D. J. (1987). Writing the empirical journal article. In M. P. Zanna & J. M. Darley (Eds.), *The Compleat Academic* (pp. 171–201). Mahwah, NJ: Lawrence Erlbaum Associates.

Dovidio, J. F., & Gaertner, S. L. (2004). Aversive racism. *Advances in Experimental Social Psychology, 36*, 1–52.

Dovidio, J. F., Kawakami, K., & Gaertner, S. L. (2002). Implicit and explicit prejudice and interracial interaction. *Journal of Personality and Social Psychology, 82*(1), 62–68.

Dovidio, J. F., Newheiser, A.-K., & Leyens, J. P. (2012). Intergroup relations: A history. In A. W. Kruglanski & W. Stroebe (Eds.), *Handbook of the History of Social Psychology* (pp. 407–430). New York: Psychology Press.

Gaertner, S. L., & Dovidio, J. F. (1977). The subtlety of white racism, arousal, and helping behavior. *Journal of Personality and Social Psychology, 35*(10), 691–707.

　(2000). *Reducing Intergroup Bias: The Common Ingroup Identity Model*. New York: Psychology Press.

Penner, L. A., Dovidio, J. F., Gonzalez, R., Albrecht, T. L., Chapman, R., . . . Eggly, S. (2016). The effects of oncologist implicit racial bias in racially discordant oncology interactions. *Journal of Clinical Oncology, 24*, 2874–2880.

Simmons, J., Nelson, L., & Simonsohn, U. (2011). False-positive psychology: Undisclosed flexibility in data collection and analysis allows presenting anything as significant. *Psychological Science, 22*(11), 1359–1366.

Tajfel, H., & Turner, J. C. (1979). An integrative theory of intergroup conflict. In W. G. Austin & S. Worchel (Eds.), *The Social Psychology of Intergroup Relations* (pp. 33–48). Monterey, CA: Brooks/Cole.

32 Symptoms, Secrets, Writing, and Words

James W. Pennebaker

I was born and reared in Midland, Texas, a small West Texas town fueled by new oil fields, optimism, ambition, alcohol, and greed. My parents, a lawyer and a *bon vivant* who were newly married, had moved there from New Orleans and Boston to take advantage of the oil boom – just like other new Midlanders. Most people we knew were temporary, coming and going once they made their fortune or were transferred by their oil companies, but my parents had come to stay. Mine was a Tom Sawyer-like childhood of adventures and social and scientific experiments and fire-setting, often bordering on delinquency.

I started college at the University of Arizona with the vague ambition of becoming a lawyer. I began as a music major but soon switched to math. Then philosophy and, after that, sociology. Oh, and anthropology. My most valuable course was meteorology (ask me about isobars and the Coriolis Effect). After two years I transferred to Florida Presbyterian College (now called Eckerd College), a hippie college at the time, with my girlfriend, Ruth.

It was in the move from Arizona to Florida that my professional life came into focus. At a stopover in Austin, I found a used copy of Krech, Crutchfield, and Livson's *Introductory Psychology*. It opened a new world. The chapter on social psychology – especially the works of Milgram, Darley and Latané, and Schachter – bowled me over. It was a discipline that celebrated a broad perspective, social dynamics, and biological processes, while keeping an eye toward addressing real-world problems, all with a sense of fun and panache.

At Eckerd, I was introduced to research by Ted Dembroski, a social psychologist, and James MacDougall, a physiological psychologist. I briefly became a True Believer in behaviorism and loved taunting my philosophy friends about the nature of meaning which was nothing more than positive reinforcement. Things were so simple. I performed brain surgery on rats and mice and was forever changed by watching a rat press a bar that stimulated its pleasure center until it collapsed.

In 1972, I applied to several graduate social programs emphasizing my interests in physiological, learning, and social psychology. None were seeking someone so unfocused. The following year, I applied again and was more successful. I still remember the letter from Elliot Aronson accepting me into the UT Austin graduate

James W. Pennebaker, University of Texas, USA.

program. Within a week, Ruth – now my wife – was accepted into UT's law school and we soon headed for Austin.

In 1973, social psychology was in flux. Motivation and drive theories were out, cold cognitive models were the rage. Freud was heresy, Lewin was a distant memory, and even dissonance was slipping from the journals. The orange attribution book by Jones et al. (1972) served as our generation's Little Red Book. This theoretical pivot was a bit of a problem for someone like me who was truly interested in physiology, learning, social behaviors, and emotions.

My path diverged from the mainstream early on. The day I arrived at UT, I met with Elliot who told me that he had accepted a job at UC Santa Cruz and wouldn't be taking students with him. A senior graduate student, David Krantz, urged me to talk with David Glass who was starting to study Type A personality, heart disease, physiology, and stress. Glass was the new chair of the psychology department who had been recruited from NYU the year before. In almost no time, he had collected a group of graduate students who were remarkable: Krantz, Karen Matthews, Charles (Chuck) Carver, Mel Snyder, Audrey Burnam, Rick Gibbons, among others. The group was beginning to study heart disease, a significant real-world problem, by focusing on personality processes, emotion, and interpersonal conflict. Unlike most labs, we had a phenomenon in search of a theory, not the other way around. None of us knew at the time but Glass had brought together some of the founding members of health psychology.

After working on Type A for almost two years, Glass announced he was leaving Texas for another job. For me, this was an opportunity to begin setting up my own research team to study the psychology of physical symptom reporting – a topic of personal relevance since I had grown up with a mother who was obsessed with her own symptoms. Rather than work with another faculty member, my strategy was to simply talk with people across all areas to get their input on the projects I was doing. Three people were particularly important mentors. Devendra Singh, a physiological psychologist, educated me about the limbic system and brain mechanisms associated with behavioral inhibition. Arnold Buss, the father of David Buss, was a powerful influence in my thinking about personality, evolution, and science in general. Bob Wicklund, a traditionally trained social psychologist, pushed me to be more theoretically focused and to think about the nature of attentional focus and the self.

One other person of great importance was Dan Wegner. Dan had just started a new job at Trinity University in San Antonio. On a visit to Austin, we met and immediately became fast friends. His ideas and demeanor were both quirky and innovative. Over the next four decades we educated and entertained each other as we developed our overlapping ideas of thought suppression, expressive writing, and much more.

The Early Years: The Psychology of Physical Symptoms

My first job was at the University of Virginia in 1977. Seven years earlier, the courts had forced UVA to admit women undergraduates. Rather than reduce the number of men, the school essentially doubled its enrollment over the next few years. In so doing, they also doubled the size of the faculty. The psychology department quickly hired a large number of eminent and, oftentimes, sketchy senior faculty, many of whom did not fit in at other universities. Although there was often great turmoil in the department, I felt free to pursue my interests surrounding physical symptoms and their links to physiological and social processes.

The symptom research soon took off. The central question was why and when do people report everyday physical symptoms such as racing heart, shortness of breath, headache, sensations associated with hunger, etc. On what internal physiological signals do people rely in making their judgments? People's perceptions of heart rate, hand temperature, hand sweatiness, blood glucose levels, and muscle tension were poorly correlated with their presumed physiological referents. Darren Newtson, my closest colleague in the early years, spent hundreds of hours talking with me about J. J. Gibson's perceptual approach, which fit nicely with what I was finding with symptoms: that is, our perception of physical symptoms was based on a host of cues – physiological and situational and whatever other information was available to us.

The symptom research was going well. My students (including Andy Skelton and Linda Gonder-Frederick) and I were publishing broadly. I began to write a book, *The Psychology of Physical Symptoms*, that came out in 1982. Just before it went to press, I realized I needed a chapter on the personality and psychological profiles of people who tended to report the most physical symptoms. With the help of a visiting faculty member, Billy Barrios, and two undergraduates, Cobie Hendler Whitten and Pam Grace, I devised an all-encompassing questionnaire that asked people about their childhoods, eating, sleeping, and dating patterns, and other topics. As we were brainstorming about possible questions, one student suggested, "Prior to the age of 17, did you have a traumatic sexual experience (e.g., rape, molestation)?"

And, like that (snap finger here), my career changed. The survey went out to 800 undergraduates. The 15 percent who endorsed the sexual trauma question were far more likely to report physical symptoms of all kinds and to have visited the university health center. Over the next three years, other surveys were completed by thousands of people of all ages and the effects were even more compelling. Both women and men who had had early traumatic sexual experiences were far more likely to have been hospitalized the previous year and to have been diagnosed with virtually every illness we asked about (e.g., cancer, high blood pressure, ulcers). Later studies found that it wasn't a sexual trauma per se that caused health problems but, rather, having any kind of major upheaval that people kept secret.

A Brief Personal Intermission

In 1982, things were coming together nicely. My wife Ruth had switched careers from being a lawyer to a journalist, writing for the local paper along with op-ed articles for the *New York Times*, *Washington Post*, and other outlets. We had a very active social life, especially with our good friends Tim Wilson and Dede Smith. In February, we had our first child, Teal, who was glorious, delightful, and oftentimes demanding. Although I was coming up for tenure in the fall, I felt secure that I'd fare well. Yes, there were some ugly rumors about data fabrication by a senior psychology faculty member that were being suppressed, but I assumed it wouldn't be a problem for me. I was mistaken. In the fall, I learned that I did not have the full support of the department and that I'd likely be turned down for tenure. Ironically, I had recently been contacted by Robert Folger at Southern Methodist University about a possible job. Three months later, I accepted a position at SMU back in my home state of Texas and Ruth landed a position with the *Dallas Morning News*.

Major life upheavals visit most of us. For an academic, being turned down for tenure is crushing and humiliating. For the first few months, I was filled with anger and bitterness, something I'd never seen in myself. With the help of Ruth, our daughter, and the move to Dallas, I was able to move on. The experience certainly taught me more about traumas and secrets than I ever expected. (Next time your life falls apart, take notes. There are some great research ideas scattered in the wreckage.)

Back to the Research Story: Expressive Writing

The secret trauma findings spurred me to talk with clinical psychologists, professional polygraphers, and trauma survivors about their experiences. Major life traumas together with overwhelming secrets appeared to undermine mental and physical health in profound ways. If holding in major secrets was such a risk factor, what would happen if we brought people in the lab and had them talk or write about their secrets?

The first SMU graduate student I met, Sandy Beall, said she wanted to do her Master's thesis on something related to health. We talked about getting students to write about major life experiences that they had kept secret. Over the next few weeks, a study emerged wherein we would randomly assign students to write about either traumatic experiences (in one of three ways) or superficial topics for four consecutive days. We got their permission to track their student health center records in the months before and after their writing.

The study worked. People who were asked to write about their thoughts and feelings about having a traumatic experience evidenced significant drops in student health center visits in the months after writing compared to controls who wrote about superficial topics. In retrospect, our findings were the result of remarkably good luck as much as anything – small sample size, borderline statistical effects, etc. Today's culture would never have accepted the paper, which we published in 1986.

Several other, more defensible studies followed from my and other labs. Most, but not all, replicated the basic patterns. The central question all of us were asking is why did writing improve physical health? Standing back now and looking at the thousands (!) of writing studies, there is a growing consensus that there are multiple overlapping processes at work, including:

- Acknowledging that the event happened.
- Translating the experience into language, including the labeling of emotions.
- Working to understand and organize the experience, perhaps constructing a story to explain it.
- Experiencing cognitive changes that help to reduce rumination, improve sleep, improve working memory, and reduce stress.
- Enjoying beneficial social changes after writing, including talking to friends about the upheaval and also greater social engagement in general.

As we and others ran more and more writing studies, we found that after writing, people went to the doctor less and had more efficient immune activity. Among students, expressive writing was associated with higher grades. Among engineers who had been laid off from their jobs, writing was linked to getting jobs more quickly compared to controls. I was occasionally stopped by students who had been in a writing study several months earlier who told me that writing had changed their lives and profusely thanked me for letting them be in my study. That had never happened before.

I've frequently asked myself why the expressive writing research caught on. In the early 1980s, concepts such as self-help, self-awareness, and self-reflection started to peak in the cultural vernacular (see https://books.google.com/ngrams/). Since its inception, psychology, and especially social psychology, had studiously avoided anything that smacked of Freud, therapy, or deep emotional processing. Expressive writing quietly entered the field at a perfect time. The method was simple and easily replicable. There was no grand theory behind it so it served as a projective test for most theoretical approaches. Above all, it brought about objective health and behavioral outcomes that were lacking in traditional paradigms.

The writing studies also changed the ways I thought about research. Most of my earlier symptom research involved self-reports. I rarely found that expressive writing affected long-term self-reports, including self-reports of exercise, drinking, smoking, talking with others, etc. It was as if people's self-views were fixed but their objective behaviors and health had changed.

Another important lesson concerned the value of theory. In the two years leading up to the first writing study, I had been developing a rather elegant theory about behavioral inhibition. The idea was that people who had had a trauma and who had kept it secret were constantly inhibiting their urges to disclose to others. The psychic work of inhibition served as a long-term, low-level stressor that exacerbated health problems. Nice, huh? The problem is that I never could find any evidence for inhibitory mechanisms at work. (Theories are quite important in guiding research questions. But theories are ultimately cheap. It's the data that is often the foundation of the story.)

Between 1986 and 1990, a number of important things happened. My wife and I had a son, Nick. I published a popular book, *Opening Up: The Healing Power of Expressing Emotion*. In 1989, Lee Ross invited me to spend part of the year at Stanford. It was a heady time.

Through all of this, I had been conducting study after study trying to identify what active mechanisms were driving the expressive writing results. Perhaps some important clues were embedded in the expressive writing samples I had collected. I enlisted many of the clinical graduate students to read and evaluate multiple writing samples. But the task was too difficult and produced ambiguous findings.

If I could just find some fast and efficient ways to analyze hundreds of expressive writing samples, my life would be perfect.

The Power of Words and Computerized Text Analysis

In the same semester I took meteorology, I also enrolled in a course on Fortran, one of the first popular computer programs. My brief background in programming gave me a sense of how a computer program might be able to analyze text. I initially called experts in cognitive science in a search for a text analysis desktop computer program. My first contact was Art Graesser who gave me names of people around the country in computer science. No luck. (Years later, I discovered that Phil Stone and his colleagues at Harvard had built a mainframe computer program twenty-five years earlier, called General Inquirer, which was largely unknown in the mainstream of psychology.)

I decided to build a text analysis program myself. Fortunately, I had a relatively new graduate student, Martha Francis, who had majored in computer science as an undergraduate. Together, over the next two to three years, we put together a program that eventually became known as Linguistic Inquiry and Word Count, or LIWC (pronounced "Luke"). The first edition of LIWC was released in 1992. The sixth edition just recently came out (Pennebaker et al., 2022).

Other than my Fortran course, I had no training in programming and no background in linguistics. My real interest was in identifying objective markers of the ways people think, feel, pay attention, and connect with others. It made sense that the words people used in everyday life would likely reflect their psychological processes.

The first LIWC studies focused on the ways people wrote in several previously published expressive writing studies. Intuitively, people who used more emotion words (such as *hurt, angry, happy*) and cognitive language (with words like *think, understand, because*) would likely benefit more than people who used these types of words at lower levels. The early studies were moderately successful. Profiles of successful expressive writing (i.e., writing samples of people who subsequently evidenced improvements in physical health) include higher use of positive emotion words, a moderate use of negative emotion words, and, most powerfully, an increasing use of cognitive words over the course of the writing exercises.

Another Personal Interlude

Between 1995 and 1997, our lives changed considerably. Ruth was diagnosed with an aggressive breast cancer when our children were 13 and 9. She underwent surgery, chemotherapy, and radiation for months. It was an upheaval that was unexpected, horrible, destabilizing, and oddly centering. I watched how Ruth's diagnosis shifted her social network. Many old friends quietly disappeared because they were so terrified by the prospect of the disease, while another set of acquaintances magically appeared because they wanted to provide support. The specter of death touched every part of our lives. Fortunately, Ruth responded well to treatment and, within a year, was reconstructing her life by writing more novels and essays.

It was about this time that my old friend Bill Swann asked me to consider moving back to Austin to join the psychology department at the University of Texas. It was a difficult choice. I loved SMU and the department was young and scrappy. In the fourteen years I'd been there, we hired a remarkable group of colleagues including David Watson, Lee Anna Clark, and the amazing Laura King. But even though Ruth and I had built strong ties in Dallas, we both had strong memories of Austin from our graduate school days. The department was exceptionally strong and there were friends to talk with in philosophy (Bob Solomon), communications (Rod Hart), linguistics (David Beaver), English (Betty Sue Flowers), computer science (Joydeep Ghosh), and other departments. Bill and UT made us an offer we couldn't refuse.

The World of Words

The move to Austin served as a transition from expressive writing research to language. Words didn't work the ways I originally thought they did. By analyzing all kinds of texts (e.g., emails, books, poetry, survey responses), I discovered that most of the social psychological information in language was apparent in *how* people expressed themselves rather than in *what* they were expressing. It was perplexing that there were large differences in personality, sex, age, and status in the linguistic styles but not the linguistic content.

It was George Miller's book *The Science of Words* that tied it together for me. He summarized centuries of work on people with different language deficits following brain damage. When their Broca's area in the left frontal lobe was damaged, people could often talk haltingly using nouns and regular verbs even though they appeared to have lost their social connections with others. Others with damage to Wernicke's area in their left temporal lobe spoke fluidly, even warmly to others, but only had access to function words such as pronouns, preposition, auxiliary verbs, and articles. They simply could not access nouns and regular verbs. This distinction between linguistic style and content was apparent in function versus content words.

The ability to use function words requires advanced social skills. The sentence, "I gave her the book," is surprisingly complex. Most anyone knows what "gave" and "book" mean. But who is "I" and "she"? If it's "the" book, it means that the speaker knows that the reader knows which book is being referred to. By analyzing people's everyday language, their function words reveal how they are paying attention to and understanding others in their social worlds, their sense of a shared identity, their interests in people and concrete objects, etc.

The power of LIWC, I finally realized, was in its ability to track social and psychological processes though people's use of function words (and, to a lesser extent, certain emotion, cognitive, and other content categories). With this knowledge, my students and I were able to begin mapping the boundaries of text analysis. Indeed, it has been my students who have helped lead the way over the last two decades.

Some examples of my former students' accomplishments include Matthias Mehl who has developed increasingly sophisticated devices to capture what people are saying as they go about their daily lives which can help foreshadow impending depression, health changes, eating behavior, and personality shifts. Richard Slatcher has found that language use in close relationships can predict breakups and the physical health of family members. Nairán Ramírez-Esparza has been a leader in tracking the language of bilingual English-Spanish speakers to understand how their personalities change as function of their language. Cindy Chung invented a new way to pull out the underlying themes of text and changed the ways our lab thought about language. These and other early findings helped spur me to summarize them in my 2011 book, *The Secret Life of Pronouns*.

My lab and I have now moved into the world of big data – a direction that has tremendous value for social psychologists. One of my central collaborators, Rada Mihalcea, is a computer science professor at the University of Michigan. She helped open my eyes about ways to think about tracking the language of hundreds of thousands of people over time, culture, and context. My former graduate student Ryan Boyd was the first person I met who represents a new generation of computational social scientists with a solid background in computer science methods with social psychology grounding. His language toolkit has helped us to identify the underlying structure of tens of thousands of stories and even identify genuine versus forged plays associated with authors such as Shakespeare and Aphra Behn.

Sarah Seraj and Kate Blackburn harnessed much of this knowledge to demonstrate the social, cognitive, and emotional shifts of thousands of people on Reddit who have undergone a major relationship breakup – from one year before to one year after the breakup. Kayla Jordan has tracked the language of US presidents and other world leaders over the last two centuries showing that the growth of mass media and democratization have changed the language styles of the people we elect. Another former student, Ashwini Ashokkumar, has identified the ways people become socially committed to groups, cults, and, during COVID, to their friends and families. Although the linguistic signals for powerful social connections and conflict are weak, big data approaches can aggregate across the noise of people's everyday lives revealing clear social processes unfolding over time.

Much to my surprise, the LIWC research is beginning to have a significant impact across several disciplines including business, medicine, computer and data science, communication, and psychology. As I stand back, I feel so grateful to so many people who shaped my thinking. My students – both graduate and undergraduate – were the muscle and brain power behind most of the ideas and methods. Some others whom I've not mentioned include Jenna Baddeley, Jason Ferrell, Molly Ireland, Youngsuk Kim, Kate Niederhoffer, Robin O'Heeron, Jason Rentfrow, Yitai Seih, Miti Shah, Lori Stone, Sanaz Talaifar, Mohini Tellakat, and Yla Tausczik. My colleagues, especially Bill Swann, Sam Gosling, Laura King, and Keith Petrie have been invaluable over the years. And, of course, Ruth and our children have been a part of all of this research – as critics, collaborators, and even participants.

What Does the Future Hold for Social Psychology?

Who knows? I got into social psychology because it was fun and offered the possibility of discovering new and exciting things that had the potential to change the world in a good way. I have been incredibly lucky. I've stumbled on some interesting findings that have occasionally yielded big payoffs.

As a discipline, social psychology is still trying to define itself. To me, it should be an endeavor where scientists are studying social behavior. It should be cross-disciplinary with researchers who study children, dogs, birds, and amoeba (at least sociable amoeba). We should embrace whatever methods help us to answer our questions. Our approaches should be deductive, inductive, and a mix of both. We should respect occasional case studies as well as population studies and laboratory experiments.

Of central importance is that we keep our eyes on the world around us. How can we help change the world? Think about the biggest challenges that people around the world are facing: social polarization, prejudice, disease, rampant fear and suspicion, the prospect for societal and/or financial collapse, global warming, paralyzed bureaucracies unable to function, and much more. These are all social psychological problems. Any solutions will require cross-disciplinary collaboration. Embedded in all of these collaborations should be experts in social and personality processes. Governments need us, businesses need us, and certainly educational institutions need us.

So, no. I don't know what the future holds for social psychology. If it acknowledges these issues and problems, the field will thrive. And we will all have fun figuring it all out.

Suggested Reading

Jones, E. E., Kanouse, D. E., Kelley, H. H., Nisbett, R. E., Valins, S., & Weiner, B. (Eds.) (1972). *Attribution: Perceiving the Causes of Behavior*. New York: General Learning Press.

Miller, G. A. (1996). *The Science of Words*. New York: Freeman.

Pennebaker, J. W. (1982). *The Psychology of Physical Symptoms*. New York: Springer-Verlag.

(1990). *Opening Up: The Healing Power of Expressing Emotion*. New York: Morrow.

(2011). *The Secret Life of Pronouns: What Our Words Say About Us*. New York: Bloomsbury Press.

Pennebaker, J. W., & Beall, S. K. (1986). Confronting a traumatic event: Toward an understanding of inhibition and disease. *Journal of Abnormal Psychology*, *95*, 274–281.

Pennebaker, J. W., Boyd, R. L., Ashokkumar, A., Booth, R. J., & Francis, M. E. (2022). *Linguistic Inquiry and Word Count (LIWC-22)*. Austin, TX: Pennebaker Conglomerates, www.liwc.net.

33 How Chance Encounters Can Foster a Career

Richard E. Petty

As a high school student in Yorktown, Virginia, I had no idea that social psychology would become my career, and understanding attitude and behavior change, my passion. In reflecting upon the influences that shaped my chosen profession and the particular research that I do, it became obvious that a series of chance meetings and events played a large role. Although as a member of my high school debate team I had a great interest in how to make the most convincing argument, it never occurred to me that one could examine persuasion as a career. Instead, it seemed that the best place to put my interest in social influence and argumentation was in the courtroom or in politics. Thus, I headed off to the University of Virginia and selected a political science major with the clear intention of eventually going to law school. That plan started to unravel when I took my first introductory psychology class. I had somehow managed to get to college without understanding that psychology was a science where you could think up interesting questions and then design research in an attempt to provide an answer. Realizing this, I was hooked, and took on psychology as a late second major largely because it also seemed highly relevant to my still intentioned law career.

Interest in Attitudes

Now, fast forward to the eventful day (for me) when a youngish assistant professor of psychology, Dr. James Lubalin, a 1970 Michigan PhD student of Herbert Kelman, came into my introductory social psychology course in the spring of my third year announcing that he was looking for undergrads who might be interested in enrolling in his graduate seminar on political attitudes. Apparently, there were not enough grad students interested, and the course could only be offered if some advanced undergrads enrolled. My good fortune of that course being offered at that particular time, and my ability to take it due to grad student disinterest, ended up having a profound influence on my life. I am quite sure that I would be a lawyer today had I not been inspired by that professor (and the course material) to consider a career in social psychology, studying attitudes. In the fall of my senior year, as applications became due, I hedged my bets by applying both to law schools and a few social psychology programs – particularly those

Richard E. Petty, Ohio State University, USA.

known to have some faculty who had published papers on attitudes and/or persuasion. High on my wish list were Ohio State University, Michigan, and Illinois.

I was very excited to be admitted to OSU (in 1973) in large part because three of the faculty, Anthony Greenwald (see his chapter in this volume), Timothy Brock, and Thomas Ostrom (1968) had edited a book called *Psychological Foundations of Attitudes*, that contained several chapters that I read in my undergraduate attitudes course. To be able to work with one or more of these prolific contributors to the literature would be fantastic.

In those days, there were no campus visits or much discussion prior to one's arrival of what the program would be like. In hindsight, had I visited before enrolling, I would have learned that these faculty were no longer interested in doing attitudes research and in fact thought that there was not much interesting left to do (i.e., the field was fully matured). So, when I got to Columbus, sight unseen, and met with each of the faculty individually, I was mortified to discover that they had all moved on from studying attitudes and persuasion to what they believed were more fruitful topics such as the self (Greenwald), interpersonal pleasuring (Brock), and person memory (Ostrom). It turned out that the OSU faculty were not alone in their assessment of the attitudes field. Reviewers of the literature published during my graduate school days said things like, "attitude change is not the thriving field it once was" (Kiesler & Munson, 1975, p. 443). The topic had lost favor in large part because so many conflicting findings had accumulated that there was no coherence. As Himmelfarb and Eagly (1974, p. 594) wrote, "after several decades of research, there are few simple and direct empirical generalizations that can be made concerning how to change attitudes."

Fortunately, a unique feature of the OSU program was that it had an NIMH training grant that allowed it to hire a new visiting faculty member each year to add some breadth to the doctoral training and to fill in for faculty who might be on leave. As luck would have it, the visiting faculty member the year I entered the program was Robert Cialdini (see his chapter in this volume). Bob had brought with him one completed study on attitude change and was looking for a student to help devise at least one more study that could render the work suitable for publication. Because my research interests did not fit well with any of the "regular" faculty's current interests, I was delighted to be assigned to work with Bob during his visiting year.

Bob was an inspiring first year advisor, but I certainly could not know at the time that he would become the amazing best-selling author, worldwide guru of social influence, and National Academy of Sciences member he is today. It was a privilege to work with him in the early days of his own career. Bob has continued to be a valued colleague and friend ever since. But, I am most grateful for his invitation to work on those data he brought with him from his recent postdoc at Columbia University. The initial study Bob had done showed that in a sample of high school girls, anticipating a discussion with a person who held a view opposite to their own led them to moderate their opinions prior to the discussion if the topic was rated as relatively low in personal importance but to polarize their opinions if the topic was rated as relatively high in importance. Furthermore, when the students learned that the discussion was canceled, those who moderated their views returned to their original positions, but those who polarized remained polarized.

The goal of the new study we planned would be to manipulate rather than measure importance and to try to understand the factors responsible for the persisting polarization but disappearing moderation. Our new study conducted on Ohio State undergraduates and using a different attitude issue replicated Bob's initial findings and also showed that the persistence of persuasion among those polarized was connected to the cognitive preparation the students did in advance of the discussion of the high importance issue. That is, these students generated more thoughts supporting their own position than students who expected to discuss a low importance issue or those not expecting to discuss the issue at all. To assess cognitive preparation, we used a "thought listing" procedure pioneered in persuasion settings by Brock and Greenwald. This work resulted in my first publication (Cialdini et al., 1976). I mention the particular aspects of this research because they were critical to much of the work on persuasion that I would conduct over the next two decades! That is, in much of my subsequent persuasion work we manipulated some variable that was presumed to impact how much people were motivated (e.g., personal responsibility) or able (e.g., message repetition) to think about an issue or message and we also assessed how the extent of thinking was tied to the overall strength of the attitude formed (i.e., how long the attitude would last over time, how much it would resist change, and how predictive it would be of behavior) – all components of what became the *elaboration likelihood model* (ELM) of persuasion (Petty & Cacioppo, 1986).

Mentioning the ELM points to another lucky aspect of beginning the OSU program the year that I did because I joined an incoming class that included Gary Wells (see his chapter in this volume) and John Cacioppo (who surely would have been a contributor if not for his premature death in 2018). Although Tim Brock became my advisor following Cialdini's visiting year, one's graduate student cohort can be as critical to the ultimate training one receives as are the faculty. John Cacioppo and I bonded quickly over our similar first-generation status, Italian-American upbringing, penchant for arguing, and our initial feeling that maybe we were in the wrong graduate program. I worried about who would advise me once Cialdini left, and John worried that none of the social psych faculty shared his interest in psychophysiology. So, we decided we would advise each other and work together to advance our individual and joint interests. I'm sure John ended up doing more persuasion work than he otherwise would have done, and the same goes for me and psychophysiology. But amazingly, we collaborated in both domains on and off for more than thirty years producing our most well-known offspring – the just mentioned ELM and the need for cognition scale (Cacioppo & Petty, 1982).

Elaboration Likelihood Model Origins

The origins of the ELM can be traced to my first graduate level class on attitudes taught by Tim Brock. The class used as the primary text a book by Chet Insko (1967).

This volume reviewed the field by describing the results of numerous studies, one after the other. In an effort to memorize these studies for Brock's infamous multiple-choice exams, John Cacioppo and I organized the research findings by categorizing them along several dimensions, such as how important the topics likely were to the participants. John had turned one of the walls in a house that we shared into a chalkboard and we used that to cluster the studies. Those scribblings likely would have remained just that had Brock not told me that my original dissertation proposal (on how memorizing one's own thoughts would enhance the persistence of persuasion over memorizing the arguments in a message) was likely a fine empirical advance (i.e., updating the Hovland/Yale "message learning" approach to persuasion to a more contemporary "cognitive response" approach) but was lacking conceptually. In particular, he stated that an acceptable dissertation required that I develop a broad theory that would account for many persuasion variables and provide a more complete account of when attitude change would persist and when it would not. Having only read one other dissertation previously, which also proposed a new theory, I took him at his word. In short, had I not had this particular advisor, or had I not taken his mandate seriously, or had I not previously collaborated with John in preparing for an exam on attitudes in the manner that we did, the ELM might not have been born (or certainly would have been delayed). The core idea of the ELM is that persuasion can take place under both high and low thinking conditions (two routes to attitude change) but that the processes and consequences will vary. The early work with Cialdini on personal importance was clearly influential as was the organization scheme Cacioppo and I developed to understand the accumulated persuasion literature.

Although John was my primary peer collaborator over the years, working with Gary Wells was also impactful and resulted in a second publication as a grad student – one that was also very important for my subsequent work over the next decades because it reported the first study to use a manipulation of *argument quality* to gauge the extent of thinking about a message (Petty, Wells, & Brock, 1976). This paper reported two studies on how external distraction affected attitude change. Some prior research had suggested that distraction would reduce persuasion because it inhibited message learning. Other research suggested that distraction might be good for persuasion because it could inhibit counterarguing or produce cognitive dissonance (i.e., this message must be valuable if I am overcoming this distraction to hear it). Building on the counterarguing notion (from Leon Festinger), we provided a more general framework. Specifically, our work showed that distraction disrupted the ongoing thinking about a message and thus could result in enhanced persuasion if it disrupted counterarguments (as would be likely if the message arguments were counterattitudinal or weak) but could also result in reduced persuasion if it disrupted favorable thoughts (as would be likely if the arguments were proattitudinal or strong). This argument quality induction has been used over the past several decades by us and many others and has shown that a wide array of variables are capable of increasing or decreasing persuasion depending on whether they enhanced or reduced thinking about the message (see Carpenter, 2015). Working with Gary was also important in influencing my career in that we conducted one of the first studies in the field to examine *embodied cognition* when we tested the impact of head movements on persuasion (Wells & Petty, 1980).

My good fortune continued after leaving OSU and taking my first faculty position as assistant professor of psychology at the University of Missouri. In that first year on the job, I got a call from Professor John Harvey, from Vanderbilt University. I first met John when he was a visiting faculty member at Ohio State, the year following Bob Cialdini. John had just contracted to produce an introductory textbook series in social psychology and was lining up potential authors for the various topics, including attitudes and persuasion. He was calling to see if Cacioppo and I might be interested.

The traditional advice for assistant professors is to steer clear of textbook writing and to focus on producing journal articles. And indeed, our department chairs at the time strongly advised us against taking on this project because it would not count much toward tenure. I do not dispute that this is generally good advice. However, Cacioppo and I decided to commit to the text for three reasons: (1) we really liked John Harvey and were flattered by the confidence he showed in us, (2) we thought a contemporary textbook on attitudes was needed and that we could produce one that would be of some value to the field and show that the topic was still a vibrant one, and (3) maybe most importantly at the time, it would give us an excuse to get together and collaborate. This book, entitled *Attitudes and Persuasion: Classic and Contemporary Approaches* (Petty & Cacioppo, 1981), was indeed a lot of work and likely reduced some journal productivity. Nevertheless, in my view it was well worth it because preparing this text forced us to thoroughly immerse ourselves in the broader literature (rather than focusing on our pet projects) and the knowledge gained paid dividends for the rest of my career. It also allowed us to introduce the ELM as an integrative persuasion framework. Had John Harvey not fortuitously been a visiting faculty member at Ohio State while Cacioppo and I were in grad school, we might not have been invited to produce this book, and one of the academic accomplishments of which I am most proud might never have been produced.

Self-Validation Theory Origins

Although experiments on the ELM dominated much of the research I did over the first two decades of my career, the two most recent decades have been dominated by research on another conceptual framework, one that also had its origins in a collaboration initiated in an unexpected way. Specifically, in December of 1998, I attended a two-day conference on "two routes to attitude change" in Salamanca, Spain. I was set to give three talks to an auditorium filled largely with faculty and students from various universities in Spain. Because my Spanish was not up to par, the organizers had arranged for an interpreter to translate my talks live to the assembled participants. All went well until my first talk was finished, and a hand went up in the audience for a question. The question was posed in Spanish and I looked up to the booth where the interpreter had been working. But, at the end of my talk, she left the room. After a bit of awkward silence, a young man in the audience, who I did not know, volunteered to translate the question to me and then my answer back to the audience member. He proceeded to do this for every question for all three talks!

Of course, after the first talk, I connected with my new translator during a break and I learned that my savior was Pablo Briñol, a doctoral student in social psychology at the Autonomous University of Madrid, who had traveled to the conference with a friend. We chatted well into the evening about our mutual research interests and how there were no faculty at his university who studied attitude change. I agreed to snail mail him some relevant papers when I returned to the United States (no email attachments at the time), but I honestly did not expect to ever reconnect with him in the future. Was I wrong! First, I ended up co-supervising his doctoral dissertation. Then, he came to Ohio State for several years in a row as a postdoctoral fellow, and we got an amazing research collaboration going. That collaboration has now lasted more than twenty years with well over 100 empirical papers produced. Although we have collaborated on a number of things, the primary focus has been on investigating what we initially called the self-validation hypothesis (Petty et al., 2002), which then became self-validation theory (Briñol & Petty, 2022). The core notion is that a large number of variables can affect which of the many thoughts people have will be translated into their attitudes and behaviors. This theory began with some surprising results from Pablo's dissertation on how nodding one's head during a persuasive message could affect attitude change by making people more confident in their thoughts (see Briñol & Petty, 2003).

I often wonder what else I would have been working on over that period of time if I had not gone to that conference in Salamanca. Indeed, I almost did not attend because my wife and I had recently become the parents to twin girls and we had agreed that both of us would swear off any multi-day or distant travel for the first two years following their birth. The Salamanca conference was two months short of our two-year moratorium, but my wife and I agreed that we were close enough to our self-imposed deadline and the conference was so intriguing, that an "exception" was OK. But what if we kept to the two-year travel ban? What if Pablo had decided not to make the trip? Apparently, this was also a close call since his friend was not a social psychologist and was a somewhat reluctant traveler. What if the translator did not leave her post after my talk? What if Pablo did not ask or I did not agree to supervise his dissertation from afar? There are so many what ifs, that my view is that our initial meeting is one of those rare happenstance events that is life changing.

Past, Present, and Future

As I look over a long career, I realize that I have had the incredibly good fortune of going to graduate school at Ohio State where there was an enviable collection of generous and expert faculty, both regular and visiting, along with two very talented classmates who became early collaborators and subsequently went on to become quite famous psychologists. Later in my career, after joining the OSU faculty after ten years away, the program provided me the opportunity to be part of an amazing collection of new colleagues and initiate a good number of collaborations with some of those faculty and my own graduate students. In fact, the greatest joy I have of continuing in the field comes from mentoring graduate students and postdocs. Although the relationships with these individuals have been very inspiring to me and have led to some long-term and joyful collaborations on topics I never would have anticipated, they seem less due to chance than the relationships I have highlighted in this essay. For example, I had nothing to do with selecting the visiting faculty at OSU or the other students in my cohort. In contrast, with my own graduate students and postdocs, I have attempted to choose people who would be a good match and they presumably did likewise. The students I have been able to mentor are truly a remarkable group and our work together has produced many empirical and conceptual contributions of which I am quite proud. Many of these papers would never have been produced without their bringing some wonderful new idea to me and soliciting my input.

Mentioning these more planned collaborations provides an important corrective to anyone who might take my earlier comments to think that successful collaborations are invariably, or even mostly, the result of happenstance. Rather, most of my collaborations have been quite deliberative. Furthermore, even when initial meetings with particular people were quite random, what followed and what sustained the collaboration surely was not.

It is often said that whereas the humanities rely on individual effort, science is collaborative. Indeed, it often "takes a village" to produce a *JPSP* paper these days. Fortunately, over the years of my career, technology has made collaborations with different people, even those on different continents, much easier. When John Cacioppo and I started our collaboration on the ELM, a painted chalkboard served as the cutting-edge technology. It is difficult to even fathom how when preparing our 1981 book, we traded hard copy drafts of typed manuscripts, writing notes in the margins and mailing them back and forth via the US Postal Service. The advance in technology is definitely the largest change to the field (and world) since my career started. Although I'm not sure modern technology has changed the thought process that goes into research, it likely enhanced the final product for no reason other than making revisions to papers now so much simpler.

Other than the technology that has impacted every field of science, perhaps the biggest change to work on attitudes compared to when I started was that although the empirical literature was in quite a mess at the time (with many different outcomes for different variables), the agreed upon goal of the field was to generate rather broad theories that could account for a wide variety of phenomena and variables under one conceptual framework (message learning theory, dissonance theory, social judgment theory, theory of reasoned action, etc.). Persuasion theories such as the ELM as well as the heuristic-systematic model (Chaiken et al., 1989) and the unimodel (Kruglanski & Thompson, 1999) were in that tradition. Over the most recent twenty years, however, the trend had been for more limited conceptualizations attempting to explain a more circumscribed set of phenomena. Also, harkening back to the days when researchers focused on single persuasion variables, there is some return to that where particular researchers become known for research on specific variables rather than following a more general conceptual framework. Although much of this work is quite good and important, there seems to be less of an attempt to incorporate the accumulated findings into either some of the existing conceptual accounts or to develop newer, more comprehensive frameworks.

Another trend is that the field of persuasion is becoming more applied, in some sense returning to its roots. As a knowledge base accumulates, it makes sense to take that information and use it to improve society and develop various interventions (e.g., getting people to adopt more environmentally sustainable behavior, reduce vaccine hesitancy, enhance acceptance of diversity and inclusion efforts). But current attempts at examining persuasion in the real world – sometimes by social scientists not versed in social psychology – occasionally point to variables and outcomes as if they are new discoveries without linking back to the relevant literature. The field of persuasion started with applied questions in mind (e.g., propaganda during World War II; Hovland, Janis, & Kelley, 1953), went through a rocky period of intense empirical and conceptual development, and now seems primed to return to application. Hopefully the current wave of applied work will lead to the development of new and improved general theories of social influence.

Suggested Reading

Briñol, P., & Petty, R. E. (2003). Overt head movements and persuasion: A self-validation analysis. *Journal of Personality and Social Psychology, 84*(6), 1123–1139.
   (2022). Self-validation theory: An integrative framework for understanding when thoughts become consequential. *Psychological Review.* https://doi.org/10.1037/rev0000340.
Cacioppo, J. T., & Petty, R. E. (1982). The need for cognition. *Journal of Personality and Social Psychology, 42*(1), 116–131.
Carpenter, C. J. (2015). A meta-analysis of the ELM's argument quality × processing type predictions. *Human Communication Research, 41*(4), 501–534.
Chaiken, S., Liberman, A., & Eagly, A. H. (1989). Heuristic and systematic information processing within and beyond the persuasion context. In J. S. Uleman & J. A. Bargh (Eds.), *Unintended Thought* (pp. 212–252). New York: Guilford Press.
Cialdini, R. B., Levy, A., Herman, C. P., Kozlowski, L. T., & Petty, R. E. (1976). Elastic shifts of opinion: Determinants of direction and durability. *Journal of Personality and Social Psychology, 34*(4), 663–672.
Greenwald, A. G., Brock, T. C., & Ostrom, T. M. (Eds.) (1968). *Psychological Foundations of Attitudes.* New York: Academic Press.
Himmelfarb, S., & Eagly, A. H (1974). Orientations to the study of attitudes and their change. In S. Himmelfarb & A. Eagly (Eds.), *Readings in Attitude Change.* New York: John Wiley & Sons.
Hovland, C. I., Janis, I. L., & Kelley, H. H. (1953). *Communication and Persuasion: Psychological Studies of Opinion Change.* New Haven, CT: Yale University Press.
Insko, C. A. (1967). *Theories of Attitude Change.* New York: Appleton-Century-Crofts.
Kiesler, C. A., & Munson, P. A. (1975). Attitudes and opinions. *Annual Review of Psychology, 26*, 415–456.

Kruglanski, A. W., & Thompson, E. P. (1999). Persuasion by a single route: A view from the unimodel. *Psychological Inquiry, 10*(2), 83–109.

Petty, R. E., Briñol, P., & Tormala, Z. L. (2002). Thought confidence as a determinant of persuasion: The self-validation hypothesis. *Journal of Personality and Social Psychology, 82*(5), 722–741.

Petty, R. E., & Cacioppo, J. T. (1981). *Attitudes and Persuasion: Classic and Contemporary Approaches.* Dubuque, IA: Wm. C. Brown

(1986). The elaboration likelihood model of persuasion. *Advances in Experimental Social Psychology, 19*, 123–205.

Petty, R. E., Wells, G. L., & Brock, T. C. (1976). Distraction can enhance or reduce yielding to propaganda: Thought disruption versus effort justification. *Journal of Personality and Social Psychology, 34*(5), 874–884.

Wells, G. L., & Petty, R. E. (1980). The effects of overt head movements on persuasion: Compatibility and incompatibility of responses. *Basic and Applied Social Psychology, 1*(3), 219–230.

34   A Multi-Decade Journey between the Lab and the Real World

Gary L. Wells

I suppose that growing up poor in a rough-and-tumble Midwestern town, replete with fist fights and run-ins with police, gave me some of my interest in the legal system and fed my willingness to "dirty" my academic research life with constant forays into the real world of criminal justice. I did not, however, start off my interest in social psychology with the legal system in mind. Bear with me. My story is a little different than most of the narratives in this book because a significant part of my story involves the application of my research findings to the real world of police investigations.

I was a first-generation college graduate, the youngest of four children. My father was a firefighter and my mother a homemaker. I attended my state university and discovered my interest in psychology when I looked up people in the name index of my psychology text and discovered that the vast majority of them were still alive. Hmmm . . . maybe I could do psychological research and someday my name would be in the name index of a psychology textbook. I applied broadly to graduate programs in 1973 but I was not sure that I could actually attend any of them because my wife and I were financially impoverished and we had a child. One of the great moments of my life, however, was when Ohio State University offered me admission to their experimental psychology program with a fellowship that paid all expenses plus a monthly living stipend. I accepted immediately.

The Ohio State University Years: 1973–1977

My first year at Ohio State was a bit rough. I was interested in the experimental study of human cognition but the questions being asked in experimental psychology in those days struck me as too trivial and divorced from the real world to be of interest. Hence, I transferred to the experimental social psychology program at the end of my first year. In those days there were only four core faculty in the social program at Ohio State, namely Tim Brock, Tony Greenwald, Bib Latané, and Tom Ostrom. The social area, however, had a slot every year for a visiting social psychologist. One year, for example, Bob Cialdini was the visiting social psychologist. Another year John Harvey was the visiting social psychologist. Harvey was an attribution researcher

Gary L. Wells, Iowa State University, USA.

and attribution theory was a very hot topic at that time. Harvey and I published some attribution articles focused on consensus information.

My initial major advisor in the OSU social program was Tim Brock. I admired Brock for his creativity; especially his creativity in operationalizing independent and dependent variables. Starting my third year, however, I switched to Tony Greenwald as my major professor. I was aware at the time that Tony's PhD advisor was Gordon Allport and one of my favorite old articles that I had read was Allport and Postman's "The Basic Psychology of Rumor" that they published in the *Transactions of the New York Academy of Sciences* in 1945. They opened the article with the following two sentences: "During the year 1942, rumor became a national problem of considerable urgency. Its first dangerous manifestation was felt soon after the initial shock of Pearl Harbor." Even if some aspects of their account of the psychology of rumor (e.g., sharpening, leveling, assimilation) did not hold up in the long run, they were at least asking questions worth answering. I liked that.

My interest in having Tony Greenwald as my advisor was not driven by my knowledge that he had been Allport's student. Instead, I had some ideas about Bayesian statistics and Tony was the only faculty member in the social area that had some familiarity with that. Also, Tony had an unusual profile that I found highly attractive because he was publishing not only in the best social psychology journals (e.g., *JPSP*) but also the best journals in cognitive psychology (e.g., *Journal of Experimental Psychology*) and the broader journals (e.g., *Psychological Review*). Moreover, Tony gave me a great deal of freedom to work on my own research projects.

A significant event for me occurred in 1975 when Elizabeth Loftus gave a colloquium on her misleading-information effect work. Loftus was probably the most sought-after speaker in cognitive psychology in those years. Her experiments, showing how post-event information changes the memory reports of eyewitnesses, remain among the best-known experiments in psychology (e.g., Loftus & Palmer, 1974). What I most admired about her was that she was able to test questions of both theoretical and practical value using rigorous methods and publish her findings in the best scientific journals. Almost no one in cognitive psychology was doing that in those days. Beth Loftus and I went on to publish the first edited book on eyewitness testimony (Wells & Loftus, 1984) and we have been dear friends and occasional collaborators ever since.

Whereas Loftus focused primarily on eyewitness *event memory*, I focused more on eyewitness *identification*, especially identifications from lineups. Eyewitness identification fascinated me because eyewitness identification is one of only two types of evidence in criminal trials that are considered *direct* evidence of guilt (the other type of direct evidence is confession evidence). Even fingerprints and DNA that match the defendant are circumstantial rather than direct evidence of guilt because they require additional evidentiary links to establish that there are no innocent ways in which the defendant's prints or DNA could have been at the crime scene (e.g., the defendant regularly visited that store, or the defendant once lived in the apartment where the crime occurred). In contrast, when an eyewitness says she saw the defendant commit the crime or the defendant confesses, that is direct evidence of guilt.

There is an interesting side story here. While I was in the Ohio State social program, I worked on the problem of how people use consensus information in causal attribution. While doing that research I was aware that there was a graduate student in the social psychology program at the University of Connecticut who was working and publishing on the same problem. It makes sense that we knew of each other given that we shared this somewhat esoteric and highly specific focus on consensus information. That graduate student was Saul Kassin. Saul went on to effectively father the scientific study of confessions and I would go on to develop the research field of eyewitness identification. In other words, we did the foundational scientific psychology work on the only two forms of direct evidence in the legal system. Many other parallels in the careers of Saul and I unfolded over time, such as winning the same distinguished career achievement awards from APA and from APS, both serving terms as President of the American Psychology-Law Society, and others too numerous to mention.

My time at Ohio State would not be complete without mentioning graduate school cohorts Richard Petty and John Cacioppo, who also started at OSU in 1973 and graduated in 1977. Petty, of course, is one of the "pillars" of social psychology who is contributing to the current book and Cacioppo would have also been one of the pillars had he not passed away just a few years ago. Imagine me, a first-generation college graduate sitting in a small graduate seminar taught by Tony Greenwald that had weekly writing assignments. Sitting at the same seminar table were Cacioppo and Petty. I had to either step up to the plate or go back to Kansas. Somehow I survived. In fact Rich and I co-authored a couple of publications from graduate school. The other graduate student colleague that I must mention is Mike Leippe. Mike and I conducted and published one of the first experimental studies of eyewitness identification (staged crimes followed by live lineups) while at Ohio State. Tom Ostrom, who was initially very supportive of my interest in eyewitness identification at the time, was a valuable co-author in that work. Strangely, the day I left OSU to assume my first academic job, Ostrom advised me to not continue to do eyewitness identification research, saying "that line of work has no future." I'm not sure where I got the nerve to ignore that advice, but I ignored it.

The Alberta Years: 1977–1988

My first academic job was at the University of Alberta where I published work on attitude change (e.g., my work on head nodding and persuasion), attribution (e.g., asymmetric attributions for reward versus punishment), counterfactual thinking (including what I believe is the first empirical journal article on counterfactual thinking), and eyewitness identification. But it was the article I wrote in the summer of 1977, at the age of 26, that set the course for what would eventually pave the way to a large impact in the legal world, land me on the CBS television news program *60 Minutes*, and earn me the Association for Psychological Science's Cattell Award for Lifetime Achievement in Research, among other things. The article, titled "Applied Eyewitness Testimony Research: System Variables and Estimator Variables" was published in the *Journal of Personality and Social Psychology* in 1978. The article described a novel distinction between system versus estimator variables and simultaneously laid the groundwork for programmatic research on the best ways to collect, preserve, and interpret eyewitness evidence.

Today, the distinction between system variables and estimator variables in the eyewitness area is so ingrained that it is in common use (often without any source attribution) not only in research articles but also in legal documents and judicial writings. A colleague recently asked me if it bothered me that my system versus estimator distinction is now often described in the psychological and legal literature without citing me. The answer is "absolutely not." In fact, it is the ultimate compliment that the distinction now needs no citation.

An eyewitness article that I published in *Personality and Social Psychology Bulletin* was one of my favorite articles because it has served as a strong guideline for understanding how police lineups *should* be conducted (versus how they too often are conducted, Wells & Luus, 1990). That article draws an analogy between police designing, conducting, and interpreting a lineup on the one hand and social psychologists designing, conducting, and interpreting a social psychology experiment on the other hand. The analogy is surprisingly rich because lineups and lineup procedures conducted by police often have confounds, demand characteristics, poor measures, experimenter expectancy effects, and confirmation biases. Indeed, lineups and lineup procedures are ripe for social influence and production of misleading results.

The analogy between police conducting lineups and social psychologists conducting experiments is extremely useful. After all, experimental psychology has a long history of developing ways to keep contaminants out of your experiments (e.g., avoiding confounds, stating our hypotheses a priori, reducing demand characteristics) that in fact were not being practiced by police investigators when designing and conducting lineups.

This lineups-as-experiments analogy was central to one of my most important contributions to criminal justice, namely the "double-blind lineup." My proposal was simple: Lineups should only be conducted by a person who does not know which person in the lineup is the person of interest and which ones are known-innocent fillers.

The Iowa State University Years: DNA Exonerations, Access to Policy Makers, and Legal System Impact

I was recruited to chair the psychology department at Iowa State University in 1988 and started there in January of 1989. I continued to pursue eyewitness identification research and by that point my work had become well known among defense attorneys. But it did not take long for me to learn that defense attorneys were by far the least powerful people in the criminal justice system as far as having any chance to impact how eyewitness evidence is collected, preserved, and interpreted. In addition, I discovered that judges were not going to impose any pressure on police in large part because of bad case law and the fact that they, like the general public, did not think that mistaken identifications were occurring. Control over system variables was going to have to come from more directly influencing police, but I was having trouble even getting past PR people in police departments, let alone getting to the policy makers.

In late 1996, I received a phone call that changed my life. (In those days, we picked up phones and answered them.) On the other end was Janet Reno, the Attorney General of the United States. She told me that she had been following news stories about new uses of forensic DNA testing that exonerated people who had been mistakenly identified by eyewitnesses and then convicted of crimes by juries, and served hard time in prison. She wanted me to come to Washington to talk with her about what is going on with eyewitness evidence. It turns out that I already knew about the unfolding DNA exoneration cases and in fact we were already cataloging them and we later published an analysis of the first forty such cases (Wells et al., 1998).

The short version of what is actually a long story is that I suggested to Reno the creation of a task force, under the auspices of the Department of Justice (DOJ), composed of eyewitness researchers, prosecutors, police, and defense attorneys. That task force was created. I was allowed to name the researchers and the Office of Justice Programs named the police, prosecutors, and defense attorneys. We met in various cities across the country over an eighteen-month period and produced a guide for law enforcement on the collection and preservation of eyewitness evidence. The recommendations in the DOJ Guide closely followed the science we had created, with one important exception. That guide was mailed to over 18,000 law enforcement agencies across the United States in 1999.

Meanwhile, DNA exonerations continued to mount around the country and propelled the visibility of my work well outside of academic psychology and even into the public eye. I appeared on *Oprah* talking about mistaken identification as well as the *Today Show*. I started to get calls from judges, police chiefs, and policy makers of various stripes. An important breakthrough occurred when the office of the Attorney General of New Jersey, John Farmer, asked me to help develop statewide guidelines. New Jersey had a DNA exoneration of someone who was mistakenly identified and the New Jersey Supreme Court was pressing for some reforms. Unlike every other US state, the Attorney General of New Jersey has administrative authority over all law enforcement agencies in the state of New Jersey. (Other states leave these issues to local police control unless their legislatures intervene with legislative law.) For eighteen months I traveled back and forth between Iowa and New Jersey helping New Jersey develop mandatory eyewitness identification procedures that included the double-blind requirement. Attorney General Farmer implemented these procedures in 2002.

North Carolina then joined in as the second state to mandate double-blind and other science-based eyewitness identification procedures. In the case of North Carolina (and other states that followed suit) it was legislative law that mandated our science-based eyewitness identification procedures. Today, as of this writing, an estimated 75 percent of the US population resides in a jurisdiction that has reformed eyewitness identification procedures largely modeled on what we recommend in a "white paper" (Wells et al., 1998), which includes double-blind administration, explicit pre-lineup instructions that reduce pressure to choose someone from the lineup, the use of known-innocent lineup fillers who fit the description given by the eyewitness (so that the suspect does not stand out), and so on. More recently, the American Psychology-Law Society (joint with the Psychology and Law Division of APA) commissioned an update of the 1998 white paper that expands the number of recommendations for properly conducted lineups (Wells et al., 2020).

Arguably, the impact of lab-based eyewitness research in reforming how the American legal system constructs, conducts, and interprets eyewitness identification evidence could be one of the top success stories of any experimental area of psychology in terms of impact on policy. But, that claim needs a couple of caveats. First, there was a lot of luck involved. Had forensic DNA testing not come along to exonerate innocent people and reveal that their convictions were commonly driven by mistaken identification, there would have been no call from US Attorney General Janet Reno, John Farmer would not have been motivated to reform New Jersey's identification procedures, North Carolina would not have been able to pass a law on reforming eyewitness identification procedures, and so on. This is something that social psychologists know very well: Experiments, data, and statistics do not move people to act; instead it is vivid individual cases that catch people's attention and motivate them. Were it not for the DNA exoneration cases and the heartbreak of these vivid wrongful convictions, my work and that of my students and colleagues would still be largely encased in the scientific journals and not penetrating the walls of police stations, police training academies, and courtrooms. Another caveat is that eyewitness identification reforms have not yet reached all jurisdictions in the United States, let alone other parts of the world.

An Advantage for Social Psychologists in Applying Our Findings? The Persuasion Process

I have long believed that social psychologists, steeped in the study of persuasion, have some advantages in being able to successfully navigate and impact real-world systems. Of course, my only experience is with impacting the legal system. Part of the key, I think, is to fully recognize that policy makers and actors in the system are just people. And we know very well in social psychology that information alone, no matter how scientific and seemingly clear, is not what moves people. Richard Nisbett and others showed us long ago that numbers and data are pallid, remote, and unpersuasive. People are more influenced by one vivid case than by thousands of data points. I took total advantage of that fact by pressing colorful, heartbreaking, individual true cases like the Jennifer Thompson and Ronald Cotton case. Jennifer Thompson mistakenly identified Ronald Cotton, resulting in his serving 11½ years in prison before DNA proved his innocence. My most effective talks to police and prosecutors was when I had Jennifer Thompson speak to the audiences before I presented them with scientific findings. Jennifer's amazing account of this mistaken identification and her vivid account of how torturous it was for her to realize years later that Cotton was innocent, always brought tears to people's eyes and makes them motivated to look at the scientific evidence and how we might gain control over reducing such tragedies.

As social psychologists we know very well that people understand issues better if they can relate it to something that they have personally experienced. I discovered a simple way at the beginning of every talk to police to help them see the eyewitness identification problem using their own experience. I simply ask law enforcement audiences for a show of hands as to how many have administered either a live lineup or a six-pack photo-lineup and observed their witness boldly identify a filler in the lineup. Inevitably, every hand goes up. The fact that detectives readily report experiencing eyewitnesses identify known-innocent fillers is not surprising. In fact, field studies of actual lineups that we have conducted in police departments show that eyewitnesses identify a known-innocent lineup filler more than one-third of the times that they make an identification.

Why Eyewitness Identification Research Was Initiated and Developed by Social Psychologists, not Cognitive Psychologists

It is interesting to note that the scientific study of eyewitness identification was launched and developed by social psychologists rather than cognitive psychologists. In addition to me, for example, early work by social psychologists Robert Buckhout, Roy Malpass, and Steve Penrod were followed by numerous other social psychologists who have totally dominated the eyewitness identification literature. So why did cognitive psychologists largely "sit it out" until just a few years ago? After all, cognitive psychology has a long history in the study of recognition memory. And isn't a lineup simply a recognition-memory test?

My take on this is that there are two somewhat-related related reasons why it was social psychologists rather than cognitive psychologists who developed the eyewitness identification area. First, for the most part cognitive psychologists steered away from testing their nuanced theories using real-world stimuli. Although James Gibson's ecological approach to perception and Elizabeth Loftus's use of real-world images to study the malleability of memory were respected, there was a strong bias (which still exists to some extent) in cognitive psychology to steer clear of questions and paradigms that smacked of applied psychology. The second reason is because I believe that cognitive psychologists saw eyewitness identification as just a recognition memory test; nothing more, nothing less, nothing special.

Social psychologists, in contrast, saw the lineup very differently. We saw the police lineup as a high-stakes pressure cooker on the eyewitness with life-changing implications for persons suspected of crimes and even for the witness who makes an identification. We saw biased lineups in which the suspect stands out so much that the fillers might as well be dogs, cats, and refrigerators. We saw the failure to give pre-lineup warnings to witnesses that the culprit might not even be in the lineup (hence the correct answer might be to identify no one) as creating dangerous psychological demands on eyewitnesses to pick someone from a lineup when they should pick no one. We saw witnesses exhibiting profound levels of deference and obedience to the case detective, making witnesses susceptible to cueing, nudges, verbal, and non-verbal influences during the identification procedure. We saw conformity effects when witnesses are told that fellow witnesses had picked a particular person. We saw witnesses making tentative, shaky mistaken identifications and then growing quickly into totally confident and highly persuasive mistaken eyewitnesses. We saw the echoes of Muzafer Sherif, Stanley Milgram, and Solomon Asch. To us in social psychology, the lineup was no ordinary recognition-memory test.

Final Observation

Improved eyewitness identification procedures developed in social psychology labs have penetrated police practices throughout the country. I have already noted how this success in impacting legal policy and practices would not have been possible were it not for the fortuitous development of forensic DNA testing. Only when the DNA exonerations unfolded did the world begin to take our lab work seriously. But it is important to keep in mind that we started this work on eyewitness identification more than two decades before DNA exonerations unfolded. Our controlled experiments had already blown the whistle on eyewitness identification evidence long before forensic DNA testing was developed. Having made so much progress before forensic DNA was developed meant that we had some pretty good answers already in place before Janet Reno called. I think this is the lesson I most want to leave for future social psychologists: Develop a strong and meaningful literature on an important social psychological problem because you can't predict when some event occurs that primes the world to be receptive to making meaningful use of your findings.

Suggested Reading

Allport, G. W., & Postman, L. J. (1945). The basic psychology of rumor. *Transactions of the New York Academy of Sciences, 8*, 61–81.

Loftus, E. F., & Palmer, J. C. (1974). Reconstruction of automobile destruction: An example of the interaction between language and memory. *Journal of Verbal Learning and Verbal Behavior, 13*, 585–589.

Wells, G. L. (1978). Applied eyewitness testimony research: System variables and estimator variables. *Journal of Personality and Social Psychology, 36*, 1546–1557.

Wells, G. L., Kovera, M. B., Douglass, A. B., Brewer, N., Meissner, C. A., & Wixted, J. T. (2020). Policy and procedure recommendations for the collection and preservation of eyewitness identification evidence. *Law and Human Behavior, 44*, 3–36.

Wells, G. L., & Loftus, E. F. (Eds.) (1984). *Eyewitness Testimony: Psychological Perspectives.* New York: Cambridge University Press.

Wells, G. L., & Luus, E. (1990). Police lineups as experiments: Social methodology as a framework for properly-conducted lineups. *Personality and Social Psychology Bulletin, 16*, 106–117.

Wells, G. L., Small, M., Penrod, S. J., Malpass, R. S., Fulero, S. M., & Brimacombe, C. A. E. (1998). Eyewitness identification procedures: Recommendations for lineups and photo-spreads. *Law and Human Behavior, 22*, 603–647.

35 A Long and Winding Road

Timothy D. Wilson

I am a child of the 1960s, raised by liberal parents and educated at a Quaker school in Philadelphia that prized social activism. I worked with kids in inner city day camps for four summers. I attended my first anti-war demonstration in Washington in 1969. I was a first-year college student in the spring of 1970 when many colleges went on strike to protest the invasion of Cambodia, and spent a week in Washington, DC attending protests. (My friends and I rolled into in DC at 11 p.m. with no place to stay, but within minutes of walking into Student Mobilization Headquarters, a stranger offered to let us sleep on the floor of her apartment.) These were heady times; we truly believed that we were helping to end the Vietnam War and maybe even fostering a revolution.

Given the current partisan divide in the United States and the existential problems staring us down, such as systemic racism and climate change, it probably seems naive to say we thought we were making such a huge difference. Nevertheless, this was the backdrop to my love affair with social psychology. I took my first social psych class in my third year in college, and was enthralled with the idea that you could do carefully designed experiments to test hypotheses about social behavior – and use what was learned to address social problems.

Although I was largely motivated by my desire to change the world, a funny thing happened along the way – I fell in love with basic research. In that first social psychology class I was intrigued by self-perception theory, and for my senior honors thesis I conducted what I thought was a critical test between self-perception and dissonance theories. The results were (not surprisingly) ambiguous, but on a lark I sent a description of my study to Daryl Bem. To my surprise, he kindly wrote back with praise over my experimental design (I still have that treasured letter). Encouraged, I applied to social psych graduate programs, which seemed like a much better alternative than being drafted and sent to Vietnam.

I've had more than my fair share of lucky breaks in my career, and the first was being admitted to the University of Michigan social psychology graduate program. My GRE scores were not stratospheric, and my background was quirky (I attended three undergraduate institutions, graduating from Hampshire College, a newly minted experimental college in western Massachusetts that did not give grades). Somehow

Timothy D. Wilson, University of Virginia, USA.

my unusual background and research experience caught their eye, for which I am forever grateful.

My second lucky break – really, the most formative one – was getting to work with Dick Nisbett. It is no exaggeration to say that Dick changed my life. I was terribly green when I started working with him, knowing little about what it took to be a successful scientist. Dick accepted me in his lab and – to my amazement – treated me as an intellectual equal in our quest to answer questions about the limits of human consciousness. By that I don't mean he abdicated his role as the expert researcher who was teaching a newbie the ropes. What was so amazing is that we would sit in his office for hours at a time talking about ideas, and he clearly valued what I had to say – or at least pretended to. I'm sure that the ratio of good to ridiculous ideas was quite low in my case, but Dick skillfully drew out the good ones and taught me how to play with them and, eventually, bottle them into experiments.

Another thing Dick taught me was that thinking like a psychologist is not just a vocation, it is a way of life. Personal experiences of all sorts were grist for hypotheses and theory, and thinking about research ideas was not just a 9–5 job. This became clear to me one Saturday morning during the time Dick and I were working on "Telling More Than We Can Know," the Nisbett and Wilson (1977) *Psychological Review* paper. I lived in a big house with several roommates, and I think we had had a party the night before, because I had just rolled out of bed, bleary eyed, when the phone rang. There was Dick on the line, wanting some feedback on a paragraph he had written for our paper. "Wow," I remember thinking, "this is serious business."

I was particularly lucky to begin working with Dick at the time he was thinking about people's awareness of their own cognitive processes. We began a series of studies assessing people's ability to verbalize the reasons for their preferences and behaviors, such as our field studies in which we asked passersby to choose which of four consumer items they liked the best (nightgowns in one version, conducted in a consumer arcade just off State Street in Ann Arbor; pantyhose in another, conducted in a general merchandise box store). We found that people showed a marked position effect in their selections, preferring items to the right of the display. But, perhaps not surprisingly, virtually no one reported that the position of the items had anything to do with their choice. These studies had their flaws (as many critics pointed out), but they showed me how simple experiments, sometimes in the field, can test important hypotheses.

Dick knew I was also interested in applied problems, and so he suggested I collaborate on a study of "attribution therapy" he was conducting with a urologist at the University of Michigan hospital. Dick had already shown that attributional principles could be used to help insomniacs (Storms & Nisbett, 1970), and wondered whether the same approach could be used to help men suffering from impotence without clear organic causes. The idea was to get the men to attribute their anxiety during sex to a placebo pill rather than to their inability to perform. I helped run the study, dutifully donning a medical lab coat over my graduate student attire and interviewing the patients about their sexual experiences. Alas, the study didn't work, in part (if memory serves) because the urologist did not quite grasp random assignment and sometimes gave the experimental instructions to participants in the control condition. This was an early lesson in the hazards of applied research.

As an aside, these studies gave me quite a reputation among my friends in Ann Arbor. None of my housemates was studying psychology (they ranged from a two-year-old to a thirty-year-old who had just been released from prison for burning draft records). Like most people, they had little understanding of what social psychology was all about. One housemate came upon Dick and me conducting the nightgown study, and another learned that I was going to the U of M hospital and interviewing men suffering from impotence. Despite my explanations, I think they were still a little unclear about what social psychologists study.

From Ann Arbor I moved to Duke University to begin my first academic job. I spent two years there getting my footing, but because it wasn't a tenure-track position, I moved on to the University of Virginia, where I have happily spent the rest of my career. UVA has been a great place to do my work, and Charlottesville has been a wonderful town in which to live and raise a family. Like any town in America, Charlottesville has its issues with equity and racial justice, though those issues have a unique flavor in Charlottesville, given its association with Thomas Jefferson and history of slavery. I've been proud to see my wife Dede Smith take on many of these issues as a social activist (and former member of both the School Board and City Council). As shown by the invasion of Charlottesville by white supremacists in August of 2017, much work needs to be done.

As I started my independent research career at Duke and UVA, I was still intrigued by applications of social psychology. One of the first articles I published after graduate school was a report of an attributional intervention with first-year college students that succeeded in improving their grades by giving them information implying that their academic struggles were likely due to temporary causes (Wilson & Linville, 1982). I was excited by these findings and conducted some follow-up studies (Wilson & Linville, 1985), but soon dropped that line of research. Why? Mainly because I applied for funding from NIMH to investigate when and why the intervention was working, and received the worst score of any grant application I ever submitted. One reviewer in particular eviscerated the project, arguing that it was unethical to suggest to participants that their problems might be due to a particular cause, when we researchers had no idea whether this was true. Discouraged by this feedback, I devoted my efforts to my basic research that was receiving better recognition (and more grant funding).

Indeed, I have spent my career investigating basic questions about self-knowledge, including the limits of introspection, the deleterious effects of engaging in too much introspection, dual attitudes, mental contamination, affective forecasting, and the difficulty of "just thinking." One of my most gratifying accomplishments was summarizing and extending this work in my 2002 book, *Strangers to Ourselves: Discovering the Adaptive Unconscious.* The book was never a best seller, but continues to attract a small audience, even twenty years after it was published. I'm told that it also inspired the rock group Modest Mouse to name their 2015 album

"Strangers to Ourselves." I guess it's true; they comped me two tickets when they performed in Charlottesville. Who says academics don't have side benefits?

Tied for my luckiest break was getting to work with Dan Gilbert, who has been my close collaborator for nearly two-thirds of my career. This wasn't entirely luck; I was a huge fan of Dan's work on Spinozan belief systems (Gilbert, 1991), and although I had only met him once or twice at conferences, I thought he would make a great collaborator. The lucky part is that by chance, we were both on leave at Stanford University in 1992 (Dan was spending the year at the Center for Advanced Studies, I was spending a sabbatical in the psychology department). We hung out, enjoyed each other's company, and became friends. We chatted about this and that, and while we didn't come up with any noteworthy research ideas at first, it was immediately clear that this guy would make a great collaborator. After all, Dan is one of the smartest people I know, one of the funniest people I know, and (as I was to learn repeatedly) one of the best writers anyone knows. Just read Dan's chapter in this volume. You'll see.

In that chapter, Dan tells the story of how we got on to the problem of affective forecasting, or people's predictions about how they will feel when events unfold in the future. In our initial studies we discovered an *impact bias*, whereby participants overestimated the intensity and duration of their emotional reactions to future events. Little did we know that these studies would spawn a decades-long investigation of the mechanisms of affective forecasting and how it influences many important phenomena (e.g., loss aversion, revenge, avoidance of intergroup contact, the pleasures of uncertainty), nor did we know that research on affective forecasting would spread to other disciplines, including the law, medicine, and behavioral economics (see Gilbert & Wilson, 2007; Wilson & Gilbert, 2003). And we certainly did not anticipate that this would be the beginning of a collaboration that has gone on for nearly three decades and has yielded over sixty joint publications on affective forecasting and many on other topics (e.g., the dynamics of conversation, self-judgments of how much one has changed over time, the difficulties of enjoying one's own thoughts, meta-science). As Dan notes, we never sat down and plotted out a long-term collaboration, and neither of us anticipated that we'd still be working together after all these years. It was just great fun, and productive.

One reason Dan's and my collaboration has been so fruitful and enduring is that we've maintained separate labs, each working on different facets of our research questions – with, of course, consultation back and forth. Each of our labs has taken the research in different directions, in no small part because we have both been blessed with terrific graduate students over the years who have taken the lead on numerous projects.

Looking back, it is hard to imagine a more ideal career path than to have been mentored by Dick Nisbett, and then getting to spend the bulk of my career working with Dan Gilbert. These two, by the way, have a lot in common, especially the joy and skill with which they talk about ideas. They are both masters at massaging an idea, picking out the most interesting threads, weaving them into personal experiences and astute observations of the world, and bottling them into experiments – with a lot of laughter along the way. To those of you considering a collaboration, ask yourself who you would most like to be stuck in a room with for three hours with nothing to do but talk. May you be as blessed as I have been in finding such great conversationalists.

* * * * * *

Sometimes I'm asked how I choose a particular problem to investigate. One answer is that I chat with Dan and see what's on his mind. For other ideas, I would like to say that I read the literature and observe social behavior, then make brilliant observations that I turn into ground-breaking hypotheses. But in truth, my research questions have rarely come about so systematically and deliberately. Instead, it is often critical to learn from one's data. Dick Nisbett taught me this early on; indeed, we did not conduct our nightgown study with the hypothesis that position would matter; we were trying to replicate an earlier study that applied fragrances to consumer goods and showed that they influenced people's choices, with the hypothesis that people would not recognize the influence of the fragrances. Alas, the fragrances had no effect on people's selections, perhaps because we were in an open-air setting with many competing odors. But Dick noticed the position effect, and the purpose of our subsequent study with pantyhose was to see if it was reliable (it was) and whether consumers themselves would notice it (they didn't; see Nisbett & Wilson, 1977).

Another example occurred early in my career. I randomly assigned participants to think carefully about why they felt the way they did about an affective experience (e.g., a movie) or to experience it without analyzing their reasons. My hunch was that people who analyzed reasons would enjoy the experience less but remember it better. (I thought of this as the paradox of the movie critic.) In fact, nothing of the sort happened. I noticed, however, that those who analyzed reasons showed less consistency between their reported attitudes and behavioral measures of those attitudes. This led to a fruitful line of research on "reasons analysis," which found that people who introspect about reasons often focus on factors that are accessible in memory and easy to verbalize, but are not necessarily the actual causes of their affective reactions. As a result, people "talk themselves into" a new attitude (Wilson et al., 1989). Sometimes, the data reveal more interesting hypotheses than the one we started with.

Another question I am asked is how I know whether a particular research question is worth pursuing. I have a simple answer to that one: Do I mull it over while walking to work? In the dark hours of the night when I can't sleep? When I'm supposed to be doing something else, such as preparing a lecture? If not, I know it's not worth spending all the time and effort to answer the question.

* * * * * *

Although I have spent most of my career conducting basic research, it has been gratifying to see others pick up my early attributional interventions and reinvent them in fascinating ways, such as Walton and Cohen's (2011) classic belonging intervention with at-risk college students. This rekindled my interest in intervention research, and I had great fun writing a trade book on social psychology's contributions to addressing a wide range of problems (*Redirect: Changing the Stories We Live By*). Greg Walton subsequently invited me to collaborate on a theory paper detailing the social psychological approach to interventions (Walton & Wilson, 2018). The crux of this paper is that theoretical and applied work in social psychology are inseparable; one can draw a straight line from basic research on attribution theory, dissonance theory, and social norms to research that translated these ideas into successful behavioral interventions. Spurred on by some talented graduate students, in recent years I have collaborated on new interventions, such as one that succeeded in improving the academic performance of minority students beginning high school (Williams et al., 2020). Thus, one could say I have come full circle: It was a desire to effect social change that initially attracted me to social psychology, which led to a long and fruitful journey into basic research, and has now wound its way back to more applied research.

It is tempting to conclude with some thoughts about how the field has changed and what is missing from the "good old days." I will demur, however, for several reasons. I have written elsewhere about the importance and uniqueness of core ideas in social psychology that date back to the origins of the field (Wilson, 2021). Others have written about the unfortunate decline of the laboratory experiment (Ross, 2020). But mostly, anyone should be wary of older scientists' complaints that the field has gone to hell; that's a sure sign that a new generation is taking off in interesting new directions. To that new generation, I say carry on, and may you be as lucky as I have been in finding great mentors and collaborators.

Suggested Reading

Gilbert, D. T. (1991). How mental systems believe. *American Psychologist, 46*(2), 107–119.
Gilbert, D. T., & Wilson, T. D. (2007). Prospection: Experiencing the future. *Science, 317*, 1351–1354.
Nisbett, R. E., & Wilson, T. D. (1977). Telling more than we can know: Verbal reports on mental processes. *Psychological Review, 84*, 231–259.
Ross, L. D. (2020). Demonstration experiments: Their value, limitations, and relevance to replicability issues. Unpublished manuscript, Stanford University.
Storms, M. D., & Nisbett, R. E. (1970). Insomnia and the attribution process. *Journal of Personality and Social Psychology, 16*(2), 319–328.
Walton, G. M., & Cohen, G. L. (2011). A brief social-belonging intervention improves academic and health outcomes of minority students. *Science, 331*, 1447–1451.
Walton, G. M., & Wilson, T. D. (2018). Wise interventions: Psychological remedies for social and personal problems. *Psychological Review, 125*, 617–655.
Williams, C. L., Hirschi, Q., Sublett, K., Hulleman, C. S., & Wilson, T. D. (2020). A brief social belonging intervention improves academic outcomes for minoritized high school students. *Motivation Science, 6*, 423–437.
Wilson, T. D. (2002). *Strangers to Ourselves: Discovering the Adaptive Unconscious.* Cambridge, MA: Harvard University Press.
(2011). *Redirect: Changing the Stories We Live By.* New York: Little, Brown.
(2021). What is social psychology? The construal principle. Under editorial review.

Wilson, T. D., Dunn, D. S., Kraft, D., & Lisle, D. J. (1989). Introspection, attitude change, and attitude–behavior consistency: The disruptive effects of explaining why we feel the way we do. In L. Berkowitz (Ed.), *Advances in Experimental Social Psychology* (Vol. 22, pp. 287–343). Orlando, FL: Academic Press.

Wilson, T. D., & Gilbert, D. T. (2003). Affective forecasting. In M. P. Zanna (Ed.), *Advances in Experimental Social Psychology* (Vol. 35, pp. 345–411). San Diego, CA: Academic Press.

Wilson, T. D., & Linville, P. W. (1982). Improving the academic performance of college freshmen: Attribution therapy revisited. *Journal of Personality and Social Psychology*, *42*, 367–376.

(1985). Improving the performance of college freshmen using attributional techniques. *Journal of Personality and Social Psychology*, *49*, 287–293.

36 Tales of a Devoted but Disillusioned Party Crasher

Roy F. Baumeister

How I Came to Be a Social/Personality Psychologist

I came to psychology in a roundabout and accidental manner. I was a math whiz in high school and chose Princeton because their math department was rated best in the country. My resident advisor pushed me to take an assortment of very different courses, and soon I realized that my math course was the dullest. At Princeton I also met some true math geniuses and quickly realized I was not one of them. Those being the hippie days, I decided I would study the grand issues of religion and philosophy. I spent a year in foreign study at Universität Heidelberg studying philosophy. While there, I happened to read some of Freud's writings on morality, which impressed me. Instead of analyzing the concepts of right and wrong, as a philosopher would, he relied on data, as to how morality emerged in early societies and how children learned right vs. wrong. Exciting!

When I got back, my parents explained that they would not pay Princeton tuition for a philosophy major, because the career and financial prospects for philosophy majors were grim – unless I agreed to go to law school afterwards. I made appointments with some lawyers to explore their career and lifestyle and decided that being a lawyer was bad karma. At a loss for what to do, I suggested psychology as a compromise. I vividly remember my father's immediate reply: "You'd be wasting your brain!" But to his credit, he did some research. It turned out that at his company (Standard Oil) there were some industrial psychologists whose salaries were higher than his, so he concluded it was possible to make a living in psychology after all. He somewhat reluctantly agreed to pay tuition for a psychology degree. The salaries of industrial psychologists in Cleveland in the mid-1970s have had no actual relevance to what I was able to earn, but the accidental circumstances were enough to steer me into the field.

My first thought was to be like Freud. I would do clinical work and write influential books elucidating the human mind. At age 19 I had no inkling that Freud's bridge had been burned long ago: If you wanted to understand the human mind, you could not specialize in psychopathology and then generalize to the so-called healthy, normal human mind. I signed up for a psychology major without having taken a single course. Many of my friends had also enrolled as psychology majors, and nearly all of us intended to do clinical. Then, gradually, information filtered down that gaining

Roy F. Baumeister, University of Queensland, Australia.

acceptance into clinical graduate programs faced horrific odds. Meanwhile, Joel Cooper's lectures inspired me, and I decided that social psychology was better for me. I could follow Freud's lead and use the scientific method to illuminate the human mind. Plus it would be easier to get into graduate school.

At the time I regarded the switch to social psychology as a compromise. The clinicians knew that if they could only get into graduate school, they would be set for life with a high-paying profession. Going into social psychology seemed like taking a vow of poverty, hoping to subsist on a professor's salary. Ironically, in the subsequent decades, clinical psychology went through a series of harsh changes, while social psychology flourished, so my ostensible vow of poverty led me to earning far more than many of my clinical friends. Just dumb luck.

A funny/sad theme of my life was that I was really good at multiple-choice tests, which buoyed my academic success for many years but rather abruptly turned into a completely useless, irrelevant skill. Probably the last time it helped was in taking the GRE. I applied to seven graduate schools and was accepted by all of them. How to choose? At the time, social psychology was growing rapidly and many eminent professors were moving around. Princeton's anti-elitist ethos discouraged me from simply choosing Harvard or Yale, and so I declined a chance to work with the great Shelley Taylor, at the time just an up-and-coming assistant professor. Edward E. Jones was a towering figure, and he had been the beloved mentor of my thesis advisor (Cooper) – plus, crucially, everyone was sure he would be at Duke forever, whereas rumors swirled around relocation by other major figures (e.g., Nisbett). So I accepted Duke's offer. Of course, this turned out to be based on completely false assumptions, because Nisbett remained at Michigan for his entire career, whereas already in my second year Jones accepted an offer to move to Princeton. I returned to Princeton as Jones's student and finished my PhD there.

All this has emphasized social psychology. Yet personality psychology was also involved. Indeed, my favorite undergraduate course was Cooper's on personality. Although personality psychology was held in low esteem at Princeton and Duke when I was there, the students were rebelling by believing that people really did differ from one another, and person × situation interactions seemed the best way to go.

To conclude: How I became a social psychologist was based on a series of accidents and false assumptions. From what I understand, many people in many walks of life likewise say they got where they are by a series of accidents. I did have a genuine and deep interest in understanding the big questions about the human mind, and social psychology appealed to me as one path, albeit a seriously flawed one, to pursue this interest. The promise of using the scientific method to explore the human mind was a big part of the appeal, but I never would have gotten here if left to my own devices.

What the Field Was Like at the Time

I graduated from high school in 1970, from Princeton with AB in 1974, MA from Duke in 1976, PhD from Princeton in 1978, and a postdoc at UC Berkeley (in sociology) in 1979, whereupon I felt myself hugely blessed to get a job at all (at Case Western Reserve University, in Cleveland). I had a fairly good record for the time (two first-author *JPSP*s and two other publications) but the job market was bleak and the competition was intense (the class of 1978 alone included Russ Fazio, Bill Swann, Susan Fiske, Caryl Rusbult, and others, all dominated by the unassailable Nancy Cantor) for very few jobs. It was a freak accident that I got a job at all, and so my entire career in social psychology almost did not happen. CWRU had no social psychologists on faculty and were struggling to hire one to round out their course offerings. I was fifth on a shortlist of three, but implausibly they interviewed the top three and decided against all of them and somehow persuaded the dean for additional interview funds. My interview was in mid-April, in the last months of my postdoc, and I was about ready to give up my academic dreams to seek an industry job. Over the years I have advised many budding researchers that getting that first job is the most chance-based phase in academic life, with myself as prime example. By rights I should not have been a social psychology professor. The field had no place for me, and only by freak accident did one open up. Yet here we are, and Saul Kassin thinks I am a pillar of the field.

Readers should perhaps be cautioned that this inauspicious start to my career has given me an idiosyncratic perspective. I have always had the sense that I "crashed the party," getting a research university job in social psychology by huge accident and thus not really belonging here. At my first job, I had no senior colleagues in social psychology to help me learn the ropes. I've always felt myself to be an outsider. Over the years I've had the pleasure of getting to know many of the elite members of the field, but it was always clear I was not one of them.

Fortunately, the research and publication process doesn't care whether authors are approved members of the field or marginal characters, so I was able to publish plenty of research (over 700 publications). Many of these have been on mainstream topics, such as the self, emotion, and aggression. But apart from a high citation count the field has not really acknowledged me. At this point in my life, none of these things matters. Still, young members of the field might like to know that if you are not a hot property at the start of your career, you may well remain on the fringe forever, as I have. Looking back, however, I also have the sense that being a fringe outsider has had its upside. I have been blessed to be able to choose my own complicated intellectual path rather than conforming to some standard script.

As for the content of social psychology: I confess I was seriously disappointed and disillusioned as a young graduate student getting to know the field. In the mid-1970s, at least where I was, the field was dominated by research on attributions and dissonance. I recall one of my undergraduate friends saying "I've never heard anything so un-profound as cognitive dissonance!" Attribution theory also seemed disappointingly simple. After spending some years studying philosophy, I could easily tell that the theorizing in social psychology was painfully simplistic, even though I respected and admired some of the innovative lab methods. We could produce interesting findings but not interpret them properly. I resigned myself to making my way there, and I had vague plans that some day I would move forward into a more competent conceptual system. It is embarrassing to confess that my leading candidate was Jungian psycho-analysis, but at the time that was still highly respected.

At Duke and Princeton, the ethos was all about doing experiments. Literature reviews, which later became a staple of my career, were ignored or derided as idle "think-pieces," and personality differences were scorned. This was the phase when Mischel's (1968) critique of personality psychology had encouraged the view that personality accounted for at most 10 percent of the variance in behavior, so the other 90 percent must be due to situational factors. Among other ostensible implications of this false but widely held view, social psychology was much more important than personality. Psychology departments were hiring social psychologists aggressively until the mid-1970s financial crisis set in, while personality psychology faculty positions were rare. We young people were aware of the hostility between the older social vs. personality faculty, though we did not share that and mostly thought that both were important.

Graduate training was about learning to conduct experiments, nothing else. A funny anecdote illustrates this narrow emphasis on running experiments. As a first-year assistant professor, I spent much time in the library reading up on recent research, to gather material for my lectures. My dissertation on self-presentation attuned me to findings that showed public/private differences in many different behaviors. In reading the literature for all the various chapters in social psychology, I kept noticing such differences. At some point I stumbled on references to something in *Psychological Bulletin*, a journal I had never heard of. It seemed this journal published only literature reviews, not experiments. I thought, what a weird journal, they must be desperate for manuscripts, so it would be easy to get a publication there. At the time I was struggling to get experiments to succeed on my own, and I thought maybe I could get an easy publication to tide me over until the experiments would start getting accepted. So I wrote up a manuscript summarizing all the public/private self-presentational effects in many fields and sent it off to them. They sent back a stern letter inviting a resubmission but requiring major revisions. I was a bit put off but I complied. And the suggestions were actually pretty intelligent, so the paper did improve. I sent it back and they accepted it (Baumeister, 1982). I had no sense this would be an important publication. I was genuinely surprised when several depart-ment colleagues, who subscribed to the journal, made a point of stopping to congratu-late me as if this were a major achievement. If I had any inkling that *Psychological Bulletin* was highly competitive with a high rejection rate, I would never have written or submitted the paper. When I went up for tenure, this was the best publication on my vita. But I wrote it by mistake.

The self-presentation paper did change my life, however. I began to realize that with literature reviews one could tackle bigger questions than with experiments. The philosopher slumbering within me woke up and said, it might be possible to address a series of grand philosophical questions by doing literature reviews of social science data. And indeed this has been half my career. I have a series of books surveying research literatures on meaning of life, identity, evil, human nature, and more. I suspect many people know me as an experimentalist, but if you delete all the original data and experiments from my vita, I have still had a reasonably good career just based on the literature reviews. Contrary to the impression I got in graduate school, literature reviews are often the most highly cited papers.

How My Ideas Emerged

I have had some successes in my research, though also plenty of failures. Reconstructing how the ideas emerged and developed is a risky undertaking. Like billionaire CEOs who write autobiographical memoirs with a triumphalist account of their path to success, a successful scientist can easily give a false impression by focusing on the successes. As a young researcher, I tried a wide variety of innovations, both with methods and theory. I did not know which would succeed. The maxim that served me best was to follow the data rather than my own theories and intuitions. I tried various things, and I stuck with the ones that turned out well. I also decided I wanted to end up knowing the truth, and I assumed I was not wise enough to know the truth in advance – so all my theories are always subject to revision. Indeed, I expected to revise.

My dissertation grew out of being a subject in an experiment. I recalled being in a false-feedback experiment and getting a negative evaluation of my personality. The study was published, and the findings were discussed in terms of effects of evaluations on self-esteem. My recollection was that my self-esteem was not much perturbed by the feedback – but I wondered whether other people, including the experimenter, had seen it. So it was the public, not the private self, that mattered. In my dissertation, I gave people identical feedback that was either private and confidential, or explicitly shared with others. Any informational effect on self-regard should be the same. But people responded much more strongly when they thought others knew about it. One theme of my career emerged from this: Inner processes serve interpersonal functions.

My most cited paper (on the need to belong, with Mark Leary) emerged in roundabout fashion. I attended multiple conferences where the Terror Management researchers repeatedly presented their theory that anxiety was rooted in fear of death. I was dubious. I thought anxiety might be about interpersonal acceptance. I did a literature review, finding that some anxieties were indeed about death and injury – but most were about being rejected, abandoned, excluded. When this was published, Leary remarked that he thought the issue went beyond anxiety. We discussed how to develop this idea, possibly a symposium or edited book, finally settling on doing a review article. We were both surprised at how strong and wide-ranging the evidence was. The manuscript managed to survive a tough review process and has gone on to garner over 25,000 citations (Baumeister & Leary, 1995). We had no idea when working on it that it would have that kind of impact. The initial success of the article then prompted me to think about what kinds of experiments I could do to develop it further. I thought perhaps laboratory-administered rejection experiences would have some discernible effects. For a while I was unable to persuade any of the graduate students to try this, but when Jean Twenge arrived for a postdoc, she liked the idea.

Her experiments on rejection worked remarkably well, and soon plenty of others started contributing also.

Ego depletion, which at present is arguably the best replicated finding in all of social psychology, likewise emerged in uncertain fashion. Back during graduate school I had decided to try to understand self and identity. During the 1980s, some of the field's smartest people were saying that self-regulation was not just another thing the self does, but rather is the key to understanding the self. That made me think, I need to read and learn about self-regulation. After a year or two of reading the literature, I noticed a pattern that seemed to suggest a limited resource. When there were multiple demands on self-regulation, the person tended to do worse at them. Back then, this was directly contrary to the prevailing views of the mind as an information-processing computer. (If the self-regulation program is already up and running, it should be more effective with new challenges, not less.) I discussed this in the book we wrote. One graduate student, Mark Muraven, thought this could be tested in the laboratory. His initial studies worked well, so we stuck with it (e.g., Baumeister et al., 1998; Muraven & Baumeister, 2000). The initial theory has been revised many times, as we follow the data, but the basic point remains valid.

The idea that bad is stronger than good also took a while. While reading diverse research literatures, I kept noticing odd findings emerging from research designs that included a good, a bad, and a neutral control condition: The bad often departed farther from the neutral control than the good. Even in my own lab, rejection reliably produced bigger changes than social acceptance. I recruited some colleagues to do a literature review (Baumeister et al., 2001). Our plan was to see where this principle was valid and where it wasn't, and that would tell us much about the power of negativity. We had many lovely theories about what the exceptions would be, such as that bad would prevail in the past but good would be more powerful when thinking of the future. But search as we might, we could not find exceptions. This was disappointing in terms of developing an interesting, complex theory, but it did fuel some excitement based on the implication that the greater power of negativity might be one of the fundamental properties of the mind.

While writing my book on evil, I read plenty about the horrible things people have done to each other (Baumeister, 1996). After a while, they ceased to bother me (desensitization), but after I finished the book I wanted to read something more uplifting. My youth during the hippie days had featured the slogan "Make love, not war," and I decided to read the sexuality literature. With few clear ideas, I started doing so. I started with the first volume of the *Journal of Sex Research* and read every abstract (and then any articles that caught my interest) from then to the present, just taking notes. One pattern that emerged was that cultural and social factors had a stronger effect on female than male sexuality. All the articles on the Sexual Revolution found that women changed more than men. I began to wonder if the nature–culture balance differed by gender, at least in sexuality. The more I read, the more evidence I found for this. The article on female erotic plasticity was accepted even despite feminist pushback, and it has gone on to be cited over a thousand times (Baumeister, 2000).

The idea of applying economic theory to sexuality goes against the grain, as I am by temperament a romantic, and economics is a decidedly unromantic discipline. The first inkling I had of the idea was in an article by feminist historian Nancy Cott. She sought to explain the prudishness of Victorian women by saying that if sex is one's main asset, then one needs the price to be high, which is achieved by restricting the supply. I immediately disliked that idea but could not find strong evidence against it. When I read through the sexuality literature, I began to notice plenty of findings that fit such an analysis, even though I continued not to like the idea. But by this point I had realized that if I wanted to know the truth, I'd have to accept plenty of things that disagreed with me. I've heard that plenty of people hate the theory, and possibly hate me and Kathleen Vohs for developing it, and I sympathize with their dislike. Nevertheless, an idea isn't wrong just because I don't like it. The evidence for sexual economics is overwhelming. In sex, women are the supply, men are the demand, and the "price" of going to bed varies just as economic theories say it should.

How the Field Has Developed

It is always instructive to compare the initial splashes that made social psychology famous with today's situation. Two different perspectives are relevant. One is the views of the researchers within the field on what they are all doing. The other is the broader impact on other fields. To illustrate the difference, consider some of the classic studies that put social psychology on the interdisciplinary map as an important advance in elucidating human behavior. The famous studies by Milgram, Darley and Latané, Schachter and Singer, Festinger and Carlsmith, and the like provoked the imagination of scholars in multiple fields, and some of that work is still discussed and debated today, more than half a century later. None of those articles would stand a chance at being published today. We social psychologists have largely repudiated our roots. Having been an upbeat booster of social psychology for decades, it pains me to say that I see the future as much less promising. If I were a young man starting out today, I do not think social psychology would strike me as an appealing field, even though in the reality of my career I have devoted my life to it.

There are two mushrooming problems. One is replicability. I think the danger is far overstated and the field has responded in unfortunate ways. The fear of failed replication has prompted social psychologists to insist on large samples. These are impractical for the kind of work that first gained respect and legitimacy for the discipline. (Can you imagine Milgram, or Latané and Darley, doing their experiment with n = 75 per cell?) The solution therefore has been to go to online data collection with large but dubious samples, such as Mechanical Turk, which is seriously infested with robots and professional participants who have already done hundreds of studies. Whether this will really improve replicability is an open question. But the watering-down of the intellectual and scientific ambitions of social psychology is enormous. Most modern research can be characterized as effects of thoughts on other thoughts. In a typical modern experiment, participants are asked to imagine something, and afterward are asked to imagine something else and say how they would rate it or what they presume they would do in such an imaginary situation. Nothing in these procedures includes "actual" behavior.

The second and more serious problem is political bias. That threat is downplayed among leaders in the field, because most of them support the prevailing bias. To me, the replication issue is an incremental problem, and we can make improvements with such innovations as preregistration, and making one's data publicly available. In contrast, the political bias is an existential crisis. I am old enough to remember that the initial call for diversity by the mainly white-male field was based on the assumption that people with different backgrounds and perspectives would make for a stronger science because they would bring in diverse viewpoints and alternative hypotheses. Over the decades, the push for diversity has morphed to become a matter of promoting liberal Democrats with different ethnic backgrounds, thus not different ideas but rather different demographic characteristics. Although I share many of their values, I fear the contribution to the health of psychological science is weakened to the extent that all researchers share the same ideological biases. Moreover, it is abundantly clear that ideological homogeneity (accompanied by editorial suppression of contrary findings) distorts the science and discourages researchers from pursuing ideas that conflict with the preferred grand narrative.

Nevertheless, if a young person is determined to make a career as a social psychologist, I can offer some advice. A first point is that the field has become much more active in left-wing politics. If you are conservative, moderate, libertarian, or apolitical, your prospects for success are limited; I advise you to seek another line of work. My second and more optimistic advice is to develop big-data skills. Big-data studies seem to me the best hope for the future of social psychology. I have said that online studies of the effects of thoughts on other thoughts have value, but this approach is limited. The amount of solid scientific knowledge that can be garnered through MTurk survey experiments is severely limited. But big data identify patterns that are genuinely there in the real world.

Perhaps the best prospect for future research would involve a combination of "small" sample social psychology experiments and big data. The sort of experiments that made social psychology famous and important can at most involve n = 10 or 20 per cell, because they are labor-intensive. The risk is that they produce false positives, yielding effects that do not exist out in the world. But big-data analyses solve that problem, given that they contain huge numbers of people and real-world differential findings. The almost inevitable drawback of big-data analyses is that they are confounded and cannot establish causality. A combination of a confounded but impressive big-data real-world finding with a couple of small-sample lab studies elucidating the causal process would be ideal.

Conclusion

Through a series of accidents, I blundered into social psychology. Up until recently, it has been a wonderful life and career. What worked for me will probably not work for young people entering the field today, and I advise them to tread carefully. It is sad for me to write this last section. I have mentored about forty researchers partly out of enthusiastic faith that social psychology is really wonderful as a life task and occupation. And it has been that, mostly, for me. Yet I have discontinued mentoring, in part because I can no longer sustain that faith.

The project of using the scientific method to study the human mind and understand human behavior strikes me as one of the greatest of all intellectual pursuits. My mentor, the iconic Edward E. Jones, once remarked on the appeal of a social psychology career as being able to earn money by indulging "one's basic curiosity about people." It is still true, though heavily constrained by dubious methodological turns and dubious ideological and political pressures. If I were a college senior today, I doubt I would choose social psychology as my life's work. The future is cloudy at best. I sincerely hope the next generations of researchers can resurrect it.

Suggested Reading

Baumeister, R. F. (1982). A self-presentational view of social phenomena. *Psychological Bulletin, 91*(1), 3–26.

(1996). *Evil: Inside Human Cruelty and Violence*. New York: W. H. Freeman.

(2000). Gender differences in erotic plasticity: The female sex drive as socially flexible and responsive. *Psychological Bulletin, 126*(3), 347–374.

(2010). The self. In R. F. Baumeister & E. J. Finkel (Eds.), *Advanced Social Psychology: The State of the Science* (pp. 139–175). New York: Oxford University Press.

Baumeister, R. F., Bratslavsky, E., Finkenauer, C., & Vohs, K. D. (2001). Bad is stronger than good. *Review of General Psychology, 5*(4), 323–370.

Baumeister, R. F., Bratslavsky, E., Muraven, M., & Tice, D. M. (1998). Ego depletion: Is the active self a limited resource? *Journal of Personality and Social Psychology, 74*(5), 1252–1265.

Baumeister, R. F., & Leary, M. R. (1995). The need to belong: Desire for interpersonal attachments as a fundamental human motivation. *Psychological Bulletin, 117*(3), 497–529.

Mischel, W. (1968). *Personality and Assessment*. New York: John Wiley & Sons.

Muraven, M., & Baumeister, R. F. (2000). Self-regulation and depletion of limited resources: Does self-control resemble a muscle? *Psychological Bulletin, 126*(2), 247–259.

37 Social Cognition, Always the Great Beyond

Susan T. Fiske

It was 1978. Having a graduate student office with a 13th story view of the Boston skyline seemed fantastic. Except that my office originally was meant to hold the secretary-receptionist for the professor within. People were always seeking directions, the use of my phone, an appointment with said professor, or change for the soda machine. But I would not trade offices. Being mistaken for the secretary was a small price to pay for having my own office, with a window, next door to my advisor, Shelley Taylor.

Until we had a fire drill. Down the dozen-plus flights of cement stairs, I carried three brown cardboard file boxes of IBM punch cards – the only copies of my coded dissertation data. If I had spilled them, it would have been almost as bad as their going up in flames. Meanwhile, my advisor, Shelley, told me that her undergrad advisor, Sara Kiesler, had persuaded a fire fighter to rescue Shelley's senior thesis data from her burning dorm room. Fortunately, our respective data survived. There was not yet a Cloud on the horizon.

More than technology has changed; having female advisors and fore-advisors would have been rare at the time. And then, there were the data and analyses recorded on those cards. All these factors – data technology, analytic methods, the theories tested, and the female role models – influenced my experience of social psychology. They were all linked: I hoped my IBM card-boxes contained the seeds of a revolution, both scientific and gendered.

Back Story

Both science and gender were prominent in my background. Although other autobiographical essays describe my suffragist fore-mothers and psychologist father's influence, a brief sketch provides context here (see Fiske, 1992, 2010, 2018a, 2022). My great-grandmother ran the Massachusetts women's suffrage movement, and my grandmother was President of the Radcliffe women's suffrage club, when she met my grandfather, President of the Harvard women's suffrage club. By the time my mother arrived at Radcliffe, women had won the vote in 1920, so she expanded her civic activities to include the civil rights of Black and Hispanic Americans. She met my

Susan T. Fiske, Princeton University, USA.

father, Donald Fiske, at a Harvard–Radcliffe mixer; he was a promising psychology major, working with Henry Murray to define personality psychology. World War II intervened, so he applied his training to the selection of spies to parachute behind enemy lines. From this came a distinguished career in psychometrics and an always attentive father who wanted to know how we would operationalize our ideas – and how we would know if we were right. "We" is me and my brother, the cultural psychologist Alan Fiske. Those dinner table debates were doubtless one reason that we followed him into the field, with lasting effects. Of his six grandchildren, three have advanced degrees in psychology.

Long before they were a twinkle in anyone's eye, and well before the boxes of IBM cards, I had decided to improve the world, for women and other oppressed people, because it was the 1970s and it seemed like we could. In my family, if you wanted to justify social change, the only credible argument in dinner table political debates required evidence. If I wanted to make a difference to women's position, civil rights, the environment, war and peace, it would require not just ideals but the right tools and the right theories. So I landed that 13th floor office, on an NSF Fellowship, with a place in Harvard's graduate program. I was determined to learn the methods necessary to win debates on evidence-based equity.

Methods Beyond Words

I took a job as a methods and computer consultant on the 13th floor's social and behavioral science computing facility. We spent a lot of time disentangling punch cards stuck in the card reader. We also got to help people think about how to analyze their data. And we checked syntax. The investment in the submitted code was considerable: Once people fed-in their data and analysis instructions, they generally had to wait overnight for their batch of analyses to run, when the mainframe traffic cleared out. Because of batch processing queues, errors routinely cost 24 hours. (Still, this was an improvement on my father's factor analyses for his dissertation. Each took three months on an adding machine. Then my mother took another three months to replicate each.)

Working as a computer consultant entailed data sets from ant colonies to primate troupes to human neighborhoods, from milliseconds to millennia. People brought us looking-time data collected with stopwatches and reaction time data collected with event recorders (these generated paper streamers with inky blips at intervals then measured with a ruler). People arrived with masses of human coding: free-response items about politics, spontaneous conversations between garbage collectors, think-aloud problem-solving. Machine learning would have been an oxymoron. We worked with a fraction of today's computing power and far simpler statistics.

Nevertheless, a methods revolution was rising. On my own punch cards were looking times and information weights – not just participants using words. The new approach aimed for the precision of measuring responses beyond self-reports on Likert scales; social psychology borrowed from the new cognitive psychology. Assistant Professor Reid Hastie was my guide here. I was interested in whether people forming impressions both attend and give weight to information that is either negative or extreme. The dissertation built an information-processing mathematical model validated by its behavioral predictions (looking time). And it identified the processes mediating between observing someone's sociable and moral behavior and reporting their likability (Fiske, 1980). Mediation was not yet on the scene, but Assistant Professor David Kenny was inventing it. I watched from my perch as his grad-stat T.A. and then literally on the ground, as he diagrammed his ideas in the dirt of the Cambridge Common; we were on the way home from an oldies bar, the Thursday night regulars being Dave, Reid, Shelley, and me (as the needed fourth; more on this later). My job-talk paper probably originated from one of those late-night walks: how to sort out the mechanisms for information in different channels as mediators (Fiske, Kenny, & Taylor, 1982).

These dry methods aimed to be precise. Social psychology was coming out of a credibility crisis that stemmed from flashy, counterintuitive studies that few could replicate (sound familiar? Fiske, 2018b). The cognitive revolution in experimental psychology had aimed to go beyond the mindless black box of classical and operant conditioning – in part because they could not account for language acquisition. Social psychology had never denied the mind, but now wanted to go beyond words to more precise, falsifiable methods and theories. The precision appealed to me in part because my father was so frustrated by the subjectivity and malleability of words as psychological measures (D. W. Fiske, 1981). But honestly, I probably wanted to do the new social cognition because all the cool, smart people were doing it.

Theories Beyond Intuition

The social cognitive revolution hinged on ideas as much as methods. The consistency theories of the 1950s and 1960s seemed to have burned out, according to us hotheads. A little orange book was circulating, not so much a manifesto, but a measured consideration by smart people of how social observers make sense of other people. Written by several gods of social psychology, when Shelley told me to read it (on a very, very long week at the beach), this book did not seem like fomenting a revolution. I had no idea of how radical it was. To my callow self, the book just seemed too abstract (people thinking about people thinking about how people make sense of people; Jones et al., 1972). But get through it I did, and I got a lot. From a mostly ignored chapter on the psychological midpoint being slightly positive, I derived the idea that negative information would be diagnostic (also extremity, for other information-value reasons). From another chapter came pieces of our Stereotype Content Model, thirty years later (Fiske et al., 2002).

Not having had a regular Psych 101 class (Harvard did not believe in superficial generalities, just deep dives, even without a map), so I played catch up, reading other psychology subfields' theories to see if they might inform social cognition. Like other social cognition researchers, my work in grad school and my first job was informed by perceptual and cognitive theories – Gestalt principles, categorization, attention to diagnostic cues, memory for incongruence, and in our case, visual salience (Taylor & Fiske, 1975) – all of these applied to people thinking about people. For me, the dilemma was achieving that level of precision, without using decidedly un-social, uninteresting stimuli. Case in point: The stimuli that generated the attention data on those IBM cards were photographs of sixteen stimulus guys, each performing eight actions along two dimensions. The social dimension, ranging from high to low, showed him picnicking with friends, picnicking but seated at the periphery, picnicking separately, or sitting with his back to all of them. The other dimension (civic responsibility? morality?) showed each guy expressing degrees of protest against child pornography: soliciting signatures for a petition, signing it himself, ignoring someone asking, and confronting someone asking. I took 128 photographs, to have standardized but ecologically valid behavior pictures. They aimed to make stimuli both rigorous and engaging. The theorist whose mathematical model I was extending, Norman Anderson, was unimpressed and advised me either to use simple stimuli such as trait words to test my attention/weight predictions *or* to see if photos acted like simple traits. I rebelled. Social cognition could be both precise and social, couldn't it? My dissertation did get published, but only after surviving three editors (one of whom lost the paper manuscript); if it hadn't been runner-up (almost a winner) of the dissertation award from the Society of Experimental Social Psychology, I would not have persisted (Fiske, 1980).

After several years of trying to own the more technical sides of these cognitive approaches, I brought my work home to emphatically *social* psychology: people interacting, whether for mutual benefit or zero-sum outcomes, getting real-time information, to make sense of each other, predict their actions, and plan their own (e.g., Erber & Fiske, 1984). Graduate school is where you learn what you can and cannot reasonably do and be. I was never going to be fluent in eye-tracking or reaction times. My identity remained social but as a go-between for social and cognitive approaches. All too often this bridging identity left me straddling the gap between boat and dock. More than once, I fell in. But mostly, I had the daily challenge of explaining each side to the other. Apparently, the new field of social cognition needed this, because when Shelley and I wrote the book in 1984 (now in its sixth edition), it became a standard resource for methods and theories (Fiske & Taylor, 1984).

Social Categories Beyond Shortcuts

Reviewing the new field revealed an especially active area: social knowledge structures. The categories that people apply to understand others – Allport's "nouns that cut slices" – have fascinated me since a project in graduate school (Taylor et al., 1978). People remembering a meeting could recall which gender made a comment but not which individual. Cognitive explanations for stereotypic information-processing seemed to offer both rigorous explanation and social relevance. I was hooked; over my career, several of our theories relevant to social categories reflected the nature of the times.

Continuum Model and Other Dual-Process Theories

Trying to reconcile category-based social cognition with the also appealing math models began in earnest when I gave my first post-PhD talk at Ohio State. An insightful grad student asked, in effect, "How can you do that clean crisp math model at the same time as that schema stuff?" Answering his question required lots of data and my first theory (Fiske & Neuberg, 1990). The continuum from category-based schemas (more immediate stereotypes) to piecemeal algebraic combinations (more deliberate individuation) depended on cognitive factors (information available, bandwidth) and on motivation (more effort into forming impressions of people who matter to you). It became one of several contemporaneous dual-process models – automatic or controlled processes depending on goals, information, time constraints – now known as thinking fast, thinking slow. Many ideas that prove popular float around the field until their time arrives.

Power as Control: Testifying for the Powerless

Another early theory came from my remembering that my science was supposed to be saving the world, so when lawyers called to ask for expert testimony on a gender discrimination case, how could I say no? As it turned out, social cognition approaches had much to offer (e.g., see Fiske et al., 1991). Everyday workplace decisions leave a paper trail of words and ratings, data that record individual and group social cognitive processes. For example, when the promotion committee counsels a "lady partner candidate" to walk, talk, and dress more femininely, the inference seems clear, namely that gender tainted their decision. The evidence that employment lawyers use (personnel ratings, written feedback) fit well with the data that social cognition uses all the time – a better fit than, say, armchair diagnoses of a decision maker's murky authoritarian motives. This fit sparked a lot of social psychology expert witnessing; after all, we've been studying prejudice since the 1930s, so we know a lot.

Nevertheless, to me the testimony also revealed that our research omits much. For example, nearly all social cognition research (impression formation, stereotyping) dealt with peers. But the most consequential decisions often rest with powerholders. None of us studied power at the time – I could not even convince anyone to join me at first – because it seemed crass and rude to admit that we're not all equal. Powerholders are prone to use categories more than other people do (because they can, in part). Now, thanks to widespread interest, we know many ways that people with power or status can be socially obnoxious.

Ambivalent Sexism: Distinct Biases

The expert witnessing on gender cases pertained to another suddenly relevant science project: Not all sexist men hate women. Granted, some do, and observations of hostile sexism were not rare forty years ago. My phone rang with many cases involving some men disliking or disrespecting women and creating a hostile work environment. In one typical case, a female security-clearance investigator was expected to make coffee for all the men, and to fill in for the secretary when she was on her lunch hour. Women who resist hostile sexists' prescribed gender roles are punished by failed promotions, for example.

Besides this obvious type, sexism can also take a seemingly benign but paternalistic form: Benevolent sexists also expect women to conform and reward those who do, for example by protecting them from other men (Glick & Fiske, 1996). Incorporating the hostile and "benevolent" types, the Ambivalent Sexism Inventory has generated a thriving literature to predict sexual harassment, intimate partner violence, workplace discrimination, and more. Overtly hostile sexism was rare in academic settings, in my experience, except when a male full professor benevolently invited two female assistant professors for a drink; when he took us to Hooters (a bar with nearly topless waitresses) he obviously enjoyed our discomfort.

Stereotype Content: Warmth and Competence as Fundamental

Hostile biases and seemingly benevolent but demeaning biases extend beyond women. This was another idea whose time had come. By the late 1990s, the field had studied more and more categories, on the assumption that they all operated according to the same principles (e.g., confirmation bias). But we had not systematically examined stereotype content; perhaps that too operated on knowable principles.

Social categories themselves locate along two dimensions; that is, social categories tend to cluster by warmth (trustworthy, friendly – or not) and competence (capable, confident – or not). So the warmth × competence space, examined as quadrants, reduces to only four kinds of people (Fiske et al., 2002): the admirable (high on both), the disgusting (low on both), the enviable (cold but competent), and the pitiable (warm but inept).

The intergroup field had begun with a focus on anti-Black racism and anti-Semitism, which Allport (1954) described as complementary stereotypes. As it turns out, the two stereotypes were opposites on the warmth and competence dimensions. Black people were stereotyped as incompetent (lazy) but warm (easygoing), landing them in the pity quadrant. Jewish people were stereotyped as competent (good with money) but cold (untrustworthy), landing them in the envy quadrant. Stereotypic warmth and competence result from groups' cooperative/competitive position and social status, which are accidents of history. Asian stereotypes had started out as the disease-laden peasants (who built US railroads), then after being banned by immigration law, the current Asian immigrant stereotype is a tech genius. So anti-Asian stereotypes went from disgust to envy. Other distinct groups also have distinctive stereotype stories: gender (competent but cold female professionals vs. warm but incompetent housewives), age (doddering but dear; well-meaning but inept). Many groups still deserve a systematic analysis of their subtypes, change over time, and regional differences.

In any case, the dimensions came into their moment, but not alone: Five of us have assembled as adversarial collaborators trying to reconcile our respective two-factor models (resulting theory: Abele et al., 2021; how-to: Ellemers et al., 2020; joint data: Koch et al., 2021). Nobody knows your work as well as a competitor. Interdependence sharpens the mind. Among other insights, you recognize your relative advantages and disadvantages.

Women Beyond Beyond

Back to the beginning: Grad school may be where you solidify your professional identity, but also where you face its intersection with other identities, in my case, gender. Gender interacts with the tension between the more precise, rigorous approaches and the more intuitive, insight-driven approaches. (Guess which gender disproportionately does which.) Sometimes women had to prove ourselves as worthy scientists. My alma mater took 100 years to hire its first female experimental psychologist, and not until years after I left.

When I was entering grad school, we had two women in the department, one in social (Shelley Taylor), one in developmental (Sonny Yando). Both role models were smart, attractive, hardworking women; once I knew Shelley well enough to know, I also learned that women could balance love and work, work and life. Psychology was appealing to women my age, judging from the number of female majors and from the often 50–50 split among grad students. One consequence of the dearth of female faculty is that female grad students were invited to join the solo female (my advisor) going for a drink with male faculty (hence my being a precocious fourth at the oldies bar). At conferences, my advisor would bring a gaggle of girl grads perhaps partly as self-protection during otherwise all-male outings.

Some of the men in charge were not so comfortable with the changing times. When grad admissions threatened to tip the balance to women, they reportedly worried openly about too many female students. In the first-year grad seminar, one of the (male) faculty assigned us *The Inevitability of Patriarchy*; we had to recapitulate its arguments. Later, as a practical part of my training, on the way to a workshop at another university, my advisor warned me about which faculty were serial harassers; she was right. During my job hunt, a male shortlist rival for the same job was told that he could have the job if he would change his sex. At another school, when I accepted an invitation to interview for a methods job, the search-committee chair asked me to interview also for a job in women's studies. "But I don't do women's studies." "Well, we just thought you might be interested."

And gendered assumptions were made not just by Americans, or just by the men. Colleagues in different countries told me that women could not be married and faculty at the same time, because no husband would tolerate the wife's long hours needed to succeed as a professor. And no department would tolerate the distracting spouse – let alone children. Faculty who were also mothers told me that even their neighbors disapproved of their choice. Being female seemed to be an example of Goffman's "master status," an identity that dominated one's other identities.

Beyond Methods, Theories, Identities

I'm no historian, but collectively, perhaps these personal histories portray the field; we've all devoted our lives to it. Admittedly, our periodic crises may land us in the disgust quadrant sometimes, publicly perceived as low on both warmth and competence. Compared to neuroscientists, we may seem incompetent, but we're involved in social issues, making us warm. Collectively, social psychology has much to recommend it, and regular people mostly appreciate us; for them, we are in the golden quadrant, warm and competent, admirable. I agree completely.

Suggested Reading

Abele, A., Ellemers, N., Fiske, S., Koch, A., & Yzerbyt, V. (2021). Navigating the social world: Toward an integrated framework for evaluating self, individuals, and groups. *Psychological Review, 128*(2), 290–314.

Allport, G. (1954). *The Nature of Prejudice*. Reading, MA: Addison-Wesley.

Ellemers, N., Abele, A., Koch, A., Yzerbyt, V., & Fiske, S. (2020). Adversarial alignment enables competing models to engage in cooperative theory-building toward cumulative science. *Proceedings of the National Academy of Sciences, 117*(14), 7561–7567.

Erber, R., & Fiske, S. T. (1984). Outcome dependency and attention to inconsistent information. *Journal of Personality and Social Psychology, 47*, 709–726.

Fiske, D. W. (Ed.) (1981). *Problems with Language Imprecision. New Directions for Methodology in Social and Behavioral Science, 9*. San Francisco, CA: Jossey-Bass.

Fiske, S. T. (1980). Attention and weight in person perception: The impact of negative and extreme behavior. *Journal of Personality and Social Psychology, 38*, 889–906.

(1992). Citation and biography, 1991 Award for Distinguished Contribution to Psychology in the Public Interest. *American Psychologist, 47*, 498–501.

(2010). Award biography and bibliography for Distinguished Scientific Contributions. *American Psychologist, 65*, 695–698.

(2018a). Not your grandparents' social cognition: A family letter about progress through crisis. In S. T. Fiske (Ed.), *Social Cognition: Selected Works of Susan T. Fiske* (pp. 1–12). New York: Routledge.

(2018b). Stereotype content: Warmth and competence endure. *Current Directions in Psychological Science, 27*, 67–73.

(2022). Love and work: How to (and not to) have both. In J. Bookwala & N. Newton (Eds.), *Reflections from Pioneering Women in Psychology* (pp. 113–126). New York: Cambridge University Press.

Fiske, S. T., Bersoff, D. N., Borgida, E., Deaux, K., & Heilman, M. E. (1991). Social science research on trial: The use of sex stereotyping research in Price Waterhouse v. Hopkins. *American Psychologist, 46,* 1049–1060

Fiske, S. T., Cuddy, A. J., Glick, P., & Xu, J. (2002). A model of (often mixed) stereotype content: Competence and warmth respectively follow from perceived status and competition. *Journal of Personality and Social Psychology, 82,* 878–902.

Fiske, S. T., Kenny, D. A., & Taylor, S. E. (1982). Structural models for the mediation of salience effects on attribution. *Journal of Experimental Social Psychology, 18,* 105–127.

Fiske, S. T., & Neuberg, S. L. (1990). A continuum model of impression formation, from category-based to individuating processes: Influence of information and motivation on attention and interpretation. *Advances in Experimental Social Psychology, 23,* 1–74.

Fiske, S. T., & Taylor, S. E. (1984). *Social Cognition.* New York: Random House.

Glick, P., & Fiske, S. T. (1996). The Ambivalent Sexism Inventory: Differentiating hostile and benevolent sexism. *Journal of Personality and Social Psychology, 70,* 491–512.

Jones, E. E., Kanouse, D. E., Kelley, H., Nisbett, R., Valins, S., & Weiner, B. (Eds.) (1972). *Attribution: Perceiving the Causes of Behavior.* Morristown, NJ: General Learning Press.

Koch, A., Yzerbyt, V., Abele, A., Ellemers, N., & Fiske, S. T. (2021). Social evaluation: Comparing models across interpersonal, intragroup, intergroup, several-group, and many-group contexts. *Advances in Experimental Social Psychology, 63,* 1–68.

Taylor, S. E., & Fiske, S. T. (1975). Point of view and perceptions of causality. *Journal of Personality and Social Psychology, 32,* 439–445.

Taylor, S. E., Fiske, S. T., Etcoff, N. L., & Ruderman, A. J. (1978). Categorical and contextual bases of person memory and stereotyping. *Journal of Personality and Social Psychology, 36,* 778–793.

38 The Accidental Social Psychologist

Brenda Major

I am honored to be included in this book among so many social psychologists whose work I respect and admire. At the risk of confirming the gender differences in attributions that Kay Deaux identified long ago – that "what is skill for the male is luck for the female" (Deaux & Emswiller, 1974) – I also feel incredibly lucky to be included here. I am, as I often tell my students, an "accidental social psychologist." Due to several strokes of good fortune, including having a supportive undergraduate mentor at the College of Wooster, who thought of me when he got notice of a last-minute opening in a PhD program due to an illness, and being in the right place at the right time with not much else to do, I managed to get into the PhD program in experimental psychology at Miami University of Ohio without going through the traditional graduate application process. There, I took two courses in social psychology, one from Richard Sherman on attribution processes, and another on the psychology of freedom and control from Art Miller, that changed the course of my life and my area of study. Those two courses hooked me on social psychology.

Thankfully, Miami let me change programs from experimental to social psychology, and my advisor, Dick Sherman, let me pursue my own research interests in gender. Luck smiled again when Kay Deaux visited at Miami University as part of a "Women in Psychology" speaker series organized by the women graduate students (not me). We had an opportunity to hear each other speak about our research, and our mutual admiration led to an offer from Kay to work with her and a transfer to Purdue, again without going through the traditional graduate school application process. I marvel at this today – given how polished, prepared, and experienced our graduate school applicants are now, I probably would never have gotten in.

After obtaining my PhD from Purdue in 1978, my first job was at SUNY/Buffalo, where I had an incredible set of supportive colleagues, including Dean Pruitt, Ed Hollander, Ed Vinacke, and Barbara Bunker. I thrived there personally and professionally and also formed a lifelong passion for the Buffalo Bills (who unfortunately have yet to win a Superbowl as of this writing). In 1993 my husband and I spent a sabbatical at the University of California, Santa Barbara and two years later we joined the faculty there. It was hard to leave the Bills and even harder to leave my colleagues at SUNY Buffalo, but when I moved to UCSB I gained another set of outstanding

Brenda Major, University of California at Santa Barbara, USA.

colleagues, as well as a beautiful environment. I feel incredibly fortunate to have been able to work in two social psychology programs that were not only excellent, but also highly collegial.

I feel most fortunate, however, for having been able to collaborate with so many outstanding graduate students, postdocs, and colleagues over the course of my career. The saying that "it takes a village" is often used, but I believe it is really true for academic research in general, and certainly for my own. My academic successes are shared with all of my students, postdocs, and collaborators, and is due in great measure to their creativity, fortitude, intelligence, and skill. My students call themselves "The Majorettes" and I am very proud of them. Unfortunately, I do not have space here to name everyone to whom I am grateful. Several people, however, deserve special mention because they had such a profound effect on my thinking and my research.

First is my graduate advisor, Kay Deaux. Kay was an exemplary role model of a successful female academic at a time when those were few and far between. She taught me countless invaluable lessons about how to approach the research process and data – lessons that I still try to hand down to my students. My enduring interest in attribution processes, identity, and perceptions of fairness and equity began with her. Our *Psychological Review* paper (Deaux & Major, 1987) presenting our model of how gender expectations and stereotypes held by "perceivers" interact with the self-perceptions and self-related goals of "targets" to create gender differences in behavior was one of the first models to integrate the self-fulfilling prophecy perspective with the newly emerging research on the self in social psychology. This theoretical model took a much more "situationist" perspective on gender differences in behavior than most theories at the time, and it framed much of my ensuing work on stigma.

Dean Pruitt, who was a senior faculty member at SUNY Buffalo when I joined the faculty there as a new assistant professor in 1978, also was especially important to my career. Dean was the epitome of what one would hope for in a senior colleague. He is one of the most generous colleagues and clearest thinkers I have ever met and my work benefited greatly from his constructive comments. We met weekly for dinner during my first year on the faculty, discussing social psychology and ideas. Dean was also a great judge of talent. He spearheaded the hiring of a terrific group of social psychologists at SUNY Buffalo who contributed greatly to my intellectual, professional, as well as personal life, including Jennifer Crocker, Lynne Cooper, Steve Spencer, Nancy Collins, Phil Shaver, and Jim Blascovich. It was a heady group of colleagues and an exciting time to be in Buffalo. The intellectual synergy I experienced there, especially with Jenny, shaped the trajectory of my professional career.

When Jennifer Crocker arrived at Buffalo, I was studying cognitive and motivational factors that could explain why groups who are objectively disadvantaged, such as underpaid working women, nevertheless often report being just as satisfied with their jobs and wages as those who are advantaged. The prevailing explanations emphasized gender differences in values – for example, that women didn't value their careers and salaries as much as men did. In contrast, I was focusing on social comparisons and attributions. Specifically, I was showing experimentally how biases to compare with similar others (e.g., members of the same sex, people in the same jobs), when combined with ideologies that legitimize status differences by attributing success and failure to internal factors (such as the belief that success is due to hard work and merit), can produce a lesser sense of entitlement among members of disadvantaged groups (Major, 1994). This lesser sense of entitlement, in turn, not only prompts subjective content in the face of objective disadvantage, but can also become self-fulfilling, thereby perpetuating disadvantage. In essence, I was studying the mechanisms by which social devaluation can lead to self-devaluation, as well as tolerance and acceptance of disadvantaged status.

Jenny's interest was in self-esteem, and she challenged me to think about responses to social devaluation through a different motivational lens – one of self-esteem protection rather than system justification. Our *Psychological Review* paper (Crocker & Major, 1989) challenged the view that disadvantage and social devaluation necessarily lead to lower self-esteem. We pointed out the attributional ambiguity that members of stigmatized groups frequently experience surrounding the causes of their negative treatment. And we proposed cognitive strategies by which members of stigmatized groups actively resist social devaluation and protect their self-esteem, such as by comparing with other disadvantaged ingroup members, rather than with advantaged outgroups, and by selectively valuing the attributes and domains in which their ingroup excels relative to other groups.

The most controversial strategy we proposed was that members of stigmatized groups can protect their personal self-esteem by attributing negative outcomes and treatment to prejudice and discrimination based on their group membership rather than to their own lack of deservingness. This hypothesis generated an enormous amount of research and theory on the antecedents and consequences of perceived discrimination. Jenny and I also stoked controversy by proposing that prejudice that is hidden behind a cloak of fairness has the potential to be more detrimental to self-esteem than prejudice that is overt, and thus more easily recognized. The seeds of much of my ensuing research career were sown in my collaboration with Jenny and the work we did together.

When I left SUNY/Buffalo to join the faculty at UCSB in 1995, Toni Schmader, who was then a first-year graduate student at SUNY/Buffalo, decided to come with me. She was soon joined in my lab at UCSB by a number of other incredible students, including Wendy Quinton, Shannon McCoy, Collette Eccleston, and Brooke Vick. Together, we launched a program of research testing predictions about how people cope with stigma and refining our ideas about the impact of prejudice attributions on self-esteem (see Major, Quinton, & McCoy, 2002). We also began to examine more intensively how beliefs about the fairness of the status system shape the ways in which people perceive and cope with stigmatized status or intergroup rejection. For example, we found that the more members of lower status groups endorse status-legitimizing ideologies the *less* likely they are to attribute rejection in an intergroup context to discrimination. In contrast, the more members of higher status groups endorse status-legitimizing beliefs the *more* likely they are to do so (Major, Gramzow, et al., 2002). I recall that when we obtained that latter finding, it seemed so counterintuitive to us that we sat on it for a couple of years to make sure it replicated. Given current events on the political scene, it now seems obvious.

In 2000 Cheryl Kaiser joined my lab as a postdoc on an NIMH RSA. That fortuitous event initiated a still-ongoing 22-year collaboration that has been not only highly generative and productive, but also a heck of a lot of fun. Cheryl is one of the most original and creative thinkers and methodologists I know. Not long after, Laurie O'Brien joined my lab as a postdoc. Together, we studied the conditions under which perceptions of prejudice do, and do not, buffer self-esteem, and documented a variety of ways in which system-legitimizing ideologies justify and maintain inequality between groups (e.g., Major & Kaiser, 2017). Most recently, Cheryl and I have been exploring the effects that organizational diversity initiatives have on perceptions of fairness and discrimination. This line of research was inspired by a legal conference we attended at Stanford on "The New Legal Realism." There, we heard sociologists provide evidence that most popular diversity initiatives do not make companies more racially or gender diverse, and legal scholars provide evidence that judges defer to diversity initiatives in deciding civil rights cases, using their mere presence as evidence of nondiscrimination, without establishing efficacy. Being experimental social psychologists, Cheryl and I set out to test whether the mere presence of diversity initiatives *causes* White people to be less sensitive to detecting discrimination against women and minorities (e.g., Kaiser et al., 2013). Our studies have repeatedly not only shown this to be the case, but also that the presence of diversity initiatives and pro-diversity values (vs. no mention) in an organization increases White people's sensitivity to reverse discrimination against Whites, and causes physiological indicators of threat and anxiety among White men engaged in a mock job interview.

Wendy Mendes is to a great extent responsible for shifting my focus from how perceived discrimination affects self-esteem to how it affects health. Wendy was a graduate student at UCSB, where Jim Blascovich was her primary advisor. Not long after Wendy received her PhD we collaborated to write an NIH grant examining how attributions to prejudice affect physiological stress responses such as cardiovascular reactivity and cortisol reactivity. It was a steep learning curve for me. But with her typical generosity, tireless energy, intelligence, and enthusiasm, Wendy guided me and my intrepid students, including Sarah Townsend, Pam Sawyer, and Dina Eliezer through the ardors of collecting, scoring, and interpreting psychophysiological measures. Tessa Dover, who joined my lab in 2011, continued this focus. Tessa not only contributed greatly to the work on diversity initiatives, but also was the brains, engine, and initiator of a five-year longitudinal study in our lab of predictors of physiological and psychological risk and resilience among low-income Latinx students.

In 2010–2011, I was fortunate to spend a year at the Center for Advanced Study in the Social Sciences at Stanford University. That year anti-fat messaging was ubiquitous on the airwaves. Everywhere I looked, it seemed, I encountered warnings about the health dangers of excess weight, and the financial burden that people with excess weight were imposing on the healthcare system. My reaction to these messages was intriguing. On the one hand, they made me more motivated to lose weight. At the same time, however, they seemed to make me eat even more! Motivated by these insights, I spent that year at the Center writing a grant proposal to examine the psychological, physiological, and behavioral effects of weight stigma. Fortunately, Jeff Hunger joined my lab as a graduate student the following year and we formed a great team. Verifying my hunch, we showed experimentally that exposure to weight stigmatizing public health messages can simultaneously both increase people's weight-loss motivation and diminish their perceived capacity to lose weight (e.g., Major et al., 2020).

I also owe a particularly deep debt of gratitude to my husband and colleague of forty-plus years, Jim Blascovich. It has been a blessing to have a brilliant spouse who shares the same values, reads the same journals, contributes methodological insights and expertise, and understands how it feels to get a paper you have worked on for years rejected, or, on occasion, accepted by *JPSP*, and a grant funded, or more commonly, denied. Jointly, we have celebrated the highs and lows of an academic career all while raising three children. Social psychology brought us together – we met at an SPSP convention - and we have grown up and both served in leadership roles in both SPSP and SESP. Jim has been my greatest cheerleader and I could not have done this without his support and encouragement.

As the above reflects, perceptions of fairness and legitimacy have been central themes in my work. Much of my work has centered around questions such as: When do people see themselves as victims of discrimination vs. when do they see their situation or treatment as fair? What are the consequences of perceiving oneself, or one's group, as a victim, or potential victim, of discrimination – for self-esteem, health, stress, motivation, job satisfaction? What are the benefits and costs of believing the system is fair? Fairness and legitimacy are timely themes in contemporary life. Is the American system fundamentally fair? Is the American Dream of upward mobility irrespective of birth or class still a reality? Or is the system fundamentally unfair, privileging those who are White or wealthy?

Our research shows clearly how believing the system is fair can justify and perpetuate group-based inequality, for example by diminishing a sense of entitlement and perceptions of discrimination among lower status groups, and increasing a sense of entitlement and perceptions of discrimination among higher status groups. However, our work also illustrates the benefits for members of disadvantaged groups of believing the system is fair and the costs of violating that belief. For example, replicating a pattern we had previously observed in the lab (Major et al., 2007; Townsend et al., 2010), we found that low income minority students who arrive at college believing the system is fair fare better over time than those who do not on measures of social and emotional outcomes, such as measures of depression, anxiety, and flourishing. But if they encounter discrimination in college, these same students fare more poorly on health-relevant markers such as measures of inflammation, blood pressure, and weight (Dover et al., 2020). This work illustrates how the belief the system is fair simultaneously can be psychologically beneficial but physically damaging for those who face systemic discrimination.

Social psychology provides powerful theories and methods for addressing important social issues. Although I did not set out purposely on this path, it is clear to me in retrospect that many of the questions I've pursued were prompted by contemporary events and perhaps also by my contrarian nature. For example, in the 1980s, prompted by the attempts of anti-abortion activists to declare abortion hazardous to women's mental health in the absence of data to support that claim, I studied how factors such as social stigma, social support, attributions, and coping expectations influence women's adjustment following an abortion. The proliferation of diversity programs in the absence of research showing their efficacy spurred me to study the effects of diversity initiatives. During the 2016 US Presidential primaries, I wondered whether the emphasis some candidates were placing on the growing ethnic diversity of the United States was increasing support for Trump among White voters. We showed that it did, but only for White voters high in ethnic identification (Major et al., 2018). For some time, I've been thinking about the potential unintended consequences of strong anti-bias norms and policies. Extending our earlier findings on the attributional ambiguity of positive feedback for minorities (Crocker et al., 1991), our studies show that minorities who believe that Whites are motivated to be nice to them because of external pressure, such as PC concerns, react to positive feedback from Whites with lowered self-esteem and increased threat, and evaluate the work of fellow minorities who receive positive feedback more harshly than those who do not share this belief (e.g., Major et al., 2016). They also perceive more discrimination at college and distrust their professors more, which in turn further increases distrust of Whites' motives and decreases well-being.

My findings often call into question what everyone assumes to be true, and challenge established dogma of the left as well as the right. I believe that in order to pursue good social psychological science, you have to be willing to ask unpopular questions and listen to and follow your data, even if you don't like what it says. It is not an easy road to follow, and seems to be getting even harder. Nonetheless, I encourage social psychologists to be brave enough to do so. Dogmatism, even if well intentioned, is the enemy of good science and inhibits advancement of our field.

Suggested Reading

Crocker, J., & Major, B. (1989). Social stigma and self-esteem: The self-protective properties of stigma. *Psychological Review, 96*, 608–630.

Crocker, J., Voelkl, K., Testa, M., & Major, B. (1991). Social stigma: The affective consequences of attributional ambiguity. *Journal of Personality and Social Psychology, 60*, 218–228.

Deaux, K., & Emswiller, T. (1974). Explanations of successful performance on sex-linked tasks: What is skill for the male is luck for the female. *Journal of Personality and Social Psychology, 29*(1), 80–85.

Deaux, K., & Major, B. (1987). Putting gender into context: An interactive model of gender-related behavior. *Psychological Review, 94*, 369–389.

Dover, T. L., Major, B., & Glace, A. M. (2020). Discrimination, health, and the costs and benefits of believing in system fairness. *Health Psychology, 39*(3), 230–239.

Kaiser, C. R., Major, B., Jurcevic, I., Dover, T., Brady, L. M., & Shapiro, J. R. (2013). Presumed fair: Ironic effects of organizational diversity structures. *Journal of Personality and Social Psychology, 104*(3), 504–519.

Major, B. (1994). From social inequality to personal entitlement: The role of social comparisons, legitimacy appraisals, and group membership. In M. Zanna (Ed.), *Advances in Experimental Social Psychology* (Vol. 26, pp. 293–355). San Diego, CA: Academic Press.

Major, B., Blodorn, A., & Major Blascovich, G. (2018). The threat of increasing diversity: Why many White Americans support Trump in the 2016 presidential election. *Group Processes & Intergroup Relations, 21*(6), 931–940.

Major, B., Gramzow, R., McCoy, S., Levin, S., Schmader, T., & Sidanius, J. (2002). Perceiving personal discrimination: The role of group status and legitimizing ideology. *Journal of Personality and Social Psychology, 82*, 269–282.

Major, B., & Kaiser, C. R. (2017). Ideology and the maintenance of group inequality. *Group Processes and Intergroup Relations, 20*, 582–592.

Major, B., Kaiser, C. R., O'Brien, L., & McCoy, S. (2007). Perceived discrimination as worldview threat or worldview confirmation: Implications for self-esteem. *Journal of Personality and Social Psychology, 92*, 1068–1086.

Major, B., Kunstman, J. W., Malta, B. D., Sawyer, P. J., Townsend, S. S., & Mendes, W. B. (2016). Suspicion of motives predicts minorities' responses to positive feedback in interracial interactions. *Journal of Experimental Social Psychology, 62*, 75–88.

Major, B., Rathbone, J. A., Blodorn, A., & Hunger, J. M. (2020). The countervailing effects of weight stigma on weight loss motivation and perceived capacity for weight control. *Personality and Social Psychology Bulletin, 46*(9), 1331–1343.

Major, B., Quinton, W., & McCoy, S. (2002). Antecedents and consequences of attributions to discrimination: Theoretical and empirical advances. *Advances in Experimental Social Psychology, 34*, 251–330.

Townsend, S. S. M., Major, B., Sawyer, P. J., & Mendes, W. B. (2010). Can the absence of prejudice be more threatening than its presence? It depends on one's worldview. *Journal of Personality and Social Psychology, 99*, 933–947.

The Power of Firmly Held Beliefs
A Troubled Child, Schachter's Incredulity, and the Roots of Extreme Behavior

William B. Swann, Jr.

I did not know it at the time, but taking a summer job at a camp for underprivileged children was one of the most important decisions of my life. There I met a seven-year-old boy named Tommy. Although it was many years ago (I had just completed my first year in college), I still have a vivid memory of our first encounter. While hurrying to a meeting with the camp director, I heard some boys fighting nearby. I ran over to find Tommy on the ground fighting two larger children. I helped break up the fight and then hurried to my meeting. When I mentioned the incident to the camp director, I was surprised when she nodded knowingly. Although it was only three days since the camp opened, the staff had already surmised that Tommy had a gift for evoking the ire of those around him. I was puzzled by his strange behavior and decided to observe him more closely.

Perhaps not surprisingly, I discovered that Tommy had terrible self-esteem. What *was* surprising was his penchant for nurturing his negative self-image by turning everyone against him: he disobeyed the counselors, taunted and teased the other kids, and generally sowed chaos everywhere he went. And it wasn't just Tommy's overt behaviors that reinforced his negative self-view. Whenever I talked to him about his experiences at the camp, he selectively recalled negative events – slights, rejections, and failed attempts to win acceptance and approval. It appeared that a host of processes, including Tommy's behaviors, thoughts, and emotions, conspired to sustain his negative self-image. The question was why. After all, most people are motivated to cultivate positive rather than negative self-views. What made Tommy different?

It would take me years before I would get a firm handle on this question, but my interest in Tommy and people like him was to have a lasting impact. Upon returning to Gettysburg College for my sophomore year, I changed my major from biology to psychology. But if I knew that I wanted to be a psychologist, I had no clue that I wanted to be a researcher.

Thane Pittman changed that. Thane had recently joined the psychology department as a new faculty member. Aside from being enrolled in his social psychology class, the only thing I knew about Thane was that he was rumored to be brilliant. Soon I discovered something else about Thane: like me, he owned a motorcycle and

William B. Swann, Jr., University of Texas, USA. Thanks to Ashwini Ashokkumar, Michael Buhrmester, Nancy Hazen, and Sanaz Talaifar for comments on this chapter.

enjoyed driving through the beautiful rolling hills surrounding Gettysburg. We began riding together. With each of us perched on top of our motorcycles it was impossible to have a conversation. Nevertheless, co-experiencing the amazing countryside with Thane simultaneously calmed and rejuvenated me. By the time we reached our destination – a river with stunning views of waterfalls below – I was always poised to ask him about the research projects on which we began collaborating. He always obliged.

In the years that followed, I recognized that Thane was not only brilliant, he was also as kind and supportive a mentor as any student could hope for. Perhaps his greatest asset was his knack for enabling students to recognize that scientific discovery was not only sublime, it was one of the best things one could do with one's life. To top it off, even a lowly undergraduate with minimal experience could help make important discoveries. Working with Thane was both inspiring and exhilarating. Through his influence, I shifted from *liking* research to *revering* it (my girlfriend at the time justifiably complained that I was *obsessed* with it, grumbling when I brought a flashlight to a movie theatre so I could read an article).

Thane also jump-started my career by shepherding our first two papers through the publication process. One paper was on the Bem dissonance debate; the other explored the overjustification effect. Both papers met stiff resistance from reviewers and multiple revisions were required. Although painful, the process of publishing them taught me invaluable lessons about the importance of believing in one's work, persistence, and having a generous and astute collaborator. Thane selflessly granted me first authorship on both papers, a choice that undoubtedly helped me gain admission to graduate school at the University of Minnesota.

At Minnesota I worked with Mark Snyder. I was fortunate to arrive just as he was about to launch an innovative new program of research on a phenomenon he called *behavioral confirmation*. My years at Minnesota were incredibly stimulating and highly productive. One of our most provocative findings was that even when asked to test hypotheses about others, people preferentially sought – and actually elicited – evidence that provided behavioral confirmation for the hypotheses they were testing (Snyder & Swann, 1978). These studies were thus among the first to demonstrate how confirmation bias can systematically influence social relationships.

The hypothesis testing studies were accepted for publication just as I was pondering a dissertation topic, and it occurred to me that someone should assess the generality of the confirmation bias. I generated a specific question: Would people seek confirmation for an hypothesis that placed them at a disadvantage? As I planned my research, I recalled my experiences with Tommy. It seemed that his negative self-views led Tommy to hypothesize that other people disliked him and he accordingly sought evidence that would confirm this hypothesis about himself. Moreover, when someone disconfirmed Tommy's self-views by treating him in a positive manner, he became even more recalcitrant than before, presumably in an effort to validate his self-view. These reflections led me to propose that people with firmly held self-views would repudiate expectations that challenged their self-views, even if their self-views were negative.

The results of my dissertation study confirmed my theorizing. Not only did people with negative self-views display more negative behaviors than targets with positive self-views, this tendency was amplified when I encouraged them to suspect that perceivers perceived them positively. I concluded that people with negative views of themselves do not subscribe to the widespread preference for positive evaluations. Instead, they prefer and seek negative evaluations that provide verification for their negative self-views. Later I would refer to this pattern as negative self-verification strivings.

Evidence of self-verification strivings both extended and qualified my previous research on behavioral confirmation. It extended the earlier work by showing that confirmation bias generalized to beliefs about the self. It qualified research on behavioral confirmation process by demonstrating that social interaction is a two-way street. As they navigate this two-way street, people engage in a process of identity negotiation wherein they come to agreements about the identities they are to assume. In this scenario, people seek confirmation for their expectancies, their partners respond by seeking verification for firmly-held identities, and eventually they come to agree on who is who (Swann, 1987). Along the way, they recognize that some parts of the two-way street are undergoing construction, other parts require zigs and zags, and they never know when they will reach their destination.

Recognizing the key role of self-views in the identity negotiation process also encouraged me to significantly revise my own identity as a researcher. Whereas I initiated my dissertation as a social cognition researcher with a casual interest in self and identity, I emerged as a self researcher with a keen interest in how identity shapes the social worlds people create around themselves.

As I was completing my dissertation, my then fiancée Nancy Hazen and I received job offers at the University of Texas at Austin. We married and headed to Austin. At UT, I launched a line of research that built on my dissertation. My first step was enlisting the assistance of Stephen Read, who was quite capable despite being very young at the time (a condition from which he later recovered). We initiated a series of studies that examined the relation of people's self-views to various cognitive and behavioral activities. Our findings indicated that the results of my dissertation study were not anomalous. Rather, the tendency for people to prefer self-confirming feedback even if their self-views were negative seemed to be robust. In fact, this preference emerged whether we examined information seeking, attention, memory, overt behavior, and even perceptions of the diagnosticity of feedback. These studies provided the empirical foundation on which self-verification theory would rest. Shortly afterwards I would flesh out the theory and begin to explore its implications for phenomena such as self-concept change, the decision to remain in abusive relationships, depression, and so on (Swann, 1983).

One thing I now wish I had done in that first self-verification chapter was to comment on the rationality of self-verification strivings. On the face of it, seeking validation for firmly-held beliefs is perfectly rational, as firmly-held beliefs are typically based on lots of evidence and are therefore likely accurate. The problem is that self-views can occasionally be firmly-held even when they are inaccurate. For example, many people with low self-esteem are convinced that they are worthless even though they have a great deal going for them. It makes no sense for worthwhile human beings to seek evidence that they are worthless. Thus, self-verification strivings are only as rational as the beliefs that regulate them are accurate.

I also wish I had spelled out the relationship between self-verification and dissonance theory in my early writings. Self-verification theory can be traced to Lecky's (1945) hypothesis that self-views give people such a profound sense of coherence. This sense of coherence is provided by negative as well as positive self-views, which means that both types of self-views will regulate behavior. More than a decade after publication of Lecky's book, Festinger's cognitive dissonance theory turned Lecky's self-consistency theory on its head. Instead of examining the ways in which stable self-views regulate behavior, Festinger emphasized the ways in which people's freely chosen behaviors shape their subsequent self-views. In addition, in the version of dissonance theory that rose to prominence within social psychology, researchers added self-enhancement strivings to the mix, producing a hybrid self-consistency/self-enhancement theory. This resulted in an additional difference between self-verification and dissonance theory: Whereas self-verification theory focused on people's efforts to maintain negative as well as positive self-views, dissonance theory emphasized efforts to maintain positive self-views – especially positive self-views that were in jeopardy. Abelson (1983, p. 43) captured it well: "the dissonance literature chiefly concerns the psychology of what people do to recover from experimentally engineered major embarrassments."

To be sure, dissonance theorists were not alone in calling on self-enhancement strivings to do the heavy lifting in their motivational framework. To the contrary, the notion that people are strongly motivated to seek self-enhancement is a bedrock assumption underlying virtually all major theoretical frameworks in social psychology. In the early days of our research on self-verification theory, I was blithely unaware of the pervasiveness of self-enhancement reasoning in social psychology. The great Stanley Schachter helpfully led me to see the light. It was 1984 and I had given a colloquium to the psychology department at Columbia (where Schachter was a resident Icon). I was excited to see him striding toward me. My excitement morphed into apprehension, however, when I noticed a scary scowl on his face. He looked so menacing that I wondered if he might be planning to take a swing at me. Stopping just short of my nose, he demanded, "You're not telling me that people with negative self-concepts actually *want* negative evaluations, are you?" The question put me in a bind. I knew that he wanted me to back down, but to do so would have been unfaithful to my data and that I could not do. So I answered "Yes, at some level, I do think that people with negative self-views want negative evaluations." For what seemed like an eternity (spectators later told me the entire interaction was less than a minute), we both stared at one another. Finally, he shook his head, announced loudly "I don't believe it" and marched off in a huff.

Schachter's reaction was deeply disconcerting yet galvanizing. Disconcerting because it was my worst nightmare to have one of the world's most eminent social psychologists cavalierly dismiss several years of work. Galvanizing because I knew in my heart that I was right and he was wrong. However brilliant he might be, he had never observed the participants with low self-esteem in my experiments let alone Tommy or other people I had encountered. I was convinced that I had discovered something important and I was determined to show the world what I had leaned.

Undaunted by the incredulity expressed by Schachter and his ilk, for the next couple of decades my students and I published more and more evidence of self-verification strivings. We encountered a great deal of incredulity along the way. Although we persisted in steering the self-verification ship through the stormy seas of scathing skepticism, I admit to feeling somewhat bewildered, for I had little understanding of the reasons for the vehemence of reviewers' resistance to our findings. It was not until four decades later that new evidence would reveal why so many people are perplexed by negative self-verification strivings. I will return to this work toward the end of this chapter.

In addition to collecting support for the robustness of self-verification strivings, my collaborators and I explored the mechanisms underlying this phenomenon. For example, we learned that self-verification requires more cognitive resources than self-enhancement. For this reason, depriving people of cognitive resources made people with low self-esteem act like people with high self-esteem (i.e., they embraced favorable evaluations). We also came to understand that Schachter's question regarding "what people with low self-esteem want" was itself misleading: In reality, people with low self-esteem are ambivalent, they want positive evaluations but eschew such evaluations because they do not find them credible. We also identified various applications of identity negotiation to diverse domains, including topics ranging from the causes of clinical depression and divorce, the mechanisms under-lying self-concept change, stereotyping and ingroup–outgroup relations, persuasion, and creativity and productivity in groups. It was my foray into group processes that caught the watchful eye of Ángel Gómez.

Ángel emailed me for assistance with a handful of studies he had conducted involving self-verification strivings on a group level (which we later dubbed "group identity verification"). I confided to him that his studies were flawed and needed to be replicated. I thought that would be the last I would hear from Ángel. I had underesti-mated him, for he would prove to be one of the most determined and resourceful individuals I have ever met. In a remarkably short period of time, he redesigned and ran all five studies again. A paper based on group identity verification would appear later. And that was just the beginning.

While the group identity verification work was still underway, Ángel invited me to Madrid to discuss potential follow-ups. At first, none of the ideas we generated were very inspiring. Then one day our conversation drifted to the 2001 terrorist attacks on the world trade towers and the 2004 attacks on the Madrid train station. We both wondered what motivated these attacks. Although we thought it must have something to do with identity, when we looked for relevant theorizing and research we came up empty-handed (e.g., social identity theory focused on ingroup–outgroup relations rather than extreme behavior on behalf of the ingroup). To fill the gap in the literature, we developed the idea of identity fusion. Later, with Jolanda Jetten and others, we would elaborate these ideas into identity fusion theory (Swann et al., 2012).

Although I was not conscious of this at the time, the identity fusion construct was a natural extension of my fascination with the power of beliefs. In particular, the idea that beliefs create reality motivated my early work on behavioral confirmation, matured in my work on self-verification and identity negotiation, and inspired the idea of pragmatic accuracy in person perception. My research on identity fusion represented the culmination of this long-standing interest in the power of beliefs, as this work made the audacious argument that people's personal identities sometimes become so "fused with" abstractions (a group or a cause) that they give their life in the service of those abstractions. From this vantage point, terrorists take self-verification to the next level. Whereas self-verifiers with negative self-views act in ways that curtail their opportunities and happiness, suicide bombers act on their beliefs in ways that actually curtail their lives. Both scenarios bear witness to the extraordinary power of beliefs.

And what of the skeptics who, in the tradition of Stanley Schachter, have doubted our evidence that people sabotage themselves in the service of maintaining their beliefs? Nearly four decades after my vexing encounter with Schachter at Columbia, Sanaz Talaifar, Michael Buhrmester, Ozlem Ayduk and I offered a novel perspective on Schachter's skepticism (Talaifar et al., 2021). We proposed that striking asymmetries occur in the levels of understanding displayed by those who differ in self-esteem (and, more broadly, status and power). Of greatest relevance here, individuals with low self-esteem understood others quite well, regardless of their self-esteem, but those with high self-esteem lacked insight into those who have low self-esteem. Specifically, whereas people with low self-esteem understood negative self-verification strivings (i.e., that people with low esteem prefer negative evaluations), people with high esteem could not fathom that *anyone* would prefer negative evaluations. These findings therefore suggested Schachter may have been more receptive to self-verification reasoning had he not "suffered from" high self-esteem. This is in no way an indictment of Schachter – Talaifar et al. even found that clinical psychology graduate students, who are trained and highly motivated to understand people with low self-esteem, registered skepticism that people with low self-esteem would prefer negative evaluations. Only high self-esteem individuals who had experienced negative identities earlier in their lives recognized that people with low self-esteem would prefer and seek negative evaluations. I was immensely gratified by these findings. Finally, after four decades of staring down skeptics of self-verification strivings, I understood why my critics could not believe that people might actually prefer negative evaluations – as did Schachter, they suffered from high self-esteem!

But surely high self-esteem is not the only factor that blinds social psychologists to the activities of people with low esteem. Another factor that impedes insight into people with low self-esteem is that such individuals are relatively rare: only 30 percent of people in the world have low self-esteem (Diener & Diener, 2009). Negative self-verification strivings come to be regarded as anomalies because they *are* somewhat anomalous. But the fact that negative self-verification strivings are not commonplace does not mean that they are unimportant. Several studies, for example, have shown that married people with negative self-views are inclined to withdraw from or even divorce spouses who perceive them more favorably than they perceive themselves (see Kwang & Swann, 2010, for a review). These findings not only offer a novel perspective on the preferences of people with negative self-views, they also call for a reconceptualization of the behaviors of people with positive self-views. Whereas past researchers have attributed the positivity strivings of people with positive self-views exclusively to a desire for self-enhancement, the research literature indicates that a desire for self-verification of their positive self-views is at least partially responsible.

More generally, it is time for the field to acknowledge that some phenomena cannot be experimentally manipulated successfully. Consider self-esteem. Experimentalists once believed that one could create low self-esteem in the laboratory by providing participants with negative feedback. In hindsight, it is stunningly naive to think that administering a dose or two of negative feedback in a laboratory can create a state of mind similar to those who suffer from chronic low self-esteem. This is especially true when it comes to the 70 percent of participants who have high chronic self-esteem. For such individuals, negative feedback will be quite surprising and will likely trigger compensatory efforts to restore their high self-esteem – precisely the opposite of the reactions of people with chronic low self-esteem. In the final analysis, although excellence in experimentation is one of social psychology's greatest assets, over-reliance on this asset could lead the field to paint an inaccurate portrait of the human condition.

Speaking of assets, in our brief history, there has been a strong tendency for social psychologists to focus on methodological innovations. Experimentation was one of the first such innovations; big data and a flurry of new statistical techniques are the current rage. I welcome such advances. Nevertheless, I sometimes fear that our focus on methods and statistics will distract us from our greatest strength: clear-headed conceptual analysis of real social problems. There are some hopeful signs that we continue to value theoretical advances – the relatively recent creation of the Wegner theoretical innovation prize being one – but I hope we do not lose sight of the critical importance of theory to our discipline.

Let me close with an important caveat: Although I have organized this chapter around a handful of positive experiences that have contributed to the modest successes I have enjoyed, I should acknowledge that I have also suffered several serious challenges that could have easily derailed my career. The fact that I escaped this fate reflected, in large measure, the chorus of voices that motivated me to persevere in the face of the obstacles I occasionally faced. The leading voice in this chorus was my wife, Nancy Hazen, who has inspired, guided, and supported me for my entire career. In addition, I have benefited enormously from support from several key colleagues, including Dave Schneider, Dan Wegner, Ned Jones, Rich Wenzlaff, and Jamie Pennebaker, and a legion of students/collaborators, including Steve Read, Robin Ely, John Griffin, Craig Hill, Lynn Miller, Brett Pelham, Al Stein-Seroussi, Greg Hixon, Shawn McNulty, Brian Giesler, Romin Tafarodi, Kate Morris, Chris De La Ronde, Stephen Blumberg, Michael Gill, Liz Pinel, Jennifer Bosson, Jason Rentfrow, Conor Seyle, Sarah Angulo, Christine Chang, Tracy Kwang, Matt Brooks, Michael Buhrmester, Brock Bastian, Bo Fraser, Sanaz Talaifar, Ashwini Ashokkumar, and

Alexi Martel. I am deeply indebted to each of them not only for their work on our collaborative projects, but more importantly for their support and intellectual cama-raderie over the years. Looking back, I have come to recognize that these relationships were not merely the vehicles that helped us move the field of social psychology forward. Rather, the relationships, the connections I formed with colleagues and students, were the true destinations, and the insights we produced together were a delicious byproduct of those relationships.

Suggested Reading

Abelson, R. P. (1983). Whatever became of consistency theory? *Personality and Social Psychology Bulletin, 9*, 37–54.

Diener, E., & Diener, M. (2009). Cross-cultural correlates of life satisfaction and self-esteem. In E. Diener (Ed.), *Culture and Well-Being: The Collected Works of Ed Diener* (pp. 71–91). Dordrecht: Springer.

Kwang, T., & Swann, W. B., Jr. (2010). Do people embrace praise even when they feel unworthy? A review of critical tests of self-enhancement versus self-verification. *Personality and Social Psychology Review, 14*, 263–280.

Lecky, P. (1945). *Self-Consistency: A Theory of Personality*. New York: Island Press.

Snyder, M., & Swann, W. B., Jr. (1978). Hypothesis testing processes in social interaction. *Journal of Personality and Social Psychology, 36*, 1202–1212.

Swann, W. B., Jr. (1983). Self-verification: Bringing social reality into harmony with the self. In J. Suls & A. G. Greenwald (Eds.), *Psychological Perspectives on the Self* (Vol. 2, pp. 33–66). Hillsdale, NJ: Lawrence Erlbaum.

(1987). Identity negotiation: Where two roads meet. *Journal of Personality and Social Psychology, 53*, 1038–1051.

Swann, W. B., Jr., Jetten, J., Gómez, Á., Whitehouse, H., & Bastian, B. (2012). When group membership gets personal: A theory of identity fusion. *Psychological Review, 119*, 441–456.

Talaifar, S., Buhrmester, M. D., Ayduk, O., & Swann, W. B., Jr. (2021). Asymmetries in mutual understanding: People with low status, power, and self-esteem understand better than they are understood. *Perspectives on Psychological Science, 16*, 338–357.

40 My Career in Social Psychology
More Than Just Fun and Games

Rupert Brown

My social psychology journey began in 1968 when I went to Edinburgh University as an undergraduate. As some may remember, that year was also memorable for other reasons. It was the year that Martin Luther King, that great civil rights leader, was assassinated. It was the year that Enoch Powell, a Conservative British politician, made a hateful speech apocalyptically predicting that unchecked immigration would lead to civil unrest and bloodshed on the streets of Britain. It was the year when "les evénements" in Paris threatened to upset the established order in several European countries. And it was the year when invading Soviet tanks brought the nascent Prague Spring to a swift and brutal end in Czechoslovakia.

I won't pretend that these events instantly inspired me to become a social psychologist interested in intergroup relations but, as they did for so many of my generation, they did awaken in me an awareness of economic inequality and social injustice. It was to be a few years before that realization found any expression in my work as a social psychologist.

One reason for this lamentably slow political development was my initial choice of degree program. At school I had always been reasonably numerate and managed to do well enough in science to gain acceptance to study mathematical physics at university. It took just a few months (and several mediocre assessment marks) to convince me that I was not cut out to be a natural scientist, still less a mathematician. To my great good fortune, I discovered that psychology at Edinburgh was in the same faculty as mathematical physics and that a transfer of degree program could be effected with a minimum of hassle. I do recall some consternation at home when I announced my change of direction. "What on earth can you do with a degree in psychology?" my father asked. It was a question to which I found I had no good answer then and was to spend the next fifty years searching for.

Early Influences

The psychology curriculum at Edinburgh in the 1960s was pretty conventional fare. Reflecting the nature of the discipline at the time, the department leaned strongly in

Rupert Brown, University of Sussex, UK.

the direction of physiological psychology, animal behavior, and psychophysics. The study of real human beings in natural settings was conspicuous by its absence. Luckily, I took three courses that convinced me that there might be more to psychology than the effects of variable reinforcement schedules on the white rat, the appetitive behavior of pigeons, or stereoscopic fusion in visual perception. One was on personality, taught by Boris Semeonoff, a kindly and wise man who also happened to be a world authority on projective tests. A second was on developmental psychology, taught by the inspirational Margaret Donaldson, who had worked with Bruner and Piaget. And the third was on social psychology, taught by Halla Beloff, who had done some interesting work on trying to quantify some aspects of Freudian theory and also on social influence. It was especially this third course which sparked my interest. It was broad in scope and, as I recall, placed much emphasis on the cultural and normative factors that influence social behavior. I remember reading Bronfenbrenner, Bettelheim, and Reisman, alongside more traditional social psychologists such as Asch and Milgram. In addition to the subject matter of the course, I was also rather inspired by Beloff herself. She was, I think, the first genuine intellectual I had ever met. She was a notable film critic and later wrote a well-received book on the role of photography in modern life.

After graduation, I embarked on a search for a PhD place. This was, I must admit, a rather haphazard process. In Britain in those days there were no such things as doctoral programs. Rather, one simply looked for a university and a faculty member willing to take you on. One then spent three years (and often longer) conducting research that culminated in a very long thesis (300 pages was not unusual!). With no clear idea of what I wanted to do, I interviewed at three places before ending up in Bristol on one fateful day in the summer of 1972.

I was interviewed there by Henri Tajfel. I remember little of the interview except that it was brief and that he offered me a place on the spot. Afterwards, I rang Halla Beloff for advice as to whether to accept the offer. She insisted that I should, telling me that Bristol was now *the* place in Britain for social psychology and that Tajfel was *the* supervisor to study with. I was quite surprised to learn this since I could not recall coming across his name in her social psychology course. But what did I know?

What did I know indeed?! Shortly after my arrival at Bristol a few months later, the truth of Beloff's description was soon apparent: I was one of four PhD students being supervised by Tajfel (one of these was John Turner, who went on to be Tajfel's most famous collaborator); his first two PhDs had recently completed and had remained as postdocs; and visits from famous social psychologists seemed to be an almost weekly occurrence. A year or so later, this sense of Bristol being the center of gravity of British (and European) social psychology was heightened still further. The first formal version of Social Identity Theory (SIT) was published (Tajfel, 1974) and Tajfel obtained a major research grant to elaborate and test some of its main tenets. This grant employed several researchers (including me), attracted still more PhD students and overseas visitors, and facilitated research trips to Paris and other exotic locations.

To a young researcher like myself, this was exciting enough. But what gave it an added frisson was the sense, very much cultivated by Tajfel himself, that we were on a mission to do social psychology in a radically different way – a more socially relevant and contextually sensitive way – than could be found (at least in our perusal) in the pages of the *Journal of Personality and Social Psychology*. Although I didn't appreciate it at the time, this had long been a preoccupation – not to say obsession – of Tajfel himself. It was that concern which had led him (together with several other European scholars) to establish the European Association of Experimental Social Psychology in the 1960s. This organization was intended to provide an intellectual counterweight to North American social psychology.

Tajfel undoubtedly played a huge part in my research apprenticeship. Like Beloff from my undergraduate days, he was a widely read intellectual with the added fascination of having a tragic personal back story. He was a Polish Jew who had evaded the worst horrors of the Holocaust, unlike the rest of his family (Brown, 2019). Although he had many deficiencies as a supervisor – not the least being that he seemed to be absent from the department more than he was present – he did have the capacity to inspire his students with his passion to understand the roots of intergroup conflict and his desire to do social psychology differently.

Another important influence on me was Muzafer Sherif. Although I never knew him personally, I was (and remain) deeply impressed by the kind of social psychology he espoused. Whether it was his pioneering Summer Camp studies or his innovative work on reference groups and social norms, it seemed to me that here was a social scientist who understood the power of group and intergroup processes to shape people's behavior. And, like Tajfel, he was someone who wanted to use social psychology to tackle important social problems but who, at the same time, recognized the discipline's limits.

At this point in my narrative, I need to say a few words about some broader developments in the field of social psychology at that time. Between 1967 and 1975, a series of articles appeared which called into question the theoretical, methodological, and political adequacy of traditional social psychology. Social psychology was criticized as having abandoned its historical Lewinian mission of theory-driven action research into important societal problems in favor of a "fun and games" approach – "clever experimentation on exotic topics with a zany manipulation" (Ring, 1967, p. 117). Worse still, according to some critics, social psychologists were deluding themselves in thinking they were scientists; rather they should be regarded as little more than journalists or cultural historians. Moreover, experiments themselves had minimal external validity, given their sterile artificiality and reliance on college students as participants. All in all, social psychology appeared to some to be a discipline ill-equipped to say anything meaningful about the big issues of the day: the Cold War, the Vietnam War, or systemic racism.

The debates sparked by those papers became known as the "crisis in social psychology" and were responsible for individual crises of confidence in many aspiring social psychologists, including me. Although I don't think I ever satisfactorily resolved that early professional life crisis, I did draw two implications from it which acted as signposts for the remainder of my career. The first was a skepticism that laboratory experimentation was the only (or best) methodological tool at our disposal.

It seemed to me then, as it still does, that many phenomena do not lend themselves easily to experimental analysis and must be investigated by other means. Moreover, if experiments were to be done, and there certainly is a place for them, they should speak to important theoretical and social questions and not just be clever demonstrations of counterintuitive findings. The second lesson I learned was an abiding concern with socially significant problems. If I studied anything, I resolved, it should matter outside Horace's "groves of academe"; social psychology should surely be more than just some laboratory fun and games.

Against such a backdrop, it is not difficult to see why I found SIT so interesting a theory. Its central premise was that, in certain situations, people did not act as autonomous individuals, influenced only by their own personal dispositions, cognitions, and motivations. Rather, when their social identities were engaged because a particular group identity was psychologically salient, they would act as group members, now influenced primarily by others in their ingroup, or by what they perceived to be ingroup norms and stereotypes, or by the nature of the intergroup relationships in which that ingroup was embedded. Moreover, it was a theory which promised to explain – if not to reduce – intergroup conflict and related phenomena like prejudice and discrimination. For someone like myself, somewhat disillusioned by what I saw as a rather arid discipline often tackling trivial issues, SIT proved seductive indeed.

How the Field of Intergroup Relations Developed During My Career

So much for my research training in the 1970s, which culminated in obtaining my PhD in 1979. After several rejections, I finally secured a temporary teaching position at the University of Sussex, followed swiftly by a tenure-track lectureship at the University of Kent. This latter position proved to be a wonderful opportunity. Psychology had not existed at Kent prior to our arrival in 1978 and so we (myself and two colleagues) were given more or less carte blanche to fashion the department to our own taste. Since we were all social psychologists, we chose to offer only a specialized degree program, focusing just on social psychology (with a smattering of general and developmental psychology thrown in to satisfy accreditation criteria imposed by the British Psychological Society). The Kent department provided a perfect launch pad for my own research career since it allowed me to pursue my interests in intergroup relations, untrammeled by any managerial expectations or constraints. I was to remain there for twenty-six years until my move back to Sussex in 2004.

How has the field of intergroup relations changed in the forty years since my PhD? I would identify four significant developments.

The first has been changes to SIT itself. During my PhD and in the decade or so thereafter, most SIT-inspired research was devoted to tests and extensions of the theory's core propositions: to delineate the conditions under which threats to group members' social identities led to enhanced attempts to differentiate the ingroup from outgroups. I did some of that work myself. In my PhD I had demonstrated the power of social identity processes to divide groups of factory workers whose objective interests should have led them to cooperate. I also tested whether enhanced intergroup similarity increased the tendency for groups to show ingroup favoritism, as predicted by SIT (by and large, it didn't). And I also investigated whether strength of group identification was correlated with intergroup differentiation, another core SIT hypothesis (it sometimes did, but not very consistently and the correlations were often quite weak). By the 1990s, research citing SIT started to do so in a more generic way. Typically, the use of SIT was to establish the potential importance of social identity processes for the phenomenon under study and then, from that point of departure, to develop some new testable ideas and applications. SIT evolved, in other words, from a quite narrowly constrained theory about ingroup favoritism to a general framework which could be usefully applied to an enormous diversity of social behaviors (Brown, 2019, ch. 8).

The second development was the emergence in the late 1980s of automatic cognitive processes as potential determinants of intergroup attitudes and behavior. This work was firmly rooted in the sociocognitive "revolution" of the preceding decade. That social cognition approach was devoted to identifying the processes which gave rise to (biased) outgroup stereotypes and which could explain their persistence even in the face of disconfirming information. The end of that decade witnessed the discovery that group stereotypes could be activated and subsequently applied by the use of subliminal priming techniques. Social cognition researchers then enthusiastically began to study the implications of unconscious mental processes for people's intergroup judgments and behavior, some even claiming that prejudice was inevitable since it could be instigated outside conscious awareness. I joined the fray, thanks to the arrival of Lorella Lepore, a clever PhD student who was able to show the weakness of that "inevitability thesis" through some ingenious experimentation. By the end of the 1990s, there were even claims that "implicit" prejudice could be measured, thus circumventing most of the social desirability issues that plagued conventional measures of prejudice. Although some of the claims of the more ardent proponents of the study of automatic processes were tempered by subsequent research, the realization that not all intergroup perceptions and behavior were under conscious control was a healthy corrective to a field which had tended to emphasize the deliberative and strategic nature of intergroup behavior.

Echoing that trend was a third development, a resurgence of interest in affective aspects of intergroup processes. A major stimulus for this was Smith's (1993) theory of intergroup emotions. Drawing on the seminal SIT idea that people sometimes act as group members (rather than as individuals), Smith argued that they could also *feel* as group members, experiencing particular emotions as a result of their appraisal of certain discomfiting intergroup situations. This analysis provoked two advances in the field. One was to extend SIT, which had hitherto concerned itself almost entirely with ingroup biases of various kinds and had overlooked a rather obvious feature of intergroup situations – that they are usually infused with emotion. The second advance was to steer the study of prejudice away from the Allportian notion that prejudice simply involves antipathy toward an outgroup. According to this new intergroup emotions approach, group-based emotions are more differentiated than that. Depending on the context, group members can feel fear, anger, disgust, shame, or guilt in their dealings with an outgroup, and will act accordingly. I was much taken with the intergroup emotions perspective. It led me to a series of collaborations with colleagues in Chile (Roberto González), Bosnia Herzegovina (Sabina Čehajić-Clancy), and elsewhere, where we sought to understand the power of group-based emotions for promoting or inhibiting intergroup reconciliation and forgiveness. Latterly, I also incorporated intergroup emotions theory into my research on hate crime, showing that members of the victims' group can also experience fear, anger, and shame after learning of a hate incident directed at their group, even though they were not directly affected themselves. The incorporation of affect into the analysis of intergroup relations proved a welcome counterbalance to some more extreme versions of the sociocognitive perspective with their metaphors of the person as a "cognitive miser" or an information processor.

The fourth development was a revival of interest in finding effective ways of reducing prejudice and discrimination. By the mid-1980s, there had been little theoretical progress on this topic since Allport's (1954) famous Contact Hypothesis. Then, just like the proverbial bus that one has almost given up waiting for, three new versions of the Contact Hypothesis appeared in quick succession. Although these new theories offered rather different – and sometimes competing – prescriptions for improving intergroup relations, their common point of departure was the insight from SIT that, once a particular social categorization becomes psychologically salient, people's behavior changes. For Brewer and Miller (1984), the implication was that in contact situations one should strive to de-emphasize the social categories and make the interaction more interpersonal. For Gaertner and his colleagues (1989), the answer lay in recategorization not decategorization, so that the ingroup and outgroup are subsumed within a common superordinate category. Miles Hewstone and I (Hewstone & Brown, 1986), concerned that neither decategorization nor recategorization offered much scope for attitude change to generalize beyond the immediate contact situation, counterintuitively argued that there were advantages in maintaining some degree of category salience in intergroup encounters. There is no doubt that these three elaborations of the Contact Hypothesis proved enormously stimulative to the field. Since their publication, we have seen a growing interest in developing practicable contact interventions that have durable effects on reducing prejudice (Brown, 2010).

Of all the developments in intergroup relations during my career, this has been the one closest to my heart since it offers an antidote to the otherwise somewhat "pessimistic" outlook provided by SIT. My work on intergroup contact began in the 1980s with Miles Hewstone and continued uninterrupted for the next three decades through several PhD students and international collaborations with colleagues in North and South America, Germany, Belgium, and Italy.

Where Is the Field Headed?

Part of our brief for these chapters was to speculate on where we see our fields heading. I must admit I have never really been one for crystal ball gazing so I will limit myself to noting what I see as two of the more interesting trends in intergroup research.

The first trend I have noticed in recent years is a willingness of researchers to design their research so they can study intergroup processes at the culture–group–individual interface. In practice, this means using large-scale samples from several different cultural or subcultural contexts. This is, I think, partly a response to warnings that our discipline has been overreliant on research participants from a narrow cross-section of humankind. But it is also – and more interestingly – instigated by a recognition that there are always multiple causal factors governing intergroup relations, and these may operate at different levels of analysis. Thus, to take the topical issue of migration. How can we best understand relationships between immigrants to a country and the receiving majority there? The dominant acculturation ideology in the society is one factor governing how immigrants will be perceived and treated (Berry et al., 2006). Within each country, there are likely to be varying patterns of neighborhood ethnic density which can greatly affect the opportunities for contact between migrant and majority groups (Christ et al., 2014). At a more granular level still, schools and classrooms within those neighborhoods may vary widely in their cultural diversity and ethos of inclusivity, which will generate different norms of acceptance or rejection. And individual students may differ in their preferred acculturation orientation (Celeste et al., 2016). Only by sampling from many schools in multiple neighborhoods in several different countries would it be possible to do justice to that multi-layered complexity.

A second trend is the growing number of attempts to conduct real or quasi-experiments in naturalistic settings. This, it seems to me, nicely combines the benefits of the causal interpretability of experiments with the advantages of contextualizing one's research in everyday settings, thus not sacrificing too much ecological validity. Despite the logistical difficulties involved in such research, social psychologists have shown remarkable ingenuity in conducting it. Three examples can suffice here. The first is Rimé and colleagues' (2011) examination of the role of Gacaca courts in Rwanda in promoting intergroup reconciliation and community cohesion after the genocide in that country. Also based in Africa is Paluck's (2010) study of the role of radio programs in improving (or deteriorating) intergroup relations in the Democratic Republic of Congo. A third example is Liebkind and McAlister's (1999) demonstration that an extended contact intervention coupled with peer modeling can have durable effects on Finnish school students' attitudes toward foreigners.

Words of Advice

The editor also invited us to offer words of advice to new generations of scholars. Again, I will be brief and limit myself to just three counsels. And I offer these with considerable hesitation since I realize they come from someone who has a relatively privileged ethnic and class background and who had the good fortune to have spent most of his career blissfully free of current institutional imperatives to maximize one's esteem indicators, citation counts, and grant income.

The first is to find a social psychological problem that genuinely interests you and that is also preferably of some social importance. Becoming a researcher can be a lonely business, especially at the early stages of your career, and so it is important to have the intrinsic motivation and curiosity to pursue the answers to that problem, wherever your inquiries take you. "Follow your nose," in other words and, whatever you do, don't become too much of a "dedicated follower of fashion ... eagerly pursuing all the latest fads and trends" (in the immortal words of the Kinks' famous 1966 song).

The second advice would be to temper the somewhat unrealistic idealism of the above with a healthy dose of pragmatism. Yes, find a worthwhile and interesting problem but then your responsibility as a social scientist is to translate that problem into some manageable research questions that can be answered by whatever methods are most appropriate. This is, in any event, an indispensable step for any researcher worth their salt and has the added benefit of making your research more amenable to funding.

The third piece of advice concerns writing style. It seems to me that much academic writing has become rather boringly uniform and sometimes downright unreadable, especially in the pages of psychology journals. Some of the blame for this homogeneity can be laid at the door of journal style guides which, while laudably exhorting us to be clear and concise, have also had the unfortunate side effect of imposing a stultifying orthodoxy on the ways we communicate our ideas and findings. In addition to this stylistic straitjacket, I sense that many authors try too hard to adopt what they believe is an appropriately formal "academese." This can lead to a tendency to use the passive voice, to hedge bets by adding too many qualifiers, and to overuse certain adverbs and phrases ("specifically" and "as such" are my personal bugbears). For role models of lucid and stylistic prose, I would urge readers to consult work by some of the discipline's foundational scholars. My personal favorites are Gordon Allport, Roger Brown, and Jerome Bruner. Much of your work as a researcher will involve expressing yourself in print. Even allowing for the necessary constraints of scientific publishing, your writing will be more interesting to read – and hence more persuasive – if you cultivate and nurture your own expository style.

Suggested Reading

Allport, G. W. (1954). *The Nature of Prejudice*. Reading, MA: Addison-Wesley.

Berry, J. W., Phinney, J. S., Sam, D. L., & Vedder, P. (Eds.) (2006). *Immigrant Youth in Cultural Transition: Acculturation, Identity and Adaptation across National Contexts.* Mahwah, NJ: Lawrence Erlbaum.

Brewer, M. B., & Miller, N. (1984). Beyond the contact hypothesis: Theoretical perspectives on desegregation. In N. Miller & M. B. Brewer (Eds.), *Groups in Contact: The Psychology of Desegregation* (pp. 281–302). Orlando, FL: Academic Press.

Brown, R. (2010). *Prejudice: Its Social Psychology*. New York: John Wiley & Sons.

(2019). *Henri Tajfel: Explorer of Identity and Difference*. Abingdon: Routledge.

Celeste, L., Meeussen, L., Verschuerren, K., & Phalet, K. (2016). Minority acculturation and peer rejection: Costs of acculturation misfit with peer-group norms. *British Journal of Social Psychology*, *55*, 544–563.

Christ, O., Schmid, K., Lolliot, S., Swart, H., Stolle, D., . . . Hewstone, M. (2014). Contextual effects of positive intergroup contact on outgroup prejudice. *Proceedings of the National Academy of Sciences*, *111*, 3396–4000.

Gaertner, S. L., Mann, J., Murrell, A., & Dovidio, J. (1989). Reducing intergroup bias: The benefits of recategorization. *Journal of Personality and Social Psychology*, *57*, 239–249.

Hewstone, M., & Brown, R. (1986). Contact is not enough: An intergroup perspective on the 'Contact Hypothesis'. In M. Hewstone & R. Brown (Eds.), *Contact and Conflict in Intergroup Encounters* (pp. 1–44). Oxford: Blackwell.

Liebkind, K., & McAlister, A. (1999). Extended contact through peer modelling to promote tolerance in Finland. *European Journal of Social Psychology*, *29*, 765–780.

Paluck, E. L. (2010). Is it better not to talk? Group polarization, extended contact and perspective taking in Eastern Democratic Republic of Congo. *Personality and Social Psychology Bulletin*, *36*, 1170–1185.

Rimé, B., Kanyangara, P., Yzerbyt, V., & Paez, D. (2011). The impact of Gacaca tribunals in Rwanda: Psychosocial effects of participation in a truth and reconciliation process after a genocide. *European Journal of Social Psychology*, *41*, 695–706.

Ring, K. (1967). Experimental social psychology: Some sober questions about some frivolous values. *Journal of Experimental Social Psychology*, *3*, 113–123.

Smith, E. R. (1993). Social identity and social emotions: Toward new conceptualizations of prejudice. In D. M. Mackie & D. L. Hamilton (Eds.), *Affect, Cognition and Stereotyping* (pp. 297–315). San Diego, CA: Academic Press.

Tajfel, H. (1974). Social identity and intergroup behaviour. *Social Sciences Information*, *13*, 65–93.

41 Chasing Self-Esteem

Jennifer Crocker

On July 3, 2021, I received an email message from Saul Kassin, which included the following:

I've been approaching high-impact scholars, many retired, who have influenced the course of social psychology and who offer unique perspectives and stories not otherwise known (e.g., Phil Zimbardo, Mahzarin Banaji, Elliot Aronson, Alice Eagly, Dan Gilbert, Richard Petty, Tom Gilovich, Carol Dweck, Herb Kelman, Bernie Weiner, Bibb Latané, Bob Cialdini, Tim Wilson, Rupert Brown, Jonathan Freedman, Bill Swann, Elaine Hatfield, Joel Cooper, James Jones, Dan Batson, Tom Pettigrew, Hazel Markus, and Susan Fiske are on board).

I am writing to you in the hope that you would be willing to contribute a chapter. Over the years, your work on self-esteem and contingencies of self-worth has proved so uniquely important that it would be an honor to bring your voice into PILLARS. Would you be interested?

Intentionally or not, this email message was devilishly designed to tickle my ego. How satisfying to see the words "uniquely important" used to describe my work! How delicious to be included in such an illustrious group of social psychologists! What an ego high to be validated in this way! Unfortunately, the pleasure lasted only moments, and was quickly followed by thoughts like, "If my work is so great, why wasn't I approached along with this earlier group?" and "Some people must have turned down the invitation, leading to an open slot that needed to be filled." How easily a preoccupation with my worth and value transformed this kind and generous invitation into a boost and then a threat to my self-esteem. Once triggered, this egosystem motivation stirred up a range of pleasant and unpleasant emotions. And then, having agreed to contribute, the task of actually writing a chapter worthy of a "pillar" became daunting, so I procrastinated; what could I say that would live up to this praise?

This is how it goes when people are motivated by their egosystems – a preoccupation with their worth and value – in their own eyes and others'. Validation feels great, but the "high" doesn't last, and is often immediately followed by anxiety – can I repeat that performance? Was it a fluke? Am I really an impostor, a fraud? In the egosystem, people seek validation from others and cringe at the thought of their ordinariness being exposed for all to see. When they do succeed in the domains in which their self-worth is invested, the bar for achieving the next ego boost gets higher. The pursuit of self-esteem becomes relentless. Much like addicts, we seek the boost to self-esteem,

Jennifer Crocker, Ohio State University, USA.

and feel great – are great! – when we get it, but it doesn't last and often leads to more anxiety and seeking the next high. One way or another, this predicament – and possible ways out of it – has captured my attention for much of the past forty years and has been explicitly the focus of my work for the past twenty or so years.

Why Self-Esteem?

The self influences how people experience, understand, and manage their lives. And self-esteem, as the judgment of the worth and value of who we are as a person, has powerful emotional consequences, affecting the quality of our everyday experience. Accordingly, the self and self-esteem have been major topics in psychology for more than a century.

From a more personal perspective, I suppose that the roots of my own interest in self-esteem lie in my childhood in Plymouth, Massachusetts. I was the middle of five children, with a father who farmed despite developing rheumatic arthritis when I was five years old and a mother who worked full time teaching while pursuing a college degree, raising her brood, and coping with her husband's illness. My role in the family and my way of securing attention and acknowledgment was to be the smart and successful child. My sense of my worth and value depended on being, seeing myself, and being seen by others as smart and successful.

It wasn't foreordained that psychology would be the domain in which I would pursue this goal. Starting in middle school, I showed an aptitude for math, and that was my focus through my first year at Reed College, where I was one of two women in my cohort placed into an accelerated math program. Because all math majors were required to take a year of physics (I suppose they thought we were all destined to become engineers), and all freshmen had to take a year-long humanities course, I had little opportunity to explore other interests. Looking around at my classmates, I had the strong feeling that I did not belong in my major. Maybe I harbored an unacknow-ledged fear that I could not be the academic star I had been in high school. In any case, I dropped out of college, and after working as a ski bum in Vermont, I found my way to Michigan State University and the psychology major, and from there to the PhD program at Harvard where I got my PhD in 1979, working with Shelley Taylor.

Looking back on those formative years, the thing that strikes me is how my academic ambitions, driven by the need to be seen as smart and successful, continually led me to choose situations where success would be validating but the bar for success kept rising, and where criticism and rejection – of ideas, research designs, analyses, drafts, manuscripts submitted for publication, grant proposals, and so on – are a constant feature.

At Harvard, I wasn't trained to be a self researcher. My work in graduate school focused on social cognition and stereotyping. In my first academic job at Northwestern, I collaborated with Naomi Tabachnik Kayne and Lauren Alloy on a study of depression and social comparison, showing that the usual tendency for people to consider themselves above average did not apply to people with symptoms of depression, who (on average) saw themselves as average, which we took as an indicator of depressive realism. This work drew me into thinking about self-esteem, and its connection to stereotyping and prejudice. With my students, I began to do studies seeking to answer questions like "Who is more prejudiced, high or low self-esteem people?" and "Does the answer depend on whether self-esteem is threatened?" Thus, it was at Northwestern that I began, however fitfully, to discover my passion for research on self-esteem. Perhaps the most formative experience of my years at Northwestern was the invitation to attend an interdisciplinary Summer Institute on Social Stigma and Interpersonal Relations at the Center for the Advanced Study of Behavioral Sciences, led by Dale Miller and Robert Scott in 1982. There, I learned about research in sociology showing that Black Americans are on average no lower in self-esteem than White Americans, which had a delayed but huge impact on my thinking and research.

Back at Northwestern, my research productivity was not sufficient to satisfy my department colleagues. The senior faculty in social psychology did not support me for tenure, and so neither did the department. At the time this felt like a sort of death – the end of my professional aspirations and ambitions. I actually called my mother one day and asked her whether she would still love me if I did not get tenure! (I realize how pathetic this was.) But in hindsight, not getting tenure at Northwestern may have been among the best things that happened in my career, because I was recruited by the University at Buffalo (with tenure), where my research on self-esteem began to flourish.

Stigma and Self-Esteem

It was during my time at Buffalo that I wrote my two most highly cited papers, both of them focused clearly on self-esteem. In 1989, Brenda Major and I published an article for *Psych Review* on the consequences of social stigma for self-esteem, and eventually had several NSF grants and published several papers on this topic. At the time, the established wisdom in the field was that being stigmatized or a target of prejudice necessarily lowers a person's self-esteem. But I knew from my summer at CASBS that it was not necessarily so. A random conversation with an undergraduate student taking my social psychology class led to conversations with Brenda, who at the time was working on women's lowered sense of entitlement with respect to pay. Anyone who has ever talked to Brenda about research knows how scintillating and creative she is, and we began a fruitful collaboration that lasted ten years, exploring how the attributional ambiguity experienced by people who are stigmatized can have self-protective consequences.

Also at Buffalo, in 1992, Riia Luhtanen and I developed a measure of collective self-esteem. This work was mainly a response to reviewers of work I had done showing that high self-esteem people derogate others following threats to their social identity. The reviewers noted that social identity theorists would have focused more on collective rather than personal self-esteem as the critical variable. Taking off from work by Tony Greenwald and Steve Breckler, Riia and I expanded the construct of collective self-esteem to include four dimensions: private (how I regard my social group), public (how I think others regard my social group), membership (how good a member of my social group I am), and importance to identity (how much membership in this group shapes my sense of self). This measure, which can be adapted to many different types of group memberships, turned out be a useful tool for the field. An unexpected and intriguing finding from our work on collective self-esteem was that for White and Asian-American students, the public and private aspects were highly correlated, but for Black students, they were not at all correlated. This perplexing finding led me to speculate about why Black subjects' private views of their identity group were so disconnected from how they believed others view their group, and the differences between people and perhaps between groups in what they base their sense of self-esteem on.

Contingencies of Self-Worth

In 1995 I moved to the University of Michigan, where working on this puzzle led me to focus in on contingencies of self-worth, or what people believe they need to be or do to have worth and value as a person. For more than a century, psychologists have observed the importance of contingencies of self-esteem in people's psychological lives. William James famously wrote about staking his self-esteem on being a good psychologist, whereas his brother Henry's self-esteem was staked on his abilities as a linguist. I began work on a measure of common contingencies of self-worth in college students, because I needed a tool to study their consequences.

In a 2001 *Psych Review* paper, Connie Wolfe and I argued that research on self-esteem has focused almost exclusively on whether trait self-esteem is high or low, and neglected other important aspects such as the contingencies on which self-esteem is based. Building on James's work, we presented a model of global self-esteem that elucidates how self-esteem is related to affect, cognition, and self-regulation of behavior, and helps resolve debates about the nature and functioning of self-esteem, among other things. I finished the final draft of that article while on a sabbatical in Berkeley, CA. The article ends by noting the double-edged nature of contingencies of self-worth: on one hand, contingencies of self-worth are highly motivating because people really want to succeed and avoid failure in these domains; on the other hand, they create psychological vulnerabilities, because failure means not only "I failed" but also "I am a failure, and therefore worthless."

Learning as Leadership

Just as I was finishing up the final edits on this paper at the end of my sabbatical, a fortuitous set of circumstances led me to a nine-day workshop in Sausalito, run by a small company called Learning as Leadership (LaL). I was finding my job at the

University of Michigan to be stressful. Impostor feelings lurked, particularly when my colleagues talked about whether various people were "Michigan material," or characterized their "quality of mind." Terms like this, along with descriptors such as "brilliant," always made me uneasy, whether they were applied to me or to others, because I doubted that I was any of those things. I tried to compensate by proving that I was, indeed, Michigan material, and took on too many projects and responsibilities, leading to self-inflicted burnout. It was in this state that I signed on to attend the LaL workshop, which promised to help participants "Be able to recognize when we are in a state of confusion by clarifying our reactions stemming from it; rediscover our aspirations and learn how to proactively fulfill them; to shift, if we decide, from the resistance of our EGOSYSTEM mechanisms to the resources of our ECOSYSTEM; and to be able, by the end of the seminar, to start creating our life rather than being at the mercy of events." I had no idea what any of this meant, but I knew I needed help and the workshop was highly recommended by a trusted friend, so I committed to do it.

The workshop was intense, nine days running from 8 a.m. to 9 p.m. It's difficult to describe the experience, but essentially it involved exploring two broad themes. The first theme involves the mechanisms of one's own *egosystem motivation* (i.e., preoccupation with self-worth), the life experiences and inferences we drew as children that shaped those mechanisms for each participant, and their consequences for oneself and other people. The most eye-opening aspect of this theme for me was the exploration of the benefits and costs of these egosystem mechanisms. For example, I quickly saw that my childhood experiences led me to conclude that I needed to be the smartest and most successful to get the love and attention I craved. It was more surprising to discover the costs for me of trying to be, or to appear to be, the smartest and most successful (stress, exhaustion, impostor feelings, and so on) and the costs for others. For example, looking at a chart I completed in 2001, I see that my reaction when I felt the need to be seen as smart, important, and competent was to take on responsibilities that are visible to others, to criticize others, to try to say smart things, and to reject others' ideas, or find flaws in their work. Rereading this twenty-year-old chart, I see that the consequences for me were, among other things, that I don't learn (because I always need to be right), my students feel inferior and are afraid to be wrong, and I create a critical and competitive environment in which people (including me) feel isolated and unsupported. This one insight was earth shattering for me. Imagine it multiplied many times over by the various exercises through which we explored these issues in the workshop; I knew I did not want to continue in this way for my sake and for others'. The goal of the workshop began to make sense. I no longer wanted to be in a state of confusion or at the mercy of events and in the resistance of my egosystem.

The second theme of the workshop involved identifying and exploring an alternative source of motivation. *Ecosystem motivation* involves goals that are not about validating self-worth, but are instead about generating, creating, or contributing to something outside of oneself, or larger than oneself, including another person or people. Each participant in the workshop explored what that would mean to them, both in a very general way, and specifically in the distinct domains or contexts of their lives (work or school, romantic relationship, friends and family, and so on). From this work, participants began to articulate an overarching goal or compass that could help them keep their lives headed in the direction they wanted to go – to start creating their lives rather than being at the mercy of events. For me, this meant identifying a goal that could help me avoid or stop seeking validation that I'm smart and successful, and take me instead toward creating (with help from others) a context that supports learning and connection for me and those in my interpersonal ecosystem.

Egosystem and Ecosystem Motivation

All of this was mind-blowing for me – both the personal part, where I saw these themes play out in my own life, and also the intellectual part, where I saw how the pursuit of self-esteem through the particular contingencies of self-worth we acquired early in life shape how we experience events in the present, how we react to them, and how those reactions affect other people and our own well-being. The most important and novel aspect for me was how a shift in motivation from egosystem to ecosystem could have profoundly beneficial effects for one's own and others' well-being, personal growth, and feeling of social connection. That insight has made a huge difference in my own life, and I wanted to bring it into the social psychological literature so it could shape how people understand the pursuit of self-esteem and its alternative.

   This workshop provided the inspiration for the next two decades of my work. The folks at Learning as Leadership are smart and widely read people, but they are not trained as psychologists. I saw things in their framework, particularly in terms of the costs of pursuing self-esteem, that I thought were not well-represented in psychological research on the self. Lora Park took the workshop and together we wrote a 2004 *Psych Bull* paper, which we titled "The Costly Pursuit of Self-Esteem." With my collaborators, I developed measures of self-image and compassionate goals that reflect egosystem and ecosystem motivation, and we explored how these motivations shape first-year college students' social experiences and psychological well-being. For example, we found that students who were higher in compassionate goals have more nonzero-sum construals of their relationships, become more growth oriented, have calm, clear, and connected feelings when interacting with other people, have less anxiety and depression symptoms, and perceive more support to be available to them. When Amy Canevello joined my lab as a postdoc, she urged me to study these processes in dyadic relationships, and we began doing longitudinal studies of interactions between strangers, and in friendships, roommate relationships, romantic relationships, and marital relationships (e.g., Crocker et al., 2017). Amy has been a highly valued friend and collaborator ever since. Over time, my students and I have gone beyond testing ideas inspired by our experiences in the LaL seminars, to asking new questions about egosystem and ecosystem motivation. This process continues today with my final two graduate students, Tao Jiang and Juan Ospina.

Despite relying heavily on the insights of the people at Learning as Leadership (thanks especially to Noah Nuer, Marc-Andre Olivier, Lara Nuer, and Carole Levy), doing this work has involved many challenges. Two have been pretty constant through the years. First, when people hear about my work, they often relate it (and reduce it) to something they are already familiar with – exactly what varies widely from person to person. Establishing what is unique about ecosystem motivation relative to every other similar-seeming construct in the field is not something I set out to do, but critics and reviewers insisted, and I thank them for it. Second, as a trained experimental social psychologist, I have long wanted to experimentally manipulate ecosystem motivation. This has proven difficult in a laboratory context where people know they are being studied and naturally want to appear a certain way to the researchers. The laboratory context pulls for egosystem motivation. Despite many years of trying, we still have not found a quick way to "manipulate" or shift people's motivational state, although Jim Abelson, Thane Erickson, and others developed a more personalized and intensive brief intervention that increases compassionate goals and decreases the physiological stress response in the Trier Social Stress Task, which was published in *Psychoneuroendocrinology* in 2014.

Appreciation

I can't conclude this little history of my work on self-esteem without acknowledging that, in addition to the many people I have already mentioned, I have benefited from the hard work, excellent insights, and constructive approaches of many graduate students, postdocs, and collaborators – too many to name individually. I hope they all know how grateful I am to have had the opportunity to work with them and explore these topics together. And none of this would have happened without my husband Charles Behling, a psychologist and intergroup dialogue expert, who gave up a tenured faculty position at Lake Forest College and followed me to the University at Buffalo, the University of Michigan, and now to Ohio. He has served as an invaluable sounding board for my work. His constant love and support has brought great joy to my quest to understand self-esteem.

Suggested Reading

Abelson, J. L., Erikson, T. M., Mayer, S., Crocker, J., Briggs, H., Lopez-Duran, N. L., & Liberzon, I. (2014). Brief cognitive intervention can modulate neuroendocrine stress responses to the Trier Social Stress Test: Buffering effects of a compassionate goal orientation. *Psychoneuroendocrinology, 44*, 60–70.

Crocker, J., Canevello, A., & Lewis, K. A. (2017). Romantic relationships in the ecosystem: Compassionate goals, nonzero-sum beliefs, and change in relationship quality. *Journal of Personality and Social Psychology, 112*(1), 58–75.

Crocker, J., & Major, B. (1989). Social stigma and self-esteem: The self-protective properties of stigma. *Psychological Review*, *96*(4), 608–630.

Crocker, J., & Park, L. E. (2004). The costly pursuit of self-esteem. *Psychological Bulletin*, *130*(3), 392–414.

Crocker, J., & Wolfe, C. T. (2001). Contingencies of self-worth. *Psychological Review*, *108*(3), 593–623.

Luhtanen, R., & Crocker, J. A. (1992). Collective Self-Esteem Scale: Self-evaluation of one's social identity. *Personality and Social Psychology Bulletin*, *18*(3), 302–318.

42 The Basement Tapes

John A. Bargh

Like any choice, my decision to go into the field was shaped by both internal and external forces. Internal, because I knew I wanted to be a psychologist as early as eight years old, with a clear memory of announcing this fact to my mother in our kitchen. Not to be a therapist, because I didn't yet know what those were, but to study people and try to figure them out. External, because current events and random occurrences played a major role in the particular area, and the specific questions, I'd spend my career studying. The *Zeitgeist* blew strong in the early 1970s, in the direction of free will and personal autonomy. I was in high school taking the one psychology class when B. F. Skinner's *Beyond Freedom and Dignity* was published to great fanfare. Skinner was on the cover of *Time* magazine – his face and skin painted in blue, implying how cold and heartless he was to claim we had no free will. Our class debated his claims for a good part of the school year. I took Skinner's side mainly to be contrarian and argue back against my classmates who naturally hated it.

Fortunately, big things were happening in psychology with the cognitive revolution and in nascent computer technology. The two went hand in glove because the technology gave us the ability to study internal mental processes using reaction times and more carefully control aspects of stimulus presentation. The revolution opened new vistas in the study of the human mind which had been forbidden to psychology students for the preceding fifty years. There was so much pent-up demand and interest in the experimental study of basic questions regarding the mind, and it was all bursting forth at once. Lucky break #1: born at the right time.

I probably don't need to say then that I was a psychology major from the get-go at Illinois. Despite the cognitive revolution, behaviorism had not suddenly disappeared, because so many of the faculty were behaviorists with tenure – in fact, it wasn't until the 1990s that the last of them finally retired. Much of experimental psychology classes at Illinois still involved running rats in mazes or shocking them. While I did not personally take any rat classes I became a lab rat myself and helped run various psychology experiments down in the basement of the new psychology building on Daniel Street. And when I wasn't in that basement, I was a few blocks away in a different one, that of a student dorm where the university's student-run FM radio station was located. Being a townie, I'd already started as a disc jockey there while in

John A. Bargh, Yale University, USA.

high school, doing the overnight "graveyard" shifts and helping out during student vacation periods. Now that I was in college myself, I took over the regular weekday nine to midnight shift.

The same advances in technology that helped enable the cognitive revolution in psychology also helped create the FM revolution in radio, and at about the same time. Our student-run station was founded in 1967, the same year as the publication of Ulric Neisser's *Cognitive Psychology*, considered the manifesto of the cognitive revolution. FM radio relied on line-of-sight transmission so it had a shorter listening range than AM but a much clearer, static-free signal, one that allowed stereo broadcasting for the first time. The spirit of this new medium was anti-AM radio which meant longer musical selections, more experimentation, and fewer commercials. The big musical groups of the era such as the Beatles and Led Zeppelin took advantage of this new broadcast medium and experimented with technology and various studio innovations. FM gave them the platform to reach audiences with longer and more progressive, experimental efforts. By the time I graduated in 1977 I had been on the air at this station for half of its existence.

But the highlight of radio days, indeed of my college years, was teaming up with two friends, Stew Oleson and Mike Pappademos, to write, create, and produce a thrice-weekly comedy show about a hapless freshman named Flush Bizbo. Three shows a week for the entire school year meant a whole lot of time in the studio, but it went by in a blur. Stew went on to form the Comedy Rangers stand-up comedy group (not his day job, he also went to law school) and Mike into a long, successful career in radio. Mike was the engineering genius who knew how to do reverb and feedback and playing reel-to-reel tapes backwards and all sorts of tricks, and helped us produce a remarkably polished, professional show. Those days and mostly nights writing and producing our show together were the most fun I've ever had. Stew, Mike, and I just fed off each other in feverishly writing each show.

Coincidentally, *Saturday Night Live* started the same year as our show, in 1975. Recently, Al Franken (2017) – an original SNL writer and cast member – wrote that those late nights with the whole cast together writing the week's skits was the most fun he had in his whole life. (And hey, that included becoming a US Senator and having drinks with Mitch McConnell!) On the much smaller stage at Illinois, our own show became so popular that at the end of the year, I was studying for finals and coming out of the undergraduate library when the last show (the "exciting conclusion") was broadcast. There at the book check-out desk, the exit of the undergraduate library, was a crowd of over 100 students, just standing there around someone's radio, all listening to our final program. It was a bittersweet moment of pride at what the three of us had done together, mixed with sadness that it was over. Mike and Stew graduated and moved on with their lives.

The teamwork at the radio station presaged the best part of my years in psychology – working together with colleagues and students on shared projects. These were long stretches of time first with Tory Higgins on the synapse model of construct accessibility, then Shelly Chaiken on automatic attitude activation, and finally Peter Gollwitzer on unconscious goal pursuit. Working so closely and intensely on a shared intellectual problem is the interpersonal (and much richer) version of private conscious thought itself, which Hannah Arendt (1978) aptly described as a "two in one" dialectic that internally mimics conversations with another person. The co-discoverer of the DNA molecule, James Watson, credited his collaboration with Francis Crick as the reason they were first to come up with the double-helix structure, before other, more brilliant minds, who tended to work alone. "If you're the brightest person in the room, you're in trouble," said Watson, noting that their most intelligent competitors seldom sought advice (see Cialdini, 2008). For me, the "dialectics" of active, intense collaboration were not only the most productive but also the most enjoyable times of my psychology career, just as working with Stew and Mike at the radio station was the best time of my college years.

Michigan

A year after they left, I moved on as well, to graduate school in Ann Arbor. This was another huge break – not the choice of Michigan over other options, mind you, given the rich traditions of the Research Center for Group Dynamics and the famous faculty in social psychology – but because I went there thinking I was going to work with Bob Zajonc on social facilitation research (the topic of my undergraduate thesis). Of course, when I got there in 1977, I quickly learned that Bob hadn't done any work on that topic in years. Instead, he was well into his new interests of mere exposure effects on attitude development, and especially the idea of "affect without cognition," or immediate affective reactions prior to any conscious reasoning about the "attitude object" (person, issue, art, food, what have you). And a good thing, too. I helped out in the lab mainly with computer programming, a then-novel skill I'd picked up in college, and was fascinated by the work going on there in subliminal mere exposure effects. The equipment Bob liked to build himself used ultra-fast camera shutters to present stimuli at speeds as fast as one-thousandth of a second.

It was my first exposure to the idea that there could be "non" or "pre" conscious influences on attitudes, preferences, and choices, the theme I'd spend the rest of my career researching and writing about, and it was happening (where else) in the basement of the Institute for Social Research on Thompson Street.

The intellectual milieu I walked into that fall of 1977 was amazing: Nisbett and Wilson's work on lack of introspective access to internal cognitive processes, Hazel Markus's seminal translation of the traditional "self" literature into cognitive terms of schemas and selective attention, plus Bob's work on affect without cognition. And these faculty and their graduate students all in the same little office bay on the third floor of ISR, offices surrounding a central meeting area where we students debated several foundational questions at the dawn of social cognition.

Looking back now on the course of psychology since that time, both Zajonc's (1980) "preferences need no inferences" paper in *American Psychologist*, and Nisbett and Wilson's (1977) *Psychological Review* article, have been tremendously influential. Bob's provocative idea, that there could be immediate affective responses prior to deliberate conscious thought and judgment about the object, was revolutionary. Across psychology, everyone assumed that judgments and preferences were formed *after* some reasoning about the various aspect of the object or issue, certainly not before. Bob's reversal of this sequence – that immediate affective reactions then *guided* reasoning (often just to find supporting reasons for how you already felt) – became the basis for seminal models of moral judgment (Haidt, 2001), for the idea of automatic attitude activation and automatic evaluation (Fazio, 1986) as well as the Implicit Associations Test of unconscious bias, which is based on immediate affective reactions (good vs. bad) to members of social groups. Today, cognitive psychology talks easily about affective priming but before Bob (and Russ Fazio), cognitive psychology treated affect as just another semantic feature, certainly nothing special (e.g., Bower, 1981; Collins & Loftus, 1975).

In its own separate way, the Nisbett-Wilson paper on introspective access was just as provocative and controversial, maybe even more so – drawing fire from the likes of Nobel Prize laureate Herbert Simon, among others. Someone once said that all of modern philosophy is a footnote to Plato – you might also say that the past forty years of research on implicit or unconscious influences in social psychology is a footnote to Nisbett and Wilson (1977). Their thesis, that people lack introspective access to their internal mental processes, was dynamite under the bridge of any research domain that depended on self-report questionnaires. It implied that people are most often unaware of the actual causal influences on their judgments and behavior, such as social norms and behavior contagion, and of the evolved goals and motives guiding what they believe are "free" choices, even regarding their political attitudes and voting behavior. Because if we are not consciously aware of and cannot report on the evident, important causes on our judgments and behavior, then they must come from some-where else, and I spent my research career looking for these "somewhere elses" (see Bargh, 2017). And the second profound implication was that our self-understanding had to be faulty because we would be misattributing the actual causes of our judgments and behavior to plausible but incorrect reasons, becoming "strangers to ourselves" as Tim Wilson (2002) concluded from his subsequent years of research on misattribution.[1]

For family reasons I spent my third year of graduate school at the University of Utah. I knew what I wanted to do. The Michigan psychology department, thanks to the kindness of Pat Gurin, generously funded me so that I could work in the lab of cognitive psychologist William Johnston. He was working on questions of selective attention, specifically preattentive processes and how unattended content (as in the to-be-ignored ear of stereo headphones) was still processed for meaning, even though conscious attention was directed elsewhere. My radio experience paid off, because as an assistant in Johnston's lab I created the stereo audio tapes used in his research,

---

[1] Tim was walking out the door at ISR as I was walking in; I literally got his old desk and office. My first day there, I opened the desk drawers and every one of them was stuffed with paper clips. Thousands and thousands, maybe even millions of paper clips! I know I have asked him why, several times since then, but I can never remember the answer.

which involved synchronized presentation (using a metronome!) of different streams of words to the left and right ears in the stereo headphones. I had kept my hand in radio while in Ann Arbor, doing overnight jazz shows for WIQB, and did the same when I moved out west, at KUER in Salt Lake City.

While helping with Professor Johnston's lab I also created the audiotapes I would use for my own dissertation the following year, back in the basement of ISR in Ann Arbor. This experiment made use of the dichotic listening technique to present self-related stimuli to the person's unattended ear – a direct influence of Hazel Markus's work on the self-schema as an attentional filter of experience (that milieu again). The other dissertation study was a collaboration with fellow graduate student and Zajonc lab member Paula Pietromonaco, who would go on to fame in relationships and emotion research at the University of Massachusetts. That study involved presenting personality trait terms outside of the person's conscious, foveal visual attention – that is, in the parafoveal visual field, based on Keith Rayner's pioneering work on preconscious "look-ahead" aspects of reading.

NYU

Jobs in social psychology were scarce in 1981, no thanks to President Reagan's cutbacks on the funding of social science research (his infamous "why fund the enemy?" line at a press conference), but I managed to score a few job interviews. In March, in a freak late snowstorm, I flew into New York City for the first time in my life, to give a job talk based on my dissertation research. My delayed flight landed at 3 a.m., the hotel had no heat, and my first meeting was at 9 a.m. That morning, I was so naive about New York I was calling cab companies for a ride downtown. At noon, on my way down the hall to give the talk, one of the faculty advised me not to talk about that new "social cognition" research, because the department didn't like it. With my transparencies and well-practiced talk in hand, there wasn't much I could do about it at that point, but fortunately it went well. One reason it did was the unknown individual stretched out on the couch at the back of the room giving me lots of supporting smiles and nods. I found out later it was Walter Mischel, who happened to be visiting NYU that year on a sabbatical from Stanford.

So what the hell, time for another lucky break, right? And that would be arriving at NYU as a little assistant professor the same year they also brought in Tory Higgins and Diane Ruble as senior faculty. Along with Jim Uleman, the four of us began to build of one of the great early centers of social cognition – bringing in Susan Andersen, Shelly Chaiken, and Yaacov Trope all over the next five years. This was about as big a career break as anyone could imagine. Diane and especially Tory were the true forces behind recruiting and establishing that program; even in those pre-Internet days the word soon got out and the stream of incredible graduate students began. Those of us who were there in those years, faculty and students alike, still have great memories of the 1980s, and then into the 1990s, on the seventh floor of 6 Washington Place in Greenwich Village. Just like we did on the third floor of ISR in Ann Arbor, the faculty and students hung out well into the evenings in our various offices and lounges discussing and debating the big questions of the time in social cognition.

There was more good luck – the annual dissertation award from the Society of Experimental Social Psychology which came with the huge bonus of immediate membership, not having to wait till five years post-PhD. That meant I was immediately able to meet colleagues from all over and hear about their current research well before it was eventually published. Another boost came from Bob Wyer, whom I'd known from my undergraduate days at Illinois, who asked me to fill in at the last minute for Richard Shiffrin and write a chapter on automaticity for the new *Handbook of Social Cognition* Bob was editing. Shiffrin, of course, was *the* expert on automatic processing, and was consequently overcommitted – Bob gave me all of two months to write the chapter, and though it meant staying in New York over Christmas break I got it done on time and so was able to be part of an influential early volume.

What followed was the hotbed of social cognition that was NYU in the 1980s – for me, it meant Tory and I working on our priming and construct accessibility model (e.g., Higgins et al., 1985), Shelly Chaiken and I putting our two research areas together and starting research on automatic attitude activation (following up on Fazio's seminal work; e.g., Bargh, Chaiken, et al., 1996), and at the end of the decade, Peter Gollwitzer combining our own two areas of expertise – motivation and automaticity – to start a decade of research on nonconscious goal pursuit (e.g., Bargh & Gollwitzer, 1994). That last one almost didn't happen because I didn't want to write a chapter that Tory had asked me to, for his (with Dick Sorrentino) second edition of the *Handbook of Motivation and Cognition*. Not only did I not know anything about motivation at the time, I didn't *want* to know (at least right then) – what I did want was to spend my first-ever sabbatical in Germany (Mannheim) traveling, seeing the sights, and enjoying the local beer (and wine) gardens. Yes, and doing a bit of work – sponsored as I was so generously as a guest of Norbert Schwarz and Fritz Strack and the Alexander von Humboldt foundation. But Tory insisted: It will be a stretch, he said, and good for you, he said. It turned out to be both.

So while I grumpily worked on this chapter, Peter Gollwitzer called and asked me down to Munich to give a talk and work with his lab group for a weekend. I had never met Peter before, and it turned out he was a motivation researcher interested in automatic components of carrying out intentions – implementation intentions. And I was an automaticity researcher, "interested" (thanks to Tory) in motivation – specifically, working on a theoretical chapter about the possibility that a person's goals might be activated automatically just as other social representations (e.g., attitudes, stereotypes) had been found to be in the 1980s. Peter and I were like two trains that started out about as far from each other as possible, but headed right at each other, and just happened to be both at the same place and time in May 1989. I've always said I learned everything I know about motivation from him. Thanks to that weekend in Munich, I even finished that chapter for Tory on time (Bargh, 1990).

Thinking back now on those years, my memories are all about people; mostly those mentioned above. The best times were when we were working closely together, doing the parts each of us could do best. For example, Peter and I did all our writing together at a computer keyboard – I was the faster typist (in English), so I did the typing and he told me what to type. It worked out great. Today people do a lot more collaboration remotely and not there together in person; while this is undoubtedly more efficient and opens many potential collaboration doors than would otherwise be available, I know (because I've done them both ways) there's something missing. Just like my radio show mates, just like Al Franken and the other *SNL* writers, just like our ISR office bay and the bean bag chair lounges on the seventh floor of the NYU psychology building, there's something magical about collaborating in person.

The Lab

Those bean bag chairs remind me that even in today's virtual age most of us still get to have in-person collaborations with the students and postdocs in our labs. I'd be remiss not to mention some of these amazing collaborations as well. There's not the space to mention all of them; the major research areas we helped initiate were the mimicry and imitation, or "chameleon effect" research with Tanya Chartrand (Chartrand & Bargh, 1999), the start of the behavioral priming research with Mark Chen (Bargh, Chen, & Burrows, 1996) and its morphing into the warmth priming research with Lawrence Williams at Yale (Williams & Bargh, 2008), where I moved in 2003, and the "power of the active goal" research first with Melissa Ferguson at NYU (Ferguson & Bargh, 2004) and then Julie Huang and David Melnikoff at Yale (Huang & Bargh, 2014; Melnikoff & Bargh, 2018). And another stroke of good fortune were the years alongside incredible postdocs: Ran Hassin, Ezequiel Morsella, Josh Ackerman, among others. They were (and still are) the best of colleagues. James Watson of double-helix fame had it right – two heads *are* better than one. Those hours with my lab members, individually and in the group meetings, were the best part of every week.

As a field, we know a lot more today than we knew back then (thank goodness) but we will also know much more forty years from now than we do today. That's a good reason both to be humble about our present theories and models, and to respect the ideas and writings of those who came before us. Just as they were, we are all just trying to do our best, and psychology is hardly a finished product. But that's no reason not to "give psychology away," as George Miller (1969) challenged us, based on our present state of knowledge, to inform and help people in their everyday lives. In my interactions with the general public, from town library talks and addresses to professional organizations, and talking with journalists, podcasters, and bloggers, they seem quite thirsty for knowledge about modern psychology. For most of them, all they know is Freud and maybe some oversimplified "two types of people" personality nonsense (see Melnikoff & Bargh, 2018).

I am looking forward to reading the other contributions to this volume. These back stories are fascinating to me, especially as they pertain to the history of psychology in our lifetimes. At annual conventions we used to gather around Ellen Berscheid or Hal

Kelley or Walter Mischel in the lounges and listen to them tell stories of back-when. I'm in touch with many of my senior colleagues and remain fascinated by their back stories. One of my favorites was when I asked Ulric Neisser – with whom I had several conversations starting as far back as 1980 when he gave a talk out at Utah, and I was still a graduate student – about his experiences writing the revolutionary *Cognitive Psychology*. After all, he wrote it right under the nose of B. F. Skinner, in a small basement office of William James Hall while Skinner had the entire twelfth floor. He said they'd see each other in the elevator sometimes, but never said a word to each other – yet Skinner knew, Neisser said, what he was up to, down in the basement.

Suggested Reading

Arendt, H. (1978). *The Life of the Mind*. New York: Harcourt.

Bargh, J. A. (1990). Auto-motives: Preconscious determinants of social interaction. In E. T. Higgins & R. M. Sorrentino (Eds.), *Handbook of Motivation and Cognition* (Vol. 2, pp. 93–130). New York: Guilford Press.

(2017). *Before You Know It*. New York: Simon & Schuster.

Bargh, J. A., Chaiken, S., Raymond, P., & Hymes, C. (1996). The automatic evaluation effect: Unconditional automatic attitude activation with a pronunciation task. *Journal of Experimental Social Psychology*, *32*, 185–210.

Bargh, J. A., Chen, M., & Burrows, L. (1996). Automaticity of social behavior: Direct effects of trait construct and stereotype priming on action. *Journal of Personality and Social Psychology*, *71*, 230–244.

Bargh, J. A., & Gollwitzer, P. M. (1994). Environmental control over goal-directed action. *Nebraska Symposium on Motivation*, *41*, 71–124.

Bower, G. H. (1981). Mood and memory. *American Psychologist*, *36*, 129–148.

Chartrand, T. L., & Bargh, J. A. (1999). The chameleon effect: The perception-behavior link and social interaction. *Journal of Personality and Social Psychology*, *76*, 893–910.

Cialdini, R. B. (2008). How to get the best solutions from your team. *Harvard Business Review*, February 29. https://hbr.org/2008/02/how-to-get-the-best-solutions-1.

Collins, A. M., & Loftus, E. F. (1975). A spreading-activation theory of semantic processing. *Psychological Review*, *82*, 407–428.

Fazio, R. H. (1986). How do attitudes guide behavior? In R. M. Sorrentino & E. T. Higgins (Eds.), *Handbook of Motivation and Cognition: Foundations of Social Behavior* (Vol. 1, pp. 204–243). New York: Guilford Press.

Ferguson, M. L., & Bargh, J. A. (2004). Liking is for doing: The effects of goal pursuit on automatic evaluation. *Journal of Personality and Social Psychology*, *87*, 557–572.

Franken, A. (2017). *Al Franken: Giant of the Senate*. New York: Hachette.

Haidt, J. (2001). The emotional dog and its rational tail: A social intuitionist approach to moral judgment. *Psychological Review*, *108*, 814–834.

Higgins, E. T., Bargh, J. A., & Lombardi, W. J. (1985). Nature of priming effects on categorization. *Journal of Experimental Psychology: Learning, Memory, and Cognition*, 11, 59–69.

Huang, J. Y., & Bargh, J. A. (2014). The selfish goal: Autonomously operating motivational structures as proximate cause of human judgment and behavior. *Behavioral and Brain Sciences*, *37*, 121–135.

Melnikoff, D., & Bargh, J. A. (2018). The mythical number two. *Trends in Cognitive Sciences, 22*, 280–293.

Miller, G. A. (1969). Psychology as a means of promoting human welfare. *American Psychologist, 24*, 1063–1075.

Neisser, U. (1967). *Cognitive Psychology*. New York: Prentice-Hall.

Nisbett, R. E., & Wilson, T. D. (1977). Telling more than we can know: Verbal reports on mental processes. *Psychological Review, 84*, 231–259.

Skinner, B. F. (1971). *Beyond Freedom and Dignity*. New York: Knopf.

Williams, L. E., & Bargh, J. A. (2008). Experiencing physical warmth promotes interpersonal warmth. *Science, 322*(5901), 606–607.

Wilson, T. D. (2002). *Strangers to Ourselves*. Cambridge, MA: Harvard University Press.

Zajonc, R. B. (1980). Feeling and thinking: Preferences need no inferences. *American Psychologist, 35*, 151–175.

43 Evolutionary Social Psychology
A Scientific Revolution in Progress

David M. Buss

My first course in social psychology in 1972 or 1973 was with Elliot Aronson, a premier social psychologist of his era. He mesmerized the class. The first edition of his book *The Social Animal* had just been published and it was our textbook for the course. My most vivid memory was learning about cognitive dissonance theory and T-groups (then popular Sensitivity Training Groups). Elliot was a big proponent of both. In front of a class of several hundred, he would hold up his book and ask: "Doesn't it read like a novel?" The class burst into applause. Some women shouted out "We love you Elliot!" He an extraordinarily charismatic lecturer, setting a high bar that was only exceeded in my experience when I heard Phil Zimbardo give a lecture in a class I was a T.A.-ing for his wife, Christina Maslach at Berkeley. During that guest lecture, students broke into applause several times *during* the lecture, and thunderously at the end. With these introductions to social psychology, nothing seemed more fascinating to me than social interactions and the prospect of uncovering our underlying social psychological machinery.

Two domains of social interaction captivated me – status hierarchies and what I later came to call "human mating strategies." As an undergraduate I wrote a paper linking the two, hypothesizing that the primary reason that men had evolved a powerful motive to claw their way up the status hierarchy was to gain sexual access to women. My professor, David Hovland (son of the famous social psychologist Carl Hovland), liked the paper. He asked me to present it to the class, which seemed like a great honor. Perhaps coincidentally, doing so raised my status among the undergraduates in the class, and in a case of life imitating art, led to interest from several of the women who sought me after class to discuss my ideas in greater depth.

It probably served me well that I attended graduate school not in a social psychology program, but rather in personality psychology (at UC Berkeley), although who knows about the road not traveled. What drew me to personality was a fascination with human nature. I wanted to understand the fundamental motives of humans, what made them tick, what determined the goals toward which they strived. Social motives, of course, particularly engaged me. Alas, I found all existing grand theories of personality to be lacking – Freud, Jung, Adler, Horney, Kelly, Maslow, etc. Although many possessed aspects that had some intuitive appeal, all lacked a solid theoretical foundation upon which to build *a science of human nature*.

David M. Buss, University of Texas, USA.

In order to develop a scientifically sound theory of human nature, it seemed to me that one had to identify the causal processes that produced that nature, whatever the constituents of that nature might be. Indeed, identifying the causes of our psychological architecture should provide insight into the nature of that architecture. During my time in graduate school (1976–1981), psychology was under the heavy theoretical influence of behaviorism and the blank slate model of the mind. The nature of human nature, it was presumed, was that humans lacked a basic nature. Adult behavior patterns, it was presumed, were caused by a history of contingencies of reinforcement, Bandurian social learning, parental socialization practices, and other social and cultural forces external to humans.

Dissatisfaction with this model of the human mind led me to search for deeper causal processes, which led me to the theory of evolution by natural and sexual selection. Alas, this interest remained one I had to pursue on the side, since none of my Berkeley professors had knowledge of evolutionary biology.

This interest was controversial then, and was to become more so in subsequent years. One manifestation in those graduate student years centered on sex differences.

Berkeley and Psychological Sex Differences

I was fortunate at Berkeley to have multiple mentors – Ken Craik, Jack Block, Jeanne Block, Harrison Gough, Richard Lazarus. I also eagerly initiated conversations with many professors, including social psychologists Cristina Maslach, Ayala Pines, and Phil Tetlock, as well as postdoc visitors such as Frank Sulloway. Berkeley also hosted a dazzling array of guest speakers, including Bob Zajonc, Mark Snyder, Walter Mischel, Beth Loftus, Daniel Kahneman (a UC Berkeley PhD) and Amos Tversky, although the latter's work on cognitive biases and heuristics had not yet had the monumental impact it was to attain later. As graduate students, we read all their papers with great alacrity.

Among my five direct mentors was Dr. Jeanne Block, who argued that existing sex differences, although few in number, were due to parental and cultural socialization practices. Parents dressed girls in pink and gave them Barbie Dolls, she argued, and dressed boys in blue and gave them trucks and toy guns. Boys were more physically aggressive than girls (one of the few well-documented sex differences), she argued, because of these forms of socialization. Her theory was published in prominent journals such as *American Psychologist*. Dr. Block even starred in a science documentary called, aptly enough, "The Pinks and the Blues."

I was dubious. Some of the sex differences, such as in rough and tumble play, seemed to emerge very early in life and appeared across cultures, suggesting both early predictable development and cross-cultural universality. Moreover, similar sex differences seemed to exist in closely related species, such as chimpanzees and gorillas. Block's theory moreover carried the implicit assumption of unidirectional causation from parents to children. But the design of the studies she cited could not rule out other causal possibilities, such as children influencing parents about their toy preferences, rejecting some toys while embracing others rather than passively accepting whatever parents gave them. She viewed humans as passive blank receptacles rather than active strategists.

My side-reading in evolutionary biology also provided a powerful alternative theory – the theory of sexual selection (about which more later). But as a graduate student whose fate was subject to the whims of a few professors who would be my letter-writers, I kept my doubts about the socialization theory of sex differences largely under wraps, revealing them only to fellow graduate students and in the most diplomatic manner I could muster to her husband, Jack Block, who dismissed it with a shrug, saying "That's Jeanne's stuff," although he too was a co-author on those papers.

One other interesting historical context for the study of sex differences is relevant. The field had assumed that males and females were essentially identical psychologically. In premier APA journals in the early 1970s, researchers were not even required to provide information about the sex of the participants (then called "subjects"). The APA mandated reporting sex of participants in the mid-1970s, and this eventually led to greater focus on the nature and origins of sex differences, as well as providing information that could be compiled in subsequent meta-analyses. As I was later to argue, males and females are not psychological clones and could not be given what we know about sex differences in reproductive biology and the differing adaptive challenges the sexes recurrently face in the domains of sexuality and mating.

I was very fortunate to have published (out or in press) ten papers during my graduate school days in premier journals (e.g., *JPSP*, *American Psychologist*, *Developmental Psychology*, *Child Development*). This is not so uncommon in modern times, but was unusual in 1981 as I was completing my PhD. My high profile as a graduate student led to my first job as assistant professor at Harvard University. The transition proved critical. For the first time, I could pursue whatever I wanted without having to worry about the approval of graduate school mentors.

Harvard and Human Mate Preferences

Although I was technically a personality psychologist, the phenomena that most interested me were inherently social. While in graduate school, I published papers on topics such as dominant acts in social interaction (developing with Ken Craik a formulation of personality as act frequencies) and links between children's activity levels and parent–child interactions. At Harvard starting in 1981, I continued this more mainstream line of personality research, but immediately returned to my interest in building a solid scientific foundation for a theory of human nature, which led me back to evolutionary theory.

This intellectual interest took two forms – in my teaching and in my research. Upon arrival at Harvard, I was assigned to teach a course on Human Motivation, previously taught by David McClelland. I used evolutionary theory as a fundamental framework for organizing the course. Then in 1982, I taught a small undergraduate seminar in evolution and human nature. These courses forced me to steep myself more deeply in the technical literature in evolutionary biology (I had no prior training in that field) and to familiarize myself with its applications to the mating strategies of other species. In turn, teaching these courses led to two other outcomes. One was an article eventually published in *American Psychologist* in 1984, called "Evolutionary Biology and Personality Psychology: Toward a Conception of Human Nature and Individual Differences."

The second outcome was that Leda Cosmides, then a graduate student in experimental psychology, knocked on my office door and was interested in talking about evolutionary theory as applied to psychology. She, in turn, introduced me to her husband, John Tooby. They knew much more about evolutionary theory than I did, although they had not yet published in that area. Their subsequent papers, which started to appear in 1987, provided a successful integration of cognitive psychology (conceptualized as information processing in computational terms) with evolutionary theory, and would prove foundational for the field. Our discussions then and in subsequent years greatly deepened my thinking, and we formed a friendship that is still vibrant some forty years later. At Harvard, I also met stellar scientists such as Irv DeVore, E. O. Wilson, Steven J. Gould, Jerome Bruner, and had the honor of serving in the same department as Professor Emeritus B. F. Skinner while he was still alive, as well as interacting frequently with prominent social psychologists such as Bob Rosenthal and Ellen Langer.

Another outcome was that my research took a dramatic turn – I started to study human mating strategies. While I was designing a study of married couples in Cambridge, it occurred to me that I could test a few evolutionary hypotheses based on the work of Robert Trivers (parental investment theory), George Williams (age and reproductive value), and Don Symons (physical attractiveness as providing a bounty of cues to fertility). At this time in the early 1980s, there existed some evolutionary speculations or predictions about human behavior, but virtually no empirical tests. Stated differently, the ratio of theory to rigorous empirical tests was poor. To my astonishment, however, the sex differences in mate preferences predicted in advance of their tests were confirmed – sex differences centering around resource acquisition ability and willingness (more preferred by women) and physical attractiveness and other fertility cues such as youth (preferred more by men).

The evolution-based hypotheses predicted universal sex differences in mate preferences, and I realized that no one would regard as convincing confirmation a study of a sample of Cambridge couples. So I launched what was to become a five-year, 37-culture study of mate preferences. I showed my Cambridge results to a dozen or so professors – psychologists mostly, but some sociologists – and asked them to make predictions. Would the sex differences I found in Massachusetts be universal across cultures? Would they be true just in Western or capitalist cultures? Nearly all those I asked predicted non-universality. These sex differences, most argued, were products of culture.

My biggest regret is that I did not ask my colleagues to sign their predictions. The reason is that after I discovered universal sex differences in mate preferences, precisely as predicted in advance by the evolutionary hypotheses, some said "I could have predicted that in advance." The hindsight bias is now well known among psychologists. But at the time, no one except those steeped in evolutionary theory predicted universal sex differences in advance of this study. It took many years to conduct, since this was pre-Internet days, and all communication with my fifty cross-cultural collaborators had to be conducted laboriously via snail mail.

The sample included many cultures that would now be described as non-WEIRD. These included the Zulu tribe of South Africa and Lagos-dwelling Nigerians; Venezuelans and Santa Caterina Brazilians; Palestinian Arabs and Israeli Jews; Chinese, Japanese, and Taiwanese; and Gujarati Indians. It included cultures that differed in political systems (e.g., capitalism, communism), religious orientation (Muslim, Christian, atheist), and mating system (presumptive monogamy versus legal polygyny). The final sample consisted of 10,047 individuals from thirty-three countries located on six continents and five islands. The study took many years to conduct and analyze, but when it was finally published in *Behavioral and Brain Sciences* (Buss, 1989), it became and remains my most cited publication (more than 6,000 as of 2021 according to Google Scholar).

While I was in the five-year process of collecting data for this study, Bob Sternberg invited me down to Yale to give a talk to their psychology department in 1984. I threw caution to the wind and decided to give my talk on human mating, my first professional talk on the topic. I think it was well received. After I returned to Cambridge I received a letter from the editor of *American Scientist*, who happened to be in the Yale audience, inviting me to write an article on human mating. This led to my first publication on the topic in 1985. An ancillary benefit was requests for reprints from different cultures around the world, since *American Scientist* had a global circulation. This allowed me to invite scholars from cultures that I did not have in my sample to join the collaboration. I'm sure the invitations, coming on Harvard stationery that had the university's name in huge, embossed letters across the top, did not hurt – forty-nine out of fifty researchers accepted my invitation, an astonishingly high rate in retrospect.

The predicted sex differences in mate preferences were fundamentally anchored in Darwin's (1871) theory of sexual selection, which deals with the evolution of adaptations due to mating advantage, not survival advantage. It identified two causal pathways by which mating success could be achieved – same-sex contests or competitions, the winners of which gained sexual access to the opposite sex; and preferential mate choice, the focus of my 37-culture study. I came to realize that sexual selection theory in general and sex differences in its causal components had profound implications for many other aspects of human mating that no one had yet explored.

This insight led to an explosion of other studies that I was to conduct in my next professional position. In 1985, four years after my PhD, I was offered a professorship with tenure at the University of Michigan. At Harvard, I had just been promoted to associate professor, but without tenure, so had another four years there and loved the intellectual vibrancy of Harvard. The undergraduates were absolutely amazing, and I formed a lab with half a dozen of them (three went on to get their PhDs in psychology – Mary Gomes at Stanford, Mike Barnes at Yale, and Niels Waller at

Minnesota). Alas, with my first child on the way and the prospect of joining one of the best psychology departments in the world at Michigan, and with the security of tenure, I reluctantly decided to leave Cambridge and move to Ann Arbor.

Michigan and Human Mating Strategies

Part of the allure of Michigan in 1985 was an interdisciplinary group of scholars whose research was guided by an evolutionary perspective. These included Richard Alexander (Biology), Richard Wrangham (Biological Anthropology), Barb Smuts (Biological Anthropology and Psychology), Randy Nesse (Psychiatry, Medical School), Bobbi Low (Natural Resources), and Warren Holmes (Psychology). The Dean gave us half a million dollars in 1986 to form an interdisciplinary group that met regularly. We seven, together with more than a dozen top-notch graduate students, became *The Evolution and Human Behavior Program*. We invited speakers and enjoyed an intellectual feast of luminaries such as W. D. Hamilton (originator of 1964 inclusive fitness theory), George C. Williams (author of the 1966 classic book *Adaptation and Natural Selection*), Martin Daly and Margo Wilson (authors of the 1988 book, *Homicide*), and Napoleon Chagnon (world expert on the Yanomamo of Brazil). I was honored to organize a symposium at Michigan in 1986–1987 with many of these intellectual giants (for a photo of our illustrious group, see www.cambridge .org/pillarsofsocialpsychology). I was the young upstart and knew less about evolutionary theory than any of them, but I soaked up the knowledge and continued to read in depth the complex technical literature in evolutionary biology.

Eventually, Richard Wrangham left Michigan for Harvard after he won a McArthur "genius" award, and Kim Hill, the world's leading expert on the Ache of Paraguay, joined our EHB group. While Richard Wrangham provided a primatological perspective on human behavior, Kim Hill provided extraordinary insights into the lives and social psychology of small-group hunter-gatherers, which were becoming increasingly rare in the world. Our annual interdisciplinary conference eventually morphed into an international scholarly organization in 1989, the *Human Behavior and Evolution Society* (HBES), with W. D. Hamilton as its first President – a society that is going strong more than thirty years later.

Although I continued to publish some mainstream articles on personality and social interaction, the bulk of my research focused on an explosion of new ideas stemming from sexual selection theory and following my 37-culture study of sex differences in mate preferences. The mate preferences I discovered had conceptual implications for intrasexual competition, since they should set the ground rules. Each sex should compete to embody the desires of the other sex, at least among heterosexuals. Among these were research projects on the psychology of *sexual jealousy* and sex differences therein, tactics of *mate competition*, tactics of *mate attraction*, *derogation of competitors*, tactics of *mate retention,* and tactics of *mate poaching*. These are all vitally important social psychological domains, yet because social psychology lacked an evolutionary lens, they were almost totally absent from the field prior to these research programs. The rare exceptions were Elaine Hatfield and Ellen Berscheid, who broke ground with some laboratory experiments on attraction, and Zick Rubin and Anne Peplau, who found that dating couples who were dissimilar in attitudes tended to break up over time.

Sexual selection theory reveals that evolved mating strategies should be center stage in understanding all sexually reproducing species. Humans are no exception. Reproductive success, the engine of the evolutionary process, cannot be attained without mating success. An evolutionary perspective suggests that our mating strategies should be complex, multifaceted, sex differentiated in some domains, and contingent on social contexts such as sex ratio in the mating pool and strategies pursued by intrasexual competitors. Human mating strategies should occupy a prominent place in social psychology. Moreover, evolutionary psychology provides a powerful metatheory for the field, a perspective I came to explore more deeply at the Center for Advanced Study in the Behavioral Sciences at Stanford.

Center for Advanced Study and Evolutionary Psychology as a Metatheory for Psychology

In 1987, I was elected to be a Fellow at the Center for Advanced Study at Stanford. Although most elected fellows opt for a year to luxuriate in scholarly activity without the usual administrative and teaching duties, the Center also provided an option to propose a group project. I proposed one, titled *Foundations for Evolutionary Psychology*. For this group, I proposed to bring in Leda Cosmides and John Tooby, who I knew from Harvard; Martin Daly and Margo Wilson, outstanding theorists and empirical scientists; and Don Symons, who had written the best book on human sexuality in 1979, *The Evolution of Human Sexuality*. Gardner Lindzey was then head of the Center, and informed me that my proposal was accepted, and that I could invite all of my proposed collaborators with the sole exception of Don Symons. Gardner never revealed why Don was not invited.

So we gathered in Palo Alto for the academic year 1989–1990. I proposed to the group that we five co-author a book on the foundations of evolutionary psychology. We met regularly. We circulated draft chapters. My intuitions about the brilliance of these scholars were amply born out, and I learned much from them.

By this point, Tooby and Cosmides had formulated a powerful integration of evolutionary theory with modern cognitive psychology within a computational information processing framework. Its centerpiece is that psychological mechanisms, housed in the brain, were the primary targets of evolution by selection. The goal, therefore, was to discover the design of these mechanisms, including the social and environmental inputs that activated them, their information processing procedures and decision rules, and their behavioral output. These psychological mechanisms are the primary products of evolution by natural and sexual selection. My work on human mating strategies fit nicely within this framework, as did Leda's work on social contract theory and cheater detection in social exchange and Daly and Wilson's work on homicide.

But I realized that the framework of evolutionary psychology provided something grander, and not just for the field of social psychology. It provided a metatheory for the entire field of psychology, and even grander, a metatheory for all social sciences. The outlines of this metatheory were spelled out by Tooby and Cosmides in their brilliant classic 1992 chapter, "The Psychological Foundations of Culture." A few years later, in 1995, I published in *Psychological Inquiry* a target article, "Evolutionary Psychology: A New Paradigm for Psychological Science," a more user-friendly outline of the metatheory with some of my own elaborations and extensions.

Alas, the co-authored book on *Foundations of Evolutionary Psychology* did not materialize. After our year at the Center, it proved impossible to coral five independent-minded scholars, each with our own research programs and now geographically scattered across North America, to focus on this grander task. So I turned my focus to developing an evolution-based theory of mating, called *Sexual Strategies Theory* (Buss & Schmitt, 1993) and to writing my first book, *The Evolution of Desire: Strategies of Human Mating*, first published in 1994, now in its third edition (2016).

After these time-intensive projects, I turned my focus back to evolutionary psychology as a metatheory for the entire field. This focus resulted in sole-authoring the first textbook in the field, first published in 1998: *Evolutionary Psychology: The New Science of the Mind*. The book remains the most widely used text in the field (now in its sixth edition, published in 2019). I eventually edited *The Handbook of Evolutionary Psychology* (2005), a collection of some thirty-two chapters on topics ranging across the entire discipline of psychology. I was honored that Steven Pinker provided the Foreword and Richard Dawkins the Afterword for the volume. That *Handbook* is now in its second edition, published in 2016, which nearly doubled in size to two volumes due to the explosion of research in the field.

The Emergence of Evolutionary Social Psychology

By far the most interesting and important modern theories in evolutionary biology center on social behavior. These include *sexual selection theory* in its modern form, which formed the foundation of my work on human mating strategies and also provides insights into status hierarchies based on intrasexual competition. They also include *inclusive fitness theory*, which provides a framework for understanding adaptations surrounding families and differing degrees of genetic relatedness. Another is *parent-offspring conflict theory*, which provides a framework for understanding adaptations in parents and children that function to influence each other. Another is *reciprocal altruism theory*, which provides one framework for understanding friendships, social exchanges, gains in trade, and social cheaters. Yet another is *sexual conflict theory*, which provides a framework for understanding the domains in which men and women predictably get into conflict with each other – the basis for my recent book, *When Men Behave Badly: The Hidden Roots of Sexual Deception, Harassment, and Assault* (Buss, 2021).

Astonishingly, these foundational evolutionary theories are almost entirely absent from mainstream social psychology, although there are some positive signs of change (e.g., Kenrick, Neuberg, & Cialdini, 2019). Why should the study of human social psychology be entirely divorced from the foundational theories that have proven so useful in understanding thousands of other social species? Indeed, many of these theories are especially relevant to humans because Elliot Aronson was right – we are, after all, *the social animal*. We live in groups. We grow up surrounded by close kin. We engage in social exchange more than any other known species. We invest in our offspring for more years than any other species. And as a species, we are obsessed with mating – with who mates with whom, who deceives whom, who cheats on whom in the form of sexual or financial infidelity, what are the many forms of sexual conflict within mating relationships, how to retain the mates we have attracted, how to fend off mate poachers, and who gets divorced.

Evolutionary theories and perspectives provide heuristic value, guiding researchers to discover features of our social psychology entirely missed. These also provide deeper illumination of some phenomena discovered by mainstream social psychologists. An example comes from *Error Management Theory* (Haselton & Buss, 2000), which provides a deeper explanation of some social-cognitive biases, such as the sexual over-perception bias (Buss, 2021), the stranger fear bias, biases stemming from Prospect Theory (Kahneman & Tversky, 1979) such as the asymmetry in affective reactions to gains and losses, and even the underlying theoretical reasons that explain why people commit the fundamental attribution error. These theories also illuminate why social psychology is so important within the social and life sciences.

Evolutionary psychology provides a metatheory for social psychology. It is an overarching conceptual framework within which all social psychological phenomena can be understood. This is extraordinarily valuable. Social psychology places prime importance on the situation. Context matters. Evolutionary psychology dovetails well with this focus, but adds the missing ingredients – the underlying psychological adaptations that evolved precisely to respond to those important situational influences, be they commands from an authority figure, the detection of cheaters in social exchange, or cues that a spouse might be committing infidelity. Evolutionary psychology enriches social psychology by specifying evolved functions, the social adaptive challenges that caused the evolution of those psychological adaptations to begin with, and the ways in which those adaptations function to solve those problems. Social psychology has been monumentally important in discovering novel phenomena, but these remain disconnected from each other, separate psychological jewels residing in their own isolated silos. From obedience to authority to conformity to group norms, from the fundamental attribution error to the sexual misperception bias, all have to be understood within the EP metatheoretical framework. If an alternative metatheoretical framework exists for social psychology, it has not been made generally known to the scientific community of psychologists.

Suggested Reading

Buss, D. M. (1989). Sex differences in human mate preferences: Evolutionary hypotheses tested in 37 cultures. *Behavioral and Brain Sciences, 12*(1), 1–14.

(1994/2016). *The Evolution of Desire: Strategies of Human Mating*. New York: Basic Books.

(Ed.) (2005). *The Handbook of Evolutionary Psychology*. Hoboken, NJ: John Wiley.

(2021). *Bad Men: The Hidden Roots of Sexual Deception, Harassment, and Assault*. New York: Little Brown Sparks.

Buss, D. M., & Schmitt, D. P. (1993). Sexual strategies theory: An evolutionary perspective on human mating. *Psychological Review, 100*(2), 204–232.

Darwin (1871). *The Descent of Man, and Selection in Relation to Sex*. London: J. Murray.

Haselton, M. G., & Buss, D. M. (2000). Error management theory: A new perspective on biases in cross-sex mind reading. *Journal of Personality and Social Psychology, 78*(1), 81–91.

Kahneman, D., & Tversky, A. (1979). Prospect theory: An analysis of decision under risk. *Econometrica, 47*(2), 263–291.

Kenrick, D. T., Neuberg, S. L., & Cialdini, R. B. (2019). *Social Psychology: Unraveling the Mystery*. Boston: Pearson.

Symons, D. (1979). *The Evolution of Human Sexuality*. New York: Oxford University Press.

44 One Man's Search for (the Assignment of) Meaning

Thomas Gilovich

Although the term wasn't in use back in the early 1970s, I was very aware throughout my college years of being a first-gen student. As a result, I thought I shouldn't veer far from the practical in choosing courses, which for me meant classes that would help me become a successful lawyer. Fortunately, a pre-law curriculum is not very constraining, so I was free to take any class that seemed interesting. (That was certainly true at Santa Clara University, where I spent my first two years because it had a good local reputation and I could save money by living at home.) And because the lawyers I read about outside of class, such as Clarence Darrow and F. Lee Bailey, were gifted amateur psychologists, I took a psychology course and loved it. Then another; same reaction.

But despite loving what I was learning in my psychology courses, the field did not seem like something to pursue because it didn't seem sufficiently practical. The clinical path didn't appeal to me and the basic research path struck me as unpromising because the answers to the most intriguing questions seemed too elusive. I believe I had some intuitive appreciation of the adage (I don't remember when I first heard it) that people don't respond to the stimuli they encounter; they respond to the meaning they assign to those stimuli. And the construction of meaning seemed so idiosyncratic that the effort to predict and understand complex human behavior appeared doomed to failure.

That changed when I transferred to UC Santa Barbara and took an Introduction to Cognitive Psychology course. The assigned reading was Ulric Neisser's magisterial *Cognitive Psychology*. Although more demanding than any textbook I'd been assigned, the book made it clear that one *could* study the construction of meaning. Sure, a good portion of meaning-making will always be a bit idiosyncratic, but Neisser's account of the lessons learned during the early years of the cognitive revolution made it clear that the information processing that gives rise to meaning obeys overarching principles. And the cleverness of the experiments conducted by the vanguard of that revolution – Broadbent, Sperling, Treisman, Sternberg – was truly inspiring.

So too was the early work on attribution theory taught by Anna Kun, a freshly-minted PhD from Bernard Weiner's lab at UCLA. That the meaning of an event changes when it is attributed to one cause versus another, and that people's causal attributions follow clear rules, furthered my growing sense that one could make real

Thomas Gilovich, Cornell University, USA.

progress in understanding how people interpret the events unfolding around them. When I then learned that giving people incentives to do things they enjoyed doing paradoxically led them to enjoy those things less, my concerns about meaning seemed less like a barrier to studying psychology than an invitation to do so. So what I most wanted, if they would have me, was to go to Stanford and work with Mark Lepper on intrinsic and extrinsic motivation.

Graduate School

Or so I thought. I did go to Stanford and had the great pleasure of working with Mark. We even ended up publishing a couple of papers on intrinsic motivation. But the papers had no impact (if it were possible for papers to *lower* one's H-index, these might do so). And my interests shifted as a result of the presence of several visitors on campus. I met the first two during an introduction-to-the-faculty seminar taught by Lee Ross, in which each week a pair of Stanford faculty would talk about their current research. I was eager to hear from the greats I had read so much about as an undergraduate – Al Bandura, Walter Mischel, Eleanor Maccoby, Gordon Bower, to name just a few of the distinguished faculty who were there at that time. But I would have to wait for those pleasures because the first session was devoted to a couple of visitors, Amos Tversky and Daniel Kahneman. It's embarrassing to admit this, but I remember being disappointed, thinking to myself "Why are we hearing from these guys; when are we going to get to the famous people?" As naive as my initial reaction was, at least I can say that when we discussed their 1974 *Science* paper, I could sense that their work was something special. So special that I gradually started to think of myself as a hybrid social psychologist/JDMer.

I did so in part because of the obvious respect (bordering on awe) that everyone had for Amos and Danny, and in part because their work addressed my initial interests with a beauty and depth I couldn't have imagined. Their work made it clear that the meaning people assign to even the most consequential information they encounter is contextually driven and often highly idiosyncratic. It is determined by what happens to spring to mind (availability), by what makes a good story (representativeness), and by the prevailing context (anchoring, framing). It was a heady time and a wonderful place to be a graduate student. Lee and Dick Nisbett were working on their book *Human Inference* so it was impossible not to get swept up in trying to understand the rules of intuitive psychology and the construction of meaning. Bob Abelson was a visitor my first year, teaching us about schemas and scripts in his *Things That Go Bump in the Mind* seminar. Later years would feature visits by Dale Miller (who was doing work on counterfactual thinking and what would later become norm theory), Phoebe Ellsworth (who taught us how to think straight about person perception – and everything else), and Bob Zajonc (who provided an influential counterpoint to the cognitive revolution underway).

An especially influential course was a seminar on Judgment Under Uncertainty taught by Amos. Beyond giving me a foundation for understanding important developments in social and cognitive psychology, the course was memorable for the presence of someone who always sat in the front, always asked a lot of questions and added his perspective on the material under discussion, and did so with an enviable self-assurance. I never saw this person anywhere other than in that seminar so I concluded that he wasn't a fellow graduate student. I asked around about who he was, but no one knew. More on him later.

My experiences at Stanford convinced me that I had stumbled on the right subject to study. But like many graduate students, I had my doubts about whether I had the right stuff to study it. One earlier experience that helped with those doubts was a time in an undergraduate course on motivation when the professor was having trouble explaining something and was being challenged by a couple of befuddled students. Out of the blue, she said to the class of eighty or so students, "Tom, I can't explain it any better; can you help me?" I don't remember whether I had any greater success than she did, but I wondered what she saw in me that I didn't see in myself that made her turn to me at that moment of desperation. Later doubts during graduate school were assuaged by the fact that the people at Stanford, especially Lee Ross, Mark Lepper, and Bob Abelson, seemed to take what I had to say seriously. It's hard to overstate how bolstering that was.

Although I didn't recognize its significance at the time, Mark, my principal advisor, was on leave for two of my four years at Stanford, Lee was gone for one of them, and he and I never did any research together back then. That meant that I worked more autonomously than I otherwise would have, which would come in handy when I left Stanford and assumed the duties of assistant professor. One of the things I worked on largely by myself, but which benefited quite a bit from conversations with Mark, Abelson, and Merrill Carlsmith, was an examination of how people come to think about a current dilemma (again, what it *means*) by drawing analogies to previous dilemmas. Whether a foreign policy crisis is seen as "another Vietnam," or as reminiscent of the run-up to World War II and the Allies' appeasement of Hitler, has a powerful influence on the decision of how forcefully to address the situation at hand. Of course, if the current situation truly is analogous to pre-WWII Europe, it's entirely reasonable to recommend a more resolute stance. But it appears that the analogies people draw can be based entirely on irrelevant similarities between the current situation and those in the past, such as whether the crisis was to be discussed in either "Winston Churchill Hall" (WWII) or "Dean Rusk Hall" (Vietnam). The paper reporting these findings (Gilovich, 1981) was my first-ever publication (the ones with Mark would come later) and provided some personal reassurance that even haphazard influences on how people decide what a given stimulus *means* could indeed be rigorously studied.

Cornell

Since getting my PhD in 1981, I have continued to pursue this topic during my forty years in the psychology department at Cornell. My efforts have included an examination of how being the second best person in the world at something can nonetheless be experienced as a failure because people can't let go of thinking about the one person who outperformed them (Medvec et al., 1995). It has also included investigations of how the meaning we assign to stimuli is determined by accessible reference points (Epley & Gilovich, 2001), by the academic training we receive (Frank et al., 1996), by the passage of time (Gilovich & Medvec, 1995), even by the color of the clothes a person is wearing (Frank & Gilovich, 1988). Perhaps the most pervasive, and the most fundamentally *social*, determinant of the meaning we assign to events is what we think others will make of them – and what those others will think of us as a result (Gilovich, Medvec, & Savitsky, 2000). I have also had the great pleasure of further exploring these in a few books intended for non-academic audiences (Belsky & Gilovich, 1999; Gilovich, 1991). Especially gratifying was one written with Lee Ross, who taught me so much of what I know about social psychology (Gilovich & Ross, 2015).

All of this work was done in an exceptionally supportive environment. Friendships with Dennis Regan and Daryl and Sandy Bem were personally gratifying and intellectually helpful. So too was being able to pick the impressive brain of Frank Keil for seventeen years until he left for Yale. (Traitor.) Especially helpful was the arrival in 1986 of a new assistant professor, David Dunning. He and I had what I consider a perfect overlap in interests, with both of us working on the border of social psychology and judgment/decision-making, with many shared interests, yet with sufficiently different flavors of those shared interests to provide balance and breadth to our department and to our graduate students. We also had different styles of working with students, which I believe worked to their benefit. It worked to mine and Dave's too, as our distinct-but-overlapping interests and styles created an identifiable Cornell brand of social psychology that played a role in our ability to win quite a few graduate student recruitment battles we waged with other esteemed departments. And what a great group of graduate students they were! One of the things that's most striking to me about having worked with so many great graduate students over my career is that I remember arriving at Cornell and thinking there were three critical components of the job: research, teaching, and graduate mentoring. I never would have guessed back then that the scariest of the three, and the one I thought I was least equipped to do, graduate mentoring, would turn out to be the most gratifying.

Another fortuitous development early on at Cornell took place in an Ithaca movie theater. Entering the theater, I recognized that guy I mentioned earlier from Amos's judgment class, and now I was *really* curious about who he was. My wife said, sensibly, that I should simply ask whether he had earlier taken a course from Tversky. But for whatever reason I demurred, and I continued to demur when we found ourselves seated directly in front of him. But my reticence finally ceased when I heard him utter the phrase "Kahneman and Tversky" to his companion. I now had my opportunity to find out who he was. "Dick Thaler" he said. "I'm in the business school here. You should come by and we should talk." I did, and that both started a friendship and gave me a front row seat at the creation of the field of behavioral economics.

The rise of behavioral economics has had many benefits. Personally, it widened the circle of like-minded behavioral scientists with whom I could discuss ideas. That included the members of what became the Cornell Center for Behavioral Economics and Decision Research, especially the economist Robert Frank. Never having taken an economics course, I received the great gift of getting an education in the discipline from Thaler and Frank, two economists who might as well be psychologists and therefore made my lessons go down easy. And I didn't even have to enter a classroom to receive those lessons: Bob and Dick taught me most of what I know about economics during weekly tennis games with each of them.

Another benefit of the rise of behavioral economics, not just to me personally but to all academic psychologists, was that it elevated the stature of psychology. Psychologists have long had some impact on policy, of course, especially when it comes to educational policy. But nowhere near the influence that economists have enjoyed. There is no White House Council of Psychological Advisors, for example. As the connections between psychologists and economists grew, psychologists found themselves with a seat at the table when it came to discussions of a broader range of issues. What psychology had to offer when it came to important societal problems suddenly became more widely recognized. And an eclectic group of economists and psychologists, of which I was proud to be a member, had a seat at the table when it came to providing input to US Presidential candidates from 2004 to 2020. We won some and lost some, but win or lose, I was consistently impressed by what my colleagues had to offer the campaign staffers.

Random Pleasures and Unintended Benefits

My participation in those campaigns exemplifies the delightful fact that being an academic psychologist can provide some unanticipated pleasures. Simply being on a college campus is one of them. People decide to become academics for many reasons, but I bet few have done so because they wanted to work in a pleasing physical environment, which most campuses are. So rather than work in a stifling office building in, say, downtown LA or Manhattan, academics in those cities get to walk around the oases that the USC and Columbia campuses are. And then there are those truly stunning work environments offered by some universities, Cornell among them.

If someone had asked me when I started at Cornell what I thought my most enjoyable professional experiences would be, it wouldn't have occurred to me that having each of my daughters take my class would top the list. I take teaching seriously and devote quite a bit of time and attention to planning my lectures. But knowing that one of them was in the audience made me attend even more to finding just the right example, just the right explanatory language, or just the right image or film clip. And anticipating how each idea would land with a member of the audience I knew extraordinarily well made the experience uncommonly rich and satisfying.

The most enduringly satisfying, did-not-plan-for-this experience of my academic life began with a phone call from an editor at Norton asking if I wanted to write a textbook with Dick Nisbett and Dacher Keltner. The editor did not know that Dick was one of my academic heroes and Dacher was one of my dearest friends. So I tried to hide my enthusiasm while we talked about terms, but I'm pretty sure I didn't succeed. Working with the two of them on the first two editions, and then with Serena Chen, a former star undergraduate at Cornell, on subsequent editions has been one of the absolute highlights of my career. When we get together somewhere and hole up for a few days to plan a new edition of the text, it's just magical. It's hard work because there's so much great research out there and only so many pages with which to cover it. But grappling with those questions of "in or out?" "what's new and exciting?" "where is the field headed?" and doing so with those three, well, that's as good as academic life gets.

Trends and Developments

Although the cognitive revolution in psychology is no longer a revolution, the emphasis on understanding the cognitive processes that underlie people's thoughts, feelings, decisions, and actions continues with great energy. But now that emphasis has been joined by robust efforts to pursue the same questions from other perspectives – including evolutionary, affective, cultural, and social influence perspectives. The addition of these other approaches, furthermore, is only one way in which the field of social psychology has broadened and become a more exciting and relevant discipline as a result. (Although referring to it as the *addition* of these perspectives is not quite right because they were always present, just obscured for many years by the long shadow of the information processing approach. *Growth* over the past quarter century is a more apt description.)

   To highlight how dominant the cognitive perspective was early in my career, I heard a joke during graduate school to the effect that those psychologists who did important work in one area of psychology and then tried to study emotion ended up looking like they lost fifteen IQ points. No one would say such a thing now. The study of emotion is as vibrant as any area of social psychology. It is also, ironically, well-suited to play the very role played by the cognitive psychologists who once mocked the study of emotion. That is, psychology is such a diverse discipline that one might wonder why all parts of it are in one department. Where's the unity among people studying income inequality, cell death during brain development, or visual perception? Since the 1960s, much of the unity was provided by the subdiscipline of cognitive psychology – and before then their predecessors, the learning theorists. For a long time, there were more cognitive social psychologists than any other kind, more cognitive developmentalists, and so on. But cognitive psychology no longer plays that unifying role; indeed, with the rise of neuroscience, it has sometimes had a divisive influence, with some psychology departments literally splitting in two, with one part occupied by one flavor or another of cognitive neuroscience, and the other part occupied by the "softer" areas.

   It's not a stretch to imagine affective science filling the unifying void left by cognitive psychology. That's because to understand emotion, it helps to know quite a bit of physiology, quite a bit of evolution, quite a bit of culture, and, of course, quite a bit of cognition. The study of emotion, then, is well suited to uniting the incredibly broad discipline of psychology.

The growth of affective approaches to supplement previously dominant cognitive approaches is only one way in which social psychology has broadened during my time in the field. Social neuroscience didn't exist until recently and is now a thriving part of our discipline. Moral psychology has also taken off, in the form of a more affectively oriented approach that looks more to Hume than to Kohlberg for inspiration. Another broadening has come from an upsurge in the amount of applied research being done, with more and more social psychologists who might not describe themselves as applied researchers nevertheless doing applied work.

Some of this applied research has taken place on the terrain shared with behavioral economics, with psychologists and like-minded economists taking what our field has learned about situational influence and the power of norms to nudge people into healthier eating, better educational habits, and wiser financial decisions. Another trend has been the application of what social psychologists have discovered about identity to make the educational environment more rewarding for members of historically marginalized groups.

This uptick in applied work will likely continue because today's most pressing problems are all problems of human behavior – climate change, the looming mass migrations resulting from a warmer planet, growing inequality, ethnocentrism, and the transformation of work as the next generation of robots-cum-AI systems proliferate. The world is turning to social psychology for solutions to these problems and social psychologists can be counted on to embrace the challenge.

In the current and looming upsurge of applied work, social psychology is more fully embracing its so-called Lewinian tradition. Broad theories and the lessons learned from laboratory experiments are put to use in trying to solve real-world problems. These efforts are usually met with some success, but almost as often with limited impact and notable shortcomings. Ideally, what is learned from these short-comings is used to modify the relevant theories and to inspire additional experimentation. But even with the most nuanced and accurate theories, there will always be gaps between what a necessarily generalized theory can offer and the particularities of the problem to which the theory is applied. Applied work is therefore necessarily a combination of science and art.

The Construction of Meaning, Continued

This interplay between the general and particular also plays out in my enduring interest in how people assign meaning to the situations, dilemmas, roadblocks, and opportunities they face. I often approach this question by considering "where the mind goes." That is, whenever we confront a stimulus, consider a prospect, or entertain a question, the mind goes somewhere. And where it goes has consequences. Even if it goes somewhere only briefly, it leaves tracks that influence the meaning we assign to the stimulus, prospect, or question at hand. We now know a lot about where the mind reflexively goes before more conscious control kicks in. All else being equal, it goes to negative prospects more readily than positive prospects. It goes to extreme targets of comparison (the happiest, most productive, and most socially connected around us) more readily than modal comparison targets. It often goes to what *can* happen (and hence, again, to extremes) when it would be more rational to go to what is *likely* to happen.

Understanding these tendencies provides considerable guidance when trying to predict and understand the meaning people assign to the stimuli they confront and the challenges and opportunities they face. But that guidance is nearly always imperfect. The particular details of any given challenge or opportunity can override those general tendencies and lead people to assign very different meanings to the stimuli before them. The general principles may be valid and generally helpful, but their influence will always be modulated by the particularities of the situation at hand.

Consider an example provided by my good friend, the economist Bob Frank. Bob is concerned about the threat posed by climate change and has thought a lot about what we might do to deal with it. Optimistic by nature, he argues that we could meet the challenge if only we would spend the money necessary to do so – by, for example, weaning the economy off fossil fuels, modernizing the electric grid, and investing in public transportation. Furthermore, he argues that it wouldn't be that painful to do so if we simply instituted a more progressive tax system. In a nutshell, his argument is that wealthy individuals whose taxes go up would be much happier on a cooler planet with higher taxes than on a hotter planet with lower taxes. Many of the rich don't see it that way, however, and they have used their influence to stifle efforts to make the tax system more progressive. But if they truly would be happier if the tax system were changed, why don't they see that way?

Well, where do their minds go when they ask themselves "how would I feel if my taxes went up?" The most natural place for their minds to go would be how they felt the last time their taxes went up. But since taxes on the wealthy have only gone *down* during the lifetime of any wealthy person living today, their minds can't go there. If they did, Bob argues, the wealthy would realize that they wouldn't be less happy in a world of higher taxes because their wealthy friends would be paying higher taxes too and their position on the ladder of wealth would not change. And our happiness is driven more by relative than absolute standing.

But if they can't think of a time when their taxes went up, where are their minds likely to go when thinking about what life would be like if they did? To other occasions when they suffered a financial loss – when they got divorced; when they suffered a medical calamity and went through a period when they couldn't work; when their estate was destroyed by a fire, etc. In those circumstances, they suffered a financial hit that was not shared by others, and their relative standing was diminished. If it's occasions like these that spring to mind, it's not surprising that wealthy people would assume they'd be less happy if their taxes increased – and therefore argue for other ways to deal with climate change.

So I find myself where I was near the beginning of my career. I remain convinced that understanding how people assign meaning to the stimuli they encounter is critical to understanding and predicting their behavior; that many of the most important drivers of the assignment of meaning can be studied empirically and used to address important real-world problems; and that those general rules will often fall short and the meaning people derive will be influenced by the nuances of the unique features of the situation at hand.

Is that latter limitation frustrating? At times, sure, but not generally. The challenge continues.

Suggested Reading

Belsky, G., & Gilovich, T. (1999). *Why Smart People Make Big Money Mistakes—and How to Correct Them: Lessons from the New Science of Behavioral Economics.* New York: Simon & Schuster.

Epley, N., & Gilovich, T. (2001). Putting adjustment back in the anchoring and adjustment heuristic: An examination of self-generated and experimenter-provided anchors. *Psychological Science, 12,* 391–396.

Frank, M. G., & Gilovich, T. (1988). The dark side of self and social perception: Black uniforms and aggression in professional sports. *Journal of Personality and Social Psychology, 54,* 74–85.

Frank, R. H., Gilovich, T., & Regan, D. T. (1996). Do economists make bad citizens? *Journal of Economic Perspectives, 10,* 187–192.

Gilovich, T. (1981). Seeing the past in the present: The effect of associations to familiar events on judgments and decisions. *Journal of Personality and Social Psychology, 40,* 797–808.

(1991). *How We Know What Isn't So: The Fallibility of Human Reason in Everyday Life.* New York: Free Press.

Gilovich, T., & Medvec, V. H. (1995). The experience of regret: What, when, and why. *Psychological Review, 102,* 379–395.

Gilovich, T., Medvec, V. H., & Savitsky, K. (2000). The spotlight effect in social judgment: An egocentric bias in estimates of the salience of one's own actions and appearance. *Journal of Personality and Social Psychology, 78,* 211–222.

Gilovich, T., & Ross, L. (2015). *The Wisest in the Room: How You Can Benefit from Social Psychology's Most Powerful Insights.* New York: Free Press.

Medvec, V. H., Madey, S., & Gilovich, T. (1995). When less is more: Counterfactual thinking and satisfaction among Olympic medal winners. *Journal of Personality and Social Psychology, 69,* 603–610.

45 Meetings with Remarkable Men: A Fortunate Journey in Social Psychology

Miles Hewstone

Happy is the man that findeth wisdom, and the man that getteth understanding. For the merchandise of it is better than the merchandise of silver, and the gain thereof than fine gold. She is more precious than rubies: and all the things thou canst desire are not to be compared unto her.

(Proverbs, 3:13–15)

Intrepid European students of my generation (1970s) were drawn to travel overland to Katmandu, as I did in 1978, just after completing my Bachelor's degree. A popular book was G. I. Gurdjieff's (1963) *Meetings with Remarkable Men*. The author, a spiritualist, set out as a young man in search of wisdom, traveling in remote regions of Central Asia to meet "Seekers of Truth" and recording their influence on him. Setting out on this chapter, I have become very aware of my own meetings with remarkable men, a series of scholars, brilliant and influential in their own distinctive ways, who guided my career, implicitly or explicitly. While writing I also came across the notion of "unusual attitudes," a certification obtained by air pilots, which teaches them what to do in the event of, for example, inadvertently flying upside down or going into a tail spin. In this chapter I record the huge debt of gratitude to those who taught me to face our field's challenges. I follow the conventional chronology of an academic career, touching on the three main areas where I hope I have made significant contributions (attribution, social influence, and intergroup relations) and some of the key people and places which are most significant to this work.

Bright College Days: Bristol

I arrived at Bristol University in the autumn of 1975 to study for my Bachelor's degree. My aim was eventually to study clinical psychology, even though that subject was not taught until our third and final year. While I waited for clinical psychology, I fell under the influence of social psychology. The three faculty in the area were Henri

Miles Hewstone is now Emeritus Professor, Oxford University, UK. I am grateful to Saul Kassin for his lapidary editing, and to Robin Martin, Hermann Swart, and Charles Judd for comments on an earlier version of this chapter.

Tajfel, Howard ("Howie") Giles, and John Turner. It was like taking a course in theology taught by the Holy Trinity. They were all brilliant, and different in their styles, and they influenced me in different ways.

Tajfel did not teach us until the final year. He was not an inspiring lecturer, but he taught a course on intergroup relations using as notes the outline for his famous 1978 volume in which he expounded his ideas about the fundamental importance of social categorization and developed his ground-breaking Social Identity Theory (Tajfel, 1978). He struck me as the quintessential European intellectual, and the impetus for his work, from his own experience of the horrors of the Third Reich, gave his words especial power, conveyed in his unique accent of one born in Poland, but who later became a French speaker. He lectured us at 9 a.m. on a Friday morning, and he was the only lecturer we would get up for at that time. Sometimes his secretary would knock on the door of the lecture room and announce, "Professor Tajfel, it's Paris [or Geneva, or Bologna ...] on the line ..." and he would head off to take the call in the middle of our lecture. This all added to his aura, his charisma, and his enigma. I was especially touched when Henri wrote to me after my final results, to congratulate me. Only three of us had obtained First Class Honors (*summa cum laude*), the first to be awarded in several years (pre-dating today's grade inflation), and to his satisfaction all three were very much students of social psychology, who all later pursued careers in our field (the other two being Stephen Reicher and Penelope Oakes). I later learned that there might have been another reason why Henri took pleasure from my achievements. At a social event he forced a glass of whiskey on me (which I don't even drink, but this was Henri Tajfel) and subtly asked me, "Miles, has your name always been Hewstone?" He really wanted me to be a *Hewstein*, a fellow Jew.

To my great good fortune Howard Giles taught us in the first year and his lectures were packed and brilliant. He imparted his wisdom with infectious enthusiasm and contagious humor, delivered in his incomparable Cardiff accent. It is some tribute to his classes that, fifty years on, when we meet occasionally, I can still tease him about his phrases and brilliant didactic devices, and his ability to turn complex ideas into simply testable propositions.

John Turner was more serious, even stern, as he introduced us to his insightful, sometimes searing, critiques of leading theories in the social psychology of groups. Bristol at this time was a wonderful place to be studying social psychology, not only because of the faculty but also because of the enthusiasm among the students. After each lecture – most of which were delivered in the elegant Georgian villa in 8–10 Berkeley Square – we would pour into "Joe's Café," and discuss over endless cups of (truly dreadful) instant coffee. My switch from clinical to social psychology was entirely due to Howard. A group of us were chatting in "Joe's" after final exams when he popped his head round the door and, worryingly, beckoned me outside. He told me about a funded doctoral position that had come up in Oxford, saying, "having read your exams, I thought you should be interested ... get your ass over there – Friday").

Because of my intention to pursue clinical psychology, I had conducted a research project in the area (using G. A. Kelly's, 1955, Personal Construct Theory to assess the impact of brief hospitalization for acute depression), a fortunate choice. I was asked to bring, and talk about, my project at the Oxford interview. And I immediately found common ground with one member of the faculty, Jos Jaspars, also a Kelly enthusiast.

Graduate School: The Dreaming Spires of Oxford

In the immortal words of Tom Lehrer's famous song, "Bright College Days," I was already at the end of those "carefree days that fly" and headed for another line in his song, "Ivy-covered professors in ivy-covered halls." Although the professor I headed for was covered in laurels, rather than ivy. I went to Oxford in the autumn of 1978. Bristol had provided me with an excellent general education in psychology, especially social psychology, and, more specifically, a detailed understanding of what caused and maintained intergroup conflict. What, I later realized, it had hardly touched upon was how to *reduce* that conflict, and that later became the major passion and commitment of my academic career.

Henri Tajfel had one final, invaluable piece of advice for me. He wrote me a second personal letter, this time emphasizing that his advice was unasked for, and strictly confidential (but I am sure I can share it by now). He told me in no uncertain terms to make sure that my supervisor would be Jos Jaspars – it was one of the best pieces of advice I have ever been given. Jos was a giant in every sense – a massive physical specimen (prevented from representing the Netherlands in the decathlon, due to the boycott of the Melbourne Olympics in 1956), he had an intellect to match. Attribution theory had not, until then, featured in my plans, but that was what Jos was working on at that time, and I followed the advice I had been given. It led, in time, to a series of publications based, on the one hand, on a rather artificial intrapersonal analysis of how we perceive causal information (for an overview, see Hewstone, 1989). This included a sophisticated and novel analysis of consensus, consistency, and distinctiveness in Kelley's (1967) "Cube" model, based on identifying necessary and sufficient conditions for the occurrence of an effect. Our model was quite different from Kelley's idea that the perceiver, somewhat implausibly, conducted an implicit analysis of variance, and was more accurate in predicting attributions. On the other hand, we considered the more social aspects of attribution, especially how explanations varied dramatically, and predictably, as a function of the social group membership of actors and perceivers.

In hindsight, my choice of attribution as a dissertation topic was fortunate in many ways. First, it allowed me to work with Jos. Second, there was an active "attribution group" in the department, which met for regular seminars, a presentation at which was a key rite of passage. I recall getting utterly confused with a new analysis and calling Jos in some desperation before my talk. He calmly said not to worry, and that I should come over to his house, where he guided me through the analyses in intricate detail. Third, the group included Frank Fincham – a brilliant, intense student – and Adrian Furnham, smart and funny; the two of them were informal graduate mentors, always generous with their time and knowledge, and helped me to settle in quickly as the only new student that year. Finally, attribution theory was "tractable" – although much of it now seems hopelessly artificial, it was a well-developed field, with established paradigms, yet still-unanswered questions – and provided a perfect environment in which to learn about and implement complex designs, develop one's research and analytic skills, accrue initial publications, and gradually move toward more social questions. Looking back, this time feels like playing the "The Glass Bead Game," depicted in Hermann Hesse's novel of that title, the pursuit of the *vita contemplativa* (or contemplative life).

One of the key things I learned from Jos was how to interrogate and interpret data. Here, I don't mean statistics, with which I have always struggled. I mean, rather, thinking about the patterns to look for in data, and how to do so. Another rite of passage for his students was for Jos to stretch up and pass down a rather ragged manuscript copy of Coombs's (1964) book, *Theory of Data*. I can't pretend to have understood much of it, but it led to many fascinating discussions with Jos, and I have, over my career, repeatedly managed to suggest analytic strategies that had not occurred to my, statistically superior, students or postdocs. Another lesson imbibed from Jos was that one should follow B. J. Winer's maxim, and always remember that "statistics is the tool and not the master."

Other anecdotes from graduate school illustrate just how much things have changed, and the value of a strong support network of fellow students. For example, running an analysis of variance, then, involved typing a stack of punch cards, cycling them round to the central computer center, and waiting until the next morning for the results (unless you had mistyped a card, in which case there wouldn't be any). Preparing questionnaires involved typing (again, faultlessly) a stencil, donning an apron as if bound for some Masonic ritual, and then spending the afternoon in a small cupboard, with only a Gestetner printing machine for company. You emerged later, if lucky, covered in ink stains, some of which would typically adorn the printed copies too. At risk of offending today's students, who doubtless have it harder in other ways, I think we did have it harder then. But I also realize that I am getting dangerously close to the Monty Python "Four Yorkshiremen" sketch, whose protagonists reminisce and retell how impossibly hard their upbringing was, ending with the immortal line, ". . . and if you tell that to the young people today, they won't believe you."

Graduate school was, of course, not all work. The *Stakhanovites* had fun too, and much of this was due to Michael Argyle, a wonderfully kind, funny, and literally colorful man. His dress sense was, at best, original – characterized by clashing colors and a striped tie with a check jacket. He invited us to his home periodically for social evenings, often after a talk by a big-league visitor, the highlight of which was the obligatory round of charades. Michael's absolute favorite, between more obvious and less testing titles, was to give the visitor the task of acting out Cook and Campbell's (1979), *Quasi-Experimentation: Design and Analysis Issues for Field Settings*. Graduate students also acted in regular Christmas time comic revues, for which all faculty were fair game. I retired early from thespianism, however, when we also performed at one of Howard Giles's international conferences. A light-hearted skit encountered a sociologist who did not share our sense of humor; he stormed out, threatening to sue.

All too quickly graduate school ended. I had applied for, and got, a tenured job, but my heart was set on trying to become more of a European social psychologist, like those "remarkable men" who had impressed me. I talked it over with Jos, and he calmly assured me that if I were good enough, which he assured me I was, then finding a safe job would not be a problem; I should tarry a while, read and write more, and keep learning. I have subsequently given this advice to all my students too.

Postdoctoral Paradise: Paris and Tübingen

I headed to Paris to work with Serge Moscovici, and to learn more about his notion of *social representations*. We used to meet over regular lunches at his local restaurant where, aided by the red wine, my French improved (at least, I relaxed) and could grill him as well as my *bavette* steak. He would roam all over the field of social science as the lunch progressed, leaning further and further back, running his hand through his distinctive long, gray, curling mop, his voice becoming ever quieter, and harder to hear. I had to respond by leaning further in, desperate to catch, and understand, his *bons mots*.

We never did any empirical research together, but we co-authored some chapters, one of which was a desperate attempt, on my part, to clarify some of the key aspects of social representations (essentially, bodies of shared social knowledge, which illustrate how society represents ideas, such as, in the prototypical study, the extent and ways in which ideas about psychoanalysis have penetrated French society) and consider how they might affect lay causal attributions. The concept was, however, too vague and descriptive for me; I could not see how you could test such a "theory." Although it had some influence on my later work (see below), I was ultimately much more influenced by Moscovici's brilliant writings on minority influence, and seeds for my own work on that topic (see below) were definitely sown in Paris.

Fifteen months later, I swapped Paris for Tübingen to work with Wolfgang Stroebe. After Jos's tragically early death in 1985 I was bereft, and Wolfgang helped to fill that gap. He welcomed me warmly and played a key role in my academic socialization. Wolfgang seemed much closer to the American scene and the American model of training, and I am grateful to him for steering me in that direction, to complement the more European approach. Wolfgang's research interests are eclectic, offering multiple opportunities to learn.

I enjoyed my work with Wolfgang, and my life in South Germany – not least because I met my wife there, assisting on his bereavement project with his wife, Maggie – and stayed for a second year. I was studying common-sense understanding of the European Community in four different countries, a project inspired by the idea of social representations – I wanted to understand how different nations understood the Community, and why the British, especially, were such reluctant Europeans (read, over thirty years later, it does not make Brexit look at all surprising).

My time with Wolfgang was also beneficial in two other ways, which had more to do with being the right (lucky) person, in the right place, at the right time. As President of what was then called the European Association of Experimental Social Psychology,

Wolfgang had proposed both an edited "European" textbook (more suitable for, and aimed specifically at, students in Europe's universities) and founding a new journal, the *European Review of Social Psychology*, as a counterpart to Berkowitz's esteemed, but more US-focused, *Advances in Experimental Social Psychology*. Through sheer good fortune I found myself co-editing both publications (for thirty years), which, somewhat, mitigated my progress toward being an academic who knows more and more, about less and less.

Paradise Lost: Time for a Job

After just over three years of a carefree life – sheltered from both teaching and administrative duties – I took my first teaching job, delightedly, at my *alma mater*, Bristol. I could not have wished for a better mentor at this stage of my career than Howard Giles. He also, generously, gave me full support, after just two years, to take up a fellowship at the Center for Advanced Study in the Behavioral Sciences (CASBS) in Palo Alto. This was, in every sense, Paradise Regained: from rubbing shoulders with approximately fifty luminaries from all fields, to daily games of volleyball when your arm ached from all that writing you could do – it was bliss. The eminent psychologist Gardner Lindzey was Director at that time and took me under his wing as not only a very youthful Fellow, but also a fellow social psychologist; but it was Bob Scott, Associate Director, who made the Center the extraordinary place it was – he was everything from mentor, to confessor, to therapist, to broker of cross-disciplinary links and, of course, volleyball coach. The Fellow I most enjoyed meeting, and gained from, another "remarkable man" on my fortunate journey, was Charles (Chick) Judd, a social psychologist and brilliant statistician. He was always generous, and patient, with his time explaining and advising, notably introducing me to the key distinction between statistical mediation and moderation, which was later crucial to my work on intergroup contact (see below).

On my return from Palo Alto to reality (Bristol), I followed the advice of Chick and others, and moved (back, after Bristol days) into intergroup relations, where I sought to develop a new approach to intergroup contact, derived from both social identity theory and studies of cognitive processes in stereotype change. This approach saw contact as the coming together of group members as representatives of, not individuals divorced from, their groups. We (Hewstone & Brown, 1986) argued, contrary to dominant views at that time, that social categories should still be salient, to some degree, when members of different groups were engaged in positive contact, or else any change in prejudicial attitudes achieved would simply not be generalized to the outgroup as a whole. I was fortunate, during this period, to be invited several times as a visiting professor to Padova, Italy by Dora Capozza, an extraordinarily kind and generous friend and colleague. We had many wonderful discussions over sumptuous meals and she sent me some great students, among whom was *amico mio*, Alberto Voci, who has made crucial contributions to our work on intergroup contact over many years (see below).

From Bristol, I then went to Mannheim, Germany, for two years, and then to Cardiff, which, at that time, was devoting huge resources to recruitment and infrastructure, and was establishing an impressive, well-resourced department, albeit one in which the achievements of social psychology were esteemed considerably less than those of other areas (a repeated experience in my well-traveled career, and one which I genuinely cannot explain). The move to Cardiff had the benefit of instigating another long-term collaboration, on social influence, with my dear friend, Robin Martin.

Moscovici's (1980) influential conversion theory of minority influence – that minorities triggered deeper message processing ("validation"), whereas majorities triggered a shallower "comparison" with the source of the message – was not consistent with the evidence. Inspired by cognitive models of persuasion, we presented respondents with messages ostensibly from numerical majority or minority sources, whose arguments were either strong or weak. We developed a series of original paradigms, often dreamed up over dangerously unhealthy all-day breakfasts in the nearby "Warm as Toast" café (though café is pushing it), to show that which source had greater influence depended on the context (see Martin & Hewstone, 2008). As Moscovici (1980) predicted, the minority could have greater influence (and its message was processed more systematically), but only under specific conditions. Under other conditions, however, the majority had greater influence (although its message was not processed more systematically). We even found that under some conditions a majority source triggered as much processing as a minority source; whereas under other conditions a minority source triggered as little processing as a majority source.

Toward the end of my time in Cardiff I felt desperate to get away, and to recharge my batteries. CASBS, incredibly, came to the rescue again, and I spent another idyllic year as part of the Millennial Class. I then returned, briefly, to Cardiff and, finally, to Oxford again, where I achieved many a graduate's dream, of returning to their (doctoral) *alma mater*, and focused my work almost entirely on intergroup contact. I established the Centre for the Study of Intergroup Conflict, thanks to uninterrupted external funding over many years, and the skills of my administrative assistant, Rachel New, who marshaled a growing group, and helped me, mostly, to manage the demands of a high undergraduate teaching load, college as well as departmental responsibilities, and a large group of graduate students.

A "don" at Oxford is blessed with clever, and some truly brilliant, undergraduate and graduate students (unnamed, because it would be invidious to name only some, when so many have established academic careers). The best of the graduates and postdocs made key contributions to the burgeoning research program on contact, especially by making it ever more sophisticated statistically (especially in the use of structural equation modeling, multilevel modeling, and social network analysis). This work involved lab experiments, large-scale surveys, and social network studies. Overall, it developed Allport's (1954) famous "Contact Hypothesis" into a fully-developed "Intergroup Contact Theory" (Hewstone, 2009) in which we, *inter alia*: (1) explored new ways to measure and validate intergroup contact (e.g., with round robin designs and social network analysis), so that it did not rely solely on self-reports;

(2) provided extensive evidence for contact effects from longitudinal studies, whereas previously cross-sectional studies had predominated; (3) identified key mediators (notably intergroup anxiety) and moderators (notably the salience of group memberships during contact) of the relationship between contact and prejudice, explaining how and when it worked; (4) accumulated evidence for secondary-transfer effects of contact, whereby contact with one outgroup reduced prejudice toward other, unrelated groups; (5) accrued evidence for forms of contact other than face-to-face contact (notably "extended contact," whereby having one or more ingroup friends who had an outgroup friend was associated with lower prejudice); and (6) demonstrated the value of living in neighborhoods where other people reported higher levels of contact (indicating the potential of contact to reduce widespread societal, not merely interpersonal, prejudice). Much of this work was carried out under challenging conditions for the Contact Hypothesis (notably in Northern Ireland), where our findings contributed to government policy. Social psychology was theoretically sophisticated, methodologically robust, and practically useful.

Looking Back: The Best of All Possible Worlds?

Writing autobiographically, the risk of a Panglossian retrospective looms, not least because one has survived, even succeeded in many respects. But a more granular analysis suggests that, as in the Book of Genesis, there were times of plenty as well as of famine, papers and grants whose rejection can still sting (even though, over my career, I have no cause for complaint on either the publication or funding front). In each of the three main areas I have worked, I hope I have left a substantial footprint.

To any student reading this piece, I can only say what worked for me, which was to find something that I not only cared about, but that had real-world importance. For this, we must begin in the real world, and identify phenomena of interest there, that are worthy of further investigation in carefully designed research studies. Failure to do things that way round we risk ending up like the "ingenious architect" Gulliver encountered on his famous "Travels," at the "Grand Academy of Lagado," who had "contrived a new method for building houses, by beginning at the roof, and working downward to the foundation" (Swift, 1950, pp. 107–108).

I feel that it is somehow my *duty* as a *social* psychologist to study, and try to contribute to, significant social issues. Failure to do so leaves us in the same bracket as the economists criticized by Nobel laureate Paul Samuelson, "highly trained athletes who never ran a race" (www.theguardian.com/politics/2009/dec/14/paul-samuelson-obituary; retrieved November 22, 2021). Far from being opposed to lab experiments, I endorse Festinger's (1953) view that an adequate social psychology should continually move back and forth between the laboratory and the field. I think this is crucial, because so much of social psychological research is, for me, still artificial, indicating little improvement since Allport's (1968) stinging rebuke over fifty years ago that: "many contemporary studies seem to shed light on nothing more than a narrow phenomenon studied under specific conditions … some current investigations seem to end up in elegantly polished triviality – snippets of empiricism, but nothing more" (p. 68).

Put more poetically, I chose to follow the route envisaged by Hermann Hesse in *The Glass Bead Game*, not "to flee from the *vita activa* to the *vita contemplativa*, nor vice versa, but to keep moving forward while alternating between the two, being at home in both, partaking of both" (Hesse, 1972, p. 223). But reliving my own career trajectory, I am fully aware how fortuitous some of the key steps have been, and I am enormously grateful for my meetings with remarkable *people* (both men and women) in many wonderful places.

Suggested Reading

Allport, G. W. (1954). *The Nature of Prejudice*. Reading, MA: Addison-Wesley.
    (1968). The historical background of modern social psychology. In G. Lindzey (Ed.), *Handbook of Social Psychology* (Vol. 1, pp. 1–80). Reading, MA: Addison-Wesley.
Cook, T. D., & Campbell, D. T (1979). *Quasi-Experimentation: Design and Analysis Issues for Field Settings*. Chicago, IL: Rand McNally.
Coombs, C. H. (1964). *Theory of Data*. New York: John Wiley & Sons.
Festinger, L. (1953). Laboratory experiments. In L. Festinger & D. Katz (Eds.), *Research Methods in the Behavioral Sciences* (pp. 136–172). New York: Dryden.
Gurdjieff, G. I. (1963). *Meetings with Remarkable Men*. London: Routledge & Kegan Paul.
Hesse, H. (1972). *The Glass Bead Game*. Harmondsworth: Penguin.
Hewstone, M. (1989). *Causal Attribution: From Cognitive Processes to Collective Beliefs*. Oxford: Basil Blackwell.
    (2009). Living apart, living together? The role of intergroup contact in social integration. *Proceedings of the British Academy, 162*, 243–300.
Hewstone, M., & Brown, R. (Eds.) (1986). *Contact and Conflict in Intergroup Encounters*. Oxford: Blackwell.
Kelley, H. H. (1967). Attribution theory in social psychology. In D. Levine (Ed.), *Nebraska Symposium on Motivation* (Vol. 15, pp. 192–238). Lincoln, NE: University of Nebraska Press.
Kelly, G. A. (1955). *The Psychology of Personal Constructs*. New York: Norton.
Martin, R., & Hewstone, M. (2008). Majority versus minority influence, message processing and attitude change: The source-context-elaboration model. *Advances in Experimental Social Psychology, 40*, 237–326.
Moscovici, S. (1980). Toward a theory of conversion behavior. In L. Berkowitz (Ed.), *Advances in Experimental Social Psychology* (Vol. 13, pp. 209–239). New York: Academic Press.
Swift, J. (1950). *Gulliver's Travels*. New York: Harper.
Tajfel, H. (Ed.) (1978). *Differentiation between Social Groups*. London: Academic Press.
Turner, J. C., & Giles, H. (Eds.) (1981). *Intergroup Behaviour*. Oxford: Basil Blackwell.

46   Dear Vera, Chuck, and Dave

Daniel Gilbert

I write these words two days before my 64th birthday, which the Beatles inadvertently defined as the beginning of old age. Boomers do not argue with the Beatles. Although I feel old enough to be a grandfather (which is presumably good news for my three grandchildren), I do not feel old enough to be a pillar of social psychology, or of anything else for that matter. A bit of Googling confirms that I am the second youngest contributor to this volume – the guy who sneaked in just before they slammed the door – so that feeling is not entirely unwarranted. It is an honor to be included in a book with the world's greatest living social psychologists, of course, but also a bit of a horror to realize that from here on out people will be asking more about my past than my present. "What are you studying these days?" is about to be replaced by "What was the world like when dinosaurs roamed?"

Oh well. Let it be.

I love writing but I hate writing about myself, and I turn down nearly all invitations to do so. The reason I agreed to tell the story of my long and winding road in this volume is that along its stretches I've had the privilege to know some *true* pillars, and this chapter is an excuse to tell you about them.

Phil Dick

Every love affair with psychology starts with a blind date. We all stumbled on it one way or another, usually by taking an introductory course in college. My blind date was blinder than most. I dropped out of high school at the age of 17. My friends and I bought a derelict 72-passenger school bus and drove it around the country, seeking truth, enlightenment, and high adventure, with emphasis on the high part. I got off the bus in 1975 in Denver, determined to become a science fiction writer because I was smitten with a woman who *was* a science fiction writer and shameless mimicry seemed like the best way to impress her. Which it did. For a short time. But more importantly, it made me realize that I loved writing. My stories included the requisite spaceships and aliens, of course, but their focus was always on humans – on their lives and hearts and minds. What would happen if a second-class citizen in a future racist

Daniel Gilbert, Edgar Pierce Professor of Psychology, Harvard University, USA.

society found a clever way to become the oppressor rather than the oppressed? What would happen if an intellectually disabled prisoner discovered a secret about the end of the world? What would happen if a robot who lusted after its owner was transformed into her human paramour – only to find true love with her computer? Those were the kinds of ideas I wanted to explore.

One day I sent a fan letter to my favorite author, Philip K. Dick. Remarkably, he wrote back. Then I wrote back and he wrote back and we corresponded for the rest of his too-short life. Phil read my early stories and offered encouragement, and in one of his letters, he wrote: "I predict that you will be a long-remembered author when the Game is finally over. Remember that you heard it from me. I want credit for having noticed." *Me? A long-remembered author? Gosh, if Phil thinks I'm going to be a long-remembered author then I probably ought to publish something.*

And so I did, selling my stories to *Amazing Stories* and *Isaac Asimov's Science Fiction Magazine* and various other magazines and book anthologies. To sharpen my writing skills, I went downtown one day to enroll in a creative writing course at the local community-college. When I arrived, the woman at the registration desk regretted to inform me that the creative writing course was full, but did so anyway. Then she leafed through a big ledger and announced that there was one course in the same time slot that still had a few empty seats: Introduction to Psychology. I said yes – or more likely, why not?

Gary Stern and Carolyn Simmons

As first dates go, that course was just okay. Some of the material was interesting, but most of it wasn't. I didn't care about the stages of cognitive development, the location of the hippocampus, the symptoms of schizophrenia, or the mechanics of color vision. I wasn't a baby or a brain surgeon, I wasn't mentally ill, and my eyes worked just fine. On the other hand, that stuff about obedience and conformity, about helping and attitude change ... now *that* was pretty cool. But the main thing I learned on that first date was that I loved school when adults weren't forcing me to go and treating me like a child when I arrived. The bad thing about high school, I now realized, had been the high part.

A few community-college courses and one GED later, I was a full-time student at the University of Colorado at Denver, and I decided to investigate psychology a bit more. Which courses should I take? I noticed that the psychology department offered two courses that were both called "Social Psychology" but that were taught by different professors, and I reasoned that any area of psychology that warranted two courses must be twice as good as the other areas. So I signed up for both.

Best. Second. Date. Ever. It was the enlightenment I never found on the school bus. It was like seeing in color for the very first time. I sat in those courses, lecture after lecture, and thought, "Yes, *this*. This is it. These are the thoughts I've always wanted to think but didn't have a name for. These are the ideas I've been exploring in fiction while social psychologists have been exploring them in fact. And they have a method for getting real answers to all the hard questions I've been asking myself since high school – not the vague, hand-wavey pseudo-answers that philosophy and religion offered me, but clear, straight answers that stand up to scrutiny and don't require me to close one eye and have a little faith. These people *really* know who we are and how we got this way – and I want to be one of them."

Is it possible to feel like you're returning home when you've never been home before? Is it possible to be homeless your entire life and not know it until you walk through the front door? My professors in these courses were Gary Stern and Carolyn Simmons, and neither of them made much of a mark on psychology. But they made a mark on me. Like Phil Dick, they noticed. They took special interest when they didn't have to. Carolyn read my science fiction stories and hired me as her T.A. the next semester, and Gary let me work in his lab. When I decided to apply to graduate school a few years later, they both helped me – and were as surprised as I was when Princeton overlooked my missing high school diploma and accepted me despite my poor graduation skills.

Phil, Carolyn, Gary. The pillars you see stand on the pillars you don't.

Ned Jones

Everyone saw Edward Ellsworth Jones. When I arrived at Princeton in 1981, Ned was perhaps the most famous and well-respected social psychologist in the world. I didn't have the slightest idea who he was. I'd applied to Princeton because I'd heard of it, and I'd accepted their offer because they had nice housing. I'd never thought about what I'd actually do there, or with whom.

Ned was 55 years old when I arrived and looking to cure his habit of working with highly qualified, well-trained graduates of prestigious universities. At least that was my theory about why he chose me as his advisee without ever having spoken to me. From the moment we met, we got along famously. I thought he was brilliant and inscrutable, he thought I was brilliant and unvarnished, so he varnished me while I scrutinized him. Ned introduced me to one foundational idea in social psychology after another (most of them his own) ranging from attribution theory to strategic self-presentation. He would give me papers to read (most of them his own) and I would read them, type out long responses filled with questions and ideas, and leave those responses in his mailbox late at night. Once a week he'd call me into his office and we'd go through my responses. "This one is fine," he'd say, turning pages. "And this one too. And this one is clever, and this one might even be right." "Well, which should we work on?" I'd ask, and he'd reply, "None of them. Keep thinking."

So I did. Ned's papers referenced other papers which referenced other papers, so I sat in the library for a year and read them all. This may be hard for modern graduate students to fathom, but it never occurred to me to worry about my career. I assumed that someday I would probably publish something because that's what psychologists seemed to do, and someday I'd probably get a job because, after all, I'd need one, but I had no idea how either of those things happened, and anyway, they weren't happening now, so I gave as much thought to them as a toddler does to puberty. Princeton seemed happy to pay me to read and talk to Ned, and Ned seemed happy about it too, so what wasn't to like? Ned sent me back to my office to "keep thinking" over and over again, and gaining his approval was the only progress I cared about making.

One day Ned called me in. "Now this one," he said, holding up one of my responses, "*this* is a good idea." Ned had taught me all about attribution theory, which described the rules by which rational people should make inferences about others. Ned was most interested in the cases in which people didn't follow those rules, and especially in the phenomenon he had discovered in 1967 and called the "observer bias," but that some sparky assistant professor named Lee Ross had recently rechristened "the Fundamental Attribution Error." Contrary to attribution theory's rational rules, people tended to attribute other people's behaviors to dispositions, even when those behaviors were clearly caused by situational constraints. Some psychologists had suggested that this was just an experimental artifact – that it happened simply because the experimenter had not made the situational constraints sufficiently salient. I suggested to Ned that we prove those psychologists wrong by designing a study in which the participants themselves *were* the situational constraints. It doesn't get more salient than that. Ned loved my idea about what we would come to call "perceiver-induced constraint," and reality loved it too because our studies worked (Gilbert & Jones, 1986). The editor at *JPSP* was last, but came to love it eventually.

Talking to Ned, reading, thinking, and publishing that paper – that's basically what I did with my four years of graduate school. When I went on the job market it was flush with good positions for newly minted social psychologists, but I got just two interviews, and just one offer. And that offer came my way only because the people who extended it – Janet Spence and Bill Swann at the University of Texas – were good friends with Ned and didn't want him to feel bad about his rather unpromising student. But a consolation prize is still a prize, so in 1985, I moved to Austin to find out what being pitied by Ned's friends might bring me.

Dan Wegner

It brought me a lot: mentoring and friendship from Bill Swann, kindness and support from a few other colleagues, and a very large department that thoroughly ignored me, leaving me to my bliss. That bliss was a group of graduate students who were barely younger than I was, and equally eager to do something big. What should it be?

Attribution theory dominated social psychology's intellectual agenda for more than a decade, but what I didn't quite realize during my time at Princeton was that interest in it had peaked and that a brand new something called "social cognition" was in ascendance – a "something" because it wasn't an idea or a theory like attribution theory was, or like cognitive dissonance theory had been before that, but rather, it was a new way of thinking about everything. Rather than studying what people did when exposed to information, we could now study what they were *doing* with it. Using the techniques and metaphors of the new cognitive psychology, we could develop and test models of the underlying cognitive processes that gave rise to all the marvelous behavioral phenomena that previous generations of social psychologists had uncovered.

Building on the work of George Quattrone (a former student of Ned's), my students and I created a model of the cognitive processes that underlie attribution. We suggested that attributions were made in a sequence of steps, the first of which was unconscious and automatic and the second of which was conscious and controlled. The first step generated a dispositional inference and the second step corrected it with information about situational constraints. Because the second process was both later and more resource-intensive, it often failed to happen, resulting in – of all things – the Fundamental Attribution Error. This was psychology's first "correction model," and we tested it in a handful of experiments that produced a handful of papers, some of which went on to become the most cited papers ever published in *JPSP* (Gilbert, Pelham, & Krull, 1988; Gilbert & Hixon, 1991). Building on this work, I produced a more general model of belief that suggested that people automatically accept every proposition they mentally represent and then "unaccept" those that require it (Gilbert, 1991). Believing is first and easy, doubting is second and hard. This "Spinozan model" met with interest and continues to be the subject of research in psychology and neuroscience.

But of all the things that happened in Texas, the most consequential was meeting Dan Wegner, a social psychologist at Trinity University in San Antonio. Dan was, quite simply, the most clever, inventive, original, and hilarious human I had ever encountered. There was no close second. Dan taught me that science was not just a way to solve problems, but a way to experience and express wonder. And the writing! Psychology papers could be interesting, but until I read Dan's, I didn't know they could also be thrilling – as rapturous, wise, witty, and fun as the greatest American novel. Here was a man who had effortlessly combined my two separate passions: writing and science. I had no idea they could be one thing. It was like discovering that my wife and my lover were actually the same woman and that everything was right with the world after all.

I spent thousands of hours in Dan's company, learning to see psychology through his eyes. Dan was just starting his seminal research on thought suppression, and watching his ideas develop and his research unfold, I realized that I wanted to do what he did: I wanted to ask *original* questions and then answer them in ways that made others quiver with insight and clap with delight. Everyone told me that scientists weren't supposed to "write that way," but I didn't care what everyone thought. I only cared what Dan thought. Kurt Vonnegut once said that all writers have a specific person in mind when they write, and that everything they write is for that person. For Vonnegut, that person was his sister. For me, it was Dan Wegner. Every word I wrote from that time on – indeed, every word I am writing right now – was and is a continuing addendum to my lifelong letter to Dan.

Tim Wilson

Writing came naturally to me, but originality did not. It was 1990, I was five years past my PhD, and my research to that point had been an extension of George Quattrone's beautiful answer to Ned Jones's beautiful question. I wanted to make something beautiful of my own. So in 1991, I went to the Center for Advanced Study in the Behavioral Sciences in Palo Alto to spend a sabbatical year sitting by myself in a little room with a lovely view while trying to be original. It wasn't very productive. One day I got an email from a fellow social psychologist whom I'd briefly met at a conference, saying that by coincidence, he too was on sabbatical in Palo Alto, and that by coincidence, he too was sitting in a little room getting nothing done. Did I want to meet for lunch?

I don't remember exactly what Tim Wilson and I talked about that day. I just remember what talking to him was like. There are people who attack your ideas and people who applaud them, but Tim did both at once, poking a hole in whatever I said and then, before all the air leaked out, filling it with something fresh and interesting that I wouldn't have thought of myself. We talked and talked that year, and I came to realize that talking to Tim was what thinking would be like if only I were twice as smart. At the end of our sabbatical years, we both went home – me to Austin and Tim to Charlottesville – where I quickly discovered what it was like to have half a brain again. Um, what kind of flowers did Charlie send Algernon?

I also discovered what it was like to lose much of what matters to you. My beloved mentor Ned died prematurely, my marriage fell apart, my son dropped out of school, and one of my most important friendships bit the dust. I went to lunch one day with a friend and told him about these calamities. He asked how I was coping. I told him that much to my surprise, I was doing pretty well – not the best year of my life, but I was holding my own. He casually asked whether I could have predicted that reaction a year earlier – and suddenly, a light went on. Can people predict what will make them happy or unhappy? Do they know how long their happiness will last? If not, then why not? And why in the world hadn't psychologists answered this question – or even asked it? After all, people's predictions about happiness are the guiding stars by which they navigate through time. Shouldn't psychologists know whether those predictions are accurate?

After lunch, I hurried back to my office and called Tim. He was intrigued by this question too and offered to run a preliminary study to see if people made mistakes when predicting their emotional responses to future events. A few weeks later he called to tell me that his data were uninterpretable. But we couldn't stop talking about the idea itself, and eventually we tried another study, which worked, as did the one after that. Soon we had enough studies to write a paper on a new topic we called "affective forecasting." In that paper (Gilbert et al., 1998), we showed that people tend to overestimate the hedonic consequences of future events – a phenomenon we ultimately dubbed "the impact bias" – and that they do so for a variety of reasons, ranging from a failure to appreciate the power of rationalization to a failure to consider how other events will compete for their attention.

We didn't know that our first paper together would be cited nearly 2,000 times in the following years, or that it would lead to an explosion of research on affective forecasting that would span disciplines from law to medicine to behavioral economics. We didn't know that our mutual interests would expand to include the pleasures of uncertainty, the fear of being alone with one's thoughts, loss aversion and discounting, meta-memory, the dynamics of conversation, and more. We just knew that we loved working together and wanted to do it again.

In 1996, I moved to Harvard, and Tim and I kept collaborating. A quarter century later, we'd published sixty or so papers together, making ours one of the most enduring collaborations in the history of social psychology. When people ask us about its parameters – about the rules and roles and mutual agreements that governed it – we sheepishly admit that it's never come up. The fact is that we never *decided* to work together for a lifetime; we just started one day and forgot to stop. Asking what my career would have been like without Tim is like asking what my life would have been like if I'd been born to different parents. There isn't a meaningful answer to either question, and for that I'm truly grateful.

Tomorrow is the Question

I once wrote that the surest sign of progress in a scientific field is the presence of grumpy old people, grousing about the good old days (Gilbert, 1998). I wrote that when I was young. Now that I'm about to be a Beatle-certified elder, I can tell you that the good old days were good indeed. But not as good as these days, and not as good as the days to come. Ned was a legend in our field, but I suspect he never saw his name in a newspaper because in those good old days that inspire so much geriatric nostalgia, social psychology was a backwater. No one took us seriously and no one paid attention. Today our science is all over the news, all over television, all over the best-seller list, and its wisdom is eagerly sought by governments, institutions, and industries across the globe. Never have we been more relevant, recognized, or richly rewarded.

But making the main stage means that for the first time we have a target on our backs. No one attacked us in the good old days because we weren't worth the bullets. Success in any human enterprise creates jobs for critics, and because social media have given a megaphone to anyone with thumbs, it is all too easy to tune into the chatter and conclude that our field is under siege. A study didn't replicate so Denmark must be rotten! What happened in Dayton didn't happen in Dubai, so kill those babies and toss out their bathwater! Meh. Ignore the hum. Social psychology has a short history but a long past, and using science to study social life at the level at which people experience it is a human enterprise that's not going away anytime soon. Our field is constantly being re-invented, re-imagined, and improved – it was happening when I came into it, and it is happening as I ease out. But that's evolution, not revolution. Growing pains are not dying pains.

"Tomorrow is the Question" is a 1959 album by the great alto saxophonist Ornette Coleman, whose invention of free jazz and harmolodics reshaped American music. How did he come upon his ground-breaking ideas? Coleman once told an interviewer, "It was when I found out I could make mistakes that I knew I was on to something." The critics derided his music as noise, but Coleman went on to win Grammys and Guggenheims, MacArthurs and Pulitzers, and more importantly, new generations of admiring musicians who continue to play his music, both experiencing and expressing its wonder. His critics are remembered by approximately no one.

Social psychology has made mistakes and should not be afraid to make more. It is, as far as anyone can tell, the only way to be on to something.

Coda

This chapter was supposed to be about me, and yet most of its sections bear the names of others. But isn't that social psychology's deepest message? Are we more than the sum of the people who teach us and touch us? The people who meet us in the "third place" that our conversations create and that neither of us can find on our own? The people who notice us, who take special interest, who read our stories and applications and articles – who overestimate our talents and in so doing, embarrass us into becoming the people they mistakenly think we are?

I've known such people in a life of happy accidents, a life spent thinking about the things that puzzle me in the warm company of fellow dreamers. Doing the garden and digging the weeds – who could ask for more?

Suggested Reading

Gilbert, D. T. (1991). How mental systems believe. *American Psychologist, 46,* 107–119.
    (1998). Ordinary personology. In D. T. Gilbert, S. T. Fiske, & G. Lindzey, (Eds.) *The Handbook of Social Psychology.* Fourth edition (Vol. 2, pp. 89–150). New York: McGraw-Hill.
Gilbert, D. T., & Hixon, J. G. (1991). The trouble of thinking: Activation and application of stereotypic beliefs. *Journal of Personality and Social Psychology, 60,* 509–517.
Gilbert, D. T., & Jones, E. E. (1986). Perceiver-induced constraint: Interpretations of self-generated reality. *Journal of Personality and Social Psychology, 50,* 269–280.
Gilbert, D. T., Pelham, B. W., & Krull, D. S. (1988). On cognitive busyness: When person perceivers meet persons perceived. *Journal of Personality and Social Psychology, 54,* 733–740.
Gilbert, D. T., Pinel, E. C., Wilson, T. D., Blumberg, S. J., & Wheatley, T. (1998). Immune neglect: A source of durability bias in affective forecasting. *Journal of Personality and Social Psychology, 75,* 617–638.

47 Always Buy the *Handbook of Social Psychology* (1968) at a Railway Station in India

Mahzarin R. Banaji

Prologue

If social psychology in the twentieth century has revealed anything stunning about human nature it is this: that individuals are created and shaped by material and social forces more than they or their observers recognize. I see my life as a textbook case of the responsiveness of bystanders who eased the path for my growth. I wrote words to this effect in the mid-1990s in an application to the John Simon Guggenheim Foundation. Notwithstanding the influence of those individuals who shaped my development (their influence even more burnished by the added twenty-five years), I neglected to mention the influences that are the hidden levers afforded by collectives – communities, institutions, governments – to regulate, both up and down, life's opportunities and outcomes. I try to rectify that lapse here.

In *Requiem for a Nun*, William Faulkner (1951) says, "The past is never dead. In fact it's not even past" (p. 73). Personality psychology (not the individual difference kind but the kind that grapples with self, consciousness, goals, motives, values) handed me a manual to make sense of the past as it has corporealized into the present. I attend to these two truths in homage to what I have learned from my fortuitous apprenticeship in these sciences.

* * *

When Drew Faust was named Harvard University's 28th and first female president in 2007, 371 years after it was established, a small group of her friends had a dinner for her. She asked me how I came to be an academic and I had to tell the story of wanting to be a secretary but being lovingly tricked into going to college. To our collective surprise, we discovered that the other four women (besides Drew), each had roughly the same story to tell. A well-known novelist reported having in fact been a secretary for a few years; an eminent historian noted that in her high school yearbook, she had in fact written that she aspired to be an "executive secretary," the "executive" she added had been emphasized because she knew she was better than the other girls. After joking that President Faust could count on a steady secretarial pool, it became clear that this discovery held deeper meaning. First, although varied in age and cultures, our

Mahzarin R. Banaji, Harvard University, USA.

similar choice of that single common path to economic freedom showed just how limited our options as middle-class women had been. But the good fortune of being where I had landed up, doing work I loved enough to do it for a nickel, made me intensely aware of all the potential, of many more amazing minds than my own, that are lost to us because they didn't experience the right intervention.

Having been "a sick child" born in 1950s India and who had largely been home schooled, I had no interest in attending college, which I saw as an extension of my intellectually dissatisfying years in high school. My mother had not attended college and although she did not speak about that loss to us, she was adamant that I go. Knowing that I had a will to match hers, she used a routine right out of social psychology's playbook: "Mahzarin, you just have to attend for a semester, to get your shy sister settled in. Then you may go off to your wonderful job." I grudgingly agreed to fulfill a filial duty for one semester, after which I would, by contract, be free to pursue the patently more daring life of a secretarial assistant.

I selected Nizam College in Hyderabad (the twin city from where we lived) not because it was the school my grandfather and father had attended nor from the recognition that my sister and I would be the first women to attend. Rather, its lure was that it was located next door to the largest cricket stadium in the city, and it was coeducational (unlike my high school). Even from the first few weeks, it was clear that college was not to be a hardship to be endured for twelve weeks before beginning a long career of snapping my secretarial heels to a boss's call for coffee. The end of the first semester came and went. Mother did not bring it up. I didn't have to admit that I had changed my mind.

It is rare that a course of action presents itself with such clarity that there is nothing to do but to follow it. While in a Master's program, I was traveling home from New Delhi to Hyderabad. At a major railway juncture, I stepped off the train to visit a bookstore on the platform where I bought a set of books that changed the course of my life. Five volumes of the *Handbook of Social Psychology* (1968) edited by Lindzey and Aronson, were being offered for the equivalent of a dollar a piece.

The printing of the *Handbook of Social Psychology* by Addison-Wesley that I bought was an independent Indian imprint. I still have the set (the binding is in red not blue, the paper is thinner and yellower, the gold lettering of lower quality). While I was the one who bought those books, no such possibility would have presented itself if the governments and publishing houses of two countries had not worked to make the handbooks economically viable in a country where academic psychology did not in any real sense even exist.

I bought the *Handbooks* out of mild interest in their content, but mostly because it seemed like a lot of book for the money. By the time I reached home twenty-four hours later, I had polished off a volume and knew with blunt clarity that this form of science was what I wanted to do. What attracted me was the combination of a focus on social processes but with an experimental approach, and this blend had a power and an appeal that I had missed in my previous encounters with psychophysics on the one hand and sociology on the other. I returned to finish the year but focused on applying to American universities. A few years later, I took great pleasure in showing Elliot Aronson the actual volumes when he visited Ohio State, where I was now a graduate student. So moved was he as he examined the imprint – he had no idea such a set even existed – that he claimed me as his student. I was delighted to accept. It would connect me symbolically to the greats whose names, like Festinger, had acquired a god-like quality while I was struggling to figure out how to get myself to graduate school.

Knowing nothing about American universities or the process, I did ask a few male engineering students in India who seemed to know exactly where they were heading, about it. Perplexed that a field called experimental psychology even existed, one of them passed on a secret to me. He had heard that American schools with the word "state" in the name "pretty much take anybody." That was all I needed to get to work. I wish I could say that I selected Ohio State over other schools because I was aware of their program in experimental social psychology. I wish I could say that I knew I wanted to go to the program that had graduated Claude Steele, Rich Petty, John Cacioppo, Gary Wells, etc. But alas, I chose Ohio State because in the letter of acceptance Tom Ostrom had included a copy of that week's college newspaper on which he had scrawled a handwritten note "I hope you will come. Tom." That pretty much sewed it up. Little wonder then that I yawn when I encounter the hyper-planning and admission carnivals that I participate in today.

An international fellowship from the American Association of University Women (AAUW) made it possible to attend graduate school in the United States, because although Ohio State had admitted me, there was so little they knew about me, and my training was so far from what was needed (I had never had a course in social psychology). AAUW covered my first year's living expenses. Why did AAUW dedicate funds each year to supporting two women from outside the United States for graduate study? In any analysis of how institutions of good will can up-regulate life's opportunities, AAUW is a front runner in my book.

It was in September 1980 that I arrived in Columbus with $80 in my pocket and no paycheck until month's end. The elderly couple (Ohio State alumni) who were there to pick me up at the airport held a sign with my name on it, but so mangled was its spelling that they and I continued to exchange smiles until nobody was left around us. I had one suitcase containing my life's belongings, mostly filled with the five volumes of the *Handbook of Social Psychology* (1968) but also one long-sleeved cotton shirt, because I had heard that it could get cold in Ohio. I cannot say that the transition to the academic environment of the United States was easy where I felt reward structures were geared toward doing things fast rather than well. As it turned out, these pains of adjustment were superficial because in spite of what today would be considered a shockingly brutal environment, I was intellectually quite happily sliding down the rabbit hole of grad school.

What made graduate school endurable were deep friendships I formed: Michael Lynn, a Texan with social and political views that were hardly "academic mainstream" and far from my own became an immediate friend and confidant and we remain close today (listen up, country!); Trish Devine, my officemate of four years, was a force of nature and outrageously fun (when I had extensive work to complete on a second-year project with a looming deadline, she persuaded me that we should first paint our office, located under the bleachers of the football stadium); Sharon Shavitt, a talented attitude theorist and on the ball in every way, could rattle off Cheese Shop and Dead Parrot sketches on cue, and she made me laugh a lot.

At the time, I was unaware of just how excellent a graduate program I had randomly landed into. Quite fortunately for me, a new approach linking the study of cognition to the study of social behavior was being formulated even as I arrived, and my advisor, Tony Greenwald, was a key player in this movement. The counter-intuitive idea underlying this approach was the notion that by studying the cognitive processes of perception, memory, and judgment, we could robustly understand repre-sentations of individual and group social behavior. It was the next step after attribution theory. This was not Leon Festinger's social psychology, and although it made for less good storytelling, it was far more to my taste of engaging more directly with tractable processes yielding reliable and robust effects.

Completing the PhD in 1986, I felt I was ready to move on to a job, but no place with a job seemed to share that opinion. I did have an offer for a one-year position from a small teaching school near beautiful Lake Seneca in upstate New York, and I would have happily taken the position and tried my luck again if not for a chance encounter with Tom Ostrom: "If you are genuinely attracted to such a job, by all means take it; but don't take it because you feel you won't be able to pursue a career in research," he said. Chance encounters like these seem so ordinary when they happen that it keeps their significance from being acknowledged. Tom's intervention was pivotal (at the level of reading of the *Handbook*).

Tom was not the only influence on this decision. My spouse, R. Bhaskar, lived in Westchester County in New York and although the job would be six hours away, it would have put us in the same state. The night before I had to make a decision regarding that idyllic college, Bhaskar spoke seriously: What if we are not together twenty years from now (we had been married for about a year) what then? How will you feel then about this choice of a one-year teaching position over taking a postdoc? What an amazing gift that long view was, shaken as I was by the suggestion of possibly not being together. But I knew immediately that I should turn down the position at that lovely college. (I should add, given the curiosity I've aroused, that Bhaskar and I have been together now for forty-one years.)

At the time, postdocs in social psychology were not considered the plum jobs they are today. You did a postdoc because you had sadly failed to get a job straight out of graduate school. But that's what I did, and of three postdoc options I had, I couldn't have chosen better. The University of Washington in Seattle was as far away as I could have traveled from New York, but the combination of collaborators in social and cognitive psychology transformed my thinking yet again and I developed a new confidence. Elizabeth Loftus, who has done pioneering work on the malleability of memory, opened her heart and her laboratory to me. Earl (Buz) Hunt reminded me that I had always been interested in the relationship between language and thought. Rumor had it that Art Lumsdaine (who had worked with Carl Hovland on experiments in mass communication during World War II) had been on Nixon's enemies list and that made him enough of a hero that I assisted with his surveys of attitudes toward nuclear disarmament.

Claude Steele was my primary mentor, and the grant that supported me was from the NIAAA and we did studies on the effects of alcohol on self-concept. After a hypermasculine and interpersonally tough environment at Ohio State, Claude provided a different model of training – that good training need not come at the expense of damage to self-worth. I would have been content to remain there, but a happy surprise came in the form of an offer of an assistant professorship from Yale University, allowing me to simultaneously be at one of the great centers of psychology and to live with my spouse of three years.

I call this offer from Yale a happy surprise because I came close to never receiving it. I had not applied for it, believing that I was not worthy of a job at such a place. But Bhaskar, had, in effect, mailed my CV to Yale (I was vaguely aware that he had, but considered it to be sufficiently a joke that I did not ask for letters of recommendation to be sent there). Yale had interviewed seven candidates before me and decided they would likely close the search for the year but decided to bring one more candidate out (me) if my unsent letters were found to be supportive. Letters were rushed, I got the job. I've encountered similar hesitancy in candidates today who do not apply for jobs they may be competitive for. I always tell the Yale story and add that in the twenty-first century women ought not to rely on their feminist husbands to mail in their CVs!

The benign neglect of junior faculty was often regarded as an unpleasant aspect of life at Yale, but for me it turned into much-needed freedom to select problems and methods without the burden of worrying about the fluctuating opinions of senior colleagues or about tenure, for Yale did not hire assistant professors into a tenure track. In 1988, an idea for an experiment on unconscious discrimination came from an unlikely source. In a weekly brown bag on memory research organized by Robert Crowder, an idea emerged that led to experiments that put me on the research path I've been on, in one form or another, ever since then.

An experiment by Jacoby and colleagues (Jacoby et al., 1989) on implicit memory used first and last names to show that familiarized names would later be mistakenly identified as famous because subjects would mistake perceptual fluency for the attribute of fame. I replicated that experiment but with carefully matched names of women added to the set of male names that Jacoby had used. The assumption was that all names should produce the false fame effect. My attempt to add female names had been motivated by a desire to simply make the stimuli more representative. But counter to expectation, the attribution of fame did not accrue to female names in the way they accrued to male names. These experiments rekindled a collaboration with my mentor from graduate school, Tony Greenwald (Banaji & Greenwald, 1995), which turned into a collaboration that then lasted for the next thirty years.

In a symposium at APS on unconscious cognition I described what was the crux of those experiments in the early 1990s:

It is remarkable that quizzing over 400 participants across six experiments about what may have caused errors in their memory elicited many hypotheses, but never, not once, the possibility that the gender of the name may have played an influencing role … Indeed, they seemed downright surprised by the suggestion. If this is true, harm can occur without the perpetrator being aware of harming and without the target becoming aware that she was harmed. If such is the power of unconscious cognition, if the source of influence on our thoughts and actions so deeply eludes us, results like these must call into question existing notions of equal treatment, individual responsibility and social justice.

I was surprised at the blatant disparity between explicit and implicit beliefs. Subjects had no idea that whatever their values may have been, the knowledge of the world they had acquired – the thumbprint of culture on their minds – had determined their behavior, rendering it to be in opposition to their own values. That these small results from laboratory experiments were speaking to the illusiveness of a just society may seem surprising. But not if you had read the *Handbook of Social Psychology* (1968) on a long train ride in India.

Of course, something called a research program had only just begun. I was surprised when in 1988 a graduate student arrived who said that he wanted to work with me, rather than all the luminaries at Yale. That was the iconoclastic Curtis Hardin. Along with him and Alex Rothman I conducted studies to show that what were assumed to be universal effects in person perception were in fact moderated by social category. We first used the term "implicit" in the title of a paper on social cognition (Banaji, Hardin, & Rothman, 1993). Later, Greenwald and I wrote a chapter for the Ontario Symposium (Banaji & Greenwald, 1994), followed by a *Psych Review* paper in which we laid out the concept of implicit social cognition and used the term "implicit bias" for the first time in our own work (Greenwald & Banaji, 1995). Toward the end of this paper, we mentioned that the field awaits a method that would allow implicit social cognition to be effectively tracked. That method turned out to be the IAT and it changed both basic research (and far more) for us and many others. It also led me to request that both universities I've been at should support an educational project that was created in collaboration with Tony Greenwald and Brian Nosek where any person with Internet access could measure their own implicit attitudes and stereotypes. That both Yale and Harvard invested substantially in this project is yet another indication of the power of institutions to step in to respond to a research need that is also a societal need. Each year over a million completed tests are collected; after the murder of George Floyd, that number more than doubled.

The singular feature of my research career and the one from which I derive the deepest gratification is the group of twenty-four PhDs and several postdocs who developed their own first research preferences and styles in my lab, and who have made formidable contributions to this and their own research programs as well as contributions well beyond academic ones. It has also been my good fortune to work with people in areas some distance from me and with whom the work on implicit social cognition advanced faster and farther. The neuroimaging work I did with Elizabeth Phelps (Phelps et al., 2000) seemed to put a stop to an odd question we were constantly being asked at the time the IAT first emerged: Why is what you are measuring an attitude? (cf. Banaji, 2001; Banaji & Heifetz, 2010).

In January 2002 I moved to Harvard, which provided me with colleagues whose work I found fascinating, especially the work on cognitive development by Liz Spelke and Susan Carey. I had thought woefully little about where implicit bias comes from, and we did studies to understand its origins by studying the minds of toddlers. My own first foray (Baron & Banaji, 2006) required us to first build a child-friendly IAT. When the results repeatedly showed that the youngest children and adults showed similar levels of bias, I had to change my mind about the nature of implicit cognition.

Being in the Boston area with its sixty-plus colleges and universities also allowed the research to reach into professional schools and my collaborations with legal scholars (Kang & Banaji, 2006), business school scientists (Banaji et al., 2003), and medical colleagues (Green et al., 2007) allowed the work to be tested in settings I could not have imagined when we first began work that I thought would teach us about the basics of implicit cognition.

It is not surprising that today, the data sets we work with are massive. Data from the public website featuring demonstration IATs (created in 1998 at Yale and now residing at Harvard: implicit.harvard.edu) continue to produce an abundance of data from volunteer participants and are available to any research scientist wishing to further analyze them. These data are unlike any other on social group attitudes as they have been collected continuously with analyzable data since 2007, and today they allow time-series analyses of attitude change. These data have produced unexpected evidence that some implicit biases are changing toward neutrality (Charlesworth & Banaji, 2019), suggesting malleability that can be detected over long time periods. Another quite different approach, one using word embeddings utilizing massive language corpora allows us to measure the presence of social group attitudes and stereotypes that are hidden in plain sight in our language (Charlesworth et al., 2021).

To think that all this began with being mesmerized by reading the 1968 *Handbook of Social Psychology* in a place far from where I ended up is unlikely and therefore surprising, but obviously possible. The creators of that possibility, I hope it is clear, are embedded in the social and political/economic networks consisting of individual others, communities, and institutions – the regulators of life.

Suggested Reading

Banaji, M. R. (2001). Implicit attitudes can be measured. In H. L. Roediger III, J. S. Nairne, I. E. Neath, & A. M. Surprenant (Eds.), *The Nature of Remembering: Essays in Honor of Robert G. Crowder* (pp. 117–150). Washington, DC: American Psychological Association.

Banaji, M. R., Bazerman, M. H., & Chugh, D. (2003). How (un)ethical are you? *Harvard Business Review, 81*(12), 56–64.

Banaji, M. R., & Greenwald, A. G. (1994). Implicit stereotyping and prejudice. In M. P. Zanna & J. M. Olson (Eds.), *The Psychology of Prejudice: The Ontario Symposium* (Vol. 7, pp. 55–76). Hillsdale, NJ: Lawrence Erlbaum.

(1995). Implicit gender stereotyping in judgments of fame. *Journal of Personality and Social Psychology*, 68(2), 181–198.

Banaji, M. R., & Heiphetz, L. (2010). Attitudes. In S. T. Fiske, D. T. Gilbert, & G. Lindzey (Eds.), *Handbook of Social Psychology* (pp. 353–393). New York: John Wiley & Sons.

Banaji, M. R., Hardin, C., & Rothman, A. J. (1993). Implicit stereotyping in person judgment. *Journal of Personality and Social Psychology*, 65(2), 272–281.

Baron, A. S., & Banaji, M. R. (2006). The development of implicit attitudes: Evidence of race evaluations from ages 6 and 10 and adulthood. *Psychological Science*, 17(1), 53–58.

Charlesworth, T. E. S., & Banaji, M. R. (2019). Patterns of implicit and explicit attitudes 1: Long-term change and stability from 2007–2016. *Psychological Science*, 30(2), 174–192.

Charlesworth, T. E. S., Yang, V., Mann, T. C., Kurdi, B., & Banaji, M. R. (2021). Gender stereotypes in natural language: Word embeddings show robust consistency across child and adult language corpora of 65+ million words. *Psychological Science*, 32(2), 218–240.

Faulkner, W. (1951). *Requiem for a Nun*. New York: Random House.

Green, A. R., Carney, D. R., Pallin, D. J., Ngo, L. H., Raymond, K. L., Iezzoni, L. I., & Banaji, M. R. (2007). Implicit bias among physicians and its prediction of thrombolysis decisions for black and white patients. *Journal of General Internal Medicine*, 22(9), 1231–1238.

Greenwald, A. G., & Banaji, M. R. (1995). Implicit social cognition: Attitudes, self-esteem, and stereotypes. *Psychological Review*, 102(1), 4–27.

Jacoby, L. L., Kelley, C., Brown, J., & Jasechko, J. (1989). Becoming famous overnight: Limits on the ability to avoid unconscious influences of the past. *Journal of Personality and Social Psychology*, 56(3), 326–338.

Kang, J., & Banaji, M. R. (2006). Fair measures: A behavioral realist revision of 'affirmative action'. *California Law Review*, 94, 1063–1118.

Lindzey, G., & Aronson, E. (Eds.) (1968). *The Handbook of Social Psychology*. Second edition. Reading, MA: Addison-Wesley.

Phelps, E. A., O'Connor, K. J., Cunningham, W. A., Funayama, E. S., Gatenby, J. C., Gore, J. C., & Banaji, M. R. (2000). Performance on indirect measures of race evaluation predicts amygdala activation. *Journal of Cognitive Neuroscience*, 12(5), 729–738.

48 Empowering People to Break the Prejudice Habit
(Re)Discovering My Inner Cialdini

Patricia G. Devine

Throughout my independent career, I have studied issues related to stereotyping, prejudice, and intergroup relations. But, my sustained interest in these issues is best understood in context and I would like to highlight two sets of early experiences that shaped how I approach my science and what ultimately became my substantive interest.

Let me start with how I first got involved in research. I went to college at SUNY Plattsburgh, where during my first year I was utterly bored and considering dropping out of school. Serendipitously, I took a course with Roy Malpass and meeting him changed the trajectory of my career. In 1978, Roy was starting a program of research on eyewitness identification issues and invited me to join his research team – which turned out was just Roy and me. The problem he wanted to tackle was the effect of lineup instructions on the likelihood that a witness would choose a lineup member and the accuracy of that choice. In real-world lineup situations, the typical instructions were leading – they essentially suggested that the culprit was in the lineup and the eyewitnesses' job was to identify that person. The rub here, however, is that often the police's suspect is innocent and the individual who committed the crime is absent from the lineup.

These realities lent themselves well to designing experiments in which we manipulated instructions (biased vs. fair) and the lineup (e.g., presence or absence of the culprit). And then we started staging crimes, namely vandalisms during large lectures, for which there would be many potential eyewitnesses. We followed the crimes with lineups conducted in the lab or in field settings. After our first big study, Roy asked me to code the data and summarize the findings in tables. Of course, in those days, everything was done by hand, so I tallied up the choosing and error rates and drew the data tables on the chalkboard. I didn't fully understand the numbers yet but Roy's reaction to the data was compelling; his eyes opened wide, and I could sense his excitement. I really wanted to understand that reaction.

As we more fully analyzed the data, I came to understand the power of randomization, carefully manipulated variables, experimental control, scripting dramas, and carefully worded dependent variables. We went on to publish three research articles

Patricia G. Devine, University of Wisconsin, USA. Preparation of this chapter was supported by a Wisconsin Alumni Research Foundation Professorship and Maximizing Investigator Research Award (R35 GM127043–01) awarded to P. G. Devine.

(e.g., Malpass & Devine, 1981). I was hooked, not so much by social psychology per se but by the process of doing research. Our findings were clear and important; they had implications for how lineups should be conducted in the world. And they led to real-world changes in how lineups are conducted! My eyewitness work with Roy was my first introduction to the importance of Cialdini's analysis of "full-cycle social psychology," whereby researchers observe a phenomenon in the real world, generate hypotheses to predict its presence, conduct experiments to test that hypothesis, and then return to naturalistic settings to corroborate the findings (Mortensen & Cialdini, 2010). I didn't yet know who Cialdini was, how this perspective would feature in my research over time, or even that I would become a social psychologist.

The second set of formative experiences occurred early and well outside the formal study of social psychology. Two puzzling experiences in particular served as preludes to issues that would ultimately consume my attention. The first was the question I was asked most frequently when I was growing up: "Are you Catholic?" Well, I was, in fact, raised Catholic, but I wondered why I was always asked that question. Over time what I came to realize is the question followed quickly on the heels of my disclosure that I have seven siblings. Apparently, the number of children in a family can lead to inferences about group membership. The second puzzling experience occurred in the context of my family relocating frequently when I was a kid. We lived in several different communities, each with a distinct ethnic identity – whether Jewish, Polish, or Italian. These experiences led me to observe that knowledge of someone's ethnic background, cued most often by a name, led people to make assumptions about these others' personalities, interests, and other qualities. These inferences, which seemed unwarranted, were made quickly and were quite often wrong.

Intellectually, each of us is a product of our environments – where we study or work, what we read, who we interact with, and the intangible "what we personally bring to the situation" (like my concern over the unwarranted inferences people form about others). After graduating from Plattsburgh in 1981, I entered the graduate program in social psychology at Ohio State. I had considered other programs at the University of Wisconsin in social and the University of Washington in cognitive. In these other programs I would have continued my study of issues related to eyewitness issues. I wanted to branch out, though, and OSU had an outstanding program. (I should note that I felt fortunate to gain entry to any program; although I had considerable research experience and a high GPA, my GRE scores were abysmal and this fact kept me out of most of the programs to which I applied.) So, how did I happen upon an interest in stereotyping and prejudice? First, I discovered what I did *not* want to study.

At OSU, I immediately established a wonderful collaborative relationship with my graduate mentor, Tom Ostrom. Tom was working on person memory-related issues and I conducted studies of how the organization of social information in the stimulus field affected memory organization and social judgment. Although I found ways to make this work interesting, and while I learned an enormous amount working with Tom, person memory failed to capture my imagination or passion. At that point,

I knew what I *didn't* want to study for my dissertation, but I had no idea what I *did* want to study. With these uncertainties in mind, during the summer after my third year, I began to read widely and the articles I found most interesting concerned stereotyping and prejudice. Within each paper I read, I checked off references that I wanted to read next (we did not have the Internet, PubMed, or Google in those days). I kept reading and reading. I found myself fully captivated by the issues and could not stop thinking about them.

There were two articles in particular that I could not stop thinking about (Billig, 1985; Crosby et al., 1980). Why? Bottom line – they bothered me. I should say at the outset that both are terrific articles, well-reasoned, thoughtful, and convincing. Nevertheless, I found the conclusions deeply disturbing and overly pessimistic.

Billig's (1985) article, following Allport (1954) among others, suggested that prejudice is an inevitable consequence of ordinary categorization (stereotyping) processes – that so long as stereotypes exist, prejudice will follow. This analysis essentially equated stereotypes with prejudice. Like me, Billig was more than a bit uneasy with this conclusion. Could it really be that easy? What if one truly believed that stereotyping was wrong? What implications did this hold for prejudice reduction?

Crosby et al. (1980) addressed the troubling paradox that although many people profess to hold egalitarian, nonprejudiced attitudes toward members of traditionally stereotyped groups, their actual behaviors often belied their egalitarian sentiments. Their position was that verbal reports of attitudes are suspect precisely because they are under the influence of controlled (strategic impression management) processes. Instead, they favored covert measures that do not involve careful, deliberate, and intentional thought. In the spirit of "actions speak louder than words," Crosby et al. (1980) interpreted the inconsistency between people's self-professed nonprejudiced attitudes and their coexisting prejudiced behaviors as evidence that people are lying about their attitudes or unable to recognize their "true" prejudices.

I found these analyses fatalistic in their implication, offering little guidance for prejudice reduction. They suggested that true change was not possible and, worse yet, claims of being nonprejudiced reflected little more than strategic impression management. The conclusions from these articles did not seem to match what I saw in people to be a genuine struggle to overcome prejudice in their everyday experience, what Myrdal (1944) had characterized as the "American Dilemma." Similarly, Poskocil (1977), a sociologist, had described the plight of well-intentioned but bumbling liberals, who, despite deliberate efforts, often failed to achieve their egalitarian ideals. Such individuals were effectively dismissed from these conceptualizations.

Throughout my career I have been concerned with the struggles people face in their efforts to reduce prejudice in their everyday lives. Is prejudice reduction possible? Could people truly change their attitudes yet remain vulnerable to prejudiced responses? Could social desirability concerns be bypassed? Is there an alternative explanation for the disparity between self-reported attitudes and less consciously monitored responses – one that would suggest that prejudice reduction is possible?

Enter the other work I was reading. Interest in social cognition was growing in the field. One set of issues that I found interesting and exciting was the distinction between automatic and controlled processes and, in particular, Neely's (1977) argument that automatic and controlled cognitive processes could operate independently. Neely demonstrated, for example, that when automatic processing would produce a response that conflicted with conscious intentions, participants inhibited the automatic response and deliberately replaced it with one consistent with their conscious intentions. However, participants could only do so if they had enough time and cognitive capacity to engage controlled processes. Without sufficient time or capacity, the automatic processes would unfold without interference. This was a powerful demonstration; the full significance for my thinking about stereotyping and prejudice would become apparent to me only later.

At the same time, I was reading articles that shaped my thinking about the activation and application of stereotypes. These articles showed that constructs activated in one setting could influence social inference processes in a subsequent setting. Bargh's work was especially influential because it suggested a strategy for activating constructs that bypassed conscious awareness and, therefore, social desirability concerns. For example, Bargh and Pietromonaco (1982) demonstrated that trait constructs, such as kindness and hostility, could be primed by repeatedly presenting trait-relevant terms in participants' parafoveal visual field. The effects of such passive priming were observed in participants' subsequent judgments of a target who engaged in ambiguous trait-relevant behaviors.

Examining the consequences of automatic stereotype activation, it seemed to me, would be a convincing way to differentiate low- and high-prejudice individuals – precisely because social desirability processes would not come into play. My thinking was that low-prejudice people renounce stereotypes whereas high-prejudice people endorse them. My goal, then, was to passively prime the stereotype at low and high levels and then to examine judgments of a race-unspecified person who engaged in ambiguously hostile behaviors (a core characteristic of the stereotype of Black people). With all this in mind, I wrote a dissertation proposal in which I argued that stereotypes could be automatically activated and that the effect would differ for low-compared with high-prejudice people. I expected prejudice level to moderate the effects of priming, such that only high-prejudice participants' hostility ratings would be strongly affected by the priming manipulation.

I wrote my proposal and confidently went to Ostrom with my ideas. I was soon to have my hopes dashed. Ostrom strongly discouraged me. He argued that he was not interested, that no one at OSU was working on stereotyping or issues of automaticity and control, and that using the new passive priming techniques was risky. His reasoning was sound, and his judgment had proved wise in other instances. Ostrom recommended I develop a new dissertation plan, one that fell more squarely in his wheelhouse. Dejected, I left his office. I didn't want to take his advice. I was excited by these ideas and wanted to take the risk.

I wasn't sure how to proceed and, in this context, I would be remiss if I didn't mention one of those intangibles that can influence one's professional development.

For me, as I suspect for many graduate students, what was critical was the unqualified and unwavering support of a fellow graduate student and for me that support came in the person of my dear friend, Mahzarin Banaji. In our early conversations I explained how I was interested in unconsciously priming stereotypic concepts of Black Americans. What I remember most about my discussions with Mahzarin was that she was keenly interested and supportive. She asked probing questions and encouraged me to explore this as yet uncharted territory. I think Mahzarin anticipated the potentially controversial nature of my proposed work (i.e., to reveal what she later wrote about – the dark side of the mind), and its potential impact much more than I did. Though she conveyed her excitement for the work, she didn't reveal her trepidations until many years later. Rather, she encouraged me to persevere. So, persevere I did. I lobbied Ostrom for his support and, in the end, he acquiesced, perhaps revealing his confidence in me.

So, I set off to run the study. I was excited to analyze the data and move forward with the write up. My excitement, however, was short-lived. The results were *not* consistent with my expectations. Rather than prejudice level moderating the effect of priming on hostility ratings, there was simply a main effect of priming. Low- and high-prejudice participants were equally affected such that hostility ratings were more extreme in the high than the low priming condition. I could not make sense of the data. It was the summer of 1985 and I was just about to start at the University of Wisconsin as an assistant professor and worried how I would be viewed.

I began to explore the possible reasons for my unexpected findings. The methodology seemed sound so I held out hope that perhaps I had miscoded something. No such luck. More discomfort. Then in a single instance, in one of those "aha" moments, everything changed, providing me with the theoretical analysis that later served as the foundation for my subsequent research. My assumption was not incorrect that high-prejudice people believe the stereotype, whereas low-prejudice people do not. Having been socialized into the same culture, however, low- and high-prejudiced people are equally *knowledgeable* about the cultural stereotype of Black people.

Recognizing the distinction between stereotypes and beliefs as knowledge structures and the possibility that they differentially involve automatic vs. controlled processes helped to make sense of my data and offer an alternative explanation for the often observed inconsistencies between self-reports and behaviors noted in Crosby et al.'s (1980) review. What I realized was that the stereotype is a frequently activated knowledge structure in our culture, so whether one endorses the stereotype or not, it is easily activated. The structures that were automatically activated in the priming task were culturally defined stereotypes that are part of one's social heritage, not necessarily one's personal beliefs.

This theorizing led me to recognize the challenges associated with reducing prejudice. The key was to recognize that the conscious decision to renounce prejudice does not immediately eliminate prejudiced responses in light of a lifetime of socialization experiences. My work suggested that stereotypes and negative feelings toward groups can be activated automatically – without awareness or intention – even among individuals who are consciously not prejudiced. The rub is that people are not always aware of when a stereotype, which is easily activated, affects their judgment – without their consent or bidding. In that sense, stereotypes operate like habits of mind. It takes conscious attention, energy, and effort to inhibit that stereotype.

I went on to publish my dissertation in an article titled "Stereotypes and Prejudice: Their Automatic and Controlled Components." In it, I suggested that prejudice reduction is akin to breaking a bad habit, that the automatic associations must be inhibited and newer responses consciously activated, lest the person "fall into old habits" (Devine, 1989). Overcoming prejudice thus represents a formidable challenge that entails internal conflict and takes a protracted period of time. From this perspective, change was difficult but possible. Prejudice was a habit that could be broken. From a Cialdinian perspective, this was very exciting.

At that point, my students and I initiated a program of research aimed at unpacking what it took to break the prejudice habit. With Margo Monteith, Julia Zuwerink, and Andy Elliot (e.g., Devine et al., 1991), we showed, for example, that those who were sincere in their renunciation of prejudice felt guilty and self-critical when they responded in biased ways. Margo Monteith and I showed that guilt led to a motivated interest in reducing bias (e.g., Devine & Monteith, 1993). Dave Amodio and I, along with Eddie Harmon Jones (e.g., Amodio et al., 2008), studied neural processes associated with activation and control of prejudiced responses. With many still doubting the sincerity of self-reported claims of nonprejudice because such claims are socially desirable, Ashby Plant and I found that internal motivation is associated with the intention to be free of prejudice and external motivation with the intention to hide prejudice. We further demonstrated the primacy of internal motivation to respond without prejudice (e.g., Plant & Devine, 2009).

Many of the issues we explored addressed concerns in the field about the trustworthiness of verbal self-reports. This issue is also important in the real world, but we also wanted to validate our conceptual analysis. As exciting as these findings were, it felt like something was missing – something big. Sometime around 2007, the enormity of what was missing became clear when the news media came calling. Unlike reluctant scientists, reporters are ready and willing to share our work with their audiences. Most often, reporters would come my way after talking with Susan Fiske, who is widely known as one of the world's foremost authorities on issues of stereotyping, prejudice, and discrimination. As the reporters broached the topic of prejudice reduction, Susan would encourage them to contact me. Our conservations always started off well; they would ask me to tell them about my work and when I talked about prejudice reduction, their ears perked up – they wanted to know what advice I had to offer for how people could reduce prejudice. I talked about how *some people*, in some cases motivated by guilt, were sincere in their desire to reduce prejudice; they were willing to work hard to reduce bias and we had evidence that some people were effective doing so. What we didn't know, I conceded, is how they got to that point. As I spoke to reporters, however, I heard the hollowness of my own words – people with sufficient motivation, if they work hard enough, can break the prejudice habit. But "*how do they do this?*" I was asked again and again. What advice could we give them, what tools or strategies can they deploy? I didn't have good answers and felt their enthusiasm (and my own) waning as our conversation proceeded.

As a scientist, these were formative experiences. Like many of my generation and those who preceded me, my self-defined role was to do elegant basic research and then leave it to practitioners (whoever they may be) to figure out how to use the accumulated knowledge to solve the practical problems. My inner Cialdini was by now bursting through. I knew at that point that I needed to demonstrate that prejudice could be reduced and that the habit could truly be broken.

I took stock of what the field was thinking about these issues. Like me, other researchers were noting that despite encouraging trends suggesting that racial prejudice in the United States had waned in the last half century, Black people continued to experience more adverse outcomes than White people across a wide range of domains related to success and well-being. This apparent paradox led to a search for factors that sustained this ongoing discrimination. Partly building on my early research, social psychologists Susan Fiske, Jack Dovidio, and John Bargh, among others, cited implicit race biases – which can be unconscious, unintentional, and automatically activated – as major contributors. These biases were powerful precisely because they occur despite the best of conscious intentions. Research showed that implicit biases predicted discriminatory outcomes in a wide range of settings. These concerns led to a clarion call for strategies to reduce implicit biases from leading scholars in the study of stereotyping and prejudice, the National Academies of Science, the National Science Foundation, and the National Institutes of Health.

I looked carefully at what those who applied our work were doing – mostly in the context of diversity and bias reduction trainings in business, healthcare, and education (see Devine & Ash, 2022, for a review) – and I discovered that typically these trainings merely described our findings. And, although they effectively made people aware of their implicit biases, they did not offer advice on how to reduce these biases. There was also little effort to evaluate the impact of such training (in fact, fieldwork has shown that such trainings often had no effect or made problems worse), which is especially concerning given that it has grown from the late 1970s to a multibillion dollar a year industry.

I went back to do a systematic analysis of the challenges people face in their everyday lives in their efforts to control prejudice. If people are motivated, as much of our empirical work suggests, why do they still respond with bias? *I had to think about it from their perspective.* They had changed their minds and consciously controlled responses. But how could they control a bias of which they are unaware? Research shows that many people don't understand the full challenge of overcoming prejudice. Many people who sincerely embrace egalitarian values are not aware of the unintended processes that lead to bias or the need to make adjustments that would prevent them from exhibiting bias in unintended ways. In short, good people can be unwittingly complicit in perpetuating the problem. Yet they won't (can't) change something they are not aware of!

These messages were not unfamiliar to me – indeed, I made many of these arguments early in my career on prejudice – mostly to academic colleagues. What

I hadn't done was to clue ordinary citizens in on the challenge or prescribe effective tools. It became increasingly evident to me that I needed to turn my attention to how to help people break the prejudice habit. As serendipity would have it, I was teaching an undergraduate seminar on stereotyping and prejudice and my efforts were helped by a student enrolled in the class, Tony Austin, who was struggling to understand his own racial biases. Tony was from a small town in Wisconsin and did not know any Black people personally, yet he observed after arriving on campus that he often had stereotypic thoughts and uneasy feelings about Black people. These biases troubled him – his values were to be fair and unbiased. Tony's struggle was real and was playing out in the real world. We had numerous discussions about why bias persisted against one's intentions and what could be done to address the problem. Hearing the echoes of my exchanges with reporters, I suggested to him that we needed to understand *why* unintentional bias persists – and *how* to reduce it.

Out of these discussions the prejudice-habit breaking intervention was born. We used Greenwald et al.'s Implicit Association Test as a tool to increase people's awareness of their racial biases. We turned the power of habit metaphor on its head to lay out what is needed to break the prejudice habit, noting that people would need to be both *aware* of their vulnerability to unintentional bias and *motivated* to reduce it. They would need to understand that such biases are consequential and lead to discriminatory outcomes. They would need *tools or strategies* to assistant in their efforts; and they would need to understand that, as in breaking any habit, *effort* over time was needed.

Tony and I spent some long hours together developing a 45-minute interactive presentation, involving the IAT, that incorporated each of these elements. Our goal was lofty one: Could this approach empower people to effect change in their own minds? To find out, Tony and I designed a twelve-week longitudinal study (Devine et al., 2012) to test the effects of the intervention on implicit bias, as measured by the IAT; explicit concern about the effects of that bias; and behavioral outcomes. This study was a monumental undertaking and its completion entirely due to Tony's dogged determination. Tony graduated before we could fully explore the data. Fortunately, Patrick Forscher, then a graduate student, analyzed the data. The study was a huge success. We observed that intervention participants showed reduced implicit bias, greater awareness of their vulnerability, and a greater concern about discrimination. It appeared that people could use the power of their conscious minds to break the prejudice habit.

Testing the efficacy of the prejudice habit-breaking intervention remains the focus of ongoing research. With Patrick Forscher, Chelsea Mitamura, Emily Dix, and Will Cox we replicated the initial findings and further found that those exposed to the intervention were more likely to challenge racial bias expressed by others. With Molly Carnes, we demonstrated the efficacy of the intervention to address gender bias in STEM departments at the University of Wisconsin, where women were underrepresented and often reported feeling like they were not respected and did not fit in. In a large-scale longitudinal study, we showed that the climate in intervention departments was improved for women with no adverse effects for men. Compared to control departments, intervention departments went on to hire woman at a substantially higher rate. My inner Cialdini was fully revealed. But we are far from done, as we continue to explore the utility of this approach in the classroom, healthcare settings, in law-enforcement, and other settings (for an overview, see Cox & Devine, 2019).

Rediscovering my inner Cialdini, born early in my eyewitness work, has enabled me to come full circle. My early observations revealed the predicament many people found themselves in when their thoughts and actions belied their values. The lab experiments that followed helped us to understand the full nature of the motivation people experienced and the challenges involved in breaking the prejudice habit. Our recent work testing our intervention delivers on the promise of empowering people to be agents of change in their own minds and to create more inclusive and equitable social environments.

My career has been long and exciting, and I've been fortunate that the work I've done has had impact. Along the way, I've learned a lot of lessons, a few of which I will share in closing. First, work on issues that you personally find exciting and important. And listen to your own reactions along the way. If I hadn't done this, I may have pursued a career studying person memory; then I may have accepted the proposition that prejudice is inevitable or that people suppress their prejudices merely for strategic impression management reasons. But I had a foothold in the real world and was attuned to people who exhibited biased responses they did not intend. In this context, for me, both discovering my inner Cialdini and the value of full cycle social psychology was critical. This approach requires that we ground our questions in the world in which the phenomenon of interest plays out. I want to be clear that this is not a model of how to do applied research but rather how to do ecologically valid basic research. Of course, the approach lends itself to applications and to translational work.

Second, in sharing your work, think beyond your own personal interest. Too often, social psychologists take for granted that the importance of their work will be obvious to others. Avoid making these assumptions; they are not valid! Lay that foundation in your papers and presentations. We saw what happened at funding agencies years ago when funding was cut for social psychology at NIH when Congress challenged the importance of our work and questioned whether federal dollars should be spent funding it.

Continuing in this vein, communication about what we do is critical. We need to "sell" our work outside the field. I'm not suggesting that we immediately shift gears and do applied work. But we do have a responsibility to communicate to a broader audiences why our work matters, how it is relevant, and how it can make a difference – in the field, for theory, and beyond. To be a good ambassador for the field, consider the role you can play with students, colleagues, the media, laypeople, granting agencies, and politicians.

Some social psychologists communicate well with the public through popular books (e.g., Elliot Aronson, Tim Wilson, Bob Cialdini, Dan Gilbert, Jamie Pennebaker among others) but we each have to find our own most effective ways to promote our discipline. I believe Hazel Markus got it right some years ago, during her Presidential Address at SPSP, when she argued that we need to help people see how our discipline is so necessary and relevant that they would notice its absence and miss it in their lives. One clear way to ensure that our work is viewed as relevant and important is to channel our inner Cialdini.

Suggested Reading

Allport, G. W. (1954). *The Nature of Prejudice*. Reading, MA: Addison-Wesley.

Amodio, D. M., Devine, P. G., & Harmon-Jones, E. (2008). Neural signals for the detection of race bias: Implications for individual differences in regulatory ability. *Journal of Personality and Social Psychology, 94*, 60–74.

Bargh, J. A., & Pietromonaco, P. (1982). Automatic information processing and social perception: The influence of trait information presented outside of conscious awareness on impression formation. *Journal of Personality and Social Psychology, 43*, 437–449.

Billig, M. (1985). Prejudice, categorization, and particularization: From a perceptual to a rhetorical approach. *European Journal of Social Psychology, 15*, 79–103.

Cox, W. T L., & Devine, P. G. (2019). The Prejudice Habit-Breaking Intervention: An empowerment-based confrontation approach. In R. Mallett & M. J. Monteith (Eds.), *Confronting Prejudice and Discrimination* (pp. 249–274). San Diego, CA: Elsevier.

Crosby, E., Bromley, S., & Saxe, L. (1980). Recent unobtrusive studies of black and white discrimination and prejudice: A literature review. *Psychological Bulletin, 87*, 546–563.

Devine, P. G. (1989). Stereotypes and prejudice: Their automatic and controlled components. *Journal of Personality and Social Psychology, 56*, 5–18.

Devine, P. G., & Ash, T. L. (2022). Diversity training goals, limitations, and promise: A review of a multidisciplinary literature. *Annual Review of Psychology, 73*, 403–429.

Devine, P. G., Forscher, P. S., Austin, A. J., & Cox, W. T. L (2012). Long-term reduction in implicit racial bias: A prejudice habit-breaking intervention. *Journal of Experimental Social Psychology, 48*, 1268–1278.

Devine P. G., & Monteith, M. J. (1993). The role of discrepancy associated affect in prejudice reduction. In D. Mackie & D. Hamilton (Eds.), *Affect, Cognition, and Stereotyping: Interactive Processes in Intergroup Perception* (pp. 317–344). New York: Academic Press.

Devine, P. G., Monteith, M. J., Zuwerink, J. R., & Elliot, A. J. (1991). Prejudice with and without compunction. *Journal of Personality and Social Psychology, 60*, 817–830.

Malpass, R. S., & Devine, P. G. (1981). Eyewitness identification: Lineup instructions and the absence of the offender. *Journal of Applied Psychology, 66*, 482–489.

Moretensen, C. R, & Cialdini, R. B. (2010). Full-cycle social psychology for theory and application. *Social and Personality Science, 4*, 53–63.

Myrdal, G. (1944). *An American Dilemma: The Negro Problem and American Democracy*. New York: Harper.

Neely, J. H. (1977). Semantic priming and retrieval from lexical memory: Roles of inhibition-less spreading activation and limited-capacity attention. *Journal of Experimental Psychology, 106*, 226–254.

Plant, E. A., & Devine, P. G. (2009). The active control of prejudice: Unpacking the intentions guiding control efforts. *Journal of Personality and Social Psychology, 96*, 640–652.

Poskocil, A. (1977). Encounters between blacks and white liberals: The collision of stereotypes. *Social Forces, 55*, 715–727.

49 Seeking the Middle Way
An Exploration of Culture, Mind, and the Brain

Shinobu Kitayama

In one of his brilliant essays, Isaiah Berlin distinguished between two types of intellectuals, the hedgehog and the fox (Berlin, 1953). Some scholars have a deep commitment to a particular framework or viewpoint. If they are good enough, they perform a penetrating analysis by using this framework. They are hedgehogs. Some prominent hedgehogs, according to Berlin, include Plato, Pascal, and Nietzsche. But if you are a hedgehog and not as good as they are, then you may easily become a victim of your commitment. Your perspective could be either too narrow, too rigid, or worse, both. Some other scholars are more diverse in orientation, entertaining a variety of ideas and phenomena. They are foxes. Some of the most brilliant scholars of this sort include Aristotle, Shakespeare, and Goethe. But if you are a fox and mediocre, your work is dispersed without any clear focus or thread. Berlin's perceptive analysis makes me realize that I have always tried to hit the middle, aspiring to be both while avoiding being fully wedded to either. I may not be completely successful, but I am trying.

In this chapter, I will discuss why I have sought the middle way and how this effort has fared. I will start with a brief memoir of where I came from and why and how I became fascinated with the study of culture. I will then illustrate, in a broad stroke, what we have accomplished. I will also explain why I have decided to take on the questions of the brain in this connection more recently. Throughout, the theme is the dialectic between the effort to see many different effects with various methods (like Berlin's fox) and the single-mindedness in how we might understand the relationship between culture and the agency (like his hedgehog).

From Yaizu to Kyoto, and then to Michigan

I grew up in the coastal town of Yaizu, near Mount Fuji in Japan. Yaizu was known for big-time tuna fishing. Once a fishing boat left the port, it would go all the way to the Atlantic chasing the schools of tuna, not coming back for more than a full year or even more. People, especially those living near the ocean – fishermen and their wives – were cordial but temperamental. They were strong people you would not want to mess with. Their kids were my friends and they shared the same character and temperament. I was a son of a Buddhist priest and had none of it. I sensed the mismatch.

Shinobu Kitayama, University of Michigan, USA.

Nevertheless, when Dick Nisbett and Dov Cohen began investigating the culture of honor in the American South (Nisbett & Cohen, 1996), I knew what they were talking about. That culture existed in my hometown.

My path to social psychology started in Kyoto in the second half of the 1970s. I was an undergraduate at Kyoto University. I majored in psychology, learning all the details of the animal learning literature (then considered "the" mainstream of psychology). The elitist aura of scientism was pleasant. And I learned quite a bit. What I learned back then proved invaluable for me as an experimental cultural and social psychologist. Nevertheless, the entire endeavor seemed out of touch with the rich reality of social life – think about the Yaizu folks! After all, the stuff was based exclusively on mice and rats.

I was drawn to Freud and Jung initially and then to more social sides of experimental psychology. My fellow students and I enjoyed interpreting each other's behaviors by using newly learned vocabularies of attribution and dissonance. Interpretation of everyday behaviors was more fun and engaging than interpretation of dreams discussed in my clinical psychology course. These social psychological ideas were news to me. They revealed, I felt, something I did not know that I had. I enjoyed learning new ways of understanding others and myself.

A Puzzle

Gradually, however, one question began to lurk in my mind: Why is it that a vast majority of scholars cited in the textbooks I read had Western names? Why is it that nowhere in these books are any Asian names to be found, let alone Japanese names? Might the field be completely underdeveloped in Japan? If so, what might it take to do research that is worthy of citation in these textbooks?

I did not formulate these questions in any sophisticated terms. I did not know that knowledge production and dissemination are part of the story. Nor did I know anything about structural inequality in material and symbolic resources that undergird the process of knowledge creation. Most of all, I had no idea that access to local culture – to its commonsense and everyday practices – is crucial to becoming a top-notch researcher in the field. You would have to know your culture well enough to act properly and impress others for sure. But in the case of psychology, this culture is part and parcel of what you study – a point I will come back to. Today, there is a welcome movement toward diversity and equity. These issues have emerged at the forefront of our field. In the United States, systemic racism is undoubtedly the most urgent issue. However, the same structural problem exists on a more global scale. With the benefit of hindsight, I would say that the discipline was and still is local and Western. There was and still is "systemic Westernism." Today, many of us have sought to find ways to globalize the discipline.

Back then, however, none of that was there to tell me why my textbooks had been loaded with Western names. To find out, I took the chance to go to the United States to learn the discipline and to find out why non-Europeans were so vastly underrepresented in it. It was 1981. I was lucky. I met Alvin Zander at a social psychology seminar held at Osaka University in his honor. Back then, "Cartwright & Zander" was the trade name for social psychology in Japan since these two scholars had edited the authoritative book on group dynamics, which had a huge impact on the development of social psychology in Japan. I still call him Zander sensei, with all affection attached to the term sensei – "teacher" in Japanese. He was kind and receptive to my ideas and plans. He nurtured me as a newcomer to the field and encouraged me to come to the United States for graduate training. Indeed, he did help me out, and soon, I received a Fulbright scholarship. Shortly afterward, I got admitted into the social psychology PhD program at Michigan.

Culture Matters

In the fall of 1982, I arrived in Ann Arbor, Michigan, to start graduate training. I took Psychology 682, Advanced Social Psychology, taught by Hazel Markus. I began working on person memory experiments with Gene Burnstein. Bob Zajonc's office was right across from the student office I shared with two other graduate students. Dick Nisbett had just published his human reasoning masterpiece with Lee Ross. James Jackson was starting his life work on the social psychology of Black Americans. And Nancy Cantor and David Buss were nearby in an adjacent building. All these individuals have since become the meat and bones of me as a psychologist. Nevertheless, the most significant moment of revelation came through numerous conversations and interactions I had with my fellow graduate students in the same cohort. This cohort had four or five individuals with extraordinary intelligence and fascinating personality.

While studying social psychology in Japan, I felt that theories such as attribution and dissonance showed what I must be doing even though I never thought I was. They were academic abstractions good for ivory-tower interpretations of others' behaviors. Perhaps, precisely because of their surreal nature, they had seemed quite profound. I had thought, for example, "I did not know that I was reasoning about social events as if I were a scientist. It's fascinating, and attribution theory is showing something I did not know." Or I had felt, "Somewhere in my mind, there must be negative emotional arousal since the two events happening to me present a cognitive conflict. Festinger pointed out to me this thing called dissonance I never felt. I must have it deep inside of my mind."

Now, I was in Michigan, watching my fellow American friends think, act, and react first-hand. I felt how true dissonance and attribution theories were to them in ways they were not to me. My American friends did show direct evidence of active thinking about social events in what they said and how they said it. They lived attribution theory. Also, they revealed their negative arousal on the face or in a spontaneous burst of frustration. The dissonance was real and visible. Neither attribution nor dissonance was a dry, academic abstraction as they had been for me. While in Japan, I felt that these abstractions showed you what you must be doing even though they do not seem real. In the United States, they showed you what people experience online. To use the jargon of cultural anthropology, both attribution and dissonance turned out much more "experience-near" for Americans than for Japanese.

Culture and the Self

Around that time, I had numerous conversations with Hazel Markus. We often joked around about how "crazy and unusual" each other was. What seemed most natural and sensible for one was not to the other. We exaggerated our cases to make fun of each other. The point of this exchange was that social behaviors have multiple layers of meanings, and these meanings are inseparable from culture. For Hazel, Americans are motivated to act freely, and behaviors based on their free choices are most genuine and powerful. They are, as we characterize them, independent from others. For me, they were merely conforming to the norm of freedom, and no behaviors would exist outside of the nexus of strong normative influences. I was so interdependent that even freedom seemed best defined as a form of conformity. Our conversations on this and numerous other topics eventually led to our 1991 paper on culture and the self, published in *Psychological Review* (Markus & Kitayama, 1991).

When this paper came out, I was on the psychology faculty at the University of Oregon. In 1993, I left Oregon to accept a faculty position at Kyoto. Over the next ten years, I worked with many Japanese students to explore many topics. We explored the cultural basis for the Fundamental Attribution Error. The main hypothesis was that this error was a manifestation of a cultural belief system that defines the self as an independent actor. In many cultures, including Japan, where an alternative cultural belief that defines the self as interdependent with others is more dominant, this effect may be attenuated. Thus, an examination of cultural variation in the Fundamental Attribution Error seemed suitable for testing the proposition that cultures vary on the dimension of independence and interdependence.

We first replicated the prior evidence that Americans draw a strong attitude inference from what another person says about a political issue under an obvious social constraint (e.g., being assigned to read a particular opinion). We then showed that this effect is much weaker in Japan. Japanese are sufficiently sensitive to the situational constraint to become agnostic about the person's attitude even if she makes a clear attitude statement (Masuda & Kitayama, 2004).

Multiple Forms of Dissonance

To tell you why I had a particular interest in this topic, I must bring you back to my earlier experience at Michigan. As noted above, I learned quite a bit about American culture through first-hand interactions with my fellow graduate students. Through these interactions, I arrived at the idea that dissonance, as formulated by Leon Festinger and his colleagues, is more "experience-near" for Americans than for Japanese. However, after spending some time in Japan, I became puzzled: Many of my fellow Japanese did show the kind of sulkiness or indignation that shared some family resemblance with the burst of frustration I had earlier identified as a direct manifestation of dissonance in my American friends. In Japanese, we do not call sulkiness or indignation "dissonance." We call it "iji（意地）."

So, I did something very simple. I had a group of Japanese undergraduates list situations in which they felt "iji." And I found something remarkable. In almost all cases, the situations listed involved someone else. For example, you may feel "iji" when someone important opposes your favorite plan. Or someone planning a thesis research project may feel "iji" when her teacher says that the plan will not work. If you know anything about dissonance theory, this observation should come across as perplexing. Didn't you know that dissonance happens when your behavior is freely chosen so that your behavior is indicative of your true attitude? Only under such conditions will you feel dissonance if the behavior is counter-attitudinal. The best way to eliminate any social interference is to make your choice in private, in the absence of any social eyes. Given this reasoning, if "iji" requires social eyes, it cannot be the dissonance as formulated by Festinger and company. However, "iji" does provide the kind of indignation or sulkiness that can be glossed as dissonance. Might it be the case that dissonance takes multiple forms depending on culture?

Armed with this theoretical framework, we carried out a series of free-choice dissonance experiments in Japan and the United States (Kitayama et al., 2004). Subjects choose between two equally attractive items. The question is whether they will end up liking the chosen item better than the rejected one. If this effect happens, cognitive dissonance must have happened. The standard dissonance theory says that the choice must be made in private since choice constrained by social pressure is not revealing the true, inner self. And there is ample evidence that Americans show this pattern. However, Japanese may not experience this dissonance since the inner self does not carry much significance in their cultural context. Instead, it is social eyes that make them worry about their choice, which could motivate them to justify it. The upshot is that Japanese will never experience dissonance in the absence of other people's eyes. In contrast, Americans will never experience their dissonance in the presence of these eyes. To manipulate social eyes, we set it up such that a poster showing several schematic faces was placed in front of each participant when the person made a choice. So, from each subject's perspective, the schematic faces were "watching" them. The results were as remarkable and "just as predicted." Overall, Americans showed more choice justification when they made a choice in the absence of this poster, but Japanese showed more choice justification when they made a choice in its presence.

A Series of Explorations

Attribution and dissonance are only two of many such effects. I was like a fox – so Berlin might have said. These effects included the following:

- Attention is more holistic in Asians than in European Americans (Kitayama et al., 2003).
- Self-enhancement (or better than average effect or self-serving bias) is much weaker for Asians than for European Americans (Kitayama et al., 1997).

- Happiness is personal for European Americans, but it is social for Japanese (Uchida & Kitayama, 2009).
- Success is a better motivator than failure for European Americans, but failure is a better motivator for Asians (Heine et al., 2001).
- When listening to a verbal message, Asians are more sensitive to vocal tone than European Americans (Ishii et al., 2003).
- European Americans actively try to feel positive emotions, but Asians do not. Consequently, feeling negative emotions constitutes a personal threat for European Americans, but not for Asians (Park et al., 2020).
- Neuroticism is a health risk for Americans, but not for Japanese (Kitayama, Park et al., 2018).
- Conscientiousness is a health-protective factor for Americans, but it is a health risk for Japanese (Kitayama & Park, 2021).
- Americans show a decrease in purpose in life as they age, but Japanese do not (Kitayama et al., 2020).

Other investigators have identified other important cultural differences, which provided the empirical backbone of the field. It is easy to encourage young scholars to go after low-hanging fruit. But it is not easy to find trees that bear such fruits. We were lucky enough to get to such trees. Surely, the time was ripe for cultural research in psychology to blossom.

Cultural Psychology's Unique Contributions

Mutual Constitution

Meanwhile, Hazel and I continued our conversation about how we might best conceptualize the relationship between culture and psychological processes (Markus & Kitayama, 2010). Not having the right word to signify what we thought about, we used hand gestures to express the idea that the two putative entities of culture and the mind are interacting with one another to such an extent that they become fused and inseparable. Hazel is an amazing intellectual who grasped the dynamic interplay between culture and the psyche even in the absence of any words to describe it. I could also immediately get it when Hazel tried to show, with her gestures, how this dynamic might work, aided perhaps by my upbringing as the Buddhist priest's son. My early experience may have given me some head start for appreciating the holism inherent in our early thinking. From the beginning, we had a commitment to this sort of holism. Berlin may well have seen two hedgehogs here.

   The effort was deeply influenced by the French philosopher Pierre Bourdieu (1977), who argued that cultural practices are internalized to form action tendencies. In combination, these tendencies constitute agency ("habitus" in his terminology). Thus, when this agency operates, it spontaneously generates behaviors that are congruent with the cultural practices from which they are derived. A similar idea was proposed by the British sociologist Anthony Giddens (1984), who noted that social structure shapes individual agency, whose actions, in turn, are instrumental in reproducing the original social structure. But most influential to us was Rick Shweder (1991), the Chicago anthropologist who drew our attention to the dialectic between culture and agency by pointing out that these two processes "make each other up."

And they are right. Let's go back to the Fundamental Attribution Error in European Americans and its near-absence among Asians. American culture emphasizes individual choice and initiatives. Hence, when seeing another person's behavior, it is reasonable to find their internal attributes, such as attitudes and personality traits, to understand why they act the way they do. On the one hand, there is a culture that emphasizes personal choice; on the other hand, there exists a psychological propensity to look for an internal attribute to explain another's behavior. These two phenomena are two sides of the same coin. One reinforces the other. They are mutually constitutive.

Or consider the two forms of cognitive dissonance. In a culture that emphasizes individual autonomy and freedom, one's unconstrained action reveals the true nature of the self. Hence, even actors themselves think their actions are not reflective of their own choice if they are under the scrutiny of others (i.e., in the presence of social eyes). This psychological propensity toward "personal" dissonance reinforces the culture of autonomy, freedom, and independence, from which it is derived. Conversely, in a culture that emphasizes social obligation, duty, and belonging, one's action is meaningful only in social situations (i.e., under the scrutiny of others). Hence, people cannot care less about their behaviors taking place in private. But they do worry profoundly about their behaviors performed under the social eyes. This psychological propensity toward "social" dissonance lends itself to the culture constituted by social obligation, duty, reputation, and the like.

Cultural Psychology in a Broader Context

The investigation of culture from a psychological perspective was exciting and surely absorbed a lot of energy from all of us involved in this effort. However, the study of culture has a respectable history that can easily be traced back for at least a few centuries (Jahoda, 1993). Hence, the study of culture in psychology discussed here is only a small part of this larger and longer history. We might ask then, what if any was the unique contribution we made to this broader scholarship.

Part of the answer to this question was discussed above. Many of us, particularly Rick Shweder and colleagues, brought to the fore the possibility that mental processes are so tied up with culture that culture is somehow internalized while at the same time mental processes are being externalized to constitute cultural processes. This idea of mutual constitution is a key piece that is fundamental to all studies of culture. I am very proud that Hazel and I contributed to the rediscovery of this idea. However, there is another piece that is implied by the idea of the mutual constitution but, strictly speaking, that is logically orthogonal to it.

This second contribution of cultural psychology to the broad scholarship on culture stems from the methods of experimental psychology we used in our investigation.

These methods enabled us to explore how deep culture might get "under the skin." Culture is embodied and perhaps "embrained." I would say, for the first time in the history of culture research, our effort provided credible evidence that culture is a fundamental constituent of the basic processes that comprise the human mind, such as cognition, emotion, and motivation. This means that the understanding of the human mind, by its very nature, would be impossible without the consideration of culture in its theoretical framework. This brings me to my last topic.

Culture and the Brain

Neuroplasticity

A lot has changed in psychology over the last several decades. Perhaps the most dramatic influence has involved the emergence and development of the science of the brain. Especially in recent decades, both functional magnetic imaging (fMRI) and the electroencephalogram (EEG) have become readily available even to those without any formal training in neuroscience. Although initially adopted by cognitive psychologists, the neuroscience approach ironically came to challenge the fundamental premise of the field, namely, that the mind is like a computer, fixed and hardwired. Studies on neuroplasticity have shown that the brain (and thus the mind) could undergo systematic structural changes through long-term "training." In one particularly impactful study, for example, Maguire et al. (2000) found that the hippocampi of London cab drivers became larger with experience. These brain regions are responsible for spatial navigation, so the finding is consistent with the notion that if you use certain brain regions to carry out a particular task, say, driving a cab in a complex city like London, these regions gain volume. This was, and still is, a remarkable finding since hippocampi typically shrink with age. Evidently, cab driving was sufficient to overcome what appears to be an inevitable neural decline due to aging and then added more.

The brain/mind is far more malleable than the computer metaphor makes it out to be. Cab driving is very specific. But we may only imagine the possible effects on the brain of other tasks within a culture. Broadly speaking, independence and interdependence may be defined by different sets of tasks. If cab driving is sufficient to change the brain, the cultural tasks of independence and interdependence may also be. Such a finding would be an ultimate vindication of the thesis that made our cultural psychology approach so unique in the entire history of the study of culture, namely, that culture is ingrained deeply into the brain (and, thus, into the "mind itself"). I was excited and could not wait to find out.

With a Little Help from My Friends

Right after my PhD, while I was at the University of Oregon, Mike Posner – a prominent cognitive psychologist at Oregon – taught me to ask questions that could be solved with the means available. But if you don't have the means needed, you must get it first. So, in addressing the question above, I wanted to learn the methods and theories of brain science.

I cannot be more thankful to several people who were willing to spend time with me, listening with patience and responding to my questions, many of which, I am afraid, might have been off target. I learned quite a bit from Brian Knutson (an affective neuroscientist at Stanford) about neuroimaging and Dave Amodio (an NYU social neuroscientist) about EEG. Steve Cole and Steve Suomi (at UCLA and NIMH, respectively) taught me how genes might be implicated in culture's influences on the brain. Back home in Michigan, Israel Liberzon, Carolyn Yoon, and Tony King – three brilliant neuroscientists and psychologists – became my indispensable collaborators in several cultural-genetic-neuroimaging projects. With great talent, intelligence, and vision, these scholars turned the brain project from something scary and daunting into pure pleasure. All conversations and social occasions I shared with every one of them have since become my enduring intellectual asset.

Cultural Neuroscience

This effort has coalesced into a new and ongoing field of inquiry called cultural neuroscience (Kitayama, Varnum, & Salvador, 2018). Indeed, a few tentative conclusions have already begun to emerge. First and foremost, we are finding what might seem obvious and even banal, namely, that the cultural variations we had documented using various measures of judgment, memory, and reaction time have a basis in the brain. We are beginning to find out exactly how cultural processes might interact with the brain to generate the cultural variations in the Fundamental Attribution Error and cognitive dissonance.

Second, we have begun to show that some aspects of brain structure are likely shaped through culture. Building on the London cab driver study, one might anticipate that regions of the brain that are repeatedly engaged by independence or interdependence may increase in volume. For example, the task of personal initiative, involving forming preferences in order to decide what to do, is prominently independent in nature. These cognitive operations are related both closely and uniquely to the frontal regions such as the orbitofrontal cortex and the medial prefrontal cortex. Is it then possible that these regions might be "bigger" for people in independent cultures than for those in interdependent cultures? Moreover, is it possible that the volume of these regions is greater for those who are relatively more independent within each culture? Our initial evidence has shown evidence for these possibilities. Last but not least, are these effects due to cultural influence? Ultimately, it requires long-term intervention studies to find that out. However, we have addressed this question by relying on a genotype known to predispose its carriers to be more "susceptible" or "sensitive" to environmental influences. If the brain difference across cultural groups is due to cultural influence – a type of environmental influence – then we may expect that cultural variation in regional brain volume to be more pronounced for the carriers than for noncarriers. This prediction has received support (Yu et al., 2019).

Seeking the Middle Way

As a fox, I have explored many topics with colleagues and students, and I have used many different methods, from surveys to behavioral experiments to neuroscience and genetics. However, many of my experiences in graduate school, in conversations with Hazel, and more, helped me form a strong conviction that culture is centrally significant in analyzing human psychology at all levels, from neural to behavioral, and all the way up to social and collective. This conviction has served as a framework for understanding social psychology, which greatly appealed to the hedgehog in me. This conviction has since been turned into the mutual constitution framework (Markus & Kitayama, 2010), which is now applied to many other domains, including cultural variation in the susceptibility to the COVID-19 pandemic (Kitayama et al., 2022).

Social psychology has transformed throughout the years. I am proud that this field has always been theory-oriented while striving to be thoroughly empirical. It has also been open to new innovative methods. As Editor of the *Journal of Personality and Social Psychology*, I have tried to reinforce this heritage (Kitayama, 2017). If Hazel and I contributed something worthy of note, that was to extend this tradition and bring culture and diversity into the field's theoretical framework. One crucial reason why we could do this, I believe, was that we did strive to be both the fox and the hedgehog simultaneously.

Suggested Reading

Berlin, I. (1953). *The Hedgehog and the Fox: An Essay on Tolstoy's View of History*. London: Weidenfeld & Nicolson.

Bourdieu, P. (1977). *Outline of a Theory of Practice*. Cambridge: Cambridge University Press.

Giddens, A. (1984). *The Constitution of Society: Outline of the Theory of Structuration*. Cambridge: Polity Press.

Heine, S. J., Kitayama, S., Lehman, D. R., Takata, T., Ide, E., Leung, C., & Matsumoto, H. (2001). Divergent consequences of success and failure in Japan and North America: An investigation of self-improving motivations and malleable selves. *Journal of Personality and Social Psychology*, *81*(4), 599–615.

Ishii, K., Reyes, J. A., & Kitayama, S. (2003). Spontaneous attention to word content versus emotional tone: Differences among three cultures. *Psychological Science*, *14*(1), 39–46.

Jahoda, G. (1993). *Crossroads between Culture and Mind: Continuities and Change in Theories of Human Nature*. Cambridge, MA: Harvard University Press.

Kitayama, S. (2017). Editorial: Attitudes and social cognition. *Journal of Personality and Social Psychology*, *112*(3), 357–360.

Kitayama, S., Berg, M. K., & Chopik, W. J. (2020). Culture and well-being in late adulthood: Theory and evidence. *American Psychologist*, *75*(4), 567–576.

Kitayama, S., Camp, N., & Salvador, C. (2022). Culture and the COVID-19 pandemic: Multiple mechanisms and policy implications. *Social Issues and Policy Review*, *16*(1), 164–211.

Kitayama, S., Duffy, S., Kawamura, T., & Larsen, J. T. (2003). Perceiving an object and its context in different cultures: A cultural look at new look. *Psychological Science*, *14*(3), 201–206.

Kitayama, S., Markus, H. R., Matsumoto, H., & Norasakkunkit, V. (1997). Individual and collective processes in the construction of the self: Self-enhancement in the United States and self-criticism in Japan. *Journal of Personality and Social Psychology*, *72*(6), 1245–1267.

Kitayama, S., & Park, J. (2021). Is conscientiousness always associated with better health? A U.S.–Japan cross-cultural examination of biological health risk. *Personality and Social Psychology Bulletin*, 47(3), 486–498.

Kitayama, S., Park, J., Miyamoto, Y., Date, H., Boylan, J. M., Markus, H. R., Karasawa, M., Kawakami, N., Coe, C. L., Love, G. D., & Ryff, C. D. (2018). Behavioral adjustment moderates the link between neuroticism and biological health risk: A U.S.–Japan comparison study. *Personality and Social Psychology Bulletin*, *44*(6), 809–822.

Kitayama, S., Snibbe, A. C., Markus, H. R., & Suzuki, T. (2004). Is there any "free" choice? Self and dissonance in two cultures. *Psychological Science*, *15*(8), 527–533.

Kitayama, S., Varnum, M. W. E., & Salvador, C. E. (2018). Cultural neuroscience. In D. Cohen & S. Kitayama (Eds.), *Handbook of Cultural Psychology*. Second edition (pp. 79–118). New York: Guilford Press.

Maguire, E. A., Gadian, D. G., Johnsrude, I. S., Good, C. D., Ashburner, J., Frackowiak, R. S. J., & Frith, C. D. (2000). Navigation-related structural change in the hippocampi of taxi drivers. *Proceedings of the National Academy of Sciences*, *97*(8), 4398–4403.

Markus, H. R., & Kitayama, S. (1991). Culture and the self: Implications for cognition, emotion, and motivation. *Psychological Review*, *98*(2), 224–253.

(2010). Cultures and selves: A cycle of mutual constitution. *Perspectives on Psychological Science*, *5*(4), 420–430.

Masuda, T., & Kitayama, S. (2004). Perceiver-induced constraint and attitude attribution in Japan and the US: A case for the cultural dependence of the correspondence bias. *Journal of Experimental Social Psychology*, *40*(3), 409–416.

Nisbett, R. E., & Cohen, D. (1996). *Culture of Honor: The Psychology of Violence in the South*. New York: Routledge.

Park, J., Kitayama, S., Miyamoto, Y., & Coe, C. L. (2020). Feeling bad is not always unhealthy: Culture moderates the link between negative affect and diurnal cortisol profiles. *Emotion*, *20*(5), 721–733.

Shweder, R. A. (1991). *Thinking through Cultures: Expeditions in Cultural Psychology*. Cambridge, MA: Harvard University Press.

Uchida, Y., & Kitayama, S. (2009). Happiness and unhappiness in east and west: Themes and variations. *Emotion*, *9*(4), 441–456.

Yu, Q., Abe, N., King, A., Yoon, C., Liberzon, I., & Kitayama, S. (2019). Cultural variation in the gray matter volume of the prefrontal cortex is moderated by the dopamine D4 receptor gene (DRD4). *Cerebral Cortex*, *29*(9), 3922–3931.

50 The Pillars, Their Stories, Retrospectives, and Signals Loud and Clear

Saul Kassin

Working on this book has been a labor of love. Grateful for a social psychology whose theories, research, and methods have proved immensely useful at identifying and preventing wrongful convictions, and inspired by the riveting stories told by the Pillars of this great field, I am eager to share this gift of memoirs with my colleagues, their students, and historians of psychology.

Having co-authored a social psychology textbook now for over thirty years (Kassin, Fein, & Markus, 2021), I mistakenly thought I knew the backstories that brought us to this point. This collection provides a treasure trove of insights and revelations. With PhD years ranging from 1956 to 1987, it is hard not to get a sense of the history that comes together in these pages (interestingly, five of our Pillars were the PhD advisors for six others – Aronson for Berscheid; Greenwald for Wells and Banaji; Nisbett for Wilson; Deaux for Major; Snyder for Swann).

Before noting the commonalities across chapters and signals that emerged in response to the questions I had presented as guideposts, I'd like to review some of the many memorable idiosyncratic stories that have emerged from the Pillars who joined this project. I learned an immense amount about them and the field they entered, often precious and personal details I was not aware of.

At the outset, I have to say, the chapters in this volume are beautifully written. Elaine Hatfield's chapter opens with the sentence, "I was born curious" – a line that took me back to "Call me Ishmael," Henry Melville's famous and famously controversial opening to *Moby Dick*.

Speaking of masterful writing, Dan Gilbert's chapter, titled "Dear Vera, Chuck, and Dave" (you'll have to figure out what that means on your own) is a treat. "I love writing," he says at the outset, "but I hate writing about myself." If that doesn't telegraph what follows, I don't know what does. Don't take my word for it. Pillar Tim Wilson, Gilbert's close friend and collaborator, refers to Gilbert as one of the best writers anyone knows. "Just read Dan's chapter in this volume. You'll see."

Substantively, too, the stories are priceless. Here's one happenstance occurrence to ponder. In 1954, Gardner Lindzey published the first edition of the *Handbook of Social Psychology*, an authoritative scholarly resource everyone in the field is familiar with. The *Handbook* was revised in 1968 in a five-edition set edited by Lindzey and Elliot Aronson – a Pillar in this book. Then in a chapter titled "Always Buy the *Handbook of Social Psychology* (1968) at a Railway Station in India," Mahzarin Banaji recounts how she "bought a set of books that changed the course of my life."

That was in 1978. Fast forward another thirty-two years and the most recent fifth edition of the *Handbook*, published in 2010, was edited by Susan Fiske and Daniel Gilbert, also Pillars in this book – and Marzu herself authored a chapter. (Heads up: a new sixth edition is scheduled to be published next year!)

From these chapters, I also learned that Robert Rosenthal stumbled into the study of experimenter expectancy effects by "over" analyzing his own 1956 dissertation data – and then he, not his colleague Stanley Milgram, received tenure in social psychology at Harvard even though he was fully immersed in the clinical program there. Speaking of Milgram, Phil Zimbardo recounts how he and Milgram were contemporary class-mates at the James Monroe High School, in Bronx, New York, in 1948. Think about that. The two social psychologists whose work most embodies a hardcore situationist perspective walked the halls of the same high school as kids. Then in 1971, Milgram thanked Zimbardo for the Stanford Prison Experiment: "Oh thanks. Now you're going to take all the ethical attacks off my shoulders, because what you did was worse than what I did in my studies."

Several disclosures made me laugh, out loud. Readers are no doubt familiar with Schachter and Singer's (1962) classic experiment testing their two-factor theory of emotion. Some subjects but not others were injected with epinephrine and informed or not about its arousing properties. They were then introduced to a "stooge," a fellow subject who proceeded to behave in a euphoric or angry manner. It turns out that Bibb Latané, while Schachter's graduate student in Minnesota, "got to play the Happy Stooge, hula hooping on a table-top." Who knew!

Anthony Greenwald was a jazz musician. While in college at Yale, he played trumpet in the University Concert Band and in the New Haven Symphony Orchestra. Before starting graduate school at Harvard, he also traveled with a couple of jazz bands. He continued to play into the early 1980s, at which point "I decided that the ten practice hours per week it was taking to keep my lip in shape were taking too much time away from work."

Robert Cialdini's first ever publication was in *Science*, a 1968 article titled "Alarm pheromone in the earthworm Lumbricus terrestris," before he discovered social psychology and field research – or to use his metaphor, "stepping from the avenues to the streets." Indeed, Patricia Devine, who has dedicated her career to studying unconscious stereotyping – and ways to reduce its pernicious effects in the real world – subtitled her chapter "(Re)Discovering My Inner Cialdini."

Dan Batson was a theological seminary student at Princeton before realizing that he wasn't cut out to be a minister and then reading Latané and Darley's newly published *The Unresponsive Bystander*. At that point, he was hooked by the promise of a scientific approach to studying ethical behavior (hence his classic 1973 paper with John Darley, "From Jerusalem to Jericho").

John Bargh, a self-described "lab rat" running experiments as an undergraduate at the University of Illinois, was also a "graveyard shift" disc jockey in college for a student-run FM rock station. This experience, followed by others, formed the basis of Bargh's funky chapter title, "The Basement Tapes."

Finally, hang on to your hat. Bibb Latané's ancestors were linked in jaw-dropping ways both to slavery and to the abolitionist movement – and he offers pictures to illustrate these connections. And Elaine Hatfield is a Hatfield – of Hatfield-McCoy feud fame. For proof, she too presents a picture of her "hard-shell Baptist" ancestors, including children, toting guns!

Common Themes

These stories just scratch the surface. Each memoir in this volume is unique in substance, style, and revelation; yet the mosaic richly formed reveals a historical image of social psychology's past, present, and projected future. I'll leave it to others, armed with a searchable electronic copy of this book, to develop a coding scheme and quantify the number of times our Pillars, perhaps as related to the year they obtained their PhD, cited the various founders (from my readings, I would unofficially estimate that Lewin, Festinger, and Gordon Allport would lead the way), how they found their way into psychology (e.g., through a purposeful master plan or by stumbling into it), the extent to which their research was inspired by existing theory or by real-world events, and whether they are generally bullish or bearish with regard to the future of the field.

Diversifications of Social Psychology

The recognition of social psychology as a once-narrow discipline, and lacking in diversity, is beyond dispute in these chapters – beginning with race and gender considerations.

Assuming you've now read this book, you would know that Professor Emeritus James Jones had a grandfather who was a slave on a plantation in North Carolina. Inspired by the legendary Kenneth Clark (whose daughter was his classmate at Oberlin College), Jones entered the social psychology graduate program at Yale in 1966 only to be told that race was not considered a legitimate variable for study! As we all know, Jones went on to have an amazing career, authoring two editions of *Prejudice and Racism* in the process. Then in 2005, thirty-nine years after his entry to Yale, he joined Tom Pettigrew (who, in his chapter, "informs" some of us and "reminds" others that in 1967 brought the Reverend Martin Luther King to speak at the Annual APA convention) in writing Dr. Clark's obituary for the *American Psychologist*.

Turning from race to gender, several female Pillars write about the rampant sexism of the "Old Boy Network" – even within the progressive bubble of academia and even during the liberated (or so I thought) 1960s and 1970s. By today's standards of conduct, and in light of current gender discrimination laws, these stories are shocking. In 1960, Ellen Berscheid was preparing to apply to Duke's PhD program until she was stopped in her tracks: "Applications accepted from men only." When Elaine Hatfield arrived as an assistant professor at the University of Minnesota in 1963, she was told by the Department Chair that women were not allowed to hang their coats in the faculty cloakroom or eat lunch in the Faculty Club.

Several male Pillars in this book similarly recall the subtle and not so subtle forms of sexism at that time. While a graduate student in 1965, Bernie Weiner recalls getting a call from the department chair at UCLA asking if he would be interested in a position. "The next thing I knew I had a job offer," he notes. "This was the old-boy network at its worst (or, for me, its best)." Jonathan Freedman recounts his early years with developmental colleague, the great Eleanor Maccoby: "Eleanor and I arrived at Stanford at the same time. She was an associate professor and already quite well known. At our first meeting of the otherwise all-male faculty, Eleanor was asked to take notes."

The narrowness of the field was also geographical. The late emergence of social psychology in Europe and Asia are prominent examples. Emeritus Professor Wolfgang Stroebe, now at the University of Groningen in the Netherlands, started working with the legendary Social Identity theorist Henri Tajfel in 1966 – the year that the European Association of Social Psychology (EASP) was founded, with Serge Moscovici as its first president. Rupert Brown, who later worked with Tajfel and John Turner in Great Britain, and Miles Hewstone, who also worked not only with Brown but with Moscovici in Paris, Stroebe in Germany, and Jos Jaspars and fellow student Frank Fincham at Oxford, both note with pride the birth of EASP and a burgeoning European perspective as they entered the field.

Social psychology's emergence in Asia is also of relatively recent vintage. In his chapter, Shinobu Kitayama, the son of a Buddhist priest from a coastal town near Mount Fuji, in Japan, recounts majoring in psychology at Kyoto University in the 1970s. "One question began to lurk in my mind: Why is it that a vast majority of scholars cited in the textbooks I read had Western names?" Then in 1982, Hazel Markus visited Japan and met Kitayama for the first time. This meeting sparked years of discussion. She and he independently describe, in ways that are both profound and entertaining, the conversations they had about cultural differences between East and West, in which they sometimes had to resort to hand gestures for lack of a better word. Of course, they went on in 1991 to publish "Culture and the Self" in *Psych Review*, one of the most highly cited papers ever in psychology.

At the University of Michigan, Richard Nisbett notes that the Culture and Cognition Program that he and Markus helped to co-found became his most important working group. His research papers with Kaiping Peng, Taka Masuda, and others soon became foundational in a field that several years prior did not exist. Separately, cross-cultural psychologist Michael Harris Bond, inspired by Harry Triandis and now at Hong Kong Polytechnic University, describes his career development from the vantage point of *Ubuntu* – an African term for humanity by which "a person becomes a person through other persons."

Remarkably, the diversification of social psychology also pertains to the acceptance of applying research. This extension of the field was oddly late in coming despite Kurt Lewin's long-accepted calls for the application of basic research to the social concerns of his day, as described in Marrow's (1969) *The Practical Theorist*. Yet just as James Jones was advised in the 1960s that race is not a legitimate variable for study (thankfully, several Pillars, such as Tom Pettigrew, Elliot Aronson, Claude Steele, and Patricia Devine, didn't get the memo), Phoebe Ellsworth recounts her arrival as a graduate student at Stanford, and how she had become interested in law only to be told: "This is Stanford. We don't do *applied* research here." As he departed Ohio State's program, Gary Wells similarly recounts advisor Tom Ostrom's friendly parting advice, in 1977, not to pursue his interest in eyewitness identification research: "That line of work has no future."

The chapters in this volume bear testament to how much the applying social psychology ethos has progressed – back to Lewin. This progress can be "measured," I would argue, by the chronologies appearing in this volume.

In 1986, Phoebe Ellsworth worked with APA on an amicus brief to the US Supreme Court in the case of *Lockhart v. McCree*, challenging the practice of "death qualification" as a biasing jury selection practice. They lost to a Court that did not seem to grasp the concept of convergent validity but they fought the battle.

Susan Fiske and Kay Deaux noted their involvement working with APA on a 1989 amicus brief in *Price Waterhouse v. Hopkins*, a sex discrimination in the workplace suit in which they cited relevant research on stereotyping – and in which the plaintiff prevailed. They describe this work in the *American Psychologist*.

In 1996, Attorney General Janet Reno called on Gary Wells to assemble an interdisciplinary Task Force aimed at the reform of eyewitness identification procedures in the wake of DNA exonerations pointing to the problem. He did, the committee published a "Guide," and procedures have reformed – and continue to be reformed – as a result.

And UCLA close relationships scholar Anne Peplau describes in her chapter how she testified as an expert witness in 2008, in a precedent-setting same-sex couples adoption case, and then again in a state case that contested the prohibition of same-sex marriage.

Of course, social psychology's involvement in the studies of physical health, happiness, and well-being has also increased over the years thanks to Jerome Singer, Shelley Taylor, Sheldon Cohen, and others. In this volume, Michael Scheier, who identifies more with personality than social psychology, describes how he and Charles Carver, who died unexpectedly in 2019, came to conceptualize, assess, and study the physical health benefits of dispositional optimism. (Scheier's wife Karen Matthews is an eminent health psychologist in her own right.) James Pennebaker, Scheier's graduate school classmate at the University of Texas, recounts how he stumbled onto the discovery that instructing people to write about a traumatic experience improved their health as measured by medical visits in the months after writing compared to controls who wrote about superficial topics. Pillar Wolfgang Stroebe describes these and other developments in the three editions of his text, *Social Psychology and Health*.

How Did You Find Your Way into Social Psychology?

Perhaps the most interesting theme that presents itself repeatedly concerns the question, how did you find your way into social psychology? Over the years, I've had countless students, undergraduate and graduate alike, disclose to me that they were anxious about not knowing exactly what they wanted to do. Looking back at generations of successful academics, they were under the impression that we all had identified our lifelong ambition early on and then proceeded on a linear track to achieve a specific goal. That certainly is not how my academic career unfolded and I told them so. "We are more like billiard balls than guided missiles" I would say. The truth probably can be found in some mix of these metaphors. But loud and clear, the Pillars of social psychology did not set out as guided missiles aiming for a prescribed destination. I think this realization should give comfort to young scholars and students just starting out.

To begin with, our Pillars entered college with varying tentative majors in mind. Roy Baumeister, a math whiz in high school, went to college initially to major in math. So too did Ellen Berscheid, Jennifer Crocker, Kay Deaux, Ed Deci, and John Dovidio. Closely related, Jonathan Freedman entered Harvard aiming to become a physicist. Bibb Latané and Tom Gilovich were initially bound for law school.

Among those who did start out in psychology, several – like Miles Hewstone and Florence Denmark – were clinically focused. Bob Rosenthal entered the clinical PhD program in 1952 with Bruno Klopfer as his advisor. Klopfer's mentor was Carl Jung. Joel Cooper of dissonance fame notes that as a graduate student at Duke, he nearly became a clinical psychologist, like his older brother. Then, as he put it, Ned Jones came to the rescue. "We do social psychology, he said, precisely because it is fun."

One particularly dramatic shift comes in the life story of Elliot Aronson, who started out majoring in economics. He was then drawn into psychology at Brandeis through a course taught by "self-actualization" psychologist Abraham Maslow, his beloved undergraduate advisor. Then he went to Stanford for a social psychology PhD working with Leon Festinger. In a chapter titled "Abe and Leon and Me," Aronson describes his lifelong struggle to bring together the humanist and the hardcore experimentalist. They hated each other, he said. Maslow was a humanist; Festinger, interested in how the mind works, "did not give a fig about making the world a better place."

One of my favorite articles was Albert Bandura's (1982) *American Psychologist* paper on how people's life and career trajectories come about through "chance encounters" and "fortuitous opportunities." Consistent with those countless conversations I've had with my students over the years, this collection of memoirs brings this perspective of Bandura's to life. Banaji's purchase of the *Handbook* volumes in a Indian train station seems like the prototype of a happenstance occurrence. Then again, Robert Cialdini was heading for a career in ethology – until he sat in on his girlfriend's social psych class!

As to what constitutes a key life-altering event, the contributors to this volume point to three types: past or present world events that highlight serious social problems (e.g., the Holocaust, the Vietnam War, the civil rights and feminist movements); reading a book or article that opened up a whole new world, or the scientific approach; and meeting someone, typically a professor, who informed, influenced, and inspired them.

Without prompting, one fascinating set of commonalities emerged with regard to influential books. Setting aside the *Handbook*, certain classics in psychology, generally, were independently and multiply cited, such as Calvin Hall's (1954) *Primer of Freudian Psychology*, Ulric Neisser's (1967) *Cognitive Psychology*, and B. F. Skinner's (1971) *Beyond Freedom and Dignity*. From within social psychology, the handful of influencers were clear: Allport's (1954) *The Nature of Prejudice* and Festinger's (1957) *A Theory of Cognitive Dissonance* led the way. These twin towers are followed by Heider's (1958) *The Psychology of Interpersonal Relations*, Roger Brown's (1955, 1985) *Social Psychology*, and later Latané and Darley's (1970) *The Unresponsive Bystander*, and Ned Jones et al.'s (1972) *Attribution: Perceiving the Causes of Behavior,* otherwise known as the orange attribution book.

Turning from influential books to individuals, it is clear that many contributors were inspired by great teachers – inside and outside the classroom. In 1950, clinically bound Florence Denmark was turned on by a course taught at University of Pennsylvania by Albert Pepitone, a student of Kurt Lewin. About his time at Duke, in the mid-1960s, Joel Cooper is emphatic: "There is no question that I owe my becoming a social psychologist to my advisor, Edward E. Jones." A few years later, a math-bound Roy Baumeister was hooked by Joel Cooper's undergraduate social psychology class, leading him to get his PhD also with Jones as his advisor.

Perhaps the most electrifying testament to the value of teaching is described by David Buss – long before his pioneering work in evolutionary psychology. Buss's first social course in 1972 or 1973 was with Elliot Aronson who "mesmerized the class" with his charismatic lectures and with the first edition of *The Social Animal.* Then he watched Phil Zimbardo give a lecture in a class he was T.A.-ing at Berkeley. During that guest lecture, students often broke into applause during the lecture and at the end. "With these introductions to social psychology," Buss writes, "nothing seemed more fascinating to me."

Attributions to luck can also be found throughout this volume. Initially on track for a career in architectural engineering, Tom Pettigrew opens his chapter by recounting his initial encounters in 1950: "You could say I fell into social psychology." Referring to herself as an "accidental" social psychologist, Brenda Major says that luck smiled on her when her future mentor Kay Deaux visited Miami University as part of a "Women in Psychology" speaker series and they met for the first time. Dan Batson titled his chapter "Getting Lucky," Joel Cooper credits "serendipity and plain old good luck," James Jones describes his journey as "meandering," John Dovidio refers to himself as a case study in how "planning is overrated," James Pennebaker uses the word "stumbled," as does Michael Scheier who describes stumbling into "pivot points," whereby one meeting or experience leads to another, which leads to another. Roy Baumeister credits his entry into the field to "a series of accidents and false assumptions." John Bargh makes several attributions to luck, beginning with "Lucky break #1: born at the right time." Similarly, Bernie Weiner reflected on luck in a broader generational sense, wondering if he would have succeeded in today's more competitive climate. And Phoebe Ellsworth – a Pillar in two subfields of social psychology – says, "My career looks more like a random walk through a candy store than a single-minded pursuit of a goal."

To sum up: Almost to a person, our Pillars bear out Bandura's perspective on life trajectories – they found themselves in the right place at the same time, read a book that opened up a new perspective, were jazzed by the field's creative "Candid Camera" laboratory experiments, or met someone, usually a professor, who lit them up inside the classroom or out. Of course this doesn't make our Pillars ordinary people who happened to catch a lucky break. Whatever the life-altering event was, the take-home moral of their stories was always the same: When an opportunity presented itself, they (1) *identified* it as such, and (2) *seized* it.

What Has Inspired and Sustained Your Career?

Common to all Pillars in this volume is their staying power. Several contributors are on lifelong missions defined by the theoretical and/or applied work they do. In a chapter titled "Seven Decades in Social Psychology," Tom Pettigrew describes the development of his work on racial prejudice and methods of improving race relations, for example, through intergroup contact. In related efforts that pertain to race, gender, and sexual orientation, Mahzarin Banaji, Kay Deaux, Patricia Devine, John Dovidio, Alice Eagly, Susan Fiske, Anthony Greenwald, James Jones, Brenda Major, Anne Peplau, and Claude Steele have dedicated themselves to grasp the causes and consequences of stereotyping and prejudice, conscious and unconscious alike.

I could go on and on, which is what makes the memoirs in this book so impressive. Phil Zimbardo's multidecade transformation from *The Lucifer Effect* to his Heroic Imagination Project designed to "convert villains into heroes" is a prime (if not primal) example. So is David Buss's role in creating an evolutionary social psychology; Susan Fiske's in defining the emerging field of social cognition, the personal motivational theories and interventions originating in Weiner's early work on attributions for success and failure, Ed Deci's work on self-determination, and Carol Dweck's work on growth mindsets; the "new" study of attraction, love, and close relationships that Ellen Berscheid, Elaine Hatfield, Anne Peplau, and Margaret Clark broke open; our current understandings of the self courtesy of Jennifer Crocker, Shinobu Kitayama, Hazel Markus, Mark Snyder, Michael Scheier, Bill Swann, and Roy Baumeister; and Nisbett, Wilson, and Gilbert's research on how humans are, to quote the title of Tim Wilson's book, *Strangers to Ourselves*.

Alongside their theoretical and empirical mission to understand people and make the world a better place, it is clear that the Pillars were sustained by a second force. We all know the core tenet of social psychology that the need to belong is, to quote Baumeister and Leary, a fundamental human motive – that people need people. Perhaps social psychologists are more socially motivated than the average person – or maybe we're all just human. Each and every chapter in this book is filled with heartwarming expressions of gratitude, friendship, and social support for colleagues and students. A message that comes through loud and clear is that people are happy, creative, and productive when they work together.

Richard Petty cites his best friend and collaborator John Cacioppo, who sadly died in 2018. Petty and Cacioppo met in graduate school at Ohio State, bonded quickly (both were first-generation students of Italian-American upbringing), sharing a house and interests in persuasion and psychophysiology. Together they devised the Elaboration Likelihood Model (ELM), which helped to transform the study of attitude change. "Amazingly, we collaborated in both domains on and off for more than thirty years."

Michael Scheier tells a similar story about meeting Charles Carver while both were in the personality program at Texas. Starting the day they met, "our professional careers would become intertwined for the next forty-six years, continuing to his death in the summer of 2019." Together, they worked on self-awareness, behavioral self-regulation, dispositional optimism, and health. Thinking back over the influences on his career, Scheier writes: "The most critical event of all, however, was meeting Carver at Texas. No Carver, no forty years of collaboration and friendship."

Richard Nisbett states in his chapter that working with Lee Ross was as important to him personally as it was intellectually. By the time Ross died in 2021, he and Nisbett had co-authored two mightily important books – *Human Inference: Strategies and Shortcomings of Social Judgment* (1980) and *The Person and the Situation: Perspectives of Social Psychology* (1991). But that was just part of the magic. "For more than fifty years," Nisbett notes, "Lee was my closest friend and personal therapist."

Michael Harris Bond reminisces about the day undergraduate Kwok Leung knocked on his door in 1979, unleashing an extended conversation about Hong Kong Chinese culture that spawned twenty-nine joint publications until Leung passed away in 2017. Looking back, Bond notes that he and Leung not only respected one another but enjoyed each other's company – playing basketball, dining out, and laughing, often about their misunderstandings. "I miss him deeply."

These kinds of sentiments can be found throughout the pages of this book. Daniel Gilbert and Tim Wilson have published sixty or so papers together. Looking back, Wilson states "it is hard to imagine a more ideal career path than to have been mentored by Dick Nisbett, and then getting to spend the bulk of my career working with Dan Gilbert." Gilbert expresses a similar sentiment about his beloved (his word) mentor Ned Jones and subsequent collaboration with Wilson. When asked about what agreements they've had in place to make their collaboration so successful, he says, "The fact is that we never decided to work together for a lifetime; we just started one day and forgot to stop."

The stories of research collaborations built upon close relationships go on and on. John Dovidio cites Sam Gaertner; Alice Eagly, the architect of Social Role Theory, cites Shelly Chaiken, Linda Carli, and Wendy Wood; Patricia Devine cites Banaji, who in turn cites Devine; so do Hazel Markus and Shinobu Kitayama. Several Pillars make it a point to pay tribute to Daryl Bem, John Darley, Ned Jones, Harold Kelley, Judson Mills, Tom Ostrom, Lee Ross, Daniel Wegner, Robert Zajonc, and others.

Personal relationships among collaborators may be particularly important for coping during times of stress. In 1975, Wisconsin Senator William Proxmire announced a "Golden Fleece" award in a frontal attack on NSF funding to relationship pioneers and friends Elaine Hatfield and Ellen Berscheid. Their grant was for the study of romantic love. Berscheid still recalls the trauma, which included death threats: "It was a terrible time for me . . . I did fear for my life." Proxmire's attack posed an indirect threat to other areas of social psychology as well. For "Ellen and Elaine," this was yet another bonding experience. Both affectionately recall the nickname they were given as the Thelma and Louise of Psychology.

The State of Things

As in any academic enterprise, individuals vary in their assessment of the status quo. Not surprisingly, several Pillars weighed in, with differences of opinion, on questions about replicability (one can pretty much discern each writer's position by whether they call it a crisis versus encase the word crisis in quotation marks or refer to it as "so-called").

Some contributors, like Jon Dovidio, credit the replication failures with stimulating important innovations, such as the Open Science Framework. Others, reflecting on the lost "golden years" of social psychology, are alarmed at the proposed solutions, beginning with samples so large that many of the field's most important experiments would no longer be tenable. As Baumeister puts it, "Can you imagine Milgram, or Latané and Darley, doing their experiment with n=75 per cell?" As for online data collection, Jonathan Freedman – whose classic foot-in-the-door field experiment (Freedman & Fraser, 1966) must have consumed hundreds of hours of data collection time – says of the MTurk paradigm, "it sure is efficient. What used to take weeks or even months can be done over the weekend." Then again, he notes, "Online manipulations rarely if ever have the power and validity of those done in person." Putting forth a third point of view, Bob Rosenthal suggests a way to make lemonade out of lemons. Ever the methodologist, he proposes "Replication-Plus-One" studies in which a new condition is added to the original design. "It would make conducting replications more interesting, more informative, more truly cumulative, and a lot more fun."

Another point of emphasis that some contributors raise concerns the hard core situationist emphasis of social psychology which has tended to plow over personality and other individual difference factors (Michael Scheier and Mark Snyder make this point repeatedly) as well as biological and evolutionary influences (David Buss is emphatic on this point). Similarly, Carol Dweck, Ed Deci, and Bernie Weiner question the emphasis of cold cognition, which sometimes overlooks hot-blooded motivational and emotional factors.

Two additional signals emerged in these chapters that should not be overlooked. Several Pillars talked about the gratification and pleasure that they derive from teaching – yes, teaching, as in a classroom. Although this group is known for the enormity of their scholarly contributions, many say they were drawn into the field by great teachers and, in turn, that they take teaching seriously.

Robert Rosenthal tells this heartwarming story: After retiring from Harvard in 1999, he moved to the University of California at Riverside, where he continued to teach because he enjoyed it – and was good at it (he received university-wide teaching awards into his 80s). Then one semester, his student course evaluations came back as barely above average. "Listening to the data, I went to the department chair that week and announced that 'I'm retiring.'"

On the question of whether they have advice for incoming social psychologists, three types of guidance can be distinguished: First, train broadly in theories and methods – not just in social but in cognitive, neuro, personality, and developmental psychology, and even outside the discipline (e.g., biology, anthropology, behavioral economics). Second, and this is a theme that comes through in several chapters:

Follow your interests, basic or applied, even if you encounter pressures not to do so ("Follow your nose," as Rupert Brown put it, rather than the "crowd," as Alice Eagly cautioned). Third, learn to communicate to the public in nontechnical terms, in speech and in writing, to achieve the Lewinian mission to solve social problems.

So, is there a bottom line? Almost to a person, contributors to this volume are thankful for having found their way into social psychology and encourage others of future generations to join. This is not a unanimous consensus, as you've seen – but it's close. I wrap this up by quoting final words from ten Pillars:

> *Social psychology is the right path for me to have chosen. Whatever combination of chance opportunities and personal inclination got me on that path, it has been a terrific journey.*
>
> > (Kay Deaux)

> *I am proud of what social psychology is and what it has become, and am very proud to be a social psychologist.*
>
> > (Florence Denmark)

> *Social psychology is a field that allows you to make a difference.*
>
> > (Carol Dweck)

> *This chapter was supposed to be about me, and yet most of its sections bear the names of others. But isn't that social psychology's deepest message?*
>
> > (Daniel Gilbert)

> *The beauty of social psychology is that virtually no problem is beyond its purview, and the methods we use to study them are constrained only by imagination, dedication, and a desire to understand and make better the world in which we live.*
>
> > (James Jones)

> *I predict a bright and practical future with careers for social psychologists in universities, governments, and corporations as this essential understanding becomes ever more apparent and widespread.*
>
> > (Hazel Markus)

> *The most striking thing to me is that social psychology has gone over the course of my career from being a small and obscure enterprise to one having a major impact on the world.*
>
> > (Richard Nisbett)

> *If I were starting over, I would do it again and become a social psychologist, perhaps this time with calling cards embossed with "social psychologist" on them!*
>
> > (Mark Snyder)

> *The field's founding Lewinian mission of helping society . . . It is what has made a life in this field, for me, always meaningful and at times exciting.*
>
> > (Claude Steele)

> *Our world needs more well-informed, broadly trained social psychologists able to contribute to the solution of these and other vital issues.*
>
> > (Philip Zimbardo)

Index

Wesner, Robert, 29
Wheeler, Ladd, 84
When Men Behave Badly (Buss, D. M.), 374–375
When Prophecy Fails (Festinger, Riecken, and Schachter), 206
White, Robert, 170
White flight, 9–10
whiteness, as point-of-view, 146–147
Whitten, Cobie Hendler, 276
Wicklund, Robert, 144–145, 249, 275
  Theory of Objective Self-Awareness, 249–250
Willerman, Ben, 72
Willerman, Lee, 249
Williams, George C., 370, 372
Williams, Lawrence, 364
Willowbrook State School, 49
Wilson, E. O., 370
Wilson, Margo, 372–373
Wilson, Timothy, 118, 261, 277
  academic career, 303–304
    at Duke University, 303–304
    at University of Virginia, 303–304
  Bem and, 301
  educational background, at University of Michigan, 301–303
  Gilbert and, 304, 400–401, 440
    on affective forecasting, 400–401
    on impact bias, 400–401
    impact bias in studies, 304
  Nisbett and, 302–303, 305
  reasons analysis, 305
  Walton and, 306
Winer, B. J., 389
Wippler, Rainer, 138
The Wisest One in the Room (Gilovich and Nisbett), 119
Witherspoon v. Illinois, 182
Witte, Wilhelm, 133
Wolfe, Connie, 353
Woman (Denmark and Unger), 29–30
Women's Realities, Women's Choices, 29–30
Wood, Wendy, 108–111
Worchel, Stephen, 144–145

Work and Motivation (Vroom), 169–170
Wortman, Camille, 239
Wrangham, Richard, 372–373
Wrightsman, Lawrence, 1, 128
Wrosch, Carsten, 254
Wurf, Elissa, 239
Wyer, Robert, 363

Yando, Sonny, 323
Yates, Dan, 167
Yeager, David, 217–218
Yoon, Carolyn, 429
Young, Danielle, 76
Youth in Ghetto, 20

Zajonc, Robert B., 45–46, 146–147, 236–237, 239, 368, 378, 423
  Bargh and, 360–361
  Markus, H. R., and, 240
  Nisbett influenced by, 118–119
Zander, Alvin, 422–423
Zanna, Mark, 116–117, 147–148, 207
Zebrowitz, Leslie, 116–117
Zeigarnik effect, 92
Zeman, Joshua, 49
Zimbardo, Philip, 50, 367, 438, 440–442
  academic career, 45–47
    Stanford Prison Experiment, 46–47
    at Stanford University, 45–47
  Bond influenced by, 153
  educational background, 44–45
    at Yale University, 44–45
  Heroic Imagination Project, 49
  The Lucifer Effect, 47–49, 439
  Milgram and, 43–45, 433
  on prison reform, 46
  on shyness, research, 50–51
    Stanford Shyness Research Program, 50
  Snyder and, 220
  Social Fitness Clinic, 50
  on time perspective, 50–51
  Zimbardo Time Perspective Inventory, 50
Zuwerink, Julia, 416

Made in United States
North Haven, CT
22 August 2023

40617891R00263